Governmental Accounting, Auditing, and Financial Reporting

Stephen J. Gauthier

GOVERNMENT FINANCE OFFICERS ASSOCIATION

Copyright 2005 by the
Government Finance Officers Association
    of the United States and Canada
203 N. LaSalle Street, Suite 2700
Chicago, IL 60601-1210
www.gfoa.org

Library of Congress Control Number: 2004114535

ISBN 0-89125-275-4

Printed in the United States of America.

Contents

List of Exhibits

Foreword

The Government Finance Officers Association (GFOA) will soon be celebrating its 100th anniversary. Throughout the past one hundred years, GFOA has been a constant and tireless promoter of transparency in financial reporting. Those efforts have included the direct promulgation of accounting standards for over half a century (e.g., the National Council on Governmental Accounting), leadership in establishing and funding the Governmental Accounting Standards Board (GASB), and the encouragement of ever higher quality financial reporting through the Certificate of Achievement for Excellence in Financial Reporting Program (which soon will mark its own 60th anniversary). In light of this history, it seems especially appropriate for GFOA to commence its centennial celebration with the release of the latest edition of its classic "Blue Book," *Governmental Accounting, Auditing, and Financial Reporting* (*GAAFR*).

Ever since its first appearance in the mid 1930s, the Blue Book has held an unrivaled position as the premier source of practical guidance on all aspects of accounting, auditing, and financial reporting for state and local governments. This latest edition marks the eighth in a series extending over almost 70 years (i.e., 1936, 1951, 1968, 1980, 1988, 1994, 2001). The text of the newest edition has been revised and updated to address a host of significant developments affecting public-sector accountants and auditors, from new rules governing auditor independence to final authoritative guidance on accounting and financial reporting for other postemployment benefits such as postretirement healthcare. It also incorporates GFOA's various recommended practices on accounting and financial reporting. In addition, this latest edition has significantly expanded references to the authoritative accounting literature, including the GASB's 2004 *Comprehensive Implementation Guide*, to facilitate direct access to source material for further research.

Serving as author of a book of the scope and substance of the *GAAFR* is a significant professional achievement. The GFOA is grateful to Stephen J. Gauthier, Director of GFOA's Technical Services Center, for the tremendous effort and dedication he brought to this important project. Indeed, this is the fourth version of the *GAAFR* for which he has served as either the author (2001 and 1994) or co-author (1988). In addition, he is the author of numerous other GFOA publications, as well as the editor of GFOA's accounting, auditing, and financial reporting periodical *GAAFR Review*.

Before joining the GFOA staff in 1987, he was in charge of research and technical review for the Office of the Comptroller of the Treasury of the State of Tennessee, Department of Audit, Division of State Audit. He also was one of the original members of the Special Review Executive Committee, which oversees GFOA's Certificate of Achievement for Excellence in Financial Reporting Program. GFOA is also grateful to those members and staff who reviewed the manuscript, helped with the appendices, or who otherwise assisted in the production process.

GFOA is pleased to take the occasion of this important milestone in its own organizational life to reaffirm its ongoing commitment to the highest standards of accounting and financial reporting. I am confident that public-sector accountants and auditors will find this latest edition of the *GAAFR* an invaluable tool in helping to achieve that same objective.

Jeffrey L. Esser
Executive Director
October 2004

Preface

In recent years, it has become increasingly challenging for busy public-sector finance professionals to keep up with an ever expanding professional literature that now includes over 50 statements and interpretations of the Governmental Accounting Standards Board (GASB), as well as hundreds of technical rulings embodied in the GASB's nine implementation guides and various technical bulletins. The goal of this publication is to provide easy access to this wealth of technical guidance with a special focus on its practical application.

This newest edition of *Governmental Accounting, Auditing, and Financial Reporting (GAAFR)* represents a through revision and updating of the text of the 2001 edition. Key changes include:

- The incorporation of all of the amendments previously contained in the *GAAFR Update Supplement;*
- The addition of entirely new material related to GASB Statements No. 39 through No. 45;
- The addition of new material based upon guidance offered in the GASB's 2004 *Comprehensive Implementation Guide*, which includes guidance published for the first time in the *Implementation Guide to GASB Statement No. 40;*
- The addition of a new section that specifically addresses school district issues;
- The significant reworking of a number of major chapters;
- A greatly expanded set of references to original source material to facilitate further research;
- An expanded and revised glossary; and
- A redesigned comprehensive index.

The new *GAAFR* benefited immeasurably from the contributions of many people. I gratefully acknowledge the following individuals who reviewed and commented on all or significant portions of the manuscript: Mr. Gregory S. Allison, Assistant Director, Institute of Government, University of North Carolina—Chapel Hill; Mr. E. Barrett Atwood, Sr., Director of Finance, County of Broward Aviation Department, Fort Lauderdale, Florida; Mr. David R. Bean, Director of Research, Governmental Accounting Standards Board; Mr. Gerry Boaz, Technical Analyst, Office of the

Comptroller of the Treasury, Department of Audit, Division of State Audit, State of Tennessee; Mr. Patrick F. Hardiman, Partner, Deloitte & Touche LLP; Mr. Robert B. Scott, Chief Financial Officer, City of Carrollton, Texas; and Ms. Phoebe S. Selden, Senior Vice President, Scott Balice Strategies. I am also grateful to Dr. Robert J. Freeman, Distinguished Professor of Accounting, Texas Tech University, for his ever generous counsel and advice.

I also wish to thank the members of a special task force that assisted in identifying and resolving a number of important financial reporting issues related to school districts: Mr. Gregory Allison; Mr. Paul Glick, Principal, Glick Consulting Group; Mr. Gary Heinfeld, Managing Partner, Heinfeld, Meech & Co.; and Mr. Gregory Holbrook, Director of Accounting, Alpine School District, Utah.

A number of members of GFOA's staff also made important contributions to the new *GAAFR*. Ms. Bonnie Ashman and Mr. James Falconer, both senior managers in GFOA's Technical Services Center, reviewed the entire manuscript and offered many valuable suggestions for improvement for which I am most grateful. I also owe a special debt of gratitude to Mr. Jake W. Lorentz, Assistant Director, Technical Services Center, who carefully reviewed significant portions of the manuscript and offered numerous useful recommendations. Mr. Lorentz also revised the illustrative comprehensive annual financial report and related appendices. In addition it was my privilege for this edition of the *GAAFR*, as for the three previous editions with which I have been associated, to work with GFOA's editor, Ms. Rebecca Russum, who supervised all aspects of production.

Finally, I am especially grateful to my wife Barbara and to my sons Marc, Paul, and Gregory for their unfailing patience and support throughout this project.

Stephen J. Gauthier
October 2004

How to Use the *GAAFR*

This newest edition of *Governmental Accounting, Auditing, and Financial Reporting* (*GAAFR*) is designed for a variety of uses and users. Some of the more important of these uses and users are as follows:

- a comprehensive introduction to public-sector accounting and auditing for experienced financial professionals new to state and local government;
- a practical reference tool for accounting and auditing staff;
- a practice-oriented textbook for college-level classes and seminars on governmental accounting, auditing, and financial reporting (a companion study guide is also available for this purpose);
- a convenient guide to current practice; and
- a practical introduction to governmental accounting and auditing for new staff members.

To make the most of the materials contained in this publication, users should become familiar with the *GAAFR*'s structure, as well as with certain underlying assumptions and conventions.

Structure and contents. The structure and contents of the *GAAFR* can be summarized as follows:

- Introduction to governmental accounting
  - *GAAP and the Governmental Environment.* Chapter 1 describes the unique environment of state and local governments and explains how environmental differences have resulted in specialized accounting and financial reporting. The chapter also explores the sources of generally accepted accounting principles (GAAP) for state and local governments.
  - *The Governmental Financial Reporting Model.* Chapter 2 reviews the origins of fund accounting and the development of an integrated governmental financial reporting model that combines traditional fund accounting with government-wide financial reporting. It also explores the different types of funds used in the public sector, as well as the measurement focus and basis of accounting applicable to each. Finally, the chapter provides an overview of the

relationship between fund financial reporting and government-wide financial reporting.

—*Classification and Terminology.* Chapter 3 examines the various classes of transactions and interfund activity and provides a brief overview of the appropriate accounting for each. The chapter also examines some of the specialized categories used for financial reporting by state and local governments.

—*The Financial Reporting Entity.* Chapter 4 examines when and how legally separate entities are incorporated into a single financial reporting entity.

- Fund accounting

—*Governmental Funds.* Chapter 5 examines both the general rules governing accounting and financial reporting for governmental funds and the application of those rules to a number of specific situations commonly encountered in connection with activities typically reported in governmental funds.

—*Proprietary Funds.* Chapter 6 focuses on differences between enterprise funds and internal service funds, as well as on the specialized application of business-style GAAP in the public sector.

—*Fiduciary Funds, Joint Ventures, and Other Multi-Party Arrangements.* Chapter 7 is devoted to fiduciary funds and other arrangements that are either excluded altogether from the government-wide financial statements, or reported there only indirectly.

—*Government-wide Financial Statements.* Chapter 8 explores in detail the relationship that exists between the fund financial statements and the government-wide financial statements, with special emphasis on converting data from the governmental fund financial statements for presentation as *governmental activities* in the government-wide financial statements and on consolidating internal balances and activity, especially in connection with internal service funds.

- Financial reporting

—*Financial Reporting Overview.* Chapter 9 examines the relationship that exists between accounting and financial reporting and outlines the various types of financial reporting encountered in practice.

—*Financial Statements.* Chapter 10 examines in detail the format and contents of each of the basic financial statements.

—*Notes to the Financial Statements.* Chapter 11 completes the discussion of the basic financial statements by examining the required disclosures that must accompany those statements.

—*Transaction-specific and Account-specific Guidance.* Chapter 12 provides specialized guidance on a variety of individual transactions and accounts reflected in the basic financial statements.

—*The Comprehensive Annual Financial Report.* Chapter 13 examines the format and contents of the comprehensive annual financial report (CAFR) other than the basic financial statements and notes.

—*Professional Recognition Programs.* Chapter 14 examines two GFOA programs to promote high quality financial reporting: the Certificate of Achievement for Excellence in Financial Reporting Program and the Popular Annual Financial Reporting Award Program.

—*States and Certain Special-purpose Governments.* Chapter 15 explores specialized guidance for states, school districts, stand- alone business-type activities, pension plans, other postemployment benefit plans, governmental external investment pools, and public-entity risk pools. It also explores situations where government-wide and fund financial reporting can be combined for special-purpose governments.

• Budgeting and its relationship to accounting and financial reporting

—*Budgetary Integration and Reporting.* Chapter 16 explores the relationship between budgeting on the one hand, and accounting and financial reporting on the other, as well as the practical implications of this relationship.

—*Performance Measurement.* Chapter 17 explores the current state of performance measurement for state and local governments and the relationship of performance measurement to budgeting and financial reporting.

• Internal controls and auditing

—*The Internal Control Framework.* Chapter 18 examines the internal control framework as it relates specifically to accounting and financial reporting.

—*Auditing in the Public Sector.* Chapter 19 examines the different types of audits, auditors, and auditing standards encountered in connection with state and local governments.

These 19 chapters are supplemented by the following appendices: (a) illustrative journal entries, (b) illustrative trial balances, (c) illustrative conversion worksheet, (d) illustrative CAFR, (e) illustrative chart of accounts, and (f) glossary. The publication also features a comprehensive index of both the narrative text and illustrative journal entries. The CD-ROM that accompanies the *GAAFR* contains the complete text of the book's 19 chapters.

Other resources. A separate *GAAFR Study Guide* is available for those desiring to use the *GAAFR* for group study or for self-study purposes. The *GAAFR Study Guide* features narrative outlines of each of the 19 chapters, along with multiple-choice and true/false questions. A separate answer booklet is also available that provides a key to the exercises, as well as an explanation of correct and incorrect responses. The *GAAFR Study Guide* is also part of a *GAAFR Self-Study Course* that may be used by certified public accountants to obtain continuing professional education credit. Also available from GFOA are the *Elected Official's Guide to the New Governmental Financial Reporting Model*; the *Elected Official's Guide to Fund Balance and Net Assets*; the *Elected Official's Guide to Auditing*; the *Elected Official's Guide to Internal Controls and Fraud Prevention*; and *Evaluating Internal Controls: A Guide For Local Government Managers*.

1

GAAP and the Governmental Environment

Accounting and financial reporting are hardly unique to the public sector.[1] Private-sector businesses and nonprofit organizations rely on accounting and financial reporting at least as much as do state and local governments. Even so, many important aspects of accounting and financial reporting for state and local governments are unique to the public sector. The differences in theory and practice between the public and private sectors often reflect significant underlying differences in the public- and private-sector environments. This chapter briefly describes the state and local government environment with a view to better understanding some of the unique features of governmental accounting and financial reporting. The chapter then details the various authoritative sources of generally accepted accounting principles (GAAP) for state and local governments.

THE GOVERNMENTAL ENVIRONMENT

General background

Under the U.S. federal system of government, each of the 50 states is sovereign, retaining all governmental powers not expressly assigned to the federal government under the U.S. Constitution. While the role of the federal government has expanded significantly over the past two centuries, states continue to play a vital role in the U.S. federal system.

The U.S. Constitution establishes only two levels of government, state and federal. Each state has its own constitution, which provides for a third (local) level of government. In effect, local governments derive their powers from the states that created them. Legally, in some states, local govern-

---

[1] Throughout this publication, the term *public sector* will refer uniquely to government. Nonprofit organizations are considered private-sector entities unless they are component units of a primary government (see chapter 4).

EXHIBIT 1-1
Types of local governments in the United States

Types of local governments	General-purpose	Special-purpose	Total
Counties	3,034		3,034
Municipalities	19,431		19,431
Towns and townships	16,506		16,506
Independent school districts		13,522	13,522
Special districts		35,356	35,356
Total	38,971	48,878	87,849

ments are presumed to enjoy no power that the state has not expressly assigned to them.

Different states have different structures of local government. All local government units are either general-purpose governments or special-purpose governments. General-purpose governments include counties, municipalities, towns, and townships. Organized county governments or their equivalent (e.g., parishes in Louisiana, boroughs in Alaska) can be found in all states but Connecticut and Rhode Island. Municipal governments are characteristic of all 50 states. Towns and townships are found in 20 states. In total, there are 38,971 general-purpose local governments in the United States (3,034 counties, 19,431 municipalities, and 16,506 towns and townships).

The most common type of special-purpose government is the independent public school district, of which there are 13,522 units in the United States.[2] There are 35,356 other types of special districts. A brief summary of the types of local governments in the United States is presented in Exhibit 1-1.[3]

General-purpose local governments differ in the range of services they provide to their citizens. Some general-purpose governments offer a limited number of basic services, such as police and fire protection; others offer a broad range of services, including schools, public housing, water and sewer services, museums, zoos, water parks, and recreational programs.

State and local governments are financed in a variety of ways. Taxation is a revenue source unique to government. At the state level, income taxes or sales taxes typically constitute the major financing sources. At the local level, property taxes and sales taxes normally play a major role. Taxes can be levied only with the approval of the people's elected representatives or by a direct vote of the people. Further, the state constitution and statute circumscribe the types and amounts of taxes that local governments can levy.

A second major source of funding is transfer payments from other levels of government. For example, the federal government often takes advantage of its broad tax base to raise revenues used to fund programs administered at the state or local level. Similarly, states frequently provide local governments with grants or shared revenues, such as state aid to school districts.

As citizens in many jurisdictions have become less receptive to tax increases in recent years, local governments are turning more often to user charges to help finance certain types of services. User charges sometimes are designed to recover all or most of the cost of providing a service (for example, charges to utility customers). In other cases, user charges are intended to recover only a portion of the actual cost of providing a service (for instance, fares charged for the use of public transportation). In this second

---

[2] An independent public school district has the power to levy taxes. In addition to independent public school systems, there are 1,508 dependent public school systems operated by state, county, municipal, or township governments.

[3] See U.S. Census Bureau, *Census of Governments* (2002).

case, the portion of the cost not recovered through user charges must be subsidized from another source, such as taxpayers or grantors.

Other sources of revenue for state and local governments include fines, fees, and permits. Fines are imposed as penalties for violating laws and regulations. Fees and permits are required in connection with certain regulated activities—for example, restaurant licenses and franchise fees. Sometimes fees and permits are intended solely to recover costs associated with the regulation of a given activity—for instance, the cost of a restaurant inspection. In other cases, they are used to help fund the government's general operations.

In summary, just as local government structure varies between states, and services vary between governments, the combination of methods used to finance services also varies.

Key environmental characteristics

Two characteristics of the governmental environment have had an important impact on the development of public-sector accounting and financial reporting practice. First, not all activities of state and local governments have the same financial objectives. Second, governments have a special responsibility to demonstrate that they have complied with restrictions on the use of resources, particularly restrictions arising in connection with the government's annual or biennial appropriated operating budget. This duty of a government to justify its actions in the context of budgetary and other legal restrictions is technically known as *fiscal accountability.*[4]

Different financial objectives for different activities

Private-sector businesses operate by selling goods or services to customers at a price sufficient to recover at least their cost. Activities supported by user charges in the public sector often operate in much this same way, giving rise to their classification as *business-type activities.* How much an individual customer pays typically will vary depending upon the quantity of goods or services received. Moreover, once the buyer and seller have agreed to a price, the seller normally cannot subsequently assess some additional amount should the price agreed upon ultimately prove inadequate to cover costs. Consequently, a key financial objective of the seller is to ensure that the price charged to customers is sufficient to cover all related costs, including those that will be paid only in future periods.

Most functions of a typical government, however, are supported by taxes rather than by user charges. These tax-supported or *governmental* functions operate quite differently from the business model just described. Normally, there is no direct relationship between how much an individual taxpayer pays and the quantity of goods or services that same taxpayer receives. For example, a family with two children in the public school system will not be asked to pay more school taxes than a family with one child or no children in the public schools. Furthermore, if some related costs are payable only in future years, taxpayers can always be assessed the additional amount needed at that time. Therefore, the financial objective of governmental functions has tended to focus on determining whether expendable resources are sufficient to cover expenditures of a given period, rather than on comparing revenues and related costs.

---

[4] Governmental Accounting Standards Board (GASB) Statement No. 34, *Basic Financial Statements—and Management's Discussion and Analysis—for State and Local Governments,* paragraph 203.

Fiscal accountability

In the American system of separation of powers, each government branch has a distinct role. The legislative branch sets policy in the form of law, which is carried out by the executive branch and enforced by the judicial branch. In a system of checks and balances, each of these three government branches is intended to act as a control on the power exercised by the other two. The legislative body, which alone has the ability to levy taxes and authorize expenditures, uses this authority as its principal tool for controlling the arbitrary exercise of executive power.

Consequently, unlike budgets in the private sector, the appropriated budget of a state or local government is much more than just a financial plan. It is the concrete manifestation of a legislative body's use of the power of the purse to set public policy. As such, the appropriated budget of a state or local government enjoys the force of law, and violations are subject to legal sanctions.

Effect of environmental differences

The reality that not all activities of a government share the same financial objectives, combined with the recognized need for governments to demonstrate fiscal accountability, explains the following three fundamental differences between private-sector practice and accounting and financial reporting for state and local governments.

Fund accounting

In the private sector, even the most complex businesses generally are presented in external financial reports as a single, unitary entity. For example, data from a parent company are merged with data from that company's subsidiaries to create a single consolidated entity for financial reporting purposes. State and local governments also prepare and report consolidated, government-wide financial statements. These government-wide presentations, however, are not deemed sufficient for assessing a government's fiscal accountability.

Accordingly, the authoritative accounting and financial reporting standards for state and local governments require that government-wide financial statements be accompanied by fund-based presentations. As described in the next chapter, a *fund* is a separate, self-balancing set of accounts used to account for resources that are segregated for specific purposes in accordance with special regulations, restrictions, or limitations.[5]

Budgetary reporting

As indicated earlier, the concept of fiscal accountability requires a government to justify its actions in the context of budgetary restrictions on the use of resources. As a result, governments, unlike private-sector businesses, are required as part of their regular financial reporting responsibilities to compare their actual results for each fiscal period against both the original and the final amended budget. At a minimum, this budget-to-actual comparison must accompany the basic financial statements as required supplementary information.[6] Alternatively, the budget-to-actual comparison may itself in most cases be presented as a basic financial statement.

---

[5] National Council on Governmental Accounting (NCGA) Statement 1, *Governmental Accounting and Financial Reporting Principles*, paragraph 2.
[6] Required supplementary information (RSI) is mandated by generally accepted accounting principles but is *not* part of the basic financial statements. Auditors are required to perform certain limited procedures in connection with RSI, but RSI is not audited as such.

Special measurement focus and basis of accounting for governmental activities

Governments use essentially the same accounting as private-sector businesses for those funds that operate as business-type activities. They also use this same accounting for purposes of preparing their government-wide financial statements. In both cases, the focus of the statement of activities is on *inflows and outflows of economic resources* (changes in net assets). Changes in net assets are recognized as soon as the cause of the change occurs, regardless of the timing of related cash flows (the *accrual* basis of accounting). That is, revenues are recognized as soon as they are earned, and expenses are recognized as soon as a liability is incurred.

As noted, however, the financial objectives associated with governmental functions differ in some important respects from those associated with business-type activities. As a result, governments have always taken an approach very different from businesses in accounting for funds that incorporate governmental functions. The measurement focus here has been on *inflows and outflows of current financial resources* (changes in net *expendable* assets). Further, changes in net expendable assets normally are recognized only to the extent that they are expected to have a near-term impact (the *modified accrual* basis of accounting). Thus, inflows are recognized only if they are available to liquidate liabilities of the current period. Similarly, future outflows typically are recognized only if they represent a drain on *current* financial resources.

In summary, the need for fiscal accountability is the reason for both the use of fund accounting and the requirement to present budget-to-actual comparisons as part of general-purpose external financial reports. Differences in the financial objectives of governmental functions and business-type activities, in turn, explain why a unique measurement focus and basis of accounting are used in connection with governmental activities.

Users of public-sector financial information

Many groups and individuals need reliable information about a government's finances. A good accounting system must meet the basic informational needs of all interested parties.

Management needs financial information for planning purposes and to ensure and demonstrate compliance with internal (budgetary) and external (e.g., grantor) restrictions on the use of resources. *Legislative and oversight bodies* need financial information to make informed decisions on the allocation of scarce resources and to monitor management's compliance with budgetary and other legal restrictions.

Investors and creditors need financial information to determine the creditworthiness of the government and whether the government is complying with finance-related legal and contractual requirements (e.g., bond covenants). *Citizens* need financial information to evaluate the financial stewardship of their elected representatives (executive and legislative) and to provide a basis for their own informed participation in the budgetary process.

Management, of course, should be able to obtain whatever financial information it needs or desires directly from the accounting system. Other interested parties seeking financial data about a government often must rely on general-purpose external financial reports, which are targeted *primarily* at meeting the needs of interested parties without direct access to financial information. Consequently, even though management, as a practical matter, may be the major user of a government's general-purpose external financial reports, it is still not ordinarily considered a *primary* user of general-purpose external financial reporting. Rather, the targets or primary users of general-purpose external financial reporting are the citizens, legislative and oversight bodies, and investors and creditors who must depend upon such reports to obtain the financial information they need.[7]

Private-sector general-purpose external financial reports are designed essentially for the benefit of investors and creditors. Public-sector general-purpose external financial reports, as just noted, must also meet the needs of citizens, legislative bodies, and oversight bodies. Because of the specialized needs of these additional report users, a general-purpose external financial report for a state or local government typically is much longer and contains more extensive note disclosures than its private-sector counterparts.

AUTHORITATIVE STANDARDS FOR STATE AND LOCAL GOVERNMENTS

Nature and purpose of GAAP

Not all users of financial reports need or desire the same types of information. A potential investor, for example, might want a different set of data than a citizen or legislator. As a practical matter, however, it is not always possible or desirable to attempt to meet all the information needs of all potential users within a single financial report. Therefore, the accounting profession has chosen instead to identify *minimum* standards governing the formatting and contents of *general-purpose* external financial reports in the public *and* private sectors. These standards, known as *generally accepted accounting principles* (GAAP), are *not* intended to meet all information needs of each of the various user groups.[8] Rather, GAAP are designed to provide all primary users of general-purpose external financial reports with the *basic* information needed to assess an entity's finances.

History of GAAP

As the term implies, *generally accepted* accounting principles have their origins in practice; however, perceptions of practice, especially of *best* practice, can vary. As a result, finance professionals concluded that there is a practical need to identify and document GAAP.

In the private sector, auditors took the leading role in the process of determining GAAP for business enterprises. Auditors established the Committee on Accounting Procedure (CAP), which issued a series of Accounting Research Bulletins (ARBs), one of which continues to play an important role in guiding private-sector practice.[9] Eventually, the CAP was replaced by the Accounting Principles Board (APB), which issued a series of opinions that defined GAAP. The APB, like its predecessor, was perceived to be closely tied to the auditing profession.

In the public sector, financial statement preparers led the first efforts to define GAAP for state and local governments. The first specific group to do so was the National Committee on Municipal Accounting (NCMA), spon-

---

[7] GASB Concepts Statement No. 1, *Objectives of Financial Reporting*, paragraph 30.
[8] For example, governments routinely are asked to provide information in addition to their GAAP-based financial statements in connection with a credit evaluation.
[9] ARB No. 43, *Restatement and Revision of Accounting Research Bulletins*.

sored by the Municipal Finance Officers Association (MFOA). The MFOA later became the Government Finance Officers Association (GFOA).

In the mid-1930s, the NCMA issued its first "Blue Book" of governmental GAAP (NCMA Bulletin No. 6, *Municipal Accounting Statements*). After the Second World War, the MFOA replaced the NCMA with the National Committee on Governmental Accounting (NCGA), which released a second Blue Book in 1951 (NCGA Bulletin No. 14, *Municipal Accounting and Auditing*). In 1968, the NCGA issued the third official Blue Book of governmental GAAP. This third edition of the Blue Book first adopted the title *Governmental Accounting, Auditing, and Financial Reporting*, which has been retained in all subsequent editions. In the mid-1970s, the National *Committee* on Governmental Accounting became the National *Council* on Governmental Accounting.

Eventually a consensus developed in the public and private sectors favoring an *independent* standard-setting process to ensure that the needs and desires of all interested parties (preparers, auditors, and users of financial statements) received full and fair consideration. This consensus resulted in the Financial Accounting Standards Board (FASB) replacing the APB in the early 1970s. Likewise, the Governmental Accounting Standards Board (GASB) replaced the NCGA in June 1984. The FASB and the GASB operate under the auspices of the Financial Accounting Foundation (FAF), which appoints the members of both boards. Both the FASB and the GASB enjoy complete autonomy from the FAF in all technical and standard-setting activities.

The GASB, like the FASB, is composed of seven members.[10] GASB members come from a variety of backgrounds, including state and local government, the public accounting profession, academe, and user groups. The GASB is aided in its work by the Governmental Accounting Standards Advisory Council (GASAC), a consultative body made up of representatives of major groups interested in governmental accounting and financial reporting (e.g., GFOA, the National Association of State Auditors, Comptrollers, and Treasurers, and the American Institute of Certified Public Accountants). The Financial Accounting Standards Advisory Council (FASAC) plays a similar role in connection with the FASB. Both the GASB and the FASB may issue guidance on the majority vote of their members. Except for the chair, GASB board members serve on a part-time basis, while their FASB counterparts serve as full-time board members.

Efforts to define GAAP for the federal government are considerably more recent than those just described for businesses and state and local governments. These efforts eventually culminated in the establishment of the Federal Accounting Standards Advisory Board (FASAB). Unlike the FASB and the GASB, the FASAB does *not* function under the auspices of the FAF. Moreover, the Treasury Department, the Office of Management and Budget (OMB), and the Government Accountability Office (GAO) each has veto power over proposed FASAB standards.

Exhibit 1-2 is a chart illustrating the authoritative standard-setting structure for GAAP.

---

[10] All FASB members serve full time; only the chair of the GASB serves on a full-time basis.

EXHIBIT 1-2
The GAAP standard-setting structure

Authoritative GAAP standard-setting body	Number of members	Responsibility for board appointments	Jurisdiction
Financial Accounting Standards Board (FASB)	7 full-time members	Financial Accounting Foundation	Business enterprises and nonprofit organizations
Governmental Accounting Standards Board (GASB)	Full-time chair and 6 part-time members	Financial Accounting Foundation	State and local governments
Federal Accounting Standards Advisory Board (FASAB)	9 part-time members	3 ex-officio members [Treasury Department, Office of Management and Budget (OMB), and Government Accountability Office (GAO)] and 6 members appointed jointly by the Secretary of the Treasury, the Director of OMB, and the Comptroller General*	Federal government

*The six jointly appointed members are public (i.e., nonfederal employees).

A special advisory committee assists with joint appointments. This committee includes the chair of the FASAB; the FASAB ex-officio members from Treasury, OMB, and GAO; and representatives of the FAF, the American Institute of Certified Public Accountants (AICPA), and the AICPA's Accounting Research Association.

Jurisdiction

The jurisdiction of the FASB extends to private-sector businesses as well as nonprofit organizations. The FASAB's jurisdiction covers all agencies of the federal government. The GASB is the ultimate authority on GAAP for state and local governments.

The *state and local governments* category includes all public corporations and bodies corporate and politic. It also includes other types of entities—including nonprofit organizations—that meet at least one of the following criteria:

- Officers of the entity are popularly elected.
- A controlling majority of members of the entity's governing body is appointed (or approved) by officials of at least one state or local government.
- A government is able to unilaterally dissolve the entity, with the entity's net assets reverting to a government.
- The entity has the power to enact *and* enforce a tax levy.
- The entity has the ability to *directly*[11] issue federally tax-exempt debt.

If the only criterion met is the ability to directly issue federally tax-exempt debt, the presumption that an entity is governmental may be rebutted based on *compelling*, relevant evidence.[12]

Some types of entities—utilities, hospitals, colleges, and universities—exist in both the public and private sectors, leading some observers to expect that all such entities would use the same authoritative standards (FASB or GASB) regardless of the sector in which they operate. Others have argued the need for consistency within the public sector, even if the result is

---

[11] Debt that is issued through a state or municipal authority is considered to be issued *indirectly*.
[12] See American Institute of Certified Public Accountants, *State and Local Governments*, Section 1.01.

differences in accounting and financial reporting between similar entities operating in different sectors.

In 1989, the FAF categorically affirmed the GASB's jurisdiction over all entities operating in the public sector, including utilities, hospitals, colleges, and universities. Therefore, the criteria for identifying governmental entities apply to these entities just as they do to all other types. So public-sector utilities, hospitals, and institutions of higher education look to the GASB for GAAP, while their private-sector counterparts turn to the FASB for authoritative guidance.

The American Institute of Certified Public Accountants (AICPA), which represents the independent auditing profession, has officially designated the FASB, the GASB, and the FASAB as the authoritative standard-setting bodies for GAAP in their respective sectors. Further, Rule 203 of the AICPA's *Code of Professional Ethics*, "Accounting Principles," makes it an ethical violation for an auditor to state that financial statements are fairly presented in conformity with GAAP if those statements materially violate FASB, GASB, or FASAB guidance.[13] The Securities and Exchange Commission (SEC), which is legally empowered by federal law to set standards of accounting and financial reporting for companies with publicly traded securities, has also used its power to mandate the use of FASB standards.

Federal law does not allow the SEC or any other agency of the federal government to set standards of accounting and financial reporting for state and local governments,[14] so the SEC does not play the same role for GASB standards that it does for FASB standards. The federal government's Single Audit Act of 1984, however, has done much to promote the use of GASB standards in the public sector.[15] Likewise, state laws mandating GAAP reporting and the GFOA's Certificate of Achievement for Excellence in Financial Reporting Program have been important factors in promoting compliance with GAAP.

The continuing role of the *GAAFR*

As noted, the first three editions of the Blue Book actually set authoritative GAAP for state and local governments. This special role for the Blue Book was eliminated, however, with the advent of the National Council on Governmental Accounting, which made clear that its own pronouncements, rather than the *GAAFR*, would henceforth serve as the official means of promulgating authoritative GAAP.[16]

The NCGA's decision by no means spelled the end of the Blue Book. Rather, the role of the *GAAFR* changed from one of *prescribing* GAAP to one of *describing* how best to implement authoritative guidance. Subsequent editions of the Blue Book were released in 1980, 1988, 1994, and 2001.[17] Moreover, the *GAAFR* continues to serve as a primary reference for the

[13] A special exception applies when unusual circumstances would make the application of an authoritative standard misleading: "If, however, the statements or data contain such a departure and the member can demonstrate that due to unusual circumstances the financial statements or data would otherwise have been misleading, the member can comply with the rule by describing the departure, its approximate effects, if practicable, and the reasons why compliance with the principle would result in a misleading statement." (AICPA, *Professional Standards*, ET 203.01.)
[14] State and local governments are, however, subject to the anti-fraud provisions of federal securities law, as administered by the SEC.
[15] The Single Audit Act does not require the use of GAAP, but it does require that an auditor's opinion be expressed on the basis of GAAP (which is set by the GASB) rather than on the basis of some "other comprehensive basis of accounting" (e.g., cash basis accounting).
[16] NCGA Interpretation 5, *Authoritative Status of Governmental Accounting, Auditing, and Financial Reporting* (1968).

GFOA's Certificate of Achievement for Excellence in Financial Reporting Program.[18]

The standard-setting process

The FASB and the GASB do not set GAAP arbitrarily. Both boards follow carefully designed due-process procedures to ensure that they adequately consider all relevant information as well as the opinions of all interested parties before reaching a final decision on any accounting or financial reporting issue.

The first stage of due process is for the board to identify specific technical issues that may need to be examined. Practical means of identifying potential technical issues include public hearings, consultation with the appropriate advisory council (FASAC or GASAC), and input from individual constituents and organizations. Once a potential issue has been identified, the board makes a preliminary assessment of whether it wishes to pursue the matter by adding the item to the board's official technical agenda, either as a separate project or as an addition to an existing project. Both the FASB and the GASB publish updated technical plans periodically throughout the year.

Once an item has been added to a board's technical agenda, the board's professional staff studies the issue, often assisted by a special task force of experts appointed by the board's chair. At the completion of initial research on a project, the board's staff may elect to issue either an Invitation to Comment (ITC) document or a Discussion Memorandum (DM). The basic purpose of these documents is to solicit the comments of interested parties to ensure that all material ramifications of the issue under study have been considered.

At this stage in due process, the board normally begins to reach its own tentative conclusions on how to address the issue at hand. These conclusions are then offered for public comment in the form of an Exposure Draft (ED). When a matter is particularly controversial or significant, the board may elect to issue a Preliminary Views (PV) document before releasing an ED.

The board actively encourages participation by all interested parties in the standard-setting process. Accordingly, copies of all GASB due-process documents are available for comment through the GASB's Web site.

The purpose of due process is not to poll the board's constituents regarding their preferences; rather, it is to ensure that the board has considered all relevant facts and viewpoints before arriving at a conclusion. While the FASB and the GASB attach great importance to comments from interested parties in response to due-process documents, the final decision on any issue reflects board members' own best judgment regarding the relative merits of the alternatives under consideration.

A chart illustrating the due-process procedures used in establishing authoritative GAAP standards is presented as Exhibit 1-3.

The GAAP hierarchy

The FASB and the GASB play a unique role in defining GAAP in the public and the private sectors. They are not, however, the *only* authoritative

---

[17] In 1998, the *GAAFR Update Supplement* amended the 1994 *GAAFR*, just as the 2002 *GAAFR Update Supplement* amended the 2001 *GAAFR*.
[18] See chapter 14.

EXHIBIT 1-3
The standard-setting process

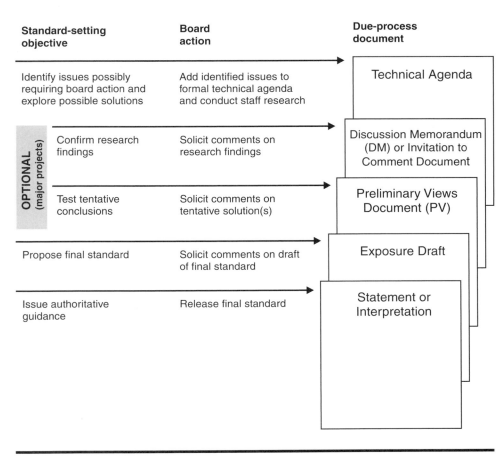

Standard-setting objective	Board action	Due-process document
Identify issues possibly requiring board action and explore possible solutions	Add identified issues to formal technical agenda and conduct staff research	Technical Agenda
Confirm research findings	Solicit comments on research findings	Discussion Memorandum (DM) or Invitation to Comment Document
Test tentative conclusions	Solicit comments on tentative solution(s)	Preliminary Views Document (PV)
Propose final standard	Solicit comments on draft of final standard	Exposure Draft
Issue authoritative guidance	Release final standard	Statement or Interpretation

OPTIONAL (major projects)

sources of GAAP. Also, not all FASB and GASB documents have the same authoritative status.

In 1992, the Auditing Standards Board of the AICPA issued Statement on Auditing Standards (SAS) No. 69, *The Meaning of "Present Fairly in Conformity with Generally Accepted Accounting Principles" in the Independent Auditor's Report.* SAS No. 69 established a hierarchy of authoritative sources of GAAP for nongovernmental entities (business enterprises and nonprofit organizations) and a separate GAAP hierarchy for state and local governmental entities.[19] Both hierarchies are composed of four levels, with higher-level sources (e.g., level 1) taking automatic preference over lower-level sources (e.g., level 4) in cases of potential conflict. Subsequently, SAS No. 69 was amended to include a similar hierarchy of authoritative sources of GAAP for the federal government.[20]

For state and local governments, the GAAP hierarchy can be summarized in the levels described here:

Level 1 GAAP

All GASB statements and interpretations enjoy automatic level 1 status to the extent that they have not been amended or superseded by subsequent pronouncements. GASB Statement No. 1, *Authoritative Status of NCGA Pronouncements and AICPA Industry Audit Guide,* extended this same status to the pronouncements of the GASB's predecessor, the NCGA. Private-sector standards also occasionally enjoy level 1 status as follows:

- *Incorporation by reference.* The NCGA and the GASB have incorporated certain specific private-sector guidance into their own standards by reference. Consequently, such private-sector guidance has level 1 status, *but only because the appropriate public-sector standard-setting body specifically adopted it.* The most important examples of private-sector guidance adopted by reference are:

---

[19] The criteria used to define a state or local governmental entity were described earlier as part of the discussion of jurisdiction.
[20] SAS No. 91, *Federal GAAP Hierarchy* (2000).

—APB Opinion No. 22, *Disclosure of Accounting Policies* (which requires the presentation of a summary of significant accounting policies);

—APB Opinion No. 30, *Reporting the Results of Operations—Reporting the Effects of Disposal of a Segment of a Business, and Extraordinary, Unusual and Infrequently Occurring Events and Transactions* (on extraordinary items);

—FASB Statement No. 5, *Accounting for Contingencies* (for guidance on recognizing a loss liability);

—FASB Statement No. 6, *Classification of Short-Term Obligations Expected to be Refinanced* (in connection with the proper classification of bond anticipation notes);

—FASB Statement No. 13, *Accounting for Leases,* as amended and interpreted; and

—FASB Statement No. 74, *Accounting for Special Termination Benefits Paid to Employees.*[21]

- *Default use of private-sector standards.* It is presumed that all applicable authoritative guidance issued by the FASB and its predecessors (the APB and the CAP) *prior to December 1, 1989,* applies to both government-wide reporting and proprietary fund[22] reporting to the extent that such guidance does not conflict with or contradict applicable GASB guidance.[23] Further, governments have the *option* of consistently following compatible FASB guidance[24] issued *after* the cutoff for those activities reported as enterprise funds (but *not* internal service funds)[25] or as business-type activities in the government-wide financial statements.[26]

Level 2 GAAP

The GASB staff is empowered to issue technical bulletins (TBs), provided a majority of the board's members does not object to their issuance. Technical bulletins normally are limited to matters not expected to cause a major change in practice or to involve significant costs. TBs also may not conflict with a broad fundamental principle or create a novel accounting practice. GASB TBs automatically have level 2 status.

The AICPA has issued Audit Guides (sometimes titled Audit and Accounting Guides) for a number of industries, including *State and Local Governments.* The AICPA also periodically issues Statements of Position (SOPs). The AICPA's Audit Guides and SOPs enjoy level 2 status if: 1) they *specifically* apply to state and local governments; *and* 2) they have been cleared for issuance by the GASB.

As a practical matter, the assertion that a given Audit Guide or SOP is applicable to all entities is *not* considered a specific application to state and local governments. Also, practitioners may presume that the AICPA's

---

[21] FASB Statement No. 74 (as amended by GASB Statement No. 27, *Accounting for Pensions by State and Local Governmental Employers*) remains in effect for state and local governments, even though it was superseded in the private sector by FASB Statement No. 88, *Employer's Accounting for Settlements and Curtailments of Defined Benefit Pension Plans and for Termination Benefits* (1985).

[22] The purpose and use of proprietary funds is examined in chapter 2.

[23] The last pronouncements issued before this December 1, 1989, cutoff were FASB Statement No. 102, *Statement of Cash Flows—Exemption of Certain Enterprises and Classification of Cash Flows from Certain Securities Acquired for Resale,* and FASB Interpretation No. 38, *Determining the Measurement Date for Stock Option, Purchase, and Award Plans Involving Junior Stock.*

[24] That is, guidance that neither conflicts with nor contradicts GASB guidance.

[25] The nature and purpose of enterprise funds and internal service funds are discussed in chapter 2.

[26] GASB Statement No. 34, paragraph 17.

Audit Guides and SOPs that specifically reference state and local governments have been cleared by the GASB absent a notice to the contrary in that same guidance.[27]

Level 3 GAAP

The AICPA's Accounting Standards Executive Committee is authorized to issue Practice Bulletins. A Practice Bulletin issued specifically for state and local governments and cleared by the GASB would merit level 3 status. Also, if the GASB were to establish an Emerging Issues Task Force, as the FASB has, the Consensus Positions reached by that group also would merit level 3 status. To date, no authoritative guidance has been issued that merits level 3 status for state and local governmental entities, nor is it likely that any such guidance will be issued in the foreseeable future.

Level 4 GAAP

The GASB staff issues Implementation Guides in question-and-answer format to help financial statement preparers implement major pronouncements.[28] These Q&As enjoy level 4 status in the hierarchy of governmental GAAP. Also, in the absence of other authoritative sources of GAAP, financial statement preparers are to follow *widely recognized and prevalent practice*, consistent with the fundamental notion of *generally accepted* accounting principles.

If the AICPA were to issue an Audit Guide, SOP, or Practice Bulletin specific to state and local government but *not* cleared by the GASB, that guidance also would have level 4 status.

Other sources

There are, of course, sources of guidance on GAAP other than those just described. These sources include professional publications, textbooks, position papers of professional organizations, and FASB guidance that is not authoritative for governments. Pride of place within this category is held by the GASB's Concepts Statements, which are considered to be more authoritative than any other source of guidance on GAAP outside of the GAAP hierarchy. As a practical matter, the *GAAFR* has been a prime source for information on the application of GAAP in the public sector, based on experience drawn from the GFOA's Certificate of Achievement for Excellence in Financial Reporting Program.[29]

Exhibit 1-4 is a chart illustrating the GAAP hierarchy for state and local governmental entities.

Enforcement

Rule 203 of the AICPA's *Code of Professional Conduct*, which was described earlier, automatically covers all sources of level 1 GAAP. Coverage of the other levels of the GAAP hierarchy is provided by Rule 202 of the *Code of Professional Conduct*, "Compliance with Standards," which places on auditors the burden of proof to justify any material departures from the guidance found in levels 2, 3, or 4 of the GAAP hierarchy.

---

[27] AICPA, *State and Local Governments*, generally repeats the authoritative guidance found in level 1 GAAP. That publication does, however, provide its own specialized guidance on a number of topics listed in Appendix B of that publication.

[28] The GASB also maintains an annually updated *Comprehensive Implementation Guide* that both consolidates and expands upon the information contained in the individual implementation guides.

[29] This program is discussed in detail in chapter 14.

EXHIBIT 1-4
GAAP hierarchy for state and local governments (per Statement on Auditing Standards No. 69)

Level of authority	GASB	AICPA	Other sources	Coverage in AICPA Code of Ethics
Level 1	Statements and Interpretations (including extant guidance of the NCGA and private-sector standards adopted by reference or by default)			Ethics Rule 203
Level 2	Technical Bulletins	Audit Guides/Statements of Position (if specific to government and cleared by the GASB)		Ethics Rule 202
Level 3	Emerging Issues Task Force Consensus Positions [*no guidance extant at this level*]	Accounting Standards Executive Committee Practice Bulletins (if specific to government and cleared by the GASB) [*no guidance extant at this level*]		Ethics Rule 202
Level 4	Implementation Guides	Audit Guides/Statements of Position (if specific to government but not cleared by the GASB) [*no guidance extant at this level*]	Widely recognized and prevalent practice	Ethics Rule 202
Other sources	Concepts Statements		Pronouncements of the FASB not otherwise applicable, textbooks, and articles	Not covered

SUMMARY

State and local governments function in a unique environment. Over the years, accounting and financial reporting for state and local governments have evolved in response to this environment. Characteristic features of governmental accounting and financial reporting include the use of fund accounting, the inclusion of budget-to-actual comparisons as part of general-purpose external financial reporting, and the employment of a special measurement focus and basis of accounting for tax-supported functions. Because there are various primary users of governments' general-purpose external financial reports, these reports tend to be longer and more complex than comparable private-sector reports. GAAP for state and local governments are not the same as GAAP for private-sector entities. The primary source of GAAP for state and local governments is the GASB. The GASB issues authoritative standards only after extensive due process. Other sources of GAAP for state and local governments are set forth in the GAAP hierarchy established by SAS No. 69.

2

The Governmental Financial Reporting Model

State and local governments employ a unique system of accounting and financial reporting commonly referred to as the *governmental financial reporting model*. This model integrates fund accounting, which has deep roots in the public and nonprofit sectors, with the more consolidated financial reporting typical of private-sector businesses. This chapter reviews the origins of fund accounting and the development of an integrated governmental financial reporting model. It then examines the various types of funds used by state and local governments, as well as the differences in the measurement focus and basis of accounting used for different types of funds. The chapter concludes by examining the relationship between fund-based presentations and government-wide financial reporting.

FUND ACCOUNTING AND THE GOVERNMENTAL FINANCIAL REPORTING MODEL

The origins of fund accounting

As a rule, government officials must comply with significant legal restrictions on the use of public resources. External resource providers, such as federal and state grantors, impose some of these restrictions. Other restrictions may be associated with resources (such as pension funds and investment pools) that a government manages in a fiduciary capacity on behalf of individuals or organizations outside the government. Still other restrictions may arise from enabling legislation that requires specific revenues to be used for particular purposes. Most pervasive are the legal restrictions embodied in the government's annual or biennial appropriated budget. Naturally, it is imperative that public-sector managers ensure and demonstrate compliance with these restrictions as well as any other legal restrictions on the use of public resources.

Historically, efforts by state and local governments to ensure and demonstrate legal compliance have not always met with success. At the start of the twentieth century, for example, a number of state and local governments were beset by charges of financial corruption and mismanagement. Critics of the period charged that financial misfeasance and malfeasance were abetted by poor accounting and financial reporting practices. In particular, critics argued that state and local governments needed to segregate their financial resources to ensure that monies were spent only for approved purposes. In response to these criticisms, many governments began to establish separate cash accounts to manage resources dedicated for various purposes.

Of course, improvements in cash management techniques have made multiple cash accounts a thing of the past for most state and local governments. Nonetheless, governments have continued to find value in *accounting* separately for financial resources that are restricted or otherwise earmarked for special purposes. In this manner, the separate cash accounts of the early twentieth century evolved into the funds still used today by state and local governments to ensure and demonstrate legal compliance.

The move to provide government-wide reporting

The Governmental Accounting Standards Board (GASB) has identified *accountability* as the paramount objective of financial reporting.[1] The GASB has further identified two essential components of accountability: *fiscal* accountability and *operational* accountability. *Fiscal accountability* is "the responsibility of governments to justify that their actions in the current period have complied with public decisions concerning the raising and spending of public moneys in the short term (usually one budgetary cycle or one year)."[2] *Operational accountability* refers to "governments' responsibility to report the extent to which they have met their operating objectives efficiently and effectively, using all resources available for that purpose, and whether they can continue to meet their objectives for the foreseeable future."[3]

Fund accounting, specifically designed to help governments ensure and demonstrate legal compliance, is naturally well-suited to achieving the goal of fiscal accountability. Over the years, however, many observers questioned whether fund accounting was equally well-suited to the task of demonstrating operational accountability. They argued that a broader, government-wide focus was needed to adequately assess operational accountability. These concerns motivated the GASB to spend more than a decade studying how the structure of governmental financial reporting (the governmental financial reporting model) could be modified to improve operational accountability without sacrificing fiscal accountability.

The GASB concluded that fund accounting continues to play an important role in helping governments achieve fiscal accountability, and that it should be retained. The board also concluded that government-wide financial statements are needed as well to allow users of financial reports to assess a government's operational accountability. The GASB does not view fund-based financial reporting and government-wide financial reporting

---

[1] GASB Concepts Statement No. 1, *Objectives of Financial Reporting*, paragraph 76.
[2] GASB Statement No. 34, *Basic Financial Statements—and Management's Discussion and Analysis—for State and Local Governments*, paragraph 203.
[3] GASB Statement No. 34, paragraph 203.

as being in conflict; rather, the GASB views both as essential, complementary components of a single integrated and comprehensive financial reporting model. This new model was officially promulgated in 1999 as GASB Statement No. 34, *Basic Financial Statements—and Management's Discussion and Analysis—for State and Local Governments.*

FUNDS AND FUND TYPES

The nature and purpose of funds

Generally accepted accounting principles (GAAP) provide the following authoritative definition of a fund:

> A fund is defined as a fiscal and accounting entity with a self-balancing set of accounts recording cash and other financial resources, together with all related liabilities and residual equities or balances, and changes therein, which are segregated for the purpose of carrying on specific activities or attaining certain objectives in accordance with special regulations, restrictions, or limitations.[4]

Funds served for many years as the focus of financial reporting for state and local governments. This focus now is shared with the government-wide financial statements that were created pursuant to GASB Statement No. 34. The principal role of funds in the new financial reporting model is to demonstrate fiscal accountability.

Number of funds

There is no limit on the number of individual funds a government may use for accounting and financial reporting purposes. In practice, a single government can have less than ten individual funds, or it can have dozens or even hundreds. Nonetheless, a basic principle of governmental accounting says that a government should use the least number of individual funds possible, consistent with its particular circumstances. This *number of funds principle* is enunciated in the authoritative literature:

> Governmental units should establish and maintain those funds required by law and sound financial administration. Only the minimum number of funds consistent with legal and operating requirements should be established, however, since unnecessary funds result in inflexibility, undue complexity, and inefficient financial administration.[5]

It is important in this regard to distinguish *accounting* from *financial reporting.* Whereas an *accounting* system must collect all of the data needed to ensure and demonstrate legal compliance, *financial reporting* is concerned with only those aspects of compliance that are of importance to users of *general purpose* external financial reports. Consequently, not every "fund" used for internal accounting purposes should automatically be classified as a *fund* in general purpose external financial reports.[6]

Fund types and classifications

No matter how many individual funds a government elects to use, all of them can be categorized into one of eleven *fund types*. These eleven fund types can be grouped into three broad classifications: governmental funds,

[4] National Council on Governmental Accounting (NCGA) Statement 1, *Governmental Accounting and Financial Reporting Principles,* paragraph 2.
[5] NCGA Statement 1, paragraph 4.
[6] Government Finance Officers Association (GFOA) recommended practice on "Improving the Effectiveness of Fund Accounting" (2004).

proprietary funds, and fiduciary funds. *Governmental funds* typically are used to account for tax-supported (governmental) activities. *Proprietary funds* are used to account for a government's business-type activities (activities supported, at least in part, by fees or charges). *Fiduciary funds* are used to account for resources that are held by the government as a trustee or agent for parties outside the government and that *cannot* be used to support the government's own programs.

Governmental funds

Five of the eleven fund types established by GAAP are classified as governmental funds: the general fund, special revenue funds, debt service funds, capital projects funds, and permanent funds.

General fund

The general fund is the chief operating fund of a state or local government. GAAP prescribe that the general fund be used "to account for all financial resources except those required to be accounted for in another fund."[7] That is, it is presumed that all of a government's activities are reported in the general fund unless there is a compelling reason to report an activity in some other fund type. This guidance is a practical application of the number of funds principle.

There are at least three compelling reasons to account for a particular activity in some type of fund other than the general fund:

- *GAAP requirements.* In certain instances, GAAP require the use of another fund type. For example, GAAP expressly require that the pension (and other employee benefit) trust fund type be used to report resources that are required to be held in trust for the members and beneficiaries of defined benefit pension plans, defined contribution plans, other postemployment benefit plans, or other employee benefit plans.[8]
- *Legal requirements.* There may be legal requirements that a certain fund type be used to account for a given activity. A government may be legally required, for instance, to establish a debt service fund to account for debt service payments on tax-supported bonded debt, even though the use of a debt service fund may not be required by GAAP in such circumstances.
- *Financial administration.* The demands of sound financial administration may require the use of a fund other than the general fund. For example, a government may find it advantageous to set up a separate private-purpose trust fund to account for its management of escheat assets, as specifically permitted by GAAP,[9] even though it is not required to do so.

GAAP prescribe that a government report only one general fund.[10] If a separate legal entity's data are blended with those of the government, the general fund of the separate legal entity should be reclassified as a special revenue fund.[11]

---

[7] NCGA Statement 1, paragraph 3.
[8] GASB Statement No. 34, paragraph 70.
[9] GASB Statement No. 34, paragraph 72.
[10] GASB Statement No. 14, *The Financial Reporting Entity,* paragraph 54.
[11] The term *component unit* is used to describe a separate legal organization that must be included within a government's financial report because of the nature of its relationship to the government (i.e., economic substance taking precedence over legal form). A *blended* component unit is one whose funds are treated as funds of the government with which it is included. A full discussion of component units and the role they play in defining the financial reporting entity can be found in chapter 4.

Special revenue funds

Often certain revenues are raised for a specific purpose. For example, a government may levy a tax on gasoline with the express purpose of using the proceeds to finance road maintenance and repair. Similarly, legal restrictions on grant proceeds often require that they be spent only for specified purposes. GAAP provide that special revenue funds may be used "to account for the proceeds of specific revenue sources (other than . . . for major capital projects) that are legally restricted to expenditure for specified purposes."[12] This definition is intended to apply to legal restrictions imposed by outside parties, although it commonly is interpreted to apply as well to restrictions imposed on specific resources by the governing body.

The use of a special revenue fund is *almost always permitted (if the criteria are met) rather than required*. That is, governments do not have to use a special revenue fund for any or all of the situations that meet the definition just cited. Indeed, several of the nation's largest local governments use no special revenue funds at all, even though they have numerous grants and earmarked revenues that meet the definition of a special revenue fund. As noted, however, GAAP *do* require the use of a special revenue fund to account for the general fund of a legally separate entity (component unit) that is blended with the government.[13]

Special revenue funds are very common even though their use is essentially voluntary. The popularity of special revenue funds seems to reflect as much a desire to avoid including restricted revenues within the general fund as to provide separate information on the sources and applications of restricted resources.

In addition, GAAP require that states use either a special revenue fund or the general fund to account for their administration of the federal food stamp program.[14]

Sometimes there is a requirement through enabling legislation that a portion of restricted resources be "permanently invested." GAAP expressly indicate that a government may use a special revenue fund in such situations. In that case, *fund balance* would need to distinguish amounts that are available for spending from those that are not.[15]

The use of a risk-financing special revenue fund is *not* appropriate, even when such activities are supported, in whole or in part, by dedicated revenues. If a single fund is to be used for risk financing activities (or for all risk financing activities of a given type), that fund should be either the general fund or an internal service fund.[16]

Debt service funds

Often governments set aside resources to meet current and future debt service requirements on general long-term debt. GAAP permit the use of debt service funds "to account for the accumulation of resources for, and the payment of, general long-term debt principal and interest."[17]

The use of a debt service fund normally is permitted rather than required. There are, however, two specific instances when GAAP require the use of a debt service fund rather than the general fund or some other type of

[12] NCGA Statement 1, paragraph 3.
[13] GASB Statement No. 14, paragraph 54.
[14] GASB Statement No. 24, *Accounting and Financial Reporting for Certain Grants and Other Financial Assistance*, paragraph 6.
[15] GASB, *Comprehensive Implementation Guide (2004)*, 7.248. As noted elsewhere, a permanent fund may be used instead for this purpose.
[16] GASB, *Comprehensive Implementation Guide (2004)*, 3.73.
[17] NCGA Statement 1, paragraph 3.

fund. First, the use of a debt service fund is required if legally mandated. Second, GAAP prescribe the use of a debt service fund "if financial resources are being accumulated for principal and interest payments maturing in future years."[18]

Of course, all debt that has not matured by the end of the fiscal year can be said to be "maturing in future years." Yet, it was clearly *not* intended that the use of a debt service fund be required in situations involving little more than the accumulation of resources for debt service payments due early in the subsequent year. Rather, this provision generally has been interpreted to apply only to accumulations of resources in excess of a full year's principal and interest payments.[19]

It does *not* follow from the decision to establish a debt service fund that all debt service payments related to general long-term debt need be accounted for in that fund. Rather, debt service payments that do not involve the advance accumulation of resources, such as capital leases, commonly are accounted for in the general fund or in a special revenue fund.

Care should be taken in applying the number of funds principle to debt service funds. Sound financial management requires that a government account for each debt issue separately in its accounting system. *General-purpose* external financial reports, however, need not necessarily provide information at this level of detail. Thus, a single debt service fund often may be sufficient for purposes of general-purpose external financial reporting, provided that detailed information on balances related to individual debt issues is properly maintained in the government's accounting system.[20]

Capital projects funds Governments often find it useful to report major capital acquisition and construction separately from their ongoing operating activities. Separate reporting enhances an understanding of the government's capital activities, and it helps to avoid the distortions in financial resources trend information that can arise when capital and operating activities are mixed.

Accordingly, GAAP provide for the use of capital projects funds "to account for financial resources to be used for the acquisition or construction of major capital facilities (other than those financed by proprietary funds and trust funds)."[21] The use of a capital projects fund is especially common for major capital acquisition or construction activities financed through borrowings or contributions. The focus of capital projects fund is on construction and acquisition; they should *not* be used as a sort of "reserve account" to accumulate resources for future capital improvements. Unless there is some legal requirement to use a capital projects fund, the use of the capital projects fund type is permitted rather than required.

It does *not* follow from the decision to establish a capital projects fund that all capital acquisition need be accounted for in that fund. For example, the routine purchase of capitalizable items such as police vehicles typically is reported in the general fund. Rather, the capital projects fund should be reserved for *major* capital acquisition or construction activities, especially

[18] NCGA Statement 1, paragraph 30.
[19] Governments may, however, voluntarily establish debt service funds to account for accumulations of resources for payments due early in the subsequent fiscal year. In practice, governments sometimes budget and accumulate resources in the current period for debt service payments due early in the subsequent period in order to avoid the need for short-term borrowings. A debt service fund may be useful to account for accumulations of resources in such cases.
[20] GFOA recommended practice on "Improving the Effectiveness of Fund Accounting" (2004).
[21] NCGA Statement 1, paragraph 3.

those that would distort financial resources trend data if not reported separately from a government's operating activities.

Once again, care should be taken in applying the number of funds principle to capital projects funds. Sound financial management requires that a government account for each capital project separately in its accounting system. Users of *general-purpose* external financial reports, however, need not necessarily have information presented at this same level of detail. Thus, a single capital projects fund may be sufficient for purposes of general-purpose external financial reporting, provided detailed information on balances related to individual capital projects is properly maintained in the government's accounting system.[22]

Permanent funds

The newest governmental fund type is the permanent fund, first introduced as part of the governmental financial reporting model established by GASB Statement No. 34. Permanent funds should be used "to report resources that are legally restricted to the extent that only earnings, and not principal, may be used for purposes that support the reporting government's programs, that is, for the benefit of the government or its citizenry."[23] Similar arrangements for the benefit of those outside the government (individuals, private organizations, other governments[24]) should be accounted for as private-purpose trust funds rather than permanent funds. A permanent fund would be used, for example, to account for the perpetual care endowment of a municipal cemetery, or for endowments relating to a municipal library or museum.[25]

Sometimes there is a requirement through enabling legislation that a portion of restricted resources be "permanently invested." GAAP expressly indicate that a government may use a permanent fund in such situations. In that case, *fund balance* would need to distinguish amounts that are available for spending from those that are not.[26]

Proprietary funds

Of the eleven fund types established by GAAP, two are classified as proprietary funds. These are enterprise funds and internal service funds.

Enterprise funds

An enterprise fund *may* be used to report any activity for which a fee is charged to external users for goods or services. GAAP also *require* the use of an enterprise fund for any activity whose *principal* external revenue sources meet any of the following criteria:[27]
  • *Debt backed solely by fees and charges.* If issued debt is backed *solely* by fees and charges, an enterprise fund must be used to account for the activity. This sole backing criterion encompasses debt secured, in part, by a portion of the debt proceeds themselves (reserve funds), but *not* debt that is also secondarily secured by the full faith and credit of the government.

---

[22] GFOA recommended practice on "Improving the Effectiveness of Fund Accounting" (2004).
[23] GASB Statement No. 34, paragraph 65.
[24] The term "other governments" is intended to apply to governments outside the financial reporting entity (i.e., *not* discretely presented component units), as described in chapter 4.
[25] The use of a permanent fund is not required for special-purpose governments that are engaged solely in business-type activities. Instead, such entities need report only a corresponding balance of restricted net assets. See GASB, *Comprehensive Implementation Guide (2004)*, 7.250.
[26] GASB, *Comprehensive Implementation Guide (2004)*, 7.248. As noted elsewhere in this chapter, a special revenue fund may be used instead for this purpose.
[27] GASB Statement No. 34, paragraph 67.

- *Legal requirement to recover cost.*[28] An enterprise fund must be used if the cost of providing services for an activity (including capital costs such as depreciation or debt service) must legally be recovered through fees or charges.
- *Policy decision to recover cost.*[29] It is necessary to use an enterprise fund if the government's policy is to establish activity fees or charges designed to recover the cost of providing services (including capital costs such as depreciation or debt service).

In addition, GAAP mandate the use of enterprise funds for the separately issued financial statements of public-entity risk pools. Public-entity risk pools also are accounted for as enterprise funds when they are included within a sponsoring government's report, provided the sponsor is *not* the predominant participant in the arrangement. Otherwise, the use of either the general fund or an internal service fund is required.[30]

GAAP specifically direct that an enterprise fund be used to account for state unemployment compensation benefit plans. This directive is the practical application of the rule discussed earlier that an enterprise fund should be used in situations where there is a legal requirement to recover the full cost of an activity.[31] Administrative costs associated with state unemployment compensation benefit plans, however, normally should *not* be reported in an enterprise fund. The reason for this difference in treatment is that the charges in the fund providing unemployment benefits are *not* designed to recover administrative costs; therefore, the inclusion of administrative costs in that fund would be inconsistent with the cost-recovery focus that led to the selection of an enterprise fund in the first place.[32]

Public colleges and universities may elect to account for their activities in an enterprise fund.[33] An advantage of using an enterprise fund for this purpose is that enterprise fund accounting in many important respects resembles the accounting and financial reporting used by private-sector colleges and universities in conformity with Financial Accounting Standards Board (FASB) Statement No. 117, *Financial Statements of Not-for-Profit Organizations*. Furthermore, public colleges and universities are free to use separate enterprise funds to report different sorts of business-type activities (e.g., auxiliary enterprises and health care facilities). In that case, however, each enterprise fund must qualify as an *activity* in its own right. It would *not* be appropriate, for example, to use separate funds for other types of disaggregation (e.g., classes of net assets).[34]

Finally, enterprise fund use is *permitted* for all governmental entities that were using traditional not-for-profit accounting as of the date of adoption

[28] Cost for this purpose means all direct costs. Thus a legal requirement to recover a specified percentage of costs does not require the use of an enterprise fund. Likewise, the exclusion of any direct cost (e.g., pension contributions) nullifies this requirement. See GASB, *Comprehensive Implementation Guide (2004)*, 7.261, 7.262, and 7.263.
[29] Cost for this purpose means all direct costs. Thus a policy decision to recover a specified percentage of costs does not require the use of an enterprise fund. Likewise, the exclusion of any direct cost (e.g., pension contributions) nullifies this requirement. See GASB, *Comprehensive Implementation Guide (2004)*, 7.261, 7.262, and 7.263.
[30] GASB Statement No. 10, *Accounting and Financial Reporting for Risk Financing and Related Insurance Issues*, paragraph 76.
[31] GASB Statement No. 34, footnote 34.
[32] GASB, *Comprehensive Implementation Guide (2004)*, 7.257.
[33] GASB Statement No. 35, *Basic Financial Statements—and Management's Discussion and Analysis—for Public Colleges and Universities*.
[34] GASB, *Comprehensive Implementation Guide (2004)*, 7.400.

of GASB Statement No. 34 (June 1999), even if their activities do not otherwise meet the criteria for using an enterprise fund.[35]

In practice, enterprise funds frequently are used to account for activities whose costs are only partially funded by fees and charges. For example, transit districts commonly are reported in enterprise funds, even though their primary source of financing often comes from subsidies rather than fare box revenues. Enterprise funds are considered useful in such cases because they focus attention on the cost of providing services, and they serve to highlight the portion of that cost being borne by taxpayers.

Combining activities that are not homogeneous in a single enterprise fund could obscure the connection between revenues and related expenses. Accordingly, separate enterprise funds normally are used to account for nonhomogeneous activities. This practice is considered consistent with the number of funds principle because it is needed for sound financial management.

Internal service funds

Governments often wish to centralize certain services (for instance, motor pool) and then allocate the cost of those services within the government. In certain cases, these centralized services also may be provided on a cost-reimbursement basis to component units or even to other governments. GAAP permit internal service funds to be used "to report any activity that provides goods or services to other funds, departments, or agencies of the primary government and its component units, or to other governments, on a cost-reimbursement basis."[36] If other governments are involved, the use of an internal service fund is only appropriate if the sponsoring government is itself the predominant participant in the activity. Otherwise, an enterprise fund should be used.

The use of an internal service fund is *never required* under GAAP. Nonetheless, internal service funds commonly are used for a wide variety of activities, including central garages and motor pools, duplicating and printing services, information systems, purchasing, and central stores.

GAAP specifically mention the internal service fund, along with the general fund, as one of two possible choices for reporting a government's risk financing activities.[37]

As noted earlier, internal service funds are specifically designed for goods or services that are provided *on a cost-reimbursement basis*. That is, the goal of an internal service fund should be to measure the *full cost* of providing goods or services for the purpose of *fully recovering* that cost through fees or charges. Full cost, for this purpose, includes the cost of capital assets used in providing goods or services to customers. If a government does *not* intend to recover the full cost of providing goods or services, *including some measure of the cost of capital assets,* the use of an internal service fund would *not* be appropriate.

---

[35] GASB Statement No. 34, paragraph 147. Before GASB Statement No. 34, the use of traditional not-for-profit standards by certain governmental entities was expressly permitted by GASB Statement No. 29, *The Use of Not-for-Profit Accounting and Financial Reporting Principles by Governmental Entities.*
[36] GASB Statement No. 34, paragraph 68.
[37] GASB Statement No. 10, paragraph 63. Governments are free to account for some types of risk in the general fund and other types of risk in an internal service fund provided all risks of a given type are reported in the same fund. Conversely, governments may choose to have each fund account for its own risks rather than to use a single fund for this purpose. See GASB, *Comprehensive Implementation Guide (2004),* 3.72.

The cost of capital assets can be charged out to internal service fund customers in a variety of ways. One method is to set the amount of the charge based on depreciation expense. If debt is used to acquire capital assets, however, the amount of the charge may be set based on debt service requirements—especially when the estimated life of the capital asset significantly exceeds the term of the related debt—to provide adequate cash flow for debt service payments. Another approach, consistent with the going-concern assumption, is to set charges for capital assets based on the replacement cost of those assets rather than their historical cost. This last approach, while suitable for managerial and financial reporting purposes, typically is *not* acceptable to grantors, who usually are unwilling to anticipate *future* funding needs.

Fiduciary funds

Four of the eleven fund types used by state and local governments are classified as *fiduciary funds*. GAAP indicate that fiduciary funds should be used "to report assets held in a trustee or agency capacity for others and therefore cannot be used to support the government's own programs."[38] Fiduciary funds include pension (and other employee benefit) trust funds, investment trust funds, private-purpose trust funds, and agency funds. The key distinction between trust funds and agency funds is that trust funds normally are subject to "a trust agreement that affects the degree of management involvement and the length of time that the resources are held." [39]

Pension (and other employee benefit) trust funds

GAAP indicate that pension (and other employee benefit) trust funds "should be used to report resources that are required to be held in trust for the members and beneficiaries of defined benefit pension plans, defined contribution plans, other postemployment benefit plans, or other employee benefit plans."[40] The mere fact that a government offers pension benefits or other benefits to its employees does *not* necessarily mean that the government should report a pension (and other employee benefit) trust fund. Rather, the critical factor is whether a government is *holding resources in trust* for that purpose. Thus, in the case of a state-administered pension system, the state, not the participating governmental employers, would report a pension (and other employee benefit) trust fund.

GAAP require the use of separate trust funds for each individual pension *plan*. A pension plan is an arrangement where all assets accumulated for the payment of benefits may legally be used to pay any member or beneficiary. If certain assets are legally restricted to the payment of certain members or beneficiaries, then there is more than one pension plan for financial reporting purposes. It is possible, of course, to have separate actuarial valuations—or even separate reserves, funds, or accounts—and still be a single pension plan, provided all assets accumulated to pay benefits may legally be used to pay any beneficiary. Conversely, resource pooling for investment purposes does not mean there is a single pension plan so long as certain assets may only be used to pay certain beneficiaries.

Resources accumulated for postemployment benefits other than pensions should be accounted for in a separate trust fund from resources accumulated for pension benefits.[41]

---

[38] GASB Statement No. 34, paragraph 69.
[39] GASB Statement No. 34, paragraph 69.
[40] GASB Statement No. 34, paragraph 70.

Sometimes governments sponsor Internal Revenue Code (IRC) Section 457 deferred compensation plans for their employees. Normally, such plans are *not* reported in the sponsoring employer's financial statements, because sponsors typically remit employee contributions directly to a third-party administrator who holds the assets in trust. In those limited instances where a sponsor of an IRC Section 457 deferred compensation plan does, in fact, hold the plan's assets as a fiduciary, the plan should be accounted for in a pension (and other employee benefit) trust fund.[42]

Investment trust funds

Governments sometimes sponsor arrangements in which legally separate governments commingle or pool their resources in an investment portfolio for the benefit of all participants. Such arrangements are commonly known as external investment pools. For example, a state may sponsor an investment pool for the benefit of its local governments. If the sponsoring government is a participant, the arrangement is referred to as a *mixed pool*.

GAAP require that a government report any external investment pool that it sponsors as an investment trust fund. In the case of mixed pools, the investment trust fund reports only the external portion of the pool's resources (the portion that does not belong to the government or its component units).[43]

Also, governments sometimes hold specific investments on behalf of units outside the government (including its component units). For example, a county treasurer may hold individual investments on behalf of local governments within the county. GAAP refers to such holdings as *individual investment accounts*,[44] which, like external investment pools, must be reported in an investment trust fund.

GAAP require the use of a separate investment trust fund for each individual external investment pool that a government sponsors.[45] Likewise, individual investment accounts should be reported in a fund separate from external investment pools when the individual accounts are offered as an alternative to a pooled position.[46]

Private-purpose trust funds

GAAP indicate that a private-purpose trust fund may be used to report any trust arrangement not properly reported in a pension trust fund or an investment trust fund "under which principal and income benefit individuals, private organizations, or other governments."[47] The use of private-purpose trust funds normally should be limited to situations where *specific* benefits accrue to *specific* individuals, organizations or governments.[48] The authoritative accounting literature provides the specific example of escheat property in situations where a government has elected to establish a separate fund for this purpose.[49] Another example of the proper use of a private-purpose trust fund would be a state-sponsored college tui-

---

[41] GASB Statement No. 43, *Financial Reporting for Postemployment Benefit Plans Other Than Pension Plans*, requires that public employee retirement systems report each individual other postemployment benefit plan they administer as a separate fund in its own right (paragraph 13).
[42] GASB, *Comprehensive Implementation Guide (2004)*, 7.268.
[43] GASB Statement No. 31, *Accounting and Financial Reporting for Certain Investments and for External Investment Pools*, paragraph 18.
[44] GASB Statement No. 31, paragraph 20.
[45] GASB Statement No. 31, paragraph 18.
[46] GASB Statement No. 31, paragraph 20, footnote 11.
[47] GASB Statement No. 34, paragraph 72.
[48] GASB Statement No. 34, paragraph 72. For this purpose, *other governments* does not include discretely presented component units. See GASB, *Comprehensive Implementation Guide (2004)*, 7.270 and 7.266.

tion savings arrangement, provided the program did not involve any form of government commitment (which would convert the arrangement into a government program).

Of course, government programs too may sometimes provide what might be described as specific benefits to specific individuals. How then are private-purpose trusts to be distinguished from such government programs (which, by definition, *cannot* be reported in a fiduciary fund)? In the case of a private-purpose trust fund, there should be virtually no discretion in determining what specific amount in the trust accrues to which specific individual.

If some resources may be used to support government programs and others may not, only the latter may be reported in a private-purpose trust fund.[50]

Agency funds

Agency funds, unlike trust funds, typically do *not* involve a formal trust agreement. Rather, agency funds are used to account for situations where the government's role is purely custodial, such as the receipt, temporary investment, and remittance of fiduciary resources to individuals, private organizations, or other governments. Accordingly, all assets reported in an agency fund are offset by a liability to the party on whose behalf they are held.

Agency funds are most commonly used to account for taxes collected by one government on behalf of other governments. For example, when multiple local governments have the power to levy taxes on the same property, it is common practice for all of the separately levied taxes to be billed and collected by a single government (for instance, the county). The collecting government commonly will use an agency fund to account for the portion of taxes collected on behalf of other governments until those amounts are eventually remitted to the governments that levied them.

GAAP *require* the use of an agency fund to account for debt service transactions involving special assessment debt for which the government is not obligated in any manner.[51] That is, property tax collections related to the repayment of no-commitment special assessment debt must be accounted for in an agency fund pending their remittance to bondholders. Likewise, GAAP *require* that postemployment benefit plans other than pension plans that do *not* qualify as trusts or equivalent arrangements be reported in an agency fund.[52]

GAAP also mandate the use of an agency fund to account for pass-through grants that are equivalent to pure cash conduits. To qualify as a pure cash conduit, a grant must meet two criteria. First, the government must have no administrative involvement with the program. Examples of disqualifying administrative involvement include monitoring subrecipients for compliance with program-specific requirements, determining eligible subrecipients (even if using grantor-established criteria), and being able to exercise discretion in how funds are allocated.

---

[49] Only that portion of escheat resources whose eventual repayment to individuals is considered probable may be reported in a private-purpose trust fund. See GASB, *Comprehensive Implementation Guide (2004),* 7.272.
[50] GASB, *Comprehensive Implementation Guide (2004),* 7.269.
[51] GASB Statement No. 6, *Accounting and Financial Reporting for Special Assessments,* paragraph 19.
[52] GASB Statement No. 43, paragraph 41.

The second criterion is that the government have no *direct* financial involvement with the grant program. Examples of direct financial involvement that would disqualify a grant from being reported in an agency fund include a requirement to finance some direct program costs (such as matching requirements) and exposure to liability for disallowed costs.

These criteria do not address *indirect* financial involvement with pass-through grants because such involvement would likely arise only in connection with administrative functions, and those functions already fall within the scope of the first criterion. As a practical matter, it is rare for a grant to qualify as a pure cash conduit based on these criteria.[53]

Because of their degree of administrative involvement with Pell Grant requirements, colleges and universities should *not* use agency funds to account for these grants.[54] Also, a provider government should not use an agency fund to account for its own unexpended resources intended to fund an expenditure-driven grant or similar arrangement (e.g., the unexpended proceeds of debt issued to finance the grant). The use of an agency fund would not be appropriate in this latter case because the unexpended resources remain the assets of the provider government until qualifying expenditures have been incurred and compliance with any other eligibility requirements related to the grant has been achieved.[55]

Finally, as a practical matter, a government may use an agency fund as an internal clearing account for amounts that have yet to be allocated to individual funds. This practice is perfectly appropriate *for internal accounting purposes*. However, *for external financial reporting purposes*, GAAP expressly limit the use of fiduciary funds, including agency funds, to assets "held in a trustee or agency capacity for others" and that, therefore, "*cannot be used to support the government's own programs*."[56] Therefore, all assets accounted for in an internal agency fund must be allocated to the appropriate funds and component units of the government in external general-purpose financial reports.[57]

MEASUREMENT FOCUS AND BASIS OF ACCOUNTING

As noted in chapter 1, governments have different financial objectives for their tax-supported (governmental) and business-type (proprietary) activities. State and local governments traditionally have provided different types of information for each type of activity. Accountants describe these disparities between governmental funds and proprietary funds as differences in *measurement focus* and *basis of accounting*.

Measurement focus

Measurement focus is commonly used to describe the types of transactions and events that are reported in a fund's operating statement. The operating statement of a proprietary fund focuses on changes in *economic* resources, much like that of a private-sector business. That is, the goal of the proprietary fund operating statement is to answer the question, "What transactions and events have increased or decreased the fund's *total economic*

---

[53] GASB Statement No. 24, paragraph 5.
[54] GASB, *Comprehensive Implementation Guide (2004)*, 7.323.
[55] GASB, *Comprehensive Implementation Guide (2004)*, 7.267.
[56] GASB Statement No. 34, paragraph 69 [emphasis added].
[57] GASB Statement No. 34, paragraph 111.

resources during the period?" Net assets (total assets less total liabilities) are used as a practical measure of economic resources for this purpose. Accordingly, a proprietary fund's operating statement includes all transactions and events that increase or decrease net assets, such as revenues, expenses, gains, and losses. Conversely, the operating statement of a proprietary fund does *not* report the following transactions:

- *The issuance of debt.* No increase or decrease in net assets occurs as the result of the issuance of debt because the assets received are offset by the related liability incurred. Therefore, the issuance of debt is not reported in the operating statement of a proprietary fund.
- *Debt service principal payments.* The repayment of the principal of debt does not increase or decrease net assets because the reduction in the amount of debt outstanding is offset by the related reduction in cash resulting from the repayment. Consequently, the repayment of the principal of debt is not reported on a proprietary fund's operating statement.
- *Capital outlay.* Capital outlay is the exchange of one asset (cash) for another (capital asset), with no ultimate effect on net assets. Thus, proprietary funds do not report capital outlays in their operating statement. A decrease in net assets does occur, however, as a capital asset is exhausted through use. This decrease in net assets is reported as depreciation expense in a proprietary fund's operating statement.

The operating statement of a governmental fund, unlike that of a proprietary fund (or private-sector business), focuses on changes in *current financial resources.* Here the goal of the operating statement is to answer the question, "What are the transactions or events of the period that have increased or decreased the *resources available for spending in the near future*?" Consequently, the operating statement of a governmental fund includes all transactions and events that affect the fund's current financial resources, even though they may have no effect on net assets. Such transactions include:

- *The issuance of debt.* While the issuance of debt does not increase or decrease a government's net assets, it does increase a government's current financial resources (cash). Indeed, it can be said that the fundamental purpose of any long-term borrowing is to provide more resources for spending in the near future. Therefore, the issuance of debt is reported in the operating statement of a governmental fund.
- *Debt service principal payments.* The repayment of the principal of long-term debt results in an equal reduction of assets (cash) and liabilities (debt principal outstanding), with no overall effect on net assets. Nonetheless, the repayment of long-term debt principal requires the use of cash, thus decreasing the resources available for spending in the near future. Consequently, the repayment of the principal of long-term debt is reported in a governmental fund's operating statement.
- *Capital outlay.* The purchase or construction of a capital asset is essentially the exchange of one asset for another. It also represents the exchange of an asset that can be spent (cash) for an asset that cannot be spent, thus resulting in a net decrease in current financial resources. This decrease is reported in a governmental fund's operat-

ing statement. Conversely, the operating statement of a governmental fund would not report depreciation on capital assets because the exhaustion of capital assets does not affect a fund's current financial resources. Viewed another way, depreciation is an allocation of previously incurred cost rather than a demand on current financial resources.

Assume, for example, that a government borrows $20,000 to acquire equipment. The equipment is expected to have a useful life of 10 years, with no anticipated salvage value. Further assume that $5,000 of the principal of the debt will be repaid at the end of each of the next four years, and that the interest rate on the borrowing is 5 percent per year. Here are the appropriate journal entries in a proprietary fund to reflect this situation during the first year:

	DR	CR
Cash	$ 20,000	
Bonds payable		$ 20,000
(To record the receipt of the proceeds of bonds)		
Equipment	20,000	
Cash		20,000
(To record the purchase of equipment)		
Bonds payable	5,000	
Interest expense	1,000	
Cash		6,000
(To record the payment of principal and interest on bonds)		
Depreciation expense	2,000	
Accumulated depreciation		2,000
(To record depreciation on equipment)		

This same situation would be recorded quite differently in a governmental fund, consistent with a governmental fund's focus on current financial resources:

	DR	CR
Cash	$ 20,000	
Other financing source[58]		$ 20,000
(To record the receipt of the proceeds of bonds)		
Expenditure—capital outlay[59]	20,000	
Cash		20,000
(To record the purchase of equipment)		
Expenditure—debt service principal	5,000	
Expenditure—debt service interest	1,000	
Cash		6,000
(To record the payment of principal and interest on bonds)		

---

[58] This is one of two categories used to describe increases in current financial resources. A detailed discussion of *other financing sources* is provided in chapter 5.

[59] Notice the distinction between *expense* (a decrease in economic resources) and *expenditure* (a decrease in current financial resources).

EXHIBIT 2-1
Illustration of the difference in measurement focus
between governmental and proprietary funds

Transaction or event	Governmental funds	Proprietary funds
Issuance of debt	+$20,000	No effect
Capital outlay	-$20,000	No effect
Debt service principal repayment	-$20,000	No effect
Depreciation expense	No effect	-$20,000
Ultimate net effect on the operating statement	-$20,000	-$20,000

As noted earlier, a governmental fund would not report depreciation expense, as the exhaustion of capital assets does not directly affect a government's current financial resources.

Eventually the *net effect* of either measurement focus on the operating statement is identical. The fact that governmental funds recognize an operating statement inflow in connection with the issuance of debt is ultimately offset by the fact that governmental funds also recognize an operating statement outflow in connection with the repayment of debt service principal. Likewise, both governmental and proprietary funds ultimately recognize identical outflows in connection with capital assets—governmental funds in the form of capital outlay expenditures, and proprietary funds in the form of depreciation expense. Exhibit 2-1 illustrates this principle using the example just discussed.

A remaining practical difference in measurement focus between governmental funds and proprietary funds involves the principle of deferral and amortization. Proprietary funds attempt to match the cost of providing goods and services with the resulting revenues received from customers. To accomplish this goal, the effect of certain transactions and events is deferred and amortized over subsequent periods. So, for example, the costs associated with debt issuance are not reported as an expense of the period in which they are incurred (i.e., deferral), but instead are reported as an adjustment to income (i.e., amortization) throughout the period during which the related debt is outstanding. A similar approach is taken in proprietary funds to prepaid items (such as rent or insurance), inventories (such as supplies and materials), and discounts and premiums on debt. A prime example of this principle is the capitalization and subsequent depreciation of capital assets (discussed earlier).

Governmental funds, of course, do not attempt to match revenues and related costs. They focus instead on increases and decreases in current financial resources, so the principle of deferral and amortization does not apply to governmental funds. Issuance costs, for example, are reported as expenditures in governmental funds as soon as they are incurred. Likewise, prepaid items and inventories may be written off when purchased.[60] In the

---

[60] As discussed in chapter 5, governmental funds have the option of reporting both prepaid items and inventories on a consumption basis, just like proprietary funds.

same way, premiums and discounts on debt are not deferred and amortized to subsequent periods in governmental funds.

Basis of accounting

A fund's measurement focus, as already discussed, has to do with the types of events or transactions reported in the operating statement (for example, expenses versus expenditures). Once it has been determined whether a fund is to measure changes in total economic resources or changes in current financial resources, the next issue to be addressed is the *timing* of the recognition of transactions and events. The technical term that describes the criteria governing the timing of the recognition of transactions and events is *basis of accounting*.

As a practical matter, a fund's basis of accounting is inseparably tied to its measurement focus. Funds that focus on total economic resources (i.e., proprietary funds) employ the accrual basis of accounting, which recognizes increases and decreases in economic resources as soon as the underlying event or transaction occurs. Thus, under accrual accounting, revenues are recognized as soon as they are earned and expenses are recognized as soon as a liability is incurred, regardless of the timing of related cash inflows and outflows.

On the other hand, funds that focus on current financial resources (governmental funds) use the *modified* accrual basis of accounting, which recognizes increases and decreases in financial resources only to the extent that they reflect near-term inflows or outflows of cash. Under the modified accrual basis of accounting, then, amounts are recognized as revenue when earned, only so long as they are collectible within the period or soon enough afterwards to be used to pay liabilities of the current period.[61] That is, revenues are only recognized under modified accrual accounting to the degree that they are *available* to finance expenditures of the fiscal period. Similarly, debt service payments and a number of specific accrued liabilities[62] are only recognized as expenditures when payment is due because it is only at that time that they normally are liquidated with expendable available financial resources.

Assume, for example, that a proprietary fund is used to report the activities of a municipal water utility. In that case, revenue would be reported as soon as services are provided (i.e., revenue recognized as earned) and vacation leave would be reported as an expense as earned by employees (i.e., expense recognized as soon as a liability is incurred). Conversely, if a governmental fund were used to account for that same municipal water utility, revenue would only be recognized to the extent that collections on billings are made soon enough to be considered *available*. Likewise, an expenditure would be recognized in connection with accrued vacation leave only to the extent that the liability for vacation leave is either liquidated or payable as of the end of the period (in the case of terminated employees who have not yet been paid for unused leave). In both cases, the net amounts of expense/expenditure ultimately recognized in the operating statement would be identical.

[61] NCGA Statement 1, paragraph 62.
[62] These liabilities include obligations for claims and judgments, compensated absences, special termination benefits, landfill closure and postclosure care costs, a government's net pension obligation as an employer, a government's net obligation for other postemployment benefits as an employer, and operating leases with scheduled rent increases.

EXHIBIT 2-2
Measurement focus and basis of accounting by fund type

Fund category	Fund type	Measurement focus		Basis of accounting	
		Economic resources	Current financial resources	Accrual	Modified accrual
Governmental funds	General fund		X		X
	Special revenue fund		X		X
	Debt service fund		X		X
	Capital projects fund		X		X
	Permanent fund		X		X
Proprietary funds	Enterprise fund	X		X	
	Internal service fund	X		X	
Fiduciary funds	Pension (and other employee benefit) trust fund	X		X	
	Investment trust fund	X		X	
	Private-purpose trust fund	X		X	
	Agency fund	Not applicable		X	

The application of measurement focus and basis of accounting to fiduciary funds

All trust funds employ the same economic resources measurement focus and accrual basis of accounting as do proprietary funds. Thus, the discussion of measurement focus and basis of accounting just provided for proprietary funds applies equally to trust funds. Agency funds, however, are unlike all other types of funds, reporting only assets and liabilities. So agency funds cannot be said to have a measurement focus (i.e., since they do not report equity they cannot present an operating statement reporting changes in equity). They do, however, use the accrual basis of accounting to recognize receivables and payables. Exhibit 2-2 summarizes how the concepts of measurement focus and basis of accounting apply to the different types of funds.

FUNDS AND GOVERNMENT-WIDE REPORTING

As noted earlier, perhaps the most salient feature of governmental accounting and financial reporting is the juxtaposition of fund-based financial statements and government-wide financial statements in a single, integrated model. The primary role of the fund-based financial statements in this model is to demonstrate fiscal accountability, while the government-wide financial statements are aimed primarily at demonstrating operational accountability. The minimum combination of 1) fund-based financial statements, 2) government-wide financial statements, and 3) accompanying note disclosures needed for fair presentation of a government's finances in conformity with GAAP is known as the *basic financial statements.*

Fund-based reporting

As already explained, all eleven fund types belong to one of three fund classifications: governmental funds, proprietary funds, and fiduciary funds. The basic financial statements include a separate set of financial statements for each of these fund classifications. In the case of governmental funds, information must be presented separately for each major governmental fund (with information on nonmajor governmental funds reported in the aggregate). Likewise, each major enterprise fund must be reported separately in the proprietary fund financial statements (internal service funds are reported by fund type). Fiduciary fund financial statements, on the other hand, report information solely on the basis of fund type.[63]

Governmental funds are required to report two basic financial statements. The balance sheet serves as the statement of position for governmental funds, while the statement of revenues, expenditures, and changes in fund balances constitutes the statement of activities for those same funds. In addition, governments normally[64] may elect to present budget-to-actual comparisons for the general fund and each individual major special revenue fund with a legally adopted annual (or biennial) budget as part of the basic financial statements rather than as required supplementary information (RSI).[65] Governmental funds do *not* present a statement of cash flows, since the modified accrual basis of accounting is sufficiently close to the cash basis of accounting to effectively eliminate the need for a separate statement of cash flows.

Proprietary funds, like private-sector businesses, are required to present three basic financial statements whose formats are somewhat different from those of their private-sector counterparts. Private-sector businesses take a capital maintenance approach to preparing their financial statements. This approach carefully distinguishes the portion of net assets provided by owners and investors (such as owner's equity, capital stock, paid-in capital in excess of par) from the portion of net assets generated from operations (retained earnings). Proprietary funds, on the other hand, focus on limitations on the use of net assets (invested in capital assets net of related debt; restricted; unrestricted) rather than on the source of those assets. Accordingly, proprietary funds report a statement of net assets and a statement of revenues, expenses, and changes in net assets rather than the balance sheet and operating statement used by private-sector businesses.[66]

Both proprietary funds and private-sector businesses report a statement of cash flows as their third basic financial statement. The statement of cash flows presented by proprietary funds, however, reports cash flows in four separate categories (operating, noncapital financing, capital and related fi-

---

[63] A detailed discussion of the criteria used to identify major funds is provided in chapter 10.

[64] The exception is situations where the framework used for budgeting cannot be meaningfully reconciled with the fund structure used for financial reporting.

[65] RSI consists of certain information that the GASB has specified must accompany the financial statements for fair presentation in conformity with GAAP. RSI is subject to certain limited procedures by the independent auditor but is not included within the scope of the audited financial statements. Conversely, budget-to-actual comparisons that are voluntarily included within the basic financial statements would be included within the scope of the independent auditor's opinion.

[66] A proprietary fund may use a balance sheet format for its statement of position. All the same, the equity section of that balance sheet would still reflect a net assets focus rather than a capital maintenance focus.

nancing, and investing), while a private-sector statement of cash flows reports only three cash flow categories (operating, financing, and investing). Also, despite the similarities in terminology, there are significant differences between the two sectors in how the various categories of cash flows are defined.

In the case of fiduciary funds, trust funds report two basic financial statements—a statement of fiduciary net assets and a statement of changes in fiduciary net assets—while agency funds report only a statement of fiduciary net assets. As a practical matter, cash flow information has been considered of limited relevance to certain entities involved primarily in the investment function.[67] Since most fiduciary funds are significantly involved in the investment function (e.g., pension trust funds, investment trust funds), the GASB has declined to make the statement of cash flows a basic financial statement for fiduciary funds.

Government-wide reporting

Government-wide financial statements are aimed at presenting a broad overview of a government's finances. There are two basic government-wide financial statements: the statement of net assets and the statement of activities. These two statements report a government's *governmental* activities[68] separately from its *business-type* activities.[69] By definition, the resources of fiduciary funds are *not* available to support government programs. Consequently, it would be confusing or even potentially misleading to include fiduciary fund resources along with a government's own resources in a broadly focused overview presentation. Therefore, fiduciary funds and fiduciary-type component units are excluded from the government-wide financial statements.

All activities included within the government-wide financial statements, both governmental and business-type, are measured and reported using the economic resources measurement focus and the accrual basis of accounting. Governmental funds, however, as noted earlier, measure and report activities using the current financial resources measurement focus and the modified accrual basis of accounting. As a result, the data reported in the governmental fund financial statements must be converted to the economic resources measurement focus and the accrual basis of accounting before those data can be reported as governmental activities in the government-wide financial statements. This conversion is presented as a reconciliation in connection with the governmental fund financial statements (either on the face of the statements or as an accompanying schedule).

Internal service funds are proprietary funds, just like enterprise funds. Unlike enterprise funds, however, internal service funds typically exist for the principal purpose of supporting activities reported in governmental funds. So the residual balances (i.e., after consolidation) of internal service funds normally are included in the governmental activities column of the government-wide financial statements rather than in the business-type activities column. The inclusion of internal service funds within the business-type activities column would be appropriate, however, in situations

[67] Thus in the private sector, the FASB exempted defined benefit pension plans, certain other employee benefit plans, and certain highly liquid investment companies from the requirement to present a statement of cash flows. These exemptions are set forth in FASB Statement No. 102, *Statement of Cash Flows—Exemption of Certain Enterprises and Classification of Cash Flows from Certain Securities Acquired for Resale.*
[68] *Governmental activities* normally include all activities reported in governmental funds.
[69] *Business-type activities* normally comprise all activities reported in enterprise funds.

where those funds do, in fact, principally support enterprise fund activities. Situations sometimes arise where fiduciary funds are the primary consumers of the goods or services produced by an internal service fund. It would be impossible to follow the example of enterprise funds (as just discussed) and include the residual balances of such an internal service fund with fiduciary activities, because the latter are not reported in the government-wide financial statements. Instead, GAAP direct that the residual balances of internal service funds that predominantly serve fiduciary funds be included as part of governmental activities.[70]

In addition to separate columns devoted to governmental and business-type activities, GAAP also require that the government-wide financial statements present a consolidated total column for the primary government.[71] Consolidation means that the effects of intragovernmental activity are eliminated from the financial statements. A special exception applies, however, to interfund services that are not equivalent to overhead (e.g., the sale of electricity from a utility to the general government). Eliminating such interfund services "would misstate both the expenses of the purchasing function and the program revenues of the selling function."[72]

Besides providing separate information on the governmental and business-type activities of the primary government, as well as consolidated data that combine both, the government-wide financial statements also present information on a government's discretely presented component units.[73]

The relationship between government-wide and fund-based financial reporting is illustrated in Exhibit 2-3.

SUMMARY

Accounting and financial reporting for state and local governments focused originally on funds, which were designed to enhance and demonstrate fiscal accountability. Gradually, however, a consensus developed that fund-based presentations needed to be accompanied by government-wide financial statements to meet the equally important objective of operational accountability. The result is today's comprehensive, integrated financial reporting model, which was especially designed to ensure and demonstrate fiscal *and* operational accountability. Authoritative guidance on the governmental financial reporting model is provided by GASB Statement No. 34.

The basic financial statements mandated by GAAP for a state or local government include separate fund-based presentations for each of the three fund classifications (governmental, proprietary, and fiduciary) used by state and local governments. Governmental funds report a balance sheet and a statement of revenues, expenditures, and changes in fund balances. Governments also normally have the *option* of reporting budgetary comparisons for the general fund and individual major special revenue funds

[70] GASB, *Comprehensive Implementation Guide (2004)*, 7.241.
[71] As discussed in chapter 4, the primary government comprises the government as legally defined and its blended component units.
[72] GASB Statement No. 34, paragraph 60.
[73] A discretely presented component unit is a legally separate organization that must be included within a government's financial statements but which does *not* operate essentially as a fund of the government. Additional information on discretely presented component units is furnished in chapter 4.

EXHIBIT 2-3
Relationship between fund-based financial reporting and government-wide financial reporting

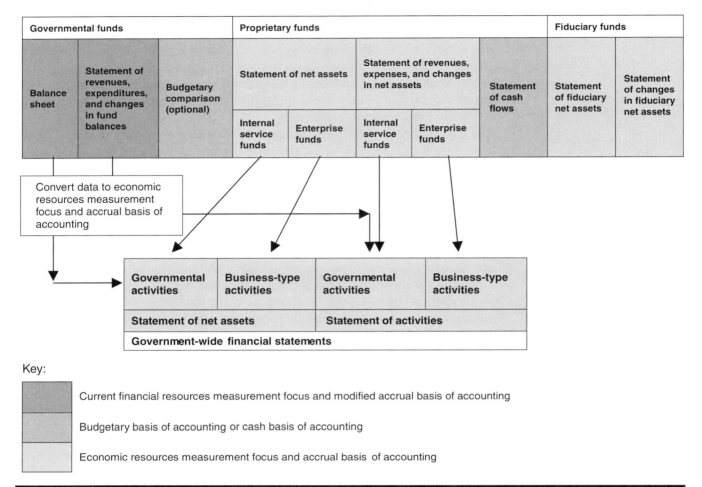

Key:

Current financial resources measurement focus and modified accrual basis of accounting

Budgetary basis of accounting or cash basis of accounting

Economic resources measurement focus and accrual basis of accounting

as a basic financial statement rather than as RSI. Proprietary funds report three basic financial statements: a statement of net assets; a statement of revenues, expenses, and changes in net assets; and a statement of cash flows. Fiduciary trust funds report a statement of fiduciary net assets and a statement of changes in fiduciary net assets, while agency funds report only a statement of fiduciary net assets.

There are two basic government-wide financial statements: the statement of net assets and the statement of activities. A government-wide statement of cash flows is not required. Fiduciary activities and fiduciary-type component units are *not* included within the government-wide financial statements because the resources reported in those funds are not available to support governmental programs.

Governmental funds use the current financial resources measurement focus and the modified accrual basis of accounting to measure and report their activities. Both emphasize near-term inflows and outflows of expendable resources, consistent with the normal focus of the annual or biennial appropriated operating budget. This measurement focus and basis of accounting differs significantly from the economic resources measurement focus and the accrual basis of accounting used for proprietary funds and private-sector businesses as well as for government-wide financial reporting. Accordingly, data from governmental funds must be converted to the economic resources measurement focus and the accrual basis of accounting before being reported in the governmental activities column of the government-wide financial statements. The reconciliation between the two measurement focuses and bases of accounting is presented either on the face of the governmental fund financial statements or as a schedule accompanying those statements.

Although internal service funds operate as proprietary funds, their residual balances normally should be consolidated as part of governmental rather than business-type activities in the government-wide financial statements (even if they primarily serve fiduciary funds). Internal service funds that primarily serve enterprise funds are an exception to this general rule and should be consolidated with business-type activities.

The government-wide financial statements include a total column that presents consolidated data for both governmental and business-type activities. Nonoverhead interfund costs are *not* eliminated as part of this consolidation, however, because eliminating them would impede the measurement of net cost for each of a government's functional activities, which is a key objective of the government-wide statement of activities.

3

Classification and Terminology

An initial step in accounting and financial reporting is to analyze transactions and events to determine their economic substance. This analytical process applies both to transactions involving parties outside the government[1] and to transaction-like activity among the various funds. Generally accepted accounting principles (GAAP) have defined specific classes of transactions and interfund activity to guide this analytical process. This chapter examines these various classes of transactions and interfund activity and provides a brief overview of the appropriate accounting for each. This chapter also examines some of the specialized categories state and local governments use for their financial reporting.

CLASSIFYING TRANSACTIONS AND INTERFUND ACTIVITY

It is an axiom among accountants that accounting and financial reporting should reflect the economic substance of transactions rather than their legal form. While this principle pertains equally to the public and private sectors, applying the principle of substance over form poses some unique challenges in the public sector. For instance, governments focus on providing services rather than on generating profits. As a result, it is not surprising that to better serve their citizens, governments sometimes enter into transactions (such as grants) that cannot be explained solely on the basis of economic self-interest. Moreover, where most private-sector transactions are voluntary, based on an agreement freely reached between a willing buyer and a willing seller, many public-sector transactions—like taxes—are essentially *involuntary*. In addition, the problem of properly analyzing the economic substance of transactions in the public sector is further complicated by the often inconsistent use of certain common terms. Thus a single term, such as "grant," may be used in practice to describe transactions that are quite different in substance.

---

[1] "Transactions," for this purpose, include events that affect the government's finances (e.g., "acts of God," litigation).

To guide the process of analysis, GAAP have defined specific classes of transactions based on economic substance rather than legal form. In defining these classes, GAAP have avoided a number of common terms that might be ambiguous as a result of inconsistent usage, preferring instead to coin new terms as needed.

Classes of transactions

The term "transaction" describes actions involving either outside parties or a government's discretely presented component units.[2] "Interfund activity" describes transaction-like activities between a government's various funds and blended component units. All transactions involving state and local governments are categorized into three classes: exchange transactions, exchange-like transactions, and nonexchange transactions. Nonexchange transactions, in turn, are categorized into four subclasses: derived tax revenues, imposed nonexchange revenues, government-mandated nonexchange transactions, and voluntary nonexchange transactions.

Exchange transactions

GAAP define an *exchange transaction* as one in which "each party receives and gives up essentially equal values."[3] In the private sector, virtually all transactions between businesses and their customers are classified as exchange transactions. Likewise, many fees and charges involving customers of proprietary funds meet this definition. Receivables, liabilities, revenues, and expenditures/expenses related to exchange transactions typically are recognized at the time the exchange takes place. In governmental funds, which use the modified accrual basis of accounting, revenue and expenditure recognition also depend on the timing of cash collections and payments.[4]

It is important to distinguish exchange transactions from the contractual arrangements that sometimes give rise to them. That is, a contract is merely a *commitment* until the goods or services contracted for are provided. Only at that point may it be said that an exchange has taken place. Thus, contracts for the transfer of assets (e.g., investment securities, capital assets) represent exchange transactions only at the point where the benefits and risks of ownership have effectively been transferred from buyer to seller.

Exchange-like transactions

In the definition provided for an exchange transaction, it was presumed that essentially *equal* values would be exchanged between parties to the transaction. In the public sector, however, situations frequently arise where "the values exchanged, although related, may not be quite equal or in which the direct benefits may not be exclusively for the parties to the transaction."[5] GAAP classify such arrangements as "exchange-*like* transactions." In most cases, fees for regulatory or professional licenses and permits qualify as exchange-like transactions, as do some types of grants and donations.

---

[2] The term *component unit* describes a separate legal unit that must be included within a government's financial report because of the nature of its relationship to the government (i.e., economic substance taking precedence over legal form). A *blended* component unit is one whose funds are treated as funds of the government with which it is included. The data of *discretely presented* component units are reported separately from the data of the primary government. See chapter 4. Note that interfund activity with the primary government is treated as a *transaction* in the separately issued report of a blended component unit.

[3] Governmental Accounting Standards Board (GASB) Statement No. 33, *Accounting and Financial Reporting for Nonexchange Transactions*, paragraph 1.

[4] See chapter 2 for an overview of modified accrual accounting.

[5] GASB Statement No. 33, footnote 1.

For all practical purposes, the accounting and financial reporting are identical for exchange transactions and exchange-like transactions, so it is not essential to be able to distinguish the two. Failure to grasp the difference, however, has sometimes led to the misclassification of certain exchange-like transactions as *nonexchange* transactions (described later), with potentially serious adverse consequences for accounting and financial reporting.

Assume, for example, that a large corporation makes a "grant" to a university to support research in product development, and that the corporation retains the right to apply for a patent on any commercial applications resulting from that research. There probably is no evidence that the values exchanged in this case are or were intended to be equal. Nonetheless, the corporation's willingness to enter into the transaction clearly is predicated on anticipating significant potential commercial benefits. Given this expectation, the substance of the arrangement is much closer to that of an exchange transaction than it is to a gift or contribution and should be treated accordingly (i.e., as an exchange-*like* transaction), even though the agreement giving rise to the transaction describes the arrangement as a "grant."

Another example demonstrates the same point. Assume a city elects to give land worth $10 million to a developer to construct an industrial park. The developer, in return, is required to construct approximately $9.8 million in infrastructure on the government's behalf to support the new industrial park. The minimal disparity between the values given and received does *not* alter the transaction's similarity to an exchange. Thus the transaction should be treated as an exchange-*like* transaction despite the disparity.

Nonexchange transactions   State and local governments, of course, engage in many transactions that do *not* involve the exchange of equal or approximately equal value. GAAP refer to such arrangements as *nonexchange transactions*. All nonexchange transactions that involve financial or capital resources can be placed into one of the four subclasses described in the following paragraphs.[6]

Derived tax revenues. Derived tax revenues result from assessments governments place on exchange transactions. Common examples include taxes on earnings or consumption (e.g., personal income tax, corporate income tax, sales tax, and motor fuel taxes). A *receivable* normally should be recognized when the transactions underlying the derived tax revenue occur. For example, a receivable for sales taxes ideally should be recognized as soon as a taxable sale takes place. Likewise, receivables related to income tax should be recognized, in principle, at the same time taxable income is earned by an individual or corporation. In general, *revenue* also should be recognized when the underlying exchange transaction takes place. In governmental funds, which use modified accrual accounting, revenue recognition (but not the recognition of the receivable) also depends on the timing of cash collections (availability).

Imposed nonexchange revenues. Imposed nonexchange revenues result from assessments by governments on nongovernmental entities, including individuals, other than assessments on exchange transactions.

[6] All guidance provided in this chapter regarding the proper accounting and financial reporting for nonexchange transactions is taken from GASB Statement No. 33. The provisions of GASB Statement No. 33 apply only to nonexchange transactions involving financial or capital resources. Consequently, contributed services and similar in-kind contributions do not fall within the scope of the guidance provided here for nonexchange transactions.

Common examples include property taxes, ad valorem taxes on personal property, and most fines and forfeits. A *receivable* normally should be recognized as soon as an enforceable legal claim arises.

Imposed nonexchange *revenues* typically are associated with the funding of one or more specific fiscal periods. For example, it may be required that certain imposed nonexchange revenues be used *during* a predetermined fiscal period. In that case, revenue would be recognized in that same period. In other cases, use of the resources provided by imposed nonexchange revenues may not be permitted *prior to* a particular fiscal period. In that situation, revenue would be recognized in the first period in which the use of the resources is permitted.

Some governments do not have an enforceable legal claim to property taxes until the period *after* the period for which the property taxes are levied. GAAP specifically direct governments in that situation to recognize property tax revenue in the period for which the taxes are levied, *even though an enforceable legal claim does not arise until the following period.*[7]

Once again, in governmental funds, which use the modified accrual basis of accounting, revenue recognition also depends on the timing of cash collections (availability).

Government-mandated nonexchange transactions. Government-mandated nonexchange transactions are essentially "funded mandates." That is, a higher level government (provider) requires a lower level government (recipient) to undertake some action and provides funding to help it do so. Examples include grants to local governments for state-mandated road upgrading and federal grants for mandated drug and alcohol abuse prevention programs. The accounting and financial reporting for government-mandated nonexchange transactions is the same as that discussed below for voluntary nonexchange transactions.

Voluntary nonexchange transactions. Voluntary nonexchange transactions result from legislative or contractual agreements, other than exchanges, entered into willingly by two or more parties. Examples include certain grants and entitlements and most donations. Resource recipients in voluntary nonexchange transactions typically recognize a receivable and revenue when all eligibility requirements have been met. In governmental funds, which use the modified accrual basis of accounting, revenue recognition also depends on the timing of cash collections (availability). Similarly, resource providers recognize expense/expenditure and a liability as soon as all eligibility requirements are met.[8]

Eligibility criteria, of course, take a variety of forms in practice. In the case of expenditure-driven (reimbursement) grants, for instance, it is an eligibility requirement that qualifying expenditures first be incurred. Similarly, matching requirements may be set as a condition of eligibility for potential resource recipients. On the other hand, purely administrative obligations (such as filing periodic grantor reports) should *not* be treated as eligibility requirements.

---

[7] GASB Statement No. 33, paragraph 18.
[8] When the resources provided or received cannot be sold, disbursed, or consumed until after a specified number of years have passed or a specific event has occurred (e.g., endowments), the eligibility criterion "is met as soon as the recipient begins to honor the provider's stipulation not to sell, disburse, or consume the resources and continues to be met for as long as the recipient honors that stipulation."(GASB Statement No. 33, paragraph 22 and footnote 12).

One condition of eligibility, which is especially common for universities, is a *time requirement*. That is, resources are provided to fund a particular period (such as a specific academic year); or, the use of resources may not be permitted prior to a particular period. Indeed, if a government is the resource provider and there is no explicit time requirement, GAAP actually mandate that such a time requirement be presumed by the recipient and that the *provider's* fiscal year be used as the applicable period. In the case of pass-through grants, this rule is to be applied to the *immediate provider* of the resources.

For example, a government with a September 30 fiscal year end might provide resources to a government with a June 30 fiscal year end. Even though the recipient's fiscal year begins July 1, the recipient could only recognize a receivable as of October 1, the start of the *provider's* fiscal year. That does *not* mean that revenues should be prorated. In this instance, as of October 1, the recipient government potentially would recognize a full year's revenue, not just the revenue for the period that the two governments' fiscal years overlap (the nine months from October 1 through June 30).[9]

It is essential to distinguish *eligibility requirements* from *purpose restrictions*. An *eligibility requirement* determines *when* the effective control of resources is transferred from one party to another, while a *purpose restriction* simply limits how resources may be used *after effective control has been transferred*. Consequently, eligibility requirements affect the recognition of receivables, liabilities, revenues, and expenses/expenditures, while purpose restrictions have no such effect.[10]

Exhibit 3-1 is a table of the different classes of transactions as well as internal activity, discussed in the next section. Exhibit 3-2 illustrates when receivables would be recognized in connection with each class of transactions. Exhibit 3-3 shows when revenues would be recognized in connection with each class of transactions.

Classes of interfund activity

Discussion so far has focused on the proper classification of *transactions*; that is, actions involving outside parties including the government's discretely presented component units. Governments, however, also engage in significant interfund activity. GAAP establish two broad classes for interfund activity: *reciprocal interfund activity* and *nonreciprocal interfund activity*. Reciprocal interfund activity is the interfund counterpart to exchange and exchange-like transactions. Nonreciprocal interfund activity, conversely, is the interfund equivalent to nonexchange transactions.[11]

Reciprocal interfund activity

Reciprocal interfund activity is divided into two subclasses: interfund loans and interfund services provided and used.

Interfund loans. Loans between funds are properly reported as increases and decreases in assets and liabilities, with no effect on activities in either government-wide or fund financial statements. Thus, the lender

---

[9] A factor that would not allow the government to recognize a full year's revenue as of October 1 would be specific grantor provisions to the contrary. Likewise, revenue recognition in governmental funds remains subject to the availability criterion of modified accrual accounting.

[10] In this regard, recall that spending requirements associated with expenditure-driven (reimbursement) grants actually are *eligibility requirements* rather than purpose restrictions.

[11] Authoritative guidance on the proper classification of interfund activity can be found in GASB Statement No. 34, *Basic Financial Statements—and Management's Discussion and Analysis—for State and Local Governments*, paragraph 112.

EXHIBIT 3-1
Classes of transactions and interfund activity

Value given/received	External	Internal
Equal	Exchange transactions	Reciprocal interfund activity: • interfund loans
Approximately equal	Exchange-like transactions	• interfund services provided/used
Not equal	Nonexchange transactions: • derived tax revenues • imposed nonexchange revenues • government-mandated nonexchange transactions • voluntary nonexchange transactions	Nonreciprocal interfund activity: • interfund transfers • interfund reimbursements

fund replaces the asset *cash* with the asset *due from other funds*, while the borrower fund reports an equal increase in both *cash* and *due to other funds*.

As always, accountants must place a premium on economic substance over legal form. It is common for governments to make interfund "loans" with little or no expectation of repayment. In substance, such a transaction is not really a loan at all (i.e., a reciprocal transaction), but rather a transfer of resources from one fund to another (i.e., a nonreciprocal transaction). Accordingly, GAAP specifically require that any portion of an interfund "loan" that is not expected to be repaid "within a reasonable time" be reclassified as a transfer.[12]

It should be noted that interfund loans are treated quite differently in some important ways from loans involving parties outside the primary government. For example, the lender fund would never treat a loan to another fund as an investment, regardless of its legal form (e.g., promissory note),[13] nor could such interfund "debt" be treated as "capital-related" for purposes of classifying net assets (as discussed later in this chapter).[14] Furthermore, governmental funds would report the issuance of a long-term interfund loan as a balance sheet item (advances payable) rather than in the operating statement (other financing source), as would otherwise be the case.[15]

Interfund services provided and used. It is common for a fund to provide services to one or more other funds, which then are charged for the services received. Sometimes the amount charged is equal to the value of the services received (similar to an exchange transaction). In other cases, the amount charged does not quite equal the value of the services received (similar to an exchange-like transaction).

GAAP direct that when the amount of an interfund charge equals or approximates the external exchange value of the services received, that charge should be classified as *interfund services provided and used*. The appropriate accounting and financial reporting for this class of interfund activity is the same as that described earlier for exchange and exchange-like transactions: the funds receiving such services should report expenses or expenditures,

---

[12] GASB Statement No. 34, paragraph 112a(1).
[13] GASB, *Comprehensive Implementation Guide (2004)*, 6.70.
[14] GASB, *Comprehensive Implementation Guide (2004)*, 7.138.
[15] GASB Statement No. 34, paragraph 112a(1).

EXHIBIT 3-2
Receivable recognition for transactions

Types of transactions	Criteria for receivable recognition			
	When exchange actually occurs	When underlying transaction occurs	When enforceable legal claim arises	When eligibility requirements met
Exchange transactions	X			
Exchange-like transactions	X			
Derived tax revenues		X		
Imposed nonexchange revenues			X	
Government-mandated nonexchange transactions				X
Voluntary nonexchange transactions				X

and the fund providing the services should report revenues, just as though the transaction had involved a party outside the government.

It is important to distinguish *interfund services provided and used* from *reimbursements,* which will be discussed later. The former category is used for *program-related services* (e.g., water provided by the water department to the parks department). Allocations of indirect costs (overhead) are properly classified as reimbursements.

Nonreciprocal interfund activity

Nonreciprocal interfund activity also can be divided into two subclasses: interfund transfers and interfund reimbursements.

Interfund transfers. GAAP define interfund transfers as "flows of assets (such as cash or goods) without equivalent flows of assets in return and without a requirement for repayment."[16] One common example would be a general fund's annual subsidy of a transit authority enterprise fund. Another good example would be the remittance of a portion of an enterprise fund's surplus to the general fund. Also, as noted previously, GAAP direct that interfund "loans" not expected to be repaid within a reasonable period be reclassified as transfers.[17]

Sometimes an enterprise fund within the primary government will be required to make *payments in lieu of taxes* (PILOTs) to the general fund. In a typical case, there is no direct relationship between the amount of the PILOTs and the value of the specific goods or services provided to the fund making the payment. Instead, the amount charged tends to be either arbitrary or related in some manner to the value of the property (modeled on property taxes) rather than to the value of the services received. In such a typical situation, PILOTs would be classified as *interfund transfers* rather than as *interfund services provided and used* because of their essentially *nonreciprocal* character.[18]

---

[16] GASB Statement No. 34, paragraph 112b(1).
[17] GASB Statement No. 34, paragraph 112a(1).
[18] GASB, *Comprehensive Implementation Guide (2004),* 7.321.

EXHIBIT 3-3
Revenue recognition for transactions

| | Criteria under accrual accounting | | | | | |
| | Criteria under modified accrual accounting | | | | | |
Type of transaction	Exchange occurs	Underlying transaction occurs	Enforeceabl e legal claim	Associate d period	Eligibility requirements met	Available
Exchange transactions	X					X
Exchange-like transactions	X					X
Derived tax revenues		X				X
Imposed nonexchange revenues			X*	X		X
Government-mandated nonexchange transactions					X	X
Voluntary nonexchange transactions					X	X

*Not required in the case of property taxes when a legally enforceable claim arises subsequent to the period with which the property taxes are associated.

Because of the difference in measurement focus and basis of accounting between governmental funds and proprietary funds,[19] reclassification may be necessary between the fund financial statements and the government-wide financial statements. Assume for example, that a capital asset of the general government is reassigned to an enterprise fund. The government-wide statement of activities would reflect the reassignment as a *transfer* between governmental activities and business-type activities. Such a transfer is not possible, however, at the fund level, because governmental funds did *not* report the capital assets being reassigned to begin with. Instead, the reassignment would be reflected at the fund level solely in the recipient enterprise fund, which would report a *capital contribution*.[20]

For the same reasons, transfers sometimes may not balance at the fund level. Assume this time that it is a capital asset of an enterprise fund that is being reassigned to the general government. Once again, there is nothing to report in the governmental funds. However, since *capital contributions* cannot, of their very nature, be negative, there is no option but to report the disposal of the capital asset as a transfer out, even though no other fund would be in a position to report a corresponding transfer in. Nonetheless, as in the previous example, *transfers in* and *transfers out* would continue to balance in the government-wide statement of activities, where everything is accounted for using a common measurement focus and basis of accounting.

In connection with financial reporting, the term *transfer* should be used exclusively in connection with interfund activities, that is, *activities between*

---

[19] See related discussion in chapter 2.
[20] GASB, *Comprehensive Implementation Guide* (2004), 7.335

funds of the primary government. Transactions between the primary government and parties outside the financial reporting entity, as well as transactions between the primary government and its discretely presented component units, should be reported as *revenues* and *expenses/expenditures* rather than as *transfers.*

Interfund reimbursements. GAAP define interfund reimbursements as "repayments from the funds responsible for particular expenditures or expenses to the funds that initially paid for them."[21] Interfund reimbursements are treated as an adjustment to expenses or expenditures; that is, an increase in expenditures or expenses in the reimbursing fund and a corresponding decrease in expenditures or expenses in the reimbursed fund. As such, interfund reimbursements are *not* reported in the financial statements. As noted, the allocation of overhead should be treated as a reimbursement rather than as interfund services provided and used. Likewise, GAAP expressly direct that payments to the general fund in connection with risk financing activities normally be treated as reimbursements.[22] Exhibit 3-1 illustrates the classes of interfund activity.

SPECIALIZED FINANCIAL REPORTING CATEGORIES FOR STATE AND LOCAL GOVERNMENTS

Various categories are used to aggregate accounting data for financial reporting purposes. State and local governments share with private-sector businesses many of these categories, such as assets, liabilities, revenues, and expenses. Other categories, such as *other financing sources/uses* and *special items,* are used solely or principally in the public sector. The following paragraphs summarize the most important specialized categories used for financial reporting by state and local governments.

Governmental funds

The specialized accounting and financial reporting used for governmental funds remain the most unique features of the governmental financial reporting model. Indeed, most of the specialized categories established for financial reporting by state and local governments involve governmental funds.

Other financing sources

As noted earlier, governmental funds focus on inflows and outflows of current financial resources.[23] Most inflows of current financial resources are reported as *revenues.* In some specific instances, however, increases in current financial resources are reported instead as *other financing sources.* Typically, this category has been used to isolate certain one-time inflows of current financial resources that might otherwise distort a governmental fund's regular ongoing revenue trends. GAAP provide for the use of the other financing sources category in five specific instances.

- *Issuance of debt.* The issuance of long-term debt increases a governmental fund's current financial resources. Nonetheless, including debt-related inflows among a government's regular revenues could distort a government's revenue trends. Accordingly, GAAP call for

---

[21] GASB Statement No. 34, paragraph 112b(2).
[22] GASB Statement No. 10, *Accounting and Financial Reporting for Risk Financing and Related Insurance Issues,* paragraph 64.
[23] See chapter 2.

the issuance of debt to be reported separately as an other financing source. The amount so reported should equal the face value of the debt.[24] If debt is issued at a premium, the premium should be reported as a separate other financing source in its own right.[25] As discussed in a later chapter,[26] the GAAP treatment to record the inception of a capital lease in a governmental fund is patterned on that just described for other long-term debt. That is, an amount equal to the present value of the net minimum lease payments is reported as an other financing source, *even though no cash is actually received in the case of a lease.*[27] Conversely, the proceeds of *no-commitment* special assessment debt are considered the functional equivalent of a grant (because the government receives resources without incurring any obligation for their repayment), and should be reported as revenue, just like other grants.[28]

- *Interfund transfers.* Inflows of current financial resources from other funds are to be distinguished from a government's regular revenues. So interfund transfers received from other funds are reported as an other financing source rather than as revenue.[29]
- *Proceeds of the sale of capital assets.* In substance, the sale of a capital asset constitutes the conversion of a non-financial economic resource (capital asset) into a current financial resource (cash). The proceeds of capital asset sales should be reported as an other financing source to avoid distorting the governmental fund's regular revenue trends.[30] Indeed, when such amounts become significant, they may need to be classified as *special items.*[31]
- *Insurance proceeds.* Insurance recoveries, if material, are properly reported in governmental funds as an other financing source if they do not meet the test for reporting as extraordinary items.[32]
- *Payments on demand bonds reported as fund liabilities.* Demand bonds are debt securities with a "put" feature that allows bondholders to demand repayment before maturity. GAAP allow demand bonds to be treated like other long-term debt, provided certain specific criteria are met.[33] Demand bonds that do *not* meet these criteria must be reported as fund liabilities in the governmental fund that receives the proceeds. GAAP require debt service principal payments on demand bonds to be reported as expenditures in either situation. Ordinarily, however, debt service principal payments on debt reported as a fund liability would be reported simply as a balance sheet transaction (i.e., an equal decrease in the appropriate liability and cash accounts). To eliminate this difficulty, GAAP direct that an other financing source

[24] GASB Statement No. 34, paragraph 88 (as amended).
[25] GASB Statement No. 34, paragraph 88.
[26] See chapter 5.
[27] National Council on Governmental Accounting (NCGA) Statement 5, *Accounting and Financial Reporting Principles for Lease Agreements of State and Local Governments*, paragraph 14.
[28] GASB Statement No. 6, *Accounting and Financial Reporting for Special Assessments*, paragraph 19. The term "proceeds" is *not* used in connection with such debt.
[29] GASB Statement No. 34, paragraph 88.
[30] GASB Statement No. 34, paragraph 88.
[31] GASB Statement No. 34, paragraph 56.
[32] GASB Statement No. 42, *Accounting and Financial Reporting for Impairment of Capital Assets and for Insurance Recoveries*, paragraph 21. The topic of insurance recoveries is also addressed in chapter 12.
[33] See chapter 5.

be reported in connection with debt service principal payments on demand bonds reported as governmental fund liabilities.[34]

Other financing uses

Just as governmental funds distinguish revenues from other financing sources, governmental funds also distinguish *expenditures* from *other financing uses*. Once again, the purpose of this distinction is to avoid potential distortions in trend data. GAAP direct governments to report other financing uses in four specific instances:

- *Issuance discounts on long-term debt.* As already noted, GAAP require that the other financing source reported for the issuance of long-term debt be equal to the face value of the debt. However, if debt is issued at a discount (i.e., because the stated rate of interest on the debt is less than the comparable market rate of interest at the time the debt is issued), the proceeds received will be less than face value. GAAP direct that an other financing use be utilized to account for this difference. This other financing use should *not* be netted against the other financing sources reported for either the debt itself or for debt-related premiums.
- *Refunding transactions.* Governments often elect to take advantage of favorable changes in interest rates by issuing new debt to refinance existing (old) debt. Likewise, a government may elect to refinance old debt to escape onerous debt covenants. Such transactions are referred to as *refundings*. In the case of a *current* refunding, the proceeds of the refunding debt are applied immediately to redeem the old debt. In the case of an *advance* refunding, the proceeds of the refunding debt are placed into an escrow account pending the call date or maturity of the old debt. Most advance refundings result in the *defeasance* of the old debt (i.e., for accounting purposes, the debt is treated as though it had been redeemed). In the case of both current refundings and advance refundings resulting in the defeasance of debt, GAAP direct that the proceeds of the refunding bonds, whether used for redemption or placed in escrow, be reported as an other financing use rather than as an expenditure. Otherwise these significant and irregular outflows of current financial resources could substantially distort a government's regular debt service expenditure trends.
- *Interfund transfers.* The transfer of resources to another fund is clearly different in substance from the consumption of those same resources, even though both situations result in a decrease in a given governmental fund's current financial resources. Hence, transfers to other funds are reported as an other financing use rather than as an expenditure.
- *Reclassification of demand bonds as a fund liability.* As noted in the discussion of other financing sources, demand bonds may be treated as long-term liabilities, despite their "put" feature and provided they meet certain specific criteria. It is possible a demand bond that originally met these criteria might at some later time cease to do so. In that case, GAAP direct that the obligation be reclassified as a fund liability

---

[34] Thus, the debits and credits for the repayment of the principal of demand bonds would be as follows: debits — 1) demand bonds payable and 2) debt service expenditures - principal on demand bonds; credits — 1) cash and 2) other financing sources - demand bond principal repayment. See GASB Interpretation No. 1, *Demand Bonds Issued by State and Local Governmental Entities (an Interpretation of NCGA Interpretation 9)*, paragraph 13.

in the governmental fund that originally received the proceeds. The journal entry used to effect this reclassification would include an other financing use equal to the amount of the demand bonds henceforth to be reported as a fund liability.[35]

Fund balance

Governmental funds report the difference between their assets and liabilities as *fund balance,* which is divided into *reserved* and *unreserved* portions. The function of *reserved fund balance* is simply to isolate the portion of fund balance that is *not* available for the following period's budget, so that *unreserved fund balance* can serve as a measure of current available financial resources.

The reservation of fund balance is necessary for two reasons:

- *Resources not available for spending.* Some of the assets reported in governmental funds are not available for spending in the subsequent year's budget. For example, a *long-term* loan receivable, such as an advance to another fund, is not available for *current* spending.[36] Likewise, governments that use the purchases method to account for their supplies inventories would need to report *reserved fund balance* for any balances reported to indicate that such amounts are not actually available for spending.[37] In the same way, if an asset is reported in a governmental fund to reflect the fund's equity interest in a joint venture, fund balance must be reserved in the same amount to indicate that an equity interest does *not* constitute an *available* current financial resource.
- *Legal restrictions on spending.* Fund balance also is reserved to indicate situations where a portion of fund balance is *not* available for spending on *any and all* purposes of the fund. That is, fund balance should be reserved in situations where legal restrictions impose a limitation *narrower than the purpose of the fund itself.*[38] One specific example cited in the authoritative standards is the case of encumbrances that a government intends to honor *and* that do not lapse at year end.[39]

Unreserved fund balance may, in turn, be subdivided into *designated* and *undesignated* portions. Designations represent management's intended future use of resources (e.g., contingencies, equipment replacement)[40] and generally should reflect actual plans approved by the government's senior management.[41] Designations essentially reflect a government's *self-imposed* limitations on the use of otherwise available current financial resources. Because designations are intended to earmark available current financial resources, they may never, by definition, exceed total unreserved fund balance.[42] Exhibit 3-4 provides an illustration of the components of fund balance.

---

[35] GASB Interpretation No. 1, paragraph 13.

[36] No portion of fund balance would be reserved for long-term receivables that are offset by a corresponding liability for deferred revenue (such as capital leases receivable, special assessments receivable).

[37] The purchases method of accounting for inventory is discussed in chapter 5.

[38] Resources legally restricted for use in capital projects could *not* properly be reported as *reserved fund balance* in a capital project fund, for instance. On the other hand, if those resources were restricted for just one of several projects accounted for in that fund, the reporting of *reserved fund balance* would be appropriate.

[39] NCGA Statement 1, *Governmental Accounting and Financial Reporting Principles,* paragraph 91(4).

[40] NCGA Statement 1, paragraph 120.

[41] American Institute of Certified Public Accountants (AICPA), *State and Local Governments,* Section 10.17.

EXHIBIT 3-4
Components of fund balance

		Governmental fund	
Financial assets	Assets available for spending and not subject to legal limitations	Liabilities normally expected to be paid from current financial resources	Fund balance
		Undesignated unreserved fund balance [*available for appropriation*]	
		Designated unreserved fund balance (management's intended future use supported by the governing body) [*available for appropriation*]	
	Assets subject to legal restrictions on spending narrower than the purpose of the fund	Reserved fund balance [*not available for appropriation*]	
	Assets not available for spending (e.g., long-term loans receivable)		

An adequate level of *unreserved fund balance* in the general fund is essential to mitigate current and future risks and to ensure stable tax rates and service levels. It also is a crucial consideration in long-term financial planning. For these reasons, laws and regulations often govern the appropriate levels of *fund balance* and *unreserved fund balance* in the general fund. Likewise, *fund balance* and *unreserved fund balance* are carefully monitored by credit rating agencies.

It is recommended that the appropriate policy-setting body within a government establish a formal policy on the level of *unreserved fund balance* to be maintained in the general fund.[43] This policy ought to provide both a temporal framework and specific plans for increasing or decreasing the level of *unreserved fund balance* if it is inconsistent with that policy.[44] If *reserved fund balance* includes resources available to finance items that typically would require the use of *unreserved fund balance*, those resources should be included as part of *unreserved fund balance* for purposes of this policy.[45]

The adequacy of *unreserved fund balance* in the general fund should be assessed based upon a government's own specific circumstances. Nevertheless, it is recommended, *at a minimum*, that general-purpose local governments, regardless of size, maintain *unreserved fund balance* in their general fund of either 1) no less than 5 to 15 percent of regular general fund operat-

---

[42] AICPA, *State and Local Governments*, Section 10.17.

[43] The adoption of similar policies is encouraged for other types of governmental funds as well. While all governmental funds report *fund balance*, the goals for fund balance will differ among fund types and individual funds. For example, a high level of fund balance may be expected in a permanent fund used to account for an endowment, whereas no fund balance at all might be anticipated in a special revenue fund used exclusively to account for expenditure-driven grants. Accordingly, a government's policy for fund balance in the general fund may differ from its policy for fund balance in other governmental fund types and individual funds.

[44] By its very nature, *unreserved fund balance* is subject to unexpected fluctuations. Therefore, a well designed policy will provide specific guidance on what actions a government will take (and over what period) to adjust levels of *unreserved fund balance* that fall outside the parameters set by policy as the result of such fluctuations.

[45] An example might be a legally required contingency reserve.

ing revenues, or 2) no less than one to two months of regular general fund operating expenditures.[46] A government's particular situation, of course, may require levels of *unreserved fund balance* in the general fund significantly in excess of these recommended minimum levels.[47]

Because fund balance is subject to unforeseeable fluctuations, it normally would be a mistake to draw conclusions based solely on fund balance at any one point in time. Furthermore, such measures should be applied within the context of long-term forecasting, thereby avoiding the risk of placing too much emphasis upon the level of *unreserved fund balance* in the general fund at any one time.

As already noted, environmental factors will affect the appropriate level of *unreserved fund balance* in the general fund. Examples of such factors include the following:

- The predictability of its revenues and the volatility of its expenditures (i.e., higher levels of unreserved fund balance may be needed if significant revenue sources are subject to unpredictable fluctuations[48] or if operating expenditures are highly volatile).
- The availability of resources in other funds, as well as the potential drain upon general fund resources from other funds (i.e., the availability of resources in other funds may reduce the amount of unreserved fund balance needed in the general fund, just as deficits in other funds may require that a higher level of unreserved fund balance be maintained in the general fund).
- Liquidity (i.e., a disparity between when financial resources actually become available to make payments and the average maturity of related liabilities may require that a higher level of resources be maintained).
- Designations (i.e., governments may wish to maintain higher levels of unreserved fund balance to compensate for any portion of unreserved fund balance already designated for a specific purpose).[49]

Naturally, any policy addressing desirable levels of unreserved fund balance in the general fund should be in conformity with all applicable legal and regulatory constraints. In this case in particular, it is essential that differences between GAAP fund balance and budgetary fund balance be fully appreciated by all interested parties.[50]

---

[46] The point of comparison for measuring *unreserved fund balance* may be either operating revenues or operating expenditures. The choice between the two is likely to be dictated by which is more predictable in a government's particular circumstances. In either case, unusual items that would distort trends (e.g., one-time revenues and expenditures) should be excluded, whereas recurring transfers should be included. A rapidly growing government that uses expenditures as its point of comparison may wish to use the current or future year's appropriation for this purpose. Once the decision has been made to compare *unreserved fund balance* to either revenues or expenditures, that decision should be followed consistently from period to period.

[47] In practice, levels of *unreserved fund balance*, expressed as a percentage of revenues/expenditures or as a multiple of monthly expenditures, typically are less for larger governments than for smaller governments because of the magnitude of the amounts involved for larger governments and because the diversification that is typical of the revenues and expenditures of larger governments often results in a lower degree of volatility.

[48] For example, state aid.

[49] Other factors that could affect the level of unreserved fund balance that is needed include 1) location in a region prone to natural disasters (e.g., hurricanes), 2) heavy reliance upon a single corporate taxpayer or upon a group of corporate taxpayers in the same industry, 3) revenues that are not level, and 4) rapidly growing budgets.

[50] GFOA recommended practice on "The Appropriate Level of Unreserved Fund Balance in the General Fund" (2002).

Government-wide reporting and proprietary fund reporting

Since proprietary fund financial statements and government-wide financial statements use the same measurement focus and basis of accounting as do private-sector businesses, there are many similarities in the categories used for financial reporting. Nonetheless, the equity categories used for both government-wide and proprietary fund financial reporting differ from those used by private-sector businesses and therefore merit special attention.

Invested in capital assets, net of related debt

A significant portion of a typical government's net assets represents the government's equity interest in its capital assets. GAAP direct that this portion of net assets be separately labeled in both the government-wide and proprietary fund financial statements. The specific amount to be so reported is calculated as follows:

> Cost of capital assets
> Less: Accumulated depreciation (if applicable)
> Less: Outstanding principal of related debt
> Invested in capital assets, net of related debt

Capital-related debt includes "bonds, mortgages, notes, or other borrowings that are attributable to the acquisition, construction, or improvement of [capital]assets."[51] Unless a significant portion of the proceeds of a given debt issue is spent for noncapitalizable purposes, the entire amount of the issue should be considered capital related.[52]

Financial assets, of course, are *not* truly "capital" until they are actually spent for some capital purpose (e.g., construction, purchase of existing assets). Accordingly, neither the unspent proceeds of debt issued for capital purposes, nor the debt itself should enter into the calculation of *net assets invested in capital assets, net of related debt*.[53] Assume, for example that a government issued $20 million in debt intended to finance construction, but that as of the end of the fiscal period only $5 million had actually been spent. In that case only the $5 million of *construction in progress* and an equivalent amount of debt would be taken into consideration as part of the calculation of *net assets invested in capital assets, net of related debt*. Meanwhile, the balance of both unspent proceeds and debt would be included as part of the calculation of either *restricted net assets* or *unrestricted net assets*, depending upon the specific circumstances.[54] Upon completion of construction, all remaining debt would henceforth be treated as "capital related."

As already explained elsewhere in this chapter, liabilities to other funds of the primary government should *not* be treated as "debt" for the purpose of calculating *net assets invested in capital asset net of related debt*.[55]

Restricted net assets

This category is designed to reflect net assets whose use is *not* subject solely to the government's own discretion. This category naturally would include resources subject to *externally imposed* restrictions (creditors, grantors, contributors, laws/regulations of other governments, constitutional provi-

[51] GASB Statement No. 34, paragraph 33.
[52] That is "governments are not expected to categorize all uses of bond proceeds to determine how much of the debt actually relates to assets that have been capitalized." GASB, *Comprehensive Implementation Guide (2004)*, 7.132.
[53] GASB Statement No. 34, paragraph 33.
[54] GASB, *Comprehensive Implementation Guide (2004)*, 7.129.
[55] GASB, *Comprehensive Implementation Guide (2004)*, 7.138.

sions).[56] It also would normally, but not always, include resources resulting from enabling legislation (i.e., legislation authorizing the raising of resources for a specific purpose).

In the case of local governments, state law often requires that resources raised by means of enabling legislation be used for the purpose for which raised. In that case, there would be no question that such amounts should be considered *restricted*, because they are subject to an *external legal constraint* (state law). State governments, however, are sovereign, and no *external* legal constraint prevents them from subsequently passing legislation to divert resources raised by means of enabling legislation to some other purpose. All the same, unless there is cause for reconsideration (e.g., the subsequent diversion of resources to some other purpose), it may reasonably be presumed that enabling legislation is tantamount to an implicit contract with taxpayers, thereby justifying the reporting of such amounts as a separate component of *restricted net assets.*[57]

Restricted assets are sometimes set aside to make debt service payments on capital-related debt. In such cases, the assets themselves, *but not the related debt*, should be considered as part of the calculation of *restricted net assets*. That is, capital-related debt, as noted earlier, is always properly taken into consideration as part of the calculation of *net assets invested in capital assets, net of related debt.*[58]

If restricted net assets include amounts related to permanent endowments or permanent fund principal, the *expendable* and *nonexpendable* components of such amounts must be reported separately.[59]

No category of restricted net assets can report a negative balance. If liabilities related to restricted net assets exceed those assets, the excess should be reported as a reduction of *unrestricted net assets.*[60]

Unrestricted net assets

Any remaining balance of net assets is to be reported as *unrestricted net assets*. Consistent with practice for proprietary funds, GASB Statement No. 34 does *not* permit the reporting of designations on the face of the government-wide statement of net assets.

Special and extraordinary items

Special items are unique to financial reporting for state and local governments and are used in connection with all types of funds, as well as in conjunction with government-wide financial reporting. Special items are closely related to *extraordinary items*, which exist in the public *and* private sectors.

Extraordinary items are *both* 1) unusual in nature (possessing a high degree of abnormality *and* clearly unrelated to, or only incidentally related to, the ordinary and typical activities of the entity); *and* 2) infrequent in occurrence (not reasonably expected to recur in the foreseeable future, taking into account the environment in which the entity operates). The primary

---

[56] GASB Statement No. 34, paragraph 34.

[57] This guidance on enabling legislation reflects a pending GASB standard on *Net Assets Restricted by Enabling Legislation (an amendment of GASB Statements No. 34 and No. 44).* "If reevaluation results in a determination that a particular restriction is no longer legally enforceable, then from the beginning of that period forward the resources should be reported as unrestricted. If it is determined that the restrictions continue to be legally enforceable, then for the purposes of financial reporting the restricted net assets should not reflect any reduction for resources used for purposes not stipulated by the enabling legislation" (paragraph 5).

[58] GASB, *Comprehensive Implementation Guide (2004),* 7.140.

[59] GASB Statement No. 34, paragraph 35.

[60] GASB, *Comprehensive Implementation Guide (2004),* Appendix 7-3, Exercise 3.

factor in applying both criteria is the environment within which an entity operates. Consequently, what is "unusual in nature" or "infrequent in occurrence" for one entity may not be so for another.[61] For example, hurricane damage may qualify as an extraordinary item in the Midwest, but not in Florida.

Special items, on the other hand, are *significant items, subject to management's control*, that meet one, *but not both* of the criteria used for identifying extraordinary items. For example, a major sale of park land might be considered unusual for a government (i.e., only incidentally related to its ordinary and typical activities), even though it would not be unreasonable to expect a similar sale sometime in the future. In that case, the sale of park land, if significant, would be reported as a special item.

It is important to emphasize that special items *must be subject to management control*. Thus, natural disasters in areas prone to such disasters, although they meet one but not both of the criteria for an extraordinary item (i.e., they are unusual in nature, but not infrequent in occurrence), may *not* be classified as special items because they are *not* subject to management's control.

Special items are treated exactly like extraordinary items for financial reporting purposes (i.e., a separate line item near the bottom of the statement of activities). When a government has both extraordinary items and special items to report, both are included within a single category, but they are identified separately, with special items being reported first.[62]

As already mentioned, the *special items* category is applicable only to items that are deemed to be *significant*. The significance of a particular transaction or event can vary considerably between the fund financial statements and the government-wide financial statements. What is properly reported as a *special item* in the one may not qualify for that same treatment in the other. Assume for example that a government sells one of its general capital assets. The general fund, under the modified accrual basis of accounting, would report the full amount of the proceeds of the sale in its statement of revenues, expenditures, and changes in fund balances. Conversely, the government-wide statement of activities, consistent with the accrual basis of accounting, would report only the gain or loss on the sale. Thus, while the proceeds of such a sale might be significant enough to qualify as a special item in the governmental fund financial statements, the related gain or loss might not be significant enough for this same classification when reported as part of governmental activities in the government-wide financial statements.[63]

SUMMARY

Accounting and financial reporting should reflect the economic substance of transactions rather than their legal form. Determining the economic substance of transactions in the public sector poses some unique challenges.

[61] Authoritative guidance on extraordinary items is provided by Accounting Principles Board (APB) Opinion No. 30, *Reporting the Results of Operations—Reporting the Effects of Disposal of a Segment of a Business, and Extraordinary, Unusual and Infrequently Occurring Events and Transactions*, which was specifically adopted for the public sector by GASB Statement No. 34.
[62] GASB Statement No. 34, paragraph 56.
[63] GASB, *Comprehensive Implementation Guide (2004)*, 7.309.

Many public-sector transactions cannot be analyzed solely on the basis of a government's economic self-interest. An additional challenge is posed by the sometimes inconsistent use of terminology. GAAP have defined specific classes of transactions to ensure that transactions are analyzed and reported based on their economic substance rather than their legal form or the terminology used to describe them.

There are three different types of transactions: exchange transactions, exchange-like transactions, and nonexchange transactions. Nonexchange transactions are subdivided into four subclasses: derived tax revenues, imposed nonexchange revenues, government-mandated nonexchange transactions, and voluntary nonexchange transactions. Exchange transactions and exchange-like transactions are considered to have occurred when the exchange actually takes place. A derived tax revenue normally is considered to exist when the underlying exchange transaction occurs. For imposed nonexchange revenues, the critical factors for their existence are the creation of an enforceable legal claim and association with a particular period, although an enforceable legal claim is *not* an essential criterion in the case of property taxes.

Government-mandated and voluntary nonexchange transactions generally are considered to have occurred when all eligibility requirements have been met. For this purpose, it is important to distinguish eligibility requirements from purpose restrictions, which do *not* affect when a nonexchange transaction is recognized.

Interfund activity can be classified as either reciprocal or nonreciprocal. Reciprocal interfund activity includes interfund loans and interfund services provided and used. Nonreciprocal interfund activity takes the form of interfund transfers and interfund reimbursements. Neither interfund loans nor interfund reimbursements are reported on a statement of activities.

Governmental funds are unique in their reporting of other financing sources and uses in addition to revenues and expenditures. These two categories are used to isolate certain items specified by GAAP that might otherwise distort a government's regular ongoing revenue and expenditure trends. The difference between assets and liabilities in governmental funds is reported as *fund balance. Unreserved fund balance* serves as a measure of the resources available for the subsequent period's budget on a GAAP basis. Designations reflect a government's self-imposed limitations on the use of otherwise available resources. An adequate level of *unreserved fund balance* in the general fund is essential to mitigate current and future risks and to ensure stable tax rates and service levels. It also is a crucial consideration in long-term financial planning.

Net assets are divided into three components for purposes of government-wide and proprietary fund financial reporting: net assets invested in capital assets, net of related debt; restricted net assets; and unrestricted net assets.

In addition to reporting *extraordinary items,* state and local governments also report *special items,* a category used to report significant transactions subject to management control that meet one but not both of the criteria used to identify extraordinary items. Except for the difference in terminology, the financial reporting for extraordinary items and special items is essentially identical.

4

The Financial Reporting Entity

Accountants place a premium on substance over legal form in financial reporting. Nowhere is the potential for conflict between form and substance greater than in the matter of defining just what constitutes "the government" as a financial reporting entity. For this reason, generally accepted accounting principles (GAAP) provide detailed guidance. This chapter reviews that authoritative guidance as well as its practical application.[1]

OVERVIEW

Government structure at the state level is determined by each state's constitution, and each state establishes its own structure for local government. As a result, the structure of state and local government varies considerably from one state to another. In some cases, general-purpose governments are responsible for providing most (if not all) services to citizens. In other cases, citizens are served by general-purpose governments *and* a range of special-purpose entities. Further, these special-purpose entities differ in the types of services they provide, in their legal structure, and in the relationships they maintain with general-purpose governments.

GAAP direct those who prepare financial statements to look beyond the legal barriers that separate these various units to define each government's financial reporting entity in a way that fully reflects the *financial accountability* of that government's elected officials. In other words, for financial reporting purposes, the entity must include the government itself (i.e., *primary government*), as well as any legally separate units for which that government's elected officials are financially accountable (i.e., *component units*). Additional legally separate units may also need to be included within the financial reporting entity as component units because their exclusion could render the financial statements misleading.

---

[1] The guidance provided in this chapter is primarily based upon Governmental Accounting Standards Board (GASB) Statement No. 14, *The Financial Reporting Entity* (as amended by GASB Statement No. 39, *Determining Whether Certain Organizations Are Component Units*).

Once all component units have been identified, the data from those units must be combined with the data of the primary government in a manner consistent with the underlying relationship that exists between each unit and the primary government. Despite their separate legal status, some component units function for all practical purposes as an integral part of the primary government. Accordingly, GAAP direct that the data of such units be *blended* with the data of the primary government to form a single, homogeneous entity. Other component units function more or less independently of the primary government, despite the ties between them. GAAP call for the data from these latter units to be presented with, but *discretely* (separately) from, the data of the primary government.

PRIMARY GOVERNMENT

The primary government serves as the nucleus and focus of the financial reporting entity as defined by GAAP. All state governments and general-purpose local governments automatically should be treated as primary governments. A special-purpose government, on the other hand, qualifies as a primary government only if it meets *all three* of the following criteria:

- *Elected governing body.* GAAP define the financial reporting entity with the express goal of highlighting the financial accountability of *elected officials*, because they alone are *directly accountable to citizens*. It is not surprising that only an entity governed by a board chosen in a *general, popular election* would qualify as a primary government under GAAP.
- *Separate legal status.* As emphasized earlier, legal form is *not* the determining factor in defining the financial reporting entity. Nevertheless, a certain degree of legal autonomy is essential to demonstrate that a separate, reportable entity exists at all. Accordingly, an entity must be legally separate to qualify as a primary government. A government is considered to function as a separate legal entity if it enjoys the corporate rights typically associated with separate legal status. Examples of such rights include the ability of the entity to have its own legal name, to sue or be sued in its own name, and to own property in its own name. If an entity is *not* legally separate, it is considered an integral part of whichever government exercises those powers.[2]
- *Fiscal independence.* GAAP attempt to focus attention on the financial accountability of elected officials. Sometimes, as a practical matter, significant limitations on the fiscal autonomy of special-purpose governments shift financial accountability to the government imposing the limitations. Accordingly, GAAP indicate that a special-purpose government fiscally dependent on another government should *not* be considered a primary government. Fiscal dependence is created when the governing board of one entity may *arbitrarily* override the financial decisions of another regarding its 1) budget, 2) tax levy or setting of rates or charges, or 3) issuance of bonded debt. Of course, not all required approvals are substantive. Frequently, the approvals that

---

[2] The offices of separately elected county officials (e.g., assessor, tax collector, sheriff, auditor) typically do not qualify as primary governments because they normally fail to meet this criterion.

special-purpose governments must obtain from other governments are essentially ministerial or compliance-oriented in character (e.g., budget review for verification of compliance with balanced-budget requirements). Such required approvals are not equivalent to substituting one board's judgment for another's and, therefore, are *not* considered to be evidence of fiscal dependence. Likewise, limitations on a special-purpose government that apply equally to all governments of the same type are not arbitrary and therefore would not be considered evidence of fiscal dependence. For example, a blanket limitation on the issuance of bonded debt by certain types of special-purpose governments would not create fiscal dependence.

COMPONENT UNITS

A component unit is a legally separate organization that a primary government must include as part of its financial reporting entity for fair presentation in conformity with GAAP. It is important to underscore that component units, by definition, must be *legally separate entities*. Otherwise, they would simply be incorporated within the financial reporting entity as an integral part of whatever government exercises corporate powers on their behalf, rather than as separate units in their own right.

There are three specific tests for determining whether a particular legally separate entity is a component unit of a primary government's financial reporting entity. Those tests involve 1) appointment of the unit's governing board (accompanied by either the potential imposition of will or ongoing financial benefit/burden), 2) fiscal dependence on the primary government, and 3) the potential that exclusion would result in misleading financial reporting. For this last test, special attention must be paid 1) to certain special financing authorities and 2) to the nature and significance of a legally separate, tax-exempt entity's relationship with the primary government and its component units.

Board appointment (accompanied by potential imposition of will or ongoing financial benefit/burden)

GAAP emphasize the ultimate accountability of *elected officials*. Consequently, when a government with elected officials appoints the board members of a legally separate unit, those elected officials may still be financially accountable for that unit, despite its separate legal status. Accordingly, GAAP provide specific guidelines for identifying situations where board appointment indicates that financial accountability lies with the appointing government's board rather than with the separate unit.

First, the appointment process must itself be substantive, reflecting a real choice on the part of the appointing government. In practice, a primary government's "power of appointment" may be quite limited. For example, the appointing government's role may be limited to approving a single list of candidates selected by others, or the appointing government may be required to select board members from a narrow list of pre-selected candidates. In such cases, board appointment would be formal rather than substantive and would not provide a sufficient basis for classifying a legally separate entity as a component unit of the primary government.

Second, the members appointed by the primary government should be in a reasonable position to exercise control over the operations of the legally separate entity. At a minimum, this means that the primary government must appoint a majority of the separate legal entity's board. In many cases, however, boards are legally structured so that certain major financial decisions must be approved by more than a simple majority. In such cases, GAAP consider true control to have been achieved by the primary government only if that government has appointed sufficient board members to produce the "voting majority" (in contrast to "simple majority") needed in such situations.

Of course, long political experience demonstrates that appointed officials do not always remain subject to the control of those who appointed them. Therefore, board appointment alone, even when substantive, is not a sufficient basis for holding elected officials financially accountable for a legally separate entity. Rather, GAAP also require evidence that the relationship established by the appointment process is an ongoing one. GAAP have identified three specific criteria for this purpose, *any one of which is sufficient* to demonstrate the existence of an ongoing relationship:

- *The ability of the appointing government to impose its will on the separate organization.* GAAP state that a government has the ability to impose its will on a legally separate organization "if it can significantly influence the programs, projects, activities, or level of services performed or provided by the organization." The emphasis here should be on the appointing government's *ability* to impose its will, regardless of the government's history in this regard, or the political feasibility of taking such action. Of course, numerous situations would provide evidence that one government has the ability to impose its will on another. The authoritative accounting and financial reporting literature specifically cites the following examples:
  —the ability to remove at will the appointed members of the separate organization's governing board;
  —the ability to modify or approve the separate organization's budget;
  —the ability to modify or approve rate or fee changes affecting revenues (e.g., water usage rate increases);
  —the ability to veto, overrule, or modify the decisions of the separate organization's governing body; and
  —the ability to appoint, hire, reassign, or dismiss persons responsible for the day-to-day operations (management) of the separate organization.

  As noted, appointment of the voting majority of a potential component unit's board is *not*, of itself, proof that the appointing government has the ability to impose its will. Board appointment would be tantamount to the ability to impose will, however, should the voting majority of a potential component unit also constitute the voting majority of the primary government.[3]
- *Financial benefit.* Sometimes the appointing government is legally entitled to the assets of the separate organization for which it appoints board members. Even if the appointing government is not legally so entitled, it may still have access in some other way to those same assets. Either situation represents a financial benefit to the appointing

---

[3] GASB, *Comprehensive Implementation Guide (2004)*, 4.47.

EXHIBIT 4-1
Indications that a primary government is obligated in some manner
for the debt of a potential component unit

The relationship between the two bodies is characterized by:

- the primary government's legal obligation to honor deficiencies to the extent that proceeds from other default remedies are insufficient;
- a requirement that the primary government temporarily cover deficiencies until funds are available from the primary repayment source or other default remedies;
- a requirement that the primary government provide funding for reserves maintained by the debtor organization, or that it establish its own reserve or guarantee fund for the debt;
- authorization for the primary government to provide funding for reserves maintained by the debtor organization, or to establish its own reserve or guarantee fund *and the primary government establishes such a fund*;
- authorization for the primary government to provide financing for a fund maintained by the debtor organization for the purpose of purchasing or redeeming the organization's debt, or to establish a similar fund of its own *and the primary government establishes such a fund*;
- explicit indication by contract, such as the bond agreement or offering statement, that in the event of default the primary government may cover deficiencies although it has no legal obligation to do so; and
- legal decisions within the state or the primary government's previous actions related to actual or potential defaults on another organization's debt that make it probable that the primary government will assume responsibility for the debt in the event of default.

government that GAAP consider to be evidence of an ongoing relationship. Moreover, GAAP expressly indicate that such a relationship can be created *indirectly* if the separate organization provides financial benefit to one or more of the appointing government's (other) component units.

Exchange transactions and exchange-like transactions, because they involve the exchange of equal or almost-equal value, are *not* considered to constitute a financial benefit, regardless of circumstances.[4] Also, the evaluation of financial benefit must be made in a manner consistent with the going-concern assumption that underlies accounting and financial reporting in general. Thus, a residual claim to the assets of a separate organization upon dissolution should not be treated as evidence of financial benefit, because it must be presumed, under the going-concern assumption, that the separate organization will continue to operate.

- *Financial burden.* Often an ongoing relationship is created between the appointing government and a separate organization because the latter imposes a financial burden on the former. GAAP identify two specific indications of such a financial burden:
  —the appointing government is legally obligated or has otherwise assumed the obligation to finance the deficits of, or provide financial support to, the organization or
  —the appointing government is obligated in some manner for the debt of the separate organization.

[4] GASB, *Comprehensive Implementation Guide (2004)*, 4.64. See chapter 3 for a discussion of the different types of transactions encountered in the public sector.

GAAP establish specific tests to determine whether an appointing government is, in fact, obligated in some manner for the debts of a separate organization. Those tests are listed in Exhibit 4-1.

The use of tax increment financing to support a separate organization is always considered evidence of financial burden. While the pledge of a tax increment is contingent on its realization, the pledge nonetheless represents a commitment of the appointing government's taxing power, much like the assumption of a contingent liability in regard to the debt of another organization.

All three of these tests *presume that another government appoints the voting majority of the separate organization's board*. That is, the tests are designed to determine whether the relationship created by board appointment is an ongoing one. Thus, in the absence of board appointment, neither the ability of the government to impose its will, nor the creation of a financial benefit, nor the imposition of a financial burden should be considered sufficient evidence that a separate organization is a component unit.[5]

In some situations, a single board governs both a government and a separate organization. For example, by virtue of election to the county board, county commissioners may also be the board members of one or more legally separate entities. In that case, it could not literally be said that the county "appointed" the boards of those other units. Nonetheless, the county, through its elected commissioners, is clearly financially accountable for those other units. Accordingly, since accounting and financial reporting stress substance over legal form, membership on dual boards is considered to be the functional equivalent of board appointment.[6]

An interesting situation arises when a government makes only the initial board appointments, and the appointees are responsible for the selection of their successors. In that case, GAAP indicate that successive boards also would be considered to meet the "board appointment" test, provided the government that made the initial appointment has the unilateral power to dissolve the organization.[7]

Fiscal dependence

The board appointment test, while perhaps most visible, is not the only test to determine whether a legally separate entity needs to be reported as a component unit. Even if a government does *not* appoint the board of a legally separate organization, that organization still needs to be included as a component unit of the government's financial reporting entity if it is fiscally dependent on the government. The issue of fiscal dependence was examined earlier in the discussion of the primary government. There it was noted that fiscal dependence is created when the governing board of one entity may *arbitrarily* override the financial decisions of another regarding its 1) budget, 2) tax levy or setting of rates or charges, or 3) issuance of bonded debt. It also was noted that ministerial or compliance-oriented reviews and blanket limitations should *not* be considered evidence of fiscal dependence.

---

[5] Of course, as discussed later, there is always the possibility that a legally separate entity that creates a financial benefit or burden, without board appointment, might still need to be included as a component unit because it would be misleading to exclude it from the financial reporting entity.

[6] GASB Statement No. 14, footnote 5; GASB, *Comprehensive Implementation Guide (2004)*, 4.7.

[7] GASB Statement No. 14, paragraph 24; GASB, *Comprehensive Implementation Guide (2004)*, 4.45.

Omission resulting in incomplete or potentially misleading financial reporting

Almost all component units are so classified because they meet the test of board appointment or are fiscally dependent on the primary government. Nonetheless, GAAP recognize that special situations may arise where legally separate organizations that meet neither of these tests might still need to be included as part of the primary government's financial reporting entity because failure to do so could render the primary government's financial statements incomplete or potentially misleading.

Special financing authorities for financially troubled local governments are a good example of just such a situation. Often the first step on the road to recovery for local governments in serious financial difficulties is the restructuring of existing obligations. Long-term debt typically must be issued for this purpose. Unfortunately, a local government in financial trouble is not in a good position to issue new long-term debt. As a result, special arrangements are sometimes made to establish a legally separate special financing authority expressly for this purpose. Potential creditors will insist that such a legally separate entity be structured to meet neither the board appointment test nor the fiscal dependency test. Nonetheless, excluding the separate financing authority—a key component of the government's financial structure—could make the government's financial statements difficult to understand, if not misleading. Therefore, such a special financing authority typically would be reported as part of the government's financial reporting entity—not because the government appointed the board or because the authority was fiscally dependent on the government, but simply because it would be potentially misleading to exclude it.

Sometimes legally separate, tax-exempt entities (e.g., university foundations) may need to be included within the financial reporting entity as component units based upon the nature and significance of their relationship with the primary government and its component units, even though they do *not* meet either the board appointment or fiscal dependency tests described earlier. Specifically, such entities must be treated as component units if they meet *all three* of the following additional criteria:

- *Direct benefit.* The economic resources received or held by the separate organization are entirely or almost entirely for the direct benefit of the primary government, its component units, or its constituents.[8]
- *Access.* The primary government, or its component units, is entitled to, or has the ability to otherwise access, a majority of the economic resources received or held by the separate organization.[9]
- *Significance.* The economic resources received or held by an *individual organization* that the specific primary government is entitled to, or has the ability to otherwise access, are significant to that primary government.[10]

---

[8] The intent of this requirement is to eliminate organizations that benefit multiple constituent groups (e.g., federated fund-raising organizations).

[9] Examples of the ability to otherwise access economic resources would include 1) the primary government's past receipt of the majority of the tax-exempt entity's economic resources, 2) the primary government's successful past requests for economic resources from the tax-exempt entity, and 3) the fact that the tax-exempt entity is financially interrelated with the primary government as defined by the Financial Accounting Standards Board in Statement No. 136, *Transfers of Assets to a Not-for-Profit Organization or Charitable Trust That Raises or Holds Contributions for Others.*

[10] The intent of this requirement is to exclude smaller organizations like booster clubs and parent-teacher organizations.

Separate, tax-exempt entities that do *not* meet all three of these criteria may still need to be considered as potential component units if the financial statements would be incomplete or misleading without them. More specifically, inclusion should be considered if these entities are closely related to or financially integrated with the primary government.[11]

POTENTIAL FOR DUAL INCLUSION

It is possible that a single legally separate organization may meet the tests to qualify as the component unit of more than one primary government. Assume, for example, that the state appoints a school board and partially finances its operations, but that the school board is fiscally dependent on the county. In that case the school board would meet the board appointment test for its relationship with the state while meeting the fiscal dependency test in regard to the county. Yet GAAP clearly state that a single entity may be the component unit of *one, and only one*, primary government. Thus, a decision would be necessary regarding the financial reporting entity in which the school board should be included as a component unit. In this case, it would probably be most appropriate to report the school board as a component unit of the county rather than of the state.[12]

FIDUCIARY REPORTING

GAAP direct that fiduciary funds be used to report assets held in a trustee or agency capacity for others.[13] Accordingly, the resources of a legally separate entity that does *not* qualify as a component unit may nonetheless still have to be included within the primary government's financial statements as a fiduciary fund.

PRESENTATION OF THE FINANCIAL REPORTING ENTITY

The manner in which component unit data are combined with the primary government's data within the latter's financial reporting entity depends on the nature of the relationship between the primary government and the component unit. The operations of some component units are so intertwined with those of the primary government that they function, for all practical purposes, as an integral part of the primary government. GAAP prescribe that the data from such integral component units be blended with the primary government's data to form a single, homogeneous entity. That is, no distinction is made between the data of the primary government and those of the component unit. Such entities are referred to in the authoritative accounting and financial reporting literature as *blended component units*.

Other component units, however, operate with a greater or lesser degree of autonomy from the primary government. According to GAAP, the data from such units are to be presented together with, *but separately from*, the data of the primary government. State and local governments use the term

---

[11] Financial integration may be evidenced by policies, practices, or organizational documents of either the primary government or the legally separate, tax-exempt entity.
[12] This specific example is given in GASB Statement No. 14, paragraph 38.
[13] GASB Statement No. 34, *Basic Financial Statements—and Management's Discussion and Analysis—for State and Local Governments*, paragraph 69.

discrete presentation to describe such separate reporting. Accordingly, the authoritative accounting and financial reporting literature refers to such entities as *discretely presented component units.*

The mechanics of blending

Data of blended component units are treated in the same way as data of the primary government, without distinction (except as described in the following paragraph). That is, each individual fund of a blended component unit is presented as though it were a fund of the primary government. Assume, for example, that a primary government reports a capital projects fund and that a blended component unit also reports a capital projects fund of its own. The combined financial reporting entity would then report two separate capital projects funds.

A practical problem arises, however, in the case of a blended component unit's general fund. As noted earlier,[14] GAAP permit the presentation of only one general fund for the entire financial reporting entity. To treat the general fund of a blended component unit as a general fund in its own right, therefore, would have the practical effect of violating this prohibition against multiple general funds. To avoid this outcome, GAAP direct that the general fund of a blended component unit be reclassified as a special revenue fund whenever the component unit is presented as part of the primary government's financial reporting entity. Of course, if the blended component unit issues a separate report, its general fund would continue to be reported as a general fund in the separately issued report.

The mechanics of discrete presentation

Discrete presentation means that the data of a component unit are reported together with, but separately from, the data of the primary government in the government-wide financial statements. This goal is accomplished by reporting the data from discretely presented component units in one or more columns at the far right side of the government-wide financial statements. The component unit data to be used for this purpose are those that appear in the entity-wide total column of the component unit's government-wide financial statements.[15]

GAAP require that information on each major discretely presented component unit be presented separately within the basic financial statements.[16] This goal can be accomplished in any of three ways:

- *Separate columns for major individual component units.* A separate column can be presented on the face of the government-wide financial statements for each individual major discretely presented component unit. In that case, data from all nonmajor units normally would be presented in the aggregate in an *other component units* column.
- *Combining statements.* If a single column is reported for discretely presented component units on the face of the government-wide financial statements, then information on major individual component units

[14] See chapter 2.
[15] The presentation of an entity-wide total column is entirely voluntary. Therefore, if a component unit that itself reports component units elects not to report such a column, the data to be used in the reporting entity's financial statements would be the data that would have appeared in the component unit's entity-wide total column had it been presented. (GASB, *Comprehensive Implementation Guide (2004)*, 7.366.)
[16] GAAP do not define a major component unit. However, GASB Statement No. 14, paragraph 51, states: "In determining which component units are major, consideration should be given to each component unit's significance relative to the other component units and the nature and significance of its relationship to the primary government."

could be presented as a separate combining statement within the basic financial statements (following the basic financial statements for the funds). With this approach, the total of the combining statements needs to support the single column reported in the government-wide financial statements. Therefore, data from all nonmajor component units normally would be presented in the aggregate in an *other component units* column on the combining presentation.[17] Once again, the data to be used are those that appear (or would have appeared) in the entity-wide total column of the component units' government-wide financial statements. Fund information for component units may *not* be presented within the basic financial statements.[18]

- *Condensed financial statements included as part of the notes to the financial statements.* If a single column is reported for discretely presented component units on the face of the government-wide financial statements, information on major individual component units could be presented as condensed financial statements within the notes to the financial statements. Again, information for all nonmajor discretely presented component units should be presented in the aggregate.[19]

As just noted, fund information normally is *not* presented for individual discretely presented component units. Instead, financial statement users desiring fund-based information on a component unit are referred to the separately issued financial statements of that unit in the notes to the financial statements. However, if a component unit that uses fund accounting does not, in fact, issue separate financial statements, then information on the underlying funds of the component unit must be provided within the comprehensive annual financial report (but not the basic financial statements) of the overall financial reporting entity at the same level of detail used for the fund financial statements that are included within the basic financial statements.

Criteria for blending   Because component units are legally separate entities, there is a basic presumption that they should be presented separately (*discretely*) from the pri-

---

[17] Many discretely presented component units are enterprise funds. The operating statement format of an enterprise fund (i.e., the format that would be used in the component unit's separately issued financial statements) differs significantly from the format of the government-wide statement of activities. This difference raises the issue of the appropriate format to be used for a combining statement for major component units. The approach to be taken depends upon the level of detail provided for component units in the government-wide statement of activities. If component units with governmental activities and component units with business-type activities are combined in a single column in the government-wide financial statements, the format used in the combining statement should be that used in the government-wide statement of activities, with the data for component units with business-type activities recast accordingly. Alternatively "the government could display a single business-type activities line on the combining statement of activities, with a supporting combining statement of revenues, expenses, and changes in net assets." If all of the component units in a given discretely presented component units column are business-type activities, "the combining statement may be presented in the statement of revenues, expenses, and changes in net assets format with the combined totals recast into the reporting entity's statement of activities." (GASB, *Comprehensive Implementation Guide (2004)*, 7.367.)

[18] Fund financial statements for component units would need to be presented elsewhere within the comprehensive annual financial report, however, if there were no separately issued component unit report providing that information.

[19] The minimal level of detail required for condensed financial statements presented in the notes is not sufficient for a government that elects to present a combining statement for individual major discretely presented component units. Rather, a combining statement, if presented, must provide essentially the same level of detail used in the component unit's separately issued statements of net assets and activities. That is, changes are permitted, but only "to combine or retitle certain accounts for consistency and comparability across component units in the combining statements." (GASB, *Comprehensive Implementation Guide (2004)*, 7.368.)

mary government. As noted earlier, though, blended component units function, for all practical purposes, as an integral part of the primary government despite their separate legal status. GAAP identify only two situations where the use of blending is appropriate:

- *Shared governing body.* Clearly, a high degree of integration is achieved when the primary government and a component unit share a common governing body. Accordingly, GAAP indicate that blending is the appropriate means of presenting the component unit's data in such cases. Further, because GAAP emphasize the importance of substance over form, the board of the primary government and the board of the component unit *need not be identical* for this purpose. Rather, GAAP require only that the boards of the two entities be "substantively the same" to qualify for blending. Boards should be considered "substantively the same" if there is "sufficient representation of the primary government's entire governing body on the component unit's governing body to allow complete control of the component unit's activities." In practice, "sufficient representation" means that *a voting majority of the component unit's board must also function as a voting majority of the primary government's board.*[20]
- *Exclusive or almost exclusive benefit to the primary government.* The data of a component unit should be blended with the data of the primary government if the component unit either 1) provides service entirely or almost entirely to the primary government; or 2) otherwise exclusively or almost exclusively benefits the primary government even though it does not provide services directly to it. These criteria are aimed at identifying situations where component units function much like internal service funds (i.e., providing goods and services to the government itself as an administrative entity rather than to citizens). Assume, for example, that a stadium authority is used to finance and construct a new facility that will belong to the primary government. Because this authority exists solely to finance and construct an asset of the primary government, it would qualify for blending based on the "exclusive benefit" criterion. Conversely, assume the stadium authority was used not only to finance and construct the facility but also to operate it upon completion. This operating component represents an ongoing service to citizens (i.e., more like an enterprise fund than an internal service fund) that would disqualify the entity from being presented as a blended component unit.[21]

Legally separate, tax-exempt entities whose relationship with the primary government meets the three addition criteria described earlier (direct benefit, access, significance) should always be discretely presented rather than blended. That is, the criteria just discussed for blending do *not* apply to such organizations.[22]

[20] GASB, *Comprehensive Implementation Guide (2004)*, 4.94.
[21] As discussed in chapter 15, states and counties that are entitled to ongoing payments from tobacco companies in connection with the Master Settlement Agreement sometimes establish special financing authorities to issue bonds secured by anticipated future payments. Such authorities typically qualify as blended component units based on the criteria just described.
[22] If legally separate, tax-exempt entities do not meet the three criteria, but are included nonetheless because their inclusion is considered necessary to avoid incomplete or potentially misleading financial reporting, the criteria for blending would be applicable. All the same, it is unlikely that entities in these circumstances would meet the criteria for blending.

SUBSEQUENT EXCLUSION/INCLUSION OF A COMPONENT UNIT

An entity that qualified as a component unit one year may no longer so qualify the next. In that case, the following year's financial statements should report *beginning net assets* as though the component unit had never been included within the financial reporting entity. The revised beginning balance would need to be labeled as "restated" and accompanied by appropriate note disclosure.[23] Conversely, if a legally separate entity did not qualify as a component unit one year, but did so the next, the following year's financial statements should report *beginning net assets* as though the component unit had always been included within the financial reporting entity. Once again, the revised beginning balance would need to be labeled as "restated" and accompanied by appropriate note disclosure. In short, 1) the exclusion or inclusion of a component unit is based entirely upon its status in relation to the primary government *as of the financial reporting date*; and 2) if a component unit is included, it must report operations for the entire period.

SEPARATE REPORTING BY COMPONENT UNITS

Component units may issue their own separate, stand-alone reports. When a component unit issues a separate report, it should present its financial statements using all the rules applicable to a primary government. That is, if the component unit has one or more component units of its own, its financial reporting entity would need to incorporate data from those units to qualify as a fair presentation in conformity with GAAP. Naturally, the relationship between the component unit issuing the separate report and its own primary government would need to be disclosed on the cover of the financial report as well as in the notes to the financial statements.

SUMMARY

General-purpose governments often work together with legally separate special-purpose governments to provide services to citizens. GAAP direct financial statement preparers to look beyond the legal barriers that separate various units of government to define the financial reporting entity in a way that fully reflects the financial accountability of elected officials.

The nucleus and focus of the financial reporting entity is the primary government. All state governments and general-purpose local governments automatically should be treated as primary governments. Special-purpose governments qualify as primary governments only if they have a popularly elected governing body, enjoy separate legal status, and are fiscally independent of other governments.

A component unit is a legally separate organization that a primary government must include as part of its financial reporting entity for fair presentation in conformity with GAAP. There are three separate tests for determining whether a legally separate entity is a component of a primary government's financial reporting entity. Those tests involve: 1) appointment of the voting majority of the potential component unit's governing

---

[23] GASB, *Comprehensive Implementation Guide (2004)*, 4.109.

board, along with evidence that the appointment process creates an ongoing relationship between the primary government and the potential component unit; 2) the potential component unit's fiscal dependence on the primary government; or 3) the likelihood that exclusion of the potential component unit from the primary government's financial reporting entity would result in misleading financial reporting. In this last instance, additional criteria apply to certain legally separate tax-exempt entities.

It is possible that a single legally separate organization may qualify as the component unit of more than one government. However, GAAP indicate that a single entity can be the component unit of *one, and only one* primary government.

The manner in which the data of component units are combined with the data of the primary government within the primary government's financial reporting entity depends on the nature of the relationship between the primary government and the component unit. The data of some component units are *blended* with the data of the primary government because their operations are so intertwined with those of the primary government that the component units function, for all practical purposes, as an integral part of the government. Blending is employed when the primary government and a component unit substantively share the same board, or when the component unit provides services or benefits exclusively or almost exclusively to the primary government, much like an internal service fund. Blending is never appropriate, however, for legally separate tax-exempt entities that are included as component units solely because of the nature and significance of their relationship with the primary government and its component units as evidenced by three criteria (i.e., direct benefit, access, and significance).

In all other situations, the data of component units are presented discretely (separately) from the data of the primary government. GAAP require that data on each separate major discretely presented component unit be included within the basic financial statements. This requirement can be met by: 1) reporting separate columns for major discretely presented component units on the face of the financial statements themselves; 2) presenting combining statements for discretely presented component units within the basic financial statements; or 3) presenting condensed financial statements for major discretely presented component units as part of the notes to the financial statements.

5

Governmental Funds

Governmental funds are used to account for most if not all of a government's tax-supported activities. The accounting and financial reporting are virtually identical for all five types of governmental funds: general fund, special revenue funds, debt service funds, capital projects funds, and permanent funds. This chapter examines the general rules governing accounting and financial reporting for governmental funds as well as the application of those rules to a number of specific situations commonly encountered in connection with activities typically reported in governmental funds.

REVENUE RECOGNITION

All governmental funds share a common measurement focus and basis of accounting. Under the *current financial resources measurement focus*, the objective of the operating statement is to report *near-term* inflows and outflows of *financial* or spendable resources. To achieve this objective, the application of the *accrual* basis of accounting must be *modified* so that the operating statement focuses on transactions and events that affect inflows and outflows of financial resources in the near future.

This special measurement focus and basis of accounting profoundly affect the recognition of revenue in governmental funds. Accrual accounting is concerned solely with establishing a claim to resources (e.g., revenue should be recognized when earned), while *modified* accrual accounting requires that the timing of revenue-related inflows of financial resources also be considered.

Generally accepted accounting principles (GAAP) direct that governmental funds recognize revenues "in the accounting period in which they become susceptible to accrual—that is, when they become both measurable and *available to finance expenditures of the fiscal period.*"[1] This availability criterion supplements rather than replaces the criteria that normally govern revenue recognition under accrual accounting. Thus, amounts that are

---

[1] National Council on Governmental Accounting (NCGA) Statement 1, *Governmental Accounting and Financial Reporting Principles*, paragraph 63 [emphasis added].

available but do not otherwise meet the criteria for revenue recognition should be reported as *deferred revenue,* a liability, rather than as revenue. The relationship between the accrual and modified accrual criteria for revenue recognition is illustrated in Exhibit 5-1.

Financial resources should be considered available only to the extent they are "collectible within the current period or soon enough thereafter to be used to pay liabilities of the current period."[2] Governments enjoy considerable discretion in determining the availability period (for instance, 30, 45, 60, or 90 days) to be used for purposes of revenue recognition under the modified accrual basis of accounting.[3] In general, however, it is recommended that governments use a single availability period.[4]

GAAP expressly recognize the need for judgment and consistency in applying the modified accrual basis of accounting to revenue recognition.[5] Accordingly, it would *not* be appropriate to apply the availability criterion in so rigid a manner as to artificially distort normal revenue patterns. Consequently, when collections are delayed beyond the normal time of receipt because of *highly unusual circumstances,* it is recommended that the amounts involved still be recognized as revenue of the current period, even if collection takes place only some time after the close of the government's regular availability period.

Assume, for example, that a local government uses a 60-day availability period for revenue recognition, and that a computer malfunction causes state-collected revenues that ordinarily would be received within 60 days to be delayed beyond that period, perhaps to within 75 days. In that case, it is recommended that the amounts in question be recognized as current-period revenue, despite the collection delays resulting from the computer malfunction.

It has been emphasized that governmental funds focus on inflows and outflows of expendable resources. From this perspective, uncollectible amounts really represent a reduction in the inflow of financial resources rather than an outflow in their own right (that is, there never *was* an inflow of financial resources). Accordingly, revenues should be reported net of estimated uncollectible amounts in governmental funds. Say, for instance, that a government books a receivable of $220,000 in a governmental fund, and $15,000 is estimated to be ultimately uncollectible. Assume that $200,000 of the $205,000 that will be collected is considered available for purposes of revenue recognition. The appropriate journal entry in that situation would be:

	DR	CR
Accounts receivable	$ 220,000	
Allowance for doubtful accounts		$ 15,000
Revenue		200,000
Deferred revenue		5,000
(To recognize receivable, allowance for doubtful accounts, deferred revenue, and revenue)		

[2] NCGA Statement 1, paragraph 62.
[3] As discussed later in this chapter, however, GAAP place important restrictions on applying the availability criterion to property tax revenues and to revenues associated with appreciation in the fair value of investments. Governments must disclose the length of time used to determine availability in their summary of significant accounting policies (Governmental Accounting Standards Board (GASB) Statement No. 38, *Certain Financial Statement Note Disclosures,* paragraph 7).
[4] As noted later in this chapter, the availability period for property tax revenue recognition is limited by GAAP to no more than 60 days.
[5] NCGA Statement 1, paragraph 62.

EXHIBIT 5-1
Revenue recognition under the accrual and modified accrual bases of accounting

Claim to resources established?	Resources available to finance expenditures of current period?	Revenue under accrual basis of accounting?	Revenue under modified accrual basis of accounting?
Yes	No	Yes	No
Yes	Yes	Yes	Yes
No	Yes*	No	No

*a prepayment, for example.

Of course, governments must rely on estimates to determine the amount to be recorded as an allowance for doubtful accounts. If it is determined in a later period that the allowance for doubtful accounts must be *decreased*, the adjustment would be reported as a corresponding increase in *revenue* (if available) or in *deferred revenue* (if still unavailable). Conversely, if it is determined in a later period that the allowance for doubtful accounts must be *increased*, the adjustment would be reported as a corresponding reduction of *deferred revenue*. Expanding on the previous example, assume that in the subsequent fiscal year it was determined that the allowance for doubtful accounts should have been $17,000 rather than $15,000. In that case, the amount of deferred revenue would be reduced by $2,000 to obtain the desired balance in the valuation account.

In theory, miscellaneous revenues—such as fines and forfeits, golf and swimming fees, inspection charges, parking fees and parking meter receipts, licenses and permits—should be recognized on a modified accrual basis ("when measurable and available"). Typically, however, when these amounts are immaterial, revenue may be recognized on a cash basis.

Exchange and exchange-like transactions

Revenues related to exchange and exchange-like transactions should be recognized as soon as the exchange has occurred and the related amounts become available to liquidate liabilities of the current period.

Investment income

In most cases, GAAP require that investments be reported at their fair value, with changes in fair value being reported as investment income of the period. In some cases, such income is directly associated with investments that the government plans to hold to maturity or otherwise intends to hold on a long-term basis. At first, it might appear that the recognition of such revenue amounts should be deferred because the government intends to hold the investments long-term. However, GAAP clearly state that "*all* investment income, including changes in the fair value of investments, must be recognized as revenue in the operating statement."[6] If a government is concerned that such an increase in revenues and fund balance might be misinterpreted by financial statement users, it is free to designate a portion of unreserved fund balance equal to the appreciation in the fair value of investments to reflect management's policy of holding the underlying investments on a long-term basis.[7]

---

[6] GASB Statement No. 31, *Accounting and Financial Reporting for Certain Investments and for External Investment Pools*, paragraph 13 [emphasis added].

In practice, the various investment income components, such as interest, dividends, and increase/decrease in the fair value of investments, typically are reported net. This net amount is always categorized as revenue, even if the amount in question happens to be negative in a given period.[8] If a government elects to separately report the various investment income components, it should *not* distinguish "realized" gains and losses from "unrealized" amounts.[9]

Arbitrage earnings

The interest paid on most debt issued by state and local governments is exempt from federal income tax. As a result, purchasers of state and municipal debt are willing to accept lower interest rates than they would on taxable debt. State and local governments sometimes temporarily reinvest the proceeds of such tax-exempt debt in materially higher-yielding taxable securities, especially during construction projects. The federal tax code refers to this practice as *arbitrage*. In certain specific situations known as "safe harbors," governments are permitted to keep the extra earnings that result from arbitrage. Otherwise, any excess earnings resulting from arbitrage must be rebated to the federal government. Federal law requires that arbitrage be calculated and rebated at the end of each five-year period that tax-exempt debt is outstanding (90 percent of the amount due), and at maturity.

Rebatable arbitrage falls within the category of *claims and judgments*. Governmental funds may not recognize a liability for claims and judgments until amounts actually become due and payable. Therefore, governmental funds should *not* report either an expenditure or a liability in connection with rebatable arbitrage until payment is actually made or the liability has become due and payable.[10]

Lease revenues

Revenues related to operating leases in which the government is the lessor should be recognized as earned over the lease period, provided the amounts also meet the availability criterion. As for capital leases, the distinction between sales and direct financing leases is not relevant under modified accrual accounting. Rather, both the principal and interest portions of lease receipts should be recognized as revenue as soon as they become available.

Special assessment revenues

Some types of public-sector capital construction produce direct benefits for individual property owners. For example, the installation of roads or sewer lines in a new subdivision typically increases the value of the properties in that subdivision. In such cases, governments may impose a special assessment on the benefiting property owners to recover all or a portion of the project costs reflected in increased property values. Typically, special assessment payments are structured over a relatively long period, perhaps five years, although payment may be due in full if the property is sold during that time.

[7] GASB, *Comprehensive Implementation Guide (2004)*, 6.70. This treatment would not apply, of course, to any net *depreciation* in the fair value of investments.
[8] GASB, *Comprehensive Implementation Guide (2004)*, 6.69.
[9] The separate reporting of "realized" and "unrealized" investment income on the face of the financial statements is permitted only in the separately issued financial statements of governmental external investment pools (GASB Statement No. 31, paragraph 13).
[10] Of course, a liability and expense must be recognized in the accrual-based government-wide financial statements as soon as rebatable arbitrage is incurred (American Institute of Certified Public Accountants (AICPA), *State and Local Governments*, Section 5.06).

As a matter of law, the amount of a special assessment normally cannot exceed the increase in value of the benefiting property (the amount of the benefit to the property owner), meaning that special assessments constitute an exchange or exchange-like transaction. Thus, upon completion of the project (exchange), related special assessments qualify as revenue in a governmental fund to the extent they are considered to be "available."[11]

Research grants

It is important that transactions be classified for accounting and financial reporting purposes based on their economic substance. From this perspective, some research "grants" actually represent the exchange of equal or almost-equal value and should therefore be treated as exchange or exchange-like transactions. For example, a commercial enterprise may provide research money to a government agency in return for the right of first refusal to any commercial applications that might result from the research. Revenue in such cases should be recognized as it is earned, subject to availability.

Conversely, research grants that do *not* involve the exchange of equal or almost-equal value should be treated as voluntary nonexchange transactions. That is, revenue should be recognized as soon as all eligibility requirements have been met and the amounts become available to finance expenditures of the current period.[12] In some instances, a single research grant may have elements of both an exchange and nonexchange transaction. In that case, the exchange and nonexchange elements of the transaction should be treated separately in accordance with the relevant revenue recognition criteria.

Derived tax revenues

Derived tax revenues result from assessments imposed on exchange transactions. The most common examples of derived tax revenues are income taxes and sales taxes.

Income taxes

Income taxes should be recognized as revenue as soon as the underlying income is earned and the related tax becomes available to finance expenditures of the current period. As a practical matter, a significant portion of amounts collected in connection with income taxes may represent "overwithholdings" that eventually must be refunded to taxpayers. GAAP direct that income tax revenues be reported net of any such refundable amounts.[13] Also, recoveries from future tax audits should be considered in estimating the receivable and the related allowance for doubtful accounts.[14]

Sales taxes

Sales taxes should be recognized as revenue as soon as the underlying sales take place and the related amounts become available to finance expenditures of the current period. Normally there is sufficient time between the end of the fiscal period and the issuance of financial statements so that governments can report the actual amount of available sales tax revenues rather than rely on estimates. Recoveries from future tax audits should be considered in estimating the receivable and the related allowance for doubtful accounts.[15]

---

[11] Of course, the entire amount would be recognized as revenue in the accrual-based government-wide financial statements.
[12] GASB Statement No. 33, *Accounting and Financial Reporting for Nonexchange Transactions*, paragraph 21.
[13] GASB Statement No. 33, paragraph 16.
[14] GASB, *Comprehensive Implementation Guide (2004)*, 7.451.
[15] GASB, *Comprehensive Implementation Guide (2004)*, 7.451.

It also is important to distinguish between sales taxes raised using a government's *own* taxing power versus *shared* sales taxes that are raised using some *other* government's taxing power. In the latter instance, the sales taxes are *not* derived tax revenues from the recipient's viewpoint, because the recipient is not actually raising the taxes. Rather, shared sales taxes are properly classified by the recipient as either a government-mandated or voluntary nonexchange transaction that should be recognized as revenue using the same criteria normally applicable to such transactions.[16]

Imposed nonexchange revenues

Assessments imposed on some basis other than an underlying exchange transaction are technically known as *imposed nonexchange revenues*. These revenues typically are associated with a particular period, such as an academic year or a budget year. Generally, a government should recognize imposed nonexchange revenues as soon as it has established an enforceable legal claim, *provided the establishment of that claim does not precede the period with which the revenues are associated.*

Property taxes

Property taxes constitute something of an exception to the general rule just described for revenue recognition for imposed nonexchange revenues. Specifically, governments are directed to recognize property tax revenues in the period for which the taxes are levied, *even if an enforceable legal claim arises only in the subsequent period*, subject to the availability criterion of modified accrual accounting.[17]

Property tax revenues may *not* be recognized before the period they are intended to finance, even if an enforceable legal claim to the resources exists and those resources are otherwise available to finance expenditures of the current period. Thus, property tax payments received in advance of the fiscal period they are intended to finance must be reported as deferred revenue, not as revenue. All the same, property taxes destined for future debt service normally should be recognized as revenue of the period for which they are levied rather than as revenue of the period in which the related debt service payment will be made.[18]

Sometimes there are several different *periods* associated with a given property tax levy (e.g., the fiscal period of the government collecting the taxes, the fiscal period of the government levying the taxes, and the period during which the taxed property was owned). In such cases, the period for which property taxes should be considered to be levied is generally the budget or fiscal period of the entity initiating the levy.[19]

Property tax revenues should be recognized net of estimated refunds and uncollectible amounts.[20]

GAAP place a limitation on the availability period that may be used for purposes of property tax revenue recognition. Specifically, property tax revenues may be considered available only if collection occurs within no more than 60 days following the end of the fiscal period. GAAP also state that "if, *because of unusual circumstances*, the facts justify a period greater

---

[16] GASB Statement No. 33, paragraph 28, (as amended by GASB Statement No. 36, *Recipient Reporting for Certain Shared Nonexchange Revenues*, paragraph 2).
[17] Sometimes governments have ignored such amounts when they have been considered unavailable (i.e., essentially netting the property tax receivable and the related liability for deferred revenue). GAAP, however, do *not* permit the application of such a netting approach.
[18] GASB, *Comprehensive Implementation Guide (2004)*, 7.454.
[19] GASB, *Comprehensive Implementation Guide (2004)*, 7.453.
[20] GASB Statement No. 33, paragraph 18.

than 60 days, the governmental unit should disclose the period being used and the facts that justify it" [emphasis added]. It is important, however, to avoid misapplying this special exception to the 60-day rule. The intent of the exception is to avoid one-time fluctuations in revenue recognition resulting from unexpected delays in collections. Accordingly, recurrent or permanent conditions (such as a statutory collection date 75 days subsequent to the end of the fiscal year) should *not* be considered an "unusual circumstance" for this purpose.[21]

Payments in lieu of taxes

Sometimes a government receives payments in lieu of taxes to compensate it for the cost of services provided to an entity that is not otherwise subject to taxation.[22] It is important to distinguish payments in lieu of taxes that are reasonably equivalent to the value of the service provided (an exchange or exchange-like transaction) from those that are levied on some other basis, such as assessed valuation (an imposed nonexchange transaction). In the former case, revenue is recognized as the related service is provided, subject to the availability criterion. In the latter case, revenue is recognized based on the establishment of an enforceable legal claim and the availability of the amounts in question.[23]

Escheat revenue

Often states take custody of private property when its legal owner cannot be found or identified (for instance, estates without heirs and abandoned bank accounts). Such property is said to *escheat,* or revert, to the state. Most often, the rightful owners of escheat property retain their legal claim to these assets in perpetuity. Despite that fact, in practice, most escheat assets are never reclaimed.

States typically remit most escheat property to the general fund, where it is used to finance the operations of the general government. Only a portion of such assets normally is retained to pay claims from property owners. A separate private-purpose trust fund may be used for escheat property that is retained for this purpose.

If a separate fund private-purpose trust fund is used, the general fund should report directly as revenue all escheat property not expected ultimately to be paid to claimants.[24] If a separate fund is *not* used, escheat revenue must be reported net of the related liability for amounts actually expected to be paid to property owners.[25]

Fines and forfeitures

Fines and forfeitures should be recognized when they are legally enforceable. A fine is considered to be legally enforceable either when the party pays the fine (thus acknowledging liability) or when imposed by a court. In the latter case, revenues should be recognized net of estimated refunds resulting from appeals, if material.[26]

---

[21] NCGA Interpretation 3, *Revenue Recognition—Property Taxes*, paragraph 8.
[22] The allocation of overhead costs constitutes a reimbursement rather than a payment in lieu of taxes.
[23] The proper treatment of payments in lieu of taxes within the primary government is discussed in chapter 3.
[24] A fiduciary fund may never report resources that will ultimately be made available to the government itself.
[25] GASB Statement No. 21, *Accounting for Escheat Property*, paragraph 5, (as amended by GASB Statement No 34, paragraph 6, and GASB Statement No. 37, *Basic Financial Statements—and Management's Discussion and Analysis—for State and Local Governments: Omnibus*, paragraph 3).
[26] GASB, *Comprehensive Implementation Guide (2004)*, 7.452.

Government-mandated and voluntary nonexchange transactions

The accounting and financial reporting are identical for government-mandated nonexchange transactions (such as funded mandates) and voluntary nonexchange transactions (such as many grants and donations). In both cases, revenue should be recognized as soon as all eligibility requirements have been met and the related amounts are available to liquidate liabilities of the current period.

It should be emphasized that eligibility requirements include *time requirements*. For example, there may be a requirement that the resources provided by a nonexchange transaction be sold, disbursed, or consumed *during a particular period*. In other cases, there may be a restriction on using the resources *prior to a particular period*. When the provider is a government and no time requirement is specified, a time restriction automatically is assumed to apply to the start of the *immediate provider's* fiscal year. If the immediate provider government budgets on a biennial basis, each year of the biennium should be treated as a separate period for this purpose.[27]

Assume, for example, that a state government with a June 30 fiscal year-end will be the immediate provider of resources from a federal grant (September 30 fiscal year-end) to a special-purpose government with a calendar fiscal year. In that case, absent a specific time restriction, the recipient special-purpose government would not recognize revenue prior to July 1, the inception of the immediate provider's (state) fiscal year.

Formula grants

Grants based on some formula (e.g., the number of full-time equivalent students) should be recognized as revenue as soon as all eligibility criteria have been met and the related amounts become available. Once again, of course, eligibility criteria would include any time restrictions imposed by (or imputed to) the provider. Assume, for example, that a school district has a fiscal year-end of August 31 but begins the fall term in mid-August. The school district receives its first installment of a state formula grant in late September. Revenue related to the September payment could be recognized in August (presuming it is considered to be available) *only if the grant could be used to cover costs of the fiscal year ending August 31*. Conversely, if the grant was *not* available to cover costs incurred prior to August 31, no revenue would be recognized in that fiscal year, *regardless of availability*.

Reimbursement grants

The defining feature of reimbursement grants is that the resources remain the property of the grantor until allowable costs are incurred.[28] Reimbursement grants, also commonly known as expenditure-driven grants, should be recognized as soon as all eligibility criteria have been met and the related amounts become available. In particular, attention should be paid to two eligibility requirements: incurrence of allowable expenditures, and compliance with any and all contingent requirements (such as matching requirements or level/maintenance of effort requirements).[29] Reimbursement grants, it should be noted, are explicitly subject to the same availability criterion normally applicable to revenue recognition under the modified accrual basis of accounting.[30]

---

[27] GASB Statement No. 33, paragraph 24.

[28] GASB, *Comprehensive Implementation Guide (2004)*, 7.455.

[29] "Recognition of assets and revenues should not be delayed pending completion of purely routine requirements, such as the filing of claims for allowable costs under a reimbursement program or the filing of progress reports with the provider" (GASB Statement No. 33, footnote 10).

[30] GASB, *Comprehensive Implementation Guide (2004)*, 7.456.

Situations also may arise where a government meets all eligibility requirements of a reimbursement grant, but the grant itself is still subject to appropriation. As a general rule, revenue related to expenditure-driven grants should *not* be recognized before appropriation by the grantor, even if the grant period has begun and eligible expenditures have been incurred.[31] An exception to this general rule occurs, however, when grant payments are legally authorized prior to appropriation. In that case, revenue should be recognized prior to appropriation, provided that the availability criterion has been met.[32]

On-behalf payments of salaries and benefits

Employers are required to reflect in their own financial statements any payments of salaries or fringe benefits made by others to a third party (such as a pension plan) on behalf of their employees, even if the employer is not legally obligated in any way for the payment. Revenue related to such on-behalf payments normally should be recognized for all amounts that were either received or receivable by the third party as of fiscal year-end. If a single fund is used to report on-behalf payments, that fund usually is the general fund.[33]

Donations of capital assets

Governmental funds are used to report *financial* or spendable assets. Accordingly, governmental funds normally do *not* report capital assets. Sometimes, however, a government receives a gift of a capital asset that it intends to sell rather than keep. Such donations of capital assets may be reported as revenues if either of the following conditions is met: the asset is sold prior to the end of the fiscal period, and the proceeds of the sale are considered available; *or* the asset is sold (or the government has entered into a contract to sell the asset) prior to issuance of the financial statements, and the proceeds of the sale are considered available.

If the proceeds of a sale of a donated capital asset are *not* considered available, then the underlying asset itself (*assets held for resale*) or the related receivable should be offset by a liability for deferred revenue.

No asset or liability would be reported in a governmental fund for donated capital assets for which there is no sale contract as of the date financial statements are issued. Instead, a receivable and revenue/deferred revenue would be recognized in the appropriate governmental fund only at the time the government finally entered into a sales contract.[34]

Endowments and similar arrangements

Permanent funds, one of the five governmental fund types, are used to account for "resources that are legally restricted to the extent that only earnings, and not principal, may be used for purposes that support the reporting government's programs." A good example of such an arrangement is an endowment for the perpetual care of a municipal cemetery. Contributions to either permanent or term endowments should be classified as revenue and recognized only when received.[35]

---

[31] GASB, *Comprehensive Implementation Guide (2004)*, 7.458.

[32] GASB, *Comprehensive Implementation Guide (2004)*, 7.459.

[33] GASB Statement No. 24, *Accounting and Financial Reporting for Certain Grants and Other Financial Assistance*, paragraph 8.

[34] The donated capital asset would, of course, be reported in the accrual-based government-wide statement of net assets. This guidance is based upon a nonauthoritative discussion found in GASB Statement No. 11, *Measurement Focus and Basis of Accounting—Governmental Fund Operating Statements*, paragraph 60.

[35] GASB Statement No. 33, footnote 12.

Pass-through grants

When governmental funds are used to account for pass-through resources provided to other governments,[36] revenue should be recognized when all eligibility requirements have been met and the resources become available, which typically is considered to occur when the resources are, in fact, transmitted to their intended final recipient.[37]

Food stamps

The federal government's food stamp program is designed to increase the food purchasing power of economically disadvantaged individuals. The use of electronic benefits transfer (EBT) systems makes it possible for program beneficiaries to charge their qualifying food purchases. Revenues and expenditures should be reported when the underlying transaction (the food purchase) occurs.[38]

Commodities programs

Sometimes the federal government sends commodities (e.g., surplus agricultural products) to state or local governments to distribute among individuals or to use in government programs (e.g., school lunch programs). Such resources technically may be classified as supplies inventories (i.e., inventories held for a purpose other than resale), in which case, revenue should be recognized at the time of receipt.[39]

OTHER FINANCING SOURCES

Theoretically, it would be possible to use the term *revenues* to describe all inflows of current financial resources in governmental funds. As a practical matter, however, financial statements for governmental funds traditionally have distinguished two categories of resource inflows: *revenues* and *other financing sources*. This latter category has been used to isolate certain nonroutine inflows that might otherwise distort the analysis of revenue trends. GAAP only permit the use of the other financing sources category in the specific situations described in the paragraphs that follow.

Issuance of long-term debt

Clearly, those wishing to analyze a government's finances need to distinguish between regular, ongoing revenues and resources provided by long-term debt. Accordingly, GAAP direct that the issuance of long-term debt be treated as an other financing source rather than as revenue. The amount so reported should equal the face value of the debt.[40] If debt is issued at a premium, the premium should be reported as a separate other financing source in its own right.[41] On account of fees and discounts (see page 81), the amount actually received by the issuer frequently will be less than the amount reported as an other financing source (i.e., face value). Therefore, it is best to avoid using terms such as *bond proceeds* to describe

---

[36] Agency funds are used to account for those rare pass-through arrangements where a government functions as a pure cash conduit (GASB Statement No. 24, paragraph 5).

[37] Pass-through grants are subject to the revenue recognition requirements of GASB Statement No. 33 (see GASB Statement No. 33, paragraph 45). Generally, pass-through grants are considered to be functionally equivalent to an expenditure-driven grant.

[38] GASB Statement No. 24, footnote 4.

[39] AICPA, *State and Local Governments*, 12.19. As noted later in this chapter, the consumption method typically is used to account for inventories of commodities rather than the purchases method.

[40] GASB Statement No. 34, *Basic Financial Statements—and Management's Discussion and Analysis—for State and Local Governments*, paragraph 88 (as amended by GASB Statement No. 37, *Basic Financial Statements—and Management's Discussion and Analysis—for State and Local Governments: Omnibus*, paragraph 16).

[41] GASB Statement No. 34, paragraph 88.

the other financing source resulting from the issuance of long-term debt, in favor of more appropriate terminology (e.g., *debt issuance*).[42]

For accounting and financial reporting purposes, a bond issuance is considered to have taken place as of the closing date (i.e., when the bonds are issued). Consequently, a government should report an other financing source for bond proceeds as of that date, even if this treatment requires the government to report a receivable.[43]

Underwriter's fees and discounts

The amount of cash actually received typically is less than the face amount of the debt (or the face amount of the debt plus premium) for one or both of the following reasons:

- A portion of the proceeds of long-term debt may be withheld for underwriter's fees due in connection with the debt issuance.
- The stated rate of interest on the debt may have been less than the market rate of interest for similar securities when the debt was issued, in which case the debt may have been sold at a discount.

As just noted, neither type of discount should be netted against the other financing source reported to record the debt issuance. Instead, discounts resulting from the withholding of underwriter's fees should be reported as *expenditures*, while discounts resulting from a disparity in interest rates should be treated as an *other financing use*.[44]

Assume that a government issues bonds with a face value of $4,700. The government receives $4,540 in proceeds from the sale. The balance of $160 represents amounts withheld for underwriter's fees ($150) and a discount resulting from a disparity between the market rate of interest and the stated rate of interest on the debt ($10). Here is the appropriate journal entry to record the receipt of the debt proceeds in these circumstances:

	DR	CR
Cash	$ 4,540	
Expenditures—issuance costs	150	
Other financing use—bond discount	10	
Other financing source—bond issuance		$ 4,700
(To record issuance of debt)		

Capital leases and similar arrangements

Governments have a variety of options for financing their capital acquisitions. One option, of course, is to obtain the needed resources from a lender and then apply those resources to acquire the desired asset(s) from the vendor. Alternatively, the vendor could itself provide the needed financing in the form of a capital lease. From the vantage point of economic substance, these situations are essentially identical, except for the identity of the lender. However, the resource inflows and outflows associated with the two situations are quite different. In the case of a third-party borrowing (such as issuance of bonds, notes, or certificates of participation), the inflows and outflows of resources are as follows:

- receipt of the proceeds of the borrowing from the third-party lender;
- purchase of the capital asset; and
- subsequent debt service payments on the borrowing.

In the case of a capital lease with the vendor, there is no initial inflow and outflow of resources equal to the value of the asset being acquired (receipt

---

[42] GASB Statement No. 37, paragraph 59.
[43] AICPA, *State and Local Governments*, 8.16.
[44] GASB Statement No. 34, paragraph 87 (as amended by GASB Statement No. 37, paragraph 16).

of proceeds and purchase of the asset). Instead, the government makes an initial down payment on the lease purchase, followed by payments over the term of the lease.

Because the two situations just described are substantially equivalent economically, GAAP require that they be treated in essentially the same way in governmental funds, despite the differences in inflows and outflows of current financial resources. Specifically, GAAP require that capital lease transactions in which the government is a lessee be accounted for as though the capital acquisition had, in fact, been financed through a third-party lender. That is, GAAP require that a governmental fund report at the inception of a capital lease both an other financing source and an expenditure equal to the net present value of the minimum lease payments.[45]

For example, a government might enter into a capital lease for equipment acquisition in the amount of $140,000. The lease agreement requires a down payment of $15,000, and scheduled lease payments are not due until the following year. Here are the appropriate journal entries in a governmental fund:

	DR	CR
Expenditures	$ 140,000	
Other financing sources—capital leases		$ 140,000
(To record capital lease acquisition)		

	DR	CR
Expenditures—debt service—principal	$ 15,000	
Cash		$ 15,000
(To record capital lease down payment)		

This same treatment logically would apply as well to situations where a government acquired a capital asset by agreeing to assume related debt.

Anticipation notes

A government's cash flow needs may require that it borrow funds in anticipation of future receipts. Thus, governments frequently issue notes in anticipation of tax and revenue collections, receipt of grant proceeds, and receipt of bond proceeds. GAAP specifically indicate that no other financing source should be reported in connection with tax anticipation notes (TANs) and revenue anticipation notes (RANs). Instead, the governmental fund receiving the proceeds of RANs and TANs should report a fund liability.[46]

The case of bond anticipation notes (BANs) is somewhat different from that of RANs and TANs. GAAP direct that the proceeds of BANs be treated as an other financing source if "all legal steps have been taken to refinance the bond anticipation notes and the intent is supported by an ability to consummate refinancing the short-term note on a long-term basis." The criteria for making this determination are provided by Financial Accounting Standards Board (FASB) Statement No. 6, *Classification of Short-Term Obligations Expected to be Refinanced*: issuing a long- term obligation after the issue date of the balance sheet; or, before the balance sheet is issued, entering into a financing agreement that clearly permits the government to refinance the

[45] NCGA Statement 5, *Accounting and Financial Reporting Principles for Lease Agreements of State and Local Governments*, paragraph 14.
[46] NCGA Interpretation 9, *Certain Fund Classifications and Balance Sheet Accounts*, paragraph 12. TANs and RANs are handled as balance sheet transactions, and only the interest related to such transactions will affect the operating statement.

BANs on a long-term basis on terms that are readily determinable.[47] These requirements are summarized as follows:

- The receipt of BAN proceeds may be treated as an other financing source only if, as of the date financial statements are issued, the BANs have been replaced by debt that extends at least one year beyond the date of the balance sheet (or a qualifying financing agreement is in place).
- Otherwise, BANs should be reported as a fund liability in the governmental fund that receives the proceeds (even if the BANs are expected to be paid with the resources of some other fund).[48]

The eventual replacement of BANs not reported as a governmental fund liability should be treated as a refunding (other financing source/use).

The appropriate treatment for grant anticipation notes (GANs) is not specifically addressed by GAAP. It is recommended, however, that GANs be treated in the same manner as TANs and RANs.

Demand bonds

Governments sometimes issue bonded debt with a provision (a *put* feature) that allows bondholders to demand repayment prior to maturity of all outstanding principal plus accrued interest. Such securities are known as *demand bonds* or *put bonds*. Typically, demand bonds are supported by a take-out agreement with a bank or investment firm ensuring that the government will be able to refinance on a long-term basis any bonds that are put by the bondholders. The issuance of demand bonds should be treated as an other financing source if all of the following criteria are met:

- The government has entered into a take-out agreement before the financial statements are issued.
- The take-out agreement does not expire within one year of the end of the fiscal period.
- Neither the take-out agreement itself, nor the obligations issued pursuant to that agreement, are cancelable by the lender within one year of the end of the fiscal period.
- The lender is expected to be financially capable of honoring the take-out agreement.

Otherwise, demand bonds are reported as a liability of the governmental fund receiving the proceeds rather than as an other financing source.

Normally, of course, the repayment of debt reported as a fund liability would *not* be reflected in the operating statement of a governmental fund. GAAP make a special provision, however, for demand bonds that are reported as liabilities of a governmental fund. In that case, financial statement preparers are directed to report an other financing source in connection

---

[47] Such a financing agreement also must meet all of the following conditions, according to FASB Statement No. 6, paragraph 11:
- The agreement does not expire within one year (or operating cycle) from the date of the balance sheet.
- The agreement is not cancelable by the lender or the prospective lender during that period.
- The obligations incurred under the agreement are not callable during that period (except for violation of provisions with which compliance is objectively determinable or measurable).
- No violation of any provision in the agreement exists at the balance-sheet date, and no available information indicates that a violation has occurred thereafter but prior to issuance of the balance sheet (or, if a violation exists a waiver has been obtained).
- The lender or the prospective lender is expected to be financially capable of honoring the arrangement.

[48] BANs in that case are handled as balance sheet transactions, and only the interest related to such transactions would affect the operating statement.

with debt service principal payments so that the full amount of those payments can still be reflected as an expenditure of the governmental funds.[49]

Assume, for example, that $2 million in demand bonds are issued in connection with a capital project, but that the terms of the arrangement require that the bonds be reported as a fund liability. In that case, the appropriate journal entries are:

	DR	CR
Cash	$2,000,000	
Demand bonds payable		$2,000,000
(To record issuance of demand bonds)		
Debt service expenditures—principal	100,000	
Debt service expenditures—interest	200,000	
Bonds payable	100,000	
Cash		300,000
Other financing sources—principal payment on		
demand bonds		100,000
(To record payment of debt service principal and interest		
related to demand bonds)		

Internal borrowings

A governmental fund sometimes will borrow resources on a long-term basis from another fund of the primary government, or from one of the primary government's *blended* component units. GAAP do *not* permit such interfund loans to be treated as an other financing source, despite their long-term character. Instead, an interfund liability should be reported.[50]

Borrowings from discretely presented component units are an entirely different matter. Even though they occur within the same financial reporting entity, they are still *external* from the perspective of the primary government, and so should be treated in the same fashion as other long-term debt.

Debt-financed capital grants

Sometimes governments, particularly at the state level, will use debt to finance grants to other governments, especially for capital purposes, such as school construction. There is no question that if the provider government were itself to receive the bond proceeds and then distribute them to the intended grant recipients, the provider would report both an other financing source and an expenditure. In practice, however, the proceeds in such cases sometimes are delivered directly to the intended grant recipients instead of passing through the provider government, which issued the debt.

There is, of course, no substantive difference between 1) receiving debt proceeds, then distributing them to other governments; and 2) directing that the proceeds of debt be delivered directly to other governments. In both cases, the government is utilizing its long-term borrowing power (an other financing source) to provide resources to one or more outside entities (an expenditure). Accordingly, the appropriate accounting and financial reporting treatment in both cases is to report an other financing source and an expenditure in the appropriate governmental fund.

---

[49] GASB Interpretation No. 1, *Demand Bonds Issued by State and Local Governmental Entities, An Interpretation of NCGA Statement 1 and NCGA Interpretation 9.*
[50] GASB Statement No. 34, paragraph 112(a) 1. Interfund borrowings are treated as balance sheet transactions, and their operating statement effect is limited to the interest-related portion of debt-service payments (if any).

Debt-financed capital contributions to proprietary funds

The situation just described for debt-financed capital contributions to other governments applies equally to debt-financed capital contributions to proprietary funds. That is, if debt is used to finance a capital contribution from the general government to a proprietary fund, the governmental funds should report an other financing source and a transfer, even if the proceeds of the debt are delivered directly to the recipient proprietary fund.[51]

Proceeds of no-commitment special assessment debt

There is essentially no difference *in form* between no-commitment special assessment debt and other long-term debt. *In substance*, however, there is a significant difference. The issuance of debt ordinarily represents a draw on a government's own future resource inflows. In the case of no-commitment special assessment debt, however, the benefiting property owners—not the government—will provide the resources needed to repay the debt. Thus, from the government's viewpoint, resources provided by no-commitment special assessment debt are essentially similar to resources provided by grantors. That is, a capital-type special assessment functions much like a property-owner-financed grant. Accordingly, the issuance of no-commitment special assessment debt should *not* be described as the receipt of debt proceeds[52] or classified as an other financing source; instead, it should be reported as revenue (like a grant) and described as "contributions from property owners" (or something similar).

Transfers

A transfer to a governmental fund is always properly reported as an other financing source. By definition, transactions with discretely presented component units are *not* considered to be interfund activity. Therefore, any amounts "transferred" from a discretely presented component unit to the primary government should be reported as revenues rather than as transfers.

Risk financing activities

Governments have the option of concentrating one or more of their risk financing activities in a single fund—either the general fund or an internal service fund. When the general fund is used to report risk financing activities, premiums received from other funds normally are treated as an interfund reimbursement by the general fund (a reduction of expenditures in the general fund and a corresponding expenditure/expense in the funds making the premium payments). The exception to this rule involves any amount of premiums paid in excess of related expenditures in the general fund. Since it is impossible to reimburse expenditures that have not yet been incurred, GAAP direct that any amount of premiums received in excess of expenditures be treated instead as an interfund transfer.[53]

Proceeds from the sale of capital assets

Governments routinely sell surplus capital assets associated with activities reported in governmental funds. Because there is the risk that sales of capital assets may distort a government's normal revenue trends, GAAP specifically direct that the proceeds of such sales be reported as an other financing

---

[51] A capital contribution presumes, of course, that taxpayers rather than the customers of the benefiting proprietary fund are expected to repay the debt. If a proprietary fund were expected to repay the proceeds of general obligation debt, that debt would be reported as a direct obligation of the proprietary fund despite its general obligation status (which would be disclosed in the notes to the financial statements), and no other financing source or transfer would be reported in the governmental funds.
[52] GASB Statement No. 6, paragraph 19.
[53] GASB Statement No. 10, *Accounting and Financial Reporting for Risk Financing and Related Insurance Issues*, paragraph 64.

source rather than as a revenue.[54] When the amounts of such capital asset sales become significant, the sales may qualify as special items.[55] In practice, however, such amounts frequently are immaterial and properly included as part of miscellaneous revenues.

Insurance recoveries

In accrual-based financial statements, insurance recoveries are normally netted against related losses. Netting is not possible in governmental funds, however, where the use of the current financial resources measurement focus prevents losses from being reported. Instead, GAAP direct that insurance recoveries be treated as an other financing source, unless they meet the criteria for classification as an extraordinary item.[56]

RECOGNITION OF RECEIVABLES AND RECOGNITION OF ASSETS RELATED TO EMPLOYEE BENEFITS

Receivables

Following are the general rules for recognizing receivables in governmental funds:

- *Exchange and exchange-like transactions.* A receivable should be recognized as soon as the underlying exchange occurs.
- *Derived tax revenues*—such as sales taxes and income taxes—are based on some underlying exchange transaction (for instance, sales taxes are based on sales transactions). A receivable for derived tax revenues ideally should be recognized at the same time the underlying transaction takes place.
- *Imposed nonexchange revenues*—such as fines and forfeits, property taxes, and other ad valorem taxes—normally should be recognized as soon as the government has obtained an enforceable legal claim.
- *Government-mandated and voluntary nonexchange transactions.* In the case of both government-mandated and voluntary nonexchange transactions, a receivable normally is recognized as soon as all eligibility requirements have been met. For this purpose, eligibility requirements include time requirements. For example, if the transaction involves a specific period, no receivable should be recognized until that period. Likewise, if the use of resources is not permitted prior to a specified date, no receivable would be reported before that date. If the resource provider is a governmental entity and no specific time requirement is stated in the agreement, a receivable should *not* be recognized prior to the start of the (immediate) *provider's* fiscal year.

Note that the concept of availability, which plays such a crucial role in revenue recognition under the modified accrual basis of accounting, has no corresponding effect on the recognition of receivables in governmental funds. For this reason, receivables in governmental funds often are offset by a liability for deferred revenue, whereas receivable and revenue recognition are essentially identical under the accrual basis of accounting.

---

[54] GASB Statement No. 34, *Basic Financial Statements—and Management's Discussion and Analysis—for State and Local Governments*, paragraph 88.

[55] Special items are discussed in chapter 3. Note that the GASB chose to use a sale of capital assets as its example of a special item in the nonauthoritative illustrative financial statements that accompany GASB Statement No. 34.

[56] GASB Statement No. 42, *Accounting and Financial Reporting for Impairment of Capital Assets and for Insurance Recoveries*, paragraph 21.

Guidance on some particular types of receivables that are sometimes problematic is offered in the paragraphs that follow.

Receivable for property taxes prior to an enforceable legal claim

Property taxes are the most common example of an imposed nonexchange revenue. Normally, receivables associated with imposed nonexchange revenues are not recognized until there is an enforceable legal claim. However, since GAAP direct that property tax revenues be recognized in the period for which levied, *even in the absence of an enforceable legal claim*, compliance with this requirement necessitates that a receivable be recognized for any such amounts levied for the period, but not yet collected as of the end of the fiscal period.

Receivable for the guaranteed reimbursement of interfund deficits

It is common for the general fund to "guarantee" the deficits of other funds. For example, the general fund may assume ultimate responsibility for all or a portion of deficits incurred in connection with capital construction accounted for in a capital projects fund. In such situations, the governmental fund benefiting from the guarantee should report a receivable (and related transfer), rather than a deficit, for whatever portion of the deficit is covered by such a guarantee.

Receivable resulting from noncompliance on the part of grant recipients

Governments that provide resources in government-mandated or voluntary nonexchange transactions typically establish eligibility requirements and purpose restrictions on the use of the resources provided. Failure to fully comply with these requirements and restrictions will reestablish the provider's claim to the assets. Accordingly, providers should recognize a receivable for recipient noncompliance with the eligibility requirements or purpose restrictions associated with a government-mandated or voluntary nonexchange transaction.[57] GAAP specifically direct that the provider recognize a receivable as soon as noncompliance is determined to be *probable* on the part of the resource recipient to correspond to the liability recognized by the latter.[58]

Receivable for bond proceeds not yet received

For accounting and financial reporting purposes, a bond issuance is considered to have taken place as of the closing date (i.e., the date the bonds are issued). Consequently, a government should report an other financing source for bond proceeds as of that date, which may require the government to report a receivable.[59]

Receivable arising from a long-term operating lease with scheduled rent increases

Sometimes operating lease contracts call for escalating rental payments. Often, such increases reflect anticipated increases in the service potential or economic value of the property being rented. In other cases, however, there is no such connection between the amount of rental payments and the value being provided to the lessee. Take, for example, the case of an initial three-month "rent holiday" offered as an inducement to enter into a lease agreement; clearly the lessee is receiving value from the use of the property despite the fact that no rent is being charged. Therefore, to ensure that

---

[57] Revenue cannot be recognized in connection with government-mandated or voluntary nonexchange transactions until all eligibility requirements have been met. Since compliance with eligibility requirements normally *precedes* expenditure recognition by the grantor, the guidance just described normally applies only to purpose restrictions. An important exception to this general rule is endowments and other gifts that cannot be sold. In such cases, the eligibility requirement is ongoing (i.e., certain resources must *not* be spent), which makes subsequent disqualifying noncompliance possible. (See GASB Statement No. 33, footnote 12.)

[58] GASB Statement No. 33, paragraph 26.

[59] AICPA, *Audits of State and Local Governments*, 8.16.

financial reporting is based upon the economic substance of such transactions rather than their legal form, GAAP indicate that whenever a long-term operating lease contains structured increases in rental payments that cannot reasonably be associated with an expected increase in the service potential or economic value of the property being rented, the lessor should report a receivable for the difference between the value provided to the lessee and scheduled lease payments. This receivable should be reported in the governmental funds, if material, because it is a financial asset. It also should be offset by a liability for deferred revenue to the extent that it is not considered to be available.[60]

Optional discounting of grant receivables

Accounting Principles Board (APB) Opinion No. 21, *Interest on Receivables and Payables,* sometimes requires that receivables be reported at their discounted present value. Discounting typically is *not* required, however, for grant receivables, because the scope of APB Opinion No. 21 encompasses only exchange transactions. That is, discounting of grant receivables normally is permitted rather than required.[61]

Prohibition against the reporting of endowment receivables

An essential eligibility requirement for an endowment is that the donated resources, once received, *not* be sold, disbursed, or consumed. Naturally this requirement cannot be met until endowment resources have actually been received. Therefore, no receivable should be reported for endowments.[62]

Assets related to employee benefits

A governmental employer's cumulative contributions to a pension plan in some situations may exceed the employer's annual required contribution (ARC) for the current and prior years. This situation may occur, for example, as the direct result of an employer's decision to issue pension obligation bonds to finance its unfunded actuarial accrued liability.[63] In that case, a net pension asset is reported as an asset on the government-wide statement of net assets. Because this net pension asset is not available for spending, it does *not* qualify as a current financial resource. Therefore, GAAP specifically preclude reporting a net pension asset in the governmental funds.[64]

The treatment just described for pensions applies equally to other postemployment benefits (OPEB). Thus, cumulative payments in excess of annual required contributions are reported as a net other postemployment benefits asset on the government-wide statement of net assets, but not on the governmental fund balance sheet.[65]

EXPENDITURE RECOGNITION

Under accrual accounting, expenses are recognized as soon as a liability is incurred, regardless of the timing of related cash flows. The same rule also generally holds true for *expenditure* recognition in governmental funds.

---

[60] GASB Statement No. 13, *Accounting for Operating Leases with Scheduled Rent Increases*, paragraph 9.
[61] GASB, *Comprehensive Implementation Guide (2004)*, 7.461. The one exception is "grants" that are actually exchange or exchange-like transactions (e.g., some research grants).
[62] GASB Statement No. 33, footnote 12, and GASB, *Comprehensive Implementation Guide (2004)*, 7.462.
[63] GASB, *Comprehensive Implementation Guide (2004)*, 7.120.
[64] GASB Statement No. 27, paragraph 16.
[65] GASB Statement No. 45, *Accounting and Financial Reporting by Employers for Postemployment Benefits Other Than Pensions.*

However, under *modified* accrual accounting, there are several important modifications to this general rule, as outlined in the paragraphs that follow.

Debt service payments

From an *economic* perspective, interest represents the rental cost of money. Accordingly, interest, like any other rental *expense*, accrues with the passage of time. Thus, a business with a fiscal year ending midway between semiannual debt service payments would report interest expense for the three months that had elapsed since the previous payment date.

Governmental funds, however, unlike businesses, focus on *expenditures* rather than expenses. From that perspective, debt service does not constitute a draw on current financial resources (an expenditure) until payment is due. Consequently, as a general rule, GAAP direct that expenditures related to debt service principal and interest payments be recognized in governmental funds in the period in which they become due.[66] Stated differently, no expenditure ordinarily should be reported in a governmental fund in connection with the unmatured principal and interest of long-term debt.[67] Thus, no expenditure or liability typically would be reported in a governmental fund at the end of the fiscal year for principal and interest payments due even as early as the first day of the following fiscal year.

There is one important exception to this general rule. In some cases, governments provide resources to a debt service fund during the current fiscal period in anticipation of debt service payments due early in the subsequent fiscal period. If the general rule on debt service expenditure recognition were to be applied in such situations, the result could be a large, short-term surplus in the debt service fund, which might be misinterpreted by some financial statement users. To avoid this potential problem, GAAP specifically *permit* governments to recognize an expenditure/fund liability in the *current* fiscal period for debt service principal and interest payments due early in the *subsequent* fiscal period if all of the following criteria are met:

- The government uses a debt service fund to account for debt service payments.
- The advance provision of resources to the debt service fund is mandatory rather than discretionary.
- Payment is due within a "short time period—usually one to several days and not more than one month."[68]

Inventories

Using the logic that normally applies to expenditure recognition, inventories of materials and supplies would be recognized immediately as an expenditure (a draw on current financial resources) when they are purchased. Accordingly, GAAP specifically provide for the use of the *purchases method* to account for inventories in governmental funds.

Since inventories commonly are consumed during a relatively short period after purchase, it may be argued that inventories should be considered a financial resource in their own right because they allow a government to avoid a near-term outlay of financial resources (an expenditure). In response, GAAP also permit inventories in governmental funds to be re-

---

[66] This treatment reflects common budgeting practice, where the entire amount of a debt service payment typically is budgeted in the year of payment.

[67] NCGA Statement 1, paragraph 72.

[68] GASB Interpretation No. 6, *Recognition and Measurement of Certain Liabilities and Expenditures in Governmental Fund Financial Statements*, paragraph 13.

ported using the *consumption approach* characteristic of accrual accounting. That is, governments may initially report the inventories they purchase as an asset and defer the recognition of an expenditure until the period in which the inventories actually are consumed. This latter approach is often encountered, for example, in the case of inventories of commodities.[69]

Under the purchases method, inventories are reported as an expenditure when purchased rather than capitalized as an asset. Some, however, expressed concern that use of the purchases method could leave financial statement users unaware of significant accumulations of inventory items. Accordingly, GAAP direct that *significant* amounts of inventory should always be reported as an asset, *even if the purchases method is used.*[70] This goal can be accomplished by making the following journal entry at the end of the fiscal period, assuming inventories on hand of $150,000:

	DR	CR
Inventories	$ 150,000	
Fund balance—reserved for inventories		$ 150,000
(To report inventories accounted for using the purchases method)		

Note that this journal entry has no effect on the amount of expenditures reported. This same journal entry would be made as well in subsequent fiscal periods to adjust the balance of the inventories account to reflect actual amounts of inventory on hand. Assume that the balance of inventories in the subsequent year was $130,000 rather than $150,000. In that case the appropriate journal entry to make the needed adjustment would be:

	DR	CR
Fund balance—reserved for inventories	$ 20,000	
Inventories		$ 20,000
(To adjust for changes in the balance of inventories)		

In both cases, the adjustment to the reserved fund balance account would be reported as a direct adjustment to beginning fund balance in the affected governmental fund.

It is especially important to note that the rule requiring the capitalization of inventories accounted for using the purchases method specifically applies only to *significant* amounts. As a practical matter, it is uncommon for inventories of materials and supplies to meet this significance threshold for capitalization.

In most cases, inventories in governmental funds are held for use rather than resale (e.g., supplies). Consequently, the cost of inventories is not "written down" to reflect market changes (i.e., "lower of cost or market") unless the usability of the inventory is affected by physical deterioration or obsolescence.[71]

Prepaid items

Certain types of services are commonly paid for in advance. Examples are insurance premiums and rent. The logic applied to such prepaid items is essentially the same as that for inventories. Accordingly, GAAP specifically allow the option of accounting for prepaid items in governmental funds

---

[69] AICPA, *State and Local Governments*, 12.19.
[70] NCGA Statement 1, paragraph 73.
[71] AICPA, *State and Local Governments*, 8.56.

using either the purchases method or the consumption method. However, in a departure from inventory accounting, GAAP do *not* require that significant balances of prepaid items be reported as assets if the purchases method is used.

Capital leases

A capital lease is treated in essentially the same way as other types of long-term debt: Both the principal and interest portions of lease payments are recognized as expenditures in the period when they are due. In addition, as noted earlier in connection with the discussion of other financing sources, GAAP direct that governmental funds report an expenditure equal to the present value of the minimum lease payments at the inception of a capital lease, to reflect the commitment of financial resources associated with acquiring a lease-financed capital asset.[72]

Debt-financed capital grants

Also as noted earlier, one government sometimes issues debt to finance a capital grant to another government. The provider government clearly is expending its own financial resources, even if the proceeds of the debt are delivered directly to the intended beneficiary rather than passing through the issuer. Consequently, the provision of debt-financed resources to another government should always be reflected in governmental funds as an expenditure, even if the issuing government does not act as a conduit for the bond proceeds.

Accrued liabilities normally financed in future periods

Governments typically liquidate their accrued liabilities with expendable available financial resources. Accordingly, an expenditure normally is recognized in a governmental fund at the same time that a liability is incurred.

Such is not the case, however, for certain long-term accrued obligations that state and local governments *in general* normally do *not* expect to liquidate with expendable available financial resources, specifically:

- compensated absences (such as vacation leave and termination payments for unused sick leave);
- claims and judgments;
- special termination benefits (special benefits offered to employees for a brief period in connection with employment termination); and
- landfill closure and postclosure care costs.

Under modified accrual accounting, expenditures and liabilities related to these obligations should be recognized in governmental funds only when they mature (*when due*). Thus, in the case of compensated absences, the only portion of the liability that would be reported in a governmental fund would be the amount of reimbursable unused vacation leave or sick leave payable to employees who had terminated their employment as of the end of the fiscal year. Likewise, a claim or judgment would only be recognized as an expenditure and a liability in a governmental fund as of the date that payment became due pursuant to the terms of a settlement agreement or court judgment. For special termination benefits, recognition would occur in a governmental fund as payments to employees who accepted the offer came due. In the case of landfill closure and postclosure costs, expenditure and liability recognition would be limited to amounts that came due each

---

[72] NCGA Statement 5, paragraph 14.

period upon receipt of goods or services used in the closing and postclosure care processes.[73]

Of course, the full amount of each of these liabilities would have to be reported in the accrual-based government-wide statement of net assets.

GAAP specifically leave open the possibility of applying this same treatment to other accrued liabilities possessing similar characteristics, but only based upon the practice of state and local governments *in general*. Thus, if state and local governments as a rule normally liquidate a given type of accrued liability with available financial resources (e.g., salaries payable), a particular government cannot avoid recognizing an expenditure and a fund liability simply by making special arrangements to liquidate the liability on a long-term basis.

Sometimes governments budget resources in advance to finance the future payment of long-term liabilities. For example, a government may elect to set aside resources as employees earn vacation leave for the eventual payment of that leave. This approach to financing future costs in no way affects the recognition of expenditures and liabilities in governmental funds, which would still report only amounts that had become due and payable upon termination.[74]

Unfunded pension contributions (net pension obligation) and unfunded OPEB contributions

Many governmental employers sponsor or participate in defined benefit pension plans on behalf of their employees. In a defined benefit pension plan, participating employees are promised pension payments based on a predetermined benefit formula that takes into account an individual employee's years of service and salary level. The estimated present value of the benefits thus promised to employees based on service already rendered is technically known as the *actuarial accrued liability*.

As the term implies, the actuarial accrued liability is an *actuarial* rather than an *accounting* liability, and so is *not* reported as a liability in either the governmental fund or government-wide financial statements. Instead, employers report a liability for accounting and financial reporting purposes only in situations where they have failed to fully fund their actuarially determined ARC to the pension plan. The liability for the cumulative effect of current and past underfunding of the ARC is known as the *net pension obligation* (NPO).[75] Because the NPO normally is not expected to be liquidated with expendable available financial resources, *no corresponding expenditure or liability is reported in the governmental fund financial statements.*[76] All the same, the NPO would still have to be reported as a liability in the accrual-based, government-wide statement of net assets.

The guidance just described for pensions applies equally to other postemployment benefits. Once again, a liability would have to be reported for the cumulative unfunded ARC (net other postemployment benefits ob-

---

[73] GASB Interpretation No. 6, paragraph 14.

[74] It may be difficult to accumulate resources (i.e., advance fund) in a governmental fund without having a liability to offset the accumulated resources. This potential problem can be alleviated by using an internal service fund or a pension (and other employee benefit) trust fund for compensated absences. Of course, the use of a trust fund requires a trust agreement with a party outside the financial reporting entity, such as employees.

[75] Sometimes, governments regularly fund their ARC, but at a date subsequent to the close of the fiscal year. Such contributions are *not* considered to be unfunded, and so do *not* give rise to an NPO.

[76] GASB Statement No. 27, *Accounting for Pensions by State and Local Governmental Employers*, paragraphs 8 and 16.

ligation—NOPEBO), but only in the accrual-based government-wide statement of net assets.[77]

Operating leases with scheduled rent increases

Earlier in this chapter, the matter of long-term operating leases with scheduled rent increases was examined from a *lessor* perspective as part of the discussion devoted to the recognition of receivables. Governments also sometimes participate in such arrangements as *lessees*. GAAP require that whenever a long-term operating lease contains structured increases in rental payments that cannot reasonably be associated with an expected increase in the service potential or economic value of the property being rented, the lessee must report a liability for the difference between value received and scheduled lease payments. However, unlike the corresponding receivable reported by lessors in these same circumstances, this liability would *not* be reported in a governmental fund because it normally would *not* be expected to be liquidated with expendable available financial resources (i.e., a typical government does not make operating lease payments earlier than required under the terms of the lease).[78] Accordingly, an expenditure would be recognized only as lease payments came due.[79]

Trade-ins involving capital assets associated with governmental funds

Governments sometimes offer to trade in an existing capital asset as part of an agreement to acquire a new capital asset. Any additional cash paid as part of such an agreement, of course, must be reported as an expenditure in the appropriate governmental fund. For instance, a government might plan to use an existing capital asset plus $5,000 cash to acquire a new capital asset with a fair value of $8,000. The $5,000 cash payment would be reported in the appropriate governmental fund as follows:

	DR	CR
Expenditures—capital outlay	$ 5,000	
Cash		$ 5,000
(To report $5,000 payment on trade-in to acquire new equipment)		

There is the argument, however, that this trade-in transaction also represents, in substance, both the sale of the existing capital asset *and* the application of the sale proceeds to the acquisition of a new capital asset. According to this argument, the following journal entry would be more appropriate for the transaction:

	DR	CR
Expenditures—capital outlay	$ 8,000	
Cash		$ 5,000
Other financing source—sale of capital assets		3,000
(To report $5,000 payment on trade-in to acquire new equipment)		

Both approaches are acceptable. As a practical matter, however, a typical budget recognizes only the cash payment of $5,000 as an expenditure for budgetary purposes. Accordingly, the first approach has the advantage of

---

[77] GASB Statement No. 45. As noted earlier in the case of pensions, sometimes governments regularly fund their ARC for OPEB, but at a date subsequent to the close of the fiscal year. Such contributions are *not* considered to be unfunded, and so do *not* give rise to a NOPEBO.

[78] GASB Statement No. 13, paragraph 9.

[79] Of course, meanwhile a liability would need to be reported in the accrual-based government-wide statement of net assets.

minimizing the differences between GAAP reporting and the basis of budgeting.

OTHER FINANCING USES

Theoretically, it is possible to use the term "expenditures" to describe all outflows of current financial resources in governmental funds. In practice, however, financial statements for governmental funds traditionally distinguish two categories of resource outflows: expenditures and *other financing uses*, a category used to isolate certain nonroutine outflows that might otherwise distort the analysis of expenditure trends. GAAP permit the use of the other financing uses category only in the specific situations described in the paragraphs that follow.

Transfers to other funds

Clearly a distinction must be drawn between the ultimate disposition of current financial resources (expenditures) and their assignment to some other fund pending their eventual disposition (transfers). Accordingly, GAAP direct that transfers of current financial resources to other funds of the primary government be classified and reported separately from expenditures as an other financing use. By definition, transactions with discretely presented component units are *not* considered to be interfund activity. Therefore, any amounts "transferred" by the primary government to a discretely presented component unit should be reported as expenditures rather than transfers.

Refundings

Governments often elect to take advantage of changes in interest rates by issuing new debt to refinance existing (old) debt. Likewise, a government may elect to refinance old debt to escape onerous debt covenants or to change the maturity of the debt. Such transactions are referred to as *refundings*. In the case of a *current* refunding, the proceeds of the refunding debt are applied immediately to redeem the old debt. In the case of an *advance* refunding, the proceeds of the refunding debt are placed into an escrow account pending the call date or maturity of the old debt. Most advance refundings result in the *defeasance* of the old debt: for accounting purposes, the debt is treated as though it had, in fact, been redeemed. For both current refundings and for advance refundings that result in defeasance, GAAP direct that the proceeds of the refunding bonds, whether used for redemption or placed in escrow, be reported as an other financing use rather than as an expenditure. Otherwise, these significant and irregular outflows of current financial resources could substantially distort a government's regular debt service expenditure trends.

Demand bonds

As noted earlier, demand bonds may be treated as long-term debt if certain specific criteria are met. In practice, it is possible that a demand bond that originally met these criteria might later cease to do so. In that case, GAAP direct that the obligation be reclassified as a fund liability in the governmental fund that originally received the proceeds. The journal entry used to effect this reclassification would include an other financing use equal to the amount of the demand bonds to be reported henceforth as a fund liability.[80]

---

[80] GASB Interpretation No. 1, paragraph 13.

RECOGNITION OF LIABILITIES

Governments recognize *all* liabilities on the government-wide statement of net assets. Governmental funds, however, only recognize liabilities to the extent that they normally are expected to be liquidated with expendable available financial resources. Accordingly, the following liabilities reported on the government-wide statement of net assets normally are *not* reported in the governmental funds:

- unmatured principal of long-term debt, such as bonds, notes, capital leases;
- accrued interest on long-term debt;
- unmatured balances of the liabilities related to compensated absences; claims and judgments; special termination benefits; and landfill closure and postclosure care costs;
- NPO/NOPEBO; and
- liabilities associated with long-term operating leases containing scheduled rent increases.

Government-mandated and voluntary nonexchange transactions

When a government is the provider in either a government-mandated or voluntary nonexchange transaction, it should recognize a liability as soon as the recipient meets all eligibility requirements. This liability should reflect not only actual claims submitted, but also estimated claims incurred, but not yet reported.[81]

When a government is the recipient in a government-mandated or voluntary nonexchange transaction, it may subsequently lose its claim to all or a portion of the resources provided as a result of its failure to continue to comply with eligibility requirements or purpose restrictions. In such cases, a liability should be recognized as soon as it is probable that the recipient has lost its claim to the assets.[82]

Income tax refunds and liability to owners of escheat property

Governments financed in part by income taxes typically must report a liability to taxpayers for anticipated refunds. GAAP specifically mandate that this liability always be reported in the appropriate governmental fund, regardless of when it is expected to be liquidated. This accounting is necessary to ensure that income tax revenues are reported net of anticipated refund payments.[83]

The same treatment just described for income tax refunds holds true as well for amounts ultimately due to the owners of escheat property accounted for in a governmental fund.[84] The topic of escheat property is examined in detail in chapter 15.

FUND ACCOUNTING AND RESTRICTED REVENUES

A government may legally restrict a portion of its revenues for specific purposes. For example, a portion of a particular property tax levy may be legally pledged to support debt service. Normally, it is recommended that

---

[81] GASB, *Comprehensive Implementation Guide (2004)*, 7.457.
[82] GASB Statement No. 33, paragraph 26.
[83] GASB Statement No. 22, paragraph 3.
[84] GASB Statement No. 21, *Accounting for Escheat Property*, paragraph 5 (as amended by GASB Statement No. 37, paragraph 3).

such restricted revenues be reported directly in the fund benefiting from the restriction. Some governments, however, prefer to report all general governmental revenues, including restricted revenues, in the general fund, and then use a transfer to move restricted resources to other funds. This preference may reflect a desire to minimize differences between GAAP financial reporting and the basis of budgeting. In such situations, it is appropriate to report restricted revenues as transfers. Note, however, that the use of transfers may result in an excess of fund expenditures over fund revenues in the funds that ultimately receive the restricted resources, because transfers are reported as an other financing source rather than as a revenue. It also may obscure the transfer of unrestricted resources.

In some cases, however, dedicated taxes are used to fund pensions. Such taxes should *not* be treated as a direct revenue of a pension (and other employer benefit) plan, because to do so would effectively preclude the employer from reporting pension cost, as required by GAAP.[85]

---

[85] GASB Statement No. 27.

6

Proprietary Funds

Proprietary funds are used to account for a government's business-type activities. Although there are two types of proprietary funds (enterprise funds and internal service funds), the accounting and financial reporting applicable to both are quite similar. Both proprietary fund types use the economic resources measurement focus and accrual basis of accounting. These are the same measurement focus and basis of accounting used for private-sector business enterprises and not-for-profit organizations, as well as for the government-wide financial statements.

Because they share a common measurement focus and basis of accounting with private-sector business enterprises, proprietary funds traditionally have used the same generally accepted accounting principles (GAAP) as similar businesses in the private sector.[1] This chapter does not attempt to review this common body of GAAP. Instead, it focuses on differences between enterprise funds and internal service funds and the specialized application of business-style GAAP in the public sector.

ENTERPRISE FUNDS VERSUS INTERNAL SERVICE FUNDS

There are three important differences between enterprise funds and internal service funds: the identity of those who benefit from the fund's services, the degree to which the costs of the fund must be recovered through fees and charges, and the application of more recent private-sector pronouncements.

Enterprise customers versus internal service fund customers

Enterprise funds and internal service funds each impose fees or charges on those who use their services. Enterprise funds are used in situations where a given fund provides services primarily to customers *outside the financial reporting entity*—citizens, for instance. Conversely, internal service funds are used when a fund primarily provides benefits "to other funds, departments, or agencies of the primary government and its component units, or to other governments."[2]

---

[1] National Council on Governmental Accounting (NCGA) Statement 1, *Governmental Accounting and Financial Reporting Principles*, paragraph 18 (2).
[2] NCGA Statement 1, paragraph 26(7).

Of course, situations arise where a single fund provides services to both types of customers. In such cases, the decision whether to classify the fund as an enterprise fund or an internal service fund depends on the *predominant* participant. If the government itself is the predominant participant in the activity, then the activity should be classified as an internal service fund; if not, the activity should be reported as an enterprise fund.

GAAP specifically state that internal service funds may be used to account for services provided to other governments outside the financial reporting entity. All the same, the use of an internal service fund is *not* appropriate in situations where other governments are the predominant participants in a given activity.[3]

The same basic rule applies to public-entity risk pools included within the financial reporting entity. Normally, GAAP direct that public-entity risk pools be reported as enterprise funds.[4] However, an internal service fund (or, alternatively, the general fund) must be used in situations where the government itself is the predominant participant in such a pool.[5]

Cost recovery through fees and charges

GAAP *mandate* the use of an enterprise fund when legal requirements or management policy require that the full cost of providing services (including capital costs) be recovered through fees and charges. GAAP also *permit* the use of an enterprise fund "to report any activity for which a fee is charged to external users for goods or services," regardless of whether the government intends to fully recover the cost of the goods or services provided.[6] Thus, it is common to encounter enterprise funds that are used to account for services (transit systems, for example) where the government intends to recover only a portion of its costs through fees or user charges.

Internal service funds, on the other hand, are expressly designed to function as *cost-reimbursement devices.* That is, an internal service fund is simply a means of accumulating costs related to a given activity on an accrual basis so that the costs can subsequently be allocated to the benefiting funds in the form of fees and charges. Accordingly, the use of an internal service fund is *not* appropriate for activities that a government only partially intends to finance through fees and charges. Otherwise, costs could be permanently stranded in the internal service funds. Consequently, internal service funds are only appropriate if a government intends to recover the full cost of providing a given activity.

Consistent with the cost-reimbursement goal of internal service funds, a significant surplus or deficit in an internal service fund could indicate that participating funds are not properly reporting the costs of the goods or services they receive from the internal service fund. Thus, a long-term, significant surplus could be evidence that user funds are being overcharged. Likewise, a long-term, significant deficit could indicate that funds are not being charged their proportionate share of costs. Indeed, in the case of internal service funds used to account for risk financing activities, GAAP state that a

[3] Governmental Accounting Standards Board (GASB) Statement No. 34, *Basic Financial Statements—and Management's Discussion and Analysis—for State and Local Governments*, paragraph 68. The authoritative accounting and financial reporting literature leaves the determination of what constitutes "predominance" to the professional judgment of financial statement preparers and auditors.
[4] GASB Statement No. 10, *Accounting and Financial Reporting for Risk Financing and Related Insurance Issues*, paragraph 18.
[5] GASB Statement No. 10, paragraph 76.
[6] GASB Statement No. 34, paragraph 67.

deficit in an internal service fund should be charged back to other funds unless needed adjustments are expected over a reasonable period of time.[7]

Governments enjoy considerable flexibility in how they calculate capital-related charges. At the simplest level, a government may choose to set charges based upon depreciation expense, which should result in a close tie between revenues and expenses each period. Frequently, however, governments calculate capital-related charges in such a way that revenues and expenses do not tie so closely. For example, if debt has been issued to acquire a capital asset, charges might be based upon debt service requirements rather than depreciation expense to ensure adequate cash flow, especially if the maturity of the debt is significantly less than the estimated useful life of the asset acquired.[8] Also, some governments prefer to base charges on the estimated replacement cost of capital assets rather than upon their historical cost (reflected in depreciation expense) to ensure that there will be adequate resources in place when an asset is retired to finance the acquisition of a replacement. In these latter two cases, an internal service fund would end up reporting an ongoing surplus. In practice, such a surplus is *not* considered to violate the rule that internal service funds should operate as cost-reimbursement mechanisms. At the same time, such methods likely will be unacceptable to grantors as a basis for establishing reimbursable costs.

Application of more recent private-sector pronouncements

Enterprise funds and internal service funds are required to follow all private-sector guidance issued prior to December 1, 1989, by the Financial Accounting Standards Board (FASB) and its predecessors (the Accounting Principles Board (APB) and the Committee on Accounting Procedure), provided such guidance does not conflict with or contradict the standards of the Governmental Accounting Standards Board (GASB).[9] However, *only enterprise funds* have the option of electing to continue consistently following more recent FASB guidance, provided it neither conflicts with nor contradicts GASB guidance.[10]

This rule applies only to the application of recent FASB pronouncements as level 1 guidance on the hierarchy of authoritative sources of GAAP for state and local governments.[11] *Both* enterprise funds *and* internal service funds remain free to make selective use of later FASB standards as an other source of GAAP to help in resolving specific issues that are not addressed in the authoritative accounting and financial reporting literature for state and local governments.

---

[7] GASB Statement No. 10, paragraph 67.

[8] Assume, for example, that an internal service fund borrows $20 million over a ten-year period to finance acquisition of a capital asset with an estimated useful life of 20 years. In that case, the fund would need to raise $2 million each year for ten years to meet its debt service principal requirements. If charges to customers were based upon depreciation expense (i.e., $20 million/20 years = $1 million/year), the result could be a cash flows shortfall of $1 million per year.

[9] The last pronouncements issued prior to this December 1, 1989, cut-off date were FASB Statement No. 102, *Statement of Cash Flows—Exemption of Certain Enterprises and Classification of Cash Flows from Certain Securities Acquired for Resale*, and FASB Interpretation No. 38, *Determining the Measurement Date for Stock Option, Purchase, and Award Plans Involving Junior Stock*.

[10] GASB Statement No. 20, *Accounting and Financial Reporting for Proprietary Funds and Other Governmental Entities That Use Proprietary Fund Accounting*, paragraphs 6-8, as modified by GASB Statement No. 34, paragraph 95.

[11] See chapter 1.

SPECIALIZED APPLICATIONS

Despite the many accounting and financial reporting similarities between proprietary funds and similar business enterprises, a number of specialized applications of GAAP are either unique to the public sector or most commonly encountered there. The remainder of this chapter covers these specialized applications.

Discounts and allowances

In the public sector, discounts and allowances normally should be netted against revenues, even in proprietary funds. Accordingly, *bad debt expense* is properly reported only in connection with non-revenue related accounts (e.g., loans receivable).[12]

Interest capitalization

Capital assets initially are recorded at their historical cost. The cost of a capital asset, for this purpose, should include any "ancillary charges necessary to place the asset in its intended location and condition for use."[13] When an enterprise fund uses debt to finance construction of a capital asset, one of these capitalizable ancillary charges is the interest expense incurred during construction.[14]

The basic private-sector guidance on interest capitalization can be found in FASB Statement No. 34, *Capitalization of Interest Cost*. That standard applies not only to construction undertaken by an enterprise fund itself (such as government work crews), but also to construction undertaken by others on the enterprise fund's behalf (such as contractors) if either deposits or progress payments are required during construction.

It is natural to think of capitalizable interest in situations where debt is issued to finance a specific project. However, under FASB Statement No. 34, interest capitalization also may be necessary even in situations where no new debt is issued to finance a project. Assume, for example, that an enterprise fund with $10 million in outstanding debt undertakes to finance a new construction project with $2 million in existing resources. If that $2 million had been applied to repay a portion of the $10 million in outstanding debt, a new borrowing would have been needed to finance the project. Accordingly, an enterprise fund's decision to use existing resources to pay for new construction rather than to repay outstanding debt effectively represents recycling of the outstanding debt to finance the new project. Consequently, under FASB Statement No. 34, interest must be capitalized on construction in an individual enterprise fund as long as there is any outstanding debt in that same fund, *even if the outstanding debt in the fund has no relationship to the new project*.

The period during which interest is to be capitalized under FASB Statement No. 34 starts when three conditions are present:
- Expenditures have been made (including deposits or progress payments to third parties).
- Activities are in progress to prepare the asset for its intended use.
- Interest is being incurred (either in connection with new debt or in connection with "recycled" outstanding debt).

---

[12] GASB Statement No. 34, footnote 41; GASB, *Comprehensive Implementation Guide (2004)*, 7.213, 7.214, 7.313.
[13] NCGA Statement 1, paragraph 48.
[14] As explained later, interest normally is *not* capitalized in internal service funds.

An expenditure occurs when an entity has either made a cash payment, transferred assets, or incurred an interest-bearing liability.

Interest is to be capitalized not only during construction but also during the preconstruction phase, provided activities are in progress to prepare the asset for its intended use (for instance, developing plans, obtaining permits). The interest capitalization period under FASB Statement No. 34 ends when an asset is "substantially complete and ready for its intended use." If nearly all activities to prepare an asset for its intended use are suspended prior to the substantial completion of a project, interest capitalization should be halted until those activities are resumed. This rule does not apply, however, to cessations of activity that are either brief, inherent in the acquisition process (such as technical problems), or externally imposed (such as strikes and litigation).

To calculate capitalizable interest under FASB Statement No. 34, the appropriate interest rate is applied to average accumulated expenditures during the capitalization period. If a specific borrowing can be identified with the project, the rate of interest on that borrowing may be used for this purpose; otherwise, the weighted average rate of interest on outstanding borrowings is used.

In the public sector, the proceeds of tax-exempt debt may be reinvested during the construction period in materially higher-yielding taxable securities (arbitrage). Although there are important federal restrictions on arbitrage, governments often are able to recover a significant portion of their interest expense during the construction phase through interest earnings on the reinvested proceeds of tax-exempt debt.[15] The FASB came to believe that strict application of Statement No. 34 to tax-exempt debt could result in overstating the cost of capital assets acquired using tax-exempt debt by not taking into account this partial recovery of interest expense through interest earnings on the reinvested debt proceeds. Accordingly, the FASB amended Statement No. 34 by issuing FASB Statement No. 62, *Capitalization of Interest Cost in Situations Involving Certain Tax-Exempt Borrowings and Certain Gifts and Grants.*

There are two important differences between how capitalizable interest is calculated under FASB Statement No. 34 and FASB Statement No. 62. First, FASB Statement No. 62 explicitly provides for capitalizing the *net effect of interest expense and related interest revenue.* Second, when debt is issued before construction activities begin, FASB Statement No. 62 moves back the start of the capitalization period to the time of the borrowing.

Applying the guidance in FASB Statement No. 62 necessarily involves a departure from the FASB Statement No. 34 approach of applying a given interest rate to average accumulated expenditures. Instead, FASB Statement No. 62 requires entities to calculate total interest on the indebtedness over the capitalization period and then offset that amount with interest revenue earned on the reinvested debt proceeds during that same period.

The FASB limited the applicability of Statement No. 62 to tax-exempt borrowings that are "*externally* restricted to finance acquisition of *specified* qualifying assets or to service the related debt" [emphasis added]. Thus general-purpose capital improvement bonds would *not* qualify for FASB

[15] Remember that the federal government permits governments to keep arbitrage earnings equal to interest expense on the underlying tax-exempt debt.

Statement No. 62, because use of the bond proceeds would not be externally restricted to *specific* projects. If bond proceeds are not externally restricted for acquisition of specified qualifying assets, interest would still need to be capitalized in accordance with FASB Statement No. 34.

FASB Statement No. 62 also supplies specialized guidance on the applicability of interest capitalization to the grant-financed portion of a construction project. Recall that under FASB Statement No. 34, interest capitalization sometimes is required *even when no new debt has been issued*. The theory in such cases was that the existing resources being used to finance new construction could have been used instead to repay the outstanding debt, thereby creating the need for a new borrowing to finance construction. This logic, however, clearly would *not* apply to any portion of a construction project financed by a restricted grant, since there would be no option in that case to apply the grant proceeds to repayment of the outstanding debt. Accordingly, FASB Statement No. 62 *prohibits* the capitalization of interest on any portion of a capital asset financed with grants (and interest on invested grant proceeds) that are *externally restricted* to the acquisition or construction of *specified* qualifying assets.

In practice, it is common to have to apply more than one approach to interest capitalization for a single public-sector project. Assume, for example, that an enterprise fund plans to finance a project partially with the proceeds of new tax-exempt debt, partially with the proceeds of a restricted capital grant, and partially with existing resources. Further assume that this same enterprise fund has other outstanding debt. In that case, the following approach would be taken:

- *Debt-financed portion of construction.* FASB Statement No. 62 would govern the capitalization of interest connected with the portion of the project being financed with proceeds of the new tax-exempt debt (presuming the proceeds are externally restricted to the acquisition of *specified* qualifying assets). Accordingly, the amount of interest capitalized would be calculated net of interest earnings on the reinvested debt proceeds, with the capitalization period to begin as early as the issuance of the debt.
- *Grant-financed portion of construction.* Under FASB Statement No. 62, no interest would be capitalized on the portion of the capital project financed with grant proceeds (and related earnings), provided they are externally restricted to the acquisition of specified qualifying assets.
- *Portion of construction financed with existing resources.* Because the enterprise fund in question has other outstanding debt, FASB Statement No. 34 requires that the interest on that other outstanding debt be imputed to the portion of the construction project financed with existing resources.

Exhibit 6-1 summarizes the authoritative guidance governing the capitalization of interest in enterprise funds.

A simplified example may help illustrate how to calculate capitalized interest. Assume that an enterprise fund borrows $4 million in tax-exempt bonds with an interest rate of 7 percent. The bond indenture specifically restricts the use of the proceeds to the construction of this specified project. No principal payments are due until five years following issuance of the

EXHIBIT 6-1
Interest capitalization requirements for enterprise funds

Source of funding	Authoritative guidance	Treatment
Tax-exempt debt externally restricted for the acquisition of *specified* qualifying assets	FASB Statement No. 62	Capitalize the difference between interest expense on debt and interest earnings on reinvested debt proceeds
Tax-exempt debt *not* externally restricted for the acquisition of *specified* qualifying assets (such as general-purpose capital improvement bonds)	FASB Statement No. 34	Capitalize weighted average construction expenditures multiplied by interest rate on the debt
Grants (and related earnings) externally restricted to the acquisition of *specified* qualifying assets	FASB Statement No. 62	Do not capitalize interest
Grants (and related earnings) *not* externally restricted to the acquisition of *specified* qualifying assets	FASB Statement No. 34	Capitalize interest *if debt is outstanding in the same enterprise fund* by multiplying weighted average construction expenditures by weighted average interest rate of outstanding debt
Existing resources	FASB Statement No. 34	Capitalize interest *if debt is outstanding in the same enterprise fund* by multiplying weighted average construction expenditures by weighted average interest rate of outstanding debt

bonds. The project also will be financed with $1 million in state grants, the proceeds of which are received before the start of the project. The grant proceeds and interest earned on invested grant proceeds are restricted by the grant contract to this specified project. Any additional funding necessary will be provided by the enterprise fund. The average interest rate on the entity's other outstanding borrowings is 8 percent. Unexpended bond and grant proceeds are placed in investments yielding 9 percent; interest earned is not reinvested. Bond and grant proceeds are presumed to be spent on a pro rata basis.

All funding is received 10 months after the start of year 1, but preconstruction activities do not commence until the beginning of year 2. Accordingly, the full $5 million is invested for two months at a 9 percent yield. Capitalizable interest is calculated by comparing interest expense on the bonds to interest income earned on the invested bond proceeds as follows:

$$\$4,000,000 \times 7 \text{ percent} \times 2/12 = \$46,667 \text{ interest expense}$$
$$\text{Less} \quad \underline{\$4,000,000 \times 9 \text{ percent} \times 2/12 = \$60,000 \text{ interest revenue}}$$
$$\text{Capitalizable interest} = (\$13,333)^{[16]}$$

Note that there is no interest capitalization related to the $1 million grant; therefore, the $15,000 interest earned on the invested grant proceeds does not enter into this calculation.

During the second year of the project, $2.5 million in average accumulated expenditures are incurred; $2 million of this amount is paid from bond proceeds. Accordingly, capitalized interest for year 2 is calculated as follows:

---

[16] Capitalized interest may be a negative amount (FASB Statement No. 62, paragraph 15).

$$\begin{array}{rl} \$4,000,000 \times 7 \text{ percent} & = \$280,000 \text{ interest expense} \\ \underline{\text{Less} \quad \$2,000,000 \times 9 \text{ percent}} & \underline{= \$180,000 \text{ interest revenue}^{17}} \\ \text{Capitalizable interest} & = \$100,000 \end{array}$$

Once again, the $500,000 paid out of grant proceeds,[18] as well as the $45,000 interest earned on the invested grant proceeds do not enter into this calculation. Accordingly, the cost of construction in progress is now reported as follows:

$$\begin{array}{rl} \$2,000,000 & \text{paid from bond proceeds} \\ 500,000 & \text{paid from grant proceeds} \\ \underline{86,667} & \underline{\text{capitalized interest (i.e., } - \$13,333 \text{ year 1} + \$100,000 \text{ year 2})} \\ \$2,586,667 \end{array}$$

During the third year of the project, average accumulated expenditures reach $6 million, leaving no invested bond or grant proceeds. Accordingly, at least $280,000 of interest expense ($4,000,000 × 7 percent) would be capitalized with no offsetting interest income. An additional factor, however, must be considered. Average accumulated expenditures exceed the total of bonds ($4 million), grants ($1 million), and interest on grants ($60,000). Therefore, interest also must be capitalized on this additional amount ($6,000,000 less $5,060,000 = $940,000) using the provision of FASB Statement No. 34:

$$\$940,000 \times 8 \text{ percent (average rate on outstanding borrowings)} = \$75,200$$

Therefore the total interest capitalization for year 3 would be $280,000 + $75,200 = $355,200. The project is substantially complete by the end of year 3. This would leave the final capitalized value of the constructed asset as follows:

$$\begin{array}{rl} \$4,000,000 & \text{paid from bond proceeds} \\ 1,000,000 & \text{paid from grant proceeds} \\ 60,000 & \text{paid from grant interest} \\ 940,000 & \text{paid from other sources} \\ \underline{441,867} & \underline{\text{capitalized interest (i.e., } - \$13,333 + \$100,000 + \$355,200)} \\ \$6,441,867 \end{array}$$

Interest capitalization for state and local governments essentially is limited to enterprise funds (and business-type activities). To capitalize interest on capital assets of the general government would be tantamount to allocating interest to individual functions indirectly through depreciation expense and GAAP, as a general rule, prohibit the allocation of interest expense among functions within *governmental activities*.[19] For this same reason, interest should *not* be capitalized on capital assets reported in internal service funds that are included as part of *governmental activities* in the government-wide financial statements.

As noted earlier, an enterprise fund should capitalize interest only on debt actually reported in the fund itself. Interest on debt issued for the benefit of an enterprise fund but expected to be repaid from *governmental activi-*

---

[17] $4 million total proceeds less $2 million spent = $2 million invested proceeds remaining.
[18] $1 million total grant proceeds less $500,000 spent = $500,000 invested proceeds remaining.
[19] GASB Statement No. 34, paragraph 46.

ties should *not* be capitalized inasmuch as the debt would be reported as a liability of *governmental activities* rather than as a liability of the benefiting enterprise fund.

Normally enterprise funds are included as part of *business-type activities* in government-wide financial reporting. Governments, however, do have the *option* of including one or more enterprise funds as part of *governmental activities* if they wish to do so. Governments that elect this option should continue to capitalize interest in the affected enterprise fund(s) and the interest thus capitalized should *not* be eliminated from the historical cost of the capital assets in the government-wide financial statements.[20] Likewise, if interest is capitalized on an enterprise fund capital asset that later is reassigned to *governmental activities*, the capitalized interest should *not* be removed from the historical cost of the reassigned asset.[21]

Proprietary fund debt

The economic resources measurement focus requires that a fund report *all* of its assets and liabilities. Debt should be reported in a proprietary fund if *both* of the following criteria are met:

- The debt is directly related to the proprietary fund (for instance, issued to finance the acquisition of a fund asset).
- The debt is expected to be paid from the proprietary fund.[22]

It is important to note that debt is *not* reported in a proprietary fund simply because it is related to that fund. For example, the general government may issue debt to finance a capital *contribution* to an enterprise fund. Clearly, such debt would be directly related to the proprietary fund; nevertheless, it would not constitute a fund liability because it is expected to be repaid from general government resources rather than proprietary fund resources.

Also important to note is that a general government's assumption of a contingent liability for debt does *not* cause the liability itself to cease being a fund liability so long as there is a reasonable expectation that the liability will be repaid with the resources of the proprietary fund. That is, the intended source of repayment rather than the security interest for debt is the factor that determines whether a liability is classified as a fund liability or as a liability of the general government.

Debt refundings

Proprietary funds sometimes issue new debt to replace existing debt. Such transactions are known as *refundings*. It is common for proprietary funds to refund debt to take advantage of more favorable interest rates. Likewise, a proprietary fund may elect to refund existing debt to free itself from onerous bond covenants associated with that debt or to change the maturity of that debt.

In some situations, the proceeds of refunding bonds (new debt) can be applied immediately to redeem the existing debt (old debt) that is to be refunded. In that case, the entire transaction is known as a *current* refunding. In other cases, it is not possible to effect an immediate redemption. For instance, the issuer may be unable to redeem the old debt prior to a contractually determined call date or maturity. In this situation, the proceeds of the new debt are placed into an escrow account, where they are used: 1) to meet periodic principal and interest payments until call date or maturity; 2) to pay the call premium (if redemption is at call date); and 3) to redeem the debt at call date or maturity. This latter type of refunding is known as an *advance* refunding because the new debt is issued *in advance* of the old debt's redemption.

Of course, in an *advance* refunding, the old debt, by definition, remains outstanding until call date or maturity. In economic substance, however, there is little practical difference between a current refunding and an advance refunding. Accordingly, GAAP direct that most advance refunding transactions be accounted for just as though the old debt had, in fact, been redeemed upon issuance of the refunding bonds, by removing both the old debt and the related escrow assets from the face of the financial statements. *Defeasance* is the technical term applied by accountants to describe this removal of outstanding debt (unredeemed old debt) and related assets (assets held in escrow).

Defeasance can be accomplished in one of two ways. In a *legal defeasance*, the issuer ceases legally to be the primary obligor for the old debt, though the issuer still remains contingently liable for repayment. In an *in-substance defeasance*, the issuer legally remains the primary obligor for the old debt, though for all practical purposes the issuer is only contingently liable for the debt. The determination of whether a legal defeasance has occurred is a matter of law. The criteria for an in-substance defeasance, however, are set by GAAP as follows:

- Assets must be placed in irrevocable escrow to be used solely for the purpose of making principal and interest payments on the old debt.
- The chance of the issuer being required to make any additional future payments must be remote.
- The assets in the escrow account must be essentially risk-free as to amount, timing, and collection of interest and principal (U.S. Government securities, securities guaranteed by the U.S. Government, or U.S. Government-backed securities).
- The timing of collections must approximately coincide in timing and amount with scheduled interest and principal payments.[23]

The concept of legal defeasance is common to private-sector and public-sector accounting, while the concept of in-substance defeasance applies only to state and local governments.[24]

There often is a difference between the carrying amount of redeemed/defeased debt and its reacquisition price. In the private sector, this difference is classified as a gain or loss and reported on the operating statement in the period in which the transaction occurs.[25] Proprietary funds, on

---

[23] GASB Statement No. 7, *Advance Refundings Resulting in Defeasance of Debt*, paragraph 4.

[24] The concept of an in-substance defeasance was first set forth in FASB Statement No. 76, *Extinguishment of Debt*, which was issued in 1983 and provided the groundwork for GASB Statement No. 7, issued in 1987. The FASB subsequently abolished the concept of an in-substance defeasance in FASB Statement No. 125, *Accounting for Transfers and Servicing of Financial Assets and Extinguishments of Liabilities*, issued in 1996. The provisions of FASB Statement No. 125 relating to in-substance defeasance may not be applied to enterprise funds because they "conflict with or contradict" GASB guidance (i.e., GASB Statement No. 7).

[25] APB Opinion No. 26, *Early Extinguishment of Debt*, paragraph 20. Later, FASB Statement No. 4, *Reporting Gains and Losses from Extinguishment of Debt*, paragraph 8, called for this gain or loss to be automatically classified as an extraordinary item. That guidance, in turn, was ultimately rescinded by FASB Statement No. 145, *Rescission of FASB Statements No. 4, 44, and 64, Amendment of FASB Statement No. 13, and Technical Corrections*, which directs that the criteria of APB Opinion No. 30, *Reporting the Results of Operations—Discontinued Events and Extraordinary Items*, be applied to refundings without modification.

the other hand, defer and amortize this amount over the remaining life of the old debt (had it not been refunded) *or* the life of the new debt, whichever is shorter. In the meantime, the unamortized difference between the carrying amount of redeemed or defeased debt and its reacquisition price should be reported as a direct reduction of (or addition to) the amount of refunding debt reported on the statement of position, much like a bond premium or discount.[26] Also like bond premiums or discounts, this unamortized balance should "follow the debt" for purposes of calculating the various components of *net assets*. Thus, any remaining unamortized balance associated with capital-related debt would be considered in the calculation of *invested in capital assets net of related debt*.[27]

Most advance refundings result in either the legal or in-substance defeasance of the old debt. An exception to this general rule occurs in the case of *crossover* refundings, which are similar to other types of advance refundings in most respects (that is, refunding bonds are issued, and their proceeds are placed into an escrow account). Unlike other types of advance refundings, however, the escrow account in a crossover refunding transaction is not immediately dedicated *exclusively* to debt service principal and interest payments on the old debt. Instead, the resources in the escrow account also are used for a time to fund principal and interest payments on the refunding bonds themselves. Only at a predetermined future date, known as the *crossover date*, do the resources in the escrow account come to be dedicated *exclusively* to the payment of principal and interest on the old debt.

Consequently, crossover refundings do *not* meet the first of the criteria discussed earlier for an in-substance defeasance. These conditions may be met later, however, at the predetermined crossover date. Until that time, both the old debt and the assets of the related escrow account must continue to be reported on the face of the financial statements, as no defeasance is considered to have occurred.

Landfill closure and postclosure care costs

Governments that operate municipal solid-waste landfills are encouraged to account for this activity in an enterprise fund.[28] Indeed, if there is a legal or managerial requirement to recover cost (including some measure of the cost of capital assets) through fees and charges, the use of an enterprise fund is required by GAAP.[29]

Various state and federal laws and regulations make governments that operate landfills financially responsible for properly closing the site at the end of its useful life and then monitoring and maintaining it afterwards, typically for 30 years. Any such costs *incurred near or after the close of a landfill* are known technically as *landfill closure and postclosure care costs*.

As noted in the discussion of interest capitalization, revenues and related expenses should be reported in the same fiscal period. In the case of municipal solid-waste landfills, revenues (such as tipping fees) occur during the useful life of the landfill. Therefore, GAAP require that landfill closure and postclosure care costs be recognized in an enterprise fund over the

[26] GASB Statement No. 23, *Accounting and Financial Reporting for Refundings of Debt Reported by Proprietary Activities*, paragraph 4.
[27] GASB, *Comprehensive Implementation Guide (2004)*, 7.130.
[28] GFOA recommended practice on "The Application of Full-Cost Accounting to Municipal Solid-Waste Management Activities (1998)."
[29] GASB Statement No. 34, paragraph 67.

useful life of the landfill, *even though such costs will only be incurred, by definition, near or after the close of the landfill.* The first step in meeting this requirement is to estimate the total cost of landfill closure and postclosure care. This estimate comprises three elements:

- the cost of equipment and facilities that will be acquired near the time the landfill stops accepting waste or after for the purpose of postclosure care and monitoring;
- the cost of applying the final cover (capping); and
- the cost of postclosure maintenance and monitoring.

This estimate should be made using *current costs* (costs that would be incurred were these services to be obtained during the current period). Naturally, this estimate must be adjusted annually to reflect the effects of inflation, advances in technology, changes in regulations, or similar changes.

Each year, the enterprise fund should determine its expense related to anticipated landfill closure and postclosure care costs by applying the following formula:

$$\frac{\left(\begin{array}{c}\text{Estimated}\\\text{total cost}\end{array}\right) \times \left(\begin{array}{c}\text{Landfill capacity}\\\text{used to date}\end{array}\right)}{\left(\begin{array}{c}\text{Total landfill}\\\text{capacity}\end{array}\right)} - \left(\begin{array}{c}\text{Amounts}\\\text{recognized in}\\\text{prior periods}\end{array}\right) = \left(\begin{array}{c}\text{Current}\\\text{period}\\\text{expense}\end{array}\right)$$

This formula, of course, is essentially the same formula used in the private sector to recognize revenue on construction contracts accounted for using the percentage of completion method. Note that the practical effect of using this formula is to recognize in the *current period* the full effect of changes in estimate as they relate to both the *current and prior periods.* Assume, for example, that a change in regulations is expected to result in an additional $1 million in total landfill closure and postclosure care costs, and that 75 percent of the landfill's capacity has already been used as of the date of this change in estimate. In that case, using the formula would result in an additional $750,000 charged to operations in the current period.

Some of the equipment and facilities needed for landfill closure and postclosure care will be acquired before the landfill is near the point where it will stop accepting solid waste. Such assets should be capitalized in the fund and depreciated over the period extending from their acquisition to the date the landfill stops accepting solid waste, even if those assets have longer useful lives. Once again, *all* costs related to landfills should be allocated to expense by the time the landfill ceases operations. Changes in estimate that occur *after* closure should be reflected in the operating statement as soon as they are probable *and* measurable.[30]

Tap fees, system development fees, and connection fees

To connect to the existing system, new customers of a utility often are charged a special fee, such as a tap fee, a systems development fee, or a connection fee. The amount of this fee frequently exceeds the actual cost to connect new customers to the system. This excess often represents a charge to new customers for their fair share of the capital cost of the system already in place, or the cost of increasing the capacity of the system to meet the additional demand created by the connection of new customers.

[30] Authoritative guidance on all aspects of accounting and financial reporting for landfill closure and postclosure care costs can be found in GASB Statement No. 18, *Accounting for Municipal Solid Waste Landfill Closure and Postclosure Care Costs.*

Tap fees and similar fees are exchange transactions for the portion of the fee that is intended to recover the cost of connecting new customers to the system. Accordingly, that portion of the fee should be recognized as a receivable and revenue as soon as the connection is made.

The portion of a tap fee or similar fee beyond the cost of connecting new customers is properly classified as an imposed nonexchange revenue. Accordingly, a receivable and revenue should be recognized as soon as the government has established an enforceable legal claim to the payment (upon connection). Such amounts should be classified either as *capital contributions* or *nonoperating revenues*, rather than as *operating revenues*.[31]

Impact or developer fees

Governments sometimes require that developers pay impact fees to help defray a portion of the costs that naturally result from increased development (construction of new parks and schools, for instance). Most often, laws or regulations require that impact fees or other similar types of developer fees be used for capital acquisition or related debt service.

Impact and similar developer fees are properly classified as an imposed nonexchange revenue. Accordingly, the full amount of the fee should be recognized as a receivable and revenue as soon as the government has established an enforceable legal claim to the resources (typically at the point the fee becomes nonrefundable). That the subsequent use of those resources is legally restricted to capital acquisition or related debt service should be reflected by the restriction of net assets rather than the deferral of revenue.

Payments in lieu of taxes

Because of their governmental character, enterprise funds most often are not subject to taxation. Therefore, some types of enterprise funds make payments in lieu of taxes to compensate the general government for public services received. In some cases, these payments are calculated to be reasonably equivalent in value to the services provided. In other cases, there is no clear link between the amounts paid and the value of services received.

When the amount of payments in lieu of taxes is reasonably equivalent in value to the services provided, the payment should be classified as *interfund services used* (a reciprocal interfund activity) and reported as an expense. Otherwise, payments in lieu of taxes should be classified as transfers (nonreciprocal interfund activity) in the enterprise fund operating statement.[32]

Naturally, discretely presented component units would report an expense rather than a transfer, regardless of how the amount of the payment in lieu of taxes was determined, since the use of transfers is strictly limited to activity between funds of the primary government.[33]

Contributions of capital assets within the primary government

Sometimes capital assets initially associated with governmental activities are later assigned to a proprietary fund. For example, a government may elect to establish a new internal service fund for an activity previously accounted for in the general fund, or it may choose to establish a new enterprise fund to account for services for which it will henceforth impose user

---

[31] AICPA, *State and Local Governments*, Section 13.23.
[32] GASB Statement No. 34, paragraph 112b(1).
[33] See the discussion of transfers in chapter 3.

charges. The rule in such cases is that the capital asset should be reported in the recipient proprietary fund at the same net book value previously reported (that is, historical cost less accumulated depreciation) in the government-wide statement of net assets.[34]

Capital assets received from the general government should be reported as *capital contributions* rather than as *transfers* in the proprietary fund operating statement. Conversely, this same event would be reclassified as a *transfer* from governmental activities to business-type activities when reported in the government-wide statement of activities.[35] Donations of capital assets to the general government would be reported as *transfers* in both the proprietary fund and government-wide financial statements.[36]

Cost of pension and other postemployment benefits

Proprietary funds use different authoritative guidance than private-sector business enterprises to account for the cost of pension and other post-employment benefits offered to employees.[37] These specialized rules are summarized as follows:

- *Single-employer defined benefit plans*. If a proprietary fund sponsors its own defined benefit plan for employees, expense normally will be the actuarially determined annual required contribution (ARC). Some adjustments to the ARC may be necessary to arrive at the amount of cost to be recognized, however, if the employer has a history of funding more or less than the ARC.[38]
- *Agent multiple-employer defined benefit plans*. An agent multiple-employer defined benefit plan is really a group of single-employer plans that are centrally administered. Such plans undergo a separate actuarial valuation for each participating employer. Accordingly, the same rules apply as for single-employer plans. That is, the ARC serves as the basic measure of expense for each period, although some adjustment may be needed if there has been a history of funding more or less than the ARC.[39]
- *Cost-sharing multiple-employer defined benefit plans*. A cost-sharing multiple-employer defined benefit plan functions as a unified plan, with a single actuarial valuation that covers all participating employers. The measure of expense for participating employers is the amount of contractually required contributions to the plan.[40]
- *Defined contribution plans*. In a defined contribution plan, the employer promises current performance (contributions now) rather than future performance (future benefit payments to employees). The

---

[34] GASB, *Comprehensive Implementation Guide (2004)*, questions 7.45 and 7.46, for (indirect) acknowledgement of this general principle.

[35] GASB, *Comprehensive Implementation Guide (2004)*, 7.335.

[36] See chapter 3 for a more detailed discussion. In the last case described, the transfer reported in the enterprise fund would *not* be matched by a corresponding transfer in the governmental funds (which do not report capital assets). Naturally, the notes would need to address this discrepancy.

[37] The authoritative private-sector guidance for employers offering pension and other postemployment benefits can be found in FASB Statement No. 87, *Employers' Accounting for Pensions* and FASB Statement No. 106, *Employers' Accounting for Postretirement Benefits Other Than Pensions*. In the public sector, the appropriate authoritative guidance is provided by GASB Statement No. 27, *Accounting for Pensions by State and Local Governmental Employers*, and GASB Statement No. 45, *Accounting and Financial Reporting by Employers for Postemployment Benefits Other Than Pensions*.

[38] GASB Statement No. 27, paragraphs 8, 11-13; GASB Statement No. 45, paragraphs 11, 14-16.

[39] GASB Statement No. 27, paragraphs 8, 11-13; GASB Statement No. 45, paragraphs 11, 14-16.

[40] GASB Statement No. 27, paragraph 19; GASB Statement No. 45, paragraphs 22-23.

measure of expense for employers participating in defined contribution plans is the amount of the required contributions for the period.[41]

- *Insured defined benefit plans.* An insured defined benefit plan is one in which an employer accumulates funds with an insurance company, and the insurance company rather than the employer unconditionally promises benefit payments upon retirement. The measure of expense for employers participating in insured defined benefit plans is equal to the annual contributions or premiums required according to the agreement with the insurance company.[42]

Passenger facility charges   Airports can obtain approval from the Federal Aviation Administration to impose a fixed fee on each departing passenger. This passenger facility charge (PFC) is collected by the ticket seller and is then remitted to the airport the next month for use in eligible construction projects or for related debt service. If the ticket is subsequently refunded, the PFC is refundable to the ticket purchaser. As a practical matter, refunds are deducted from subsequent remittances by sales agents.

PFCs qualify as exchange-like transactions and should be recognized as a nonoperating item when earned.[43] Since airports depend on third-party remittances for their information on PFCs, the amount to be recognized may need to be estimated.

Regulated enterprises   The FASB provides specialized accounting guidance for rate-regulated enterprises. This guidance is contained in FASB Statement No. 71, *Accounting for the Effects of Certain Types of Regulation*, and several related pronouncements.[44] These are the principal features of this specialized guidance:

- In certain instances, charges of the current period may be deferred (capitalized) if they will be recovered through future rates.
- The recognition of revenues associated with rates levied in anticipation of future charges may be deferred until the anticipated charge is incurred.
- If a gain reduces allowable costs, and this reduction will be reflected in lower future rates for customers, then the gain itself may be deferred and amortized over this same period.

As noted earlier, enterprise funds normally are *required* to apply FASB guidance issued prior to December 1, 1989, unless that guidance conflicts with or contradicts GASB standards. Compliance is purely *voluntary*, however, in the case of FASB Statement No. 71 (and related pronouncements through FASB Statement No. 101). To qualify for the voluntary use of specialized regulated enterprise accounting, an enterprise fund[45] must meet *all* of the following criteria:

- Rates for regulated services or products are established by or subject to approval by either an independent, third-party regulator or the

---

[41] GASB Statement No. 27, paragraph 25; GASB Statement No. 45, paragraph 29.

[42] GASB Statement No. 27, paragraph 23; GASB Statement No. 45, paragraph 28.

[43] GASB Statement No. 34, paragraphs 102 and 436.

[44] FASB Statement No. 90, *Regulated Enterprises—Accounting for Abandonments and Disallowances of Plant Costs*, FASB Statement No. 92, *Regulated Enterprises—Accounting for Phase-in Plans*, and FASB Statement No. 101, *Regulated Enterprises—Accounting for the Discontinuation of Application of FASB Statement No. 71*.

[45] The use of specialized regulated enterprise accounting is limited to enterprise funds per GASB Statement No. 34, paragraph 94.

governing board itself, if it is empowered by statute or contract to establish rates that bind customers.

- The regulated rates are designed to recover the specific enterprise's costs of providing regulated services or products.
- It is reasonable to assume that the regulated activity can set and collect charges sufficient to recover its costs.[46]

Risk financing premiums received from other funds

Governments may use either the general fund or an internal service fund if they wish to use a single fund to account for all risk financing activities of a given type. If a government chooses to use an internal service fund to account for its risk financing activities, interfund premiums should be classified as *interfund services provided* (a reciprocal interfund activity). As a result, premiums received by the internal service fund should be reported as *revenues*.[47] This treatment, however, can only be applied to the extent that any excess of premiums charged over probable and measurable losses is justified by one of the following conditions: The excess represents a reasonable provision for anticipated catastrophe losses; or the excess is the result of a systematic funding method designed to match revenues and expenses over a reasonable period of time (for instance, an actuarial funding method based on historical cost data). Otherwise, any portion of premiums in excess of probable and measurable losses incurred must be reported as a transfer (a nonreciprocal interfund activity) rather than as revenue.[48]

Changes in accounting principle

In the private sector, changes in accounting principle or changes in the application of an accounting principle are treated in accordance with the provisions of APB Opinion No. 20, *Accounting Changes.* That statement calls for the cumulative effect of a change in accounting principle (including a change in the application of an accounting principle) to be identified separately in the operating statement.

Generally, the provisions of APB Opinion No. 20 apply to proprietary funds. GAAP specifically indicate, however, that changes in accounting principles or changes in the application of an accounting principle "should be reported as restatements of beginning net assets/fund equity, not as a separately identified cumulative effect in the current-period statement of activities or proprietary fund statement of revenues, expenses, and changes in fund net assets."[49] This treatment reflects the fact that the concerns prompting this provision of APB Opinion No. 20 in the private sector (potential manipulation of "earnings per share") have been largely nonexistent for proprietary funds.[50]

---

[46] This last criterion sometimes is erroneously overlooked.

[47] Recall from chapter 5 that a similar premium payment to the general fund would be reported as an *interfund reimbursement* (a nonreciprocal interfund activity).

[48] GASB Statement No. 10, *Accounting and Financial Reporting for Risk Financing and Related Insurance Issues*, paragraph 66.

[49] GASB Statement No. 34, note 13.

[50] GASB Statement No. 34, paragraph 309.

7

Fiduciary Funds, Joint Ventures, and Other Multiparty Arrangements

Agovernment's core activities are reported as *governmental funds* and *proprietary funds* in the fund financial statements, and as *governmental activities* and *business-type activities* in the government-wide financial statements. A government also may participate in arrangements that are *not* reported as governmental or proprietary funds, and which are either *excluded* altogether from the government-wide financial statements or *reported* there only *indirectly*. Such arrangements—which include fiduciary funds, joint ventures, and other multiparty arrangements—are the subject of this chapter.

FIDUCIARY FUNDS

Generally accepted accounting principles (GAAP) prescribe the use of fiduciary funds "to report assets held in a trustee or agency capacity for others and therefore cannot be used to support the government's own programs."[1] Those for whom assets are held in a trustee or agency capacity commonly include individuals (such as pension plan participants and beneficiaries), private organizations (such as university foundations), and other governments (such as local government investment pools). Because the resources of fiduciary funds, by definition, cannot be used to support the government's own programs, such funds are specifically *excluded* from the government-wide financial statements.[2] They are reported, however, as part of the basic fund financial statements to ensure fiscal accountability.

---

[1] GASB Statement No. 34, *Basic Financial Statements—and Management's Discussion and Analysis—for State and Local Governments*, paragraph 69.
[2] GASB Statement No. 34, paragraph 12.

Fiduciary responsibilities versus fiduciary funds

Not all fiduciary arrangements are properly reported as fiduciary funds. Rather, GAAP explicitly state that trust funds and agency funds are to be used solely to account for resources that are *held* by the government. For example, a local governmental employer participating in a statewide, multiple-employer pension plan would *not* report a pension trust fund to account for its share of assets accumulated by the statewide plan, even though that employer has fiduciary responsibilities to its employees in connection with its participation in the statewide pension plan. Instead, the state government, which actually holds the assets, would report a pension trust fund.

Two criteria may be used to determine whether a government is, in fact, holding assets in connection with its fiduciary responsibilities to individuals, private organizations, or other governments. A government is considered to be holding any assets: 1) for which it performs the investment function; or 2) with which the government has *significant* administrative involvement (for example, involvement that goes beyond the remittance of predetermined amounts[3] to a third party).

Specialized guidance for pension (and other employee benefit) trust funds

Detailed specialized guidance on accounting and financial reporting for pension plans and other postemployment benefit plans is provided elsewhere in this book.[4] All the same, several aspects of pension (and other employee benefit) trust fund accounting will be addressed here as part of a general examination of fiduciary fund accounting.

Deferred compensation plans

Many state and local governments sponsor Internal Revenue Code (IRC) Section 457 deferred compensation plans for the benefit of their employees. In many cases, the governments that sponsor such plans remit the amounts withheld from employees directly to a third-party administrator (such as an investment firm or insurance company). In most situations involving third-party administrators, the sponsoring government's practical involvement in administering the plan is essentially limited to remitting the amounts collected from employees to the plan administrator. In that case, the use of a fiduciary fund to account for the assets of the deferred compensation plan would *not* be appropriate, because the government is not properly considered to be holding the assets.

There are instances, however, where state and local governments do, in fact, hold the assets of IRC Section 457 plans. For example, the state treasurer may directly invest the assets of the state's own IRC Section 457 plan on behalf of employees; or, a government may hire investment managers to perform the investment function while the government maintains significant oversight of the managers' activities. In that case, the sponsoring government is considered to be holding the plan's assets and would need to report its stewardship of those assets in a pension (and other employee benefit) trust fund.[5]

Governments also may participate in other types of deferred compensation arrangements, such as 401(k) and 403(b) plans. While GAAP provide no specific guidance on the appropriate accounting and financial reporting for such plans, the approach described for IRC Section 457 plans appears equally suitable for other types of deferred compensation arrangements.[6]

---

[3] For example, amounts calculated in conformity with a predetermined formula.
[4] See chapter 15.
[5] See GASB, *Codification of Governmental Accounting and Financial Reporting Standards*, D25.101.

Recognition of contributions receivable for pension plans and other postemployment benefit plans

GAAP require that employers participating in *single employer* and *agent multiple employer* defined benefit pension plans and other postemployment benefit (OPEB) plans report a liability on the face of their financial statements if they fail to fully fund their actuarially determined annual required contribution. The employer's act of reporting such a liability, however, is *not* sufficient basis to justify the pension (and other employee benefit) trust fund reporting a corresponding receivable on the statement of plan net assets and a related addition on the statement of changes in plan net assets. Rather, GAAP specifically indicate that a pension (and other employee benefit) trust fund may report a contribution receivable only "pursuant to formal commitments as well as statutory or contractual requirements." For example, recognition of a receivable from a contributing employer would be appropriate if the employer's governing body had appropriated the contribution. Similarly, a receivable should be recognized in situations where a contributing employer has demonstrated a consistent pattern of making required payments for the previous year subsequent to the plan's reporting date.[7]

In the case of *cost-sharing multiple-employer* defined benefit pension or OPEB plans, a receivable is recognized by the plan for any contractually required contributions from employers.

Exclusion of the actuarial accrued liability

The estimated present value of the benefits owed to participants and beneficiaries in pension plans and other postemployment benefit plans based on services already rendered is known as the actuarial accrued liability. As its name implies, this amount is an *actuarial* obligation rather than an *accounting* liability, and so is *not* reported on the face of the statement of fiduciary net assets. GAAP require, however, that trend data on the actuarial accrued liability be presented as required supplementary information. Furthermore, in the case of other postemployment benefit plans, one year's data from the most recent actuarial valuation must also be included within the notes to the financial statements.[8]

Reassignment of employee asset balances

When a single pension system administers multiple individual pension plans, member account asset balances sometimes may be reassigned among plans to reflect employment changes, such as employees being reassigned to another department or agency. Such reassignments should be reported as additions and deductions for each plan involved rather than as transfers among plans.[9]

---

[6] GASB Statement No. 32, *Accounting and Financial Reporting for Internal Revenue Code Section 457 Deferred Compensation Plans*, paragraphs 17-18.

[7] GASB Statement No. 25, *Financial Reporting for Defined Benefit Pension Plans and Note Disclosures for Defined Contribution Plans*, paragraph 22 and GASB Statement No. 43, *Financial Reporting for Postemployment Benefit Plans Other Than Pension Plans*, paragraph 20.

[8] GASB Statement No. 43, paragraph 101. The aggregate actuarial cost allocation method does not produce all of the data needed to present a schedule of funding progress because it does not identify or separately amortize unfunded actuarial liabilities. Accordingly, *pension plans* that use the aggregate method need not present a schedule of funding progress (although they may do so using the approach described below, per GASB, *Comprehensive Implementation Guide (2004)*, 5.82). In the case of *other postemployment benefit plans*, however, a schedule of funding progress is required even if the aggregate method is used. To comply with this requirement, financial statement preparers for other postemployment benefit plans are directed to use the entry-age actuarial cost allocation method to provide the missing data. See GASB Statement No. 27, paragraph 22 and GASB Statement No. 43, paragraph 30d(1).

[9] GASB, *Comprehensive Implementation Guide (2004)*, 5.69.

Specialized guidance for investment trust funds

GAAP direct that external government investment pools be reported in investment trust funds.[10] Not all pooling arrangements, however, constitute an external investment pool for this purpose, so it is important to clearly identify situations that require the use of an investment trust fund.

Four key criteria must be met for an arrangement to qualify as an external investment pool.[11]

- *Commingling of assets.* An investment *pool* necessarily involves the *commingling* of assets from more than one source. If individual participants can be identified with specific investments, there is an absence of commingling, and the arrangement does not constitute a *pool*.
- *External participation.* To qualify as an *external* government investment pool, a pooling arrangement must include *at least one legally separate participant from outside the financial reporting entity.* When a single arrangement pools internal and external resources, creating a mixed pool, only the portion of pool assets attributable to participants outside the financial reporting entity is treated as an *external* investment pool.
- *Investment focus.* The *primary purpose* of an investment pool is to *generate income.* When investment pooling is strictly ancillary to some other purpose—such as investment pooling during the construction phase of a joint venture—the arrangement does not qualify as an *investment* pool.
- *Participants as beneficiaries.* Sometimes all income from commingled moneys accrues to the benefit of the investing government rather than to participants from outside the financial reporting entity. An example is a situation involving a county treasurer acting as custodial agent for the investments of governments within the county's jurisdiction. Such arrangements do not qualify as *external investment* pools because, from the perspective of the outside participants, positions in such pools are not investments.

It is important to note that pools need not be permanent arrangements. For example, moneys may be pooled and invested temporarily during the year. In such cases, an investment trust fund must be used, *even if no pooled resources are outstanding at the end of the fiscal period.* In this case, the investment trust fund would report only a statement of changes in fiduciary net assets to account for activity related to the investments of outside parties during the period.[12]

Property taxes, sales taxes, and gas taxes often are collected by one government on behalf of other governments. Typically, there is a delay between when the taxes are collected and when they are remitted to the appropriate governments. These amounts may be invested in a pool during this period. The collecting government should *not* report an investment trust fund in connection with these assets because they do not qualify as investments; that is, the assets are not pooled primarily to generate income on behalf of participants.[13]

---

[10] GASB Statement No. 34, paragraph 71.
[11] GASB Statement No. 31, *Accounting and Financial Reporting for Certain Investments and for External Investment Pools.*
[12] GASB, *Comprehensive Implementation Guide (2004)*, 6.89.
[13] GASB, *Comprehensive Implementation Guide (2004)*, 6.90.

A number of other arrangements that include investing activities also do not qualify as external investment pools because their primary purpose, once again, is something other than the generation of income. For example, sometimes governments establish joint ventures for constructing and operating certain facilities, such as a sewage treatment plant. Such an arrangement should *not* be considered an external investment pool even if, during the construction phase, the joint venture realizes significant investment income from idle construction funds. Investment activities, though substantial during the construction phase, ultimately remain incidental to the joint venture's basic purpose, which is the construction and operation of a plant.[14]

Public-entity risk pools[15] and venture capital limited partnerships[16] are other examples of arrangements that would *not* qualify as external investment pools because their primary purpose is not the generation of income. The primary purpose of a public-entity risk pool is to manage liability exposure; a venture capital limited partnership is intended primarily to serve as a mechanism for raising capital.

Specialized guidance for private-purpose trust funds

Some clarifications may be useful regarding the proper use of private-purpose trust funds.

Private purpose versus indirect private benefit

Private-purpose trust funds are used to report all trust arrangements (other than pension and investment trust funds) "under which principal and income benefit individuals, private organizations, or other governments."[17] In light of this definition, it might be tempting to classify as private-purpose trust funds any number of arrangements that provide direct or indirect benefits to individuals. For example, a perpetual care endowment for a municipal cemetery certainly provides very tangible benefits to the families of individuals buried in the cemetery. Remember, however, that all fiduciary funds are also subject to the general limitation that fund resources "cannot be used to support the government's own programs." Thus, although a municipal cemetery provides services to specific individuals and their families, the cemetery also is a government program and therefore cannot properly be accounted for in a fiduciary fund.[18] Therefore the term "private-purpose" is best understood as referring to the *absence of a public purpose* rather than to the presence of a private benefit.

Specific benefits for specific individuals, organizations, or governments

The use of private-purpose trust funds normally should be limited to situations where *specific* benefits accrue to *specific* individuals, organizations, or governments. For example, it would not be appropriate to use a private-purpose trust fund to account for the revenues of prison pay phones that will provide benefits to inmates generally.[19]

Of course, government programs too may sometimes provide what might be described as specific benefits to specific individuals. How then are private-purpose trusts to be distinguished from such government pro-

---

[14] GASB, *Comprehensive Implementation Guide (2004)*, 6.92.
[15] GASB, *Comprehensive Implementation Guide (2004)*, 6.93.
[16] GASB, *Comprehensive Implementation Guide (2004)*, 6.94.
[17] GASB Statement No. 34, paragraph 72.
[18] GAAP indicate that a perpetual care endowment for a municipal cemetery should be reported in a permanent fund (GASB Statement No. 34, paragraph 65, note 32).
[19] GASB, *Comprehensive Implementation Guide (2004)*, 7.266.

grams (which, by definition, *cannot* be reported in a fiduciary fund)?   In the case of a private-purpose trust fund, there should be virtually no discretion in determining what specific amount accrues to which specific individual.

Escheat resources

States may report escheat resources held on behalf of individuals or private organizations in a private-purpose trust fund[20] rather than in the fund(s) to which those resources normally escheat (e.g., general fund). When escheat resources are reported in the fund(s) to which those resources normally escheat, a liability for amounts expected to be paid to individuals or private organizations would have to be reported. If a private-purpose trust fund is used, however, no such liability is necessary because the use of a trust fund by itself is considered sufficient to demonstrate the ultimate disposition of the fund's resources. Consistent with the definition of a fiduciary fund, only that portion of escheat resources whose eventual payment to claimants is considered to be probable may be reported in a private-purpose trust fund.[21] Likewise, escheat resources not expected eventually to be paid to claimants would be reported directly as revenue of the general fund.

Specialized guidance for agency funds

Some clarifications may be useful regarding the proper use of agency funds.

Internal agency funds

As a practical matter, a government may use an agency fund as an internal clearing account for amounts that have yet to be allocated to individual funds.[22] This practice is perfectly appropriate *for internal accounting purposes*. However, for *external financial reporting purposes*, GAAP expressly limit the use of fiduciary funds, including agency funds, to assets "held in a trustee or agency capacity *for others*" and that, therefore, "*cannot be used to support the government's own programs.*[23] Therefore, all assets accounted for in an internal agency fund must be allocated to the appropriate funds and component units of the government in external general-purpose financial reports.[24]

No-commitment special assessment debt

A government may issue special assessment debt for which it is not obligated in any manner. Even though the government is not obligated to repay the debt, typically it still is responsible for collecting the amounts from property owners in connection with the property tax levy, and then subsequently remitting to bondholders the amounts collected. GAAP prescribe that an agency fund be used to account for assessments collected prior to remittance.[25]

When agency funds are used in connection with no-commitment special assessment debt, no asset is reported for receivables not yet due. To report such an asset would result in a liability equal to the amount of the outstanding debt, and GAAP specifically prohibit governments from reporting no-commitment special assessment debt on the face of the financial statements.[26] Instead, agency funds should report only cash collected (whether

---

[20] Escheat assets held for other governments would be reported in an agency fund rather than in a private-purpose trust fund. Alternatively both assets and liabilities could be reported in a governmental or proprietary fund.
[21] GASB, *Comprehensive Implementation Guide (2004)*, 7.272.
[22] For example, the government's own portion of combined tax collections.
[23] GASB Statement No. 34, paragraph 69 [emphasis added].
[24] GASB Statement No. 34, paragraph 111.
[25] GASB Statement No. 6, *Accounting and Financial Reporting for Special Assessments*, paragraph 19.
[26] GASB Statement No. 6, paragraph 17c.

on hand or with the government's paying agent) and any delinquent receivable balances.

Unexpended proceeds to be used to finance reimbursement grants

By definition, the resources that are to be used to finance a reimbursement or expenditure-driven grant or similar arrangement do *not* become the property of the grantee until qualifying expenditures are incurred. Therefore, until that time, the use of an agency fund to account for such resources would *not* be appropriate.[27]

Escheat resources held for other governments

Sometimes a government will hold escheat resources on behalf of another government. In that case, the use of an agency fund, rather than a private-purpose trust fund, would be appropriate.[28] Alternatively, both the assets and the liabilities could be reported in a governmental or a proprietary fund.

JOINT VENTURES

Governments commonly enter into special arrangements with each other to jointly obtain or provide needed services. A common type of special arrangement is the joint venture. A multigovernment arrangement qualifies as a joint venture only if it meets *all four* of the following criteria:

- *Contractual basis.* A joint venture is always the direct product of a contractual arrangement. Sometimes the contract underlying a joint venture will clearly define each participating government's claim to some or all of the resources of the joint venture. In other cases, the contract either does not include such a provision or only addresses disposition of the joint venture's resources upon dissolution.
- *Separate identity.* A joint venture must function as a separate and specific activity in its own right. That is, the joint venture contract must create a separate activity that did not previously exist.[29]
- *Joint control.* A joint venture implies two or more participants and must involve at least some degree of joint control. If one participant is able to unilaterally control the joint venture's financial or operating policies, the arrangement is not a joint venture from that participant's point of view,[30] although the other participating governments may still consider the arrangement a joint venture.
- *Ongoing financial relationship.* A joint venture must create either an ongoing financial interest or an ongoing financial responsibility for the participating governments. An ongoing financial interest can be either direct (such as a right to the joint venture's surpluses) or indirect (such as the ability to cause the joint venture to undertake desired projects). Ongoing financial responsibility can take the form of being "obligated in some manner" for the joint venture's debt. Financial responsibility also arises when a joint venture's continued existence depends on a government's continuing participation. This consideration is particularly important in arrangements with only a small number of participants, or in situations where one or a small number

---

[27] GASB, *Comprehensive Implementation Guide (2004)*, 7.267.
[28] GASB, *Comprehensive Implementation Guide (2004)*, 7.272.
[29] This would include previously existing activities of a government that are spun off as joint ventures.
[30] It probably would qualify instead as a component unit.

EXHIBIT 7-1
Accounting and financial reporting for joint ventures

```
                    ┌─────────────┐
                    │    Start    │
                    └─────────────┘
                          │
                          ▼
              ◇ Explicit,          ◇   YES    ◇ Equity            ◇   YES    ┌────────────────┐
              measurable                      interest in                    │ Report in       │
              equity interest? ───────────▶   the capital      ───────────▶  │ government-wide │
              ◇                   ◇           assets of the     ◇            │ and proprietary │
                                              venture?                       │ fund financial  │
                          │                       │                          │ statements      │
                          │ NO                    │ NO                       │ as an asset     │
                          ▼                       ▼                          └────────────────┘
              ┌──────────────┐       ┌──────────────────┐                          │
              │ Disclose in  │       │ Report in        │                          │
              │ the notes to │       │ government-wide  │                          │
              │ the financial│       │ and fund financial│                         │
              │ statements   │       │ statements as    │                          │
              │              │       │ an asset         │                          │
              └──────────────┘       └──────────────────┘                          │
                      │                       │                                    │
                      │                       ▼                                    │
                      │                ┌─────────────┐                             │
                      └───────────────▶│    Stop     │◀────────────────────────────┘
                                       └─────────────┘
```

of participants accounts for a significant proportion of the total participation in the joint venture.

If all four of these criteria are met, the arrangement is properly classified as a joint venture.[31]

It is essential to conform to the going concern assumption in applying these criteria. Thus, a residual claim to the assets of a joint venture upon dissolution should *not* be considered evidence of an ongoing financial interest for this purpose.[32]

The criteria for identifying joint ventures do *not* supersede other relevant authoritative guidance.[33] Using these criteria, for example, it is possible to argue that participation in a public-entity risk pool or external investment pool should be accounted for as a joint venture. However, GAAP have provided specific guidance on the proper accounting and financial reporting for participation in both public-entity risk pools[34] and external

---

[31] GASB Statement No. 14, *The Financial Reporting Entity*, paragraph 69.
[32] GASB Statement No. 14, footnote 10.
[33] As a rule, GAAP should be interpreted in accordance with the principle that "the specific governs the general." That is, it must be presumed that the authoritative standard-setting body considered all relevant general principles in making decisions regarding specific applications.
[34] GASB Statement No. 10, *Accounting and Financial Reporting for Risk Financing and Related Insurance Issues* and GASB Interpretation No. 4, *Accounting and Financial Reporting for Capitalization Contributions to Public Entity Risk Pools (an interpretation of GASB Statements No. 10 and 14).*

investment pools[35] and that specific guidance takes precedence over the more general GAAP guidance on joint ventures.

The proper accounting and financial reporting for joint ventures depends on whether the underlying contract creates an *explicit, measurable equity interest* in some or all of the joint venture's resources. If there is an explicit, measurable equity interest in the joint venture, the government's investment in the joint venture should be reported as a single line item in the government-wide statement of net assets. Likewise, changes in the government's investment in the joint venture should be reported as a single line item in the government-wide statement of activities. The same treatment applies to the proprietary fund financial statements.

The amount of the asset reported in conjunction with participation in a joint venture may change for any one of three reasons:

- as the result of additional capital contributions by the participating government;
- as the result of distributions from the joint venture to the participating government; or
- as the result of any portion of the joint venture's net income or loss that affects the participating government's explicit measurable equity interest.

The first two items, of course, would not be reflected in the operating statement of the participating government as they affect only asset and liability accounts. The last item would affect the operating statement and its proper treatment would depend on the reason why the government participates in the joint venture. If the government's participation is for investment purposes, the change would be reported as an element of general revenue. Conversely, if the government's participation in the joint venture is intended to assist in the provision of services, the change would be treated as a program item.[36]

In the case of governmental funds, an investment in the joint venture should be reported in a governmental fund only to the extent that it represents a *financial* asset rather than an interest in the underlying capital assets of the joint venture.[37] Joint ventures *not* involving an explicit, measurable equity interest are reported simply as note disclosures. Exhibit 7-1 illustrates the appropriate accounting and financial reporting for joint ventures.

OTHER MULTIPARTY ARRANGEMENTS

In addition to joint ventures, a number of other types of multiparty arrangements are commonly encountered in the public sector. Such arrangements include jointly governed organizations, undivided interests in joint operations, and cost-sharing agreements.

Jointly governed organizations

Governments often use contracts to establish separate activities for their mutual benefit that are beyond the control of any single participating government. For example, all governments of a similar type in a similar region may form a council of governments to deal with common planning issues. While such arrangements meet three of the criteria for classification as a

[35] GASB Statement No. 31.
[36] GASB, *Comprehensive Implementation Guide (2004)*, 7.176.
[37] GASB Statement No. 14, paragraphs 73-74.

joint venture (contractual basis, separate identity, and joint control), they ultimately fail to qualify as a joint venture because they typically create neither an ongoing financial interest nor an ongoing financial responsibility for the participants. Financial reporting for such jointly governed organizations is limited to disclosure in the notes to the financial statements.[38]

Undivided interests in joint operations

In some joint operations, individual participating governments retain their claim to specific assets and continue to be responsible for specific liabilities. When an individual participating government can be thus associated with a specific asset or liability of a joint operation, that government has an undivided interest in that asset or liability. Undivided interests are always reported simply as assets and liabilities in their own right in the appropriate government's financial statements rather than as an asset or liability of the joint operation itself.

A single multiparty arrangement may possess aspects of both a joint venture and an undivided interest in a joint operation. In that case, the separate components of the arrangement should be accounted for separately. Assume, for example, that two governments decide to combine their separate water and sewer systems into a single joint venture, but that each will retain title to the capital assets initially provided to the joint venture. All subsequent capital assets will be financed from the earnings of the joint venture and will be the property of the joint venture rather than of either participating government. In that case, each government's undivided interest in the capital assets initially provided to the joint venture would be reported separately from its investment (if any) in the joint venture itself.[39]

Cost-sharing agreements

Two or more governments that wish to share costs effectively need not always establish a separate activity. For example, arrangements such as jointly financed highway projects or joint purchasing agreements represent contractual commitments rather than joint ventures because they do *not* create a separate activity. Accounting and financial reporting for cost-sharing agreements is limited to disclosure in the notes to the financial statements.[40]

Participation in pools

GAAP specifically exclude both public-entity risk pools and external investment pools from the defined scope of a joint venture. Instead, as noted earlier, specialized authoritative guidance preempts the requirements of joint-venture accounting and financial reporting.[41]

Public-entity risk pools

The proper accounting for a government's participation in a public-entity risk pool depends on the nature of the pool. Specifically, the appropriate accounting and financial reporting for participation in a public-entity risk pool depends on whether there is a transfer or pooling of risk.

Some public-entity risk pools, such as risk-sharing pools, in fact transfer or pool the risk of participating governments. In that case, required premiums to the pool should be treated in the same way as an insurance premium paid to a private insurance enterprise. If it is probable that additional pay-

---

[38] GASB Statement No. 14, paragraph 77.
[39] Recall that a reportable investment in a joint venture requires an explicit, measurable equity interest based on the underlying contract.
[40] GASB Statement No. 14, paragraph 81.
[41] GASB Statement No. 14, paragraph 79.

EXHIBIT 7-2
Accounting for capitalization contributions made to public-entity risk financing pools

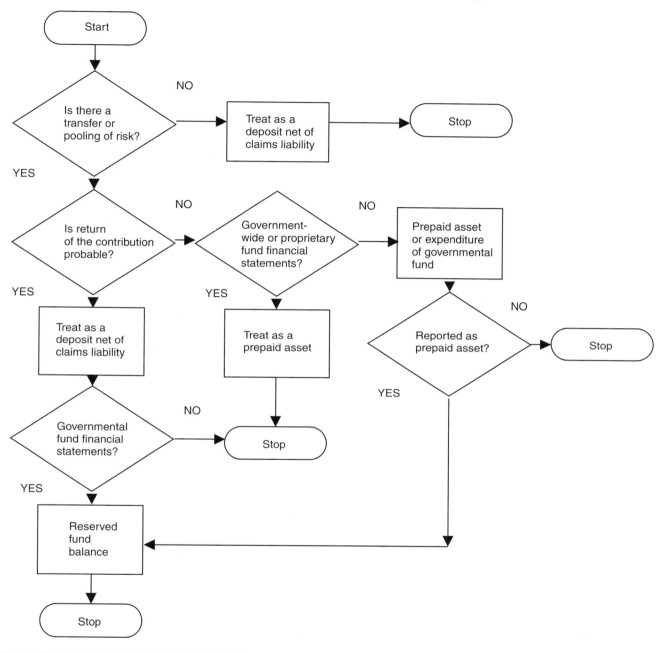

ments will be required (for instance, if the pool agreement provides for additional assessments), a liability for that amount should also be recognized, if it can be estimated.

Other public-entity risk pools do *not* transfer or pool the risk of participating governments. A banking pool, for example, is simply an arrangement for making loans available to pool participants in the event of loss. Likewise, a claims-servicing pool is an administrative convenience whereby a pool manager pays each individual pool member's losses out of that same pool member's own separate account. In these and similar arrangements, payments to the pool essentially amount to deposits that should be reported as an asset, net of any related liability for estimated claims payable.[42]

Participants in a public-entity risk pool often are asked to provide start-up capital or "seed money" in the form of a capitalization contribution. The proper accounting and financial reporting for such contributions depends, once again, on whether the contribution is made to a pool that transfers or pools the risk of participating governments. If there is no transfer or pooling of risk, then the capitalization contribution should be reported as a deposit, net of any related liability for estimated claims payable. If the capitalization contribution is made to a pool that does transfer or pool the risks of participating governments, then the appropriate accounting depends on whether it is probable that the contribution eventually will be refunded.

If return of the capitalization contribution is probable, then the contribution should be treated by the participating government as a deposit (asset). In a governmental fund, a portion of fund balance should be reserved to indicate that the capitalization contribution is not available for spending.

If return of the capitalization contribution is not considered probable, the amount should be reported as a prepayment in the government-wide statement of net assets and amortized over the period coverage is to be provided. (This coverage period should be consistent with the period during which the contribution is factored into the pool's determination of premiums. If that period is not readily determinable, amortization should occur over a period not to exceed ten years.) This same treatment applies equally to proprietary funds. The amount of the capitalization contribution may be reported using either the consumption method or the purchases method in governmental funds. If the consumption method is used, a portion of fund balance must be reserved to indicate that such contributions are not available for spending.[43]

Exhibit 7-2 illustrates the appropriate accounting and financial reporting for capitalization contributions to public-entity risk pools.

External investment pools   Positions in external investment pools normally should be reported at the fair value of the participant's share of the underlying portfolio. If the participating government's share is guaranteed not to fall below a certain level, and that guarantee is considered reliable, then the participating government may report the guaranteed share value even if its share of the underlying portfolio is a lesser amount. When a government participates in a pool that operates in accordance with Securities and Exchange Commission Rule 2a7, a participating government should report its position in the pool based on the pool's share price, which may be based on the amortized cost of the portfolio.[44]

---

[42] GASB Statement No. 10, paragraphs 69-71.
[43] GASB Interpretation No. 4, *Accounting and Financial Reporting for Capitalization Contributions to Public Entity Risk Pools (an interpretation of GASB Statements No. 10 and 14)*.
[44] GASB Statement No. 31, paragraphs 11 and 12.

8

Government-wide
Financial Reporting

As chapter 2 described, perhaps the single most visible characteristic of accounting and financial reporting for state and local governments is the unique combination of fund accounting and government-wide financial reporting. This chapter more closely examines the nature of the relationship between these two essential components of the governmental financial reporting model.

BACKGROUND

Government-wide financial reporting involves more than simply aggregating the various balances reported in each individual governmental and proprietary fund. It also requires the following:

- *Conversion of governmental fund data.* The data reported in governmental funds using the current financial resources measurement focus and the modified accrual basis of accounting needs to be converted to the economic resources measurement focus and the accrual basis of accounting.[1]
- *Consolidation of fund data.* The effects of interfund activity within the primary government normally need to be eliminated from government-wide presentations.
- *Removal of indirect costs from functional expense.* Except for *general government*, individual functions within governmental activities normally should report only direct costs. If any indirect costs were allocated to a given function in the fund financial statements, that allocation must be reversed for purposes of government-wide financial reporting.

---

[1] The concepts of measurement focus and basis of accounting are closely related. As a matter of convenience, this chapter sometimes uses the term *basis* to refer to both. Thus, the term *modified accrual basis* is sometimes used to describe the combination of the current financial resources measurement focus and the modified accrual basis of accounting, while the term *accrual basis* may be used to describe the combination of the economic resources measurement focus and the accrual basis of accounting.

- *Assignment of unallocated direct costs to the appropriate functional expense category.* Often significant direct costs associated with governmental activities are included within the *general government* function in the fund financial statements. All such direct costs must be allocated to the appropriate function within governmental activities for purposes of government-wide financial reporting.

CONVERSION OF GOVERNMENTAL FUND DATA

Preparers of government-wide financial statements must convert data presented in the basic governmental fund financial statements from the current financial resources measurement focus and the modified accrual basis of accounting to the economic resources measurement focus and the accrual basis of accounting. Our discussion will begin with a conceptual examination of each of the different modifications needed, first from the perspective of the statement of position (i.e., *governmental fund balance sheet* versus *government-wide statement of net assets*) and then from the viewpoint of the statement of operations/activity (i.e., *governmental fund statement of revenues, expenditures, and changes in fund balances* versus *government-wide statement of activities*). Our consideration will then turn to how financial statement preparers go about the practical task of converting governmental fund data for incorporation in the governmental activities column of the government-wide financial statements.

From the governmental fund balance sheet to the government-wide statement of net assets

Governmental funds report only those assets and liabilities that are considered relevant to flows and balances of current financial resources. The government-wide statement of net assets, on the other hand, reports *all* assets and liabilities associated with governmental activities, regardless of whether they are relevant to flows and balances of current financial resources. Thus, *governmental activities* in the government-wide statement of net assets will report a number of *additional* assets and liabilities *not* reported in the governmental funds. Conversely, one particular liability commonly reported in a modified accrual balance sheet (*deferred revenue* for amounts considered to be unavailable) does *not* qualify as a liability under the accrual basis of accounting and must therefore be eliminated for purposes of government-wide reporting.

The specific adjustments needed to reflect the differences just described can be summarized as follows (see also Exhibit 8-1):

- *Include capital assets of the general government.* Governmental funds focus on current *financial* resources. Therefore, *not* reported in the governmental funds are capital assets used in the operations of a government, such as land, buildings and improvements, equipment, infrastructure, intangibles, and certain investments in joint ventures. Such assets must be included in the government-wide statement of net assets (net of depreciation or amortization, as applicable).
- *Include deferred charges for debt issuance costs.* Governmental funds report debt issuance costs as an expenditure when those costs are first incurred because they require the use of current financial resources. However, debt issuance costs must be included as a deferred charge

EXHIBIT 8-1

Conversion from the governmental fund balance sheet to the government-wide statement of net assets

Assets and liabilities	Reported in governmental fund financial statements?	Reported in government-wide financial statements?	Action required	Adjustments to reconcile *fund balance – governmental funds* and *net assets – governmental activities*
				Start: *Fund balance*
Capital assets of the general government (e.g., land, buildings and improvements, equipment, infrastructure, intangibles)	No	Yes	Report capital assets net of accumulated depreciation/ amortization	Add: Carrying value of capital assets
Deferred charges for issuance costs	No	Yes	Report unamortized balance of deferred charge for issuance costs	Add: Unamortized balance of deferred charge for issuance costs
Inventories and prepaids	No*	Yes	Report inventories outstanding and unamortized portion of prepaid items	Add: Inventories outstanding and unamortized portion of prepaid items
Unmatured long-term debt (e.g., bonds, notes, capital lease obligations, certificates of participation) net of unamortized premiums, discounts, and similar items	No**	Yes	Report unmatured long-term debt net of unamortized premiums, discounts, and similar items	Less: Net unmatured long-term debt
Accrued interest	No***	Yes	Report liability for accrued interest payable	Less: Accrued interest payable
Certain accrued obligations *not* normally expected to be liquidated with expendable available financial resources unless they are due for payment in the current period (i.e., claims and judgments, compensated absences, special termination benefits, landfill closure and postclosure care costs, operating leases with scheduled rent increases, and a government's net pension obligation or net other post-employment benefit obligation as an employer)	No	Yes	Report accrued liabilities outstanding	Less: Certain accrued liabilities not reported in governmental funds
Assets of internal service funds that primarily serve governmental funds	No	Yes	Report assets of internal service funds	Add: Assets of internal service funds qualifying as governmental activities
Liabilities of internal service funds that primarily serve governmental funds	No	Yes	Report liabilities of internal service funds	Less: Liabilities of internal service funds qualifying as governmental activities
Internal receivable/payable representing cumulative "crossover" effect of involvement with business-type activities	No	Yes	Report "crossover" internal receivable/payable	Add: Crossover internal receivable Less: Crossover internal payable
Liability for *earned* but deferred revenue	Yes	No	Remove liability	Add: Earned but deferred revenue
Liability for *unearned* deferred revenue	Yes	Yes	No change required	No effect
				End: *Net assets – governmental activities*

*Inventories and prepaids are reported in the governmental fund balance sheet if the consumption method is used. Likewise, material balances of inventories accounted for using the purchases method must also be reported on the governmental fund balance sheet.
**The unmatured principal of debt may be reported as a debt service fund liability if amounts are transferred to that fund during the current fiscal year for payments due early in the subsequent year.
***Accrued interest may be reported as a debt service fund liability if amounts are transferred to that fund during the current fiscal year for payments due early in the subsequent year.

(much like a prepaid item) in the government-wide statement of net assets.

- *Include inventories and prepaids as assets.* Governmental funds have the option of accounting for inventories and prepaids using the *purchases method* (that is, recognizing an expenditure at the time of purchase rather than based on consumption). Whenever this option is taken, it is important to ensure that inventories and prepaids are reported as assets nonetheless in the government-wide statement of net assets.[2]
- *Include unmatured long-term debt.* Governmental funds report only those liabilities that are normally expected to be liquidated with current available financial resources. Thus, governmental funds typically report no liability for the unmatured principal of bonds, notes, capital lease obligations, and similar debt obligations (such as certificates of participation and certificates of obligation).[3] All debt, however, must be reported in the government-wide financial statements.
- *Include liability for accrued interest.* Consistent with the treatment described for long-term debt, governmental funds typically do not report a liability for accrued interest until it is due and payable.[4] Accrued interest must be reported as a liability in the government-wide financial statements.
- *Include liabilities for certain accrued obligations not recognized in governmental funds.* Certain specific accrued obligations are *not* recognized in governmental funds until they are due and payable, because they are not considered to be uses of current financial resources until that time. Those specific liabilities arise in connection with compensated absences, claims and judgments, special termination benefits, landfill closure and postclosure care costs, and operating leases with scheduled rent increases. Likewise, governmental funds do not report any liability for the government's net pension obligation (NPO) or net other postemployment benefit obligation (NOPEBO) as an employer.[5] All of these accrued liabilities, however, must be included as part of the government-wide financial statements.

---

[2] GAAP require that *material* balances of inventories accounted for using the purchases method still be reported as an asset in the appropriate governmental fund. There is no similar GAAP requirement for reporting material balances of prepaid items (see chapter 5).

[3] The one exception to this general rule involves voluntary recognition of debt service principal expenditures in the current year when dedicated resources have been transferred to debt service funds for debt service principal payments due early in the following year. If this option is taken, a liability is reported in the debt service fund for the amount of the principal payment thus anticipated. As described in the following note, this same treatment also applies to the interest portion of the debt service payment (see chapter 5). Also, revenue anticipation notes and tax anticipation notes are always reported as fund liabilities in governmental funds.

[4] Once again, there is an exception to this general rule that allows voluntary recognition of debt service interest expenditures in the current year when dedicated resources have been transferred to debt service funds for debt service interest payments due early the following year. If this option is taken, a liability is reported in the debt service fund for the amount of the interest payment thus anticipated. As described in the previous note, this same treatment also applies to the principal portion of the debt service payment (see chapter 5).

[5] In this regard, it is important to distinguish a NPO/NOPEBO from a *short-term difference* in making the annual required contribution. GAAP define a short-term difference as "one that the employer intends to settle by the first actuarial valuation date after the difference occurred or, if the first valuation is scheduled within a year, not more than one year after the difference occurred." A short-term difference should *not* be treated as a NPO/NOPEBO unless the amount remains unfunded at the end of the term just cited (Governmental Accounting Standards Board (GASB) Statement No. 27, *Accounting for Pensions by State and Local Governmental Employers*, paragraph 11, and GASB Statement No. 45, *Accounting and Financial Reporting by Employers for Postemployment Benefits Other Than Pensions*, paragraph 14).

- *Eliminate liability for earned but unavailable deferred revenue.* Under the modified accrual basis of accounting, revenue cannot be recognized until it is *available* to liquidate liabilities of the current period; under accrual accounting, revenue must be recognized as soon as it is earned, regardless of its availability. Accordingly, any liability for earned but *unavailable* deferred revenue must be eliminated for purposes of government-wide financial reporting. Conversely, unearned deferred revenue is not recognized under either the modified accrual basis of accounting or the accrual basis of accounting.[6] Therefore, any liability reported in the governmental funds for *unearned* deferred revenue should *not* be removed when preparing the government-wide statement of net assets.

From the governmental fund statement of revenues, expenditures, and changes in fund balances to the government-wide statement of activities

Governmental funds report *expenditures* (changes in net *current* financial resources), whereas governmental activities report *expenses* (changes in *total* net assets). Also, the timing of related cash flows often plays a crucial role in revenue and expenditure recognition for governmental funds, but *not* in revenue and expense recognition for governmental activities.

As a result of these differences, the following specific adjustments are needed (see also Exhibit 8-2):

- *Eliminate expenditures that represent the acquisition of capital assets.* From an accrual perspective, the acquisition or construction of a capital asset does *not* affect *net* assets.[7] Accordingly, *expenditures* to acquire or construct capital assets are not *expenses,* and should *not* be included in the government-wide statement of activities.[8]
- *Eliminate expenditures for debt service principal payments.* From an accrual perspective, the payment of debt service principal has no effect on net assets.[9] Consequently, debt service *expenditures* for principal payments are not *expenses* and should *not* be included in the government-wide statement of activities.[10] The same approach should be taken to other financing uses reported in connection with current or advance refunding transactions.
- *Eliminate other financing sources, uses, and expenditures associated with debt issuance.* From an accrual perspective, debt issuance has no impact on net assets, but rather affects only accounts reported on the statement of position (debt payable, premiums, discounts, issuance costs, difference between the carrying value and reacquisition cost of refunded debt).[11] Accordingly, other financing sources, uses, and ex-

---

[6] See the discussion of revenue recognition under the modified accrual basis of accounting in chapter 5.

[7] The increase in capital assets (debit) is matched by either a reduction in cash (credit) or an increase in liabilities (credit), all "balance sheet" accounts.

[8] As noted in the previous discussion, the assets resulting from such expenditures are, of course, reported in the government-wide statement of net assets.

[9] The decrease in debt principal outstanding (debit) is matched by a decrease in cash (credit), both "balance sheet" accounts.

[10] As noted in the previous discussion, these expenditures should reduce the amount reported as debt payable in the government-wide statement of net assets.

[11] In the private-sector, debt issued to finance a refunding may affect the operating statement in the form of a gain or loss on the extinguishment of debt. In the public sector, however, this amount is deferred as a contraliability (difference between the carrying value and the reacquisition cost of refunded debt) and subsequently amortized as an adjustment to the amount of interest expense reported in the operating statement. GASB Statement No. 23, *Accounting and Financial Reporting for Refundings of Debt Reported by Proprietary Activities,* paragraphs 4-5.

EXHIBIT 8-2
Conversion from the governmental fund operating statement to the government-wide statement of activities

Transaction/Event	Reported in governmental fund financial statements?	Reported in government-wide financial statements?	Action required	Adjustments to reconcile *net change in fund balances– governmental funds* and *change in net assets – governmental activities*
				Start: *Net change in fund balances – governmental funds*
Capital outlays	Yes	No	Remove capitalizable expenditures incurred for the acquisition or construction of capital assets	Add: Capitalizable expenditures incurred for the acquisition or construction of capital assets
Debt service principal payments and refunding payments	Yes	No	Remove expenditures and other financing uses incurred for debt service principal payments and refunding payments	Add: Expenditures and other financing uses incurred for debt service principal payments and refunding payments
Other financing sources, uses, and expenditures resulting from debt issuance	Yes	No	Remove other financing sources, uses, and expenditures resulting from debt issuance	Less: Other financing sources for debt and related premiums
				Add: Other financing uses for discounts
				Add: Expenditures for issuance costs
				Add: Excess of reacquisition cost of refunded debt over carrying value of refunded debt
				Less: Excess of carrying value of refunded debt over reacquisition cost of refunded debt
Donations of capital assets	No	Yes	Record donations of capital assets	Add: Donations of capital assets
Sales of capital assets	Yes, in the amount of the proceeds of the sale	Yes, but only in the amount of the gain or loss on the sale	Replace amount of proceeds by gain or loss on transaction	Less: Sale proceeds *less* gain
				Less: Sale proceeds *plus* loss
Sales of fund assets (e.g., foreclosure assets held for resale)	Yes, but reported as revenues or expenditures (or reduction of revenue)	Yes, but reported as gains or losses	Reclassify revenues and expenditures (or reduction of revenue) related to sales of fund assets as gains or losses	No effect
Revenues and expenditures related to prior periods	Yes	No	Remove revenues and expenditures related to prior periods	Less: Revenues related to prior periods
				Add: Expenditures related to prior periods
Revenues earned during the period but not yet available	No	Yes	Record revenue earned during the period but not yet available	Add: Revenue earned during the period but not yet available
Expenses incurred during the period, but not normally expected to be liquidated with expendable available financial resources unless they are due for payment in the current period	No	Yes	Record expenses incurred during the period related to liabilities that are still outstanding at year-end that are not normally expected to be liquidated with expendable available financial resources unless they are due for payment in the current period	Less: Expenses incurred during the period related to liabilities that are still outstanding at year-end for: • accrued interest • compensated absences • claims and judgments • special termination benefits • landfill closure and postclosure care costs • operating leases with scheduled rent increases • net pension obligation • net other postemployment benefit obligation

EXHIBIT 8-2 *(continued)*
Conversion from the governmental fund operating statement to the government-wide statement of activities

Transaction/Event	Reported in governmental fund financial statements?	Reported in government-wide financial statements?	Action required	Adjustments to reconcile *net change in fund balances– governmental funds* and *change in net assets – governmental activities*
Depreciation	No	Yes	Record depreciation expense	Less: Depreciation expense
Amortization of issuance costs, premiums, discounts, and similar items	No	Yes	Adjust revenues and expenses for amortizations	Less: Amortization of issuance costs and discounts (and net refunding difference if a debit)
				Add: Amortization of premiums (and net refunding difference if a credit)
Inventories and prepaids	No*	Yes	Record expense for inventories consumed and prepaids amortized during the period	Less: Inventories consumed and prepaids amortized during the period
Activities of internal service funds properly included within governmental activities	No	Yes	Record internal service fund revenues and expenses not subject to consolidation and adjust functional expenses to reflect "look-back" adjustment	Add: Net profit (after look-back consolidation)
				Less: Net loss (after look-back consolidation)
				End: Change in *Net Assets – Governmental Activities*

*This treatment does not apply to governments using the consumption method to account for inventories and prepaids reported in governmental funds.

penditures associated with the issuance of debt should *not* be included in the government-wide statement of activities.[12]

- *Include donations of capital assets.* Governmental funds do *not* report the donation of capital assets not held for resale. Such donations are, however, a transaction that must be reported in the accrual-based government-wide statement of activities.
- *Restate sales of capital assets on an accrual basis.* Governmental funds report the *full amount* of the proceeds from a capital asset sale as either *other revenue* (if immaterial) or as an *other financing source* or *special item*. From an accrual perspective, however, the sale of capital assets should be reported on the government-wide statement of activities only to the extent that there is a disparity between the amount of the sale proceeds and the carrying value of the asset sold (a gain or loss). Accordingly, other revenue, other financing sources, and special items arising from the sale of capital assets in governmental funds should be replaced by gains or losses in the government-wide statement of activities. Because the gain or loss associated with a sale may be significantly less than the amount reported in the governmental fund operating statement, a sale that was properly reported as a special item in the governmental fund operating statement may not qualify for reporting as a special item in the government-wide statement of activities.[13]

---

[12] As noted in the previous discussion, such amounts should be reported as liabilities, contraliabilities, and deferred charges in the government-wide statement of net assets.
[13] GASB, *Comprehensive Implementation Guide (2004)*, 7.309.

- *Restate sales of fund assets on an accrual basis.* The difference between the carrying value of a fund asset (such as foreclosure assets held for resale) and the related sale proceeds typically is reported as either a revenue or an expenditure (or reduction of revenue) in the governmental fund operating statement. This same amount must be reclassified as a gain or loss for purposes of government-wide financial reporting.
- *Eliminate revenues and expenditures related to prior periods.* Governmental funds report revenue in the current period for amounts deferred in prior years because they were not considered available at that time. Likewise, governmental funds report expenditures during the current period in connection with accrued liabilities that arose in prior periods, including accrued interest, compensated absences, claims and judgments, special termination benefits, landfill closure and postclosure care costs, operating leases with scheduled rent increases, and the government's NPO/NOPEBO as an employer. Revenues and expenditures related to transactions and events of prior periods should *not* be included as revenues and expenses in the accrual-based government-wide statement of activities.
- *Make all regular accrual adjustments.* The regular closing process to prepare accrual-based financial statements routinely involves the following adjustments:
  - recognition of revenues earned but not yet available (that is, earned but *unavailable* deferred revenue);
  - recognition of expenses incurred during the period but not yet paid (including interest payable, claims and judgments, compensated absences, special termination benefits, landfill closure and postclosure care costs, operating leases with scheduled rent increases, and the government's NPO/NOPEBO as an employer);
  - recognition of depreciation expense on depreciable capital assets;
  - recognition of the amortization of issuance costs, premiums, discounts, and the difference between the carrying amount and reacquisition cost of refunded debt; and
  - recognition of expense for inventory consumed and prepaids amortized during the period.

Conversion worksheet and adjusting entries

Governments do not maintain separate accounting systems for fund financial statements and government-wide financial statements. Instead, they normally use a fund-based system for their day-to-day accounting needs and then manipulate the fund-based data at the end of the fiscal period to make whatever adjustments are needed to prepare the government-wide financial statements.

Of course, the government-wide statement of net assets must include certain assets and liabilities that are *not*, in fact, reported in *any* fund—specifically, those associated with activities reported in governmental funds (*general government* assets and liabilities). Governments typically track these assets and liabilities from period to period to provide the additional information needed for government-wide financial reporting.

The governmental financial reporting model, as noted elsewhere,[14] is unique in mandating *both* fund *and* government-wide financial reporting.

Because fund financial statements are not replaced by government-wide financial statements, but rather continue from one period to the next, nothing in the process used to prepare the government-wide financial statements can alter the underlying fund data. Instead, the adjustments needed to convert fund data for incorporation into the government-wide financial statements typically are made on a special worksheet.

A typical conversion worksheet will combine 1) the *preclosing trial balance* for the governmental funds and 2) the *opening balances* of the various accounts used to track general government assets and liabilities (and associated equity[15]). Adjustments are then made for each of the items mentioned in the discussion of the differences between the governmental fund operating statement and the government-wide statement of activities. For example, the following adjustment would be needed to convert a capital outlay expenditure (modified accrual) to the appropriate capital asset account (accrual):

	DR	CR
Buildings	$ 100	
Expenditures—capital outlay		$ 100

Two things should be noted regarding this sample worksheet adjustment. First, in virtually all cases, the adjustments needed to convert modified accrual temporary accounts[16] to their accrual equivalent will automatically restate the permanent accounts[17] on an accrual basis.[18] That is why the worksheet adjustments proceed on the basis of what needs to be changed in the temporary accounts. Similarly, the worksheet must start out with the *beginning balances* for the general government asset and liability accounts because the automatic restatement of permanent accounts just described captures the activity in those accounts during the period (which would be duplicated if the year-end balances were used instead).[19]

Once all adjustments have been made, accounts originally described as *expenditures* will actually represent *expenses* instead. Thus, there is no need to establish separate expense accounts on the worksheet to distinguish expenditures from expenses. All that is needed is to change the title used in the government-wide financial statements to reflect the change.

Some adjustments will involve revenues and expenditures associated with prior periods (e.g., delinquent property tax collections, expenditures involving the liquidation of liabilities incurred in prior periods, *deferred revenue* related to prior periods). As a matter of convenience, the worksheet adjustment in such cases can be made simply to the *fund balance* account, which ultimately will be included as a component of *net assets*.

The equity associated with general government assets and liabilities is commonly labeled **NET ASSETS**.[20] It must be emphasized that this account

---

[14] See chapter 2.
[15] One component of the *net assets* reported for *governmental activities* in the government-wide financial statements.
[16] *Temporary accounts* are those reported in a statement of operations/activity.
[17] A *permanent account* is one that is reported on the statement of position.
[18] An important exception is donations of capital assets that will be used in operations. Governmental funds do not report such donations and so provide no indication that they have taken place.
[19] As a practical matter, a government will likely make changes to general government asset and liability accounts throughout the period. In that case, the beginning balances after adjustment on the worksheet should equal the balances actually reported at the end of the current period.

is *not* equivalent to *net assets-governmental activities*. The latter amount would include not only **NET ASSETS**, but also *fund balance* (after the various adjustments made on the worksheet), as well as the *net assets* of any internal service funds (or enterprise funds) consolidated as part of *governmental activities.*[21]

Appendix C presents the illustrative conversion worksheet used to prepare the *governmental activities* columns reported in the government-wide financial statements illustrated in appendix D.

CONSOLIDATION OF FUND DATA

As explained earlier,[22] funds of the primary government often engage in interfund activity. For example, one fund may loan money to another fund, or charge another fund for goods and services that it provides. Likewise, one fund may simply transfer resources to another fund. Such interfund activity poses no special problems for fund financial reporting; it does, however, create the risk that inflated numbers might be reported in the government-wide financial statements. To avoid this potential problem, generally accepted accounting principles (GAAP) direct that the effects of interfund activity be eliminated from the government-wide financial statements by means of consolidation.

Consolidating governmental and enterprise fund data in the government-wide statement of net assets

As a rule, the primary government total column in the government-wide statement of net assets should report no interfund receivables or payables. Instead, interfund balances should be eliminated by means of a two-step process:

Intra-activity eliminations

All interfund receivables and payables between governmental funds should be netted in the *governmental activities* column, while all interfund receivables and payables between enterprise funds should be netted in the *business-type activities* column. This netting may be accomplished in either of two ways. One approach is to include an eliminations column immediately preceding the total column in the fund financial statements so that a zero balance is reported in the latter, as follows:

	Fund 1	Fund 2	Eliminations	Total
Interfund receivables	$ 500	$ 0	$ (500)	$ 0
[Other assets]	19,500	10,000		29,500
Interfund payables	0	(500)	500	0
[Other liabilities]	(10,000)	(2,000)		(12,000)
[Equity]	(10,000)	(7,500)		(17,500)

Alternatively, interfund receivables and payables between governmental funds and between enterprise funds could be left in the total columns of the respective fund financial statements and simply not carried forward to the government-wide financial statements.

---

[20] This publication uses the convention of **ALL CAP BOLD ITALIC** for accounts associated with general government assets and liabilities.
[21] The amount reported as *net assets-governmental activities* also may be affected by the allocation of direct costs and the disallocation of indirect costs (discussed later in this chapter).
[22] See chapter 3.

Interactivity eliminations   It is a simple matter to eliminate interfund receivables and payables between governmental funds or between enterprise funds. In both cases, the receivables and payables in question appear in the same fund financial statements and in the same activities column, making netting possible. It is another matter entirely to eliminate interfund receivables and payables between governmental funds and enterprise funds. In this latter case, netting is impossible in either the fund financial statements (since the receivable and payable appear in different sets of financial statements) or in the activities columns (since the receivable and payable appear in different activities columns). Rather, such amounts should be classified as *internal balances* and reported in the appropriate activities column in the government-wide financial statements.

Internal balances still ultimately need to be netted/eliminated from the primary government total column. This goal can be accomplished in one of two ways. The simplest approach is simply to report both the receivable and payable on the same line, so that a zero balance is automatically reported in the primary government total column, as follows:

	Governmental activities	Business-type activities	Total primary government
Internal balances	$5,000	$(5,000)	$ 0

Alternatively, a government could report the internal receivable and payable as separate line items, provided a zero balance was still reported in the primary government total column, as follows:

	Governmental activities	Business-type activities	Total primary government
Internal receivables	$5,000		[blank]
Internal payables		$(5,000)	[blank]

If this latter approach is taken, the amounts reported for internal receivables and payables will not cross foot. Therefore, GAAP direct that financial statement preparers taking this latter approach provide appropriate disclosure *on the face of the government-wide statement of net assets.*[23]

Of course, if the primary government includes a blended component unit with a different fiscal year end, complete consolidation may be impossible. Assume for example that a blended component unit borrows money from a fund of the primary government on November 1. Further assume that the fiscal year end of the primary government is December 31, whereas the fiscal year end of the blended component unit is September 30. In that case, no interfund payable would be reported for the blended component unit (which would report only balances as of September 30), while the primary government would report an interfund receivable for the November borrowing. Consequently, it would be impossible to net/eliminate the internal receivable from the government-wide statement of net assets.[24]

---

[23] GASB Statement No. 34, *Basic Financial Statements—and Management's Discussion and Analysis—for State and Local Governments*, paragraph 312.
[24] GASB, *Comprehensive Implementation Guide (2004)*, 7.125.

Consolidating governmental and enterprise fund data in the government-wide statement of activities

Two different types of interfund activity could potentially affect the government-wide statement of activities: *transfers* and *interfund services provided and used*.[25] The proper treatment for these two different types of interfund activity is radically different.

The rules for consolidating transfers are virtually identical to those described earlier for interfund receivables and payables. Transfers must be eliminated between governmental funds and between enterprise funds (intra-activity elimination), either by the use of an eliminations column in the fund financial statements, or by reporting the transfers in the total column of the fund financial statements and then simply not carrying those same amounts forward to the government-wide statement of activities. Likewise, transfers between governmental funds and enterprise funds would need to be reported in the appropriate activities columns and then eliminated from the primary government total column.

Of course, for the same reasons explained earlier, the complete consolidation of transfers may not be possible if one or more transfers involve a blended component unit with a different fiscal year end than the primary government.

A completely different approach must be taken to interfund services provided and used. As explained elsewhere,[26] this category is used for interfund activity that would qualify as an exchange or exchange-like transaction if it involved an outside party. The netting/elimination of such transactions could seriously distort the cost data reported for a government's various functions. Assume , for example, that a government's water department sells water to the government's parks department for its swimming pools and water park, just as it would to its regular customers. If this interfund activity were netted/eliminated in the process of consolidation, the water department would appear less efficient than it really is, because it would report the cost of providing water to the parks department, but not the revenue it received from doing so. Conversely, the parks department would appear more efficient than it really is, because it would avoid reporting a major operating cost. Accordingly, GAAP *prohibit* the elimination of interfund services provided and used between different governmental activities.[27]

Consolidating internal service funds

As cost allocation devices, internal service funds necessarily involve a high degree of redundancy. Thus, virtually all of the expense incurred by a typical internal service fund will be recognized as expense once again in the various funds that are billed. Naturally, such redundancy must be eliminated from the government-wide financial statements as part of the process of consolidation.

The first step in consolidating internal service funds is to determine whether a given internal service fund should be included as part of governmental activities or business-type activities. The rules to follow in making this determination can be summarized as follows:

- It should be presumed that internal service funds will be consolidated as part of governmental activities.

---

[25] Both of these categories of interfund activity are described in detail in chapter 3.
[26] See chapter 3.
[27] GASB Statement No. 34, paragraph 60. All the same, interfund services provided and used *within the same function* would need to be eliminated as part of the process of consolidation if material (see GASB, *Comprehensive Implementation Guide (2004)*, 7.235).

- If an internal service fund provides services exclusively to enterprise funds, it should be consolidated as part of business-type activities.
- If an internal service fund provides services to both governmental funds and enterprise funds, it should be consolidated in the same activities column as its predominant customers.[28]
- A given internal service fund must be consolidated either entirely within governmental activities or entirely within business-type activities.

Once that determination has been made, the process of consolidation should proceed as follows:

Direct incorporation of amounts not to be consolidated. Revenues and expenses that involve parties *external to the primary government* should *not* be eliminated in the process of consolidation (e.g., revenues from *external* customers and the expense of providing goods or services to those same customers; external grants and contributions). The same is true for items not properly reported as program revenue or functional expense (e.g., most interest revenue and interest expense). Rather, they should be incorporated directly into the appropriate activities column of the government-wide statement of activities.[29]

Assume, for instance, that an internal service fund received $1,100 from external customers and that the related cost of goods sold/services provided was $1,000.[30] Also assume that the fund received grants and contributions of $600 and incurred interest expense of $250. In that case, all of these amounts would be added directly to the numbers reported in the appropriate activities column of the government-wide statement of activities, with a resulting increase in net assets of $450:

Added to program revenues (fees and charges)	$1,100
Added to program revenues (grants and contributions)	600
Subtotal	$1,700
Added to functional expenses	($1,000)
Added to *interest expense* line item	($250)
Net increase in net assets	$450

Look-back adjustment. For purposes of consolidation, it is always assumed that an internal service fund operates on a "break-even" basis for its internal customers. Thus, a surplus is presumed to be the result of overcharging internal customers, and a deficit is presumed to demonstrate that internal customers were undercharged. Accordingly, if the remaining revenue and expense accounts are not in balance, any resulting surplus or deficit must be eliminated in the process of consolidation by adjusting the amounts reported as expense by internal customers.[31] This process of ad-

---

[28] Of course, transactions with functions reported in the other activities column need to be consolidated, which will affect that column as well, as discussed later in this chapter.

[29] GASB, *Comprehensive Implementation Guide (2004)*, 7.231.

[30] If the cost of goods sold/services provided to external parties is not separately maintained in the accounting system (job order costing), it could be estimated on the basis of the overall profit margin. In this example, assume total revenues from customers amount to $56,100 ($55,000 from internal customers +$1,100 from external customers) and that the total cost of goods sold/services provided comes to $51,000. If the specific cost associated with external customers is not otherwise discernable, it could be calculated thus: $56,100/$51,000 = 1.1; $1,100/1.1 = $1,000.

[31] This adjustment affects only the worksheet used to prepare the government-wide financial statements. An operating surplus or deficit would not be eliminated from the internal service fund itself.

justing functional expense to eliminate a surplus or deficit is commonly known as a "look-back" adjustment.

Assume, for example, that the internal service fund in question also reports operating revenues from internal customers of $55,000, related operating expenses of $50,000, and a resulting net profit of $5,000. Further assume that the proportionate share of goods and services purchased was as follows for each participating function:

Function	Proportionate participation (percent)
A	65
B	25
C	5
D	3
E	2
	100

Based on these assumptions, the amount of the surplus attributable to each function could be calculated as follows:

Function	Proportionate reduction of expenses	
A	65 percent × $5,000 =	$3,250
B	25 percent × $5,000 =	$1,250
C	5 percent × $5,000 =	$ 250
D	3 percent × $5,000 =	$ 150
E	2 percent × $5,000 =	$ 100
		$5,000

This surplus would be eliminated for purposes of consolidation by *reducing* functional expense by means of the following closing entry:

Revenues (internal service fund)	$ 55,000	
Expenses (internal service fund)		$ 50,000
Expense (Function A)		3,250
Expense (Function B)		1,250
Expense (Function C)		250
Expense (Function D)		150
Expense (Function E)		100

Of course, had the $5,000 been a net loss rather than a net profit, the effect of the look-back adjustment would have been to *increase* functional expense, as follows:

Revenues (internal service fund)	$ 50,000	
Expense (Function A)	3,250	
Expense (Function B)	1,250	
Expense (Function C)	250	
Expense (Function D)	150	
Expense (Function E)	100	
Expenses (internal service fund)		$ 55,000

A slightly different approach must be taken for any customer functions reported in the opposite activities column, because a surplus or deficit cannot just be netted against functional expense if the latter is reported elsewhere. Assume, for example, that the internal service fund is consolidated as part of governmental activities, but that Function E is part of business-

EXHIBIT 8-3
Consolidation of internal service fund activities

Internal service fund activity		Report in governmental activities	Exclude from governmental activities
Operating revenues:			
Internal customers	$55,000		$55,000
External customers	1,100	$1,100	
Total:	$56,100		
Operating expenses:			
Internal customers	($50,000)		($50,000)
External customers	(1,000)	($1,000)	
Total:	($51,000)		
Operating profit/(loss)	$5,100	$100	$5,000
Nonoperating:			
Grants and contributions	$600	$600	
Interest expense*	($250)	($250)	

*The same approach would apply to interest revenue.

type activities. In that case the adjusting entries needed to remove the $5,000 surplus posted earlier would be as follows:

Governmental activities:

Revenues (internal service fund)	$ 55,000	
Expenses (internal service fund)		$ 50,000
Expense (Function A)		3,250
Expense (Function B)		1,250
Expense (Function C)		250
Expense (Function D)		150
Internal payable		100

Business-type activities:

Internal receivable	$ 100	
Expense (Function E)		$ 100

The internal balance thus produced is commonly referred to as the "crossover amount."

Typically, consolidation is based exclusively on amounts reported in an internal service fund's preclosing trial balance. The crossover amount is an important exception. The crossover amount reported in the government-wide statement of net assets will be the *cumulative total* of both current year and prior year adjustments.[32] Using the example just considered, assume that the cumulative amount reported last year in the government-

---

[32] The internal balances reported from year to year in connection with the look-back adjustment are worksheet adjustments only, and so are *not* reflected in the internal service fund's preclosing trial balance.

wide statement of net assets was $50. In that case, the amount to be reported this year would be $150 (i.e., $50 past years + $100 current year adjustment), which would require an adjustment to beginning *net assets* equal to the cumulative amount for past years.[33]

Incorporation of fund assets, liabilities and net assets. The final step of consolidation for internal service funds is to directly incorporate fund assets, liabilities, and net assets, following the adjustments just described, into the appropriate column of the government-wide statement of net assets.

REMOVAL OF INDIRECT COSTS FROM FUNCTIONAL EXPENSE

Accountants commonly distinguish *direct* costs from *indirect* costs (overhead). A practical way of distinguishing direct costs from indirect costs is that a formula is necessary to assign the latter to specific functions. When both direct and indirect costs are reported for a given function, the presentation is said to be on a *full-cost* basis. The basic rule is that functional costs for governmental activities may include *only* direct costs. Governments desiring to provide full-cost information for their various functions are free to do so, but only in the form of a separate column.[34]

As far as GAAP are concerned, governments may allocate indirect costs in their fund financial statements if they wish to do so, as is often the case for at least a portion of overhead costs. In that case, the allocations must be reversed as part of the process of preparing the government-wide statement of activities so that *only* direct costs are reported in each of the governmental functions.[35] For example, if the cost of operating a personnel department was charged out to various functions in the fund financial statements, that charge, if not directly attributable to the various functions, would need to be reversed as part of the process of preparing the government-wide statement of activities.[36]

GAAP provide one specific exception to the general rule that indirect cost allocations to governmental functions at the fund level must be reversed for purposes of government-wide financial reporting. If a government has centralized a given service and the charges made to the various benefiting functions include an administrative overhead component, that component need not be eliminated as part of the process of consolidation.[37]

Governments are *not* required to remove indirect costs of the general government charged to enterprise funds, although they are free to do so.[38]

[33] GASB, *Comprehensive Implementation Guide (2004),* 7.229. It should be noted that the cumulative amount need reflect only adjustments actually made since the implementation of GASB Statement No. 34.
[34] GASB Statement No. 34, paragraph 42.
[35] GASB, *Comprehensive Implementation Guide (2004),* 7.162.
[36] GASB, *Comprehensive Implementation Guide (2004),* 7.225.
[37] GASB Statement No. 34, paragraph 43; GASB, *Comprehensive Implementation Guide (2004),* 7.226.
[38] If indirect costs incurred by the general government and allocated to business-type activities are subsequently removed in the process of preparing the government-wide financial statements, an annual cumulative adjustment is required similar to that described earlier in connection with the crossover amount.

ASSIGNMENT OF UNALLOCATED DIRECT COSTS TO THE APPROPRIATE FUNCTIONAL EXPENSE CATEGORY

It is essential that *all* direct costs be assigned to the appropriate functional category of governmental activities for purposes of government-wide financial reporting, *regardless of how those costs are treated in the fund financial statements.* Examples of the practical application of this principle include the following:

- Many of the costs of a centralized city-wide vehicle maintenance operation accounted for as part of the *general government* function will be identifiable with specific functions. Such direct costs should be reported in the appropriate functional line in the government-wide statement of activities rather than as part of *general government.* Conversely, costs of the vehicle maintenance operation that cannot be identified with specific functions (e.g., depreciation on maintenance facilities) are indirect costs and should *not* be allocated to individual functions (unless a separate column is used for this purpose).[39]
- Employee benefits typically are identifiable with specific functions and, therefore, should be reported as direct costs of the benefiting functions. As a practical matter, a formula could be used to assign employee benefits to individual functions.[40]
- If a telephone bill can be assigned to individual functions based on actual usage, it should be treated as a direct cost of the benefiting functions.[41]

Interest expense rarely qualifies as a direct functional cost within governmental activities, even if the related debt is legally limited for use in a single function.[42] Instead it is almost always reported as a separate line item in its own right within governmental activities.[43] Nonetheless, in those rare instances "when borrowing is essential to the creation or continuing existence of a program and it would be misleading to exclude the interest from direct expenses of that program,"[44] it should be treated as a functional expense. An example of such a situation, cited in the authoritative literature, is interest on state bonds used to finance reduced-rate loans to school districts.[45]

Governments are *not* required to charge direct costs incurred by the general government on behalf of enterprise funds to business-type activities, although they are free to do so.[46]

---

[39] GASB, *Comprehensive Implementation Guide (2004)*, 7.158.

[40] It is important to underscore that this suggestion is offered purely as a practical expedient based upon considerations of materiality (i.e., if a given cost could not be identified with a specific function without using a formula it would be an indirect cost). See GASB, *Comprehensive Implementation Guide (2004)*, 7.159.

[41] GASB, *Comprehensive Implementation Guide (2004)*, question 7.224.

[42] GASB, *Comprehensive Implementation Guide (2004)*, 7.173.

[43] In contrast, interest is always a functional cost within business-type activities. (GASB, *Comprehensive Implementation Guide (2004)*, 7.172.)

[44] GASB Statement No. 34, paragraph 6.

[45] GASB, *Comprehensive Implementation Guide (2004)*, 7.170.

[46] If direct costs incurred by the general government are subsequently allocated to business-type activities in the process of preparing the government-wide financial statements, an annual cumulative adjustment is required similar to that described earlier in connection with the crossover amount.

SUMMARY

Government-wide financial reporting involves more than simply aggregating the various balances reported in each individual governmental and proprietary fund. Up to four separate operations may be necessary to transform fund data to meet the requirements of government-wide financial reporting.

First, the data in governmental funds must be converted from the current financial resources measurement focus and modified accrual basis of accounting to the economic resources measurement focus and the accrual basis of accounting. Because financial reports for state and local governments include both fund financial statements and government-wide financial statements, the process of preparing the latter can in no way alter the data used for the former. Instead, all of the adjustments needed to convert governmental fund data into the form needed for government-wide financial reporting typically are made on a special worksheet.

Second, the effect of interfund activity must be removed to avoid redundancy in the government-wide financial statements. Interfund receivables and payables must be netted/eliminated, first between governmental funds and between enterprise funds (intra-activity consolidation) and then between governmental funds and enterprise funds (interactivity consolidation). Transfers must be eliminated from the government-wide statement of activities using this same two-step approach. Interfund activities provided and used between functions, however, must *not* be eliminated, as to do so would distort the cost data reported by the functions involved.

Internal service funds should be consolidated as part of governmental activities unless they primarily benefit enterprise funds. Any operating surplus or deficit should be eliminated as part of the consolidation process by decreasing/increasing functional expenses by the same amount, a procedure commonly referred to as the "look-back adjustment." The look-back adjustment should not include items directly related to external parties, nor should it reflect amounts not properly reported as part of functional expense (e.g., interest expense).

Third, any indirect costs allocated among governmental functions at the fund level must be removed from the amounts reported as functional expense in the government-wide statement of activities. The one exception to this rule is that an indirect cost component of a charge for centrally managed services need not be removed.

Finally, the amounts reported for functional expense for governmental activities must include *all* direct costs, which may be defined as those costs that can be reasonably identified with a given function without using a formula. Accordingly, any direct costs treated as overhead (*general government*) in the fund financial statements must be assigned to the appropriate governmental activities functional category for purposes of government-wide financial reporting.

The rules just discussed regarding the allocation of direct costs and the disallocation of indirect costs are mandatory only for governmental activities. Their application to costs incurred by the general government on behalf of enterprise funds is optional.

9

Financial Reporting Overview

Accounting aims to collect, analyze, and classify all data relevant to an entity's finances. To do so, accounting systems must maintain detailed data on each transaction that affects the entity and on the entity's individual asset, liability, and equity accounts. Even the smallest governments routinely engage in numerous individual transactions involving many separate accounts.

The raw data that an accounting system collects and maintains are too detailed to be practical for most potential users. Financial reporting must contend with this situation by aggregating the detailed data produced by the accounting system and then presenting those data in a format that facilitates use by decision makers.

TYPES OF FINANCIAL REPORTING

There are at least three types of financial reporting: internal financial reporting, special-purpose external financial reporting, and general-purpose external financial reporting.

Internal financial reporting

Management is primarily responsible for the effective and efficient handling of a government's operations. To fulfill this important responsibility, government managers need reliable financial data. Because managers are part of the government itself, accountants commonly classify them as *internal users* of financial data, and financial reports prepared for their benefit are referred to as *internal financial reports*.

Internal financial reporting typically is designed to accomplish two goals. First, internal reports allow management to monitor compliance with legal and contractual provisions applicable to the management of public funds (the appropriated budget and grant contracts, for instance). Second, internal reports provide management with information on current performance needed to make future financial plans (such as preparing the operating budget).

Internal financial reporting is designed expressly to meet management needs, so management is free to select whatever format or contents it finds most suitable for its internal financial reports. In most cases, internal financial reports are prepared using the basis of budgeting, a logical approach considering how important it is to monitor compliance with the annual or biennial appropriated operating budget.

As decision makers, managers need financial information while there is still time for decisions to be made. For example, if actual sales tax revenues are proving to be significantly less than estimated sales tax revenues, corresponding reductions in expenditures may be necessary to keep the budget in balance. Timeliness is a critical consideration in internal financial reporting. As a result, internal financial reports are issued periodically (perhaps biweekly, monthly, or quarterly) rather than just annually, as is often the case for external financial reports.

Special-purpose external financial reporting

Sometimes parties outside the government are in a position to require that financial data be provided to meet their specific needs. For example, as a condition of making a grant award, a federal agency may require that the recipient government periodically submit specialized financial reports on grant activity and balances. Similarly, state governments may take advantage of their sovereign power over local governments to make them file specialized financial data collection forms. Such reports are known technically as *special-purpose external financial reports*. The contents, format, and timing of these reports depend on the outside party that imposes the requirement.[1]

General-purpose external financial reporting

Accountants presume that those inside a government are capable of making their own decisions regarding the contents, format, and timing of the financial reports they receive. The same presumption holds true for outside parties that are able to require submission of special-purpose external financial reports. Many other interested parties, however, are *not* in a position to prescribe the types of financial information they are to receive. Rather, they must rely on *general-purpose external financial reporting* to meet their need for information on a government's finances.

In the public sector, there are three classes of potential users of general-purpose external financial reports:[2]

- those to whom the government is primarily accountable (citizens, taxpayers, voters, service recipients);[3]
- those who directly represent the citizens (legislative and oversight bodies); and
- those who lend to the government or participate in the lending process (such as individual and institutional investors and creditors, municipal security underwriters, bond rating agencies, bond insurers, and financial institutions).

---

[1] Note that special-purpose external financial reports are *not* intended for the general public and their widespread distribution normally should be avoided. See American Institute of Certified Public Accountants (AICPA), *Professional Standards*, AU 623.

[2] Governmental Accounting Standards Board (GASB) Concepts Statement No. 1, *Objectives of Financial Reporting*, paragraphs 30-31.

[3] This category also includes those who directly or indirectly attempt to serve the needs of the citizenry, such as the media, advocacy groups, and public finance researchers.

Frequently, internal users of financial data also use general-purpose external financial reports. Indeed, as a practical matter, public-sector financial managers probably use general-purpose external financial reports at least as much as any other user group. Nevertheless, management is *not* considered a *primary* user of general-purpose external financial reports because it has direct access to the underlying financial data in the accounting system and, therefore, need not rely on general-purpose external financial reports.[4] Consequently, the needs of primary users of general-purpose external financial reports always take precedence over the needs of management in setting the standards that govern preparation of these reports.

Different user groups have different information needs and preferences. There is no single workable financial report capable of accommodating all of these varying needs and preferences. Instead, accountants have designed a report aimed at meeting the *common information needs* of those desiring to assess a government's finances.[5] The criteria used to determine those common information needs are known as *generally accepted accounting principles* (GAAP).

In most cases, governments prepare just the annual general-purpose external financial report in conformity with GAAP. This public-sector practice varies from the private sector, where publicly traded business enterprises routinely issue quarterly general-purpose external financial reports in conformity with GAAP.[6] While governments also often issue quarterly financial reports, these are primarily for internal use, and normally are prepared in conformity with the basis of budgeting rather than GAAP.[7]

Sometimes confusion arises over what relationship should exist between GAAP and any conflicting demands that may develop in connection with legal compliance. Ideally, general-purpose external financial reporting should *both* provide financial data presented in conformity with GAAP *and* demonstrate compliance with finance-related legal and contractual provisions. If GAAP financial reporting is not sufficient to achieve this latter goal, then *additional* schedules should be provided as needed. In no case, however, do legal requirements justify supplanting GAAP information with information presented on some other basis.[8]

---

[4] GASB Concepts Statement No. 1, paragraph 30.

[5] Exposure draft of a Proposed GASB Concepts Statement on *Communication Methods*, Paragraph 8 (June 2004).

[6] There are two key factors that drive the demand for quarterly GAAP reporting in the private sector. First, the price of equity securities is especially susceptible to market fluctuation since equity securities, unlike debt securities, have no guaranteed cash flow, but are ultimately worth only as much as someone else is willing to pay for them. Consequently, relatively small changes in earnings per share can have serious and disproportionate ramifications if they shake the confidence of potential purchasers. Second, debt securities, despite their guaranteed cash flows, may lose substantial value if serious concerns arise concerning their issuers' ultimate viability.

The first factor, of course, is irrelevant to state and local governments as they do not issue equity securities. Likewise, the second factor, as a practical matter, is much less important in the public sector than in the private sector, given the taxing power and permanence of governments, as well as the fact that (other than technical) defaults by state and general-purpose local governments are all but unknown.

[7] The failure to issue quarterly GAAP financial reports undoubtedly adds to the time needed to prepare annual financial reports.

[8] National Council on Governmental Accounting (NCGA) Statement 1, *Governmental Accounting and Financial Reporting Principles*, paragraphs 9-15.

EXHIBIT 9-1
Objectives of general-purpose external financial reporting

General objectives	Specific objectives	Type of accountability primarily associated with objective
Financial reporting should assist in fulfilling government's duty to be publicly accountable and should enable users to assess that accountability.	Financial reporting should provide information to determine whether *current-year revenues were sufficient to pay for current-year services.* This also implies that financial reporting should show whether current-year citizens received services but shifted part of the payment burden to future-year citizens; whether previously accumulated resources were used up in providing services to current-year citizens; or, conversely, whether current-year revenues not only were sufficient to pay for current-year services, but also increased accumulated resources.	Operational accountability
	Financial reporting should demonstrate whether *resources were obtained and used in accordance with the entity's legally adopted budget.* It should also demonstrate compliance with other finance-related legal or contractual requirements.	Fiscal accountability
	Financial reporting should provide information to *assist users in assessing the service efforts, costs, and accomplishments of the governmental entity.* This information, when combined with information from other sources, helps users assess the economy, efficiency, and effectiveness of government and may help form a basis for voting or funding decisions. The information should be based on objective criteria to aid interperiod analysis within an entity and comparisons among similar entities. Information about physical resources should also help to determine cost of services.	Operational accountability
Financial reporting should assist users in evaluating the governmental entity's operating results for the year.	Financial reporting should provide information about *sources and uses of financial resources.* Financial reporting should account for all outflows by function and purpose, all inflows by source and type, and the extent to which inflows met outflows. Financial reporting should identify material nonrecurring financial transactions.	Fiscal accountability
	Financial reporting should provide information about *how the governmental entity financed its activities and met its cash requirements.*	Fiscal accountability
	Financial reporting should provide information necessary to *determine whether the entity's financial position improved or deteriorated* as a result of the year's operations.	Operational accountability
Financial reporting should assist users in assessing the level of services that can be provided by the governmental entity and its ability to meet its obligations as they become due.	Financial reporting should provide information about *the financial position and condition* of a governmental entity. Financial reporting should provide information about resources and obligations, both actual and contingent, current and noncurrent. The major financial resources of most governmental entities are derived from the ability to tax and issue debt. As a result, financial reporting should provide information about tax sources, tax limitations, tax burdens, and debt limitations.	Operational accountability
	Financial reporting should provide *information about a governmental entity's physical and other nonfinancial resources* having useful lives that extend beyond the current year, including information that can be used to assess the service potential of those resources. This information should be presented to help users assess long- and short-term capital needs.	Operational accountability
	Financial reporting should disclose *legal or contractual restrictions on resources* and risks of potential loss of resources.	Fiscal accountability

GENERAL-PURPOSE EXTERNAL FINANCIAL REPORTING

Having clarified the relationship that exists between general-purpose external financial reporting and other types of financial reporting, the stage is set for examining general-purpose external financial reporting in greater detail.

Objectives

The paramount objective of general-purpose external financial reporting is *accountability.*[9] Public-sector financial statements traditionally have focused on two essential aspects of accountability. *Fiscal accountability* is "the responsibility of governments to justify that their actions in the current period have complied with public decisions concerning the raising and spending of public moneys in the short term (usually one budgetary cycle or one year)." *Operational accountability* is "governments' responsibility to report the extent to which they have met their operating objectives efficiently and effectively, using all resources available for that purpose, and whether they can continue to meet their objectives for the foreseeable future."[10] These aspects of accountability are the ultimate source of the specific objectives of general-purpose external financial reporting identified in Exhibit 9-1.

In examining the specific objectives of general-purpose external financial reporting, it is useful to distinguish *financial position* from *economic condition*. *Financial position* is concerned with a government's *existing resources* and claims to those resources. *Economic condition* involves *both existing and future resources* and claims to those resources (including the commitment to provide services). Assume for example that two governments temporarily have identical assets and liabilities, and one of them faces the possibility of a significant drain on its resources resulting from the loss of a major local employer. In that case, both governments would be in the same *financial position*, while the government that lost a major employer could be in a worse *economic condition*.

Traditionally, general-purpose external financial reporting has focused almost exclusively on financial position. More recently, the specific objectives identified for general-purpose external financial reporting have drawn increased attention to economic condition.[11]

Essential characteristics of accounting data

Decisions can be only as good as the information on which they are based. For general-purpose external financial reports to be useful to decision makers, the accounting data in the reports must possess certain essential characteristics:

- *Understandability*. Ideally, the information in general-purpose external financial reports should be easily comprehensible to all intended primary users. This level of understandability is virtually impossible, however, because many potential users of state and local government financial reports have limited familiarity with financial matters. Therefore, *understandability* should be sought in a narrower sense: financial statements legitimately demand that users obtain "a reasonable under-

---

[9] GASB Concepts Statement No. 1, paragraph 76.
[10] GASB Statement No. 34, *Basic Financial Statements—and Management's Discussion and Analysis—for State and Local Governments*, paragraph 203.
[11] This fact is evidenced by the release of GASB Statement No. 44, *Economic Condition Reporting: The Statistical Section (an amendment of NCGA Statement 1)* in May 2004.

standing of government and public finance activities and of the fundamentals of governmental financial reporting," study reports "with reasonable diligence," and apply "relevant analytical skills."[12]

- *Reliability.* Financial data are valuable only if they are *reliable*, which means they must be verifiable (reproducible) and free of bias. Accounting data also must faithfully reflect the substance of what they represent (rather than legal form, for instance). In addition, data must be comprehensive.
- *Relevance.* Information is useful to financial report users only if it can make a difference in how the users assess a problem, condition, or event. Therefore, all data contained in financial reports should be relevant for such purposes. Irrelevant data impair rather than enhance more relevant data.
- *Timeliness.* Information is valuable to decision makers only if it is available in time for decision making. Financial reports should be issued quickly enough following the close of the fiscal period so that the information they contain can still affect decisions.[13]
- *Consistency.* An accounting principle, once adopted, should be applied consistently over time. Consistency is essential to the soundness of trend data, which are particularly important for many forms of financial analysis.
- *Comparability.* Similar events, transactions, and activity should be treated similarly. Conversely, different financial treatment of transactions, events, or activity should result from underlying differences in substance rather than from differences in accounting.[14]

Basic financial statements   Basic financial statements are the core of general-purpose external financial reporting for state and local governments. Basic financial statements have three components:

- *Government-wide financial statements.* GAAP require that state and local governments provide a government-wide statement of net assets and a government-wide statement of activities that are to include all of the primary government's governmental activities, business-type activities, and (nonfiduciary) component units. These government-wide financial statements are to be presented using the economic resources measurement focus and the accrual basis of accounting, the same measurement focus and basis of accounting employed by private-sector business enterprises and nonprofit organizations.
- *Fund financial statements.* GAAP require that the government-wide financial statements be accompanied by separate sets of financial statements for governmental funds, proprietary funds, and fiduciary funds. The financial statements for proprietary funds and fiduciary funds use the same measurement focus and basis of accounting used

---

[12] Exposure draft of a Proposed GASB Concepts Statement on *Communication Methods*, Paragraph 20 (June 2004).

[13] The Government Finance Officers Association's (GFOA) Certificate of Achievement for Excellence in Financial Reporting program requires that financial reports submitted to that program be published no later than six months following the end of the fiscal year. GFOA strongly encourages even earlier reporting.

[14] The essential difference between *consistency* and *comparability* is that consistency is concerned with multiple periods while comparability is concerned with one or more entities during the same period.

for government-wide financial reporting. The financial statements for governmental funds, on the other hand, are prepared using the current financial resources measurement focus and the modified accrual basis of accounting. Accordingly, the governmental fund financial statements must present a summary reconciliation to explain differences between the data reported in the governmental funds and the data reported for the corresponding *governmental activities* columns in the government-wide financial statements.

- *Notes to the financial statements.* The data displayed on the face of the government-wide and fund financial statements must be accompanied by various disclosures to ensure that a complete picture is presented. This additional disclosure is presented in the form of a single set of notes (or separate summary of significant accounting policies and notes) placed immediately following the government-wide and fund financial statements.

As described, the basic financial statements represent the *minimum* information that must be included within a financial report of a state or local government for an independent auditor to issue a "clean" audit opinion, assuring report users that the government has complied with GAAP.

Required supplementary information

GAAP also call for certain information to accompany the audited basic financial statements. The technical term for this additional material, which need not be audited, is *required supplementary information* (RSI). There are five types of RSI for state and local governments:

- *Management's discussion and analysis (MD&A).* MD&A are intended to provide the narrative introduction and overview that users need to interpret the basic financial statements. MD&A also provide analysis of some key data presented in the basic financial statements.
- *Budgetary comparisons.* Governments are required to compare actual results (using the basis of budgeting) with the original budget and the final amended budget for the general fund and each individual major special revenue fund with an annual (or biennial) appropriated budget.[15] (GAAP specifically permit the budgetary comparison(s) to be included as part of the basic financial statements for governmental funds rather than presented as RSI.)[16]
- *Trend data on infrastructure condition.* Some governments elect to use the *modified approach* to account for certain networks or subsystems of infrastructure assets. Using the modified approach eliminates the need to report depreciation expense in connection with those particular infrastructure assets. GAAP require that governments electing to use the modified approach for infrastructure assets provide two types

---

[15] Sometimes a given fund will be classified in one manner for financial reporting purposes and in another manner for budgetary purposes. Budgetary reporting requirements apply based solely upon how a fund is classified for financial reporting purposes. Thus, no budgetary comparison should be presented in the basic financial statements (or as RSI) for a budgetary special revenue fund that is classified as an enterprise fund for financial reporting purposes (GASB, *Comprehensive Implementation Guide (2004)*, 7.380).

[16] This option is *not* available, however, whenever there is a perspective difference between the framework used for budgeting and the fund structure used for financial reporting so serious as to make a meaningful reconciliation between the two problematic. In that case, the budgetary comparison must be presented as RSI. (See GASB Statement No. 34, footnote 53, as amended by GASB Statement No. 41, *Budgetary Comparison Schedules—Perspective Differences, an amendment of GASB Statement No. 34*, paragraph 3).

EXHIBIT 9-2
Relationship between the basic financial statements and RSI

Management's discussion and analysis				RSI	
+					
Government-wide financial statements	Fund financial statements			Audited basic financial statements	Mandatory reporting
	Governmental funds	Proprietary funds	Fiduciary funds		
Notes to the financial statements					
+					
Other required supplementary information				RSI	

of trend data as RSI. First, they must provide information on the condition of their infrastructure assets over time. Second, they must provide a comparison over time of the estimated and actual annual expense to preserve and maintain infrastructure assets at the government's selected condition level.

- *Trend data on the funding of pension and other postemployment benefits (OPEB)*. GAAP require governments to provide certain information on the funding of pension benefits and OPEB, typically presented as RSI, if the governments: 1) sponsor single-employer defined benefit plans, 2) participate in agent multiple-employer defined benefit plans, or 3) include a trust fund for a defined benefit plan in their financial reporting entity.[17] The schedule of funding progress compares over time the actuarial accrued liability for benefits with the actuarial value of accumulated plan assets. The schedule of employer contributions compares over time the employers' actuarially determined annual required contribution with actual contributions.

- *Claims development data for public-entity risk pools*. GAAP require that public-entity risk pools provide trend data on pool revenues as well as estimated and actual claims.

Although RSI by definition need not be audited, auditors are required to perform certain limited procedures in regard to RSI.[18] Because RSI is not part of the basic financial statements, its absence does not affect the auditor's opinion on the fair presentation of the basic financial statements. Nonetheless, the independent auditor's report still must be modified to signal: 1) the absence of RSI, 2) any deficiency in RSI that is discovered as the result of the limited procedures performed by the auditor, or 3) the auditor's inability to perform satisfactorily the limited procedures normally required in connection with RSI.[19]

---

[17] RSI must also be presented by employers participating in a cost-sharing multiple-employer defined benefit OPEB plan if a separate report containing the information is not available. (GASB Statement No. 45, *Accounting and Financial Reporting by Employers for Postemployment Benefits Other Than Pensions*, paragraph 27.

[18] AICPA, *Professional Standards*, Section 558.06-.07.

EXHIBIT 9-3
The comprehensive annual financial report and its relationship to the basic financial statements and RSI

General information on the government's structure, services, and environment	Introductory section

+

Mandatory reporting:

Management's Discussion and Analysis
Government-wide Financial Statements
Governmental Fund Financial Statements
Proprietary Fund Financial Statements
Fiduciary Fund Financial Statements
Notes to the Financial Statements
Additional Required Supplementary Information

Financial section

Information on individual funds and discretely presented component units and other supplementary information not required by GAAP

+

Trend data and nonfinancial data	Statistical section

CAFR

Because MD&A are designed, in part, to introduce the basic financial statements, they are presented *before* the basic financial statements. Other RSI is presented immediately following the notes to the financial statements.[20]

Exhibit 9-2 illustrates the relationship between the basic financial statements and RSI.

Comprehensive annual financial report

GAAP have established the basic financial statements and RSI as the *minimum* standard for financial reporting. Governments are expressly encouraged to go beyond these minimum requirements and to present a *comprehensive* annual financial report (CAFR).[21] A CAFR has three major sections: introductory, financial, and statistical. The introductory section furnishes general information on the government's structure, services, and environment. The financial section contains all basic financial statements and RSI, as well as information on all individual funds and discretely presented component units *not* reported separately in the basic financial statements. Sometimes governments also use the financial section to provide supplementary information not required by GAAP (e.g., information needed to demonstrate compliance with finance-related legal or contractual provi-

[19] AICPA, *Professional Standards*, Section 558.08-.10.
[20] In one specific instance, RSI may be reported in the statistical section of the comprehensive annual financial report (CAFR) rather than immediately following the notes to the financial statements. Specifically, GASB Statement No. 30, *Risk Financing Omnibus*, paragraph 7, states: "Public entity risk pools that are included as part of a sponsoring government's financial reporting entity and that do not issue separate financial reports should present the required supplementary information after the notes to the reporting entity's financial statements. However, if the reporting entity issues a CAFR, those pools may present the required supplementary information as statistical information."
[21] NCGA Statement 1, paragraph 135.

sions). The statistical section provides trend data and nonfinancial data useful in interpreting the basic financial statements and is especially important for evaluating economic condition.

The CAFR and its relationship to the basic financial statements and RSI are illustrated in Exhibit 9-3.

Popular annual financial reporting

The CAFR provides a wealth of information for those interested in a state or local government's finances. Unfortunately, the very comprehensiveness of the CAFR can make it a forbidding document for many potential users. Consequently, a number of governments voluntarily issue some form of popular report designed to meet the needs of average citizens or others who may be unable or unwilling to use the CAFR.[22]

In a recommended practice, the GFOA provides the following guidance on preparing a popular annual financial report:

- The popular annual financial report should be issued on a timely basis, no later than six months after the close of the fiscal year, so that the information it contains is relevant.
- The scope of the popular report should be clearly indicated (for instance, the report should indicate whether component units have been included).
- The report should mention the existence of the CAFR for the benefit of readers desiring more detailed information.
- The report should attract and hold readers' interest, convey financial information in an easily understood manner, present information in an attractive and easy-to-follow format, and be written in a concise and clear style.
- The report should avoid technical jargon to meet the needs of a broad, general audience; and the report's message should be underscored, as appropriate, by photographs, charts, or other graphics.
- Narrative should be used, as appropriate, to highlight and explain items of particular importance.
- Comparative data should be used constructively to help identify trends useful in interpreting financial data.
- Popular annual financial reports should be distributed in a number and manner appropriate to their intended readership (such as newspaper or magazine inserts, sample copies provided to libraries, sample copies provided to professional offices).
- Popular annual financial report preparers should strive for creativity.
- Users of popular annual financial reports should be encouraged to provide feedback.
- Most important, the popular annual financial report should establish its credibility with intended readers by presenting information in a balanced and objective manner.

There is no requirement that a popular annual financial report be accompanied by the independent auditor's report. Nonetheless, some issuers of popular annual financial reports wish to associate their independent auditors with their popular reports in order to lend those reports added credibility in the eyes of citizens and other users. Generally accepted auditing

---

[22] As discussed in chapter 14, the GFOA sponsors a program to encourage governments to prepare popular annual financial reports and to recognize governments that have issued such reports.

standards (GAAS) treat popular financial reports as summary financial information (SFI). Because of its summary character, SFI is *not* sufficient for fair presentation in conformity with GAAP, and an auditor is not able to render an opinion on SFI. However, an auditor may give an opinion regarding whether SFI is fairly stated "in all material respects in relation to the general-purpose financial statements from which it has been derived."[23] At a minimum, SFI must:

- be informative of matters that may affect its use, understanding, and interpretation (for example, significant subsequent events, significant contingencies, significant restrictions on resources);
- be prepared using the same measurement focus and basis of accounting as the basic financial statements;
- be classified, summarized, and presented in a reasonable manner;
- reflect the underlying transactions and events within limits that are reasonable for a *summary* report;
- be clearly labeled as *summary financial information*;[24]
- disclose the availability of the CAFR or separately issued basic financial statements;
- disclose the method of aggregation used; and
- disclose how the method of aggregation materially differs from GAAP (such as formal reconciliation, narrative explanation).[25]

SUMMARY

Financial reporting is the process of aggregating and formatting the detailed information collected and maintained in an accounting system so that it can be used effectively by decision makers. *Internal financial reporting* is aimed at managers and other interested parties within the government. Because internal financial reports are designed specifically to meet management needs, it is appropriate that management decide the appropriate contents, scope, and timing of these reports. *Special-purpose external financial reporting* is imposed on governments by outside parties and must be tailored to meet those parties' specific information needs. *General-purpose external financial reporting* is aimed at parties that are interested in a government's finances but that do *not* have direct access to accounting data. Such primary users of general-purpose external financial reports include citizens, legislative and oversight bodies, and investors and creditors.

The paramount objective of general-purpose external financial reporting is accountability, both *fiscal* and *operational*. The data contained in general-purpose external financial reports must have certain essential characteristics. Specifically, such data must be understandable, reliable, relevant, timely, consistent, and comparable.

The core of general-purpose external financial reporting is the *basic financial statements*. These include both government-wide financial statements and separate sets of financial statements for governmental funds, proprietary funds, and fiduciary funds. The basic financial statements also include various accompanying disclosures presented in the form of notes

---

[23] This type of opinion is commonly referred to as an *in-relation-to* opinion.
[24] The words *consolidated* and *condensed* may *not* be used in connection with SFI because they might create the impression that the data are presented in conformity with GAAP.
[25] AICPA, *State and Local Governments*, Section 14.68.-75.

(or summary of significant accounting policies and notes) to the government-wide and fund financial statements.

GAAP also require that the basic financial statements be accompanied by RSI. By definition, RSI need not be audited, but it is subject to certain limited procedures to be performed by the independent auditor.

GAAP encourage governments to present basic financial statements and RSI as part of a larger CAFR. The CAFR contains three major sections: introductory, financial (including the basic financial statements and RSI), and statistical.

Some governments prepare separate popular annual financial reports to meet the special needs of those unable or unwilling to use the CAFR's detailed financial data. The GFOA provides certain recommendations regarding the contents of popular annual financial reports, and GAAS govern the independent auditor's involvement with those reports.

10
Financial Statements

The governmental financial reporting model is characterized by a distinctive blend of fund accounting and government-wide financial reporting. As a result, a typical government may need to present as many as four types of financial statements:
- government-wide financial statements;
- governmental fund financial statements;
- proprietary fund financial statements; and
- fiduciary fund financial statements.

These various presentations combine to form a single, integrated set of financial statements that together with appropriate note disclosure constitute the basic financial statements for state and local governments.

This chapter examines the format and content of each basic financial statement. The notes, which are also integral to the basic financial statements, are addressed separately.[1]

GOVERNMENT-WIDE FINANCIAL STATEMENTS

Generally accepted accounting principles (GAAP) for state and local governments prescribe two basic government-wide financial statements: the government-wide statement of net assets and the government-wide statement of activities.

The government-wide financial statements include all governmental and business-type activities of the primary government but *not* its fiduciary activities. Likewise, the government-wide financial statements include discretely presented component units, but *not* those that are fiduciary in character.[2]

Government-wide statement of net assets

The government-wide statement of net assets is the basic government-wide statement of position.

---

[1] See chapter 11.
[2] For a detailed discussion of component units, see chapter 4.

Format	By definition, a statement of position presents all of an entity's *permanent accounts* (assets, liabilities, and equity/net assets). GAAP allow these accounts to be presented in one of two ways:

assets – liabilities = net assets (net assets approach)

assets = liabilities + net assets (balance sheet approach)

In either case, the presentation is referred to as the *statement of net assets* (rather than *balance sheet*), and the difference between assets and liabilities is referred to as *net assets* (rather than *equity*).[3]

Activity columns

GAAP require that the primary government's governmental activities be reported separately from its business-type activities. In general, governmental activities include activities reported in the governmental fund financial statements, and business-type activities include activities reported as enterprise funds in the proprietary fund financial statements.[4]

It is presumed that the residual balances of internal service funds will be included as part of governmental activities. However, if an internal service fund provides services exclusively to enterprise funds, its residual balances should be included as part of business-type activities. If an internal service fund provides services to both governmental funds and enterprise funds, its residual balances should be reported in the same activities column as its predominant customers.[5] Thus, *all* of the residual balances of an internal service fund that predominantly served governmental funds, but also served enterprise funds, would be reported as part of governmental activities. In no case, would residual balances of an internal service fund be divided between governmental and business-type activities.[6]

Situations sometimes arise where fiduciary funds are the primary consumers of the goods or services produced by an internal service fund. In that case, the internal service fund should be consolidated as part of *governmental activities*.[7]

In certain situations, a government may conclude that it would better reflect public policy to include an activity reported in a governmental fund as part of business-type activities, or to include an activity reported in an enterprise fund as part of governmental activities. For example, a government may prefer to report enterprise fund activities that are intended to be only partially self-supporting (public transportation, for instance) as governmental activities in the government-wide financial statements. The reason, in this case, would be to avoid potentially misleading comparison with activities intended to be entirely self-supporting (such as a public utility). In such situations, GAAP allow an exception to the general rule that governmental funds are reported as part of governmental activities and that enterprise funds are reported as part of business-type activities. Of course, governments that elect this option would need to provide an appropriate reconciling item in the reconciliation associated with the fund financial statements.[8]

---

[3] GASB Statement No. 34, *Basic Financial Statements—and Management's Discussion and Analysis—for State and Local Governments*, paragraph 30.
[4] GASB Statement No. 34, paragraph 12d, 15.
[5] GASB Statement No. 34, paragraph 62.
[6] The other column, of course, could still be affected by the look-back adjustment discussed in chapter 8.
[7] GASB, *Comprehensive Implementation Guide (2004)*, 7.241.
[8] GASB, *Comprehensive Implementation Guide (2004)*, 7.27.

Total column—primary government

GAAP require that the government-wide statement of net assets provide a total column for the primary government.[9] With one exception, all internal balances (payables and receivables between governmental activities and business-type activities) must be eliminated from this total column.[10]

The exception just referred to can arise in connection with internal receivables and payables associated with blended component units that have a different fiscal year than the primary government. For example, a loan from the primary government to a blended component unit that occurs between the close of the blended component unit's fiscal year (e.g., September 30) and the close of the primary government's fiscal year (e.g., December 31) would result in the financial reporting entity reporting the primary government's receivable, but not the component unit's related payable. In that case, the internal balance would be reported in the primary government's total column in the government-wide statement of net assets.[11]

Although removing internal balances has no net effect on the overall statement of net assets, it does prevent the affected account lines (internal payables and internal receivables) from adding across to the total column, which could prove confusing for some financial statement users. To minimize this difficulty, GAAP provide two options to financial statement preparers. One approach is to report all internal balances (receivables and payables) on a single line (within the assets section of the statement, for instance), making the zero balance in the total column self-evident. The alternative is to attach a notation to the separate lines for internal receivables and internal payables, explaining to readers that the total column has been adjusted to remove the effect of internal balances.[12]

Component units column

Governments should present their nonfiduciary discretely presented component units as one or more separate columns immediately after the total column for the primary government.[13] The data for these component units should be taken from each component unit's government-wide presentation.[14]

Sometimes a discretely presented component unit properly prepares its financial statements using a different financial reporting model (e.g., a nongovernmental nonprofit organization associated with a public college or university). In that case, there may be a requirement that the component

---

[9] GASB Statement No. 34, paragraph 14.

[10] GASB Statement No. 34, paragraph 58.

[11] GASB, *Comprehensive Implementation Guide (2004)*, 7.125. Another situation can arise in connection with interfund receivables and payables involving fiduciary funds. Technically speaking, such balances are *external* rather than *internal* from the perspective of government-wide financial reporting (i.e., because fiduciary funds are external to the government-wide financial statements). Consequently, receivables and payables involving fiduciary funds should be reported separately from *internal balances* in the government-wide statement of net assets. To avoid the appearance of inconsistency between the government-wide financial statements and the fund financial statements, governments may wish to classify interfund balances involving fiduciary funds separately from other interfund balances in the fund financial statements. (GASB, *Comprehensive Implementation Guide (2004)*, 7.265.)

[12] GASB Statement No. 34, paragraphs 58 and 312. See also the related discussion in chapter 8.

[13] Data on fiduciary-type component units are included within the fiduciary fund financial statements, where no distinction is made between component units and fiduciary funds of the government, even in the case of otherwise "discretely" presented component units.

[14] If a discretely presented component unit itself reports one or more discretely presented component units, the amounts presented should be the entity-wide totals for the component unit, even if no entity-wide total column is presented in the component unit's separately issued financial statements. (GASB, *Comprehensive Implementation Guide (2004)*, 7.366.) Any fiduciary funds or fiduciary-type component units of a component unit would *not* be included.

unit format its financial statements in a way that is incompatible with the governmental financial reporting model, or there may be a requirement to present additional financial statements not mandated by the governmental model. In such a situation, any incompatible or additional financial statements should be included within the basic financial statements but presented separately from the primary government and labeled "component units."[15]

GAAP require that the basic financial statements include separate information for each major discretely presented component unit.[16] This requirement can be met in one of three ways:

- Include separate columns for each major discretely presented component unit on the face of the statement of net assets (with a single aggregated column for nonmajor component units).
- Within the basic financial statements, immediately following the fund financial statements, include a combining statement of net assets for major discretely presented component units (with a single aggregated column for nonmajor component units and a total column that supports the presentation on the face of the government-wide statement of net assets).
- Include condensed financial statements for each major component unit in the notes to the financial statements.[17]

Usually, governments with two or three component units most likely will present multiple component unit columns on the face of the government-wide statement of net assets, thus avoiding the need for an additional combining or condensed presentation within the basic financial statements (including notes). Conversely, governments with numerous component units typically elect to present information on individual major units as combining or condensed presentations.

Debt may *not* be assigned from the primary government to a discretely presented component unit even if the component unit is expected to repay the debt. Rather, a discretely presented component unit should report only debt that it is legally obligated to repay.[18] Thus, debt issued by the primary government to finance capital acquisition by a discretely presented component unit would need to be reported as a liability of the primary government in the absence of a legal obligation for the component unit to repay the debt.[19]

Total column—financial reporting entity

If they wish, governments may present a total column for the entire financial reporting entity. If a government elects to provide an entity-wide total column, items may need to be reflected differently in that column than in the total column of the primary government. Assume, for example, that the primary government issued debt to finance capital acquisition by a dis-

---

[15] GASB, *Comprehensive Implementation Guide (2004)*, 7.376.

[16] GASB Statement No. 34, paragraph 126.

[17] The minimal level of detail required for condensed financial statements presented in the notes is *not* sufficient for a government that elects to present a combining statement for individual major discretely presented component units. Rather, a combining statement, if presented, must provide essentially the same level of detail used in the component unit's separately issued statements of net assets and activities. (GASB, *Comprehensive Implementation Guide (2004)*, 7.368.)

[18] Contrast this treatment with general obligation debt of the primary government that is expected to be repaid by an enterprise fund of the primary government. In that case, the enterprise fund expected to repay the debt would report it as a fund liability.

[19] GASB, *Comprehensive Implementation Guide (2004)*, 7.127.

cretely presented component unit. Further assume that the component unit is not legally obligated to repay the debt. The contrast in treatment between the primary government's total column and the entity-wide total column would be as follows:

- The primary government's total column would treat the debt as an element in the calculation of *unrestricted net assets* (i.e., the debt is not capital-related from the primary government's perspective because the related capital asset is not reported in the primary government's total column).
- The entity-wide total column would treat the debt as an element in the calculation of *invested in capital assets net of related debt* (i.e., the debt is considered to be capital-related from the entity-wide perspective because both the capital asset and the related debt are reported in the entity-wide total column).

A reclassifications/eliminations column or a note disclosure in this situation could be useful to avoid confusion.[20]

Comparative data

Governments are required to present comparative data only in connection with management's discussion and analysis (MD&A).[21] If they wish, governments also may present comparative data on the face of the government-wide statement of net assets. Such data may be presented for the primary government alone or for both the primary government and the entire financial reporting entity.

It is useful to distinguish comparative *data* from comparative *financial statements*. Comparative financial statements provide *all of the information needed for a full GAAP presentation for each individual year*. For example, a comparative government-wide statement of net assets requires comparative data for governmental activities, business-type activities, the total primary government, and discretely presented component units. Alternatively, a separate government-wide statement of net assets could be presented for each period. When comparative financial statements are issued, the independent auditor normally renders an opinion on both periods presented (for instance, " . . . for the fiscal years ended December 31, 2009, and December 31, 2010").

Order for presenting assets and liabilities

GAAP prescribe two approaches for ordering the presentation of assets and liabilities on the government-wide statement of net assets. The preferred approach is to present assets and liabilities in the relative order of their liquidity. Alternatively, assets and liabilities may be classified simply as *current* or *noncurrent*. The preferred approach is applied to *classes* of assets and liabilities, while the alternative approach is applied to *individual* assets and liabilities.[22]

Relative order of liquidity. The relative liquidity of an asset class depends on how readily items within the class are expected to convert to cash. Relative liquidity also is affected by any restrictions placed on assets within the class. Thus, receivables typically would be more liquid than capital assets, while cash on hand would be more liquid than cash in restricted accounts.

---

[20] GASB, *Comprehensive Implementation Guide (2004)*, 7.29.
[21] GASB Statement No. 34, paragraph 11b.
[22] GASB Statement No. 34, paragraph 31 (including footnote 23).

For liability classes with fixed maturities, relative liquidity depends on the maturity date of the liabilities within the class. In the absence of a maturity date (or if liquidation is expected prior to maturity), relative liquidity of a liability class depends on when liabilities within that class are expected to be liquidated.

The relative order of liquidity for each class of assets and liabilities is determined on the basis of the *average liquidity of the entire class*, even though individual items within the class may be significantly more or less liquid than the class average. If a reported *liability* account (*bonds payable*, for instance) has an average maturity of greater than one year, GAAP require that the current and noncurrent portions be reported separately *within that reported liability account*, as follows:[23]

Bond payable:
Due within twelve months $5,000
Due beyond twelve months $45,000

Note how this treatment differs from the classified approach, where the current portion would have been reported elsewhere on the statement of position (i.e., along with other current liabilities) rather than next to the noncurrent portion.

Classified presentation. GAAP encourage the presentation of assets and liabilities based on their relative liquidity. Alternatively, governments may elect to use the same classified approach taken by private-sector business enterprises. Under the classified approach, individual assets and liabilities typically are categorized as either *current* or *noncurrent* based on whether they are expected to generate or use cash within twelve months of the end of the fiscal period.[24]

When restricted assets are being used to repay maturing debt, the appropriate portion of each should be treated as a current asset and a current liability. To report the debt as current, but the restricted assets that will be used to repay it as noncurrent, would distort *working capital* (i.e., current assets less current liabilities = working capital).

Presentation of capital assets

While most capital assets are subject to depreciation, some are not (land, infrastructure accounted for using the modified approach, certain collections, construction-in-progress). Capital assets that are being depreciated must be reported separately *on the face of the statement of net assets* from those that are not being depreciated.[25] It would *not* be appropriate, for example, to report both land and buildings as a single line item, *even if the necessary detail is provided in the notes to the financial statements.*[26]

Categories of net assets

The difference between assets and liabilities in the government-wide statement of net assets must be labeled as *net assets*. GAAP further require that

[23] The practical effect of this provision is to ensure that the most important single piece of information provided by the classified approach is also available to financial statement users when the relative order of liquidity approach is taken.
[24] Authoritative guidance on classifying assets and liabilities as *current* or *noncurrent* can be found in chapter 3 of Accounting Research Bulletin No. 43, *Restatement and Revision of Accounting Research Bulletins*.
[25] GASB Statement No. 34, paragraph 20; GASB, *Comprehensive Implementation Guide (2004)*, 7.49.
[26] GASB Statement No. 34, paragraph 116, requires that this same distinction be made as well in the notes to the financial statements; GASB, *Comprehensive Implementation Guide (2004)*, 7.352.

net assets be subdivided into three categories: net assets invested in capital assets, net of related debt; restricted net assets; and unrestricted net assets.

Net assets invested in capital assets, net of related debt. Because the government-wide statement of net assets reports *all* government assets, a significant portion of the net assets reported there typically reflect a government's investment in capital assets. To draw financial statement users' attention to this important information, GAAP require the portion of net assets invested in capital assets to be reported as a separate category of *net assets*. The specific amount to be reported is calculated as follows:

	Capital assets
Less:	Accumulated depreciation
Less:	Outstanding principal of related debt[27]
	Net assets invested in capital assets, net of related debt

The outstanding principal of related debt should be calculated net of the unamortized balance of any debt-related accounts (i.e., deferred issuance costs; discount or premium; difference between the reacquisition price of refunded debt and its book value).[28]

GAAP exempt some governments in some circumstances from reporting certain types of capital assets (e.g., certain small governments are exempt from the requirement to report infrastructure assets acquired prior to the implementation of GASB Statement No. 34). Outstanding debt related to these unreported capital assets still should be considered to be capital-related for purposes of calculating *invested in capital assets net of related debt*.[29] In extreme circumstances, the situation just described may result in an overall negative balance in the category. In that case, the title *invested in capital assets net of related debt* should still be used, despite the deficit balance.[30]

The unspent proceeds of capital debt are *not* considered to be a capital asset until they are actually spent.[31] Therefore, only construction-in-progress and a portion of debt equal to that amount should be part of the calculation of *net assets invested in capital assets net of related debt* until construction is actually completed. Meanwhile, unspent debt proceeds would be included in the calculation of *restricted net assets*. Upon completion of the project, all of the remaining debt (including any portion used to fund restricted debt service accounts[32]) would be considered to be capital-related and included as part of future calculations of *net assets invested in capital assets net of related debt*.

It is common for a small portion of the proceeds of capital-related debt to be expended on items that are ultimately not capitalized. Such amounts need not be deducted from the amount treated as capital-related debt.[33]

A government's equity interest in a joint venture is *not* properly classified as capital for this purpose, even if it reflects an interest in the joint ven-

---

[27] The GASB does not provide criteria for identifying capital-related debt because "the Board believes that most governments can readily distinguish between debt that is 'capital related' and debt that is not" (GASB Statement No. 34, paragraph 322).
[28] GASB, *Comprehensive Implementation Guide (2004)*, 7.130.
[29] GASB, *Comprehensive Implementation Guide (2004)*, 7.135.
[30] GASB, *Comprehensive Implementation Guide (2004)*, 7.136.
[31] GASB Statement No. 34, paragraph 33.
[32] GASB, *Comprehensive Implementation Guide (2004)*, 7.140.
[33] GASB, *Comprehensive Implementation Guide (2004)*, 7.132.

ture's capital assets. Instead, such amounts should be classified as unrestricted net assets.[34]

Governments may have no outstanding debt related to their capital assets. In that case, the title of this category should change to *net assets invested in capital assets*.[35]

Finally, it should be noted that whenever a level debt service payment schedule is used, asymmetry will occur between the rate of asset reduction (straight-line) and the rate of liability reduction (increasing with time as interest becomes an increasingly smaller portion of each debt service payment). In some extreme cases, the result may be a negative balance of *net assets invested in capital assets net of related debt*.

Restricted net assets. Restrictions may be imposed on a portion of a government's net assets by parties outside the government (such as creditors, grantors, contributors, laws or regulations of other governments).[36] An amount equal to these restricted assets, less any related liabilities (other than capital-related debt), should be reported as *restricted net assets*.

As discussed above, until a project is actually completed only construction-in-progress and an equal portion of capital-related debt may be considered in the calculation of *net assets invested in capital assets net of related debt*. Meanwhile, the remaining debt, as well as the unspent proceeds, are part of the calculation of *restricted net assets* (assuming there are, in fact, legal restrictions on the use of the proceeds).

Also as discussed above, sometimes restricted assets are to be used to service capital-related debt. In that case, only the restricted assets themselves would enter into the calculation of *restricted net assets*. The capital-related debt itself would remain part of the calculation of *net assets invested in capital assets net of related debt*.[37]

A restriction that the government itself can remove is not really a restriction. Accordingly, assets subject to self-imposed "restrictions" ("earmarking," for example) do not qualify as part of *restricted net assets*. There are two technical exceptions to this rule, constitutional restrictions and enabling legislation.

Constitutional restrictions, while technically self-imposed, clearly cannot be removed easily. Therefore, resources restricted pursuant to constitutional provisions are properly included as part of *restricted net assets*.[38]

Enabling legislation authorizes money to be raised for a specific purpose. In the case of local governments, state law often requires that resources raised by means of enabling legislation be used for the purpose for which raised. In that case, there would be no question that such amounts should be considered *restricted*, because they are subject to an *external legal constraint* (state law). State governments, however, are sovereign, and no *external* legal constraint prevents them from subsequently passing legislation to divert resources raised by means of enabling legislation to some other purpose. All the same, unless there is cause for reconsideration (e.g., the subsequent diversion of resources to some other purpose), it may reasonably be presumed that enabling legislation is tantamount to an implicit

---

[34] GASB, *Comprehensive Implementation Guide (2004)*, 7.151.
[35] GASB, *Comprehensive Implementation Guide (2004)*, 7.134.
[36] Encumbrances are not a factor in the calculation of restricted net assets.
[37] GASB, *Comprehensive Implementation Guide (2004)*, 7.140.
[38] GASB Statement No. 34, paragraph 34b.

contract with taxpayers, thereby justifying the reporting of such amounts as a separate component of *restricted net assets.*[39]

A related issue arises in connection with special revenue funds. Special revenue funds, by definition, should be used only "to account for the proceeds of specific revenue sources …that are *legally restricted* to expenditure for specified purposes" [emphasis added].[40] As explained elsewhere,[41] however, the term "restricted" in this particular case has been understood to encompass self-imposed restrictions. Therefore, the fact that resources are reported in a special revenue fund is not, of itself, sufficient evidence to justify their being reported as *restricted net assets.*

A true restriction must impose a real limitation on the use of resources. For example, a grant to a school district that may be used only for educational purposes should not be considered restricted, since the purpose of the grant is as broad as that of the school district itself. More precisely, GAAP specify that "restricted" should be interpreted as meaning that the permitted use of resources is narrower than the purpose of the reporting unit in which those resources are reported.[42] Thus, a general transportation grant could be considered to be restricted from the perspective of *business-type activities* in the government-wide financial statements but unrestricted from the perspective of the underlying transportation enterprise fund.[43]

While the balance reported in *net assets invested in capital assets net of related debt* may be negative, such is *not* the case for *restricted net assets.* Indeed, no category within *restricted net assets* may have a negative balance.[44]

If both restricted and unrestricted resources are available for the same purpose, a flow assumption is necessary for calculating *restricted net assets* (e.g., restricted assets considered to be used first or restricted and unrestricted assets considered to be used on a pro rata basis). There is no GAAP preference regarding the flow assumption to be used when determining the balance of restricted resources[45]

GAAP require that a distinction be drawn between *permanent* and *temporary* restrictions on net assets. Thus, the *nonexpendable* net assets related to permanent endowments must be reported separately from the (ultimately) *expendable* net assets associated with term endowments. Likewise, the expendable resources generated by a permanent endowment, if restricted, must be distinguished from the endowment proper, which is permanently restricted (nonexpendable).[46]

GAAP also require that the major categories of restrictions be disclosed *on the face* of the statement of net assets.[47]

[39] This guidance on enabling legislation reflects a pending GASB standard on *Net Assets Restricted by Enabling Legislation, an amendment of GASB Statements No. 34 and No. 44.*
[40] National Council on Governmental Accounting (NCGA) Statement 1, *Governmental Accounting and Financial Reporting Principles*, paragraph 26 (as amended).
[41] See chapter 2.
[42] GASB, *Comprehensive Implementation Guide (2004)*, 7.142.
[43] The amount reported as *restricted net assets-business-type activities* typically will be more than the sum of the amounts reported as *restricted net assets* in the various enterprise funds combined to form *business-type activities.*
[44] "No category of restricted net assets can be negative—that is, if liabilities that relate to restricted assets exceed those assets, no balance should be reported; the negative amount should be reported as a reduction of unrestricted net assets." GASB, *Comprehensive Implementation Guide (2004)*, appendix 7-3, exercise 3.
[45] GASB, *Comprehensive Implementation Guide (2004)*, 7.147.
[46] GASB Statement No. 34, paragraph 35.

EXHIBIT 10-1
Calculation of net asset components

Assets	Capital assets	Capital-related debt	Liabilities
		Net assets invested in capital assets, net of related debt	Net assets
	Restricted resources	Liabilities related to restricted resources (other than capital-related debt)	Liabilities
		Restricted net assets	Net assets
	Other assets	Other liabilities	Liabilities
		Unrestricted net assets	Net assets

Unrestricted net assets. GAAP direct that the difference between total net assets and the two categories just discussed (*invested in capital assets net of related debt* and *restricted net assets*) be reported as *unrestricted net assets*. This amount may be a deficit to the extent that a government has elected to fund certain long-term liabilities (vacation leave, for instance) as they come due rather than when they are incurred.

Debt that is unrelated to either capital assets or restricted assets (e.g., debt issued by a state to finance a capital grant to local governments) should be included in the calculation of *unrestricted net assets*.[48] Once again, the outstanding principal of any such debt should be calculated net of the unamortized balance of any debt-related accounts (i.e., deferred issuance costs; discount or premium; difference between the reacquisition price of refunded debt and its book value).[49]

The various categories used to report net assets on the government-wide statement of net assets are illustrated in Exhibit 10-1.

Government-wide statement of activities

The government-wide statement of activities is used to report changes in the net assets reported on the government-wide statement of net assets.

Format

Unlike the operating statement of a private-sector business enterprise, the government-wide statement of activities presents expenses *before* revenues.[50] This order is designed to emphasize that in the public sector, revenues are generated for the express purpose of providing services rather than as an end in themselves. That is, governments do not seek to maximize revenues as such; instead, they identify the service needs of citizens and then raise the resources needed to meet those needs.

Direct expenses

The first column of the government-wide statement of activities should present the direct expenses associated with each of the government's functional activities.[51] GAAP do not define the term *function*. Common examples of functions encountered in practice include general government, public safety, public works, engineering services, health and sanitation, culture

---

[47] GASB, *Comprehensive Implementation Guide (2004)*, 7.122.
[48] GASB, *Comprehensive Implementation Guide (2004)*, 7.137.
[49] GASB, *Comprehensive Implementation Guide (2004)*, 7.130.
[50] GASB Statement No. 34, paragraph 38.
[51] A more detailed presentation of direct expenses (e.g., by program) is encouraged.

and recreation, and community development.[52] For a government's business-type activities, direct expenses should be presented separately, at a minimum, for *different identifiable activities*. A business-type activity is *identifiable* if it has a specific revenue stream and related expenses, gains, and losses that are accounted for separately. The determination of whether an activity is *different* typically can be made on the basis of the types of goods, services, or programs provided. For example, providing natural gas is different from supplying water or electricity,[53] even though all three activities might be described as "utility services."[54] Conversely, there is no need to treat separate water districts as different activities for this purpose,[55] since all provide the same service.[56] A more detailed presentation (by program, for instance) is encouraged but not required.[57]

Each function included in governmental activities should report *all* its direct costs and *only* its *direct costs*. A direct cost is one that is clearly identifiable with a specific function. As a general rule, the need to use a formula for allocation purposes is an indication that a given cost is indirect rather than direct.[58]

As explained elsewhere,[59] indirect costs assigned to governmental functions in the fund financial statements must be reversed for purposes of government-wide financial reporting. Only then will functional expenses report *all* and *only* direct costs.

Direct expenses include depreciation on capital assets that are clearly associated with a given functional activity. Accordingly, direct expenses include not only depreciation on capital assets associated exclusively with a given function, but also depreciation expense on any shared capital assets whose use can directly be identified with specific functional activities (such as a shared office building).

On the other hand, it would *not* be appropriate to allocate depreciation expense on capital assets that serve essentially all of a government's functional activities (city hall, for example). Instead, depreciation on such overhead capital assets should be reported either as part of the *general government* functional activity, or as a separate line item. In the latter case, the amount so reported should be labeled "*unallocated* depreciation expense" to make it clear that a portion of total depreciation expense has been reported elsewhere (i.e., as part of the direct expenses of the various functional activities).[60]

Depreciation on a government's infrastructure assets normally is reported in the functional activity associated with the acquisition and maintenance of those assets (such as public works). Alternatively, it may be

---

[52] Smaller governments often report their departments as their functional categories, or they report their departments or programs separately within functions.
[53] GASB, *Comprehensive Implementation Guide (2004)*, 7.156.
[54] Commonly grouped services like water and sewer could be treated as a single activity for this purpose if accounted for in the same fund.
[55] GASB, *Comprehensive Implementation Guide (2004)*, 7.155.
[56] Institutions of higher education that use the business-type activities model often have a variety of operations (e.g., food service, bookstore, residence halls, student union) that support their primary purpose of instruction. All of these different operations may be considered to form part of a single identifiable activity for purposes of government-wide financial reporting. (GASB Statement No. 37, paragraph 10, footnote c.)
[57] GASB Statement No. 34, paragraphs 39-40.
[58] See chapter 8.
[59] See chapter 8.
[60] GASB Statement No. 34, paragraph 44.

reported as *unallocated depreciation expense*. In no instance, however, should depreciation on infrastructure be allocated to the various functional activities of the government.[61]

Gains and losses resulting from the impairment of capital assets should be treated as an adjustment to expense in the affected function, unless they qualify as special or extraordinary items.[62]

In almost all cases, interest on debt associated with governmental activities cannot meaningfully be associated with individual functions, and so should be reported as a separate line within *governmental activities* on the government-wide statement of activities.[63] This same treatment applies as well to interest associated with capital leases, even when the asset acquired can be directly associated with one or more individual functional activities.[64] Likewise, interest on debt legally restricted for use in a given governmental function also most likely would *not* qualify as a functional expense.[65] Nonetheless, in those rare instances "when borrowing is essential to the creation or continuing existence of a program and it would be misleading to exclude the interest from direct expenses of that program" it should be treated as a functional expense. An example of such a situation, cited in the authoritative literature, is interest on state bonds used to finance reduced-rate loans to school districts.[66] In contrast, note that interest expense is *always* included as part of individual functional expenses for business-type activities.[67]

The practical effect of capitalizing interest incurred during the construction of capital assets used in *governmental activities* would be to allocate interest cost to whatever function reported the related depreciation expense. As just noted, however, the allocation of interest to individual functions within *governmental activities* normally is *not* appropriate. Consequently, no interest should be capitalized in connection with the construction of capital assets used in *governmental activities*. For the same reason, interest should *not* be capitalized in connection with capital assets reported in internal service funds that are included within *governmental activities* for purposes of government-wide financial reporting.

Losses on the sale of capital assets used in governmental activities, *if material*, should be reported as an expense in the general government function rather than in the function reporting related depreciation expense. Immaterial losses may be handled as an adjustment to the current period's depreciation expense.[68] In contrast, losses on the sale of capital assets used in business-type activities should be reported in the appropriate functional category,[69] because there is no equivalent to the functional category *general government* for business-type activities.

---

[61] GASB Statement No. 34, paragraph 45.

[62] GASB Statement No. 42, *Accounting and Financial Reporting for Impairment of Capital Assets and for Insurance Recoveries*, paragraphs 21 and 56.

[63] As discussed later in this paragraph, in exceptional circumstances a portion of interest expense may properly be included as part of functional expenses within governmental activities. In that rare situation, the separate line ordinarily reported for *interest expense* would need to be relabeled to put users on notice that a portion of interest expense was reported elsewhere (i.e., *unallocated* interest expense).

[64] GASB, *Comprehensive Implementation Guide (2004)*, 7.169.

[65] GASB, *Comprehensive Implementation Guide (2004)*, 7.173.

[66] GASB, *Comprehensive Implementation Guide (2004)*, 7.170.

[67] GASB, *Comprehensive Implementation Guide (2004)*, 7.172.

[68] GASB, *Comprehensive Implementation Guide (2004)*, 7.204.

[69] That is, identifiable activity.

Expenses involving discretely presented component units should be reported in the appropriate functional category rather than presented as a separate line item.

Indirect expenses

GAAP do *not* require governments to allocate *indirect* expenses to their various functional activities. Rather, indirect expenses may be either included as part of the *general government* functional activity (or its equivalent) or, in the case of unallocated depreciation expense and unallocated interest expense, reported as a separate line item. GAAP, however, *permit* governments to allocate their indirect expenses. If a government elects to do so, it should use a separate column for this purpose. That column should present a *decrease* for each line that reports an expense to be allocated (such as general government) and a corresponding *increase* for each line to which that expense is being allocated (such as public safety). The presentation of a full cost column (direct expenses by function +/− indirect expense allocation = full cost by function) is permitted but not required.[70] Governments may allocate indirect costs to business-type activities as well as to governmental activities if they wish to do so.

Ideally, indirect cost allocation would be strictly limited to the separate column just described. As a practical matter, however, functional charges for *direct* costs related to centralized activities may include a component to recover administrative overhead, which is an *indirect* cost. For example, billings from a central stores operation often will include an element of administrative cost recovery. GAAP specifically do *not* require the removal of such incidental indirect costs from the column used to report the direct costs of functions and activities.[71]

Program revenues

Some functional programs are directly financed, in whole or in part, by resources *other than taxes and other general revenues*. GAAP require that such *program revenues* be presented separately on the face of the statement of activities. Program revenues include all of the following:

- amounts received from those who purchase, use, or directly benefit from a program (charges) as well as amounts received from those who are *otherwise directly affected* by a program (e.g., fees, permits, licenses, fines, and forfeitures).[72] ("Fees" based on property value or gross receipts are really *taxes* and should *not* be classified as program revenue.[73]) Charges for services include payments received for services provided to other functions (i.e., interfund services provided and used).[74]

- grants, contributions, donations, and similar items *that are restricted to one or more specific programs*. While reimbursement-type grants automatically qualify,[75] other types of multipurpose grants do so only if the amount attributable to each program is identified in either the grant award or the grant application.[76] Note that single-program

---

[70] GASB Statement No. 34, paragraph 42.

[71] GASB Statement No. 34, paragraph 43 and GASB, *Comprehensive Implementation Guide (2004)*, 7.226.

[72] GASB Statement No. 34, paragraph 49 (as amended by GASB Statement No. 37, paragraph 13; GASB, *Comprehensive Implementation Guide (2004)*, 7.174.

[73] See GASB, *Comprehensive Implementation Guide (2004)*, 7.182, for a practical application of this principle.

[74] Such amounts should be combined with other program revenues of a given function rather than presented separately.

[75] GASB, *Comprehensive Implementation Guide (2004)*, 7.183.

[76] GASB Statement No. 34, paragraph 50.

grants are always reported as program revenues, even if the program happens to be reported in more than one function in the government-wide statement of activities.[77] Also note that contributions of infrastructure automatically qualify as program revenue, even in the absence of a legal restriction, because the use of such assets is considered to be inherently restricted.[78]

- Earnings on investments that are legally restricted for a specific program (such as certain endowments and permanent funds, invested grant proceeds).[79]

As a rule, most revenues of component units that function as business-type activities will qualify as *program revenues*, even though they typically are not reported as *program revenues* in the component unit's separately issued financial statements.[80]

Charges for services[81] should be reported separately from *grants and contributions* on the face of the statement. Likewise, *operating grants and contributions* should be reported separately from *capital grants and contributions* on the face of the statement.[82] *Grants and contributions* that may be used for either capital or operating purposes should be treated as *operating grants or contributions.*[83] Pass-through grants to finance capital acquisition by a subrecipient should be treated as operating grants and contributions by the primary recipient.[84]

Charges for services are always reported as program revenue of the function in which they are *generated*, even if they are used for some other purpose.[85] Determining which particular function *generates* a given charge for services may not always be simple (e.g., Are traffic fines generated by the public safety function or by the judicial function?). In such instances, a government should adopt a classification policy and apply it consistently.[86] In the case of tuition, the entire amount should be treated as program revenue of the *instructional* function, even if a portion is intended to recover administrative costs.[87]

---

[77] A reasonable allocation method should be used to assign the program revenues to the appropriate functions–for instance, relative percentages of expenses. Thus, a grant restricted to special education could be allocated to "Instruction," "Administration," and "Transportation," even if that level of categorization is not provided for in the grant application or award. GASB, *Comprehensive Implementation Guide (2004)*, 7.185.

[78] GASB, *Comprehensive Implementation Guide (2004)*, 7.190.

[79] GASB Statement No. 34, paragraph 51.

[80] Component units that function as business-type activities typically qualify as a single activity, thus eliminating the need for the separate reporting of *program revenues* in their separately issued financial statements (GASB, *Comprehensive Implementation Guide (2004)*, 7.157).

[81] Which includes amounts received by those merely affected by a program (e.g., fines).

[82] These three categories are intended to serve as the *minimum* level of detail for presenting program revenues. Governments may present more than one column to display different components of the various categories of program revenues. Likewise, governments are free to adopt more descriptive category headings if they believe those headings would better explain the range of program revenues reported in a given column. For example, a government might elect to use the heading *operating grants, contributions, and restricted interest* rather than the more generic *operating grants and contributions* (GASB Statement No. 34, paragraph 48, as amended).

[83] GASB Statement No. 34, paragraphs 48-51.

[84] GASB, *Comprehensive Implementation Guide (2004)*, 7.189.

[85] Thus lottery revenues would be reported in the function responsible for the lottery, even if the revenues were dedicated to another function (for example, education).

[86] GASB Statement No. 34, paragraph 48, as amended by GASB Statement No. 37, paragraph 12, footnote e.

[87] Tuition is *generated* by an institution's instructional activities, and *generation* is the determining factor when classifying program revenues from *charges for services*. (GASB, *Comprehensive Implementation Guide (2004)*, 7.210.)

Reimbursements of indirect costs by grantors should be reported in the same functional category as the expense being reimbursed (for example, *general government*).[88]

It is important to underscore that "all taxes, even those that are levied for a specific purpose, are general revenues."[89] For this purpose, special assessments are *not* considered to be taxes, even if collected in connection with the property tax levy. Rather, operating-type special assessments should be treated as *charges for services* and capital-type special assessments should be treated as *capital grants and contributions.*[90] In contrast, tax revenues associated with tax-increment financing, despite certain superficial similarities with special assessments, remain taxes and should be classed as general revenue rather than as program revenues.[91]

Other examples of items that would *not* be classified as program revenue because they are considered to be taxes are developer fees based upon a formula applied to the assessed value of property[92] and taxes on alcoholic beverages sold at government outlet stores.[93]

Investment income (including changes in the fair value of investments) normally does *not* qualify as program revenue because it is *not* considered to be generated by the function associated with the underlying investments. One exception, referred to earlier, is investment income that is legally restricted for use in a particular function or program (e.g., endowment income). Such restricted investment income is considered to be tantamount to a restricted grant and thus should properly be classified as program revenue.[94]

Net (expense) revenue

A key goal of the government-wide statement of activities is to highlight the *net* (expense)/revenue of each functional activity. Accordingly, program revenues should be subtracted from total functional expenses to arrive at the net expense or revenue for each functional activity.[95]

General revenues

All revenues that do *not* qualify as program revenues should be reported as *general revenues*, even taxes whose use is limited to particular functions (e.g., road maintenance).[96] Moreover, governments may *not* voluntarily reclassify *program revenues* as *general revenues*, regardless of their significance to the government.[97]

General revenues should be presented immediately following the total net expense of the government's functions. Tax revenues should be reported by type of tax (sales taxes, gas taxes, property taxes, franchise taxes, income taxes).

Gains on the sale of capital assets associated with governmental activities, *if material*, should be reported as general revenue (unlike gains on the sale of capital assets of enterprise funds, which would be reported as part of

---

[88] GASB, *Comprehensive Implementation Guide (2004)*, 7.209.
[89] GASB Statement No. 34, paragraph 52.
[90] GASB, *Comprehensive Implementation Guide (2004)*, 7.199 and 7.200. Note that under accrual accounting, revenue related to capital-type special assessments is recognized as soon as the project has been completed. Revenue recognition is deferred in governmental funds, but only because it is not *available* (a modified accrual concept).
[91] GASB, *Comprehensive Implementation Guide (2004)*, 7.198
[92] GASB, *Comprehensive Implementation Guide (2004)*, 7.195.
[93] GASB, *Comprehensive Implementation Guide (2004)*, 7.197.
[94] GASB, *Comprehensive Implementation Guide (2004)*, 7.203.
[95] GASB Statement No. 34, paragraph 38.
[96] GASB, *Comprehensive Implementation Guide (2004)*, 7.192.
[97] GASB, *Comprehensive Implementation Guide (2004)*, 7.181.

the appropriate functional expense within business-type activities). Immaterial gains may be handled as an adjustment to the current period's depreciation expense.[98] Conversely, gains resulting from the impairment of capital assets[99] should be reported as an adjustment to program expense in the affected function, if they do not qualify as a special or extraordinary item.[100]

Endowment and permanent fund contributions

Contributions to term endowments, permanent endowments, and permanent fund principal should be reported as a separate line item, immediately following general revenues. For this purpose, no distinction is necessary between contributions to *term* endowments and contributions to *permanent* endowments, even though the two types of endowments are distinguished on the government-wide statement of net assets (i.e., *expendable* versus *nonexpendable*).

Special and extraordinary items

Special and extraordinary items should be reported on a separate line after endowment and permanent fund contributions. If special items and extraordinary items occur in the same period, the two should be reported separately within a single category, with special items reported before extraordinary items.[101]

Transfers

Transfers is the last item reported on the government-wide statement of activities before the total change in net assets. Except in the case of certain transfers involving blended component units with a different fiscal year end than the primary government,[102] no transfers should be reported in the primary government's total column.

Changes in accounting principle

The net cumulative effect of a change in accounting principles should be reported as a restatement of *beginning net assets.*[103]

Activity columns

GAAP require that the primary government's governmental activities be reported separately from its business-type activities on the statement of activities, just as on the government-wide statement of net assets. This distinction is particularly important in connection with the government-wide statement of activities in order to avoid inappropriate comparisons between the net costs of business-type activities (which are intended to recover a significant portion of their costs from customers) and governmental activities (which are *not* intended to recover a significant portion of their costs from customers).

This distinction between governmental and business-type activities must be made in two ways. First, separate *line items* must be reported to distinguish individual governmental functional activities from individual business-type functional activities[104] and to show the program revenues associated with each. Second, separate *columns* must be used for governmental and business-type activities to report net program cost and other changes in net assets (general revenues; endowment and permanent fund

[98] GASB, *Comprehensive Implementation Guide (2004),* 7.204.
[99] Impairment *losses* frequently produce *gains* for accounting purposes, because losses are netted against related insurance recoveries, which are often based on a value that is higher than depreciated historical cost (e.g., fair value, replacement value).
[100] GASB Statement No. 42, paragraphs 17, 56.
[101] GASB Statement No. 34, paragraph 55. For a discussion of special items see chapter 3.
[102] See chapter 8.
[103] GASB Statement No. 34, footnote 13. This treatment departs from that set forth in Accounting Principles Board Opinion No. 20, *Accounting Changes.*
[104] That is, identifiable activities.

contributions; special and extraordinary items; transfers; and changes in accounting principles).

Total column—primary government

GAAP require that the government-wide statement of activities, like the government-wide statement of net assets, provide a consolidated total column for the primary government.

Component units column

Governments should present their discretely presented component units as one or more separate columns immediately after the total column for the primary government. The data for these component units should be taken from each unit's government-wide presentation.[105] The considerations governing the number of columns presented for discretely presented component units on the government-wide statement of activities are the same as those described earlier for the government-wide statement of net assets.[106]

Total column—financial reporting entity

Also like the government-wide statement of net assets, the government-wide statement of activities may include a total column for the entire financial reporting entity.

Comparative data

Governments are required to present comparative data only in connection with MD&A.[107] If they wish, governments also are free to present comparative data on the face of the government-wide statement of activities. Such data may be presented for the primary government alone, or for both the primary government and the entire financial reporting entity.

The structure of the government-wide statement of activities is illustrated in Exhibit 10-2.

Interpreting cost data

The cost data provided in the government-wide statement of activities are invaluable for assessing the cost of functions and programs on an accrual basis and the degree to which that cost is being recovered through program revenues. Still, care must be taken to ensure that those data are interpreted appropriately. For example, in considering privatization or other forms of external competition, a government should distinguish avoidable costs from unavoidable costs, because only the former are relevant to a privatization decision.[108]

---

[105] If a discretely presented component unit itself reports one or more discretely presented component units, the amounts presented should be the entity-wide totals for the component unit, even if no entity-wide total column is presented in the component unit's separately issued financial statements. (GASB, *Comprehensive Implementation Guide (2004)*, 7.366.) Any fiduciary funds or fiduciary-type component units of a component unit would not be included.

[106] Many discretely presented component units are enterprise funds. The operating statement format of an enterprise fund (i.e., the format that would be used in the component unit's separately issued financial statements) differs significantly from the format of the government-wide statement of activities. This difference raises the issue of the appropriate format to be used for a combining statement for major component units. The approach to be taken depends upon the level of detail provided for component units in the government-wide statement of activities. If component units with governmental activities and component units with business-type activities are combined in a single column in the government-wide financial statements, the format used in the combining statement should be that used in the government-wide statement of activities, with the data for component units with business-type activities recast accordingly. Alternatively "the government could display a single business-type activities line on the combining statement of activities, with a supporting combining statement of revenues, expenses, and changes in net assets." If all of the component units in a given discretely presented component units column are business-type activities, "the combining statement may be presented in the statement of revenues, expenses, and changes in net assets format with the combined totals recast into the reporting entity's statement of activities." (GASB, *Comprehensive Implementation Guide (2004)*, 7.367.)

[107] GASB Statement No. 34, paragraph 11b.

[108] The concept of avoidable cost, for this purpose, encompasses not only those costs that can be eliminated immediately, but also costs that can be eliminated after a transition period.

EXHIBIT 10-2
Structure of the government-wide statement of activities

Total direct expenses by functional activity	Less: Program revenues			Net expenses (or revenues) by functional activity (i.e., "net program cost")
	Fees and charges	Operating grants and contributions	Capital grants and contributions	
[A]	[X]	[Y]	[Z]	A – (X+Y+Z) = [A1]

Key

    Inflows

    Outflows

    Net change

General revenues **[B]**	
Endowment and permanent fund contributions **[C]**	
"Special" and extraordinary items **[D]**	"Special" and extraordinary items **[E]**
Transfers in **[F]**	Transfers out **[G]**
Increase or (decrease) in net assets (B+C+D+F) – (A1+E+G)	

Care also must be taken when comparing cost information between governments to ensure that such comparisons are valid. The use of historical cost depreciation, for example, may significantly distort the costs reported for capital-intensive activities (e.g., activities with older assets may appear more efficient than activities with newer assets because of the lower asset costs being depreciated[109]).

Furthermore, accrual accounting, by definition, does not take the timing of cash flows into consideration for purposes of revenue and expense recognition. Therefore, accrual-based data cannot be used indiscriminately for purposes of setting rates and charges. For example, rates set to recover the cost of a debt-financed capital asset through the funding of depreciation expense may not be adequate to make timely debt service payments if the service life of the asset is longer than the maturity of the debt.[110]

GOVERNMENTAL FUND FINANCIAL STATEMENTS

GAAP prescribe, at a minimum, two basic governmental fund financial statements: the governmental fund balance sheet and the governmental fund statement of revenues, expenditures, and changes in fund balances.

Both statements should include the government's general fund as well as all of its special revenue funds, capital projects funds, debt service funds, and permanent funds.

GAAP also require that a budgetary comparison be presented for the general fund and any major special revenue funds for which annual (or biennial) budgets have been legally adopted.[111] While GAAP require only

---

[109] Conversely, older assets may be expected to result in higher maintenance costs than newer assets.
[110] GFOA recommended practice on "Measuring the Cost of Government Services" (2002).

that this budgetary comparison be presented as required supplementary information (RSI), governments are specifically permitted to include this presentation as an integral part of the basic financial statements for their governmental funds.[112] Indeed, the Government Finance Officers Association formally recommends that budgetary comparisons be reported as basic governmental fund financial statements.[113] This option is not available, however, if the framework used for budgeting differs so significantly from the fund structure used for financial reporting that a reconciliation between the two would not be meaningful. In that case, the budgetary comparison would need to be presented as RSI.[114]

Governmental fund balance sheet

The governmental fund balance sheet is the basic statement of position for the governmental funds.

Excluded assets

Governmental funds focus on *current financial resources*. Accordingly, only *financial* assets are properly reported in governmental funds. An asset is considered *financial* if it satisfies any of the following conditions:

- *The asset is a form of cash.* Because it is liquid, cash is the ultimate financial asset. For this purpose, cash includes currency on hand as well as demand deposits with banks or other financial institutions. Cash also includes deposits in other kinds of accounts or cash management pools that have the general characteristics of demand deposit accounts (the depositor may deposit additional cash at any time and effectively may withdraw cash at any time without prior notice or penalty).[115]

- *The asset will convert to cash in the ordinary course of operations.* Some noncash assets are acquired with the intention of being converted to cash in the ordinary course of operations. Examples include receivables and investments as well as capital-type assets acquired for the express purpose of resale (such as foreclosure properties, economic development properties, certain gifts of capital assets). These assets are also considered *financial* because they will eventually be available for spending, even though they do not have the same high level of liquidity as cash.

- *The asset represents inventories (such as materials or supplies) or a prepayment.* Because the governmental funds focus on current financial resources, it might be expected that inventories and prepayments would be reported as expenditures immediately when purchased. Indeed, GAAP permit the use of the purchases method for inventories and prepaids.[116] However, GAAP also allow governments to record inventories and prepaids as assets in the governmental funds, thereby deferring the recognition of an expenditure until the period that

---

[111] Sometimes a given fund will be classified in one manner for financial reporting purposes and in another manner for budgetary purposes. Budgetary reporting requirements apply based solely upon how a fund is classified for financial reporting purposes. Thus, no budgetary comparison should be presented for a budgetary special revenue fund that is classified as an enterprise fund for financial reporting purposes. (GASB, *Comprehensive Implementation Guide (2004)*, 7.380.)

[112] GASB Statement No. 34, footnote 53.

[113] GFOA recommended practice on "Budget to Actual Comparison Statements" (1999).

[114] GASB Statement No. 34, paragraph 130, as amended by GASB Statement No. 41, *Budgetary Comparison Schedules—Perspective Differences (an amendment of GASB Statement No. 34)*, paragraph 3.

[115] GASB Statement No. 9, *Reporting Cash Flows of Proprietary and Nonexpendable Trust Funds and Governmental Entities That Use Proprietary Fund Accounting*, footnote 5.

[116] See chapter 5.

directly benefits from the outlay. The rationale for this option is that inventories and prepayments may be considered *financial* assets in the indirect sense that they allow a government to avoid what otherwise normally would be an expenditure (the use of current available financial resources).

Examples of assets that should *not* be reported in governmental funds because they are *not* financial in nature include general capital assets and intangible assets used in the government's operations. General capital assets might include land, construction-in-progress, buildings and improvements, equipment, and infrastructure. Water rights are an example of an intangible asset.

An equity interest in the capital assets of a joint venture also is not a current financial resource and so should *not* be reported in a governmental fund.

Excluded liabilities

All liabilities must be liquidated with *financial* resources, but not necessarily with *current* financial resources. Accordingly, governmental funds, with their focus on current financial resources, do *not* report liabilities for the following:

- unmatured principal and interest of long-term debt (except for amounts due early in the subsequent year in a debt service fund and reported in accordance with the early recognition option);[117]
- compensated absences (except for unused balances payable to employees separated from service as of the end of the fiscal year);
- claims and judgments (until due and payable);
- landfill closure and postclosure care costs (until due and payable);
- obligations under long-term operating leases with scheduled rent increases (until payments are due in accordance with the contractual payment schedule);
- net pension obligation; and
- net other postemployment benefit obligation. [118]

The treatment described above for unmatured debt applies solely to debt associated with parties outside the primary government, *including the primary government's discretely presented component units.* Any amount due to another fund of the primary government must be reported as a fund liability, regardless of when repayment is expected.[119]

Presentation of equity

The difference between the assets and liabilities of governmental funds is reported as *fund balance.* As discussed previously,[120] fund balance is divided into *reserved* and *unreserved* components, with *unreserved* representing amounts considered available for new spending. Common examples of reserved fund balance include the following:

- *Reserved for long-term loans and advances.* Receivables related to long-term loans[121] are always matched by a reservation of fund balance to alert financial statement users that the receivable reported in the governmental fund, while representing a *financial* resource, does not con-

---

[117] See chapter 5.
[118] GASB Interpretation No. 6, *Recognition and Measurement of Certain Liabilities and Expenditures in Governmental Fund Financial Statements*, paragraph 14.
[119] GASB Statement No. 34, paragraph 112(a) 1.
[120] See chapter 3.
[121] *Advance* is commonly used to describe long-term loans within the primary government.

stitute a *current* financial resource because receipt is not expected in the near future. Fund balance should *not* be reserved for long-term receivables that are already offset by a liability for *deferred revenue* (such as *special assessments receivable, capital leases receivable*).[122]

- *Reserved for legal restrictions.* Current financial resources are not considered available for general spending if they are *legally restricted to some use that is narrower than the purpose of the fund* itself. Therefore, a portion of fund balance should be reserved to reflect any such legally restricted resources. Generally, it is accepted practice that only restrictions enforceable by an outside party qualify as restrictions for this purpose. A good example would be the corpus of an endowment reported in a permanent fund.[123]

- *Reserved for inventories and prepaids.* As noted earlier, inventories and prepaids are reported as assets in governmental funds whenever the consumption approach is used. Such assets technically are available to liquidate the related expenditures that will be recognized when those assets are eventually consumed.[124] However, financial statement users typically are most interested in the balance of current financial resources available for *new* spending. Therefore, inventories and prepaids are quite similar to assets subject to legal restrictions in the sense that their use is narrower than the purpose of the governmental fund in which they are reported. Accordingly, in practice, governments typically choose to report *reserved fund balance* for material balances of inventories and prepaids reported in governmental funds using the consumption method. Of course, GAAP also require governments that use the purchases method for inventories to report an asset on their balance sheet if the amounts are considered material.[125] In this latter case, an equivalent amount of fund balance *must* be reserved, because no related *future* expenditure will ever be recognized (i.e., the expenditure was already recognized at the time of purchase).

- *Reserved for equity in joint ventures.* Governmental funds sometimes report an equity interest in joint ventures. Any such amounts should be offset by *reserved fund balance* to indicate that they are not, in fact, available for spending.

- *Reserved for encumbrances.* Often, governments enter into contracts and purchase orders that will be fulfilled in a subsequent fiscal period. Although the contract or purchase order creates a legal *commitment*, the government incurs no *liability* until performance has occurred on the part of the party with whom the government has entered into the arrangement. When a government intends to honor outstanding commitments in subsequent periods, such amounts are said to be *encumbered*.[126] In some cases, governments keep their current budget open for some time following the close of the fiscal year

---

[122] American Institute of Certified Public Accountants (AICPA), *State and Local Governments*, Section 10.10. Fund balance is the difference between fund assets and fund liabilities. Accordingly, if there is a liability for deferred revenue that offsets the receivable, then there is no net fund balance to reserve.
[123] GASB, *Comprehensive Implementation Guide (2004)*, 7.188.
[124] Even then, it can be argued that an amount equal to any minimum balances of inventories that must be maintained would need to be reserved. See NCGA Statement 1, Illustration 1, footnote 2 (b).
[125] See chapter 5.
[126] Chapter 16 features a complete discussion of encumbrances.

(this is commonly known as a *lapse period*) to allow for liquidation of these encumbrances. When the encumbrances are finally liquidated, they are charged against the prior year's budget rather than against the budget of the year in which the expenditure is actually incurred. In such cases, GAAP require that fund balance be reserved for encumbrances.[127] More commonly, governments avoid the potential complications of keeping two budgets open simultaneously by automatically reappropriating encumbrances outstanding at the end of the current fiscal year as part of the subsequent year's budget. In this latter situation, it cannot be said that the resources are unavailable for the subsequent year's budget, since the encumbrances will, in fact, be included in that budget. Accordingly, fund balance should *not* be reserved for encumbered amounts that are reappropriated as part of the following year's budget.[128]

The financial statements (or accompanying notes) should provide "sufficient detail to disclose the purposes of the reservations (for example, "reserved for debt service" or "reserved for encumbrances")."[129]

Unreserved fund balance, in turn, may be divided into *designated* and *undesignated* portions. Designations represent management's intended future use of available resources (e.g., contingencies, equipment replacement)[130] and generally should reflect actual plans approved by the government's senior management.[131] Designations essentially reflect a government's *self-imposed* limitations on the use of otherwise available current financial resources. For example, a designation would be used to reflect outstanding encumbrances at the end of the fiscal year that will be reappropriated as part of the subsequent year's budget. A designation also is an appropriate way to highlight that a portion of unreserved fund balance reflects an increase in the fair value of investments that the government does not intend to liquidate in the following year.[132]

Reservations of fund balance are intended to reflect *demands* or *limitations* on net current financial resources. Consequently, it is possible for a government to have reservations of fund balance in excess of total fund balance (reflecting commitments of current financial resources in excess of amounts available). To the contrary, designations of fund balance *are intended to represent accumulations of resources*. Therefore, it is *not* appropriate to report designations in excess of available resources (that is, unreserved fund balance).[133] Naturally, any reservations or designations reported must have a positive balance.

It might be tempting to assume a close relationship between the amounts reported for *reserved fund balance* in the governmental funds and the amounts reported for *restricted net assets* in the governmental activities column of the government-wide statement of net assets. These two amounts, however, are likely to differ for several reasons:
- There is a difference in measurement focus and basis of accounting between the two statements.

---

[127] NCGA Statement 1, paragraph 91.
[128] As discussed below, however, a *designation* would be appropriate.
[129] GASB Statement No. 34, paragraph 84.
[130] NCGA Statement 1, paragraph 120.
[131] AICPA, *State and Local Governments*, Section 10.17.
[132] GASB, *Comprehensive Implementation Guide (2004)*, 6.70.
[133] AICPA, *State and Local Governments*, 10.17.

- *Reserved fund balance* focuses on availability as well as restrictions.
- No *reserved fund balance* is reported for restrictions unless they are narrower than the purpose of the fund itself. Thus resources that are not considered reserved from the narrow perspective of an individual governmental fund may be considered restricted from the broader perspective of *governmental activities*.[134]

Major fund reporting

A key function of fund accounting is to segregate resources, a purpose frustrated to some extent when different individual funds are combined for financial reporting purposes. On the other hand, governments typically have too many funds to include information on each individual fund within the basic financial statements. GAAP resolve this potential financial reporting dilemma by requiring that governmental fund data be presented separately for *each individual major governmental fund*. That is, the financial statements for governmental funds report a separate column for each individual major fund, with data from all nonmajor governmental funds aggregated into a single *other governmental funds* column, regardless of fund type.[135]

By definition, the general fund[136] is always considered a major fund. In addition, governments may report as major funds whatever other individual governmental funds they believe to be of particular importance to financial statement users (for instance, because of public interest).[137] At a minimum, governmental funds other than the general fund *must* be reported as major funds if they meet *both* of the following criteria (as applied to the final adjusted balances reported in the funds):

- *Ten percent criterion*. An individual governmental fund reports at least 10 percent of *any* of the following: a) total governmental fund assets, b) total governmental fund liabilities, c) total governmental fund revenues, or d) total governmental fund expenditures.[138]
- *Five percent criterion*. An individual governmental fund reports at least 5 percent of the aggregated total for both governmental funds *and enterprise funds* of any one of the items for which it met the 10 percent criterion.[139]

If an individual fund is expected to meet the minimum criteria for mandatory major fund reporting in some years but not in others, a government might elect to always report it as a major fund to enhance consistency from year to year. Also, it should be remembered that events occurring near the end of the fiscal year (e.g., debt issuance) may require reclassification of a previously nonmajor fund as a major fund.

GAAP require, that the column used to report nonmajor governmental funds report *unreserved fund balance* separately by fund type, rather than

---

[134] GASB Statement No. 34, footnote 24 and AICPA, *State and Local Governments*, Section 10.15.

[135] Governments do *not* have the option of reporting separate fund-type columns for their nonmajor governmental funds.

[136] Or the principal operating fund if the government does not report a *general fund*.

[137] Because auditors must assess materiality separately for each major fund, an expansion in the number of major funds will provide increased audit coverage, along with potentially higher audit costs.

[138] Other financing sources and uses are excluded for purposes of this calculation.

[139] In applying the 10 percent and 5 percent criteria to assets and liabilities, governments have the *option* of netting internal balances for both individual funds and the combined totals, provided they do so consistently from year to year. In the context of enterprise funds, *revenues* and *expenses* should be understood to encompass all revenues and expenses (operating and nonoperating) reported on the operating statement (including *capital contributions, additions to permanent endowments,* and *special items*) except *extraordinary items*. (GASB, *Comprehensive Implementation Guide (2004)*, 7.288.)

just in the aggregate.[140] These fund-type balances should be further subdivided into their *designated* and *undesignated* components. Also, the amounts reported by fund type must be *exactly the same* as those reported in the combining financial statements. [141]

If a government has only one nonmajor governmental fund, that fund will necessarily have to be reported in its own separate column. The presentation of a separate column is *not* equivalent to classification as a major fund in such cases. To avoid potential misunderstandings, financial statement preparers are advised to use columnar labels that make it clear whenever a separate fund column is not a major fund, as in the following example:[142]

Major Funds			Nonmajor Fund	
General Fund	Special Revenue Fund 1	Special Revenue Fund 2	Special Revenue Fund 3	Total

Total column and reconciliation

GAAP require that like the government-wide statement of net assets, the governmental fund balance sheet also report a total column.[143] Still, there is an important difference between these two requirements. In the case of the government-wide statement of net assets, GAAP require eliminating internal balances. There is no similar GAAP requirement for eliminating interfund balances from the total column reported on the governmental fund balance sheet, although governments are free to do so. Governments choosing to eliminate interfund balances may wish to consider presenting a separate *eliminations* column immediately preceding the total column.[144]

For the most part, the activities reported in the governmental funds are the same as those reported in the governmental activities column of the government-wide statement of net assets. However, the amounts reported in the two locations often differ significantly for two reasons:

- *Classification differences.* The residual balances of internal service funds, as noted earlier, typically are included as part of governmental activities in the government-wide financial statements, even though internal service funds are themselves proprietary funds. Accordingly, one difference between the total column for the governmental fund balance sheet and the governmental activities column of the government-wide statement of net assets is the amount of the residual balances of internal service funds included in the latter. Likewise, governments have the *option*, as discussed previously, of selectively classifying individual governmental funds as business-type activities or of selectively classifying individual enterprise funds as governmental activities. If this option is taken, there will be a difference similar to that described for internal service funds.
- *Measurement focus and basis of accounting.* Governmental funds use the current financial resources measurement focus and the modified accrual basis of accounting, while the government-wide financial

---

[140] GASB Statement No. 34, paragraph 84.
[141] GASB, *Comprehensive Implementation Guide (2004)*, 7.305.
[142] GASB, *Comprehensive Implementation Guide (2004)*, 7.286.
[143] GASB Statement No. 34, paragraph 83.
[144] See chapter 8.

statements use the economic resources measurement focus and the accrual basis of accounting. As a result, there are important differences between the assets and liabilities reported on the governmental fund financial statements and those reported on the government-wide financial statements. For example, as explained earlier, many nonfinancial assets and long-term liabilities are excluded from the governmental fund balance sheet. Conversely, the government-wide financial statements do not report a liability for deferred revenue in connection with amounts that are not yet considered available for appropriation.

Because the government-wide and fund presentations are designed to function as a single, integrated set of financial statements, GAAP require that a summary reconciliation be provided between the total column reported on the governmental fund balance sheet and the governmental activities column reported in the government-wide statement of net assets. This reconciliation may be presented on the face of the governmental fund balance sheet or as an accompanying schedule.[145] A government may choose to present more detailed information on the various elements of this reconciliation in the notes to the financial statements.[146] Such additional detail is required if "aggregated information in the summary reconciliation obscures the nature of the individual elements of a particular reconciling item."[147]

Governmental fund statement of revenues, expenditures, and changes in fund balances

The governmental fund statement of revenues, expenditures, and changes in fund balances is the basic statement of activities for the governmental funds. Because of the unique measurement focus and basis of accounting of governmental funds, the terminology used for this statement varies considerably from that used for other statements of activities.

Basic elements

Consistent with the current financial resources measurement focus, the governmental fund statement of activities reports *expenditures* rather than *expenses*. Likewise there is no distinction in governmental funds between revenues and gains or between expenditures and losses. On the other hand, GAAP require that certain transactions and events be reported separately as *other financing sources* or *other financing uses* rather than as revenues or expenditures, to avoid the potential distortion of revenue and expenditure trend data.[148] Like the government-wide statement of activities, the governmental fund statement of revenues, expenditures, and changes in fund balances reports special items and extraordinary items separately from revenues, expenditures, and other financing sources/uses.[149]

---

[145] GASB Statement No. 34, paragraphs 77 and 85. The term "accompanying" should be interpreted to mean the page immediately following the statement it supports.

[146] GAAP do not specify the minimum level of detail required to constitute a *summary reconciliation* for this purpose. It is recommended, however, that this summary reconciliation be at least as detailed as that found in paragraph 85 of GASB Statement No. 34. That is, the summary reconciliation should separately address each of the following items: 1) reporting capital assets at their historical cost and depreciating them instead of reporting capital acquisitions as expenditures when incurred; 2) adding general long-term liabilities not due and payable in the current period; 3) reducing deferred revenue for those amounts that were not available to pay current-period expenditures; and 4) adding internal service fund net asset balances.

[147] GASB Statement No. 34, paragraph 77. Potential obscurity requiring note disclosure occurs whenever 1) a single reconciling item is a combination of several similar balances or transactions (e.g., different types of long-term liabilities) or 2) a single reconciling item is a net adjustment. (GASB, *Comprehensive Implementation Guide (2004)*, 7.295.)

[148] A thorough discussion of other financing sources and uses is found in chapters 3 and 5.

Level of detail

Revenues should be presented by source in sufficient detail to be meaningful.[150] Expenditures should be presented by function and character. Additional detail (such as department, object of expenditure) may be presented but is not required by GAAP.[151]

In theory, the character of an expenditure is based on the periods it is presumed to benefit. Expenditures that primarily benefit the present period (current expenditures) are distinguished from those presumed to benefit both the present and future periods (capital outlay expenditures) and from those presumed to benefit periods past, present, and future (debt service expenditures). GAAP also provide for a fourth character classification, *intergovernmental expenditures*, for situations where one governmental entity provides resources to another.[152] The capital outlays character classification often is used solely for capital outlays reported in capital projects funds. In other words, capital outlays of the general fund often are included as part of the *current* expenditures reported for each functional activity within that fund.

Order of presentation

The various components of the governmental fund statement of revenues, expenditures, and changes in fund balances should be presented in the following order:[153]
- revenues;
- expenditures;
- excess (deficiency) of revenues over expenditures;
- other financing sources and uses (including transfers);
- special items;
- extraordinary items;
- net change in total fund balance;
- fund balance beginning of period; and
- fund balance end of period.

Major fund reporting

The governmental fund statement of revenues, expenditures, and changes in fund balances is subject to the same major fund reporting requirements as the governmental fund balance sheet.

Total column and reconciliation

GAAP require that the governmental fund statement of revenues, expenditures, and changes in fund balances report a total column. Once again, there is no requirement that interfund activities be eliminated from this total column. Governments are free to consolidate interfund activity if they wish, but only to the extent that such consolidations do not have the practical effect of removing interfund services provided or used between functions from the government-wide statement of activities, thereby distorting the functional cost data reported in that statement. Governments choosing to eliminate interfund activity from the governmental fund statement of revenues,

---

[149] Because of the difference in measurement focus and basis of accounting between the government-wide financial statements and the governmental fund financial statements, an item may appear as a special item or an extraordinary item in one but not the other. (GASB, *Comprehensive Implementation Guide (2004)*, 7.309.)

[150] For example, typically there should be no less detail in the statement of revenues, expenditures, and changes in fund balances than in the government-wide statement of activities.

[151] The level of detail presented in the fund financial statements may be different than the level of detail presented in the government-wide financial statements. (GASB, *Comprehensive Implementation Guide (2004)*, 7.153.)

[152] NCGA Statement 1, paragraphs 110-116.

[153] GASB Statement No. 34, paragraph 86.

expenditures, and changes in fund balances may wish to consider presenting a separate *eliminations* column immediately preceding the total column.[154]

The government-wide statement of activities and the governmental fund statement of revenues, expenditures, and changes in fund balances exhibit the same types of differences in classification and differences in measurement focus and basis of accounting as those described for the government-wide statement of net assets and the governmental fund balance sheet. Accordingly, the amounts reported on the two statements often differ significantly.

For example, the governmental funds report capital outlay expenditures, while the government-wide financial statements report depreciation expense. Likewise, the governmental funds report an other financing source for the issuance of debt and an expenditure for debt service principal payments, while the government-wide financial statements report neither. Similarly, under *modified* accrual accounting, governmental funds often defer the recognition of revenues and expenditures until periods subsequent to that in which the underlying event or transaction occurred, while the government-wide statement of activities does not.

Again, GAAP require that a summary reconciliation between the two statements be provided, either on the face of the governmental fund statement of revenues, expenditures, and changes in fund balances, or as an accompanying schedule.[155] A government may provide detailed information on the various elements of this reconciliation in the notes to the financial statements.[156] Such additional detail is required if "aggregated information in the summary reconciliation obscures the nature of the individual elements of a particular reconciling item."[157]

Budgetary comparison statement

A budgetary comparison must be presented for the general fund and for each major individual special revenue fund for which an annual (or biennial) budget is legally adopted.[158] Governments do *not* have the option of presenting budgetary comparisons for other funds in conjunction with the basic financial statements or RSI.[159] This budgetary comparison may be presented either as the third of the basic governmental fund financial statements or as RSI.[160] When the budgetary comparison is presented as part of the basic governmental fund financial statements, it is properly referred to as a *statement*, while the term *schedule* describes this same information when it is presented

---

[154] See chapter 8.

[155] The term "accompanying" should be interpreted to mean the page immediately following the statement it supports.

[156] GAAP do not specify the minimum level of detail required to constitute a *summary reconciliation* for this purpose. It is recommended, however, that the level of detail be at least equal to that found in paragraph 90 of GASB Statement No. 34. That is, the summary reconciliation should separately address: 1) reporting revenues on the accrual basis; 2) reporting annual depreciation expense instead of expenditures for capital outlays; 3) reporting long-term debt proceeds in the statement of net assets as liabilities instead of other financing sources; also, reporting debt principal payments in the statement of net assets as reductions of liabilities instead of expenditures; 4) reporting other expenses on the accrual basis; and 5) adding the net revenue (expense) of internal service funds.

[157] GASB Statement No. 34, paragraph 77. Potential obscurity requiring note disclosure occurs whenever 1) a single reconciling item is a combination of several similar balances or transactions or 2) a single reconciling item is a net adjustment. (GASB, *Comprehensive Implementation Guide (2004)*, 7.295.)

[158] Sometimes a given fund will be classified in one manner for financial reporting purposes and in another manner for budgetary purposes. Budgetary reporting requirements apply based solely upon how a fund is classified for financial reporting purposes. Thus, no budgetary comparison would be mandated for a budgetary special revenue fund that is classified as an enterprise fund for financial reporting purposes. (GASB, *Comprehensive Implementation Guide (2004)*, 7.380.)

[159] GASB, *Comprehensive Implementation Guide (2004)*, 7.381.

as RSI.[161] Otherwise, the requirements regarding form and content are identical, whether the budgetary comparison is presented as a basic financial statement or as RSI. The budgetary comparison must be presented at least at the same degree of detail as the statement of revenues, expenditures, and changes in fund balances (by function).[162]

At minimum, the budgetary comparison must include the following:

- *Original budget.* GAAP define the *original budget* as "the first complete appropriated budget."[163] Amounts automatically carried over from one budget to the next—such as encumbrances that are subject to automatic reappropriation—should be included as part of this original budget. Likewise, the original budget should be adjusted to reflect reserves, transfers, allocations, and supplemental appropriations that occur prior to the start of the fiscal year. Sometimes a government fails to adopt a budget prior to the start of the new fiscal year. In that case, the law may provide some temporary funding expedient until a budget can be adopted. In those circumstances, the complete budget that is eventually adopted constitutes the original budget for purposes of the budgetary comparison presentation.
- *Final amended budget.* The final amended budget should reflect the ultimate appropriation authority for the period, even if, as sometimes permitted by law, some or all of the amendments occur after the close of the fiscal period.[164]
- *Actual amounts.* Because a goal of the budgetary comparison is to demonstrate legal compliance, the actual amounts of revenues and expenditures reported on that comparison should be presented using the same basis of budgeting used to present both the original and the final amended budget, *even when the basis of budgeting differs from GAAP.*

GAAP encourage governments to present a variance column to highlight differences between actual amounts and the final amended budget. Governments also have the option of presenting a variance column for differences between the original budget and the final amended budget.

There is nothing inherently favorable about reducing expenditures in the public sector if a reduction results from cutting services. Likewise, there is nothing inherently favorable about generating revenues in excess of a government's needs. Therefore, it is recommended that governments minimize the potential for misunderstanding by using neutral or mathematical terminology—such as *over/under*—to describe variances rather than the more subjective terms *favorable/unfavorable* commonly encountered in private-sector cost accounting.

A government can take one of two approaches to format the budgetary comparison: the budget document approach or the financial statement approach.

---

[160] A government must present all required budgetary comparisons in the same manner (i.e., basic financial statement or RSI). As already noted, the GFOA has formally recommended that this budgetary comparison be presented as a basic governmental fund financial statement. Also as noted previously, RSI must be used if a perspective difference (difference between the framework used for budgeting and the fund structure used for financial reporting) is so significant as to render a reconciliation between the basis of budgeting and GAAP of limited value.

[161] GASB, *Comprehensive Implementation Guide (2004)*, appendix 7-1, illustration A.

[162] GASB Statement No. 34, paragraph 131.

[163] GASB Statement No. 34, paragraph 130a.

[164] GASB Statement No. 34, paragraph 130b

- *Budget document approach.* Many practitioners directly concerned with the budgetary comparison are more familiar with the budget document than they are with the GAAP financial statements. Accordingly, the budgetary comparison may be presented using the same format, terminology, and classifications used in the budget document.
- *Financial statement approach.* Often the presentation method used for the budget document differs substantially from that used for the basic financial statements. Since the budgetary comparison is presented in connection with the basic financial statements, financial statement preparers are permitted to emphasize the link between the two by using the same format, terminology, and classifications used for the governmental fund statement of revenues, expenditures, and changes in fund balances.

With either approach, when the basis of budgeting differs from GAAP, a reconciliation must be provided between the two bases.[165]

PROPRIETARY FUND FINANCIAL STATEMENTS

GAAP prescribe three basic financial statements for proprietary funds: statement of net assets/balance sheet; statement of revenues, expenses, and changes in fund net assets/equity; and statement of cash flows.

Proprietary fund statement of net assets/balance sheet

The statement of net assets/balance sheet is the basic statement of position for proprietary funds.

Format

A government may present its government-wide statement of position using either a net assets format or a balance sheet format. The same two options also apply to presenting the statement of position for proprietary funds. In the case of the government-wide financial statements, the statement title (statement of net assets) and the terminology used to describe the difference between assets and liabilities (net assets) should be the same, regardless of the formatting option selected. In the case of proprietary funds, however, the basic statement of position may be described as a *balance sheet* if the balance-sheet format is used. Likewise, the difference between proprietary fund assets and liabilities may be described as *equity* rather than as *net assets*.[166] In either case, the terminology and categories used for *net assets/equity* are the same as those described for the government-wide statement of net assets.

GAAP *require* that the proprietary fund statement of net assets/balance sheet classify assets and liabilities as *current* and *noncurrent*, while use of the relative order of liquidity approach is encouraged for the government-wide statement of net assets.[167]

In the private sector, the accumulated balance of certain items associated with the notion of *comprehensive income* must be displayed separately in the

---

[165] When the budgetary comparison is presented as a basic financial statement, this reconciliation is included as part of the notes to the financial statements. When the budgetary comparison is presented as RSI, the reconciliation is presented as part of the separate notes to RSI. Alternatively, the reconciliation may be presented on the face of the budgetary comparison itself or as an attached schedule. Chapter 11 includes a detailed discussion of this reconciliation.

[166] GASB Statement No. 34, paragraph 91.

[167] GASB Statement No. 34, paragraph 97.

equity section of the statement of position.[168] This formatting approach is inconsistent with GASB standards and therefore is not applicable even to those enterprise funds/business-type activities that elect to follow private-sector standards issued subsequent to November 30, 1989, as permitted by GASB Statement No. 20, *Accounting and Financial Reporting for Proprietary Funds and Other Governmental Entities That Use Proprietary Fund Accounting.*[169]

Major fund reporting for enterprise funds

GAAP require the same major fund reporting for enterprise funds described earlier for governmental funds. However, GAAP also indicate that internal service funds are *never* to be reported as major funds. Accordingly, the 10 percent criterion and the 5 percent criterion should be applied to the total for all enterprise funds and to the total for all governmental funds plus enterprise funds, respectively (based on the final adjusted balances reported in the funds).[170] When applying these criteria to enterprise funds, *revenues* and *expenses* should include *all* operating statement revenues and expenses (both operating and nonoperating) including *capital contributions, additions to endowments,* and *special items,* but not *extraordinary items.*[171] Each individual major enterprise fund must be reported in a separate column on the face of the proprietary fund statement of net assets/balance sheet. Nonmajor enterprise funds, if any, should be reported in a separate, aggregated *other enterprise funds* column.

If a government has only one nonmajor enterprise fund, that fund will necessarily have to be reported in its own separate column. The presentation of a separate column is *not* equivalent to classification as a major fund in such cases. To avoid potential misunderstandings, financial statement preparers are advised to use columnar labels that make it clear whenever a separate fund column is not a major fund.[172]

Separate reporting for internal service funds/total column enterprise funds

Data from enterprise funds normally are incorporated as business-type activities in the government-wide statement of net assets, just as data from governmental funds normally are incorporated as governmental activities in that same statement. Internal service funds, however, are in a unique situation. Although internal service funds are proprietary funds (like enterprise funds), they normally are consolidated as part of governmental activities because their primary customers typically are the governmental funds. Therefore, internal service funds should be reported in a separate aggregated column on the proprietary fund statement of net assets/balance sheet, immediately following the total column for all enterprise funds, so that the amounts reported in this latter column may be traced more easily to the business-type activities column of the government-wide statement of net assets.[173]

There is no GAAP requirement to eliminate interfund balances from the total column for enterprise funds reported on the proprietary fund statement of net assets/balance sheet, although governments are free to eliminate such internal balances if they desire to do so. Governments choosing to eliminate interfund balances may wish to consider presenting a separate

---

[168] See the Financial Accounting Standards Board's Statement No. 130, *Reporting Comprehensive Income.*
[169] GASB, *Comprehensive Implementation Guide (2004),* 7.315.
[170] GASB Statement No. 34, paragraph 96.
[171] GASB, *Comprehensive Implementation Guide (2004),* 7.288.
[172] GASB, *Comprehensive Implementation Guide (2004),* 7.286.
[173] GASB Statement No. 34, paragraph 96.

eliminations column immediately preceding the enterprise fund total column.

Reconciliation to the government-wide statement of net assets

Because proprietary funds use the same measurement focus and basis of accounting as the government-wide financial statements, there typically will be fewer differences between the amounts reported in the total column for enterprise funds and the amounts reported for business-type activities in the government-wide statement of net assets. The most likely reasons for differences are the following:

- "crossover" internal balances resulting from the "look-back" adjustment made both in the current year and in past years in connection with the consolidation of internal service funds;[174]
- voluntary assignment to *business-type activities* of direct costs incurred by governmental funds on behalf of enterprise funds reported as *business-type activities;*[175] and
- election to report one or more enterprise funds as *governmental activities* rather than as *business-type activities* for purposes of government-wide financial reporting.[176]

In all these cases, a reconciliation would be required between the total column for the enterprise funds and the business-type activities column of the government-wide statement of net assets, either on the face of the statement or as an accompanying schedule. Detailed information on the elements of this reconciliation should be provided, if needed, in the notes to the financial statements.[177]

Proprietary fund statement of revenues, expenses, and changes in fund net assets/equity

The proprietary fund statement of revenues, expenses, and changes in fund net assets/equity is the basic statement of activities for the proprietary funds. Unlike the governmental fund statement of activities, the focus here is on *expenses* rather than *expenditures.*

Format

In the private sector, certain items must be reported separately as *other comprehensive income* (immediately following *net income*).[178] This formatting approach is inconsistent with GASB standards and therefore is not applicable even to those enterprise funds/business-type activities that elect to follow private-sector standards issued subsequent to November 30, 1989, as permitted by GASB Statement No. 20.[179]

Operating versus nonoperating revenues and expenses

GAAP require that the statement of revenues, expenses and changes in fund net assets/equity for proprietary funds distinguish operating from nonoperating revenues and expenses. The goal of this requirement is to display the extent to which an enterprise's operating expenses were covered by revenues generated by its principal ongoing operations.[180] GAAP do not provide an authoritative definition of *operating* and *nonoperating* revenues and expenses for this purpose, although GAAP suggest that financial state-

---

[174] See discussion of internal service fund consolidation in chapter 8.
[175] See discussion of assignment of direct costs in chapter 8.
[176] See previous discussion of activity columns.
[177] Detailed information is necessary if aggregated information in the summary reconciliation obscures the nature of the individual elements of a particular reconciling item.
[178] FASB Statement No. 130, *Reporting Comprehensive Income.*
[179] GASB, *Comprehensive Implementation Guide (2004),* 7.315. For example, despite FASB Statement No. 133, *Accounting for Derivative Instruments and Hedging Activities,* a gain or loss associated with the hedging of a foreign currency exposure may *not* be treated as part of comprehensive earnings.
[180] GASB, *Comprehensive Implementation Guide (2004),* 7.330.

ment preparers consider the authoritative guidance on identifying *cash flows from operating activities* in arriving at their own definition.[181] Items commonly included in the *nonoperating* category include the following:

- taxes;
- certain nonexchange fees and charges;
- interest;
- appropriations (note that GAAP expressly indicate that a state appropriation to a university may *not* be classified as an operating revenue);[182]
- contributions; and
- operating grants.

Investment income should only be classified as operating revenue if an entity's primary activity is investing. Thus, investment income of a public-entity risk pool would not qualify as operating revenue because the primary purpose of such a pool is to provide risk financing.[183] Likewise, income on a college's endowment would not qualify as operating revenue.[184]

Presentation of revenues   Revenues should be reported by major source. GAAP also require that revenues used as security for revenue bonds be identified separately. All the same, no special indication of pledged revenues is required if essentially all revenues of a given proprietary fund are pledged. Also, if different revenues are pledged to support different debt issues, there is no requirement that the different revenues be reported separately (which is the function of segment disclosure).

The presentation of revenues should reflect the effect of discounts and allowances, to be accomplished in one of two ways. One approach is to report revenues on a net basis, with discounts and allowances disclosed separately, either parenthetically or in the notes to the financial statements. The other approach is to report gross revenues followed immediately by deductions for discounts and allowances to arrive at net revenues.[185] Either way, any subsequent adjustments needed to obtain the appropriate balance in a revenue-related allowance for doubtful accounts would be made directly to revenue.[186]

Order of presentation   The following order should be followed in presenting the statement of revenues, expenses, and changes in fund net assets/equity:
- operating revenues;
- operating expenses;
- operating income (loss);
- nonoperating revenues and expenses;
- income before . . . (as appropriate);[187]
- capital contributions (for instance, from grantors and developers);[188]
- additions to endowments;

---

[181] GASB Statement No. 34, paragraph 102.
[182] GASB, *Comprehensive Implementation Guide (2004)*, 7.330.
[183] GASB, *Comprehensive Implementation Guide (2004)*, 7.329.
[184] GASB, *Comprehensive Implementation Guide (2004)*, 7.331.
[185] GASB Statement No. 34, footnote 41.
[186] GASB, *Comprehensive Implementation Guide (2004)*, 7.316. Note that adjustments to an allowance for doubtful accounts unrelated to revenue (e.g., loans receivable) would be treated as an expense. (GASB, *Comprehensive Implementation Guide (2004)*, 7.313.)
[187] This line should be labeled based on a government's specific situation. For example, a government with only capital contributions following this line would report *income before capital contributions*, while a government with both capital contributions and extraordinary items would report *income before capital contributions and extraordinary items*.

- special items;
- extraordinary items;
- transfers;
- increase (decrease) in net assets/equity;
- net assets/equity – beginning of period; and
- net assets/equity – end of period.

Major fund reporting

Governments should apply major fund reporting to the proprietary fund statement of revenues, expenses, and changes in fund net assets/equity in the same way described for the proprietary fund statement of net assets/ balance sheet.

Separate reporting for internal service funds/total column enterprise funds

Internal service funds should be reported separately on the statement of revenues, expenses, and changes in fund net assets/equity, immediately following the total column for enterprise funds, to facilitate tracing amounts between the fund financial statements and the government-wide financial statements.

Again, there is no requirement that interfund activities be eliminated from the total column for enterprise funds. If they wish, governments are free to consolidate interfund activity to the extent that such consolidations do not have the practical effect of removing interfund services provided or used between functions from the government-wide statement of activities, thereby distorting the cost data for functional activities reported in that statement. Governments choosing to eliminate interfund activity from the proprietary fund statement of activities may wish to consider presenting a separate *eliminations* column immediately preceding the enterprise fund total column.

Reconciliation to the government-wide statement of activities

The numbers appearing in the proprietary fund statement of revenues, expenses, and changes in fund net assets/equity for *total enterprise funds* may differ from those reported in the *business-type activities* column of the government-wide statement of activities.[189] A reconciliation of such differences should be provided, either on the face of the statement or as an accompanying schedule. Detailed information on the elements of this reconciliation should be provided, if needed, in the notes to the financial statements.[190]

Proprietary fund statement of cash flows

The statement of cash flows is the third basic financial statement for proprietary funds. It is also required as a third basic financial statement for virtually all private-sector business enterprises and nonprofit organizations. Nonetheless, there are critical differences between the statement of cash flows prepared for such entities and that prescribed for governmental entities.[191]

---

[188] GAAP do not define a *capital contribution*. GAAP do mention, however, that the reassignment of a general government capital asset to an enterprise fund would fall into this category in the proprietary fund financial statements, although it would be reclassified as a transfer in the government-wide financial statements. (GASB, *Comprehensive Implementation Guide (2004)*, 7.335.) Technically speaking, capital contributions are a subcategory of nonoperating revenues.

[189] As noted earlier, reasons for the difference might include 1) "cross-over" internal balances produced by a look-back adjustment connected with the consolidation of an internal service fund, 2) an assignment to *business-type activities* of direct costs incurred by governmental funds on behalf of enterprise funds reported as *business-type activities*, and 3) the election to report one or more enterprise funds as *governmental activities* rather than as *business-type activities* for purposes of government-wide financial reporting.

[190] Detailed information is necessary if aggregated information in the summary reconciliation obscures the nature of the individual elements of a particular reconciling item.

A statement of cash flows is never a required basic financial statement for discretely presented component units when they are included within the financial reporting entity.[192] However, if a component unit does not provide required cash flows information in a separately issued report, that information would need to be reported elsewhere within the reporting entity's comprehensive annual financial report.[193]

Focus

The focus of the statement of cash flows may be either *cash* or *cash and cash equivalents*. *Cash* includes:

- cash on hand;
- cash on deposit;
- cash in restricted accounts; and
- a position in a cash and investment pool that has the same characteristics as a demand deposit (resources can be deposited or withdrawn without notice or penalty).

GAAP define a *cash equivalent* as a short-term, highly liquid investment that is readily convertible to known amounts of cash and matures within three months of the date it is acquired by the entity. For example, a six-month U.S. Treasury bill bought within three months of maturity would qualify as a cash equivalent. However, that same U.S. Treasury bill bought six months before maturity would *not* become a cash equivalent as it entered its last three months. Whether an asset is a cash equivalent is determined only once, when the asset is first acquired.

Including cash equivalents is optional. If they wish, governments may choose to focus on cash alone. Furthermore, governments may adopt their own definition of *cash equivalents*, provided their definition is *more restrictive* than the GAAP definition. For example, a government is free to define cash equivalents so as to eliminate resources held in restricted accounts. Governments enjoy no similar flexibility regarding the definition of cash. Thus, for example, a government must include cash held in restricted accounts as part of the *cash* balance it reports on the statement of cash flows.

As its name implies, the statement of cash flows is concerned solely with flows of cash (and cash equivalents). Consequently, *only transactions that affect an entity's cash account typically should be reported in the statement of cash flows*. Accordingly, the following transactions would *not* be reflected in the statement of cash flows:

- receipt of the proceeds of refunding bonds if the refunded debt qualifies for defeasance and the cash is placed directly in escrow;
- receipt of bond proceeds related to financing authorities if the proceeds are delivered directly to the intended recipients rather than to the financing authority;
- commodities and similar noncash items (for example, federal surplus food used in school lunch programs), even though they may be reported as revenues and expenses in the statement of revenues, expenses, and changes in fund net assets/equity; and
- rollovers of certificates of deposit.[194]

---

[191] The authoritative guidance for the private-sector statement of cash flows can be found in FASB Statement No. 95, *Statement of Cash Flows*. The authoritative guidance in the public sector is provided by GASB Statement No. 9, *Reporting Cash Flows of Proprietary and Nonexpendable Trust Funds and Governmental Entities That Use Proprietary Fund Accounting* (as amended).

[192] GASB, *Comprehensive Implementation Guide (2004)*, 2.2 and 7.374.

[193] GASB, *Comprehensive Implementation Guide (2004)*, 7.373. See also chapter 13.

There are some exceptions to the basic rule that only cash (and cash equivalents) are reported on the statement of cash flows. One exception is checks and warrants, which, as a matter of convenience, are considered cash flows when issued rather than when presented for payment.[195] Likewise, a cash balance cannot be less than zero; therefore a negative position in a cash account should be treated as tantamount to a borrowing and reported as a cash flow.[196] Finally, changes in the fair value of investments subject to fair value reporting and classified as cash equivalents should be recognized as cash flows from investing activities when they occur.

Gross versus net reporting   In most instances, GAAP require that cash flows be reported *gross* rather than *net*. Special exceptions apply to the following situations, where cash flows may be reported at their *net* rather than their *gross* amounts:
- items whose turnover is quick, whose amounts are large, and whose maturities are short (certain investments, loans receivable, and debt), provided the original maturity of the asset or liability is three months or less, or[197]
- governmental enterprises whose assets for the most part are highly liquid investments and that have little or no debt outstanding during the period.[198]

Format   GAAP require that cash flows be classified into one of four categories:
- cash flows from operating activities;
- cash flows from noncapital financing activities;
- cash flows from capital and related financing activities; and
- cash flows from investing activities.

Cash flows from operating activities generally include all cash flows related to transactions and events reported as components of *operating income* in the statement of revenues, expenses, and changes in fund net assets/equity. In addition, the operating activities category is used for any cash inflow or outflow that cannot properly be classified in one of the other three categories (for example, the receipt and return of customer deposits[199]).[200] Cash flows in this category must be reported by major categories of receipts and payments.[201] At minimum, the amounts that should be reported separately are receipts from customers, receipts connected with interfund services, payments to suppliers of goods or services, payments to employees for services, and payments connected with interfund services.[202]

---

[194] For this purpose, a *rollover* is the extension of the maturity date of a certificate of deposit.

[195] GASB, *Comprehensive Implementation Guide (2004)*, 2.11.

[196] An inflow in *cash flows from noncapital financing activities* would be reported the year of the "borrowing," and an outflow the following year. (GASB, *Comprehensive Implementation Guide (2004)*, 2.11.)

[197] Such items function essentially as cash equivalents, even though they might be classified as investments. GASB Statement No. 9, paragraph 13.

[198] GASB Statement No. 9, paragraph 14.

[199] GASB, *Comprehensive Implementation Guide (2004)*, 2.50.

[200] GASB Statement No. 9, 16-19.

[201] In the private sector, cash flows from operating activities *may* be presented in the form of a reconciliation between *net income* and *cash flows from operating activities*. In this case, the entity is said to be using the *indirect method* of reporting cash flows from operating activities. This option is *not* available to governmental entities under GASB Statement No. 9, as amended by GASB Statement No. 34, paragraph 105. As described later, estimation techniques based on changes in receivables and payables may be used if the accounting system does not provide information on major categories of receipts and payments.

[202] GAAP require separate reporting of *cash flows from operating activities* involving other funds of the primary government (GASB Statement No. 9, paragraph 31). This specific provision does *not* extend to transactions with discretely presented component units. All the same, note disclosure may be necessary pursuant to the requirement to disclose, for each major component unit, the nature and amount of sig-

Interest receipts rarely qualify for inclusion as part of cash flows from operating activities.[203] The exception to this rule is loans that: 1) are made to fulfill government social programs rather than for income or profit; *and* 2) directly benefit individual constituents of the government (examples are low-income housing loans and student loans).[204] *Program loans* typically refer to loans that meet *both* of these criteria. The making and collection of program loans also are classified as *cash flows from operating activities.*

Cash flows from noncapital financing activities include borrowing and repayments (principal and interest) of debt that is *not* clearly attributable to capital purposes.[205] For example, borrowings to finance program loans would properly be reported in this category, even though the loans themselves would be treated as part of cash flows from operating activities, as just discussed. Similarly, this category is used to report grant proceeds not specifically restricted to capital purposes, as well as grant payments (both capital[206] and otherwise) to other entities.[207] In addition, the noncapital financing category includes transfers to and from other funds (except when a transfer is *received* for capital purposes). Finally, tax receipts not attributable to capital purposes also are reported in this category, along with any interest paid on noncapital-related vendor payables.[208]

Cash flows from capital and related financing activities include the borrowing and repayment (principal and interest) of debt clearly attributable to capital purposes. This category also is used to report the proceeds of capital grants and contributions, as well as transfers from other funds for capital purposes. Payments related to the acquisition, construction, or improvement of capital assets also are reported in this category.[209]

In addition, the capital and related financing activities category serves to report cash flows resulting from the sale or involuntary conversion of capital assets (such as insurance proceeds resulting from the loss of a capital asset). Likewise, cash flows from capital-type special assessments are reported in this category. Also, tap fees in excess of the actual cost of connection are reported in this category if they are to be used for capital purposes, as are taxes levied specifically for capital purposes or related debt service.[210]

Interest capitalization is ignored for purposes of the statement of cash flows. In other words, interest payments should be reported as *interest payments* rather than as *capital acquisition*, even though the payments may be capi-

nificant transactions with the primary government and other component units. (GASB, *Comprehensive Implementation Guide (2004),* 7.338.)

[203] This is in contrast to the treatment accorded both interest revenue and interest expense under FASB Statement No. 95.

[204] GASB Statement No. 9, paragraph 19, and GASB, *Comprehensive Implementation Guide (2004),* 2.55.

[205] Capital purposes include capital acquisition, construction, or improvement, including capital lease repayments.

[206] From the perspective of the fund reporting cash flows, a transaction is only "capital-related" if the fund itself acquires a capital asset as a result.

[207] For this purpose a *grant* would *not* include payments in furtherance of a proprietary fund's own operating activities. Thus, cash flows related to a "grant" that reimbursed a nonprofit organization for services it provided in furtherance of the proprietary fund's operations would be properly classified as cash flows from *operating* activities.

[208] GASB Statement No. 9, paragraphs 20-22.

[209] Once again, this treatment differs substantially from that prescribed under FASB Statement No. 95, where capital outlays are classified as cash flows from investing activities (investment in property, plant, and equipment).

[210] GASB Statement No. 9, paragraphs 23-25.

talized in the statement of position and not reported as *interest expense* in the statement of revenues, expenses, and changes in fund net assets/equity.[211]

Cash flows from investing activities include receipt of interest (except on program loans),[212] loan collections (except for program loans),[213] proceeds from the sale of investments, receipt of interest on customer deposits, and changes in the fair value of investments subject to fair value reporting and classified as *cash equivalents.* Cash outflows in the investing activities category include loans made to others (except for program loans)[214] and the purchase of investments.[215]

Exhibit 10-3 summarizes the various categories of cash flows. It should be noted that *prior* period adjustments do *not* result in cash flows in the *current* period. If a prior period adjustment affects the opening balance of *cash and cash equivalents*, it should be reflected as a restatement of that balance.

Reconciliation

Ordinarily, there is a difference between cash flows from operating activities (as reported on the statement of cash flows) and operating income (as reported on the statement of revenues, expenses, and changes in fund net assets/equity). GAAP require that the financial statements draw users' attention to this important difference by providing a reconciliation of these two amounts. This reconciliation should be presented either on the face of the statement of cash flows or as a schedule accompanying that statement. The most common elements of this reconciliation are illustrated in Exhibit 10-4.

Noncash investing, capital, or financing transactions

It is understandable, as noted earlier, that the statement of *cash* flows would be limited to actual inflows and outflows of *cash* (and cash equivalents). Nonetheless, financial statement users still need information on certain noncash activities that otherwise would fail to be reported either in the statement of revenues, expenses, and changes in fund net assets/equity or in the statement of cash flows.[216] Specifically, information is needed regarding noncash transactions that meet two criteria: the transaction affects recognized assets or liabilities; *and,* had it involved cash, the transaction would *not* properly have been classified as cash flows from operating activities.

This information may be presented in either narrative or tabular form on a separate schedule accompanying the statement of cash flows. When a single transaction involves both cash and noncash components (for instance, the initiation of a capital lease involving a down payment) this schedule should "clearly describe the cash and noncash aspects" of the transaction.[217] A good example of a noncash transaction that would require disclosure on this schedule but that might easily be overlooked: net appreciation/depreciation in the value of investments reported at fair value (but *not* classified as cash equivalents).

---

[211] GASB, *Comprehensive Implementation Guide (2004),* 2.67.

[212] Interest collected on program loans is reported as a cash inflow in the *cash flows from operating activities* category.

[213] Principal collected on program loans is reported as a cash inflow in the *cash flows from operating activities* category.

[214] The cash outflows related to program loans made to individuals are reported in the *cash flows from operating activities* category.

[215] GASB Statement No. 9, paragraphs 26-28.

[216] These items are commonly known as *balance-sheet transactions* (for instance, a government acquires an asset in return for agreeing to assume the related debt).

[217] GASB Statement No. 9, paragraph 37.

EXHIBIT 10-3
Common inflows and outflows reported on the statement of cash flows

Cash inflows			
• cash sales of goods and services • collections of receivables related to sales of goods and services • collection of principal and interest on program loans • collection of customer deposits	• debt proceeds other than from capital debt (including debt used to finance program loans) • grants available for operating purposes • transfers available for operating purposes • taxes available for operating purposes	• capital debt proceeds • capital grant proceeds • capital contributions • transfers received for capital acquisition • proceeds of the disposition of capital assets • proceeds of capital-type special assessments • taxes restricted for capital purposes or capital-related debt service	• loan collections (except for program loans) • sales of investments • interest received (except on program loans) • increase in fair value of investments subject to fair value reporting and classified as cash equivalents
↓	↓	↓	↓
Cash flows from operating activities	Cash flows from noncapital financing activities	Cash flows from capital and related activities	Cash flows from investing activities
↑	↑	↑	↑

Cash outflows			
• payments to vendors • payments to employees • payments of benefits on behalf of employees • liquidation of liabilities related to the provision of goods and services • payments of taxes, duties, fines, fees and penalties • return of customer deposits • program loans	• debt service on debt used for other than capital or related purposes • grants to others (including capital grants) • transfers to other funds (including transfers for capital or related purposes)	• debt service on capital-related debt • payments related to the acquisition, construction, or improvement of capital assets	• loans made to others (except for program loans) • purchase of investments • decrease in fair value of investments subject to fair value reporting and classified as cash equivalents

Traceability to statement of fund net assets (balance sheet)　GAAP specifically indicate that "the total amounts of cash and cash equivalents at the beginning and end of the period shown in the statement of cash flows should be easily traceable to similarly titled line items or subtotals shown in the statements of financial position as of those dates."[218] Accordingly, one of four approaches must be taken when cash and cash equivalents are included as part of restricted assets:

- Report the portion of restricted assets that represents cash and cash equivalents as a separate line item on the statement of position.
- Report the amount of cash and cash equivalents included as part of restricted assets parenthetically on the statement of position.[219]
- Report the amount of cash and cash equivalents included as part of restricted assets parenthetically on the statement of cash flows.[220]
- Provide a reconciliation on the face of the statement of cash flows.

Estimating cash flows from operating activities　As noted in the previous discussion, cash flows from operating activities need to be reported by major categories of receipts and payments. Esti-

---

[218] GASB Statement No. 9, paragraph 8.
[219] For example: "Restricted assets (including $5,800 of cash and cash equivalents)."
[220] For example: "Cash and cash equivalents – end of period (including $5,800 reported as part of restricted assets)."

EXHIBIT 10-4
Common differences between operating income and cash flows from operating activities

Transaction	Effect on operating income	Effect on cash flows from operating activities	Necessary adjustment to *operating income* in reconciliation	Elements of reconciliation
				Start: *Operating income*
Sales on credit (i.e., creation of accounts receivable)	Increase	None	Subtract to arrive at net cash flows	Subtract net increase in receivables (or add net decrease in receivables)
Collection of receivables	None	Increase	Add to arrive at net cash flows	
Incurrence of payables and other operating liabilities	Decrease	None	Add to arrive at net cash flows	Subtract net decrease in liabilities (or add net increase in liabilities)
Liquidation of payables and other operating liabilities	None	Decrease	Subtract to arrive at net cash flows	
Purchase of inventories	None	Decrease	Subtract to arrive at net cash flows	Subtract net increase in inventories (or add net decrease in inventories)
Consumption of inventories	Decrease	None	Add to arrive at net cash flows	
Depreciation expense	Decrease	None	Add to arrive at net cash flows	Add back depreciation expense and amortization expense
Amortization expense	Decrease	None	Add to arrive at net cash flows	
				Finish: *net cash flows from operating activities*

mates may be used for this purpose, based upon changes in related receivable and payable accounts. Assume, for example, that an enterprise fund reported the following items on its operating statement:

Revenues:	
Operating revenues	$ 639,744
Other revenues	34,506
Total operating revenues	$ 674,250
Expenses:	
Salaries and benefits	$ 545,201
Supplies and materials	86,950
Repairs and maintenance	385,489
Utilities	11,460
Bad debt expense	16,696
Other operating expenses	134,518

Depreciation	405,132
Total operating expense	$1,585,446
Operating Income (loss)	$ (911,196)

Two of these items, by definition, do not involve cash flows: *bad debt expense* and *depreciation expense*, and so may ignored. Furthermore, rather than trying to separate cash flows related to *operating revenues* from cash flows relating to *other revenues*, it will simply be assumed, as a matter of convenience in this illustration, that all of the *other revenues* were received in cash. That leaves a need to estimate three specific types of cash flows from operating activities: cash received from customers, cash paid to employees, and cash paid to suppliers.

Cash received from customers can be estimated by 1) treating all revenues of the period and the beginning balance of customer receivables as cash inflows, 2) treating all customer payables at the end of the period as reductions of cash inflows, and 3) treating an increase/decrease in the allowance account related to customer receivables as a reduction/increase in cash inflows, as follows:

Operating revenues	$639,744
Customer receivables – beginning	152,641
Customer receivables – ending	(195,595)
Increase in bad debt reserve	(16,696)
Cash receipts from customers (estimate)	$580,094

Cash paid to employees can be estimated by 1) treating all salaries and benefits expense of the period and the beginning balance of salaries and benefits payable as cash outflows, 2) treating the beginning balance of compensated absences payable as a cash outflow, and 3) treating the ending balance of both salaries and benefits payable and compensated absences payable as reductions of cash outflows, as follows:

Salaries and benefits	$545,201
Salaries and benefits payable – beginning	23,533
Compensated absences – beginning	18,160
Salaries and benefits payable – ending	(27,721)
Compensated absences – ending	(26,320)
Cash paid to employees (estimate)	$532,853

Cash paid to suppliers can be estimated by 1) treating all vendor-related expenses of the period and the beginning balance of accounts payables as cash outflows and 2) treating the ending balance of accounts payable as a reduction of cash outflows, as follows:

Supplies and materials	$ 86,950
Repairs and maintenance	385,489
Utilities	11,460
Other operating expenses	134,518
Accounts payable – beginning	90,336
Accounts payable – ending	(106,870)
Cash paid to suppliers (estimate)	$601,883

The net result of these calculations would be to report the following amounts as *cash flows from operating activities*:

Cash received from customers	$ 580,094
Other operating cash receipts	34,506
Cash paid to employees	(532,853)
Cash paid to suppliers for goods and services	(601,883)
Net cash used in operating activities	$(520,136)

FIDUCIARY FUND FINANCIAL STATEMENTS

GAAP prescribe up to two basic financial statements for fiduciary funds:
- Statement of fiduciary net assets (required for all fiduciary funds).
- Statement of changes in fiduciary net assets (required for all fiduciary funds except agency funds).[221]

Statement of fiduciary net assets

The statement of fiduciary net assets is the basic statement of position for the fiduciary funds.

Format

The fiduciary fund statement of position must employ the net assets format. Unlike the government-wide statement of position and the proprietary fund statement of position, there is no option of substituting a balance sheet format. No total column should be presented as the statement does *not* support amounts reported in the government-wide statement of net assets.

Presentation of assets and liabilities

Assets should be subdivided into major categories (such as cash and cash equivalents, receivables, investments, assets used in operations). In the case of pension plans and other postemployment benefit plans, the principal subdivisions of receivables and investments also should be reported.[222]

Liabilities

The statement of fiduciary net assets should include only *accounting* liabilities. Accordingly, no liability should be reported for the unfunded *actuarial* accrued liability of pension trust funds.[223]

Presentation of net assets

GAAP prescribe that net assets be reported in three categories on both the government-wide and proprietary fund statements of position: invested in capital assets, net of related debt; restricted; and unrestricted. This requirement specifically does *not* apply to the fiduciary fund statement of position.[224] Instead, net assets should be reported as "assets held in trust for pension/other postemployment benefits [if a pension (and other employee benefit) trust fund is reported], pool participants [if an investment trust fund is reported], and other purposes [if a private-purpose trust fund is reported]." Of course there should be no net assets associated with agency funds, because all assets reported in agency funds must be offset by a corresponding liability.[225]

---

[221] GASB Statement No. 34, paragraph 110.

[222] GASB Statement No. 25, *Financial Reporting for Defined Benefit Pension Plans and Note Disclosures for Defined Contribution Plans*, paragraph 21, and GASB Statement No. 43, *Financial Reporting for Postemployment Benefit Plans Other Than Pension Plans*, paragraph 19.

[223] If all or a portion of this amount has been converted into a pension-related liability, that liability must be reported, since it would then qualify as an *accounting* liability rather than an *actuarial* liability.

[224] GASB Statement No. 34, paragraph 108.

[225] GASB Statement No. 34, paragraph 110.

Reporting by fund type

GAAP require that governmental and enterprise fund financial reporting focus on major individual funds. Fiduciary funds, however, are never reported as major funds. Therefore, the focus of reporting for the fiduciary fund statement of position should be the various fiduciary fund types [pension (and other employee benefit) trust funds, investment trust funds, private-purpose trust funds, and agency funds]. That is, the statement should present one column for each fund type reported.[226] Fiduciary-type discretely presented component units are treated no differently than other fiduciary funds (i.e., they are combined into the appropriate fund-type column).

Statement of changes in fiduciary net assets

The statement of changes in fiduciary net assets is the basic statement of activities for fiduciary funds.

Format

The statement of changes in fiduciary net assets is unique in that all changes in net assets are classified simply as either *additions* or *deductions*.[227] The difference between additions and deductions is then reported as the net increase (or decrease) in fiduciary net assets.[228] In the case of pension plans and other postemployment benefits plans, GAAP prescribe that contributions be reported separately by source (contributions from employer(s), contributions from plan members,[229] and contributions from other sources[230]). Likewise, the following components of net investment income should be reported within the *additions* category for both pension (and other employee benefit) trust funds and investment trust funds:

- Net appreciation (depreciation) in the fair value of investments. Realized and unrealized gains and losses should not be separately displayed in the financial statements.
- Interest income, dividend income, and other income not included as part of the net appreciation (depreciation) in the fair value of investments. For this purpose, interest income would be based exclusively on the stated rate of interest.[231]
- Total investment *expense* (such as investment management fees, custodial fees, and all other significant investment-related costs).[232]

GAAP allow governments to report the first two components as a single amount.[233]

The deductions section of the statement of changes in fiduciary net assets should include all items that reduce fiduciary net assets except for *investment-related expenses*, which, as explained, are properly reported as a *reduction in the additions category rather than as a deduction in their own right*. Deductions of pension plans and other postemployment benefit plans would include benefit payments, refunds, and administrative costs.[234]

---

[226] Separate columns would be acceptable for individual pension and other postemployment benefit plans in the absence of a separately issued financial report providing the necessary individual plan information.

[227] Although the terms *revenues* and *expenses* would be acceptable for describing certain items within these broader categories, it is recommended that the use of these terms be avoided in connection with fiduciary funds.

[228] GASB Statement No. 34, paragraph 109.

[229] This amount would include employee contributions transmitted by the employer.

[230] For example, a state pension contribution on behalf of a local school district's teachers.

[231] Interest adjustments due to the amortization of premiums, discounts, and issuance costs would already be reflected in the net appreciation (depreciation) in the fair value of investments.

[232] GASB Statement No. 25, paragraph 29.

[233] GASB Statement No. 25, paragraph 29d, GASB Statement No. 43, paragraph 27d.

Examples of deductions for investment pools could include dividends to shareholders, shares redeemed, and administrative costs.

No total column should be presented as the statement does *not* support amounts reported in the government-wide statement of activities.

Reporting by fund type

As with the statement of fiduciary net assets, the statement of changes in fiduciary net assets reports information separately by fund *type* rather than by major fund. Fiduciary-type discretely presented component units are treated no differently than other fiduciary funds (i.e., they are combined into the appropriate fund-type column).[235]

Agency fund reporting

Agency funds are excluded altogether from this presentation because they do *not* report *net assets* (and therefore cannot report changes in net assets). All the same, agency funds *must* include a statement of changes in assets and liabilities within the comprehensive annual financial report, although they may *not* do so within the basic financial statements.[236]

[234] GASB Statement No. 25, paragraph 30, and GASB Statement No. 43, paragraph 28.
[235] Separate columns would be acceptable for individual pension and other postemployment benefit plans in the absence of a separately issued financial report providing the necessary individual plan information.
[236] GASB, *Codification of Governmental Accounting and Financial Reporting Standards,* 2200.181e(3).

11

Notes to the Financial Statements

The basic financial statements for state and local governments comprise three essential elements: the government-wide financial statements, the fund financial statements, and the notes to the financial statements. Chapter 10 focused on the first two elements. This chapter completes the discussion of the basic financial statements by examining the requirements of generally accepted accounting principles (GAAP) regarding the disclosures to be furnished in the notes to the financial statements.

SUMMARY OF SIGNIFICANT ACCOUNTING POLICIES

GAAP require that the basic financial statements be accompanied by a summary of significant accounting policies (SSAP).[1] The SSAP may be formatted either as the first note to the financial statements, or as a separate presentation immediately preceding the notes.[2] (In practice, governments rarely use the separate presentation.)

The basic guidance governing SSAP contents appears in Accounting Principles Board (APB) Opinion No. 22, *Disclosure of Significant Accounting Policies.* As a basic rule, APB Opinion No. 22 requires that the SSAP address the following situations:

- any selection of an accounting treatment when GAAP permit more than one approach (for instance, selection of the consumption method or the purchases method to account for inventory reported in governmental funds);

---

[1] National Council on Governmental Accounting (NCGA) Statement 1, *Governmental Accounting and Financial Reporting Principles,* paragraph 158.
[2] NCGA Interpretation 6, *Notes to the Financial Statements Disclosure,* paragraph 8. GAAP require that each basic financial statement include a reference to the notes to the financial statements (for example, "See notes to the financial statements" or "the notes to the financial statements are an integral part of this statement"). If the SSAP is formatted separate from the notes, then this reference should be to both the SSAP and the notes.

- accounting practices unique to state and local governments (such as using the modified accrual basis of accounting for governmental funds); and
- unusual or innovative applications of GAAP.

Consistent with these general principles, the SSAP should provide all disclosures discussed in the following paragraphs that are relevant to a government's circumstances.

Description of the government-wide financial statements

Despite their name, the government-wide financial statements do not, in fact, incorporate all funds and component units of a government. Specifically, GAAP direct financial statement preparers to exclude fiduciary funds and fiduciary-type component units from the government-wide presentations.[3] Therefore, to avoid any potential confusion regarding the scope of the government-wide presentations, the SSAP should disclose the omission of fiduciary funds and fiduciary-type component units.[4]

Description of the financial reporting entity

Because accounting and financial reporting place a premium on economic substance over legal form, the financial reporting entity often includes more than one legally separate entity.[5] To ensure that financial statement users understand what has or has not been included within a given financial report, GAAP require that the SSAP provide the following information concerning the financial reporting entity:

- description of the component units included within the financial reporting entity;
- description of the relationship between the component units and the primary government;
- discussion of the criteria for including component units within the financial reporting entity;
- discussion of how component units are reported (i.e., blended versus discrete presentation);[6] and
- information on how to obtain the separately issued financial statements of component units.[7]

If the government is a component unit of a larger financial reporting entity, the primary government should be identified and the nature of the relationship disclosed.[8]

Sometimes a government may appoint the voting majority of board members for another entity without establishing a bond of financial accountability with that entity that would justify its inclusion as a component unit. GAAP refer to entities that meet this description as *related organizations*. The SSAP should briefly disclose the nature of the relationship between the primary government and the related organization Likewise, a related organization should disclose its relationship with the primary government in its own separately issued financial statements.[9]

---

[3] See the discussion of the government-wide financial statements in chapter 10.
[4] Governmental Accounting Standards Board (GASB) Statement No. 34, *Basic Financial Statements—and Management's Discussion and Analysis—for State and Local Governments*, paragraph 115a.
[5] The financial reporting entity is the subject of chapter 4.
[6] GASB, *Comprehensive Implementation Guide (2004)*, 4.113.
[7] GASB Statement No. 14, *The Financial Reporting Entity*, paragraph 61.
[8] GASB Statement No. 14, paragraph 65.
[9] GASB Statement No. 14, paragraph 68.

Columnar descriptions

The basic fund financial statements focus on major governmental funds and major enterprise funds. Nonmajor governmental funds and nonmajor enterprise funds are reported in the aggregate, regardless of fund type. Other sorts of funds (i.e., internal service funds and fiduciary funds) are reported by fund type.

GAAP require that governments provide a description of the types of activities reported in each major fund column and in each fund-type column appearing in the basic fund financial statements unless the caption of the related column makes the nature of those activities self-evident. In the case of the general fund, this description may be more or less generic. For other major funds, however, the description must be specific to the government's circumstances.[10] Specific descriptions also are required for each of the fund-type columns reported in the basic fund financial statements. No description is required for columns that aggregate data from nonmajor governmental and enterprise funds.[11]

Measurement focus and basis of accounting for government-wide financial statements

Governmental *activities* are accounted for in the government-wide financial statements using the economic resources measurement focus and the accrual basis of accounting. Conversely, governmental *funds* employ the current financial resources measurement focus and the modified accrual basis of accounting for these same activities. As a result, there are usually significant differences between the governmental activities columns reported in the government-wide financial statements and the corresponding total columns reported in the governmental fund financial statements. GAAP require that the SSAP specifically address the measurement focus and basis of accounting used in preparing the government-wide financial statements, thereby explaining, in part, why a reconciliation is necessary between the government-wide and the governmental fund presentations.[12]

Revenue recognition policies

Under the modified accrual basis of accounting, revenues are recognized only as they become *susceptible to accrual* (measurable and available). Because of differences in circumstances (differences in the property tax calendar, for instance) and because of the inherent flexibility of this criterion, the timing of revenue recognition for a given revenue source may vary considerably among governments. Accordingly, GAAP direct governments to disclose in the SSAP their own policy on applying the *susceptible to accrual* criterion for major revenue sources.[13] This disclosure should address the availability period used for revenue recognition purposes and the specific types of major revenue sources that meet this criterion.

Policy for eliminating internal activity from the statement of activities

GAAP require that governments disclose their policy for eliminating internal activity from the statement of activities. The general intent of this disclosure is to "give readers a general understanding of how internal activity is reported in the statement of activities." That is, the *policy* intended here is essentially a description of how a government has exercised its professional judgment in implementing the GAAP *requirement* to consolidate internal

---

[10] It is recommended that the fund's classification by fund type also be disclosed if not otherwise discernable.
[11] GASB Statement No. 38, *Certain Financial Statement Note Disclosures*, paragraph 6.
[12] GASB Statement No. 34, paragraph 115b.
[13] NCGA Statement 1, paragraph 69, and GASB Statement No. 38, paragraph 7.

activities in the government-wide statement of activities. Specific elements of this disclosure could include the following:

- an explanation that direct expenses are not eliminated from the various functional categories, whereas indirect expenses are (presuming a separate column is not used to allocate indirect expenses);
- a discussion of the types of internal payments that are treated as program revenue (i.e., interfund services provided and used); and
- a discussion of the types of internal payments that are treated as a reduction of expense (i.e., reimbursements).[14]

Policy for capital assets   GAAP require that policies related to accounting for capital assets be disclosed. Examples of policies that might be disclosed under this rule include the following:

- the monetary threshold for capitalization (for instance, capital assets with an initial cost of $5,000 or more);[15]
- the method(s) used for estimating historical cost or fair value, when estimates are required;[16]
- the extent of infrastructure reporting for networks and subsystems acquired prior to fiscal periods ending after June 30, 1980;[17]
- the method used to calculate depreciation expense (straight line, for example) and the estimated useful lives of its capital assets for purposes of allocating depreciation expense to the appropriate periods; and
- the decision to follow the modified approach for one or more networks or subsystems of its infrastructure assets.

Furthermore, GAAP specifically require governments that elect to use the modified approach for one or more networks or subsystems of infrastructure assets to describe that approach.[18] Although not specifically addressed by GAAP, such a description of the modified approach might include the following elements:

- a statement that the government has made the commitment to preserve and maintain certain networks or subsystems of infrastructure assets at a condition level determined by the government;
- identification of the party or parties within the government responsible for determining the appropriate condition level at which such assets are to be maintained;
- a statement that no depreciation expense is reported for such assets, nor are amounts capitalized in connection with improvements that lengthen the lives of such assets, unless the improvements also increase their service potential;
- a statement that the government maintains an inventory of these infrastructure assets and performs periodic condition assessments to establish that the predetermined condition level is being maintained; and

[14] GASB Statement No. 34, paragraph 115c and GASB, *Comprehensive Implementation Guide (2004)*, 7.350.
[15] Government Finance Officers Association (GFOA) recommended practice on "Establishing Appropriate Capitalization Thresholds for Tangible Capital Assets" (2001).
[16] GASB, *Comprehensive Implementation Guide (2004)*, 7.354.
[17] Also, for certain small governments, the extent of infrastructure reporting for networks or subsystems acquired prior to the implementation of GASB Statement No. 34. (GASB, *Comprehensive Implementation Guide (2004)*, 7.355.)
[18] GASB Statement No. 34, paragraph 115e.

- a statement that the government makes annual estimates of the amounts that must be expended to preserve and maintain these infrastructure assets at the predetermined condition level.

Description of program revenues

GAAP require that the government-wide statement of activities be presented using a net-cost format. That is, in the statement of activities, revenues from nontax sources directly related to individual functions (user fees and charges, restricted grants, and restricted contributions) are to be presented as a reduction of the total cost of providing program services. This format enables a government to arrive at the net amount of program cost to be financed from the government's own resources.[19]

Governments frequently dedicate a portion of their own resources to support specific functions (e.g., dedicated taxes). Such amounts do *not* constitute program revenues, despite their close relationship with specific functions. Therefore, to avoid any potential confusion, GAAP require that a government describe in the SSAP the types of transactions that are reported as program revenues.[20]

Allocation of indirect expenses

There is a presumption that all of the expenses reported in governmental functions represent *direct costs* of those functions. Sometimes charges to governmental functions for centralized services will automatically include a component designed to recover administrative (overhead) costs, which are *indirect costs*. As a practical concession, GAAP do not require governments to identify and eliminate such incidental indirect costs from functional expense. Governments that take advantage of this concession must disclose in the SSAP that functional expenses include an element of indirect cost.[21]

Also, if governments elect to allocate costs (in a separate column) in the government-wide statement of activities, the basis for making the allocations to individual functions should be disclosed.[22]

Definition of operating and nonoperating revenues

GAAP require that proprietary funds distinguish between *operating* and *nonoperating* revenues and expenses. While GAAP provide no definitive guidance on how to make this distinction, governments are advised that they may wish to *consider* the criteria used for identifying *cash flows from operating activities* in the statement of cash flows.[23] The definition of *operating* and *nonoperating* revenues and expenses ultimately selected needs to be disclosed.[24]

Applicability of optional private-sector guidance

Governments have the *option* of consistently implementing private-sector guidance issued after November 30, 1989, for both business-type activities and enterprise funds, provided the standards so adopted do not conflict with or contradict the Governmental Accounting Standards Board's (GASB) own guidance.[25] GAAP specifically indicate that the SSAP should mention whether this option has been selected.[26]

---

[19] Program revenues are discussed in chapter 10.
[20] GASB Statement No. 34, paragraph 115f.
[21] GASB Statement No. 34, paragraph 43.
[22] GASB Statement No. 34, paragraph 115f.
[23] GASB Statement No. 34, paragraph 102.
[24] GASB Statement No. 34, paragraph 115g.
[25] GASB Statement No. 34, paragraphs 17 and 93-95.

Cash and cash equivalents

GAAP specifically allow a government to choose either *cash* or *cash and cash equivalents* to serve as the focus of the statement of cash flows. Moreover, GAAP allow considerable flexibility in the definition of what constitutes a *cash equivalent*.[27] A government's election of either focus should be disclosed in the SSAP, consistent with the general principle of APB Opinion No. 22 that a selection among GAAP options must always be disclosed in the SSAP. If *cash equivalents* are reported, they should be defined.

Flow assumption for restricted resources

Net assets are segregated into three categories on the government-wide statement of net assets: 1) invested in capital assets, net of related debt; 2) restricted; and 3) unrestricted. In practice, it is common for governments to have the option of using either restricted or unrestricted resources to make certain payments (such as capital construction costs being financed partially from restricted grants and bond proceeds and partially from the government's own resources). Accordingly, governments must select a flow assumption to determine which assets (restricted or unrestricted) are being used when both restricted and unrestricted assets are available for the same purpose. GAAP require that this flow assumption be disclosed in the SSAP.[28]

Investment basis

The SSAP should indicate the valuation basis used for investments. In general, governments are required to report their investments at fair value. However, governments also typically have the *option* of reporting certain investments at cost or amortized cost rather than at fair value.[29] The SSAP should indicate whether the government has made use of this option and, if so, for which specific categories of investments. Also, if a government uses some basis other than quoted market prices to estimate the fair value of its investments, the methods and significant assumptions used for this purpose should be disclosed.[30] Likewise, if an entity must estimate the fair value of its position in a governmental external investment pool because it cannot obtain the information it needs from the pool sponsor, the entity should disclose the methods and significant assumptions used for making the estimate, as well as the reason an estimate was needed.[31]

Allocation of investment income among funds

It is presumed under GAAP that investment income is reported in the same fund that reports the underlying investment. However, it is common for income on investments to legally accrue to the benefit of some other fund. In that case, the investment income is reported directly in the fund to which it accrues.[32] GAAP require that a government disclose whenever the income from investments reported in one fund is assigned directly to another fund.[33] It is recommended that this disclosure be made in the SSAP.

[26] GASB Statement No. 34, paragraph 115d. Naturally, governments that do not report enterprise funds or business-type activities should not make this disclosure.

[27] See chapter 10.

[28] GASB Statement No. 34, paragraph 115h. Note that arbitrage regulations typically make it desirable for a government to assume that the proceeds of tax-exempt debt are used first in a project funded from bond proceeds and other sources, because such an assumption reduces the amount of *excess arbitrage earnings* that otherwise would be rebatable to the federal government. Also, see GASB's *Comprehensive Implementation Guide (2004)*, 7.147.

[29] See the discussion of investment valuation in chapter 12.

[30] GASB Statement No. 31, *Accounting and Financial Reporting for Certain Investments and for External Investment Pools*, paragraph 15a.

[31] GASB Statement No. 31, paragraph 15e.

[32] GASB Statement No. 31, paragraph 14.

Inventories and prepaid items

GAAP specifically allow governments to account for inventories and prepaid items in governmental funds using either the purchases method or the consumption method.[34] Consistent with the requirements of APB Opinion No. 22, the option selected must be disclosed in the SSAP. Also disclosed should be the basis used to value inventories (cost basis, for instance), as well as the method used to apply that basis (specific identification, weighted average, first-in-first-out, last-in-first-out).

TOPICAL NOTE DISCLOSURES

In addition to the SSAP, the notes to the financial statements must provide all other disclosures necessary for an adequate understanding of the government-wide and fund financial statements.

Budgetary information

Four basic disclosures must be made in the notes to the financial statements regarding the annual appropriated budget:

1. *Budgetary expenditures in excess of appropriations.* GAAP require the disclosure of the excess of budgetary expenditures over appropriations in individual funds. This requirement applies only to budgetary comparisons required in conjunction with the basic financial statements (i.e., general fund and major special revenue funds).[35]

2. *Material violations.* GAAP require the disclosure of all "material violations of finance-related legal and contractual provisions."[36] Violations of the annual (or biennial) appropriated budget, if material, clearly fall within this category, even for funds other than the general fund and major special revenue funds. Disclosure should include the actions taken to address budgetary violations.[37]

3. *Basis of budgeting.* Governments often adopt budgets using a basis of budgeting that differs from GAAP (for instance, cash basis, cash basis plus encumbrances, modified accrual basis plus encumbrances). Naturally, *legal compliance* can only be demonstrated if both budgetary and actual amounts are presented using the basis of budgeting, even if it differs from GAAP. Therefore, GAAP require that the notes to the financial statements disclose the basis of budgeting.[38]

4. *Reconciliation between the basis of budgeting and GAAP.* When there is a difference between the basis of budgeting and GAAP, a reconciliation must be provided for the general fund and for any major individual special revenue funds for which budgetary comparisons are presented. The reconciliation should be provided either on the face of the budgetary comparison statement or in the notes to the financial statements.[39]

Whenever budgetary comparisons are presented as required supplementary information (RSI) rather than as a basic governmental fund financial

---

[33] GASB Statement No. 31, paragraph 15f.

[34] See chapter 5.

[35] GASB Statement 34, paragraph 131 as interpreted by GASB, *Comprehensive Implementation Guide (2004)*, 7.390.

[36] NCGA Statement 1, paragraph 11. This requirement is addressed in more detail later in this chapter.

[37] GASB Statement No. 38, paragraph 9, and GASB, *Comprehensive Implementation Guide (2004)*, 7.390.

[38] NCGA Interpretation 6, paragraph 5. If the basis of budgeting is GAAP, that fact should be disclosed. It is *not* appropriate to describe the basis of budgeting as GAAP if there are significant modifications of GAAP for specific items (e.g., encumbrances, capital leases, on-behalf benefit payments).

[39] NCGA Interpretation 10, *State and Local Government Budgetary Reporting,* paragraph 15.

statement, disclosures 1, 3, and 4 on the previous page would be reported as notes to RSI rather than as part of the notes to the financial statements. The disclosure of material violations, on the other hand, would always be included in the notes to the financial statements.

At least two approaches can be taken to preparing the reconciliation between GAAP and the basis of budgeting. One approach is to reconcile the budgetary and GAAP operating statements. The other is to reconcile fund balance as reported on a GAAP basis and fund balance as reported on the basis of budgeting. In some cases, governments elect to provide both types of reconciliation, although a dual presentation is not required.

The budget-to-GAAP reconciliation must be presented in sufficient detail to be meaningful. GAAP indicate that an adequately detailed reconciliation should at least provide separate information on each of the following differences between the basis of budgeting and GAAP:

- *Basis differences* occur when the basis of budgeting (cash basis plus encumbrances, for instance) differs from the basis of accounting prescribed by GAAP for governmental funds (modified accrual basis).
- *Timing differences* occur when the period used for budgeting differs from the period used for GAAP reporting (for example, a special revenue fund that uses a grant-year budget rather than a fiscal-year budget).
- *Perspective differences* occur when the framework used for budgeting differs from the fund structure used for financial reporting (for example, a single unified budget for the entire government).
- *Entity differences* occur when the budget includes programs or entities that do not fall within the financial reporting entity as defined by GAAP, or vice versa.

Again, these categories provide the *minimum level of detail* required by GAAP. That is, if a fund had items from each of these categories, the reconciliation would need to present *at least* four reconciling amounts.[40] For instance, it would be inappropriate to combine basis and perspective differences into a single reconciling amount. Financial statement preparers, however, need not employ the terminology used by GAAP (*perspective difference,* for instance) if they believe that some other terminology would be more readily understandable to financial statement users.

If no budgetary comparison is presented for a major special revenue fund because it does not have an annual (or biennial) appropriated budget, it is recommended that fact be disclosed in the notes. It also is recommended that the notes disclose for which governmental funds annual (or biennial) appropriated budgets are adopted.

Cash deposits with financial institutions

GAAP require five types of disclosure regarding cash deposits with financial institutions:

- legal and contractual provisions governing deposits;
- policies governing deposits;
- exposure to custodial credit risk as of the date of the statement of position;
- defaults and recovery of prior-period losses; and

---

[40] "More comprehensive budgetary presentations are generally to be preferred over the minimum standards." (NCGA Interpretation 10, paragraph 13.)

- exposure to foreign currency risk.

Legal and contractual provisions governing deposits

The notes to the financial statements should disclose any legal restrictions governing cash deposits with financial institutions (such as insurance and collateralization requirements). Naturally, any material violations of these requirements during the period also must be disclosed, as well as actions the government has taken to address those violations.[41]

Policies governing deposits

The notes should disclose a government's policies concerning foreign currency risk (if exposed) and custodial credit risk. If a government does *not* have a policy for one of these risks to which it is exposed, that fact must, itself, be disclosed.[42]

To qualify as an *investment policy*, a given item must either be formally adopted in some way by the governing body or be incorporated into a contract. Managerial "policies" that have not been approved by the board or past practice alone are *not* sufficient to constitute a *policy* for this purpose.[43]

Sometimes governments adopt the state law or regulation governing deposits as their policy. In such cases, it is not enough simply to provide a citation of the relevant state law or regulation without also providing a reasonable description of its specific provisions.[44]

Exposure to custodial credit risk as of the date of the statement of position

"The *custodial credit risk* for deposits is the risk that, in the event of the failure of a depository financial institution, a government will not be able to recover deposits or will not be able to recover collateral securities that are in the possession of an outside party" [emphasis added].[45]

Any portion of a deposit *not* covered by depository insurance[46] is exposed to custodial credit risk in *any* of the following three situations:
- deposits are uncollateralized;
- collateral for deposits is held by the pledging financial institution; and/or
- collateral for deposits is held by the pledging institution's trust department or agent, but not in the name of the depositor government.[47]

When deposits are exposed to custodial credit risk at the end of the period, a government must disclose the fact that balances are uninsured, the nature of the exposure (i.e., one of the three situations just described), and the amount thereby exposed.[48]

Typically there is a difference between the amount reported for deposits on a government's books of account (the *book balance*) and the corresponding amount reported on the books of the financial institution holding the deposit (the *bank balance*). For example, if a government issues a check, the amount of the check is deducted immediately from the government's book

---

[41] GASB Statement No. 3, *Deposits with Financial Institutions, Investments (including Repurchase Agreements), and Reverse Repurchase Agreements*, paragraphs 65-66. GASB Statement No. 38, paragraph 9.
[42] GASB Statement No. 40, paragraph 6.
[43] GASB, *Comprehensive Implementation Guide (2004)*, 1.20.
[44] GASB, *Comprehensive Implementation Guide (2004)*, 1.23.
[45] GASB Statement No. 40, *Deposit and Investment Risk Disclosures*, glossary.
[46] Some governments use irrevocable standby letters of credit to secure uninsured deposits. The scope of an irrevocable standby letter of credit normally is substantially the same as insurance, in which case the two situations should be treated the same way for purposes of custodial credit risk disclosure. Naturally, this treatment would not be appropriate if the letter of credit were issued by the bank itself or by one of the bank's affiliates. (GASB, *Comprehensive Implementation Guide (2004)*, 1.96.)
[47] GASB Statement No. 3, paragraph 67, as amended.
[48] GASB Statement No. 40, paragraph 8.

balance; the financial institution deducts the amount from the bank balance only when the check is presented for payment. In the same way, a government will increase its book balance for deposits as soon as additional resources are sent to the financial institution, while the financial institution will increase the bank balance only when those additional resources are actually received. For purposes of disclosing custodial credit risk, the bank balance rather than the book balance is relevant. For example, if a government has written a check for $100, but that check has not yet been cashed, it could still lose the $100 if its deposit is uninsured and the bank fails. Therefore, GAAP require that custodial credit risk be disclosed for the *bank balance* of deposits with financial institutions.[49]

Cash deposit applies to any government resources that could qualify for federal depository insurance. Thus, cash deposits encompass negotiable order of withdrawal (NOW) accounts, nonnegotiable certificates of deposit (CDs),[50] and bank investment contracts.[51] Conversely, cash deposits do *not* encompass guaranteed investment contracts[52] or *negotiable* CDs. (Negotiable CDs are much less common than their nonnegotiable counterparts and typically are issued in denominations of $1 million).[53]

Sometimes a single financial institution establishes a collateral pool to secure multiple governmental depositors. The amount of this single-institution collateral pool may be insufficient to protect the full amount of uninsured deposits of all governmental depositors in the event of a default. For example, a collateral pool of $2 million may be intended to cover $2.5 million in uninsured governmental deposits. In this case, a government depositor should consider its uninsured deposits to be collateralized only to the extent of its pro rata claim to the pool's assets ($2 million/$2.5 million = 80 percent collateralization).[54]

Conversely, several financial institutions may join together to form a single collateral pool for the benefit of all of their governmental depositors. Once again, the pooled collateral may be insufficient to cover the full amount of uninsured deposits of all governmental depositors. However, unlike the situation described for a single-institution collateral pool, it is unlikely that all depositors covered by a multiple-institution collateral pool would need coverage simultaneously (it is unlikely that all participating banks would go bankrupt at the same time). Therefore, a government with uninsured deposits covered by a multiple-institution collateral pool may consider itself collateralized to the extent that the pool's resources are sufficient to cover all uninsured deposits of the particular participating financial institution in which it keeps its deposits.[55]

Furthermore, a statute or pooling agreement may provide for additional assessments on a pro rata basis against members of a multiple-institution collateral pool in the event that the pool's resources prove insufficient to cover the losses of a member financial institution that fails. If the ability to make these pro rata assessments exists, the deposits covered by the multi-

[49] GASB, *Comprehensive Implementation Guide (2004)*, 1.73.
[50] GASB, *Comprehensive Implementation Guide (2004)*, 1.1.
[51] GASB, *Comprehensive Implementation Guide (2004)*, 1.105.
[52] GASB, *Comprehensive Implementation Guide (2004)*, 1.105.
[53] GASB, *Comprehensive Implementation Guide (2004)*, 1.103.
[54] GASB, *Comprehensive Implementation Guide (2004)*, 1.100.
[55] GASB, *Comprehensive Implementation Guide (2004)*, 1.102.

ple-institution collateral pool would be considered insured, and therefore not exposed to custodial credit risk.[56]

Defaults and recovery of prior-period losses

If the government incurs a loss as a result of a default on its deposits, this loss should be disclosed in the notes if it is not separately visible on the face of the financial statements. Likewise, the subsequent recovery of prior-period losses should be disclosed if not otherwise visible in the financial statements.[57]

Exposure to foreign currency risk

When a government maintains deposits denominated in a currency other than the U.S. dollar, it exposes itself to the risks associated with currency fluctuation. Therefore, in addition to the disclosures already described, governments maintaining deposits denominated in a foreign currency must disclose the value of such deposits in U.S. dollars. Separate disclosure is necessary for each foreign currency in which deposits are maintained.[58]

Investments

GAAP require the following types of disclosures regarding investments:
- participation in external investment pools;
- information concerning realized gains and losses (when disclosed);
- legal and contractual provisions governing investments;
- investment policies;
- exposure to custodial credit risk as of the date of the statement of position;
- defaults and recovery of prior-period losses; and
- other credit risk exposure.

Participation in external investment pools

GAAP set two specific disclosure requirements for governments that participate in external investment pools. First, if the pool is *not* registered with the Securities and Exchange Commission (SEC), the government should describe any regulatory oversight of the pool and state whether the fair value of its position in the pool is the same as the value of the pool shares. Also, a government's involuntary participation in a pool should be disclosed.[59]

Information concerning realized gains and losses

Except for separately issued financial statements of governmental external investment pools, governments are *not* permitted to distinguish realized gains and losses from unrealized gains and losses on the face of the financial statements. Nonetheless, GAAP *permit* governments to disclose information on realized gains and losses in the notes to the financial statements. When this option is selected, governments must accompany their disclosure of realized gains and losses with the following additional interpretive information:
- an indication that the calculation of realized gains and losses is independent of the calculation of the net change in the fair value of investments; and
- an indication that realized gains and losses of the current year include unrealized gains and losses on those same investments that were recognized in previous periods as part of the net appreciation or depreciation in the fair value of investments.[60]

---

[56] GASB Statement No. 3, paragraph 11.
[57] GASB Statement No. 3, paragraph 75.
[58] GASB Statement No. 40, paragraph 17.
[59] GASB Statement No. 31, paragraph 15c and 15d.
[60] GASB Statement No. 31, paragraph 15.

Legal and contractual provisions governing investments

The notes should disclose any legal restrictions on investments (such as types of investments permitted). Any material violations of these requirements during the period also must be disclosed, as well as actions the government has taken to address those violations.[61] Investment polices (see below) may be framed more narrowly than legal or contractual provisions, so that compliance with the former implies compliance with the latter as well. In such cases, disclosure of the broader legal or contractual provisions is still required, nonetheless.[62]

Investment policies

The notes should disclose a government's policies concerning credit risk (including custodial credit risk), concentration risk, interest rate risk, and foreign-currency risk whenever it is, in fact, exposed to such risks. If a government does not have a policy that addresses one of these risks to which it is currently exposed, that fact must, itself, be disclosed.[63]

To qualify as an *investment policy*, a given item must either be formally adopted in some way by the governing body or be incorporated into a contract. Managerial "policies" that have not been approved by the board or past practice alone are *not* sufficient to constitute a *policy* for this purpose.[64]

Sometimes governments adopt the state law or regulation governing investments as their investment policy. In such cases, it is not enough simply to provide a citation of the relevant state law or regulation without also providing a reasonable description of its specific provisions.[65]

Exposure to custodial credit risk as of the date of the statement of position

"The *custodial credit risk* for investments is the risk that, in the event of the failure of the counterparty to a transaction, a government will not be able to recover the value of investment or collateral securities that are in the possession of an outside party" [emphasis added].[66]

Any investments that are both uninsured and unregistered are exposed to custodial credit risk in *either* of the following situations:
- investments are held by the counterparty; or
- investments are held by the counterparty's trust department or agent, but not in the name of the investor government.[67]

When investments are exposed to custodial credit risk at the end of the period, a government must disclose 1) their type, 2) their reported amount, and 3) how they are held.[68]

All deposits are potentially subject to custodial credit risk. Investments, however, are subject to custodial credit risk *only if they are evidenced by securities that exist in physical or book entry form.* Thus the following types of investment would *not* be subject to custodial credit risk disclosure because they do not meet this test:
- positions in external investment pools;
- positions in open-end mutual funds;
- securities underlying reverse repurchase agreements;
- limited partnerships;
- real estate;

---

[61] GASB Statement No. 3, paragraphs 65-66; GASB Statement No. 38, paragraph 9.
[62] GASB, *Comprehensive Implementation Guide (2004)*, 1.27.
[63] GASB Statement No. 40, paragraph 6.
[64] GASB, *Comprehensive Implementation Guide (2004)*, 1.20.
[65] GASB, *Comprehensive Implementation Guide (2004)*, 1.23.
[66] GASB Statement No. 40, *Deposit and Investment Risk Disclosures*, glossary.
[67] GASB Statement No. 3, paragraphs 68-69, as amended.
[68] GASB Statement No. 3, paragraphs 68-69, as amended..

- direct investments in mortgages and other loans;
- annuity contracts; and
- guaranteed investment contracts.[69]

In the case of securities lending arrangements, the notion of custodial credit risk applies either to the collateral (when reported as an asset) or to the underlying securities (when collateral is not reported as an asset).[70]

Custodial credit risk disclosure does *not* apply to investments that are held for purposes other than income or profit. Common examples would include interfund loans, equity in joint ventures, and interest-bearing receivables (e.g., tax receivables or student loans).[71]

Normally, custodial credit risk disclosure applies only to investments that are actually reported as assets in the financial statements. Thus, investments in escrow accounts associated with advance refundings that result in the defeasance of debt are *not* subject to custodial credit risk disclosure.[72]

There may be an interval between when a government purchases an investment (the trade date) and when it actually acquires that investment (the settlement date). Investment transactions should be recorded as of the trade date.[73] A government faces no custodial credit risk for investments prior to settlement (except to the extent that the counterparty holds a deposit or margin account against those investments). Therefore, purchases recorded on the balance sheet prior to settlement date are *not* subject to custodial credit risk disclosure. Conversely, governments continue to face custodial credit risk in connection with sold investments prior to settlement. Accordingly, such securities remain subject to custodial credit risk disclosure, even though they no longer appear on the balance sheet (an exception to the general rule described in the previous paragraph).[74]

As discussed earlier, custodial credit risk arises whenever uninsured and unregistered securities are either 1) held by the counterparty, or 2) held by the counterparty's trust department or agent, but not in the government's name. Several clarifications may be useful in this regard.

A government's custodial financial institution occasionally may purchase investments on a government's behalf. In such cases, the financial institution is actually playing two roles simultaneously. In one role, the custodial institution is the counterparty for investments it has purchased on the government's behalf (subject to custodial credit risk disclosure); its second role is to remain the government's agent for investments it holds, but did not purchase, on the government's behalf (*not* subject to custodial credit risk disclosure).[75] For this purpose, a *purchase* must be distinguished from a *settlement*. In the latter case, the financial institution is simply concluding a transaction initiated by the government, rather than initiating a transaction itself (compare, for example, a bank honoring a check presented

---

[69] GASB, *Comprehensive Implementation Guide (2004)*, 1.44. Investments that would be subject to custodial credit risk include U.S. Treasury bills, notes, and bonds; federal agency and instrumentality obligations, including asset-backed securities; corporate debt instruments, including commercial paper; corporate equity instruments; negotiable certificates of deposit; bankers' acceptances; shares in closed-end mutual funds (mutual funds that have a limited number of shares); and shares of unit investment trusts.

[70] GASB Statement No. 40, paragraph 10.

[71] GASB, *Comprehensive Implementation Guide (2004)*, 1.1-1.3.

[72] GASB, *Comprehensive Implementation Guide (2004)*, 1.4.

[73] GASB, *Comprehensive Implementation Guide (2004)*, 6.64.

[74] GASB, *Comprehensive Implementation Guide (2004)*, 1.108.

[75] GASB, *Comprehensive Implementation Guide (2004)*, 1.46.

for payment), and therefore is *not* considered to be acting as the counter-party.[76]

Many investments exist only in book-entry form, which is electronic form rather than paper securities. Book-entry securities typically are held by a custodial financial institution in the latter's Federal Reserve account or in a Depository Trust Company (DTC) account. The Federal Reserve or the DTC should *not* be treated as the custodian of book-entry securities; instead, they should be viewed as a "vault" for the participating custodial agent.[77]

Sometimes both the counterparty and a government's custodial agent are subsidiary banks of the same bank holding company. In such situations, both institutions are considered to constitute a single entity for purposes of assessing custodial credit risk, thereby making it necessary that the government's custodial agent be treated as a counterparty.[78]

In some situations, county treasurers purchase specific investments on behalf of individual government units and then hold those investments in the county's name. The county treasurer is *not* considered a counterparty in such a situation, provided that the county's underlying records identify the individual governments as owners.[79]

Book-entry securities are considered to be held *in the name of the government* if 1) they are held in a pledge account rather than a trading account, and 2) the government's claim to the collateral or investments is supported by the custodian's underlying records.[80]

In practice, securities are commonly held in *street name* or *nominee name* by financial institutions, brokers, and dealers on behalf of their clients. For classifying custodial credit risk, securities held in street or nominee name may be considered held *in the name of the government*, provided the custodian's underlying records adequately establish the government's interest in the securities.[81]

Defaults and recovery of prior-period losses

A government that incurs a loss as a result of a default on its investments should disclose this information in the notes if it is not separately visible on the face of the financial statements. Likewise, the subsequent recovery of prior-period losses should be disclosed if not otherwise visible in the financial statements.[82]

Other credit risk exposure

Credit ratings. The notes must disclose the credit ratings of all investments in debt securities, whether held directly or indirectly (i.e., through positions in external investment pools, money-market funds, bond mutual funds, or similar pooled investments of fixed-income securities). If no rating is available from a nationally recognized statistical rating organization (Fitch Ratings, Moody's Investors Service, Standard & Poor's), that fact should be disclosed.[83]

Financial statement preparers may consolidate their presentation of credit ratings by aggregating their disclosure by investment type or by

---

[76] GASB, *Comprehensive Implementation Guide (2004)*, 1.47.
[77] GASB Technical Bulletin 87-1, *Applying Paragraph 68 of GASB Statement 3*, paragraph 9.
[78] GASB Technical Bulletin 97-1, *Classification of Deposits and Investments into Custodial Credit Risk Categories for Certain Bank Holding Company Transactions*.
[79] GASB, *Comprehensive Implementation Guide (2004)*, 1.118.
[80] GASB Technical Bulletin 87-1, question 2.
[81] GASB, *Comprehensive Implementation Guide (2004)*, 1.64.
[82] GASB Statement No. 3, paragraph 75.
[83] GASB Statement No. 40, paragraph 7.

credit quality.[84] If issuers of securities obtain credit ratings from more than one nationally recognized statistical rating organization they must, at a minimum, disclose the least favorable rating issued. (They are permitted, but not required, to disclose other, more favorable ratings as well).[85]

It is not enough simply to indicate the different categories of credit ratings applicable to debt securities of a given type (e.g., "all mortgage bonds held by the government are rated either AAA or AA"). The dollar value in each ratings category must also be disclosed (e.g., "60 percent of the total dollar value of the government's mortgage bonds are rated AAA, while the remaining 40 percent are rated AA").[86]

In recent years, rating agencies have taken to using modifiers to "fine tune" credit ratings of AA/Aa or less. Moody's Investors Service, for instance, uses numerical modifiers (i.e., 1, 2, 3), while Fitch Ratings and Standard and Poor's use a plus or minus sign (+/-) for this same purpose. Governments are *not* required to disclose such modifiers as part of their credit risk disclosure.[87]

Naturally, the requirement to disclose credit ratings does not apply to debt securities of the U.S. government or obligations of U.S. government agencies that are *explicitly* guaranteed by the U.S. government. Examples of the latter include obligations of the Government National Mortgage Association (GNMA), the Export-Import Bank (EXIMBANK), and the Small Business Administration (SBA). Conversely, this exception does not extend to obligations of U.S. government instrumentalities, which are only *implicitly* guaranteed by the U.S. government. Examples of such securities would include those of the Federal National Mortgage Association (FNMA), the Federal Home Loan Banks (FHLB), the Federal Home Loan Mortgage Corporation (FHLMC), the Federal Farm Credit Banks (FFCB), and the Student Loan Marketing Association (SLMA).[88]

Not all of the debt securities of a particular issuer may be rated (e.g., guaranteed investment contracts). The issuer's credit rating is *not* equivalent to a rating for an individual debt security. Therefore, any debt security for which an individual rating has not been obtained should be disclosed as unrated.[89]

Typically, repurchase agreements function essentially as collateralized loans in which the government is the lender. In that case, the requirement to disclose credit ratings technically applies to the underlying debt securities offered by the borrower as collateral. As a practical matter, however, the securities underlying repurchase agreements often are either securities of the U.S. government or securities explicitly guaranteed by the U.S. government, which would not be subject to the requirement to disclose a credit rating.[90]

As noted earlier, the requirement to disclose credit ratings for debt securities applies regardless of whether those securities are held directly or indirectly. Thus, credit ratings for positions in pools or mutual funds that hold debt securities must be disclosed. When a debt security is held by a pool or

---

[84] GASB, *Comprehensive Implementation Guide (2004)*, 1.30.
[85] GASB, *Comprehensive Implementation Guide (2004)*, 1.29.
[86] GASB, *Comprehensive Implementation Guide (2004)*, 1.37.
[87] GASB, *Comprehensive Implementation Guide (2004)*, 1.33.
[88] GASB, *Comprehensive Implementation Guide (2004)*, 1.35.
[89] GASB, *Comprehensive Implementation Guide (2004)*, 1.31.
[90] GASB, *Comprehensive Implementation Guide (2004)*, 1.38.

mutual fund, it is the rating of the pool or fund that should be disclosed, not the rating of the underlying debt securities. Thus, rated investments in an unrated pool should be disclosed as unrated by pool participants.[91] Furthermore, the narrow restrictions placed on the types of investments that can be held by pools that elect to operate in accordance within the guidelines set by SEC Rule 2a7 do not eliminate the requirement to disclose a credit rating for the pool.[92]

Concentration risk. Credit risk also can arise in the wake of a failure to adequately diversify investments. Accordingly, the notes must disclose *concentration risk,* which is defined as positions of 5 percent or more in the securities of a single issuer. For this purpose, the term *issuer* should be understood as referring to the underlying investments themselves rather than to the investment-company manager or pool sponsor in the case of mutual funds, external investment pools, and other similar pooling arrangements. Furthermore, because of the minimal risk associated with U.S. government obligations and obligations explicitly guaranteed by the U.S. government, this requirement does not apply to concentrations in those particular types of investments.[93]

Affiliates and subsidiaries of parent companies engaged in similar activities and having similar economic characteristics may need to be treated as a single issuer for purposes of concentration risk disclosure.[94]

Interest-rate risk. Interest-rate risk arises because potential purchasers of debt securities will not agree to pay face value for those securities if interest rates subsequently increase, thereby affording potential purchasers more favorable rates on essentially equivalent securities. Accordingly, holders of debt securities in the situation just described face the prospect of a loss should those securities be sold prior to maturity, even though cash flows under the debt contract remain unaffected by changes in interest rates. Therefore, direct or indirect holders of debt securities must use one of five specified methods to disclose interest-rate risk.[95]

- *Specific identification.* Under this method, the notes provide an actual list of the maturities for different individual investments. As explained below, the maturity assigned to variable-rate debt should be the next reset date and this fact should be disclosed either as part of the narrative or in the form of a footnote to a schedule presenting interest-rate risk.[96] The same disclosure options (i.e., narrative or footnote) should be applied as well to any call options on debt securities held by the government.[97]

- *Segmented time distribution.* Under this approach the notes to the financial statements provide a schedule of maturities for debt securities grouped by period (e.g., maturities within six months, maturities within six months to one year, maturities within one to three years, maturities over three years). The maturity to be assigned a position in

[91] GASB, *Comprehensive Implementation Guide (2004),* 1.41.
[92] GASB, *Comprehensive Implementation Guide (2004),* 1.34.
[93] GASB Statement No. 40, paragraph 11.
[94] GASB, *Comprehensive Implementation Guide (2004),* 1.124.
[95] GASB Statement No. 40, paragraph 15.
[96] GASB, *Comprehensive Implementation Guide (2004),* 1.132.
[97] GASB, *Comprehensive Implementation Guide (2004),* 1.127.

a bond fund is the average maturity or duration of the underlying bonds.[98]

Participants in mutual funds and external investment pools often can liquidate their position on demand. Such a demand provision in no way changes the fact that the earnings of the participant will be affected by the interest-rate risk exposure of the underlying securities in the fund or pool. Thus, the maturity to be assigned to a position in a mutual fund or external investment pool is the duration or weighted average maturity of the underlying debt securities.[99]

As explained earlier, interest-rate risk is really the risk of being "trapped" for an extended period with an interest rate that is lower than market. A variable-rate feature on debt can eliminate much of this risk by assuring purchasers of debt securities that the interest rate they will be paid will be periodically adjusted to reflect changes in the market rate of interest. Consequently, the maturity assigned to a pure variable-rate debt security would be its next reset date. For example, a 10-year bond due contractually to mature in 10 years but scheduled to have its interest rate reset daily, weekly, or monthly, would be classified as having a maturity as of the next reset date for purposes of interest-rate risk disclosure.[100]

As just explained, variable-rate debt can significantly reduce an investor's exposure to interest-rate risk. Certain features in a variable-rate debt contract, however, could alter this effect. For example, a maximum interest rate provision (i.e., "cap") could have the practical effect of reducing or eliminating altogether the variability of variable-rate debt. Thus, variable-rate debt securities that are approaching a cap in a rising interest-rate environment would behave, for all practical purposes, much like fixed-rate securities from the perspective of interest-rate risk and the disclosure would need to be adjusted accordingly.[101]

- *Weighted average maturity.* Under this method, the focus of disclosure is the average maturity of outstanding debt, taking into account not only the timing of maturities, but also the amounts. When investments are callable, a government needs to make assumptions regarding their effective maturity as well as disclose those assumptions.[102]

- *Duration.* Duration allows for one of three different approaches: *Macauley duration, modified duration,* and *effective duration.* Only the last of these approaches, however, reflects the timing and amount of variable cash flows. Consequently, the use of the third approach, effective duration, may be desirable or even necessary in the case of debt securities involving call options and prepayment provisions (e.g., collateralized mortgage obligations).[103]

- *Simulation model.* A fifth alternative is to focus directly on the potential effect of an eventual change in interest rates by using a simulation model (e.g., anticipated effect of a 100 basis-point change, anticipated

---

[98] GASB, *Comprehensive Implementation Guide (2004)*, 1.129.
[99] GASB, *Comprehensive Implementation Guide (2004)*, 1.130.
[100] GASB, *Comprehensive Implementation Guide (2004)*, 1.131.
[101] GASB, *Comprehensive Implementation Guide (2004)*, 1.131.
[102] GASB, *Comprehensive Implementation Guide (2004)*, 1.133.
[103] GASB, *Comprehensive Implementation Guide (2004)*, 1.134.

effect of a 200 basis-point change, etc.). A simulation model can involve either sensitivity analysis (e.g., market value models and option-adjusted spread models) or value-at-risk (e.g., variance/ co-variance, historical simulation, or Monte Carlo simulation). Normally, interest-rate risk results from increases in interest rates. However, the less traditional structure of some debt securities can have just the opposite effect (i.e., securities may lose value when interest rates decrease). Accordingly, while governments are permitted to make a presentation that shows the effect of changes in interest rates in both directions, they are only required to show changes in whichever direction would result in a loss of value.[104]

The method selected to disclose interest-rate risk should reflect how that risk is actually managed within the government. As a practical matter, investment managers may take different approaches for different types of investments. For example, managers may be satisfied with a less sophisticated method for short-term securities than for long-term securities, given the more limited exposure of the former to interest-rate risk. Likewise, different methods may be used for different types of investments. A government's interest-rate risk disclosure should properly reflect such differences. That is, a government is not required to use a single method of disclosing interest-rate risk for all of its debt securities.[105]

Furthermore, differences in the methods used to manage interest-rate risk may naturally occur over time or may follow a change in managers. Governments should change their method of disclosing interest-rate risk to reflect such changes as they occur. Such a change in disclosure would *not* violate the rule on the consistent application of accounting policies set by APB Opinion No. 20, *Accounting Changes*, because in such situations it is the object of reporting that has really changed (i.e., the method of managing investments) rather than the method of reporting, as such.[106] All the same, it is still necessary to disclose, in the period the change occurs, the nature of the change and the reason for it.

Disclosure is also required of any contractual terms (e.g., coupon multipliers, benchmark indices, reset dates, embedded options)[107] or other special factors that make debt investments highly sensitive to interest-rate changes. Such special factors might include, for example, the intent to hold long-term, fixed rate debt to maturity, the likelihood that embedded options may be exercised,[108] the expectation that caps or floors on variable-rate debt may be reached, the size of the portfolio relative to the gov-

---

[104] GASB, *Comprehensive Implementation Guide (2004)*, 1.135.

[105] GASB, *Comprehensive Implementation Guide (2004)*, 1.128.

[106] GASB, *Comprehensive Implementation Guide (2004)*, 1.126.

[107] GASB Statement No. 40, paragraph 16.

[108] Prepayments on collateralized mortgage obligations (CMOs) are affected by changes in interest rates. This fact alone, however, does not make every CMO "highly sensitive" to interest-rate risk. The reason is that CMOs can be structured to assign specific payment streams (e.g., principal, interest) to the holders of specific securities in a specific order. Thanks to these specialized groupings known as *tranches* (i.e., French for *slices*) some holders of CMOs will be highly exposed to interest-rate risk, while others will be effectively shielded from such risk. Thus, interest-only and principal-only tranches are, by nature, highly sensitive to interest-rate risk, as are Z tranches (typically paid indiscriminately from principal and interest payments received after all other tranches have been retired). Conversely, many planned amortization class tranches, targeted-amortization class tranches, and sequential-pay tranches can be fairly insensitive to changes in interest rates. (GASB, *Comprehensive Implementation Guide (2004)*, 1.142-1.145.)

ernment's cash flow needs, anticipated liquidity tightening, or the investment objectives of the portfolio.[109]

Foreign currency risk. When a government holds investments denominated in a currency other than the U.S. dollar, it exposes itself to the risks associated with currency fluctuation. Therefore, in addition to the disclosures already described, governments holding investments denominated in a foreign currency should disclose the value of such investments in U.S. dollars. Separate disclosure is necessary for each different foreign currency denomination. Furthermore, if a government has a position in more than one type of investment in a given foreign currency denomination, disclosure at that level of detail is required (i.e., by investment type in a given foreign currency denomination).[110] Foreign currency risk need not be a separate disclosure, as such, but may be combined with other disclosures related to foreign-denominated investments.[111] No special disclosure normally is required in connection with limited partnerships (unless the investment in the partnership is itself an investment in foreign currency investments) or international mutual funds (whose very name may be sufficient to alert financial statement readers to potential foreign currency risk).[112]

Derivatives

The public sector has adopted the private-sector definition of a *derivative*.[113] As the name implies, a *derivative* is a contract that *derives* its existence from the behavior of some variable, technically described as an *underlying* (e.g., a published interest rate), that is associated with a potential payment in one of two ways: 1) as a function of some other number ("notional/face/contract amount") in a formula, as in "underlying x notional amount = payment" or 2) as a trigger ("payment provision"), as in "if underlying exceeds threshold, then payment." Since many simple price calculations technically would meet the definition of a derivative as described thus far (e.g., a contract to purchase so many bushels of wheat [notional amount] at the price quoted on a given exchange [underlying]), a second requirement to qualify as a derivative is that the initial net investment (if any) be less than the notional amount (or the result of applying the notional amount to the underlying) *and* that the contract *not* require actual delivery (i.e., a derivative must be derived from something rather than the thing itself).

Some of the more common examples of derivative contracts encountered in the public sector include interest-rate swaps (i.e., exchanging fixed-rate interest payments for variable-rate interest payments or vice versa), basis swaps (e.g., exchanging a variable interest rate based on one index for a variable interest rate based on a different index), and swaptions (i.e., the option to participate in an interest-rate swap at some future date). Governments also sometimes use derivatives to protect themselves from swings in the price of commodities (e.g., electricity) and foreign exchange rates (e.g., in connection with foreign-denominated investments).

---

[109] GASB, *Comprehensive Implementation Guide (2004)*, 1.138.
[110] GASB Statement No. 40, paragraph 17.
[111] GASB, *Comprehensive Implementation Guide (2004)*, 1.152.
[112] GASB, *Comprehensive Implementation Guide (2004)*, 1.154-1.155.
[113] GASB Technical Bulletin, 2003-1, *Disclosure Requirements for Derivatives Not Reported at Fair Value on the Statement of Net Assets*, paragraph 3, adopts the definition of a derivative set forth in FASB Statement No. 133, *Accounting for Derivative Instruments and Hedging Activities*, as amended.

GAAP require five types of disclosure for governments with derivatives outstanding as of the end of the fiscal period:

- objectives;
- significant terms;
- fair value;
- associated debt; and
- risks.

These requirements do *not* apply to derivatives already reported on the face of the statement of position at fair value.[114] They also generally do *not* apply to derivatives that are embedded in a contract that is not itself a derivative (e.g., a call option that is written into a bond contract rather than written separately).[115]

Objectives

A government must explain why it is has entered into a derivative contract. In doing so, it should provide whatever context is necessary to explain the government's objectives and strategies in using derivatives. It also should indicate the specific types of derivatives used, including options purchased or sold.[116]

Significant terms

The significant terms of derivatives should be disclosed, including the following:[117]

- notional, face, or contract amount;
- underlying indexes or interest rates, including terms such as caps, floors, or collars (i.e., combination of cap and floor);
- options embedded in the derivatives;
- the date when the derivative became effective and when it is scheduled to terminate or mature; and
- the amount of cash paid or received when the derivative was initiated.

Fair value

A government needs to disclose the fair value of derivatives and the method used to determine that value (zero-coupon method, par-value method, option pricing model for derivatives that are themselves embedded in derivatives contracts), as well as any significant assumptions made if estimates are used (i.e., in the absence of quoted market prices).[118]

Associated debt

When the intended effect of a derivative is to create a synthetic interest rate (e.g., a variable-to-fixed interest rate swap), a government needs to disclose both the derivative's net cash flow and the debt service requirements of the associated debt.[119]

Assume, for example, that a government with variable-rate debt outstanding of $100 million and a current interest rate of 1.5 percent ($100 million x 1.5% = $1.5 million interest) wishes to enjoy the advantages of fixed-rate debt without actually redeeming its variable-rate bonds. It can accomplish this objective by entering into a contract to "swap" current and future variable-rate interest payments for another government's (counterparty) future 3.0 percent fixed-rate interest payments (i.e., $100 million x

---

[114] GASB TB 2003-1, paragraph 1.
[115] GASB TB 2003-1, paragraph 18.
[116] GASB TB 2003-1, paragraph 6.
[117] GASB TB 2003-1, paragraph 7.
[118] GASB TB 2003-1, paragraph 8.
[119] GASB TB 2003-1, paragraph 9.

3.0% = $3.0 million interest). The result would be a *synthetic* interest rate of 3.0 percent, calculated as follows:

Actual interest payments on debt	$1.5 million
Amount due to counterparty under swap contract $3.0 million	
Amount due from counterparty under swap contract ($1.5 million)	
Net payment under swap contract	$1.5 million
Total payments	$3.0 million
Synthetic interest rate (payments/notional amount)	3.0 percent

The appropriate disclosure in the situation just described is illustrated in the following (truncated) example:

Variable-rate bond		Interest rate	
Principal	Interest	swap, net	Total
$ 0	$1,500,000	$1,500,000	$3,000,000

Risks

Six different types of risk can arise in connection with derivatives. Disclosure should be limited to just those types of risks actually faced by the reporting government in connection with derivatives outstanding as of the end of the fiscal period.

It is important to emphasize that all of the information required in connection with risk disclosure for derivatives needs to be presented in this specific context. That is, information already presented elsewhere in some other context needs to be repeated once again as part of this disclosure.[120]

Credit risk. "Credit risk is the risk that a counterparty will not fulfill its obligations." There are five specific disclosures for credit risk:[121]
- credit ratings;
- maximum amount of loss (excluding collateral or other security);
- collateral or other security;
- information on any master netting arrangements to mitigate credit risk (a master netting agreement allows the parties to a contract to offset amounts they owe each other); and
- extent of diversification among counterparties.

Interest rate risk. If the practical effect of a derivative is to increase the risk of loss resulting from changes in interest rates (e.g., a swap from a fixed rate to a variable rate), the relevant facts should be disclosed.[122]

Basis risk. Basis risk arises when different indexes are used in connection with a derivative (e.g., both LIBOR and BMA[123]). In such cases, the government needs to disclose both the derivatives' payment terms and the payment terms of the government's associated debt.[124]

Termination risk. Termination risk arises when the unscheduled termination of a derivative could have an adverse effect on the government's asset or liability strategy or could lead to potentially significant unscheduled payments. When termination risk is present, a government needs to disclose the following:[125]
- any termination events that have occurred;

---

[120] GASB TB 2003-1, paragraph 10.
[121] GASB TB 2003-1, paragraph 10a.
[122] GASB TB 2003-1, paragraph 10b.
[123] LIBOR = London Inter-Bank Offering Rate; BMA = Bond Market Association.
[124] GASB TB 2003-1, paragraph 10c.
[125] GASB TB 2003-1, paragraph 10d.

- dates that a derivative may be terminated; and
- out-of-the-ordinary termination events contained in contractual documents.

Rollover risk. Rollover risk arises when a derivative associated with a government's variable-rate debt does not extend all the way to the maturity date of the associated debt, thereby creating a gap in the protection otherwise afforded by the derivative. When rollover risk arises, a government needs to disclose both the maturity of the derivative and the maturity of the associated debt.[126]

Market-access risk. Market-access risk arises when a government enters into a derivative in anticipation of entering the credit market at a later date, but may ultimately be prevented from doing so, thereby frustrating the purpose of the derivative. When market-access risk is present it should be described.[127]

Significant contingent liabilities

GAAP require that the notes to the financial statements disclose any situation where there is at least a reasonable possibility that assets have been impaired or that a liability has been incurred (pending litigation, for instance). Likewise, GAAP require disclosure if it is probable that an asset has been impaired or a liability has been incurred, but the effect of the impairment or liability has not been reflected in the financial statements because it cannot be estimated.

Sometimes it is *reasonably possible* that a loss or asset impairment falls somewhere within a monetary range, but only the low end of the range is considered *probable* and so is reflected on the balance sheet. In that case, the amount within the range that was not booked would be disclosed as a contingent liability in the notes to the financial statements.[128]

Any guarantee of indebtedness should be disclosed, even if there is only a remote chance that the government will be called on to honor its guarantee.[129] Likewise, disclosure should be made of any intra-entity guarantees of indebtedness (such as the general government guaranteeing the debt of a proprietary fund or a discretely presented component unit). Also, incurred but not reported claims (IBNRs) should be disclosed if 1) it is *probable* that the claim will, in fact, be asserted, *and 2)* it is *reasonably possible that the claim will prevail.* In practice, these criteria typically are applied to IBNRs based on a government's experience (trend data on claims filings) rather than on specific situations encountered.[130]

Encumbrances outstanding

Many governments allow encumbrances to lapse at year-end and then automatically reappropriate them as part of the subsequent year's budget. In that situation, GAAP require that the balance of encumbrances outstanding be disclosed in the notes to the financial statements (if not reported as a designation).[131]

---

[126] GASB TB 2003-1, paragraph 10e.
[127] GASB TB 2003-1, paragraph 10f.
[128] FASB Statement No. 5, *Accounting for Contingencies*, paragraph 10.
[129] FASB Statement No. 5, paragraph 12.
[130] GASB Statement No. 10, *Accounting and Financial Reporting for Risk Financing and Related Insurance Issues*, paragraph 58.
[131] NCGA Statement 1, paragraph 91(3); NCGA Interpretation 6, paragraph 4c.

Subsequent events

Sometimes it is important for readers of the financial statements to be aware of events and transactions that occur after the end of the fiscal period but prior to issuance of the financial statements. GAAP require that such subsequent events be disclosed in the notes to the financial statements. The most common subsequent events reported by state and local governments are debt issuances (such as the ultimate issuance of bonds to replace bond anticipation notes outstanding at year-end), the settlement of litigation, the initiation of litigation, and natural disasters. Of course, subsequent events that shed light on the amounts of transactions and balances of the fiscal period should also be reflected in the financial statements. An example of such an event is a settlement of litigation that was still pending at the end of the fiscal year.[132]

Employer participation in defined benefit pension and other postemployment benefit plans

The disclosures required of employers participating in defined-benefit pension plans are quite similar to those required of employers participating in defined-benefit other postemployment benefit (OPEB) plans.

Employers participating in defined benefit pension plans

Employers that participate in *defined benefit* pension plans[133] are required to provide the following note disclosures:[134]
- a description of the plan
  - the name of the pension plan, the name of the entity administering the plan, and the identification of the plan as either 1) a single- employer defined benefit plan, 2) an agent multiple-employer defined benefit plan, or 3) a cost-sharing multiple-employer defined benefit plan
  - a brief description of the types of benefits offered by the plan and the authority for establishing and amending benefits
  - information on any separately issued pension plan report (or separately issued public employee retirement system report in which the pension plan is included) and how it can be obtained
- funding policy
  - the authority for establishing and amending the funding policy
  - the required contribution rate(s) of active members
  - the employer's required contribution rate(s) in dollars or as a percentage of current-year covered payroll
  - how the contribution rate is determined if it differs significantly from the   actuarially determined annual required contribution (ARC)[135]
  - the required contributions in dollars and actual contributions as a percentage of that amount for the current and the preceding two years[136]
- additional disclosures for employers that participate in either single-employer or agent multiple-employer defined benefit plans
  - the annual pension cost and the contributions made (in dollars)

---

[132] NCGA Interpretation 6, paragraph 4d; American Institute of Certified Public Accountants (AICPA), *Professional Standards*, AU 560.06.
[133] As noted later in this chapter, this disclosure does *not* apply to *insured* defined benefit plans.
[134] GASB Statement No. 27, *Accounting for Pensions by State and Local Governmental Employers*, paragraphs 20-21.
[135] This requirement applies only to employers that participate in single-employer or agent multiple-employer plans.
[136] This requirement applies only to employers that participate in cost-sharing multiple-employer plans.

- in situations where there is a net pension obligation (NPO),[137] the three components of annual pension cost (the ARC, interest on the NPO, and the actuary's adjustment of the ARC based on the existence of the NPO); also, the increase or decrease in the NPO at the end of the year
- annual pension cost, the percentage of annual pension cost contributed, and the NPO at the end of the year for the current year and the two preceding years
- the date of the actuarial valuation and the identification of the actuarial methods and significant assumptions used. These disclosures should include the following:
  - ¤ the actuarial cost method (entry age, frozen entry age, attained age, frozen attained age, projected unit credit, or aggregate)
  - ¤ the actuarial method used for valuing assets
  - ¤ the assumptions regarding the inflation rate, investment return, projected salary increases, and post-retirement benefit increases
  - ¤ the amortization method (level dollar or level percentage of projected payroll)
  - ¤ the amortization period (or equivalent single amortization period if multiple periods are used)[138]
  - ¤ identification of the amortization periods as open or closed[139]
  - ¤ if the aggregate method is used, a statement that the actuarial cost method does *not* identify or separately amortize unfunded actuarial accrued liabilities.[140]

Employers participating in defined benefit OPEB plans

The disclosures for employers participating in defined benefit OPEB plans were modeled on those just described for employers participating in defined benefit pension plans. Those disclosures, however, were modified and amplified as follows:

- *Modifications.* In several instances, the disclosures just described for pension plans were only slightly modified for OPEB.
  - *Employer contribution rates.* Also disclose any legal or contractual maximum contribution rates.
  - *Required and actual contributions to cost-sharing plans.* Also disclose how the rate is determined. If the plan uses pay-as-you-go funding, state that fact.
  - *Actuarial assumptions.* Also disclose healthcare cost trend data, as applicable.
  - *Economic assumptions.* If different rates are used for different years, disclose initial and ultimate rates.

---

[137] An NPO results when a government funds less than its actuarially determined annual required contribution to the pension plan. When a government funds more than its actuarially determined annual required contribution, the result is a negative NPO.

[138] The amortization period (or equivalent single amortization period) may not exceed 30 years. The equivalent single amortization period (ESAP) is calculated by dividing the total unfunded actuarial accrued liability by the sum of the amounts amortized for each component.

[139] GAAP allow the use of both closed and open amortization periods. Closed amortization periods systematically reduce the amount to be amortized. With a 30-year closed amortization period, for example, there would be nothing left to amortize at the end of 30 years. Open amortization periods, however, work quite differently. With an open amortization period, the actuary works backward from the contribution rate so that the difference between the current year's total contribution and normal cost is treated as the current year's amortization of the unfunded actuarial accrued liability. The amount of amortization so calculated is only then expressed in terms of an amortization period. As a result, there is no set period at the end of which amortization will necessarily be complete.

[140] GASB Statement No. 27, paragraphs 20 and 21.

- *Investment return assumption.* If a blended rate is used because a plan is only partially funded, disclose the method used to determine the blended rate.
- *Aggregate method.* Explain that data on funding progress are presented using the entry age actuarial cost method.
- *Amplifications.* The following additional disclosures must also be included in the notes to the financial statements of employers participating in defined-benefit OPEB plans.
  - *Funding progress.* Include in the notes to the financial statements the data from the most recent period presented in the schedule of funding progress.
  - *Background information.* Explain that:
    - Actuarial valuations involve estimates and assumptions about the distant future that are continually revised.
    - The schedule of funding progress, located following the notes, provides multi-year trend data to help determine whether net plans assets are increasing or decreasing over time.
    - Benefits are projected based on benefit levels and cost-sharing arrangements as of the date of the valuation and do not explicitly reflect the potential effects of legal or contractual funding limitations.
    - Actuarial valuations take a long-term perspective that involves the use of techniques designed to reduce volatility.[141]

Employer participation in defined contribution pension and OPEB plans

GAAP set the following disclosure requirements for employers that participate in defined contribution pension plans or defined contribution OPEB plans:

- the name of the plan;
- the entity administering the plan;
- an indication that the arrangement is a defined contribution plan;
- a brief description of the plan's provisions and the authority for establishing or amending the plan's provisions;
- contribution requirements (either as a dollar amount or as a percentage of salary) for the employer, participating employees, and other contributors;
- the authority for amending contribution requirements; and
- contributions actually made by the employer and plan members.[142]

Employer participation in insured pension and OPEB plans

An insured plan is a defined benefit arrangement where employers transfer the legal responsibilities and risks associated with future benefit payments to an insurer in return for a premium. From a participating employer's perspective, such plans function much like defined contribution plans, even though they provide defined benefits to employees. As a result, the following disclosures required by GAAP resemble those for defined contribution plans:

- description of the plan and authority for establishing and amending provisions;

[141] GASB Statement No. 45, *Accounting and Financial Reporting by Employers for Postemployment Benefits Other Than Pensions*, paragraphs 24-25.
[142] GASB Statement No. 27, paragraph 27; GASB Statement No. 45, paragraph 31.

- a statement that the responsibility for making payments to employees has effectively been transferred to the insurer;
- an indication whether the employer has guaranteed benefits in the event of default by the insurer;
- amount of current-year pension cost (the amount of contributions or premiums due); and
- contributions or premiums actually paid.[143]

Employer participation in a special funding situation

In a *special funding* situation, one government is legally responsible for making pension or OPEB payments on behalf of the employees of another entity. In such cases, the paying government should treat the plan just like a plan offered to its own employees. If the government is the only contributor, the plan would qualify as a single-employer plan, even if the employees of several entities participate.[144]

Information on individual pension plans and individual OPEB healthcare plans

Fiduciary funds are reported in the basic financial statements by fund type. Therefore, a government may report only a single column for all of its pension (and other employee benefit) trust funds in the basic financial statements. GAAP, however, require that information be reported separately for each individual pension plan and OPEB plan. Ordinarily, this goal is accomplished by means of a reference to a separately issued report, which provides the needed detail on individual plans. If not, GAAP require that data on individual plans be presented as part of the notes to the financial statements.[145]

Material violations of finance-related legal and contractual provisions

GAAP require that the financial statements disclose any material violations of finance-related legal and contractual provisions, as well as actions the government has taken to address those violations.[146] As discussed earlier, the issue of compliance violations may arise in connection with a government's annual or biennial appropriated budget. Reportable violations also may occur in connection with grant requirements, bond covenants, regulations governing deposits and investments, and a variety of other common situations.

Governments must be careful in applying the concept of materiality to violations of legal and contractual provisions. Specifically, it is especially important in such cases to consider the *qualitative* as well as the quantitative aspects of materiality.[147]

---

[143] GASB Statement No. 27, paragraph 23; GASB Statement No. 45, paragraph 28.
[144] GASB Statement No. 27, paragraph 28; GASB Statement No. 45, paragraph 32.
[145] GASB Statement No. 34, paragraph 106.
[146] GASB Statement No. 38, paragraph 9.
[147] In this regard, it may be useful to cite the following discussion taken from GASB, *Comprehensive Implementation Guide (2004)*, 1.157:

> What constitutes a *significant* violation is a matter of judgment for the financial statement preparer. However, *significant* connotes qualitative as well as quantitative features. A significant violation would not necessarily be restricted to one that involves a large dollar investment or a large dollar risk of loss. Preparers need to look at the specific wording of the legal or contractual provisions, the reason for the provisions, the current political environment, whether such a violation would affect the actions or accountability assessment of the financial statements users, and whether the lack of control that allowed a small dollar violation potentially could allow a future violation involving a much larger dollar investment or larger dollar risk of loss. For example, suppose a government that is required by law to fully collateralize uninsured deposits had a small amount of uncollateralized deposits during the reporting period because it has no procedures to monitor the value of collateral. This situation could be considered a significant legal violation because the lack of procedures could result in higher levels of uncollateralized deposits in the future. Moreover, some believe any violations of legal provisions relating to collateral requirements and the use of

Debt service requirements to maturity

GAAP require that a government disclose debt service to maturity for all outstanding debt. This disclosure should present debt service principal and interest separately for each of the succeeding five fiscal years, and in at least five-year increments thereafter.[148] GAAP direct that interest payments on variable-rate debt be calculated using the rate in effect at the financial statement date (even though some different rate might be in effect at the time the financial statements are issued). To avoid any misunderstanding concerning the potential volatility of debt service connected with variable-rate debt, GAAP specifically require that the terms by which interest rates change for variable rate debt be disclosed.[149]

Lease obligations

Governments are required to provide the same disclosures as their private-sector counterparts for leases in which they participate as lessees. In the case of capital leases, GAAP require the following disclosures:
- general description of leasing arrangements;
- the gross amount of assets recorded under capital leases presented by major asset classes;
- minimum future lease payments for each of the next five years, and for at least each five-year increment thereafter, presenting a deduction for the amount of imputed interest to reduce the net minimum future lease payments to their present value;[150]
- total minimum future sublease rentals;
- total contingent rentals incurred; and
- amortization of leased assets (if not displayed) or statement that it is included as part of depreciation expense.[151]

For operating leases, GAAP set the following note disclosure requirements:
- general description of leasing arrangements;
- future minimum rental payments for each of the next five years and for at least each five year increment thereafter (only for noncancelable leases of more than one year);[152]
- minimum future sublease rentals (only for noncancelable subleases); and
- current-year rental costs (with separate amounts for minimum rentals, contingent rentals, and sublease rentals).[153]

Lease receivables

GAAP require the same disclosures of governments that are lessors and of private-sector enterprises in the same situation. For capital leases, these disclosure requirements are summarized as follows:
- general description of leasing arrangements;
- the total future minimum lease payments receivable (with separate deductions for executory costs and uncollectibles);
- unguaranteed residual values accruing to the government;
- initial indirect costs (direct financing leases only);

---

unauthorized investment types are inherently significant in a qualitative sense and should be disclosed, regardless of the dollar amount involved.
[148] The details of debt service to maturity need not be presented separately for each individual debt issue. (GASB, *Comprehensive Implementation Guide (2004)*, 7.357.)
[149] GASB Statement No. 38, paragraph 10.
[150] GASB Statement No. 38, paragraph 11.
[151] FASB Statement No. 13, *Accounting for Leases*, paragraphs 13 and 16.
[152] GASB Statement No. 38, paragraph 11.
[153] FASB Statement No. 13, paragraph 16.

- unearned income;
- minimum lease payments for each of the five succeeding fiscal years; and
- total contingent rentals of the period.[154]

For operating leases, the disclosure requirements are summarized as follows:

- general description of leasing arrangements;
- cost and carrying amount of leased assets by major asset class and accumulated depreciation in total;
- for noncancelable leases, minimum future rentals in the aggregate and for each of the five succeeding fiscal years; and
- total contingent rentals of the period.

Construction and other significant commitments

GAAP require that material commitments, such as construction contracts, be disclosed.[155] Commitments are defined as "existing arrangements to enter into future transactions or events, such as long-term contractual obligations with suppliers for future purchases at specified prices and sometimes at specified quantities."[156] Encumbrances, which technically meet this definition, typically are disclosed separately, as discussed earlier (unless reported as a designation).

Capital assets

Most governments have a significant investment in their capital assets. GAAP require governments to disclose 1) the historical cost of capital assets (or their fair value at the time of donation), 2) accumulated depreciation, 3) additions during the period, and 4) deletions during the period in a format that demonstrates the change between the beginning and ending book values. In doing so, a government must make the following distinctions for all four items:

- capital assets related to governmental activities must be reported separately from those related to business-type activities;
- different major classes of capital assets (e.g., land, buildings and improvements, equipment, infrastructure, construction-in-progress) must be reported separately from one another;
- capital assets that are *not* being depreciated (land, construction-in-progress, certain art collections, and infrastructure reported using the modified approach) must be reported separately from those that are being depreciated; and
- accumulated depreciation must be reported separately for each major class of depreciable capital assets (rather than just in total).

Furthermore, the notes must disclose how much depreciation has been included in each line of functional expense reported for *governmental activities*. This rule, however, does *not* apply to depreciation expense indirectly charged to the various functions of *governmental activities* by way of internal service fund charges. Rather, the total amount of depreciation expense included in internal service fund charges to *governmental activities* may be reported as a single item in its own right.[157]

---

[154] FASB Statement No. 13, paragraph 23; FASB Statement No. 91, *Nonrefundable Fees & Costs Associated with Originating or Acquiring Loans and Initial Direct Costs of Leases*, paragraph 25(d).
[155] NCGA Interpretation 6, paragraph 4j.
[156] AICPA, *State and Local Governments*, Section 8.82.
[157] GASB Statement No. 34, paragraph 117; GASB, *Comprehensive Implementation Guide (2004)*, 7.239.

Whenever a capital asset is out of service at the end of the year as the result of either a permanent or temporary impairment, that fact must be disclosed.[158]   Furthermore, the notes should provide any information not visible on the face of the financial statements regarding the nature, amount, and financial statement classification of capital asset impairments recognized during the period.[159]

Insurance recoveries

Governments sometimes qualify for insurance recoveries, most often in connection with the impairment of capital assets. The notes must disclose the amount and classification of any such recoveries if not otherwise visible in the financial statements.[160]

Long-term liabilities

GAAP specify note disclosure requirements for the primary government's long-term liabilities. The required disclosures should provide information separately for each major class of long-term liabilities (for example, bonds and notes, leases payable, claims and judgments, compensated absences). Also, a clear distinction should be drawn between long-term liabilities associated with governmental activities and long-term liabilities associated with business-type activities.

GAAP also require that information be presented on changes in long-term liabilities by major class. Note that additions and deductions must be reported separately, rather than netted. This presentation also should specifically indicate the portion of each liability balance that is due within one year of the date of the statement of net assets. Finally, in the case of long-term liabilities other than debt, disclosure should be made of the governmental funds that typically have been used in prior years to liquidate such amounts.[161]

Deficits in individual funds

The basic financial statements provide information on individual funds only for 1) *major* governmental funds, 2) *major* enterprise funds, 3) a nonmajor governmental or enterprise fund that is the only one of its kind, and 4) internal service funds and fiduciary funds that happen to be the only fund of their respective fund type. However, if a given activity is considered sufficiently important to merit separate reporting as a fund, it is assumed under GAAP that a deficit in that fund would interest users of the basic financial statements. Accordingly, GAAP require that the notes to the financial statements disclose all material instances where there is a deficit of fund balance/net assets/equity in an individual fund that is not otherwise visible on the face of the basic financial statements.[162] Sometimes a deficit in an individual fund constitutes a violation of finance-related legal or contractual provisions, in which case the disclosures normally required for material violations (including actions taken to address the violation), would apply.

Interfund receivables, payables, and transfers

GAAP require that the details of interfund receivables and payables be disclosed in the notes to the financial statements at the level of detail of the col-

---

[158] GASB Statement No. 42, *Accounting and Financial Reporting for Impairment of Capital Assets and for Insurance Recoveries*, paragraph 20.
[159] GASB Statement No. 42, paragraph 17.
[160] GASB Statement No. 42, paragraph 21.
[161] GASB Statement No. 34, paragraph 119.
[162] NCGA Interpretation 6, paragraph 4n.

umns that appear in the basic financial statements (e.g., major governmental funds, nonmajor governmental funds in the aggregate, fiduciary funds by fund type).[163] The notes also must disclose the purpose of interfund balances, as well as any amounts not expected to be paid within one year.[164]

A parallel requirement applies to interfund transfers. Once again, the minimum level of detail is that of the columns that appear in the basic fund financial statements. The principal purpose of interfund transfers also must be disclosed, as well as the purpose and amount of significant transfers that are either nonroutine or inconsistent with the activities of the fund making the transfer.[165]

Significant transactions involving major discretely presented component units

By definition, transactions between the primary government and its discretely presented component units are properly classified as *external* activity, while similar situations involving the various funds of the primary government are classified as interfund activity. Nonetheless, a distinction clearly must be made between transactions involving parties outside the financial reporting entity and those involving discretely presented component units. Accordingly, GAAP direct that the notes to the financial statements disclose the nature and amount of any significant transactions between the primary government and its major discretely presented component units (as well as the nature and amount of any significant transactions between discretely presented component units).[166]

Donor-restricted endowments

Governments sometimes receive endowments that are subject to donor-imposed restrictions. GAAP require several specific disclosures regarding donor-restricted endowments:
- the amounts of net appreciation on investments of donor-restricted endowments that are available for expenditure authorized by the governing board, and how those amounts are reported in net assets;
- the state law regarding the ability to spend net appreciation; and
- the policy for authorizing and spending investment income, such as a spending-rate or total-return policy.[167]

Risk financing activities

GAAP require the following disclosures regarding a government's risk financing activities:
- a description of the types of risk a government faces and how it is handling those risks;
- any significant reduction in insurance coverage from the previous year (by risk category); and
- an indication whether the amount of settlements exceeded insurance coverage for each of the past three fiscal years.

In addition, if the government participates in a risk pool, it should describe that arrangement. The description should specifically address the rights and responsibilities of the government and the pool.

Finally, if a government retains some risk of loss, it should make the following disclosures:

---

[163] Some combining is permitted, however, when amounts in a column are immaterial.
[164] GASB Statement No. 38, paragraph 14.
[165] GASB Statement No. 38, paragraph 15.
[166] GASB Statement No. 34, paragraph 128.
[167] GASB Statement No. 34, paragraph 121.

- a description of what the liability for unpaid claims represents and how it is calculated (this discussion should mention whether non-incremental claims adjustment expenses have been included as part of the liability for claims and judgments);
- if a government exercises its option to discount claims liabilities or has entered into any structured settlements, the nondiscounted carrying amount of any liabilities reported at a discounted value and the range for interest rates used for discounting;
- claims *defeased* through annuity contracts (unless beneficiaries have signed an agreement releasing the government from all further obligation, and the likelihood of further payments is remote); and
- a tabular reconciliation of the claims liability for both the current fiscal year and the prior fiscal year,[168] using the following format:
  - claims liability (beginning of year)
  - claims incurred during the year
  - changes in the estimate for claims of prior periods
  - payments on claims
  - other (for example, change in the methodology used to estimate claims)
  - claims liability (end of year).[169]

Component units participating in the primary government's risk financing internal service fund are not required to provide all of these disclosures in their separate reports. Instead, the financial reports of such component units need disclose only the following information:

- types of risks to which the component unit is exposed and how it is dealing with those risks;
- significant reductions in insurance coverage from the previous year (by major risk categories);
- an indication whether settlement amounts exceeded insurance coverage for each of the past three fiscal years; and
- a statement that the unit participates in the primary government's risk financing fund and a description of the nature of the participation, including the rights and responsibilities of the component unit and the primary government.[170]

Governments that use an internal service fund for risk financing activities sometimes include a reasonable provision for future catastrophe losses in the internal service fund's charges to other funds. GAAP direct that the notes to the financial statements disclose a *designation* for the portion of equity that represents resources thus accumulated in the internal service fund.[171]

Property taxes

GAAP require that the notes to the financial statements disclose lien dates, levy dates, due dates, and collection dates on the government's property tax calendar.[172]

---

[168] For example, a report for the fiscal year ended December 31, 2010, would provide: 1) a reconciliation of the amounts reported at December 31, 2010, and December 31, 2009; and 2) a reconciliation of the amounts reported at December 31, 2009, and December 31, 2008.
[169] GASB Statement No. 10, paragraph 77.
[170] GASB Statement No. 10, paragraph 79.
[171] GASB Statement No. 10, paragraph 67. This designation is a note disclosure only and may *not* appear on the face of the financial statements.
[172] NCGA Interpretation 3, *Revenue Recognition—Property Taxes*, paragraph 11.

Segment information

GAAP sometimes require segment disclosures for activities associated with enterprise funds or stand-alone business-type activities. A *segment* is an activity or grouping of activities that meets all three of the following criteria:

- *The activity must be identifiable.* An activity is *identifiable* if it has a specific revenue stream and related expenses and gains and losses that are accounted for separately.
- *The activity must have revenue-supported debt outstanding.* As of the end of the fiscal period, the activity must have one or more bonds or other debt instruments (e.g., certificates of participation) outstanding with a revenue stream pledged in support of that debt.[173] (Conduit debt is not a consideration for this purpose).[174]
- *The activity must be externally required to maintain separate accounts.* An *external* party (e.g., pursuant to a bond indenture) must require separate accounting for *all* of the following items related to the activity: revenues, expenses, gains, losses, assets, and liabilities.[175]

The specific disclosures to be provided for each identified segment are as follows:

- the types of goods or services provided by the segment
- a condensed statement of net assets
  - total assets—distinguishing between current assets, capital assets, and other assets; amounts receivable from other funds or component units should be reported separately
  - total liabilities—distinguishing between current and long-term amounts; amounts payable to other funds or component units should be reported separately
  - total net assets—distinguishing restricted amounts (separately reporting expendable and nonexpendable components); unrestricted amounts; and amounts invested in capital assets, net of related debt
- condensed statement of revenues, expenses, and changes in net assets
  - operating revenues (by major source)
  - operating expenses; depreciation (including any amortization) should be identified separately
  - operating income (loss)
  - nonoperating revenues (expenses)—with separate reporting of major revenues and expenses
  - capital contributions and additions to permanent and term endowments
  - special and extraordinary items
  - transfers
  - change in net assets
  - beginning net assets
  - ending net assets
- condensed statement of cash flows

---

[173] In contrast to the criterion governing the mandatory use of enterprise funds, there is no requirement that revenue-backed debt be supported *solely by* the revenue in question.

[174] GASB Statement No. 34, footnote 48.

[175] It is important to emphasize that the external requirement for separate accounting must apply to *all* of the elements mentioned. Thus, a "coverage" requirement that mandated separate accounting for only revenues and expenses would not be sufficient for segment reporting. (GASB, *Comprehensive Implementation Guide (2004)*, 7.360.)

- net cash provided (used) by operating activities
- net cash provided (used) by noncapital financing activities
- net cash provided (used) by capital and related financing activities
- net cash provided (used) by investing activities
- beginning cash and cash equivalents balances
- ending cash and cash equivalents balances.[176]

Naturally, only the disclosure concerning the types of goods and services provided (if not evident from the fund's name) is required in the case of segments that are already reported as a separate column (e.g., major enterprise funds) in the basic financial statements.[177]

For governments that wish to present more detailed disaggregated information concerning multiple-function enterprise funds, GAAP encourage presenting a statement of activities as supplementary information. GAAP also encourage this same presentation for special-purpose governments engaged only in business-type activities.[178]

Governments may have enterprise-related activities that are similar to segments, but that do *not* meet all of the criteria discussed earlier for segment reporting. GAAP specifically preclude governments from voluntarily including information on such "segment-like" activities as part of their regular segment disclosure note. They are not precluded, however, from furnishing segment-like disclosures for such activities in a separate note or as supplementary information, if they wish to do so, provided that they refrain from describing the activities in question as *segments* (e.g., "disclosures concerning other revenue-supported debt of enterprise funds").[179]

Information on major discretely presented component units

GAAP require that financial information be provided within the basic financial statements for each major individual discretely presented component unit. This requirement may be met in one of three ways:

- presenting separate columns on the face of the government-wide financial statements for each major discretely presented component unit;
- presenting combining statements with separate columns for major individual discretely presented component units within the basic financial statements; or
- presenting condensed financial statements for major individual discretely presented component units within the notes to the financial statements.[180]

If the last option is selected, GAAP prescribe the following minimum level of detail:

- a condensed statement of net assets
  - total assets
    - distinguish capital assets from other assets
    - report separately amounts receivable from the primary government or from other component units
  - total liabilities

---

[176] GASB Statement No. 34, paragraph 122.
[177] GASB Statement No. 34, footnote 48.
[178] GASB Statement No. 34, paragraph 123.
[179] GASB, *Comprehensive Implementation Guide (2004)*, 7.362.
[180] GASB Statement No. 34, paragraph 127. See chapter 13 regarding requirements for combining statements.

- ¤ distinguish long-term debt outstanding from other liabilities
- ¤ report separately amounts payable to the primary government or to other component units
- – total net assets
  - ¤ distinguish restricted amounts; unrestricted amounts; and amounts invested in capital assets, net of related debt
- • condensed statement of activities
  - – expenses by major functions (and for depreciation, if reported as a separate line item)
  - – program revenues by type
  - – net program (expense) revenue
  - – tax revenues
  - – other nontax general revenues
  - – contributions to endowments and permanent fund principal
  - – special and extraordinary items
  - – change in net assets
  - – beginning net assets
  - – ending net assets.[181]

Short-term debt instruments and liquidity

GAAP require that the notes to the financial statements describe a government's short-term debt instruments and liquidity. Short-term debt for this purpose would include anticipation notes, uses of lines of credit, and similar loans. The disclosure should discuss the purpose for which short-term debt was issued and provide a schedule of changes in short-term debt that presents 1) balances at the beginning of the period, 2) increases, 3) decreases, and 4) balances at the end of the period. This schedule is required even if no short-term debt is outstanding at the close of the fiscal year.[182] The disclosure also might address how the government intends to finance the payment of short-term debt outstanding at the end of the period (for instance, repayment from operating revenues, a rollover of the obligations, or replacement with long-term debt).

Related party transactions

Most transactions are of the "arm's-length" variety. That is, it is reasonably assumed that both parties to the transaction are acting solely on the basis of their self-interest. Occasionally, however, in the public and the private sectors, parties enter into transactions that an informed observer might reasonably believe reflect considerations other than self-interest. GAAP use the phrase *related party transactions* to describe such arrangements.

While there is nothing inherently undesirable about related party transactions, they raise potential concerns regarding 1) the reasonability of the terms of the arrangement, and 2) the eventual collectibility of related receivables.[183] Accordingly, the notes to the financial statements should disclose the terms of material related party transactions, as well as the balances of any related receivables if not separately reported on the face of the basic financial statements.[184]

---

[181] GASB Statement No. 34, paragraph 127.
[182] GASB Statement No. 38, paragraph 12.
[183] For example, a government might be expected to use less aggressive collection efforts with a related party than with a party to an arm's-length transaction.
[184] NCGA Interpretation 6, paragraph 5; FASB Statement No. 57, *Related Party Disclosures*, paragraph 2.

Joint ventures

GAAP require that the notes to the financial statements include a general description of each joint venture that includes the following basic elements:
- description of any ongoing financial interest;
- description of any ongoing financial responsibility;
- information to allow users of the financial statements to evaluate whether the joint venture is accumulating significant financial resources or is experiencing fiscal stress that may cause an additional financial benefit or burden for the participating government in the future;
- information on how to obtain the separate financial statements of the joint venture; and
- information on related party transactions.[185]

Jointly governed organizations

A variety of multigovernmental organizations share many characteristics of joint ventures but do not involve an ongoing financial interest or responsibility for participating governments. GAAP refer to such entities as *jointly governed organizations*. Disclosure requirements for participating governments are limited to related party transactions, if any.[186]

Debt refundings

When governments enter into either a current or an advance refunding transaction, GAAP require that they present the following disclosures in the notes to the financial statements:
- a brief description of the refunding transaction;
- the aggregate difference in debt service between the refunded debt and the refunding debt;[187] and
- the economic gain or loss on the transaction.

The economic gain or loss on a refunding transaction is calculated in the manner described below.
- The present value of the debt service payments related to the refunding debt is calculated using the following formula:

	Face amount of refunding bonds
+/−	Premium/original issue discount
+	Accrued interest
−	Costs *not* recoverable through escrow earnings
	Present value of debt service payments on refunding debt

- A calculation is made to determine what effective interest rate applied to the debt service payments on the *refunding* bonds would result in the present value determined in the previous calculation.
- The effective interest rate calculated for the refunding bonds is then applied to the debt service on the *refunded* bonds to calculate the present value of debt service on the refunded bonds.
- The difference between the present value of the two debt service streams (refunding debt and refunded debt) constitutes the economic gain or loss on the transaction.

---

[185] GASB Statement No. 14, paragraph 75.
[186] GASB Statement No. 14, paragraph 77.
[187] This is essentially the arithmetic difference between the two debt service streams. For this purpose, the debt service stream used for the refunded debt is the original debt service stream (debt service to maturity).

Any amounts of debt defeased *in substance*, but still outstanding as of the end of each fiscal year, should be disclosed in the notes.[188]

Transactions not reported because not measurable

Sometimes nonexchange transactions or events cannot be recognized in the financial statements because they are not *measurable*. In that case, note disclosure of the transaction or event is required.[189]

Reserved and designated unreserved fund balance

The basic financial statements should provide information on the nature and purpose of each major component of reserved fund balance for major[190] and nonmajor[191] governmental funds. They also should provide the same type of information about designations.[192] The notes to the financial statements should disclose this information when it is not discernible on the face of the financial statements.

Interfund eliminations

As noted elsewhere,[193] governments generally have the *option* of eliminating interfund balances and transactions in the fund financial statements, whereas eliminations are *required* in the governmental and business-type activities columns of the government-wide financial statements. If a separate column is *not* used for this purpose in the fund financial statements, a disclosure that eliminations have been made in the governmental and business-type activities columns should be included in the notes to the financial statements.

Pension and OPEB trust funds

When a government includes a pension or OPEB trust fund, that fund typically also is the object of a separately issued report. In that case, the financial reporting entity is required to provide only the following information regarding each pension or OPEB trust fund:

- identification of the plan type (such as single-employer defined benefit plan) and the number of participating employers and other contributors;
- the basis of accounting used (specifying when contributions, benefits, and refunds are recognized);
- the method used to determine the fair value of investments;
- the terms of any long-term contracts for contributions and the amount outstanding as of the plan's reporting date;[194]
- concentrations of 5 percent or more of net assets in securities of a single issuer. (This rule does *not* apply to U.S. government securities; securities explicitly guaranteed by the U.S. government; and investments in mutual funds, external investment pools, and other pooled investments.)
- information on how to obtain the stand-alone plan report.[195]

---

[188] GASB Statement No. 7, *Advance Refundings Resulting in Defeasance of Debt,* paragraphs 11-12, 14.

[189] GASB Statement No. 33, *Accounting and Financial Reporting for Nonexchange Transactions,* paragraph 11, as amended.

[190] NCGA Interpretation 6, Appendix, IIID2.

[191] GASB Statement No. 34, paragraph 84.

[192] NCGA Statement 1, paragraph 120.

[193] See chapter 8.

[194] Long-term contracts may arise when participating employers enter into an agreement to convert their share of the plan's unfunded actuarial accrued liability (an *actuarial* liability) into a contract to pay the plan a fixed amount (an *accounting* liability). Such a situation may occur, for instance, when a single-employer plan joins an existing multiple-employer plan.

If a separate plan report is not issued, then the financial reporting entity is required to provide all disclosures ordinarily required of stand-alone plan reports.[196]

Bond anticipation notes

Bond anticipation notes (BANs) may be considered long-term obligations, and therefore be excluded from the governmental funds if they meet either of the following criteria:

- the BANs have been replaced by a long-term obligation subsequent to the close of the fiscal period, but prior to issuance of the financial statements; or
- the BANs are backed by a financing agreement that ensures their long-term character.[197]

If the second criterion is the basis for classifying BANs as long-term liabilities, the details of the financing agreement must be disclosed in the notes to the financial statements. The notes also should disclose the terms of any new obligation incurred or expected to be incurred as a result of the refinancing.[198]

Fiscal-year inconsistencies

A primary government may not share a common fiscal year with all of its component units. In such cases, GAAP require the financial reporting entity to *present component unit data based on the component unit's fiscal year.* As a result of the disparity in fiscal years, some amounts reported by the primary government may be inconsistent with related amounts reported by component units. For example, assume that a primary government with a calendar fiscal year-end made a loan in November to a component unit with a September 30 fiscal year-end. The primary government would report a receivable, but the component unit would *not* report a payable, because the transaction occurred *after* the close of the component unit's fiscal year. The amount of any such resulting inconsistency would need to be disclosed and explained in the notes to the financial statements.[199]

Reverse repurchase agreements

Governments that participated in reverse repurchase agreements during the fiscal period should provide the following disclosures in the notes to the financial statements:

- the relevant legal or contractual provisions;
- reverse repurchase agreements in force as of the end of the fiscal year;
- the source of legal or contractual authorization;
- significant violations of legal or contractual provisions;
- credit risk (except for agreements of the yield-maintenance variety);[200]
- for agreements of the yield-maintenance variety, the fair value of the securities to be repurchased as of the end of the fiscal year and the terms of the agreement;

---

[195] GASB Statement No. 25, *Financial Reporting for Defined Benefit Pension Plans and Note Disclosures for Defined Contribution Plans,* paragraph 32, as amended; GASB Statement No. 43, *Financial Reporting for Postemployment Benefit Plans Other Than Pension Plans,* paragraph 30.
[196] These requirements are discussed in chapter 15.
[197] See chapter 12 for a detailed discussion of the requirements for such a financing agreement.
[198] NCGA Interpretation 9, *Certain Fund Classifications and Balance Sheet Accounts,* paragraph 12.
[199] GASB Statement No. 14, paragraph 60, as amended.
[200] Credit risk is the difference between 1) the aggregate amount of the obligations under the agreement, and 2) the aggregate fair value of the securities underlying the agreement. Interest should be included in calculating both of these elements.

- losses recognized during the period due to default and amounts recovered from prior-period losses (if not discernible on the face of the financial statements); and
- an indication whether the maturities of the investments made with the agreements' proceeds generally are matched to the agreements' maturities, as well as the extent of such matching at the end of the fiscal period.[201]

Securities lending transactions

Governments with large investment portfolios sometimes enter into securities lending arrangements. GAAP require the following disclosures for all securities lending arrangements, regardless of their structure:

- the source of legal or contractual authorization
- significant violations of legal or contractual provisions
- a general description to include
  - the types of securities on loan
  - the types of collateral received
  - ability to pledge or sell collateral without a default
  - the amount by which collateral is to exceed the amount of securities on loan
  - restrictions on the amount of securities that may be lent
  - loss indemnification to be provided by agents (if applicable)
  - carrying amount and fair value of securities on loan
- whether the maturities of the investments made with the cash collateral generally match the maturities of securities loans and the extent of such matching as of the end of the fiscal year
- credit risk (how much more does the broker or dealer owe the government than vice versa?) or the absence of credit risk
- losses of the period resulting from default and recoveries of prior-period losses.[202]

Special assessment debt

A government's note disclosure requirements related to special assessment debt depend on whether the government is obligated in some manner for the debt.

If the government is obligated in some manner for special assessment debt, the notes to the financial statements should disclose the following information:

- the nature of the government's obligation (including the identification and description of any guarantee, reserve, or sinking fund established to cover defaults by property owners);
- amount of delinquent special assessment receivables (if not discernible on the face of the financial statements); and
- all other disclosures ordinarily required in connection with long-term debt.[203]

If the government is not obligated in any manner for special assessment debt, then the notes should disclose the amount of the debt, as well as the

---

[201] GASB Statement No. 3, paragraphs 63 and 76-80; GASB Interpretation No. 3, *Financial Reporting for Reverse Repurchase Agreements (an interpretation of GASB Statement No. 3)*, paragraph 6.
[202] GASB Statement No. 28, *Accounting and Financial Reporting for Securities Lending Transactions*, paragraphs 11-15.
[203] GASB Statement No. 6, *Accounting and Financial Reporting for Special Assessments*, paragraph 20.

information that the government is only acting as an agent and is in no way liable for the debt.[204]

Demand bonds

GAAP require the following disclosures of governments that have demand bonds outstanding at the end of the fiscal year:

- a general description of the demand bond program;
- the terms of any letters of credit or other liquidity facilities outstanding;
- commitment fees to obtain the letters of credit and any amounts drawn on them outstanding as of the balance sheet date;
- a description of the take-out agreement, commitment fees to obtain that agreement, and the terms of any new obligation incurred or expected to be incurred as a result of the take-out agreement; and
- debt service requirements to maturity that would result if the take-out agreement were exercised.[205]

Landfill closure and postclosure care costs

GAAP require the following disclosures for governments that are legally responsible for closure and postclosure care costs associated with the operation of a municipal solid-waste landfill:

- the nature and source of landfill closure and postclosure care requirements (federal, state, or local laws or regulations);
- an explanation that the cost of landfill closure and postclosure care is allocated based on landfill capacity used to date;
- the liability for landfill closure and postclosure care costs reported on the statement of position (if this liability is not visible on the statement of position because it is combined there with other liabilities);
- the portion of the estimated total current cost of landfill closure and postclosure care that has not yet been recognized in the financial statements;
- the percentage of the landfill's total capacity that has been used to date;
- the estimated remaining life of the landfill (in years);
- an explanation of how financial assurance requirements, if any, connected with landfill closure and postclosure care are being met;
- any assets restricted for payment of closure and postclosure care costs (if not apparent on the face of the statement of position); and
- a statement that the total current cost of landfill closure and postclosure care is an estimate and subject to changes resulting from inflation/deflation, technology, or changes in applicable laws or regulations.[206]

On-behalf payments for fringe benefits and salaries

When a government makes payments for fringe benefits or salaries to a third party on behalf of another government's employees, the employer government is required to disclose in the notes to its financial statements the related amounts recognized in its financial statements.

Also, if on-behalf benefits take the form of contributions to a pension or OPEB plan for which the employer government is *not* legally responsible,

---

[204] GASB Statement No. 6, paragraph 21.

[205] GASB Interpretation No. 1, *Demand Bonds Issued by State and Local Governmental Entities (an Interpretation of NCGA Interpretation 9)*, paragraph 11.

[206] GASB Statement No. 18, *Accounting for Municipal Solid Waste Landfill Closure and Postclosure Care Costs*, paragraph 17.

the employer government should disclose the name of the plan and the name of the entity that makes the contributions.[207]

Conduit debt

GAAP define conduit debt as "certain limited-obligation revenue bonds, certificates of participation, or similar debt instruments issued by a state or local governmental entity for the express purpose of providing capital financing for a specific third party that is not a part of the issuer's financial reporting entity." Governments that have issued conduit debt are required to make the following disclosures in the notes to the financial statements:
- a general description of the conduit debt transactions;
- the aggregate amount of all conduit debt obligations outstanding at the balance sheet date; and
- a clear indication that the issuer has no obligation for the debt beyond the resources provided by related leases or loans.[208]

Sponsors of governmental external investment pools

When governmental external investment pools issue separate financial reports, the notes to the sponsor's financial statements need only mention how to obtain a copy of the separate report. However, if a separate report is *not* issued, the notes to the sponsor's financial statements must provide all disclosures normally required in a separate pool report, as well as condensed statements of net assets and changes in net assets.[209]

Interest included as direct expense

Interest normally is reported as a separate line item in the governmental activities column of the government-wide statement of activities. However, when a borrowing is "essential to the creation or continuing existence of a program," it is properly included as part of direct program costs. In such situations, the notes should disclose the amount of any such direct program interest excluded from the general *interest* line, if not already disclosed on the face of the statement of activities.[210]

Detail on reconciliations

Governments are required to provide a summary reconciliation at the bottom of the governmental fund financial statements (or in an accompanying schedule) to explain differences between the amounts reported in those statements for *total governmental funds* and the amounts reported for *governmental activities* in the government-wide financial statements. A similar summary reconciliation is required to explain any differences between the amounts reported in the proprietary fund financial statements for *total enterprise funds* and the amounts reported for *business-type activities* in the government-wide financial statements. The summary character of these reconciliations could obscure the nature of individual elements of the reconciliations. In that case, GAAP require that additional information be disclosed in the notes to the financial statements.[211] Specifically, note disclosure is required whenever 1) a single reconciling item is a combination of several similar balances or transactions (e.g., different types of long-term liabilities) or 2) a single reconciling item is a net adjustment (e.g., substitution of depreciation expense for capital outlay). [212]

---

[207] GASB Statement No. 24, *Accounting and Financial Reporting for Certain Grants and Other Financial Assistance,* paragraph 12.
[208] GASB Interpretation No. 2, *Disclosure of Conduit Debt Obligations (an interpretation of NCGA Statement 1),* paragraph 3.
[209] GASB Statement No. 31, paragraph 19.
[210] GASB Statement No. 34, paragraph 46.
[211] GASB Statement No. 34, paragraph 77.

Discounts and allowances   GAAP require that revenues be reported net of discounts and allowances. One approach to meeting this requirement is to report revenues gross on the face of the financial statements with related discounts and allowances shown directly following as deductions from this amount. A second approach is to report net revenues on the face of the financial statements with a parenthetical disclosure of the discounts and allowances that reduced the original gross amount. If neither of these approaches is taken, GAAP require that information on discounts and allowances be disclosed in the notes to the financial statements.[213]

Disaggregation of receivables and payables   The various components of significant receivables must be disclosed separately in the notes to the financial statements if not visible on the face of the statement of position. In addition, GAAP require the disclosure of any significant receivable balances not expected to be collected within one year.

GAAP also mandate the disaggregation of the various components of significant payables if these components are not displayed separately on the statement of position. In the case of payables, however, there is no special requirement to report amounts due beyond one year, as is the case for receivables.[214]

Collections   Collections (works of art and historical artifacts, for example) meet the definition of a capital asset and normally should be reported in the financial statements.[215] The requirement for capitalization is waived, however, for collections that meet *all* of the following conditions:

- the collection is held for reasons other than financial gain;
- the collection is protected, kept unencumbered, cared for, and preserved; and
- the collection is subject to an organizational policy requiring that the proceeds from sales of collection items be used to acquire other items for collections.[216]

GASB Statement No. 34 *encourages* but does not *require* the capitalization of collections that meet all of the above criteria.

If a government elects *not* to capitalize a collection because it meets the criteria described, the government must provide a description of the collection and an explanation of the reasons it has elected *not* to capitalize it (essentially a disclosure of the criteria that qualify the collection for exemption from the capitalization requirement). Of course, capitalized collections are subject to all of the note disclosure requirements described earlier for capital assets.[217]

---

[212] GASB, *Comprehensive Implementation Guide (2004)*, 7.295.

[213] GASB Statement No. 34, footnote 41.

[214] GASB Statement No. 38, paragraph 13.

[215] GAAP set special rules governing the capitalization of collections, but offer no definition of that term. Those interested in a definition may wish to refer to paragraph 128 of the Financial Accounting Standards Board's (FASB) Statement No. 116, *Accounting for Contributions Received and Contributions Made*, which states that collections "generally are held by museums, botanical gardens, libraries, aquariums, arboretums, historic sites, planetariums, zoos, art galleries, nature, science and technology centers, and similar educational, research, and public service organizations that have those divisions; however, the definition is not limited to those entities nor does it apply to all items held by those entities." (GASB, *Comprehensive Implementation Guide (2004)*, 7.105)

[216] GAAP do *not* require such a written statement of policy in the case of collections that are permanently installed and that cannot be removed without destroying the items (e.g., murals). (GASB, *Comprehensive Implementation Guide (2004)*, 7.110.)

[217] GASB Statement No. 34, paragraph 118.

Extraordinary gains and losses, special items, and similar situations

When a government reports extraordinary gains or losses or special items in its financial statements, an explanation of the underlying event ordinarily is reported in the notes to the financial statements. Also, disclosure is required of any situations that would otherwise qualify as special items except for the fact that they are not subject to management control (if not presented separately as revenues or expenditures/expense).[218]

Prior-period adjustments and accounting changes

When a government reports a prior-period adjustment or a change in accounting principles (or a change in the application of accounting principles), an explanation of the adjustment or change ordinarily is reported in the notes to the financial statements.

Details of restricted asset accounts

Restricted assets sometimes arise in connection with the issuance of revenue bonds. Since an objective of state and local government financial reporting is to demonstrate compliance with finance-related legal and contractual provisions, it is recommended that the detail of restricted asset accounts (both purpose and amount) be disclosed in the notes to the financial statements if not otherwise visible on the face of the financial statements.[219]

Deferred revenue reported in governmental funds

A government may wish to disclose the separate components of the liability for deferred revenue reported on the governmental fund balance sheet. It also may wish to distinguish amounts that are deferred because they are not available, from amounts that are deferred because they are unearned.

Additional recommended disclosures for debt

In addition to the GAAP-required disclosures in connection with long-term debt, it also is recommended that governments provide a description of each outstanding debt issue. Such a description could include all of the following information:
- purpose for which the debt was issued;
- original amount of the debt;
- type of debt (revenue bonds or general obligation bonds, for instance);
- amounts of installments;
- interest rate;
- maturity range; and
- applicability of federal arbitrage regulations.

The government also may wish to provide readers with summary information on bond covenants entered into by the government in connection with revenue bonds.

Governments subject to a legal debt margin may wish to disclose information on their legal debt limit in the notes to the financial statements. Also, governments may wish to disclose that additional debt has been authorized but not yet issued.

---

[218] APB Opinion No. 30, *Reporting the Results of Operations–Reporting the Effects of Disposal of a Segment of a Business, and Extraordinary, Unusual and Infrequently Occurring Events and Transactions*, paragraph 11; GASB Statement No. 34, paragraph 56.
[219] The inclusion of interfund receivables as part of restricted assets should be considered a likely indication of noncompliance with legal or contractual provisions requiring asset restriction. AICPA, *Audits of State and Local Governments*, Section 2.56.

NOTES FOR COMPONENT UNITS

The note disclosure requirements described thus far potentially apply to discretely presented component units as well as to the primary government and blended component units. Two factors must be considered:

- whether a given disclosure is needed for a particular discretely presented component unit depends on 1) the component unit's significance relative to discretely presented component units in the aggregate, and 2) the nature and significance of the component unit's relationship to the primary government; and[220]
- data related to discretely presented component units may not be aggregated with data of the primary government.

AVOIDANCE OF *NEGATIVE* DISCLOSURE

A set of financial statements is presumed to include all required disclosures applicable in the circumstances. So ordinarily there is no need to state that a particular disclosure is *not* applicable to the government (for instance, "there are no subsequent events to report"). Indeed, such *negative disclosures* normally should be avoided because they add length and complexity to a financial report without providing any added benefit, thus detracting from the efficiency of the report presentation. An exception might be made in unusual situations where financial statement users are likely be confused by the absence of certain information for a given government (e.g., the only government of its size and type in a state not to offer other postemployment benefits to employees).

The rule just described does *not* apply to the rare disclosure requirements introduced by the term "whether" (rather than "if") in the authoritative accounting literature. For example, in conjunction with risk financing, GAAP require governments to disclose *"whether* the amount of settlements exceeded insurance coverage for each of the past three fiscal years." In that case, either an affirmative or negative statement must be made to comply with the requirement.

MATERIALITY

Note disclosure requirements, like all other GAAP requirements, apply only to *material* items. A material note disclosure, for this purpose, is described as one whose omission would be considered important by some financial statement users, either because of its size (quantitative materiality) or inherent interest (qualitative materiality). It is useful to recall that "the notes should focus on the primary government—specifically, its governmental activities, business-type activities, major funds, and nonmajor funds in the aggregate."[221]

---

[220] GASB Statement No. 14, paragraph 63.
[221] GASB Statement No. 34, paragraph 113.

12

Transaction-specific and Account-specific Guidance

The preceding chapters have examined the format and contents of the basic financial statements, including the accompanying notes. This chapter provides specialized guidance on selected transactions and accounts.

ASSET-RELATED ISSUES

Traceability of cash and cash equivalents

Governments are required to present a statement of cash flows for proprietary funds. The focus of the statement of cash flows may be either *cash* or *cash and cash equivalents*. Whichever focus is selected, generally accepted accounting principles (GAAP) state that "the total amounts of cash and cash equivalents at the beginning and end of the period shown in the statement of cash flows should be easily traceable to similarly titled line items or subtotals shown in the statements of financial position as of those dates."[1]

The term *cash* properly encompasses *all* cash items, regardless of any restrictions that may attach to them. Accordingly, the amounts reported in the statement of cash flows may not tie to similar amounts reported in the statement of position if cash and noncash items are commingled indiscriminately as *restricted assets* in the statement of position. There are four practical ways to avoid this discrepancy and thereby comply with the GAAP requirement for traceability:

- report the different components of restricted assets separately on the statement of position (distinguish *cash and cash equivalents* from noncash items);[2]

---

[1] Governmental Accounting Standards Board (GASB) Statement No. 9, *Reporting Cash Flows of Proprietary and Nonexpendable Trust Funds and Governmental Entities That Use Proprietary Fund Accounting*, paragraph 8.
[2] GASB, *Comprehensive Implementation Guide (2004)*, 2.71.

- parenthetically disclose the cash and cash equivalents component of restricted assets on the statement of position: "Restricted assets (including $X of cash and cash equivalents);"
- parenthetically disclose the amount of restricted cash and cash equivalents in the statement of cash flows: "Cash and cash equivalents–end of period (including $X of cash and cash equivalents included in restricted assets);" and
- provide a reconciliation on the face of the statement of cash flows.

As noted earlier, GAAP specifically require traceability *to the statement of position*. A simple reconciliation disclosed in the notes to the financial statements does *not* meet this requirement.

Positions in internal investment pools[3]

It is common for governments to pool the cash and investments of various funds and component units to improve investment performance. It is *not* appropriate to report the pool itself as a separate fund in such circumstances. Rather, each fund and component unit's position in the pool should be reflected in the participating fund or component unit as an asset.[4] This same approach applies in situations where a government sponsors a single pool that has both internal and external[5] participants (a mixed pool). That is, the portion of the pool representing the reporting entity's own investments should be reported as a line item across its various funds and component units, while the portion of investments belonging to outside parties should be reported in a separate investment trust fund.[6]

Sometimes an individual fund overdraws its share of pooled cash. If so, the overdraft should be reflected as an interfund liability rather than a credit balance in an asset account (negative cash). Likewise, an equivalent amount of some other fund's position in the pool should be reclassified as an interfund receivable. Management is responsible for determining the specific fund that will report this receivable. If the pool itself is overdrawn, the overdraft should be reported as an external liability rather than an interfund liability.[7]

Valuation of investments

For entities other than governmental external investment pools, the following types of investments normally must be reported at fair value:[8]

- interest-earning investment contracts, such as guaranteed investment contracts and bank investment contracts;
- positions in external investment pools;
- positions in mutual funds;
- debt securities;
- equity securities;*
- option contracts;*

---

[3] The concept of an *internal* investment pool covers not only the primary government, but also its discretely presented component units. (GASB Statement No. 31, *Certain Investments and External Investment Pools*, paragraph 22, definition of an *internal investment pool*.)

[4] GASB Statement No. 31, *Accounting and Financial Reporting for Certain Investments and for External Investment Pools*, paragraph 14.

[5] That is, participants outside the financial reporting entity.

[6] GASB Statement No. 31, paragraph 18.

[7] American Institute of Certified Public Accountants (AICPA), *State and Local Governments*, Section 5.26.

[8] GASB Statement No. 31, paragraph 2. *Fair value* is used instead of *market value* because not all investments are traded on a market. When an investment is traded on a market, its fair value (as discussed later) normally is its market value.

- stock warrants;* and
- stock rights.*

(*if fair value is readily determinable)

The use of cost or amortized cost is appropriate for valuing other types of investments, such as real estate, venture capital limited partnerships, loans receivable, trade accounts receivable, and restricted stock.

Note that *investments* in this context describes assets held primarily to generate income or profit. Thus, the following categories are *not* subject to fair value reporting because they are *not* considered investments for investment-valuation purposes: seized debt securities, performance deposits, securities held in trust by a bank regulator, worker's compensation deposits, equity securities representing a component unit, and investments accounted for using the equity method of accounting.[9]

Fair value is the amount the seller would be paid for an investment if it were to be sold currently in a transaction between a willing buyer and a willing seller.[10] Typically, the measure of fair value is the last quoted market price of an investment on the principal exchange on which it is traded (on the last day of trading) as of the date of the financial statements. If no trade occurred on the date of the financial statements, the bid or asked price may be used as a measure of the investment's fair value.[11] For thinly traded securities, other measures may be used in the absence of a quoted market price (such as market value for similar securities, discounted cash flows, matrix pricing, fundamental analysis, option-pricing models, option-adjusted spread models).[12]

Special considerations arise when investments are associated with purchased *put* options or written *call* options. A *put* option allows the investment holder to demand that the investment be purchased at a predetermined price by some third party. Conversely, a *call* option requires that the investment holder sell the investment at a predetermined price to some third party. Naturally, holders of investments with purchased put options use those options when the market price of the investment is *below* the strike price of the option. In the same way, call options are exercised when the market price of an investment is *above* the option price. In either situation, the fair value of investments associated with purchased put options and written call options should reflect the strike price. For example, assume that a government has purchased a put option that allows it to sell an investment with a current market price of $8 for the predetermined strike price of $10. The fair value of the investment plus the purchased option is $10. Similarly, assume that a government has written a call option on an investment with a current market price of $10 that allows a third party to demand that the investment be sold for $8. In this instance, the fair value of the investment is equal to the strike price of $8.[13]

The fair value of a government's position in an external investment pool is equal to the fair value of the government's proportionate share of the pool's underlying assets. An estimate should be used when the pertinent

---

[9] GASB Statement No. 31, paragraphs 5 and 40; GASB, *Comprehensive Implementation Guide (2004)*, 6.12.
[10] GASB Statement No. 31, paragraph 7.
[11] GASB, *Comprehensive Implementation Guide (2004)*, 6.27, indicates that "practice generally is to use bid prices, because they are the amounts at which transactions presumably will be completed."
[12] GASB, *Comprehensive Implementation Guide (2004)*, 6.32 and 6.78.
[13] GASB Statement No. 31, paragraphs 7 and 75; GASB, *Comprehensive Implementation Guide (2004)*, 6.63.

information is not available as of the date of the participating government's financial statements. An exception to the general rule occurs when a government's position in an external investment pool is guaranteed. In that case, investments may be reported at guaranteed value if the fair value of the participating government's share of the pool's portfolio falls below the guaranteed amount. Naturally, the valuation of investments at a guaranteed value that exceeds actual market value presumes that the guarantor will be able to honor the guarantee; if not, the use of the guaranteed value is *not* appropriate.[14]

Sometimes governmental external investment pools voluntarily comply with guidelines established by Securities and Exchange Commission Rule 2a7, which places narrow constraints on the types and maturities of investments that a pool may hold. In response to these constraints, the market value of the portfolio of a 2a7-like pool does not differ appreciably from the amortized cost of the investments it contains. Accordingly, governments that participate in 2a7-like pools may value their position in the pool based on the price of their shares, even if share price is a function of the amortized cost of the underlying investments rather than of fair value. This option of using share price rather than fair value to report positions in pools is strictly limited to 2a7-like pools and may not be used for other similar pooling arrangements, such as money-market funds of regulated banks.[15]

Described below are some important exceptions to the general rule that investments in the categories listed earlier must be reported at fair value.
- *Nonparticipating interest-earning investment contracts.* Not all interest-earning investment contracts are affected by changes in market values. For example, a fixed-rate contract that cannot be negotiated or transferred to a third party (a nonnegotiable certificate of deposit, for instance) is not susceptible to gains or losses as a result of interest rate changes. GAAP permit such *nonparticipating* interest-earning investment contracts to be reported at amortized cost.[16]
- *Short-term money-market securities.* Governments often invest in highly liquid, short-term debt instruments commonly known as money-market securities, including commercial paper, banker's acceptances, and U.S. Treasury and agency obligations. Any such securities may be reported at amortized cost rather than at fair value, *provided the government acquires them within one year of maturity.*[17]
- *Short-term interest-earning investment contracts.* In contrast to *nonparticipating* interest-earning investment contracts, which always may be valued at amortized cost rather than at fair value, *participating* interest-earning investment contracts may be reported at amortized cost *only if the government acquires them within one year of maturity.*[18]

Of course, the amount of any investments reported at amortized cost must be reduced whenever those investments' value *to the government* is ultimately impaired (as in situations where a government may have to sell the investments before they recover their full value). On the other hand, purely

---

[14] GASB Statement No. 31, paragraph 11.
[15] GASB Statement No. 31, paragraph 12.
[16] GASB Statement No. 31, paragraph 8.
[17] GASB Statement No. 31, paragraph 9.
[18] GASB Statement No. 31, paragraph 9.

temporary declines in the market value of investments reported at amortized cost need *not* be recognized.

For example, assume that a government intends to hold a *temporarily* impaired investment to maturity *and* it is not reasonably possible that the government will sell the investment before that time (e.g., to meet unforeseen cash flow needs). In this case the investment's value *to the government* is not ultimately impaired, because payment is expected to be made in full at maturity, *and* the government is expected to still be holding the investment at that time. Accordingly, the government would continue to report the investment at its amortized cost, even though that amount temporarily exceeds the investment's net realizable value.[19]

Investment-related income

It normally is presumed that income on investments is to be reported in the same fund as the underlying investments. In some situations, however, the income on certain investments may legally accrue directly to the benefit of some other fund. In those cases, the investment income should be reported directly in the fund to which it legally accrues rather than in the fund that reports the underlying investment, with an appropriate note disclosure to avoid confusing financial statement users.[20]

Normally, governments report investment income as a net amount, but they retain the option of reporting separately the various components of investment income.[21] If a government chooses to report separately, the amount of interest income reported should be the stated rate of interest on the underlying investments in the case of investments reported at fair value. That is, interest income in this case should *not* be adjusted for the effect of amortizing issuance costs, premiums, or discounts, as all of these items are already reflected indirectly in the change in the fair value of the investments.[22]

Occasionally the balance of net investment income for the period is negative. In such cases, GAAP direct that investment income be reported as *negative revenue* in the statement of activities rather than as an expense or expenditure. This treatment is consistent with the fact that governments typically consider investments in the context of revenue analysis.[23]

Assets associated with securities lending arrangements

Governments with large investment portfolios sometimes enter into securities lending arrangements in which a government "lends" selected investment securities from its portfolio to brokers and dealers to fill client orders. The government's interest in the lent securities is secured either by collateral (cash or securities) or by a letter of credit until the same or similar securities are returned, per the agreement. If cash is used as collateral for the agreement, the government is obliged to rebate interest on the collateral to the broker or dealer at a rate specified by the agreement.

Governments enter into securities lending arrangements to increase their investment income. They accomplish this goal in one of two ways,

---

[19] GASB Statement No. 31, paragraphs 9 and 76; GASB, *Comprehensive Implementation Guide (2004)*, 6.29; AICPA, *State and Local Governments*, section 5.21.

[20] GASB Statement No. 31, paragraph 14.

[21] Of course, only the separately issued reports of external investment pools are permitted to report realized gains and losses separately from unrealized amounts on the face of the financial statements. (GASB Statement No. 31, paragraph 13.)

[22] GASB Statement No. 31, footnote 7.

[23] GASB, *Comprehensive Implementation Guide (2004)*, 6.69.

depending on the structure of the particular securities lending arrangement in which they participate:

- *Reinvestment of collateral at a higher rate of return.* If a government receives cash collateral to secure its lent securities, it may be able to increase its investment income by reinvesting the collateral at a higher rate of return than it is contractually obligated to rebate to the broker or dealer. The same situation holds true when the government receives securities as collateral that can be sold or pledged, even without a default by the broker or dealer.
- *Loan premium or fee.* If a securities lending agreement is backed by a letter of credit, there is no collateral available for reinvestment to obtain additional investment income for the lending government. Instead, the broker or dealer agrees to pay a loan premium or fee to compensate the government for its assistance.

Regardless of the type of securities lending agreement, the underlying or "lent" securities continue to be reported on the lending government's statement of position.[24] Furthermore, in the case of securities lending agreements that are collateralized by cash or by securities that can be sold or pledged even without a default by the broker or dealer, these additional amounts (and subsequent reinvestments) must also be reported as assets in the statement of position, along with a corresponding liability.[25]

As noted earlier, governments frequently pool the cash and investments of their various funds. In such cases, each fund typically reports only a single amount on the face of the statement of position to reflect its net position in the pool. As a result, the statement of position normally does *not* furnish information on the pool's underlying investments. However, GAAP specifically require that an asset and liability be reported on the face of the statement of position for securities lending arrangements of the reinvested-collateral type. Accordingly, when an internal investment pool participates in a securities lending arrangement of the reinvested-collateral type, the related assets and liabilities must be allocated among the participating funds in the financial statements based on each fund's risk of loss on the collateral assets.[26]

Assets associated with reverse repurchase agreements

A reverse repurchase agreement is an arrangement whereby a government "sells" securities to a third party, with an agreement that the government will later buy back those same (or similar) securities at a future date on terms specified by contract. Typically, such an arrangement transfers neither the risks nor the benefits of ownership to the purchaser. Instead, the arrangement functions essentially as a form of collateralized loan with the government in the role of borrower. That is, the amount received as "payment" by the government really represents the loan proceeds, and the "purchased" securities function essentially as collateral.[27] Because GAAP direct that transactions be classified and reported based on economic substance rather than legal form, reverse repurchase agreements of the type

---

[24] GASB Statement No. 28, *Accounting and Financial Reporting for Securities Lending Transactions*, paragraph 5.
[25] GASB Statement No. 28, paragraph 6.
[26] GASB Statement No. 28, paragraph 9.
[27] Such agreements typically involve the return of identical securities (plain vanilla reverse repurchase agreements) or the return of securities that have the same stated interest rate as, and maturities similar to, the securities transferred (fixed-coupon reverse repurchase agreements).

just described are properly reported as collateralized loans. In other words, the borrowing government should continue reporting the securities provided to the broker or dealer as collateral in the statement of position, at the same time reporting the cash proceeds of the loan (and any resulting investments) as an asset, along with a corresponding liability to the lender ("obligations under reverse repurchase agreements").[28]

As noted in the discussion of securities lending arrangements, the specific investments of internal investment pools typically are not reported as such on the face of the statement of position. Instead, each fund simply reports its net position in the pool. GAAP, however, specifically require that assets and liabilities arising in connection with reverse repurchase agreements be reported separately on the face of the statement of position. Accordingly, when an internal investment pool participates in a reverse repurchase agreement, the related assets and liabilities must be allocated among the participating funds in the financial statements based on each fund's relative risk of loss associated with the assets.[29]

There are situations where a reverse repurchase agreement does, in fact, transfer the risks and benefits of ownership to the purchaser. These reverse repurchase agreements of the *yield-maintenance* variety[30] should be handled in exactly the same manner as any other sale and purchase of investments.[31]

Gross reporting for securities lending arrangements and reverse repurchase agreements

Recall from the discussion of securities lending arrangements secured by cash collateral that a government produces income in such situations by reinvesting the collateral at a higher rate of interest than it is paying as a rebate to the party that provided the collateral. Similarly, reverse repurchase agreements are sometimes used in this same manner to generate additional income through leverage. Governments participating in such transactions like to focus attention on the net difference between the interest rate on the borrowing and the income generated by the reinvestment. GAAP, however, specifically prohibit the netting of these amounts.[32] All the same, as explained elsewhere,[33] GAAP do permit financial statement presentations that allow governments to demonstrate this relationship.

Restricted assets

It is common for a creditor to create and retain a security interest in *specific assets* (for instance, a mortgage on real property) to ensure repayment. This situation poses no particular financial reporting problem in the case of capital assets. However, such a security interest raises financial reporting issues in connection with assets that normally are highly liquid, such as cash. Specifically, the restrictions created by the security interest may fundamentally alter the liquidity of the assets concerned, thereby affecting, for example, the presentation of those assets in a classified statement of position (such as the statement of net assets for proprietary funds). Accordingly, GAAP require that restricted assets be reported separately in the statement of posi-

---

[28] GASB Statement No. 3, *Deposits with Financial Institutions, Investments (including Repurchase Agreements), and Reverse Repurchase Agreements*, paragraph 81. The structure described is essentially that of securities lending arrangements of the reinvested-collateral type.

[29] GASB Interpretation No. 3, *Financial Reporting for Reverse Repurchase Agreements: An Interpretation of GASB Statement No. 3*, paragraph 3.

[30] In a yield-maintenance agreement, the securities returned provide the seller-borrower with a yield specified in the agreement; they are not necessarily the same or similar securities.

[31] GASB Statement No. 3, paragraph 83.

[32] GASB Statement No. 3, paragraph 82; GASB Statement No. 28, paragraph 8.

[33] See chapter 15.

tion "when restrictions . . . on asset use change the nature or normal understanding of the availability of the asset."[34] In practice, restricted assets are encountered most commonly in connection with the various special accounts mandated by revenue bond indentures.[35]

Assets held in connection with financial assurance requirements associated with landfills

Owners of municipal solid-waste landfills may be required to provide financial assurance that they will meet their legal obligation to close, monitor, and maintain the landfill site properly once it is no longer in active use. Governments that operate municipal solid-waste landfills may place assets in trust for this purpose. In that case, the assets should be labeled appropriately (for example, "amounts held by trustee") and reported in the same fund used to report the landfill's regular operations (typically an enterprise fund).[36]

Receivables for pension and OPEB contributions

Employers are required to report a liability for their net pension obligation (NPO) or net other postemployment benefits obligation (NOPEBO). An employer incurs an NPO/NOPEBO upon failure to fully fund its actuarially determined annual required contribution.[37] The existence of an employer liability for an NPO/NOPEBO is *not* a sufficient basis for a pension plan or other postemployment benefits (OPEB) plan to report a corresponding receivable. Rather, GAAP indicate that a receivable for employer contributions may only be recognized if the employer shows a formal commitment to make the contribution. Examples of a formal commitment include the employer appropriating a specific contribution, or the employer exhibiting a consistent pattern of making payments after the plan's reporting date pursuant to an established funding policy that attributes those payments to the preceding plan year.[38]

Capital assets held for resale in governmental funds

Governmental funds properly report only *financial* assets.[39] Accordingly, governmental funds routinely exclude capital assets such as land and buildings, because those assets normally are meant to be used in operations rather than converted to cash. However, there are situations where capital assets are acquired for the express purpose of sale rather than for use in government operations. In such cases, capital assets may properly be reported in a governmental fund as financial assets ("assets held for

---

[34] GASB Statement No. 34, *Basic Financial Statements—and Management's Discussion and Analysis—for State and Local Governments*, paragraph 99.

[35] Common examples of restricted assets associated with revenue bond indentures include: 1) the revenue bond construction account (cash, investments, and accrued interest segregated by the bond indenture for construction); 2) the revenue bond operations and maintenance account (accumulations of resources equal to operating costs for a specified period); 3) the revenue bond current debt service account (accumulations of resources for principal and interest payments due within one year); 4) the revenue bond future debt service account (accumulations of resources for principal and interest payments beyond the subsequent 12 months); and 5) the revenue bond renewal and replacement account (accumulations of resources for unforeseen repairs and replacements of assets originally acquired with bond proceeds).

[36] GASB Statement No. 18, *Accounting for Municipal Solid Waste Landfill Closure and Postclosure Care Costs*, paragraph 15.

[37] GASB Statement No. 27, *Accounting for Pensions by State and Local Governmental Employers*, paragraph 11; GASB Statement No. 45, *Accounting and Financial Reporting by Employers for Postemployment Benefits Other Than Pensions*, paragraph 14.

[38] GASB Statement No. 25, *Financial Reporting for Defined Benefit Pension Plans and Note Disclosures for Defined Contribution Plans*, paragraph 22; GASB Statement No. 43, *Financial Reporting for Postemployment Benefit Plans Other Than Pensions*, paragraph 20.

[39] See chapter 10.

resale"). The following common situations are among those in which capital assets are acquired for resale:

- *Foreclosure assets.* Governments sometimes must foreclose on real property to collect amounts due to the government for back taxes, penalties, and interest. Such assets almost always are sold rather than retained by the government. Accordingly, foreclosure assets may be reported in the governmental funds. Normally, these assets would be valued in the governmental fund at the amount of the related lien on the property. However, if sale of the property likely will not generate sufficient proceeds to cover the full amount of the liens, the assets should be reported at their lower, net realizable value.
- *Redevelopment properties.* Governments occasionally acquire property in economically depressed areas, intending to render the property suitable for economic development (by razing vacant buildings, for instance) and then reselling it to private-sector purchasers meeting certain criteria. Because such properties are acquired with the express intent of resale, they may properly be reported at cost in the governmental funds. Again, however, care must be taken to ensure that the properties are not reported at an amount higher than their expected net realizable value.
- *Donated capital assets.* Various parties outside the government may contribute land, buildings, or other capital assets to a government. Such assets may be reported in the governmental funds if the government intends to liquidate the assets rather than retain them for use in operations. In this instance, the government's intent should be supported by a contract for sale prior to issuance of the financial statements.[40] Otherwise, the donated asset should be treated like a capital asset used in the government's operations until a sale occurs.

Fund balance should be reserved in connection with these assets to the extent that they are not considered available to liquidate liabilities of the current period and are not otherwise offset by deferred revenue.[41]

Capital assets to be reported

Capital assets are tangible and intangible assets acquired for use in operations that will benefit more than a single fiscal period.[42] Typical examples are land, improvements to land, easements, water rights, buildings, building improvements, vehicles, machinery, equipment, works of art and historical treasures, infrastructure, and various intangible assets. (Land associated with infrastructure should be reported as land rather than as part of the cost of the related infrastructure asset).[43]

As a general rule, governments should report all and only those capital assets that they own. Ownership typically is evidenced by title. However, situations do occur where one party has the risks and benefits of ownership associated with a given capital asset, while another party actually holds title to the asset (e.g., capital leases). In such a situation, it is the party that

---

[40] This recommendation is based on the inherent difficulty of arriving at a reliable estimate of the fair value of many capital assets donated to governments. It also is consistent with the position in GASB Statement No. 11, *Measurement Focus and Basis of Accounting—Governmental Fund Operating Statements,* paragraph 60. Although GASB Statement No. 11 never took effect, none of the board's subsequent positions are inconsistent with the specific guidance cited here.

[41] AICPA, *State and Local Governments,* Section 10.10.

[42] GASB Statement No. 34, paragraph 19.

[43] GASB, *Comprehensive Implementation Guide (2004),* 7.423.

has the risks and benefits of ownership that should report the capital asset on its statement of position.[44]

Sometimes the ownership of a capital asset may not be clear, particularly in the case of networks or subsystems of infrastructure assets. In that case, the item in question should be reported as an asset of the government that is primarily responsible for the asset's management and maintenance.[45] It must be emphasized, however, that management and maintenance are relevant considerations *only in situations where actual ownership is unclear*. That is, a government that owns an infrastructure asset should report that asset on its statement of position even if some other government is responsible for managing and maintaining it.[46] To take the matter a step further, one government may be responsible for managing a given infrastructure asset, while another government may be responsible for eventually replacing that same asset. In that situation, presuming the ownership of the asset is not evident, it is the government that manages the infrastructure that should report an asset on its statement of position.[47]

The federal government may retain a reversionary interest (i.e., a claim to an asset upon disposal) in capital assets that state and local governments acquire with federal funding. A federal reversionary interest is *not* tantamount to ownership and, therefore, should not prevent state and local governments from reporting a capital asset on their statement of position.[48]

In some instances, not only may the government's ownership of certain infrastructure assets be unclear, but responsibility for their management may rest with others, such as property owners (e.g., sidewalks in some circumstances). Governments should *not* report such items as capital assets on their statement of position.[49]

Collections (works of art and historical artifacts, for example) meet the definition of a capital asset and normally should be reported in the financial statements.[50] The requirement for capitalization is waived, however, for collections that meet all of the following conditions:

- the collection is held for reasons other than financial gain;
- the collection is protected, kept unencumbered, cared for, and preserved; and
- the collection is subject to an organizational policy requiring that the proceeds from sales of collection items be used to acquire other items for collections.[51]

---

[44] GASB, *Comprehensive Implementation Guide (2004)*, 7.41.
[45] GASB Statement No. 34, footnote 67.
[46] GASB, *Comprehensive Implementation Guide (2004)*, 7.52.
[47] GASB, *Comprehensive Implementation Guide (2004)*, 7.54.
[48] GASB, *Comprehensive Implementation Guide (2004)*, 7.42.
[49] GASB, *Comprehensive Implementation Guide (2004)*, 7.53.
[50] GAAP set special rules governing the capitalization of collections, but offer no definition of that term. Those interested in further clarification may wish to refer to paragraph 128 of the Financial Accounting Standards Board's (FASB) Statement No. 116, *Accounting for Contributions Received and Contributions Made*, which states that collections "generally are held by museums, botanical gardens, libraries, aquariums, arboretums, historic sites, planetariums, zoos, art galleries, nature, science and technology centers, and similar educational, research, and public service organizations that have those divisions; however, the definition is not limited to those entities nor does it apply to all items held by those entities." (GASB, *Comprehensive Implementation Guide (2004)*, 7.105.)
[51] GAAP do *not* require such a written statement of policy in the case of collections that are permanently installed and that cannot be removed without destroying the items (e.g., murals). (GASB, *Comprehensive Implementation Guide (2004)*, 7.110.)

GAAP encourage but do not require the capitalization of collections that meet all of the above criteria. With rare exceptions (e.g., successful breeding colonies), zoo animals do *not* meet the criteria for a collection exempt from capitalization and therefore should be capitalized and depreciated like other capital assets.[52]

Capital asset valuation

Capital assets should be reported at their historical cost. In the absence of historical cost information, the asset's *estimated* historical cost may be used. Assets donated by discretely presented component units or by parties outside the financial reporting entity should be reported at their fair value on the date the donation is made.[53] When capital assets are moved from one fund or activity to another, the recipient fund or activity should continue to report those assets at their historical cost as of the date they were acquired by the primary government.[54]

The historical cost of a capital asset should include all of the following:[55]
- ancillary charges necessary to place the asset in its intended location (freight charges, for example);
- ancillary charges necessary to place the asset in its intended condition for use (installation and site preparation charges, for example); and
- capitalized interest (only for enterprise funds and internal service funds that are reported as part of *business-type activities*).[56]

The historical cost of a capital asset should *include* the cost of any subsequent additions or improvements but *exclude* the cost of repairs. An addition or improvement, unlike a repair, either enhances a capital asset's functionality (effectiveness or efficiency), or it extends a capital asset's expected useful life. For example, periodically resurfacing a road, (assuming that the road surface was not treated as a separate asset in its own right), would be treated as a repair (i.e., the cost *would not* be capitalized), whereas adding a new lane would constitute an addition (i.e., the cost *would* be capitalized).

A variety of methods can be used to estimate the historical cost of capital assets for which invoices and similar documentation of historical cost (*direct costing*) are no longer available. One method is to use historical sources, such as old vendor catalogs, to establish the average cost of obtaining the same or a similar asset at the time of acquisition (*standard costing*). Another approach is to deflate the current cost of the same or a similar asset using an appropriate price index (*normal costing* or *backtrending*).[57] In either case, the estimated historical cost of the capital asset, once calculated,

---

[52] GASB, *Comprehensive Implementation Guide (2004)*, 7.107.

[53] GASB Statement No. 34, paragraph 18. It may be difficult to determine the fair value of donated assets resulting from developer contributions because there often is no ready market for such assets. One practical solution to this potential problem is to use the developer's own costs as a surrogate for fair value. (GASB, *Comprehensive Implementation Guide (2004)*, 7.55.)

[54] Thus, capitalized interest on assets constructed in enterprise funds should *not* be removed if those assets are later reassigned to *governmental activities*, even though interest is *not* capitalized on capital assets acquired for *governmental activities*. (GASB, *Comprehensive Implementation Guide (2004)*, 7.45.)

[55] GASB Statement No. 34, paragraph 18.

[56] Interest capitalization is discussed in detail in chapter 6. Interest is *not* included as part of the cost of the general government's capital assets because interest is reported as a separate non-functional line item in the government-wide statement of activities. Interest also is *not* capitalized in connection with capital assets reported in internal service funds that are included within *governmental activities* in the government-wide financial statements for that same reason. (GASB, *Comprehensive Implementation Guide (2004)*, 7.44.)

[57] Appropriate adjustments should be made, as necessary, to reflect significant changes in construction methods or specifications since the date of acquisition (e.g., as the result of changes to applicable codes, standards, or ordinances). (GASB, *Comprehensive Implementation Guide (2004)*, 7.442.)

would need to be reduced by an appropriate amount of accumulated depreciation.[58]

Assume, for example, that a government wishes to estimate the price of a piece of equipment that was acquired ten years ago and has a remaining useful life of five years. The current cost of the same or a similar asset acquired new is $9,740, and the price index for that class of equipment over the past ten years is 1.87 (that is, an 87 percent increase). In that case, the estimated historical cost of the capital asset could be calculated as follows:

$$\frac{\$9,740 \text{ (cost of a new asset)}}{1.87 \text{ (price index)}} = \$5,209 \text{ (estimated historical cost)}$$

Alternatively, assume that the equipment manufacturer has disclosed that ten years ago, the asset in question sold for approximately $5,400. In that case, the $5,400 quoted by the manufacturer could serve as the asset's estimated historical cost.

In either case, the amount of estimated historical cost must be adjusted for accumulated depreciation as follows:

$$\frac{10 \text{ years (past service life)}}{15 \text{ years (total service life)}} \times \text{(estimated historical cost)} = \text{(accumulated depreciation)}$$

Normal costing/backtrending example:

$$\frac{10}{15} \times \$5,209 \text{ (estimated historical cost)} = \$3,473 \text{ (accumulated depreciation)}$$

$$\$5,209 \text{ (historical cost)} - \$3,473 \text{ (accumulated depreciation)} = \$1,736 \text{ (net book value)}$$

Standard costing example:

$$\frac{10}{15} \times \$5,400 \text{ (estimated historical cost)} = \$3,600 \text{ (accumulated depreciation)}$$

$$\$5,400 \text{ (historical cost)} - \$3,600 \text{ (accumulated depreciation)} = \$1,800 \text{ (net book value)}$$

The example assumes the use of the straight-line method of depreciation, which is the method commonly used in the public sector. Also acceptable are other depreciation methods such as the double-declining balance method and the sum-of-the-years'-digits method.

As noted earlier, land under infrastructure must be reported as part of the *land* account rather than as part of the cost of infrastructure.[59] For this purpose, an easement qualifies as *land*.[60] When the land under infrastructure is donated by developers, the developers' actual costs normally would be an acceptable basis for valuation, as would an estimate made by the government's own public works department.[61] A developer's actual costs could *not* be used for valuation purposes, however, if the land was acquired by the developer a substantial period of time before it was donated to the gov-

---

[58] Depreciation is discussed in more detail later in this chapter.
[59] GASB, *Comprehensive Implementation Guide (2004)*, 7.423.
[60] "An easement for a road is, in substance, equivalent to ownership of the land because the grantor of the easement retains virtually no right of use." (GASB, *Comprehensive Implementation Guide (2004)*, 7.56.)
[61] GASB, *Comprehensive Implementation Guide (2004)*, 7.55.

ernment, since GAAP require that donations be reported at their fair value *as of the date of donation*.

Some have argued that only a nominal value should be assigned to the land under infrastructure. That is, they interpret *fair value* as equivalent to *market value* and take the position that there is no real market for the typically oddly shaped parcels of land that underlie infrastructure. GAAP, however, expressly reject this argument.[62] Instead, *fair value*, in the case of donations of land and infrastructure, ought to be interpreted as applying to the fair value of *acquisition* rather than to *resale* value.

Capitalization thresholds

By definition, any asset that benefits more than one fiscal period potentially could be classified as a capital asset. As a practical matter, however, governments capitalize only their higher-cost assets. That is, governments specify a dollar value or *capitalization threshold* that assets must exceed if they are to be capitalized. Governments are free to select different capitalization thresholds for different capital asset classes, just as they are free to apply different depreciation methods to different capital asset classes.

Governments must, of course, maintain adequate control over all assets, including lower-cost capital assets. Capitalization, however, which necessarily focuses on a government's *financial reporting needs*, is neither designed for nor particularly suited to this purpose. There are means more effective and efficient than capitalization for ensuring control over a government's lower-cost assets. Indeed, the capitalization of numerous small items can have a deleterious effect by overburdening the overall capital asset management system. Accordingly, governments are urged to choose their capitalization thresholds based exclusively on their financial reporting needs, and to use alternative means to ensure control over lower-cost assets. Likewise, the Government Finance Officers Association (GFOA) recommends that capitalization thresholds never be less than $5,000.[63] In setting capitalization thresholds, a government also should consider any restrictions imposed by grantors.[64]

Governments often group assets together for purposes of capitalization. For example, infrastructure assets such as roads, bridges, tunnels, drainage systems, water and sewer systems, dams, and lighting systems normally are grouped into networks or subsystems rather than reported as individual items. This approach can greatly simplify accounting and financial reporting for capital assets, thereby increasing effectiveness and efficiency.

Consistent with the recommendation on capitalization thresholds discussed earlier, governments normally are discouraged from capitalizing as a group smaller items that would not individually meet their capitalization threshold (school desks, for instance). Too strict an application of this approach, however, could result in significant classes of capital assets not being reported (e.g., library books in the case of a library district). Accordingly, GAAP advise that governments strive for "an appropriate balance

---

[62] GASB, *Comprehensive Implementation Guide* (2004), 7.56.

[63] See GFOA recommended practice on "Establishing Appropriate Capitalization Thresholds for Capital Assets" (2001). Naturally, this recommendation should be implemented only to the extent that it is consistent with constitutional, statutory, and other state and local provisions regarding capitalization thresholds.

[64] For example, grantors may prohibit capitalization levels in excess of $5,000 for certain classes of assets acquired with grant funds.

between ensuring that all material capital assets, collectively, are capitalized and minimizing the cost of record keeping for capital assets."[65]

Depreciation

Depreciation is the systematic and rational allocation of the cost of a capital asset over its estimated useful life. Because of the absence of tax incentives for accelerated depreciation methods in the public sector, most governments depreciate their capital assets on a straight-line basis.

Governments may elect to use composite depreciation methods for certain types of capital assets rather than depreciate them individually.[66] It is important to note in this regard that composite depreciation can be applied to groups of dissimilar assets within the same capital asset class (e.g., buildings), but *not* to different classes of capital assets (e.g., buildings and equipment). For this purpose, infrastructure networks or subsystems are considered to constitute a single asset class.[67]

Because depreciation is intended to allocate the cost of a capital asset over its entire useful life, it normally is *not* appropriate to report assets still in service as fully depreciated. Instead, the annual amount of depreciation expense should be reduced prospectively as soon as it becomes clear that an asset's useful life will be longer than originally estimated.[68] In practice, however, the use of *average* estimated useful lives for entire classes of assets means that at least a few fully depreciated capital assets typically will be reported (i.e., those whose actual lives exceed the group estimate). Such reporting of fully depreciated capital assets is acceptable, *but only if such balances do not become material*, in which case the estimated useful life for the group would need to be changed.[69]

Depreciation is *not* appropriate for land[70] and other assets that are considered to be inexhaustible (e.g., certain art treasures held by a museum).

Depreciation accounting requires that governments estimate the useful service lives of their depreciable capital assets, a process commonly known as "lifing." It is recommended that governments profit to the greatest extent possible from the experience of other governments and private-sector enterprises when estimating the useful lives of their own capital assets. At the same time, governments should make whatever adjustments are needed to any estimates obtained from others to ensure that such estimates are appropriate to their particular circumstances, as evidenced by their own experience.[71] It is especially important that governments consider the potential effect of each of the following factors on the estimated useful lives of their capital assets:

- *Quality.* Similar assets may differ substantially in quality, and hence in their useful lives, because of differences in materials, design, and

---

[65] GASB, *Comprehensive Implementation Guide* (2004), 7.43.

[66] Composite depreciation methods, for instance, can be based on: 1) the weighted average of the estimated useful lives of the assets that make up the group; 2) the unweighted average of the estimated useful lives of the assets that make up the group; or 3) an estimate of the useful life of the group of assets *as a group*. The depreciation rate calculated for a group of assets using a composite method must be adjusted to reflect any significant changes in either the composition of the group of assets or in their estimated lives.

[67] GASB, *Comprehensive Implementation Guide* (2004), 7.75.

[68] GASB, *Comprehensive Implementation Guide* (2004), 7.409.

[69] GASB, *Comprehensive Implementation Guide* (2004), 7.67.

[70] Land used for certain purposes (e.g., toxic waste disposal) does lose its value through use and should be depreciated.

[71] Information from a government's own public works department is particularly valuable in this regard.

workmanship. For example, an asphalt road will not have the same useful life as a concrete road. Likewise, the depth of the material used for paving purposes, as well as the quality of the underlying base, will also affect the useful life of a road.

- *Application.* The useful life of a given type of capital asset may vary significantly depending upon its intended use. For example, a vehicle used in the public safety function may have a different useful life than a similar vehicle used in the parks and recreation function.
- *Environment.* Environmental differences among governments can have an important impact on the useful lives of their respective capital assets. For instance, the useful life of a road in a climate subject to extremes in temperature is likely to be different from that of a similar road located in a more temperate climate. Also, regulatory obsolescence may shorten the service life of some capital assets used in connection with highly regulated activities (e.g., utilities).

Naturally, the weight to be assigned to each of these specific factors will depend upon how a government manages its capital assets. The potential effect of each of the factors just described may be mitigated or exacerbated as a consequence of a government's maintenance and replacement policy. For example, the potential for road damage is increased in a cold environment when cracks are not promptly repaired, because water settling in the cracks will expand and contract, thereby accelerating the initial deterioration represented by the crack itself.

Once established, estimated useful lives for major categories of capital assets should be periodically compared with a government's actual experience and appropriate adjustments should be made to reflect this experience.[72]

As in the private sector, changes in the estimated useful life of a capital asset should always be handled *prospectively.*

Modified approach for infrastructure

In some regards, infrastructure assets resemble land to the extent that many infrastructure assets may reasonably be expected to continue to function indefinitely if they are adequately preserved and maintained. Accordingly, GAAP allow a government to forego reporting depreciation in connection with networks or subsystems of infrastructure assets, provided that the government has made a commitment to maintain those particular networks or subsystems at a predetermined condition level of its own choosing and has established an asset management system that is adequate for that purpose. Governments that elect to follow this method are said to be using the *modified approach* to infrastructure reporting.

GAAP set the following specific requirements that must be met by a network or subsystem of infrastructure assets to qualify for using the modified approach:

- The government must have an up-to-date inventory of infrastructure assets within the network or subsystem for which the modified approach is adopted.
- The government must perform or obtain condition assessments on infrastructure assets and summarize the results using a measurement scale. This required condition assessment must be performed at least

---

[72] GFOA recommended practice on "Establishing the Estimated Useful Life of Capital Assets" (2002).

once every three years.[73] It is essential that such condition assessments be replicable (conducted using methods that would allow different measurers to reach substantially similar results). Statistical sampling may be used for condition assessments, provided that each item in a network or subsystem of infrastructure assets has an equal chance of being selected for sampling purposes.[74]

- Each year the government must estimate the amount needed to maintain and preserve infrastructure assets at a condition level established and disclosed by the government.[75]
- The government must document that infrastructure assets are being preserved at or above the condition level established and disclosed by the government.[76]

Governments that use the modified approach for one or more networks or subsystems of infrastructure assets are required to present certain data as required supplementary information to demonstrate that they are, in fact, maintaining their commitment to adequately preserve and maintain those assets at an appropriate condition level.[77]

The modified approach is available for all infrastructure networks and subsystems, including those of business-type activities. If a government that has been using the modified approach for a network or subsystem of infrastructure assets subsequently fails to preserve and maintain that network or subsystem at the predetermined condition level (as indicated by the periodic condition assessment), it must then begin to depreciate the affected network or subsystem *on a prospective basis.*[78] Alternatively, the government could elect to lower the predetermined condition level.[79]

It was noted earlier that normally the historical cost of a capital asset should include the cost of any subsequent additions or improvements. However, because the modified approach presumes an indefinite asset life, the only additions or improvements that should be capitalized when this approach is used are those that enhance the asset's functionality.[80]

Governments may convert from the modified approach to depreciation accounting or from depreciation accounting to the modified approach (assuming the criteria for using the modified approach have been met) if the change is considered to result in a *preferable* accounting treatment. In either case, the change must be handled *prospectively* (as just described for the involuntary conversion from the modified approach to depreciation accounting). Assume, for example, that a government originally estimated that a subsystem of infrastructure that cost $40 million would have an estimated useful life of 40 years and that 20 years after acquisition the govern-

[73] A government may adopt the modified approach for a given network or subsystem as soon as at least one complete condition assessment has been performed for that network or subsystem. (GASB, *Comprehensive Implementation Guide (2004)*, 7.430.)
[74] GASB, *Comprehensive Implementation Guide (2004)*, 7.99.
[75] Disparities between estimated and actual maintenance and preservation expense would not, of themselves, disqualify a government from continuing to use the modified approach. Only an actual decline in the condition of infrastructure assets below targeted levels (which is the likely ultimate outcome of habitually deferred maintenance) would disqualify a government from the continued use of the modified approach. (GASB, *Comprehensive Implementation Guide (2004)*, 7.103.)
[76] GASB Statement No. 34, paragraphs 23-26.
[77] See chapter 13 for a discussion of required disclosures.
[78] GASB, *Comprehensive Implementation Guide (2004)*, 7.88.
[79] GASB, *Comprehensive Implementation Guide (2004)*, 7.90.
[80] That is, it is impossible to extend the life of a capital asset for which an indefinite useful life is presumed. (GASB, *Comprehensive Implementation Guide (2004)*, 7.82.-7.83.)

ment decided to convert to the modified approach for that subsystem. In that case, the $20 million undepreciated book value of the asset (i.e., $40 million - $20 million accumulated depreciation) would be the value henceforth reported using the modified approach. Conversely, if the asset had originally been accounted for using the modified approach and the decision was made at the end of 20 years to convert to depreciation accounting with an estimated remaining useful service life of 20 years, the full $40 million cost would need to be depreciated over the remaining 20 years.[81]

GFOA advises governments that are considering the possibility of adopting the modified approach for one or more of their networks or subsystems of infrastructure assets to carefully weigh a number of factors before making a decision one way or the other.[82]

Capital asset impairments

Normally capital assets used in operations are reported at their historical cost (or estimated fair value as of the date of donation), less accumulated depreciation. Capital assets that are *permanently removed from service*, for whatever reason, must be written down to their fair value (if lower than carrying value).[83] The carrying value of a capital asset must also be adjusted, *even though it will remain in service*, if its service utility has been significantly impaired in any of the following circumstances:

- physical damage;

[81] GASB, *Comprehensive Implementation Guide (2004)*, 7.88; GASB Statement No. 37, *Basic Financial Statements—and Management's Discussion and Analysis—for State and Local Governments: Omnibus*, paragraphs 8-9.

[82] Per GFOA's recommended practice on "Considerations on the Use of the Modified Approach to Account for Infrastructure Assets" (2002), a balanced and informed decision on whether a government should use the modified approach for a given network or subsystem of infrastructure assets should take into consideration all of the following factors:

- *Usefulness of data for managerial purposes.* The modified approach provides information on capital assets that clearly is of value for the budget process and for asset management purposes. It also has the advantage of avoiding the costs associated with the depreciation of infrastructure assets.
- *Potential impact of prospective depreciation.* There is a de facto "penalty" on governments that choose the modified approach but later convert to depreciation accounting, either by choice or necessity (i.e., failure to achieve targeted condition levels). Specifically, governments making the conversion to depreciation accounting are required to depreciate the full cost of the network or subsystem over its estimated remaining service life (i.e., prospective application of depreciation as a change in accounting estimate). Consequently, a change to depreciation accounting late in the life of a network or subsystem of infrastructure assets could result in elevated levels of annual depreciation expense for an extended period.
- *Inherent capital bias.* As just noted, the modified approach creates a de facto accounting "penalty" for governments that fail to maintain their infrastructure assets at selected condition levels. No such penalty applies, however, for failure to adequately fund other essential services. This disparity in treatment creates an inherent bias in favor of capital-related outlays. As a result, the use of the modified approach could distort the process used by governments to set budget priorities.
- *Unmatched debt.* Under regular depreciation accounting, capitalizable improvements include expenditures that either 1) lengthen the useful life of a capital asset or 2) increase the efficiency or effectiveness of a capital asset. If a government selects the modified approach, however, only the second type of improvement may be capitalized. Consequently, a major, debt-financed project designed to lengthen the life of a network or subsystem of infrastructure assets accounted for using the modified approach would result in a government's reporting a significant liability with no corresponding asset related to the construction. Furthermore, the debt would be included as part of the calculation of *unrestricted net assets* rather than as part of the calculation of *invested in capital assets net of related debt*, which could produce a deficit balance in *unrestricted net assets*.
- *Reliance upon interested parties.* It is to be expected that officials responsible for maintaining infrastructure assets will play a major role in selecting condition level targets and in performing condition assessments. As a result, those with the greatest interest in encouraging infrastructure investment are in a unique position to promote that agenda.
- *Decreased comparability.* The use of the modified approach decreases the comparability of cost data among governments.

[83] GASB Statement No. 42, *Accounting and Financial Reporting for Impairment of Capital Assets and for Insurance Recoveries*, paragraph 16.

- changes in legal or environmental factors;
- technological changes or obsolescence;
- changes in manner or duration of use; and
- construction stoppage.[84]

In that case, an impairment needs to be recognized if the situation meets *both* elements of the following *test of impairment:*
- The magnitude of the decline in service utility is significant.
- The decline in service utility is unexpected. (It is only natural that capital assets will lose service capacity with age and use. Such foreseeable changes do *not* constitute an impairment).[85]

Situations that can properly be said to meet both of these criteria would in all likelihood have been the subject of discussion by management or the governing board, or would otherwise have been the topic of press coverage.[86]

Temporary impairments of capital assets should not be recognized in the financial statements. In this regard, the burden of proof is on the government to demonstrate that a given impairment is only temporary. Furthermore, if a government recognizes an impairment because it cannot meet this burden of proof, it may not recognize a subsequent recovery in value should the impairment ultimately prove to be temporary. Assume, for instance, that a school district believed two years ago that its pending conversion of a middle school building from instructional use to storage (i.e., change in manner of use) would only be temporary, but did not have sufficient evidence at the time to overcome the presumption that the resulting impairment was permanent. In that case, no recovery would be reported later if the school district ultimately proved correct and the middle school was reconverted to instructional use.[87]

Sometimes the level of demand for a capital asset is significantly less than anticipated. Such reduced demand should *not*, of itself, be treated as a capital asset impairment. All the same, a reduction in demand resulting from one of the types of circumstances described earlier (e.g., obsolescence) would constitute a capital asset impairment.[88]

The amount of an impairment loss should be calculated using one of three methods. Which method is used in a particular case will depend upon the circumstances that gave rise to the impairment, as follows:
- *Restoration cost approach.* Used in situations involving evidence of physical damage.
- *Service units approach.* Used for impairments arising from 1) changes in legal or environmental factors, 2) technological changes or obsolescence, or 3) changes in the manner or duration of use.
- *Deflated depreciated replacement cost approach.* An alternative method available for impairments involving changes in the manner or duration of use.[89]

---

[84] GASB Statement No. 42, paragraph 9.
[85] GASB Statement No. 42, paragraph 11.
[86] GASB Statement No. 42, paragraph 8.
[87] GASB Statement No. 42, paragraph 18.
[88] GASB Statement No. 42, paragraph 10.
[89] GASB Statement No. 42, paragraphs 12-15.

EXHIBIT 12-1
Methods of calculating capital asset impairments and their applicability

Situation creating Impairment	Method of calculating impairment		
	Restoration cost approach	Service units approach	Deflated depreciated replacement cost approach
Physical damage	X		
Changes in legal or environmental factors		X	
Technological changes or obsolescence		X	
Changes in the manner or duration of use		X	X

This relationship between the method used to determine the amount of a capital asset impairment and the cause of the impairment is illustrated in Exhibit 12-1.

Note that capital assets that are impaired as the result of a work stoppage are reported at the lower of their carrying value or fair value.[90]

Restoration cost approach   This method uses the cost of restoring a capital asset's service potential as a basis for calculating the relative portion of the historical cost of the asset that has been impaired. The application of this method involves several steps.

- identify the cost to restore the physical damage;
- calculate a damage ratio by comparing either 1) restoration cost (today's dollars) to replacement cost of the entire asset (today's dollars) or 2) deflated restoration cost (acquisition year dollars) to original historical cost (acquisition year dollars);
- apply the damage ratio just calculated to the carrying value of the impaired capital asset; and
- reduce the gross impairment loss (as just calculated) by the amount of any insurance recoveries to arrive at the net impairment loss/gain.

Assume, for example,[91] that a building with a carrying value of $21,466,667 (i.e., $28,000,000 historical cost - $6,533,333 accumulated depreciation = $21,466,667) sustains structural damage as the result of an earthquake. The restoration costs are estimated to amount to $3,500,000. Further assume that the appropriate factor to discount current year dollars to acquisition year dollars is .81309 (i.e., 3 percent per year for seven years), and that the loss will qualify for an insurance recovery of $2,500,000. In that case, the impairment loss would be calculated as follows:

$3,500,000	restoration costs (today's dollars)
× .81309	deflation factor
$2,845,815	restoration costs (acquisition year dollars)

$$\frac{\$2,845,815 \quad \text{restoration costs (acquisition year dollars)}}{\$28,000,000 \quad \text{historical cost (acquisition year dollars)}} = 10.1636\%$$

$21,466,667	carrying value (historical cost less accumulated depreciation)
× .101636	damage ratio

[90] GASB Statement No. 42, paragraph 16.
[91] GASB Statement No. 42, illustration 2.

$2,181,786   gross impairment loss
($2,500,000)   less insurance recovery
($318,214)   gain on capital asset impairment[92]

Service units approach

The service units approach compares productivity before and after an impairment to determine the relative portion of the historical cost of the capital asset that has been impaired. There are at least three different ways to apply this approach:

- calculate the ratio of total lost units to total units originally projected and apply that ratio to *total historical cost*;
- calculate the ratio of lost annual production to projected annual production and apply that ratio to *carrying value*; and
- apply the unit cost as originally calculated to remaining units of service.

Total lost units/total projected units.[93] Assume that a government constructed underground storage tanks at a historical cost of $700,000. Further assume that originally the tanks were expected to have a total useful life of 40 years, but recent changes in environmental regulations have now reduced their estimated useful life to just 11 years (i.e., impairment through a change in legal or environmental factors). If each year of service is treated as a "service unit," the impairment caused by the change in regulations could be calculated as follows:

$$\frac{29 \ (\text{total lost units})}{40 \ (\text{total projected units})} \times \$700{,}000 \ (\text{total historical cost}) = \$507{,}500 \ \text{loss}$$

Lost annual production/projected annual production. Assume that a city constructed a stadium for its major league baseball team, but then later lost the team.[94] As a result, the stadium must henceforth be used for activities other than major league baseball games (i.e., impairment through a change in the manner or duration of use of the asset). Further assume that other activities typically bring in only 20 percent of the revenue of a major league baseball game and that it is the latter that will serve as the basic service unit for purposes of the impairment calculation. The original cost of the stadium was $120 million and its carrying value at the time the city lost its team was $52 million (i.e., $120 million cost - $68 million accumulated depreciation = $52 million). Before the team's departure, annual usage was 81 baseball games and 24 other activities. Following the departure, the stadium will be able to book an additional 12 other activities (i.e., total of 36). Based on these assumptions, the impairment loss could be calculated as follows:

81.0   baseball games (81 games)
4.8   other activities (24 x .2 = 4.8)

7.2   other activities (36 x .2 = 7.2)

85.8   projected annual production
(7.2)   actual annual production
78.6   lost annual production

$$\frac{78.6 \ \text{lost annual production}}{85.8 \ \text{total annual production}} \times \$52{,}000{,}000 \ \text{carrying value} = \$47{,}636{,}364 \ \text{loss}$$

---

[92] Since the insured value (fair value/replacement cost) of a capital asset will often exceed its carrying value (historical cost), an impairment "loss" may result in a gain for financial reporting purposes.
[93] GASB Statement No. 42, illustration 3.
[94] GASB Statement No. 42, illustration 6.

Cost of remaining units.[95] Assume that demand for traditional enclosed MRI equipment ($2.25 million original cost - $964,286 accumulated depreciation = $1,285,714 carrying value) has decreased substantially as the result of the introduction of more patient-friendly open-unit technology. Further assume that each individual patient test counts as a service unit. Finally, assume that the original level of usage was projected to be ten tests per day each weekday over the seven-year estimated useful life of the asset, whereas usage during the four remaining years of the asset's useful life following the impairment is now projected to be one test per day each weekday. Based on these assumptions, the original unit cost could be calculated as follows:

$$\frac{10 \text{ tests}}{\text{day}} \times \frac{5 \text{ days}}{\text{week}} \times \frac{52 \text{ weeks}}{\text{year}} \times 7 \text{ years} = 18{,}200 \text{ total tests}$$

$$\frac{\$2{,}250{,}000 \text{ total historical cost}}{18{,}200 \text{ total tests}} = \$124 \text{ / test unit cost}$$

This unit cost could then be applied to the estimated number of tests remaining to calculate the adjusted carrying value of the asset after the impairment, as follows:

$$\frac{1 \text{ test}}{\text{day}} \times \frac{5 \text{ days}}{\text{week}} \times \frac{52 \text{ weeks}}{\text{year}} \times 4 \text{ years} = 1{,}040 \text{ total tests remaining}$$

$$1{,}040 \text{ total tests remaining} \times \$124/\text{test} = \$128{,}960$$

The impairment loss would then be the difference between the carrying value immediately prior to the impairment and the new carrying value just calculated:

$1,285,714	carrying value (prior to impairment)
($128,960)	carrying value (after impairment)
$1,156,754	impairment loss

Deflated depreciated replacement cost

This method calculates what the depreciated cost of a capital asset acquired at the same time, but for a different purpose, would have been in order to determine the relative portion of the carrying value of the capital asset that has been impaired. Assume, for example,[96] that a school building had an original cost of $10 million and has a current carrying value of $7.6 million (i.e., $10 million - $2.4 accumulated depreciation = $7.6 million carrying value). Further assume that the school district recently decided to use the school building for storage rather than for instructional purposes and that the replacement cost for equivalent warehouse space today would be $4.2 million. Finally, assume that what cost $1 in the year the school building was acquired would cost $1.50 today. In that case, the impairment loss could be calculated as follows:

$$\frac{\$7{,}600{,}000 \text{ carrying value}}{\$10{,}000{,}000 \text{ original cost}} = 76\% \text{ remaining carrying value}$$

---

[95] GASB Statement No. 42, illustration 4.
[96] GASB Statement No. 42, illustration 5.

$4,200,000	equivalent warehouse space (today's dollars)
× .76	ratio of remaining carrying value
$3,192,000	equivalent depreciated warehouse space (today's dollars)

$3,192,000	equivalent depreciated warehouse space (today's dollars)
× .67	discount factor to deflate to acquisition-year dollars
$2,128,000	deflated depreciated replacement cost

$7,600,000	carrying value (prior to impairment)
($2,128,000)	carrying value (after impairment)
$5,472,000	impairment loss

Classification of impairment losses

In some cases, a capital asset impairment will qualify as an extraordinary item. Capital asset impairments that are subject to management control (e.g., change in manner or duration of use) may qualify as special items. Otherwise, capital asset impairments should be treated as a component of net program cost in the appropriate functional category.[97]

Insurance recoveries

All insurance recoveries, not just those associated with the impairment of capital assets, should be reported net of the related loss as soon as the recovery is realized or realizable. In governmental funds, recoveries are an other financing source or an extraordinary item.[98]

Computer software

Governments often acquire or develop computer software for internal use (for example, general ledger systems and accounts receivable systems). It is recommended that internal-use computer software be capitalized as an intangible capital asset and amortized (normally on a straight-line basis) over its anticipated useful life.[99]

Not all costs associated with the acquisition of internal-use software qualify for capitalization. For example, costs associated with the preliminary project stage should be expensed as incurred. Such costs could include the conceptual formulation of alternatives, the evaluation of alternatives, the determination of existence of needed technology, and the final selection of alternatives. Likewise, training costs and data conversion costs normally should be expensed as incurred.

Capitalizable costs include external *direct* costs of materials and services consumed in developing or obtaining internal-use software, payroll and payroll-related costs devoted *directly* to the project, and interest costs incurred during development.[100] Examples of such costs include those associated with the design of a chosen path (including the software configuration and the software interfaces), coding, installation to hardware, and testing (including the parallel processing phase). Upgrades and enhancements should be capitalized only to the extent that they increase the functionality of the product.

Capitalization should occur only *after* the preliminary project stage is complete. Likewise, capitalization is appropriate only if management has authorized and committed to funding the project, and it is considered probable that the project will be completed and put to its intended use. The capi-

---

[97] GASB Statement No. 42, paragraph 17.
[98] GASB Statement No. 42, paragraph 21.
[99] This recommendation would not apply, of course, to governmental funds, which do not report intangible assets. It is still recommended, however, that software related to governmental funds be capitalized and amortized in the government-wide financial statements.
[100] Interest is *not* capitalized on capital assets of the general government.

talization of costs related to internal-use software should cease once testing is complete.[101]

Joint venture assets

Governments do *not* report an asset in connection with all joint ventures in which they participate. Rather, governments report an asset for participation in a joint venture only when they have an explicit, measurable equity interest in the joint venture based on the joint venture agreement.[102]

For practical reasons, a government's interest in a joint venture often represents its interest in the capital assets of the joint venture. To the extent that a government's explicit, measurable equity interest in a joint venture is not a *financial* asset (because it represents the government's underlying interest in the capital assets of the joint venture), that interest should *not* be reported as an asset in the governmental funds. It should, however, still be reported in connection with governmental activities in the government-wide statement of net assets.[103] In this case, the relevant portion of government-wide net assets should *not* be reported as *invested in capital assets, net of related debt,* because an interest in a joint venture, even when it represents an interest in the joint venture's capital assets, is still not a *capital* asset, properly speaking, from the perspective of the participating government.[104]

Capitalization contributions

Governments that participate in public-entity risk pools often are asked to provide start-up capital or "seed money" in the form of a capitalization contribution. Capitalization contributions to public-entity risk pools should *not* be treated as an equity interest in a joint venture. Instead, the proper accounting and financial reporting for capitalization contributions depend on two factors: 1) whether the contribution is made to a public-entity risk pool that truly pools or transfers risk; and 2) whether it is probable that the contribution will be returned to the participating government upon dissolution of the public-entity risk pool or upon the government's withdrawal from the pool.

If a capitalization contribution is made to a public-entity risk pool that does *not* pool or transfer risk (a claims servicing pool is an example), the capitalization contribution should be treated as a deposit or, if there is a liability for claims and judgments, as a reduction of that liability.

If the capitalization contribution is made to a public-entity risk pool that *does* pool or transfer risk, the appropriate treatment depends on whether the government considers it probable that the capitalization contribution will be returned.

- If the return of the capitalization contribution is considered probable, then it should be treated by the participating government as a deposit (an asset or, if there is a liability for claims and judgments, as a reduction of that liability). If the deposit is reported in a governmental fund,

---

[101] The guidance presented here is based on the AICPA's Statement of Position (SOP) 98-1, *Accounting for the Costs of Computer Software Developed or Obtained for Internal Use.* This guidance is only a recommendation, as SOP 98-1 specifically does *not* apply to state and local governments (a practical example of the use of "other sources" of generally accepted accounting principles [GAAP] mentioned in the discussion of the GAAP hierarchy in chapter 1).
[102] GASB Statement No. 14, *The Financial Reporting Entity,* paragraph 72.
[103] GASB Statement No. 14, paragraph 74.
[104] GASB, *Comprehensive Implementation Guide (2004),* 7.151.

fund balance should be reserved to indicate that the amount is not available for expenditure.

- If the return of the contribution is *not* considered probable, the appropriate accounting and financial reporting depends on the fund or unit making the contribution. Governmental funds have the option of reporting the contribution either as a prepaid asset or as an expenditure of the period.[105] Proprietary funds should report a prepaid asset. Whenever a prepaid asset is reported, an expenditure or expense should be recognized over the period coverage is to be provided. This period should be consistent with the period during which the contribution is factored into the pool's determination of premiums; if this period is not readily determinable, expenditure or expense should be reported over a period not to exceed 10 years. If a governmental fund is used, fund balance must be reserved to indicate that the amount is not available for expenditure.[106]

Split-interest agreements

Colleges and universities sometimes are participants in split-interest agreements. A typical split-interest agreement operates as follows:

- a donor provides assets to a college or university that agrees to act as trustee of those assets for a predetermined period;
- as trustee, the college or university agrees to make an annual distribution to a beneficiary specified by the donor; and
- at the end of the predetermined period (e.g., the lifetime of the beneficiary specified by the donor), the remaining assets of the trust revert to the institution/trustee.

A college or university should recognize an asset equal to the fair value of the assets held in trust at the inception of a split-interest agreement. The initial difference between the fair value of the assets held in trust and the liability to the beneficiary should be recognized as gift revenue. Subsequent changes should be reflected in operations in the period in which they occur.[107]

LIABILITY-RELATED ISSUES

Matured debt associated with governmental funds

State and local governments generally do make timely debt service payments, so an individual government's failure to make a debt service payment when due does not alter the reality that such payments *normally* are expected to be liquidated with current available financial resources. Consequently, governmental funds should always report an expenditure and a liability for *matured* long-term debt and related accrued interest.[108]

Interfund debt

Governmental funds typically do *not* report unmatured long-term debt. For this purpose, *long-term debt* properly applies only to debt associated with parties *outside the primary government*, including the government's discretely presented component units. Interfund borrowings, regardless of the

---

[105] *Governmental activities* in the government-wide financial statements, of course, must report a prepaid asset regardless of the option selected for the governmental funds.
[106] GASB Interpretation No. 4, *Accounting and Financial Reporting for Capitalization Contributions to Public Entity Risk Pools.*
[107] GASB, *Comprehensive Implementation Guide (2004)*, 7.324.
[108] National Council on Governmental Accounting (NCGA) Statement 1, *Governmental Accounting and Financial Reporting Principles*, principle 8.

terms of the loan, must always be treated as a liability of the governmental fund that receives the proceeds.[109]

Early recognition of debt service expenditures in debt service funds

Debt service funds offer an exception to the general rule that governmental funds should *not* report expenditures and liabilities in connection with unmatured long-term debt. Specifically, governments have the *option* of recognizing an expenditure and a liability in a debt service fund in the current period if "debt service fund resources have been provided during the current year for payment of principal and interest due early in the following year."[110] This *early recognition option* is designed to allow governments to avoid inflating fund balance in their debt service funds by allowing them to recognize an expenditure and a liability in the current period to balance the other financing source and asset associated with the transfer of resources to the debt service fund.

Several points must be emphasized regarding the application of this early recognition option for debt service payments:

- *The early recognition approach is only an option.* Governments are free to apply the general rule on debt service expenditure recognition to all of their long-term debt, including amounts due early in the subsequent year for which resources have been transferred to a debt service fund during the current fiscal year. Like any other GAAP option, this one must be applied consistently from period to period.
- *The early recognition option for debt service applies only to situations where debt service payments are made from a debt service fund.*[111] Some governments do not use debt service funds, or they make debt service payments from other funds as well.
- *The early recognition option applies only to the nondiscretionary transfer of dedicated resources to a debt service fund.*[112] Governments often transfer resources to debt service funds because they are legally obligated to do so. In other cases, however, governments voluntarily provide resources to a debt service fund. Such voluntary transfers do *not* qualify for the early recognition option.
- *The early recognition option applies only to payments due within one month.*[113] The option was intended to apply only to payments due *early in the following fiscal year,* typically within several days of the current fiscal year-end. While governments enjoy some flexibility in determining what constitutes *early in the following year,* GAAP indicate it is not acceptable to include debt service payments due more than one month after the close of the current fiscal year.

Proprietary fund debt

Proprietary funds use the economic resources measurement focus, which requires those funds to report *all* assets and liabilities, including long-term debt. Debt is properly considered a proprietary fund liability only if it meets *both* of the following criteria:

- *Direct relationship.* Debt must be *directly related* to a given proprietary fund to be reported as debt of that fund.

---

[109] GASB Statement No. 34, paragraph 112.
[110] NCGA Statement 1, paragraph 72.
[111] GASB Interpretation No. 6, *Recognition and Measurement of Certain Liabilities and Expenditures in Governmental Fund Financial Statements,* paragraph 13.
[112] GASB Interpretation No. 6, paragraph 13.
[113] GASB Interpretation No. 6, paragraph 13.

- *Proprietary fund financing.* Not all debt associated with proprietary funds will necessarily be repaid from the resources of those funds. For example, governments often issue debt that will be repaid out of general revenues to finance capital contributions to proprietary funds. Only when debt is intended to be repaid from the resources of a proprietary fund should it be classified as debt of that fund.

The underlying security interest for debt should *not* be the determining factor in whether a given debt issue is reported as an obligation of the general government or as proprietary fund debt. Assume, for example, that a government issues debt backed by the full faith and credit of the government for the benefit of a given proprietary fund. The proprietary fund is expected to fully repay this debt from its own resources. In that case, the debt would be properly reported as a liability of the proprietary fund, even though it is backed by the full faith and credit of the general government. The reasons: 1) The debt is *directly related* to the proprietary fund; and 2) the debt is *intended to be repaid from the resources of the proprietary fund.*[114] If only a portion of a given debt issue is to be repaid from the resources of a proprietary fund then only that portion should be reported as proprietary fund debt.

Capital leases and fiscal funding/appropriations clauses

Governments use the same criteria for capital leases as do private-sector enterprises. One unique factor, however, needs to be taken into account when applying these criteria in the public sector. As a matter of public policy, legislative bodies often are prevented legally from entering into obligations extending beyond the current budget year. Accordingly, it is common for a public-sector lease contract to contain a *fiscal funding clause* or a cancellation clause that makes the continuation of the agreement subject to future appropriations.

Normally, a lease agreement must be noncancellable to qualify as a capital lease. For all practical purposes, however, fiscal funding clauses are essentially a legal fiction given the effect that invoking such a provision would have on a government's credit. Since GAAP emphasize the need to classify transactions based on their economic substance rather than their legal form, the presence of a fiscal funding clause in a lease contract should not prevent the agreement from qualifying as a capital lease, provided that the likelihood of invoking the provision is considered to be remote.[115]

Deferred revenue

There are two meanings for *deferred revenue* in the public sector.
- *Unearned revenue.* Under both the accrual and the modified accrual basis of accounting, revenue may be recognized only when it is earned. If assets are recognized in connection with a transaction before the earnings process is complete, those assets must be offset by a corresponding liability for *deferred revenue* (commonly referred to as *unearned revenue* in the private sector). Such deferred revenue can be found in government-wide financial reporting as well as in governmental fund, proprietary fund, and fiduciary fund financial statements.
- *Unavailable revenue.* Under the modified accrual basis of accounting, it is not enough that revenue has been earned if it is to be recognized as

---

[114] NCGA Statement 1, paragraph 42.
[115] NCGA Statement No. 5, *Accounting and Financial Reporting Principles for Lease Agreements of State and Local Governments,* paragraphs 18-21.

revenue of the current period. Revenue must also be susceptible to accrual (it must be both measurable and *available to finance expenditures of the current fiscal period*). If assets are recognized in connection with a transaction, but those assets are not yet available to finance expenditures of the current fiscal period, then the assets must be offset by a corresponding liability for deferred revenue. This type of deferred revenue is unique to governmental funds, since it is tied to the *modified* accrual basis of accounting, which is used only in connection with governmental funds.

Compensated absences

Compensated absences commonly describe paid time off made available to employees in connection with vacation leave, sick leave, and similar benefits. For financial reporting purposes, *compensated absences* are strictly limited to leave that 1) is attributable to *services already rendered,* and 2) is *not contingent* on a specific event (such as illness) that is outside the control of the employer and employee. GAAP require that employers report a liability for compensated absences that meets both of these criteria.[116]

Vacation leave

A government should recognize a liability for vacation leave if it meets two conditions: the vacation leave is related to employee services already rendered, and it is probable that the leave will be paid.

The term *vested* commonly describes employee benefits that are *not* dependent on continued employment. GAAP require that in addition to vested amounts, vacation leave also must be reported for *nonvested* amounts that are expected to vest. Assume for example that new employees earn one day of leave per month but may not take any leave before completing a six-month probationary period. Employees not completing the probationary period forfeit any leave accumulated during that period. In this situation, the employer must accrue leave earned by new employees to the extent that those employees are expected to successfully complete the probationary period. Conversely, the liability for vacation leave should *not* include accumulated amounts of vacation leave that are expected to lapse (such as vacation leave accumulated in excess of the maximum carry-forward amount).[117]

The liability for vacation leave should include salary-related payments, which are payments *directly and incrementally related to the amount of salary paid* to the employee. Typical salary-related payments include the employer's share of Social Security, Medicare taxes, employer contributions to cost-sharing multiple-employer public employee retirement systems, and employer payments to defined contribution pension arrangements.

Salary-related payments do not include contributions paid to single-employer pension and other postemployment benefit plans or to an agent multiple-employer plan. Similarly, life-insurance premiums and healthcare premiums paid on behalf of employees do not normally qualify as salary-related payments. In practical terms, governments need to establish a salary-related benefit rate to use in the calculation of the total leave liability.[118]

---

[116] GASB Statement No. 16, *Accounting for Compensated Absences*, paragraph 7.
[117] GASB Statement No. 16, paragraph 7.
[118] GASB Statement No. 16, paragraph 11.

The liability for vacation leave should be calculated using pay or salary rates in effect at the date of the statement of position. Current salary costs are used for this purpose because they are considered "objective, easily measurable, and not affected by the timing of pay increases."[119]

In some unusual situations, employees may not be compensated for leave on the basis of current salary. In such cases, the rate that should be used to value the liability is the applicable contractual rate rather than the rate in effect at the date of the statement of position.[120]

Sick leave

Sick leave does not qualify as a compensated absence because it is contingent on a future event (namely, illness) that is beyond the control of both the employer and the employee. Accordingly, sick leave should *not* be accrued as a liability. It is common, however, for governments to make a payment to employees upon termination for a portion of their balance of unused sick leave. When unused sick leave is payable upon termination, it is no longer contingent on a future event outside the control of both the employer and the employee and, consequently, must be included as part of the liability for compensated absences. Either of two approaches can be taken to measure the amount of the liability for unused sick leave payable upon termination:

- *Termination payments method.* Under this approach, a government estimates the amount of sick leave that will be paid out upon termination based on its experience in making such payments. Three methods of applying the termination payments method are illustrated in Exhibit 12-2.
- *Vesting method.* Financial statement preparers following this approach estimate the liability for sick leave payouts by calculating the amount of sick leave that is expected to become eligible for payment at termination. This calculation, of course, must take into account caps on the amount of sick leave eligible for payout (for instance, 30 days), as well as any special rates that apply to sick leave payouts (perhaps 30 percent of normal pay). Application of the vesting method is illustrated in Exhibit 12-3.

Several observations must be made regarding use of the two approaches for measuring the amount of the liability for unused sick leave payable upon termination. The vesting method may be more practical in situations where a government does not have adequate historical data to establish sick leave payout patterns. Similarly, sick leave payout patterns may be of limited benefit in estimating future payouts for governments with a relatively small number of employees.

Of course, some of the leave that is eligible for payout upon termination may eventually be used during an illness. Consequently, the liability calculated using the vesting method is likely to include a certain amount of sick leave that will, in fact, be used to compensate employees for time taken off on account of illness. Although GAAP normally prohibit the recognition of a liability for sick leave as such, the incidental inclusion of sick leave under the vesting method is permitted based on cost-benefit considerations.

It also should be noted that the time focus is different for the two methods. The termination payments method focuses on several past periods,

---

[119] GASB Statement No. 16, paragraphs 10 and 46.
[120] GASB Statement No. 16, paragraph 10.

EXHIBIT 12-2

Application of the termination payments method to calculate the liability for sick leave payable upon termination

"Days paid" approach*	"Amount paid" approach*	"Ratio" approach
Prepare a list of employees who have terminated during the past several years (e.g., preceding five years)	Prepare a list of employees who have terminated during the past several years (e.g., preceding five years)	
Calculate total years of employee service for terminated employees (e.g., 60 years)	Calculate total years of employee service for terminated employees (e.g., 60 years)	Prepare a list of year-end sick leave balances during the past several years (e.g., preceding five years), including both vesting and nonvesting sick leave.
Calculate total **unused sick leave days paid** at termination (e.g., 70 days)	Prepare a list of the **amounts of unused sick leave paid** during the past several years (e.g., preceding five years)	Prepare a list of the **amounts of unused sick leave paid** during the past several years (e.g., preceding five years)
Multiply unused sick leave days paid by average daily pay for *current* employees (e.g., $95/day x 70 days = $6,650)	Convert the amounts of unused sick leave paid during the past several years into current year's dollars (e.g., $2,494)**	Calculate the sum of sick leave payments (e.g., $8,026)
Reduce to pay rate in effect for termination payments (e.g., $6,650 x 30% = $1,995)	Adjust amount of unused sick leave paid to reflect lower average salary levels of current employees (e.g., $2,494 x 80% = $1,995).	Calculate the sum of year-end sick leave balances (e.g., $167,840)
Calculate sick leave payout rate per year of service (e.g., $1,995/60 years of service = $33.25/year of service)	Calculate sick leave payout rate per year of service (e.g., $1,995/60 years of service = $33.25/year of service)	Calculate the ratio of sick leave payments to year-end sick leave balances (e.g., $8,026/$167,840 = 4.8%)
Apply sick leave payout rate to the years of service of *current* employees (e.g., 38 years; $33.25 x 38 years = $1,263.50)	Apply sick leave payout rate to the years of service of *current* employees (e.g., 38 years; $33.25 x 38 years = $1,263.50)	Apply the ratio of sick leave payments to year-end sick leave balances to the current balance of sick leave (e.g., $42,710; 4.8% x $42,710 = $2,050)
Adjust for salary-related payments (e.g., 8.5%; $1,263.50 x 1.085 = $1,370)	Adjust for salary-related payments (e.g., 8.5%; $1,263.50 x 1.085 = $1,370)	Adjust for salary-related payments (e.g., 8.5%; $2,050 x 1.085 = $2,224)

* Governments may wish to consider using samples to eliminate the need to provide detailed information for numerous employees.
** The rate used for this purpose should reflect the average rate of pay increases during the period.

while the vesting method focuses primarily on data as of the date of the statement of position.[121]

In some situations, unused sick leave balances may not qualify for payout upon termination; instead, they may be credited to an employee's length of service for purposes of calculating the employee's pension benefits. Such amounts should *not* be accrued as part of the leave liability, because they are considered instead in connection with calculating pension cost.[122] Likewise, unused sick leave that converts to a defined benefit OPEB (e.g., retirement healthcare) is properly taken into consideration as part of the calculation of

[121] GASB Statement No. 16, paragraph 8.
[122] GASB Statement No. 16, footnote 6.

EXHIBIT 12-3
Application of the vesting method to calculate the liability for sick leave payable upon termination

Steps	Assumptions	Calculation
Determine the point in employment ("milestone date") where it becomes probable that payment for an employee's unused sick leave will vest	Public safety: 8 years Other employees: 10 years	N/A
List unused sick leave for only those employees who have passed the milestone date	N/A	N/A
Reduce balances to reflect the maximum number of unused sick leave days eligible for payment at termination	30 day maximum	N/A
Multiply days of unused sick leave eligible for payment upon termination by the employee's daily pay rate	$75/day	30 days x $75/day = $2,250
Reduce this amount to reflect reduced pay rate in effect for sick leave payments	30% payment rate for sick leave payments	$2,250 x 30% = $675
Calculate total for individual employees	$5,438	N/A
Adjust amount to reflect salary-related payments	8.5% extra for salary-related payments	$5,438 x 1.085 = $5,900

the cost of OPEB. Conversely, unused sick leave that is credited to an *individual account* to be used to pay for OPEB constitutes a termination payment that should be part of the calculation of the leave liability.[123]

Sabbaticals

There are two different types of sabbaticals for accounting and financial reporting purposes. Some sabbaticals are given in expectation of service to be rendered by employees on leave. For example, a university professor may be granted a sabbatical to complete a monograph. Other sabbaticals require no service from the employee while on leave; instead, they function as a reward for past service. GAAP require that sabbatical leave given as a reward for past service be accrued like any other vacation leave. Sabbatical leave requiring current service, on the other hand, should not be accrued in advance.[124]

Recognition of an expenditure and liability in governmental funds

State and local governments normally do not liquidate their liability for compensated absences until leave is actually taken by employees. Accordingly, no expenditure or liability should be reported in the governmental funds in connection with compensated absences until they are paid or, in the case of separation payments for unused leave, due for payment (i.e., at separation).[125] If a government is advance funding its vacation leave as it is earned by employees, it may wish to consider using an internal service fund or a pension (and other employee benefit) trust fund so that it can report a corresponding fund liability to match the resources accumulated for future payments.[126]

Claims and judgments

Governments should recognize a liability for claims and judgments as soon as it appears *probable* that a loss has been incurred and the amount in question can be reasonably estimated.[127] The liability thus accrued should

---

[123] GASB Statement No. 45, paragraph 9.
[124] GASB Statement No. 16, paragraph 9.
[125] GASB Interpretation No. 6, paragraph 14.
[126] GASB Interpretation No. 6, footnote 7.
[127] GASB Statement No. 10, *Accounting and Financial Reporting for Risk Financing and Related Insurance Issues*, paragraph 53.

include an amount for incurred but not reported claims (IBNRs) if two criteria are met: 1) It is probable that a successful claim will be asserted; and 2) the amount can be reasonably estimated.[128]

As a practical matter, the portion of the liability for claims and judgments representing IBNRs typically is calculated based on the government's claims history. Assume, for example, that a government has determined that in the recent past an average of only 65 percent of eventually successful claims against the government were filed as of the end of the year in which the underlying event occurred. In that case, the government could extrapolate its liability for the current year's known claims and judgments (for instance, $10,000) to arrive at an estimate of total claims and judgments for the year that includes IBNRs (in this example, $10,000/.65 = $15,384).[129]

In settling claims and judgments, governments incur claims adjustment costs. Normally, such costs do not arise in connection with particular claims but instead represent the allocation of existing resources (for example, the salary of the city attorney's office staff). Occasionally, however, certain claims adjustment costs are directly and incrementally associated with individual claims. GAAP require that these costs be included as part of the estimated liability reported for claims and judgments. Indirect costs may also be included as part of the estimated liability for claims and judgments, but their inclusion is not required by GAAP.[130]

For example, assume that the city attorney's office normally is responsible for the legal work involved with claims and judgments, and that a particular case requires specialized legal expertise in environmental law. In this instance, there would be no requirement to accrue in advance the staff time of the city attorney's office as part of the estimate of the liability for claims and judgments. The estimated liability, however, would need to reflect the anticipated costs of hiring outside legal counsel to deal with the environmental law issues.

Claims and judgments often are settled years after the event that prompted the claim. Accordingly, the issue arises whether the liability for claims and judgments should reflect the anticipated final gross amount of the payments or the present value of that amount. Normally, governments have the option of valuing their liability for claims and judgments using either approach. The one exception is the case of a *structured settlement,* a settlement that involves a series of payments over time rather than a single payment. Typically, governments that are involved in structured settlements purchase annuity contracts in the name of the claimants to settle the claim. In such cases, both the liability and the value of the related annuity contract are removed from the financial statements. In other cases, however, a government will choose to make the series of prescribed payments over time based on the agreed-upon payment schedule. In these cases, GAAP direct that governments report the liability related to this stream of payments at its present value.[131]

---

[128] GASB Statement No. 10, paragraph 56.

[129] GASB Statement No. 10, footnote 5. Estimates of IBNRs based on trend data depend for their reliability on the reliability of each year's estimate. Larger governments often use actuarial estimates for this purpose.

[130] GASB Statement No. 30, *Risk Financing Omnibus: An Amendment of GASB Statement No. 10,* paragraphs 9-10. A government's policy regarding the inclusion of nonincremental claims adjustment costs as part of the liability for claims and judgments should be disclosed in the notes to the financial statements because it constitutes the exercise of an option under GAAP (see chapter 11).

Normally, governments liquidate liabilities associated with claims and judgments only as they become due and payable. Accordingly, governmental funds should *not* report a liability for claims and judgments until that time.

Liability for rebatable arbitrage

Governments may incur a liability to the federal government for rebatable arbitrage if they earn more interest on the reinvested proceeds of tax-exempt debt than they incur on the underlying debt itself. Although rebatable arbitrage need only be calculated for tax purposes every fifth year that debt is outstanding and at maturity, a liability must be recognized in accrual-basis financial statements (i.e., the government-wide statement of net assets and the proprietary fund statement of net assets) as soon as the underlying event has occurred (i.e., interest earnings in excess of interest expense).[132]

Consistent with the modified accrual basis of accounting, no liability would be recognized in a governmental fund until rebatable amounts were actually due and payable (i.e., every fifth year and at the maturity of the debt).[133] Accordingly, governmental funds cannot treat rebatable arbitrage as a reduction of related interest revenue, because to do so would require reporting the liability for arbitrage in a governmental fund before it was due and payable.

Net pension obligation/net other postemployment benefits obligation

Employer governments should *not* report on their statement of position their unfunded actuarial accrued liability for pension benefits or other postemployment benefits (OPEB) earned by employees (that is, the difference between the actuarial value of the assets set aside to meet future pension/OPEB obligations and the present value of those obligations). Instead, a liability should only be reported for an employer's net pension obligation (NPO) or net OPEB obligation (NOPEBO). A NPO/NOPEBO arises when an employer fails to fully fund its annual required contribution (ARC) to a single-employer plan or to an agent multiple-employer plan.[134] In the case of OPEB, it is important to underscore that only payments to beneficiaries, insurers, and trusts (or equivalent arrangements) constitute a *contribution* for this purpose.[135]

The balance of the NPO/NOPEBO might be expected to equal the arithmetic sum of current and prior underfunded amounts. In reality, however, the calculation of the NPO/NOPEBO also must take into account interest associated with prior underfunding, as well as the necessity to consider prior underfunding in calculating the ARC for the current period. Therefore, the increase/decrease in the NPO/NOPEBO for a given period is the difference between actual employer contributions and pension/OPEB cost for the period, with pension/OPEB cost calculated as follows:

---

[131] GASB Statement No. 10, paragraph 24. This requirement is consistent with the principle that liabilities generally should be reported at their present value if both the exact amount of the liability and the exact timing of the payments are known (see Accounting Principles Board Opinion No. 21, *Interest on Receivables and Payables*).

[132] AICPA, *State and Local Governments*, Section 5.06.

[133] Governments *normally* do not liquidate their arbitrage obligations until they are due and payable; therefore such obligations do *not* qualify as fund liabilities consistent with the provisions of GASB Interpretation No. 6.

[134] In an agent multiple-employer plan, each participating employer has a separate actuarial valuation and contribution rates based on that valuation.

[135] GASB Statement No. 45, paragraph 13g.

```
     ARC (the normal measure of pension/OPEB cost)
  +  Interest on the NPO/NOPEBO at the beginning of the
     period
  -  Adjustment (reflected in the ARC)
     Pension/OPEB cost for the period
```

Assume that in the previous year, a governmental employer had reported an NPO of $1,000, and that the ARC for the current year is $5,117.[136] Had there not been a previous underfunding, the amount of the current-year ARC would be the measure of pension cost. However, the following adjustment is needed to reflect the effect of prior underfunding:

- Pension cost must be *increased* to reflect interest on the NPO. If the interest rate assumption used for the pension plan is 8 percent, then pension cost must be increased by $80 ($1,000 NPO x 8 percent = $80).
- Pension cost must be *reduced* by the portion of the current-period ARC that represents the actuary's adjustment for prior underfunding. If the actuary uses an amortization factor of 8.56, then pension cost must be reduced by $117 ($1,000/8.56 = $117).
- The result of these adjustments would be a net pension cost for the current period of $5,080 ($5,117 ARC + $80 interest - $117 actuarial adjustment = $5,080).
- Any amount paid in excess of pension cost would reduce the NPO reported at the end of the period. Thus, if the government paid the full amount of the ARC for the current period, the NPO would decrease by $37 ($5,117 - $5,080 = $37).

The NPO/NOPEBO arises from a government's ultimate failure to fully fund its ARC. Accordingly, an NPO should *not* be reported in connection with temporary delays that result merely from the timing of payments, such as a governmental employer's routine of paying its current-year ARC in the subsequent fiscal year.[137] Because an NPO/NOPEBO by nature is a long-term liability, it is *not* properly reported as a liability in the governmental funds. Instead, an expenditure is recognized in the governmental funds only as the NPO/NOPEBO is actually liquidated. An NPO/NOPEBO should, however, be reported as a liability in the government-wide statement of net assets and in connection with proprietary and fiduciary funds.

It is possible for a government to overfund its ARC, creating a *negative* NPO/NOPEBO (a NPO/NOPEBO with a debit balance). A negative NPO/NOPEBO should be reported as an asset in the government-wide statement of net assets and in connection with proprietary and fiduciary funds. Conversely, a negative NPO/NOPEBO is *not* considered to represent a *financial* asset and therefore is *not* properly reported in a governmental fund.[138] The existence of a negative NPO/NOPEBO, like that of a positive NPO/NOPEBO, must be taken into account in calculating annual pension/OPEB cost, as described earlier.[139]

---

[136] This example is taken from GASB Statement No. 27, paragraph 197, example 1.
[137] GASB Statement No. 27, paragraph 11; GASB Statement No. 45, paragraph 14. A pension/OPEB payment is considered simply delayed if the employer intends to settle by the first valuation date after the difference occurred or, if the first valuation is scheduled within a year, not more than one year after the difference occurred.
[138] GASB Statement No. 27, paragraphs 16-17.

In some cases dedicated taxes are used to fund pensions. Such taxes should *not* be treated as a direct revenue of a pension (and other employer benefit) plan, because to do so would effectively preclude the employer from reporting pension cost, as required by GAAP.[140]

Pension-related debt/OPEB-related debt

Governmental employers sometimes convert a portion of what would have been their actuarial accrued liability into *a fixed contractual liability to the plan* (perhaps upon first entering a multiple-employer plan). Such *pension-related debt/OPEB-related debt* must be reported on the government-wide statement of position, even though the obligation it replaced (the unfunded actuarial accrued liability) would not be reported there. The reason for this difference in treatment is that the unfunded actuarial accrued liability is merely an *actuarial* liability, while pension-related debt/OPEB-related debt is an *accounting* liability. Pension-related debt/OPEB-related debt converts what was an "off balance-sheet" obligation into a liability that must be reported on the face of the statement of position.[141]

Pension-related debt and *OPEB-related debt* should be distinguished from *pension obligation bonds* and *OPEB obligation bonds*. Pension-related debt/OPEB-related debt is an obligation to the plan itself, while pension obligation bonds/OPEB obligation bonds are a *liability to a third party other than the plan.*

Pension obligation bonds/OPEB obligation bonds

Pension obligation bonds/OPEB obligation bonds can be issued for one or more of the following reasons: to reduce or eliminate the employer's NPO/NOPEBO, to pay the employer's ARC for the year, and/or to reduce or eliminate the plan's unfunded actuarial accrued liability.

Pension obligation bonds and OPEB obligation bonds issued by the government should be reported as a liability in the government-wide statement of position, even though an obligation they replaced (i.e., the unfunded actuarial accrued liability) was *not* reported in that statement. The payment to the plan to reduce or eliminate the unfunded actuarial accrued liability would be reflected in the government-wide statement of position as an asset (i.e., negative NPO/negative NOPEBO), and would affect the calculation of pension/OPEB cost in subsequent years, as discussed earlier. Internal payments to a debt service fund for debt service on pension obligation bonds and OPEB obligation bonds would be reported as transfers rather than expenditures.[142]

It is important that contributions funded from the proceeds of pension obligation bonds and OPEB obligation bonds be reflected on the schedule of employer contributions in a manner consistent with the specific purpose for which the bonds were issued. Thus, *only amounts specifically borrowed to finance the ARC should be reported in that schedule.*[143]

Special termination benefits

Governments sometimes offer special incentives to employees during a brief period to encourage early retirement. Such special termination benefits are properly accounted for in accordance with FASB Statement No. 74,

---

[139] Of course, interest related to a *negative* NPO/NOPEBO *decreases* pension/OPEB cost, while the adjustment for prior overfunding *increases* pension/OPEB cost.
[140] GASB Statement No. 27.
[141] GASB Statement No. 27, paragraph 30; GASB Statement No. 45, paragraph 20.
[142] GASB, *Comprehensive Implementation Guide (2004),* 7.120.

Accounting for Special Termination Benefits Paid to Employees, even though this guidance has been superseded in the private sector. FASB Statement No. 74 requires that employers recognize a liability as soon as employees accept the offer and the liability amount can be reasonably estimated. The liability for special termination benefits should reflect any lump-sum payments and the present value of any expected future payments.

The cost of pension benefits and OPEB typically is affected by special termination benefits (employees taking advantage of the offer will retire earlier than they would have otherwise, resulting in more years of pension and other postemployment benefits payments). Under FASB Statement No. 74, this increase in cost was to be included as part of the liability for special termination benefits. However, this specific provision of FASB Statement No. 74 is now inoperative. Instead, the increase in cost resulting from special termination benefits automatically is taken into account as part of the ARC calculations for pension benefits and OPEB.[144]

Once again, governments normally liquidate special termination benefits only when they become due. Therefore no expenditure or liability is recognized in governmental funds in connection with special termination benefits until the benefits become due and payable.[145] A liability is recognized, however, in the government-wide statement of net assets and in connection with the proprietary fund and fiduciary fund statements of net assets.

Operating leases with scheduled rent increases

Sometimes governments enter as lessees into operating leases with scheduled rent increases (*escalator clauses*). To the extent that there is a reasonable connection between the scheduled rent increases and corresponding changes in the economic value of the leased property, no liability would be reported. The situation is the same as having an operating lease without an escalator clause. In some cases, however, there is no reasonable connection between the economic value of the leased property and scheduled increases in lease payments. Assume that a lessor offers a temporary "rent holiday" as an inducement for a potential lessee to enter into a lease agreement. Clearly, the lessor is not offering free use of the rental property during the rent holiday; rather, the lessor is simply making the lease financing more attractive to the potential lessee by deferring payment to a later period. Accordingly, if accounting and financial reporting are to reflect economic substance rather than legal form in this situation, then a portion of the future lease payment stream must be attributed to the use of the rental property during the rent holiday.

GAAP require that lease rentals be accrued on a systematic and rational basis in connection with operating leases having scheduled rent increases. To the extent that scheduled increases in operating lease payments reflect

---

[143] "The purpose of the schedule of employer contributions is to disclose the trend of the employer's contributions in relation to the ARC. In order to avoid distorting the trend, the plan should include in the percentage contributed column only the contributions (whether special or regular) that the employer and the plan agree are ARC related. The total amount of the county's contribution from the proceeds of pension obligation bonds and the treatment of the proceeds (for example, the portions applied to payment of the ARC, reduction of the unfunded actuarial accrued liability, or payment of pension-related debt) should be disclosed in a note to the required schedules, as a factor affecting users' interpretation of trends, in accordance with Statement 25, paragraph 40b." (GASB, *Comprehensive Implementation Guide (2004)*, 5.91.)

[144] NCGA Interpretation 8, *Certain Pension Matters*, paragraph 12, as amended by GASB Statement No. 27, paragraph 6 and GASB Statement No. 45, paragraph 8.

[145] GASB Interpretation No. 6, paragraph 14.

economic factors related to the leased property (such as anticipated cost increases or anticipated increases in property values), the rental schedule is considered a systematic and rational basis for recognizing rental cost. If no such economic justification can be offered, however, rental cost should be recognized on the straight-line basis over the term of the lease, or on some other systematic and rational basis consistent with the fair value of the rental property. Accordingly, an expense and liability is recognized in such cases in both the government-wide financial statements and in proprietary fund and fiduciary fund financial statements.

Governments, of course, normally make operating lease payments only as they come due, regardless of the use value of the underlying leased property. Accordingly, no expenditure or liability should be recognized in governmental funds related to operating leases having scheduled rent increases until payments become due and payable.[146]

Tax anticipation notes and revenue anticipation notes

The key issue that arises in connection with tax anticipation notes (TANs) and revenue anticipation notes (RANs) is their proper classification as a liability (current or long-term). GAAP indicate that both TANs and RANs, by nature, are considered to function as current liabilities. Accordingly, they should be classified as current liabilities whenever a classified statement of position is presented for either the government-wide financial statements or the proprietary fund financial statements. For the same reason, TANs and RANs associated with governmental funds should be reported as fund liabilities in the governmental fund that initially received the proceeds (rather than as an other financing source).[147] GAAP provide no similar guidance on the proper treatment for grant anticipation notes (GANs). It is recommended, however, that the treatment described for TANs and RANs be applied to GANs as well.

Bond anticipation notes

Bond anticipation notes (BANs), unlike RANs and TANs, may properly be classified as long-term obligations if certain conditions are met. That is, BANs may be reported as a long-term liability (in government-wide and proprietary fund financial statements) or as an other financing source (in governmental funds) if "all legal steps have been taken to refinance the bond anticipation notes and the intent is supported by an ability to consummate refinancing the short-term note on a long-term basis." The criteria for making this determination are provided by FASB Statement No. 6, *Classification of Short-Term Obligations Expected to be Refinanced*, which may be applied specifically to BANs as follows:
- *Subsequent issuance of replacement debt.* A BAN may be treated as a long-term liability/other financing source if it is actually replaced in the subsequent period, prior to issuance of the current period's financial statements, by some form of long-term debt (for instance, if the BANs are replaced by the bonds they were originally intended to anticipate).
- *Demonstrated ability to issue replacement debt.* A BAN may be treated as a long-term liability/other financing source if the government has entered into a financing agreement before the statement of position is

[146] GASB Statement No. 13, *Accounting for Operating Leases with Scheduled Rent Increases.*
[147] NCGA Interpretation 9, *Certain Fund Classifications and Balance Sheet Accounts.*

issued that clearly permits the government to refinance the BAN on a long-term basis on terms that are readily determinable.[148]

These requirements may be summarized as follows:

- The receipt of BAN proceeds may be treated as a long-term liability/other financing source only if—as of the issue date of the financial statements—the BANs have been replaced by debt that extends at least one year beyond the date of the balance sheet (or a qualifying financing agreement is in place).[149]
- Otherwise, BANs should be reported as a current liability (government-wide and proprietary fund financial statements) or as a fund liability in the governmental fund that received the proceeds (even if the BANs are expected to be paid with the resources of some other fund).[150]

Naturally, BANs that qualify as long-term obligations should *not* be reported as liabilities in the governmental funds. Also, the rollover of a BAN that is properly classified as long-term is *not* reflected in the statement of revenues, expenditures, and changes in fund balances.

Demand bonds

Governments have been known, under certain limited market conditions, to issue bonded debt with a specific provision that allows bondholders to demand repayment prior to maturity of all outstanding principal plus accrued interest (this is a *put* feature).[151] Such securities are known as *demand bonds* or *put bonds.* Typically, demand bonds are supported by a *take-out agreement* with a bank or investment firm that ensures that the government will be able to refinance on a long-term basis any bonds that are *put* by the bondholders.

GAAP direct that the receipt of demand bond proceeds be treated as a long-term liability (government-wide and proprietary fund financial statements) or as an other financing source (governmental fund financial statements) if all four of the following criteria are met:

- The government has entered into a take-out agreement before the financial statements are issued.
- The take-out agreement does not expire within one year of the fiscal-period end.
- Neither the take-out agreement itself nor the obligations issued pursuant to that agreement are cancelable by the lender within one year of the fiscal period end.

---

[148] Such a financing agreement also must satisfy all of the following conditions:
- The agreement does not expire within one year (or operating cycle) from the date of the balance sheet.
- The lender or the prospective lender cannot cancel the agreement during that period.
- The obligations incurred under the agreement are not callable during that period (except for violation of provisions with which compliance is objectively determinable or measurable).
- No violation of any provision in the agreement exists at the balance-sheet date, and no available information indicates that a violation has occurred thereafter but prior to issuance of the balance sheet (or, if a violation exists, a waiver has been obtained).
- The lender or the prospective lender is expected to be financially capable of honoring the arrangement. [FASB Statement No. 6, paragraph 11.]
[149] This would include *rollovers* of the BANs themselves, provided rollovers outstanding at the time the financial statements were issued had maturities beyond 12 months of the close of the fiscal year.
[150] BANs in that case are handled as balance sheet transactions, and only the interest related to such transactions will affect the operating statement.
[151] Demand bonds may be used to entice investors in volatile markets characterized by the expectation of rising interest rates. The government's long-term interests typically are protected by a call provision.

- The lender is expected to be financially capable of honoring the take-out agreement.

If these four criteria are not met, demand bonds should be reported as a current liability (government-wide and proprietary fund financial statements) or as a liability of the governmental fund receiving the proceeds rather than as an other financing source.

Normally, of course, the repayment of the principal of debt reported as a fund liability is *not* reflected in the operating statement of a governmental fund. GAAP make a special provision, however, for demand bonds that are reported as liabilities of a governmental fund. In that case, financial statement preparers are directed to report an other financing source in connection with debt service principal payments so that the full amount of those payments can still be reflected as an expenditure of the governmental funds.[152]

Assume, for example, that $2 million in demand bonds are issued in connection with a capital projects fund, but that the terms of the arrangement require that the bonds be reported as a fund liability. In that case, the appropriate journal entries would be as follows:

	DR	CR
Cash	$2,000,000	
Demand bonds payable		$2,000,000
(To record the issuance of demand bonds)		
Debt service expenditures—principal	100,000	
Debt service expenditures—interest	200,000	
Demand bonds payable	100,000	
Cash		300,000
Other financing sources— principal payment on demand bonds		100,000
(To record the payment of debt service principal and interest related to demand bonds)		

Conduit debt

Sometimes a state or local government issues limited-obligation debt (for example, revenue bonds or certificates of participation) for the express purpose of helping a specific third party outside the financial reporting entity to finance capital asset acquisition. Such obligations are commonly referred to as *conduit debt*.

In practice, two approaches have been taken to accounting and financial reporting for conduit debt obligations. Sometimes governments report both the conduit debt and the related asset (the receivable from the third party that obtained the proceeds) on their statement of position. More commonly, neither conduit debt nor the related asset is reported.[153] GAAP specify that both approaches are acceptable.[154]

Special assessment debt

Governments often issue debt to finance capital improvements that will benefit individual property owners by increasing the fair value of their properties. In such cases, the government may impose a special assessment on the benefiting property owners to recover all or a portion of the cost of the improvement (but not to exceed the resulting increase in the fair value

[152] GASB Interpretation No. 1, *Demand Bonds Issued by State and Local Governmental Entities: An Interpretation of NCGA Statement 1 and NCGA Interpretation 9,* paragraph 13.
[153] GASB Interpretation No. 2, *Disclosure of Conduit Debt Obligations: An Interpretation of NCGA Statement 1.*
[154] As discussed in the next section, a special rule applies to conduit debt associated with special assessments.

of the benefiting property). Debt that is secured by such anticipated payments from property owners is known as *special assessment debt*. The proper treatment of special assessment debt depends on whether the government is obligated in some manner, *however limited*, for the debt repayment.

A government should *presume* it is obligated for all special assessment debt it has issued *unless* the government meets one of the following tests:

- *Prohibition of repayment*. Sometimes governments are legally prohibited (perhaps by constitution, charter, statute, ordinance, or contract) from making payments to bondholders to cover delinquent special assessments.
- *Legal immunity*. A government may be considered immune from the obligation to repay defaulted special assessments if the government is not legally liable for the debt *and* it has not compromised this immunity from liability by making a statement or otherwise indicating that it either will or may honor the debt in the event of a default.

GAAP specifically indicate that a government would *not* meet these conditions in *any* of the following circumstances:

- The government is obligated to honor deficiencies to the extent that lien foreclosure proceeds are insufficient.
- The government is required to establish a reserve, guarantee, or sinking fund with resources other than the proceeds of the special assessment debt itself.
- The government is required to cover delinquencies with other resources until foreclosure proceeds are received (*up-fronting* payments to bondholders).
- The government must purchase all properties foreclosed for delinquent assessments that were not sold at public auction.
- The government is authorized to establish a reserve, guarantee, or sinking fund, and it establishes such a fund.
- The government may establish a separate fund with resources other than the proceeds of the special assessment debt itself for the purpose of purchasing or redeeming special assessment debt, and it establishes such a fund.
- The government explicitly indicates by contract—such as the bond agreement or offering statement—that in the event of default it may cover delinquencies, although it has no legal obligation to do so (this is *moral obligation debt*).[155]
- Legal decisions within the state or previous actions by the government related to defaults on other special assessment projects make it probable that the government will assume responsibility for the debt in the event of default.

GAAP direct governments to refrain from reporting on the statement of position any special assessment debt for which they are not obligated in any manner, although the disclosure of such debt is required in the notes to the financial statements. Conversely, special assessment debt for which a government is obligated in some manner must be reported on the face of

---

[155] For example, a government could commit itself to include an amount for the repayment of delinquent special assessments in all future budgets prepared by the executive branch over the life of the special assessment debt, although the legislative branch would be under no obligation to include those amounts as part of the final appropriated budget.

the statement of position as "special assessment debt with governmental commitment."

Of course, property owners often are not the exclusive beneficiaries of capital improvements financed through special assessment debt. Accordingly, a government may agree to finance a portion of a special assessment project out of general revenues. In that case, the portion of any debt related to the project that will be repaid from general revenues should be reported as general obligation debt rather than as special assessment debt.[156]

Split-interest agreements

As discussed earlier, colleges and universities sometimes are participants in split-interest agreements that require them to pay benefits for a specified period to a designated beneficiary out of assets held in trust for this purpose. At the end of the period, the assets revert to the college or university.

When trust assets are first received in connection with a split interest agreement, the college or university should recognize a liability for its obligation to the beneficiary. At the end of the specified period, any remaining liability should be removed and the related increase in net assets reported as a revenue of that period.[157]

EQUITY-RELATED ISSUES

Purpose restrictions

Resources received in connection with nonexchange transactions often come with limitations on how they may be used by the recipient. To the extent that prior compliance with such limitations is not a condition of eligibility (as in the case of reimbursement or expenditure-driven grants), such *purpose restrictions* do *not* affect revenue recognition and therefore should *not* be reported as a liability for deferred revenue. Instead, purpose restrictions should be reflected in the equity section of the statement of position. In governmental funds, a reservation of fund balance would be appropriate for this purpose. In government-wide and proprietary fund financial statements, such amounts would be reflected as part of *restricted net assets*.[158]

Designations

Designations are used to reflect a government's *intended* use of current available financial resources. The focus on current financial resources is unique to governmental funds. Accordingly, designations should be reported only on the governmental fund balance sheet. There is no equivalent equity designation that may be used for government-wide financial reporting or for proprietary fund and fiduciary fund financial reporting to reflect the intended use of resources.[159]

Direct adjustments to equity

It is presumed that *all* changes to equity (such as changes in net assets, net changes in fund balances) should be reported as part of the results of operations for the current period rather than treated as a direct adjustment to *equity—beginning of the fiscal year*. There are, however, several important exceptions to this rule:

[156] GASB Statement No. 6, *Accounting and Financial Reporting for Special Assessments.*
[157] GASB, *Comprehensive Implementation Guide (2004),* 7.324.
[158] GASB Statement No. 33, *Accounting and Financial Reporting for Nonexchange Transactions,* paragraph 14.
[159] In the private sector, the *appropriated retained earnings* account has been established for this purpose, although its use in practice is quite limited.

- *Prior-period adjustments* are the net effect of changes resulting from the correction of an error. Because such amounts are the product of errors from a *prior period*, they are *not* properly included as part of the results of operations of the current period, even though they are reported in the current period (or, in the case of comparative financial statements, in the earliest period for which GAAP financial statements are presented). Instead, such adjustments are properly reported as a direct adjustment to *equity—beginning of the fiscal year* to restate that amount to what it would have been had the error not occurred.

- *Changes in accounting principle,* which occur when: 1) a new GAAP standard is implemented; 2) a government decides to use an alternative accounting principle permitted by GAAP because it believes that principle is preferable to the one previously employed; or 3) a government changes its *application* of an accounting principle. In the private sector, the cumulative effect of either of changes 2 or 3 would be reported as a component of the results of operations for the period.[160] GAAP for state and local governments, however, direct that all three of these changes in accounting principles be treated as a direct adjustment to beginning equity, essentially in the same manner as a prior-period adjustment (although the term *prior-period adjustment* would *not* be used to describe such changes).[161]

- *Changes in inventory balances accounted for using the purchases method.* Governmental funds may report an expenditure for inventories when these items are purchased (the *purchases method*). Nonetheless, GAAP require that *material* balances of inventories accounted for under the purchases method are reported as an asset on the governmental fund balance sheet. To accomplish this goal, the initial capitalization of such inventories, as well as all subsequent changes in the balance of the inventories account, must be reported as a direct adjustment to beginning equity rather than as a component of the results of operations of the period.[162] To do otherwise would effectively negate the purchases method by removing expenditures for inventories for the period.

---

[160] Accounting Principles Board Opinion No. 20, *Accounting Changes.*

[161] GASB Statement No. 34, footnote 13 and paragraph 309.

[162] The initial journal entry would be *inventories* (debit) and *reserved fund balance–inventories* (credit). Creation of the reserved fund balance account and all subsequent changes would be reported on a separate line between beginning and ending fund balance in the governmental fund statement of revenues, expenditures, and changes in fund balances.

13

The Comprehensive Annual Financial Report

Generally accepted accounting principles (GAAP) provide the criteria for judging whether a financial report is fairly presented. In defining the minimum standard of acceptable financial reporting for state and local governments, GAAP mandate a complete set of basic financial statements, including accompanying note disclosures, as well as the presentation of certain required supplementary information (RSI). GAAP encourage governments to imbed this minimum presentation within the broader framework of a comprehensive annual financial report (CAFR).[1]

At a minimum, every CAFR comprises three basic sections (in addition to the report cover, title page, and table of contents):

- *The introductory section* provides general information on the government's structure and the services it provides.
- *The financial section* contains the basic financial statements and RSI (including management's discussion and analysis), as well as the independent auditor's report. In addition, the financial section provides information on each individual fund and component unit for which data are not provided separately within the basic financial statements. The financial section also may include supplementary information of interest to financial statement users.
- *The statistical section* provides a broad range of financial and demographic information useful in assessing a government's economic condition, much of it in the form of ten-year trend data.

REPORT COVER AND TITLE PAGE

To describe the report, the cover should use the terminology "comprehensive annual financial report" rather than less specific language, such as "annual report." If the government preparing the CAFR is a component unit of another government, the cover should include a reference to the pri-

---

[1] National Council on Governmental Accounting (NCGA) Statement 1, *Governmental Accounting and Financial Reporting Principles*, paragraph 135.

mary government (for example, "The Comprehensive Annual Financial Report of the XYZ School District – A Component Unit of the City of XYZ").[2] Since some potential users of the CAFR may be far removed geographically from the government preparing the report, the state in which the government is located also should be indicated. Finally, the report cover should disclose the fiscal period covered by the report (for example, "for the fiscal year ended December 31, 2005").

The title page should present all information included on the cover of the report. In addition, the title page should indicate the department responsible for preparing the CAFR ("prepared by the finance department of the City of XYZ"). Sometimes, governments also use the title page of the CAFR to list their principal officials, although it is more common for the CAFR to contain a separate list of principal officials, as described later.

TABLE OF CONTENTS

A general table of contents should clearly divide the CAFR into its basic sections. Further, the listing for the financial section should be subdivided, distinguishing clearly between 1) the basic financial statements, including the accompanying notes, 2) RSI, and 3) other contents of the financial section (combining and individual fund presentations and supplementary information).

The table of contents should identify each statement and schedule by its full title and indicate the page or pages of the CAFR where each can be found. If statements and schedules are identified by exhibit numbers, these also may be presented in the table of contents to supplement (but not replace) page number references.

INTRODUCTORY SECTION

This section is designed to provide the background and context that financial report users need to profit fully from the information presented in the financial section of the CAFR. The information in the introductory section is *not* included within the scope of the independent audit; however, the independent auditor is responsible for reading the contents of the introductory section to ensure that none of the information presented there is misleading or inconsistent with the audited financial statements.[3]

Certificate of Achievement for Excellence in Financial Reporting

Many governments of all types have met the demanding requirements of the Government Finance Officers Association's (GFOA) Certificate of Achievement for Excellence in Financial Reporting (Certificate of Achievement) Program. When a government has earned the Certificate of Achieve-

---

[2] Governmental Accounting Standards Board (GASB) Statement No. 14, *The Financial Reporting Entity*, paragraph 65.

[3] "Other information in a document may be relevant to an audit performed by an independent auditor or to the continuing propriety of his report. The auditor's responsibility with respect to information in a document does not extend beyond the financial information identified in his report, and the auditor has no obligation to perform any procedures to corroborate other information contained in a document. However, he should read the other information and consider whether such information, or the manner of its presentation, is materially inconsistent with information, or the manner of its presentation, appearing in the financial statements." (American Institute of Certified Public Accountants (AICPA), *Professional Standards*, AU550.04.)

ment in the year immediately preceding the issuance of the CAFR, the government should reproduce that award in the current year's CAFR. The photographic reproduction of the Certificate of Achievement typically is placed somewhere after the letter of transmittal.

Because the Certificate of Achievement is specifically associated with a government's CAFR, it is inappropriate to reproduce the certificate in any other type of document (such as an offering statement or popular report).[4] Nonetheless, in other types of documents, a government may mention that its CAFR has been awarded the Certificate of Achievement.[5]

List of principal officials

The CAFR's introductory section normally contains a list of the government's principal officials. A number of approaches may be taken in preparing this list. For instance, elected officials may be identified separate from appointed officials, or each official's length of service may be disclosed. As noted earlier, some governments choose to incorporate the names of their principal officials on the CAFR's title page rather than presenting them as a separate list.

Typically, the principal officials listed are those who were in office during the fiscal period covered by the report. Alternatively, the individuals listed may be those in office at the time the report is issued. To avoid potential misunderstandings, a government may wish to specify the period for which the list of officials is being presented.

Organizational chart

Included in the CAFR's introductory section, an organizational chart typically appears somewhere after the letter of transmittal. The organizational chart provides useful information concerning the assignment of responsibilities within the government. In some cases, governments merge the organizational chart and the list of principal officials by incorporating the names of responsible officials at the appropriate locations on the organizational chart. Often organizational charts graphically illustrate that all of the government's powers derive ultimately from its citizens. Likewise, governments frequently present the organizational chart so that it reflects the various functional categories reported in the government-wide statement of activities.

Letter of transmittal

As discussed later in this chapter, management's discussion and analysis (MD&A) is designed to "introduce the basic financial statements and provide an analytical overview of the government's financial activities."[6] The role of the letter of transmittal is not to reproduce information already available in MD&A, but rather to provide a way for management to express "more subjective information than would be acceptable for MD&A."[7]

It is recommended that the letter of transmittal contain the following four sections:

- formal transmittal of the CAFR;
- profile of the government;

---

[4] Consistent with this approach, it would be appropriate for a government to reproduce the Certificate of Achievement on its Web site if the entire CAFR were reproduced there as well.
[5] The GFOA provides participating governments with standard language that may be used to refer to the Certificate of Achievement in a setting other than a CAFR.
[6] GASB Statement No. 34, *Basic Financial Statements—and Management's Discussion and Analysis—for State and Local Governments*, paragraph 6a.
[7] GASB Statement No. 34, paragraph 294.

- information useful in assessing the government's economic condition; and
- awards and acknowledgements.

Formal transmittal of the CAFR

The first objective of the letter of transmittal, as its name implies, is to formally convey the CAFR to its intended users. In the process, management is afforded an excellent opportunity to educate recipients as to why and to what extent they can rely upon the information contained in the report. Specific items that ought to be addressed are as follows:

- *Legal requirements.* Management should mention any legal requirements that the CAFR is intended to fulfill.
- *Assumption of responsibility.* Many potential users of financial statements are unaware of the fact that the financial statements are the representations of management rather than of the independent auditors. Management should assume full responsibility for the contents of the CAFR.
- *Internal control.* Management must have some reasonable basis for assuming responsibility for the information contained in the basic financial statements. That basis is provided by a comprehensive framework of internal control. Management should allude to the role played by internal control, as well as to its inherent limitations.
- *Independent audit.* Because management can be directly affected by the information it reports in the financial statements, users of those statements need some form of independent assurance that the financial statements can be relied upon. Accordingly, management should mention the independent audit.
- *Reference to MD&A.* MD&A provides much information that might otherwise be included as part of the letter of transmittal. Consequently, the letter of transmittal should refer readers to the complementary information offered in MD&A.

Discussion of the items just mentioned should be kept to an absolute minimum to avoid creating a "boilerplate" effect that serves only to discourage potential readers.

Profile of the government

It is hard to understand a government's finances without knowing something about the government and how it operates. Given the CAFR's wide potential audience, it is not reasonable to simply assume that anyone who may eventually come across the report will possess this requisite background. Accordingly, the letter of transmittal ought to provide the minimal context needed to appreciate the government's specific circumstances. That discussion should address all of the following topics, as appropriate in the government's specific circumstances:

- *Basic information.* Basic information about a government would include its structure (e.g., city manager) and the specific types of services it provides. Information about the government's geography, population, and history could also be provided.
- *Component units.* Readers are often unaware that the financial reporting entity may differ from the primary government as the latter is legally defined. Therefore, the letter of transmittal should explain the inclusion of component units as well as the exclusion, as appropriate,

of potential component units that an average reader might reasonably have expected to see included within the financial reporting entity.

- *Budget.* Because of the importance of the budget to public finance, the letter of transmittal should summarize (rather than describe in detail) the budget process, identify the governmental funds for which budgets are annually (or biennially) appropriated, and briefly and simply describe the legal level of budgetary control.

Information useful in assessing the government's economic condition

The third basic element of the letter of transmittal is information useful in assessing a government's *economic condition*, which focuses not only on existing resources and claims to resources (financial position), but also on *future* resources and claims to resources (including the commitment to provide services). That is, economic condition reflects not only today's financial position, but also the prospects that today's financial position will improve or deteriorate.

The analysis of economic condition inherently involves a substantial degree of subjectivity, well beyond what would be appropriate in MD&A. Accordingly, it is the letter of transmittal, rather than MD&A, that must provide this type of information. Specific topics to be addressed in this regard are as follows:

- *Local economy.* The letter of transmittal should include a brief description of the local economy (e.g., major industries, unemployment) that addresses financial trends for the previous five- to ten-year period. Management also ought to offer its assessment of the local economy's prospects. Ideally, the discussion would situate the local economy within the broader context of the regional economy.

- *Long-term financial planning.* The letter of transmittal should briefly review those aspects of a government's long-term financial planning (e.g., capital budget, revenue and expenditure forecasts) most likely to have a future impact on the government's financial position. For example, capital acquisition typically will result in long-term increases in operating costs connected with the operation and maintenance of new facilities. Similarly, a government could choose to explain that it is deliberately building up fund balance in the general fund because its capital budget calls for future construction to be advance funded rather than financed by debt. Likewise, a government could refer to its long-term revenue and expenditure forecast to explain how it plans to deal with an unusually low level of unreserved fund balance in the general fund.

- *Relevant financial policies.* GFOA encourages governments to establish a comprehensive set of financial policies as guidelines for the budget process (e.g., policy on the use of one-time revenue sources).[8] The letter of transmittal should describe situations directly affected by one or another of those policies (e.g., application of one-time revenues of the current period).

- *Major initiatives.* The budget document typically highlights major initiatives of the fiscal year. These initiatives also should be addressed in the letter of transmittal to the extent that they are expected to affect future financial position.

---

[8] See GFOA's recommended practice on "Adoption of Financial Policies" (2001).

Awards and acknowledgements

The principal objective of this fourth and last section of the letter of transmittal is to refer to objective indicators of the quality of the government's financial management and to acknowledge those who have made a significant contribution to the preparation of the CAFR or to the government's financial reporting generally. Thus, it is recommended that a government mention its successful participation in GFOA's Certificate of Achievement for Excellence in Financial Reporting or other similar forms of recognition for the quality of the government's financial management (e.g., GFOA's Award for Distinguished Budget Presentation). The letter of transmittal also should recognize those who helped to produce the CAFR, as well as the governing body's support.

Authorship, dating, and format

Ideally the letter of transmittal should be a joint communication of the chief financial officer (CFO) and either the chief executive officer (e.g., mayor or county board president) or the chief operating officer (e.g., city manager or county executive). If a joint communication is not possible, the CFO and the chief executive officer/chief operating officer could issue separate letters, both of which could be included in the introductory section of the CAFR. If neither of these first two possibilities is feasible, then the letter of transmittal should, at a minimum, be signed by the CFO.

The letter of transmittal should be dated, ideally on the date the CAFR is first made available to the public (referred to as the "date of transmittal"). In practice, it is common to use some earlier date. Naturally, it would not be appropriate for the date of the letter of transmittal to precede that of the independent auditor's report, even though the letter of transmittal is not itself audited.

As an official communication of the government, the letter of transmittal should be printed on the government's official letterhead. At a minimum, the letter of transmittal should be addressed to the government's citizens. It is both appropriate and common to include others in the address as well (e.g., governing board, chief executive officer).

Less sophisticated users of the CAFR are perhaps more likely to consult the letter of transmittal and MD&A than any other parts of the CAFR. A letter of transmittal, therefore, must be short and to the point if it is to capture and maintain the interest of such users. Also, given the strong likelihood that less sophisticated users will be drawn to the letter of transmittal, it could particularly benefit from the judicious use of charts and graphs to communicate information.

FINANCIAL SECTION

The second basic section of a CAFR is the financial section, which should provide the following information (in this order):
- independent auditor's report on the financial statement audit;
- MD&A;
- basic financial statements;
- RSI (other than MD&A); and
- combining and individual fund presentations and supplementary information.

Independent auditor's report

Management is primarily and ultimately responsible for the fairness of the basic financial statements. Understandably, however, users of the basic financial statements desire *independent* assurance that the basic financial statements are reliable. To provide such assurance, the CAFR's financial section should begin with the independent auditor's report on the fair presentation of the financial statements.

At a minimum, the independent auditor's report offers an opinion on the fair presentation of the various "opinion units" that make up the basic financial statements: governmental activities, business-type activities, individual major governmental funds, individual major enterprise funds, and all other funds/discretely presented component units in the aggregate.[9]

The independent auditor sometimes issues an opinion on the fair presentation of the combining and individual fund financial presentations that follow the basic financial statements. With this additional opinion, the independent auditor indicates that the scope of the audit was sufficiently broad to provide assurance that the various combining and individual fund presentations are fairly presented *in their own right*. More commonly, the independent auditor is not engaged to offer an opinion on the fair presentation of the combining and individual fund presentations as such. Instead, the auditor is engaged to provide what is commonly referred to as an *in-relation-to* opinion on those presentations. In other words, the auditor states that 1) the scope of the audit was limited to the basic financial statements; and 2) based on the audit of the basic financial statements, it is possible to assert that the combining and individual fund statements and schedules are fairly presented *in relation to the basic financial statements*. Either approach is acceptable for GFOA's Certificate of Achievement for Excellence in Financial Reporting Program. GFOA encourages the additional opinion, although the *in-relation-to* approach is more commonly encountered in practice.[10]

In most cases, the independent auditor's report does *not* specifically address information reported in the introductory and statistical sections of the CAFR, because those sections are neither included within the scope of the audit of the financial statements nor are they normally the potential object of an *in-relation-to* opinion based on the financial statement audit. Nonetheless, in certain instances the independent auditor may specifically indicate that such information is "unaudited" to avoid potential confusion for financial report users regarding the degree of responsibility that the independent auditor assumes for such information. Likewise, RSI need *not* be mentioned in the independent auditor's report unless it has been inappropriately omitted or the auditor's limited procedures associated with RSI indicate that the presentation might in some way be deficient.[11] All the same, many auditors voluntarily choose to describe their association with RSI in their report.[12]

---

[9] Normally, 1) all other funds in the aggregate and 2) discretely presented component units in the aggregate are treated as separate opinion units. They may be combined into a single opinion unit, however, if either is not quantitatively or qualitatively material to the primary government, in which case the combined opinion unit is known as "aggregate discretely presented component unit and remaining fund information." (AICPA, *State and Local Governments*, Section 4.25.)

[10] See GFOA's recommended practice on "Audit Procurement" (1996).

[11] AICPA, *Professional Standards*, AU558.08. Nonetheless, a government may engage its independent auditor to provide an in-relation-to opinion on RSI.

[12] AICPA, *State and Local Governments*, Appendix A, example A.9.

MD&A

The purpose of MD&A is to provide users of the basic financial statements with a narrative introduction, overview, and analysis of those statements. Like RSI itself, the concept of MD&A originated in the private sector, where the Securities and Exchange Commission (SEC) has long required MD&A in connection with the financial reports of publicly traded companies.

Contents of MD&A

GAAP identify a list of specific topics that a government should address in its MD&A to the extent that those topics are relevant to a government's particular circumstances.[13] Because MD&A constitute *required* supplementary information, a government may *not* address additional topics not found on this list as part of MD&A, although a government is free to provide whatever level of detail it deems appropriate in addressing the specific topics identified by GAAP.[14] The letter of transmittal provides an appropriate place for addressing topics not identified by GAAP for inclusion within MD&A.

Discussion of the basic financial statements. A key feature of the governmental financial reporting model is its unique combination of government-wide financial statements and fund financial statements. MD&A should describe both types of financial statements and explain the significant differences in the kinds of information that each provides. The analytical component of this discussion should focus on how fund financial statements either reinforce the information provided in the government-wide financial statements (for instance, proprietary funds), or provide additional information (for instance, governmental funds and fiduciary funds). In particular, this discussion should focus on the relationship between *governmental funds* and *governmental activities* (as reported in the government-wide financial statements).

Condensed comparative data. MD&A should include condensed, government-wide comparative financial data for both the current fiscal period and the prior fiscal period,[15] *regardless of whether comparative data are presented on the face of the basic financial statements.* Such comparative data should be presented separately for governmental activities and business-type activities at the following minimum level of detail:
- total assets, distinguishing between capital assets and other assets;
- total liabilities, distinguishing between long-term liabilities and other liabilities;
- total net assets, distinguishing amounts invested in capital assets, net of related debt; restricted amounts; and unrestricted amounts;
- program revenues, by major source;
- general revenues, by major source;

[13] All of the requirements described in the paragraphs that follow are based on GASB Statement No. 34, paragraphs 8-11, as amended. Separately issued departmental reports should include MD&A that address each of the required topics to the extent that it is relevant to the report. See GFOA recommended practice on "Voluntary Reporting of Management's Discussion and Analysis" (2004).
[14] GASB Statement No. 37, *Basic Financial Statements—and Management's Discussion and Analysis—for State and Local Governments: Omnibus—an amendment of GASB Statements No. 21 and No. 34*, paragraph 4.
[15] When comparative financial statements are presented, three years of data must be presented. That is, meeting the requirement to provide comparative information for *both* years necessitates presenting data for three years, as follows:
1) Comparative data for year X = year W (preceding year) + year X
2) Comparative data for year Y = year X (preceding year) + year Y
3) Comparative data for both = year W, year X, year Y.
See GASB, *Comprehensive Interpretation Guide (2004)*, 7.14.

- total revenues;
- program expenses, at minimum by function;[16]
- total expenses;
- excess (deficiency) before contributions to term and permanent endowments or permanent fund principal, special and extraordinary items, and transfers;
- contributions to term and permanent endowments;
- special and extraordinary items;
- transfers;
- change in net assets; and
- ending net assets.

Overall analysis. MD&A should analyze the government's overall financial position and results of operations and specifically address whether the government's overall financial position has improved or deteriorated. Analysis, properly speaking, necessarily will focus on the *reasons* for significant changes rather than simply on their size (amount or percentage of change). This analysis also should separately address governmental and business-type activities. Finally, an adequate analysis must take into account any important economic factors that significantly affected the government's operating results for the current fiscal period. Although comparative data are presented in MD&A, the overall financial analysis should emphasize the current fiscal period.

Fund analysis. In addition to providing an analysis of the overall government, MD&A also should analyze significant balances and operations of individual major funds, focusing on reasons for significant changes in fund balances (governmental funds) or fund net assets (proprietary funds). An adequate analysis should include information on any significant limitation on the future use of fund resources. Governments are free to discuss significant balances and operations of nonmajor funds in MD&A as well, but are not required to do so.[17]

Budget variances in the general fund. MD&A should address significant differences between 1) the original budget for the general fund and the final amended budget; and 2) the final amended budget for the general fund and actual amounts (presented using the basis of budgeting). If these variances are expected to significantly affect either future services or liquidity, the analysis should include the reasons for the variances (if currently known). A reasonable level of specificity is required when discussing the causes of budgetary variances. It would not be sufficient, for example, to "explain" that the original budget was increased because of "higher than anticipated expenditures."[18]

Capital asset and long-term debt activity. MD&A should describe significant changes in capital assets and long-term debt, including commitments for capital expenditures, changes in credit ratings, and debt limitations that could affect the financing of planned facilities or services. This

---

[16] This requirement may not apply to special-purpose governments reported as business-type activities (i.e., because the entire unit may constitute a single function). Accordingly, "if an organization reports its expenses using natural classifications, the comparative information in MD&A should be presented in the same manner as that included in the basic financial statements." (GASB, *Comprehensive Implementation Guide (2004)*, 7.319.)

[17] GASB, *Comprehensive Implementation Guide (2004)*, 7.17.

[18] GASB, *Comprehensive Implementation Guide (2004)*, 7.20.

discussion should not repeat the information on capital assets and long-term debt provided in the notes to the financial statements. Rather, it should summarize that information and refer the reader to the more detailed information provided in the notes.

Special assessment debt for which the government is not obligated in any manner need not be addressed as part of the discussion of long-term debt because it is not debt of the government. Management may wish to address no-commitment special assessment debt, however, as part of its discussion of capital asset activity.[19]

Infrastructure. Governments have the option of not reporting depreciation on one or more networks or subsystems of their infrastructure assets. Governments that elect to use this optional "modified approach" to infrastructure reporting should discuss all of the following in MD&A:
- significant changes in the condition levels of infrastructure assets;
- how current condition levels compare with target condition levels established by the government; and
- significant differences between the amount estimated to be necessary for maintaining and preserving infrastructure assets at target condition levels and the actual amounts of expense incurred for that purpose during the current fiscal period.

Other potentially significant matters. MD&A also should address any other "currently known facts, decisions, or conditions that are expected to have a significant effect on financial position (net assets) or results of operations (revenues, expenses, and other changes in net assets)." For this purpose, "currently known" should be interpreted as known by management as of the date of the independent auditor's report on the financial statements (the date of the end of audit field work). This discussion should address governmental activities separate from business-type activities. Examples of the types of situations envisioned for such reporting include the following:
- award and acceptance of a major grant;
- adjudication of a significant lawsuit;
- reassessment of taxable property;
- completion of an agreement to locate a major manufacturing plant in a city;
- an adopted increase in a state's sales tax rate;
- an increase in a university's tuition;
- a flood that caused significant damage to a government's infrastructure; and
- a renegotiated labor contract with government employees.[20]

Note that each of these examples involves something that has actually happened (a known matter) rather than something that simply *might* happen (such as the *possible* award of a major grant, the *anticipated* reassessment of taxable property, or the *potential* negotiation of an agreement to locate a major manufacturing plant in a city).[21]

---

[19] GASB, *Comprehensive Implementation Guide (2004)*, 7.21.
[20] GASB, *Comprehensive Implementation Guide (2004)*, 7.22.
[21] The more subjective information could properly be included in the letter of transmittal, as discussed earlier.

Location of MD&A	MD&A falls within the broader category of RSI. In most cases, RSI is located immediately following the notes to the financial statements. However, because MD&A is specifically intended to serve as a narrative *introduction* to the basic financial statements, it should be placed in front of those statements rather than behind them.[22]
Charts, graphs, and tables	Charts, graphs, and tables can serve as important aids in making MD&A accessible to a wide range of potential users of financial statements. The role of charts, graphs, and tables, however, should be to enhance rather than replace the required presentations of financial data. A bar graph of total revenues and expenses, for example, may not serve as a substitute for reporting the actual amounts of total revenues and expenses.[23]
Component units	MD&A should focus on the primary government. The decision whether to address matters related to component units in MD&A depends on the size of a particular component unit (in comparison with other discretely presented component units) and the nature of its relationship with the primary government (essentially the same rules governing note disclosures for component units). Naturally, any discussion in MD&A involving both the primary government and its discretely presented component units must distinguish between the two. When necessary, reference may be made to the separately issued reports of component units.[24]
Basic financial statements	The basic financial statements, including the accompanying notes, constitute the core of the CAFR's financial section. Chapter 10 details the format and contents of the basic financial statements, and chapter 11 addresses required note disclosures. Each basic financial statement should contain a reference to the notes to the financial statements ("See notes to the financial statements" or "The notes to the financial statement are an integral part of this statement").

The fiscal year of the financial reporting entity is always the same as the fiscal year of the primary government. If one or more component units included within the financial reporting entity has a different fiscal year-end than that of the primary government, then the data presented for such units should be the data for the last fiscal year ended prior to the fiscal year of the primary government. Assume that the primary government has a December 31 fiscal year-end, but that one of its component units has a September 30 fiscal year-end. In that case, the data presented for the component unit would be the data for the fiscal year that ended the previous September 30.

The one exception to this general rule occurs when a component unit has a fiscal year that ends within three months of the primary government's fiscal year-end. In that case, the financial reporting entity has the option of either 1) using the data for the component unit's fiscal year that ended during the primary government's fiscal year; or 2) using the data for the component unit's fiscal year that ended during the first quarter of the primary government's subsequent fiscal year.

Assume that the primary government has a September 30, 2010, fiscal year-end and a component unit has a December 31 fiscal year-end. The data presented in the reporting entity's report could be either the data for the

[22] GASB Statement No. 34, paragraphs 6c, 8.
[23] GASB, *Comprehensive Implementation Guide (2004)*, 7.19.
[24] GASB Statement No. 34, paragraph 10.

component unit's December 31, 2009, fiscal year-end (nine months prior to the close of the primary government's fiscal year) or the data for the component unit's December 31, 2010, fiscal year-end (three months after the close of the primary government's fiscal year). The second option should be adopted only if its application would not unreasonably delay issuance of the reporting entity's financial statements.[25] As with the application of any accounting principle, this option, once adopted, must be applied consistently from period to period.

RSI other than MD&A

Depending on a government's specific circumstances, four types of RSI, other than MD&A, must be presented, normally immediately following the notes to the financial statements:[26]

- *budgetary comparisons* (for the general fund and major individual special revenue funds for which annual (or biennial) appropriated budgets are adopted[27] if not presented elsewhere as a basic governmental fund financial statement);
- *infrastructure condition and maintenance data* (for governments using the modified approach for one or more networks or subsystems of infrastructure assets);
- *pension/other postemployment benefits (OPEB) trend data* (for certain pension/OPEB plans and participating employers); and
- *revenue and claims development trend data* (for public-entity risk pools).

Note that the RSI category is strictly limited to these specific items. That is, just because *supplementary information* is *required* to be presented (e.g., per statute or regulation) does not necessarily mean that it qualifies as *required supplementary information* for financial reporting purposes. Rather, this category may be used only for items specifically designated as RSI by the GASB. Other mandated presentations of supplementary information should be presented elsewhere within the CAFR, as described later in this chapter.

Budgetary comparisons

The format and contents of required budgetary comparisons for the general fund and major individual special revenue funds are the same regardless of whether those comparisons are presented as a basic governmental fund financial statement or as RSI.[28] However, budgetary comparisons presented as RSI are properly described as *schedules* rather than as *statements*.[29] Likewise, disclosures related to budgetary comparisons presented as RSI must be presented as *notes to RSI* rather than as part of the notes to the financial statements. The one exception to this latter rule is budget-related legal violations, which are always properly reported in the notes to the financial statements, even when the comparisons themselves are presented as RSI.[30]

---

[25] GASB Statement No. 14, paragraph 59.
[26] Notes to RSI follow the RSI presentation itself.
[27] Sometimes a given fund will be classified in one manner for financial reporting purposes and in another manner for budgetary purposes. Budgetary reporting requirements apply based solely upon how a fund is classified for financial reporting purposes. Thus, no budgetary comparison should be presented in the basic financial statements (or as RSI) for a budgetary special revenue fund that is classified as an enterprise fund for financial reporting purposes. (GASB, *Comprehensive Implementation Guide (2004)*, 7.380.)
[28] See discussion in chapter 10.
[29] GASB Statement No. 34, footnote 53.
[30] GASB, *Comprehensive Implementation Guide (2004)*, 7.390.

Infrastructure condition and maintenance data

Normally, infrastructure assets are treated in the same way as other capital assets. That is, infrastructure assets are capitalized at their historical cost and subsequently depreciated over their estimated useful life. All the same, GAAP allow governments the *option* of avoiding the requirement to report depreciation expense for networks or subsystems of infrastructure assets that meet certain specified criteria (this is the *modified approach*).

GAAP set the following specific requirements that must be met by a network or subsystem of infrastructure assets to qualify for using the modified approach:

- The government must have an up-to-date inventory of infrastructure assets within the network or subsystem for which the modified approach is adopted.
- The government must perform or obtain condition assessments on infrastructure assets and summarize the results using a measurement scale. This required condition assessment must be performed at least once every three years.[31] It is essential that such condition assessments be replicable (conducted using methods that would allow different measurers to reach substantially similar results). Statistical sampling may be used for condition assessments, provided that each item in a network or subsystem of infrastructure assets has an equal chance of being selected for sampling purposes.[32]
- Each year the government must estimate the amount needed to maintain and preserve infrastructure assets at a condition level established and disclosed by the government.[33]
- The government must document that infrastructure assets are being preserved at or above the condition level established and disclosed by the government.[34]

A government that elects to follow the modified approach for one or more networks or subsystems of infrastructure assets is required to present two types of information regarding those infrastructure assets. First, the government must present the results of the three most recently completed condition assessments to demonstrate that those assets have, in fact, been maintained at or above the condition level established by the government. Second, the government must disclose its estimate of the amount needed to maintain or preserve infrastructure assets at the level established by the government *and* actual amounts of expense for each of the past five reporting periods. While actual amounts must be presented on an accrual basis, estimated amounts may be presented using some other basis of accounting.[35] These schedules should be accompanied by the following disclosures as *notes to RSI*:

- the basis for the condition measurement and the measurement scale used to assess and report condition;

---

[31] A government may not adopt the modified approach for a given network or subsystem until a complete condition assessment has been performed for that network or subsystem.
[32] GASB, *Comprehensive Implementation Guide (2004)*, 7.99.
[33] Disparities between estimated and actual maintenance and preservation expense would not, of themselves, disqualify a government from continuing to use the modified approach. Only an actual decline in the condition of infrastructure assets below targeted levels (which is the likely ultimate outcome of habitually deferred maintenance) would disqualify a government from the continued use of the modified approach. (GASB, *Comprehensive Implementation Guide (2004)*, 7.103.)
[34] GASB Statement No. 34, paragraphs 23-26.
[35] GASB, *Comprehensive Implementation Guide (2004)*, 7.104.

- the condition level at which the government intends to preserve its infrastructure assets;
- factors that significantly affect trends in the information reported in the required schedules;
- if there is a change in the condition level at which the government intends to preserve eligible infrastructure assets, an estimate of the effect of the change on the estimated annual amount to maintain and preserve those assets (for the current period only);[36] and
- the basis used in calculating the amounts estimated to be necessary to maintain and preserve infrastructure assets at the condition level selected by the government if the estimated amounts are *not* presented on an accrual basis.[37]

Pension/OPEB trend data

Two schedules of actuarial[38] trend information typically must be presented in connection with defined benefit pension plans (six most recent years) and defined benefit OPEB plans (three most recent valuations): a schedule of funding progress and a schedule of employer contributions.

The schedule of funding progress. The schedule of funding progress is designed to show the extent to which a pension/OPEB plan has been successful over time in setting aside assets sufficient to cover its actuarial accrued liability. The actuarial accrued liability for this purpose is the amount calculated using the pension/OPEB plan's *funding method* (assuming it is consistent with the funding parameters established by GAAP). For pension plans, no schedule of funding progress need be presented when a pension plan uses the aggregate actuarial cost method, because that method does *not* identify or separately amortize unfunded actuarial liabilities.[39] In the case of OPEB plans, however, this schedule must still be provided even if the aggregate actuarial cost method is used, in which case the entry-age actuarial cost method should be used to provide the additional data needed to produce the schedule.[40]

It is common for pension/OPEB plans to issue separate, stand-alone reports that contain the required schedule of funding progress. In such cases, there normally is no need to present the schedule yet again in a sponsoring government's financial report that includes the pension/OPEB plan as a pension (and other employee benefit) trust fund or component unit. Instead, it ordinarily is sufficient for the sponsoring government's financial report to indicate how users may obtain a copy of the pension/OPEB plan's separately issued financial report. All the same, a schedule of funding prog-

[36] GASB Statement No. 34, paragraphs 132-133.

[37] GASB, *Comprehensive Implementation Guide (2004)*, 7.104.

[38] OPEB plans with a total membership (including employees in active service, terminated employees who have accumulated benefits but are not yet receiving them, and retired employees and beneficiaries currently receiving benefits) of fewer than one hundred have the option of using a simplified alternative measurement method instead of obtaining actuarial valuations. The same option is available for sole employers in an OPEB plan with fewer than one hundred total plan members, as well as for employers with fewer than one hundred plan members in an agent multiple-employer OPEB plan in circumstances in which the plan itself was not otherwise required to obtain an actuarial valuation for plan financial reporting purposes and does not, in fact, do so for purposes of separate financial reporting. The essential difference between this simplified alternative measurement method and a regular actuarial cost allocation method is the use of simplified assumptions. For convenience sake, the term *actuarial*, as it is used throughout this discussion, will encompass data generated by this simplified alternative method.

[39] GASB Statement No. 25, *Financial Reporting for Defined Benefit Pension Plans and Note Disclosures for Defined Contribution Plans*, paragraph 37.

[40] GASB Statement No. 43, *Financial Reporting for Postemployment Benefit Plans Other Than Pension Plans*, paragraph 30d(1).

ress for the past *three actuarial valuations* is always required in the case of single-employer pension/OPEB plans.[41]

This same schedule of funding progress for the past three actuarial valuations is required of *employers* who sponsor single-employer defined benefit pension/OPEB plans (regardless of whether those plans are included within the sponsoring government's report). It also is required of employers who participate in agent multiple-employer defined benefit pension/OPEB plans.[42]

The schedule of employer contributions. The schedule of employer contributions is designed to show the extent to which employers have actually funded their actuarially determined annual required contribution (ARC) over time.

The separate, stand-alone reports commonly issued by pension/OPEB plans typically contain the required schedule of employer contributions. As in the case of the schedule of funding progress, there is no need to present the schedule of employer contributions yet again in a sponsoring government's financial report that includes the pension/OPEB plan as a pension (and other employee benefit) trust fund or component unit. Instead, it is sufficient for the sponsoring government's financial report to indicate how users may obtain a copy of the pension/OPEB plan's separately issued financial report.[43]

Revenue and claims development trend data

GAAP require the presentation of certain revenue and claims development data as RSI in connection with public-entity risk pools. The format and contents of this presentation are addressed as part of the discussion of risk-pool accounting and financial reporting.[44]

Combining and individual fund statements, schedules, and supplementary information

The basic financial statements and RSI are immediately followed by a series of subsections devoted to each of the fund categories and to discretely presented component units. These subsections offer combining and individual fund statements and schedules, as well as related supplementary information.

Combining statements

To be truly *comprehensive*, the CAFR must provide information on each individual fund and component unit. As a rule, the basic financial statements provide detailed information only on individual major governmental funds, individual major enterprise funds, and individual major component units. Accordingly, it is the role of the combining and individual fund presentations to provide the needed level of detail for 1) nonmajor governmental funds, 2) nonmajor enterprise funds, 3) individual internal service

---

[41] GASB Statement No. 25, paragraph 34 and GASB Statement No. 43, paragraph 32. If there is no publicly available, separately issued pension/OPEB plan report, then the required schedule of funding progress must be presented in the sponsoring government's report when the pension/OPEB plan is included as a pension (and other employee benefit) trust fund or component unit. Detailed information on the format and contents of the schedule of funding progress can be found in chapter 15.

[42] GASB Statement No. 25, paragraph 34; GASB Statement No. 27, *Accounting for Pensions by State and Local Governmental Employers*, paragraph 22; GASB Statement No. 43, paragraph 32; GASB Statement No. 45, *Accounting and Financial Reporting by Employers for Postemployment Benefits Other Than Pensions*, paragraph 26.

[43] GASB Statement No. 25, paragraph 34; GASB Statement No. 43, paragraph 32. If there is no publicly available, separately issued pension/OPEB plan report, then the required schedule of employer contributions must be presented in the sponsoring government's report when the pension/OPEB plan is included as a pension (and other employee benefit) trust fund or component unit. Detailed information on the format and contents of the schedule of employer contributions can be found in chapter 15.

[44] See chapter 15.

EXHIBIT 13-1
Location of individual fund data within the CAFR

Governmental funds	Proprietary funds	Fiduciary funds	Component units
General fund	Major enterprise funds	Private-purpose trust funds	Major component units
Other major governmental funds	Nonmajor enterprise funds	Pension (and other employee benefit) trust funds	
		Investment trust funds	Nonmajor component units
Nonmajor governmental funds	Internal service funds	Agency funds	

Key:

☐ Basic financial statements

▨ Combining and individual fund subsection of the financial section of the CAFR

---

funds and fiduciary funds, and 4) *nonmajor* individual discretely presented component units (see Exhibit 13-1).

The CAFR should include a combining statement to support each column in the basic financial statements that aggregates data from more than one fund or discretely presented component unit. Thus, a government with the full complement of fund types and component units could have up to eight sets of combining financial statements, as follows:

- combining statements – nonmajor governmental funds;
- combining statements – nonmajor enterprise funds;
- combining statements – internal service funds;
- combining statements – private-purpose trust funds;
- combining statements – pension (and other employee benefit) trust funds;
- combining statements – investment trust funds;
- combining statements – agency funds; and
- combining statements – nonmajor discretely presented component units.[45]

Of special note, the combining statements for agency funds also need to include a *combining statement of changes in assets and liabilities—all agency funds*, even though this statement does *not* support one of the basic financial statements.[46]

Naturally, combining statements are unnecessary in situations where there is only one individual fund in any of these categories (for instance, no combining statements for investment trust funds are needed if a government reports only a single such fund).

---

[45] As discussed in chapter 10, GAAP require information on individual major discretely presented component units to be included within the basic financial statements, either as a separate column on the government-wide financial statements, as a combining statement, or as a note disclosure of *condensed* financial information. If this last option is selected, it is required that full (rather than condensed) combining statements for major discretely presented component units be included in the combining section.

[46] See GASB, *Codification of Governmental Accounting and Financial Reporting Standards,* Section 2200.181e(3), including footnote 40. Note that this requirement applies even if there is only a single agency fund, in which case the information would be presented as an individual fund statement rather than as a combining statement.

A unique characteristic of the combining statements for nonmajor governmental funds is that they combine individual funds from different fund types in a single financial statement. Because the fund type of an individual fund is important to financial statement users, columnar headings are useful to clearly identify the fund type of each individual fund presented in that statement.

Sometimes a government has so many individual nonmajor governmental funds that it is difficult to present all of the individual fund data on a single financial statement. In such cases, a government may elect to present subcombining statements to support the combining statements. Assume that a government has twenty individual nonmajor special revenue funds, in addition to several nonmajor capital projects funds, debt service funds, and permanent funds. The government could elect to present a combined column for all of the nonmajor special revenue funds in the combining statement for nonmajor governmental funds, provided this combined column is supported, in turn, by a subcombining statement that presents a separate column for each nonmajor special revenue fund.

GAAP emphasize that "only the minimum number of funds consistent with legal and operating requirements should be established . . . since unnecessary funds result in inflexibility, undue complexity, and inefficient financial administration."[47] If a government is hesitant to report information on each individual fund in its CAFR, this hesitation may itself be an indication that such "funds" are not, in fact, funds at all *for external financial reporting purposes*, even though they may be treated as such for internal accounting purposes. At the same time, it must be remembered that an important objective of the CAFR is to demonstrate compliance with finance-related legal and contractual requirements, and that the presentation of individual funds may be necessary for this purpose, especially in the case of funds with their own annual appropriated budget. Accordingly, a government should carefully consider the proper application of the number of funds principle to its particular situation before proceeding to present a large number of individual funds in its CAFR.[48]

Normally, a government has considerable flexibility in determining what constitutes a "fund" for external financial reporting purposes. Such is *not* the case, however, for funds that represent blended component units. In such cases, the activity's status as a separate fund for external financial reporting purposes is established automatically by virtue of its status as a legally separate entity.[49]

Individual fund statements and schedules

By definition, information on each individual fund and component unit will be provided either in the basic financial statements themselves or in the combining financial statements that support them. Accordingly, there is no reason to provide individual fund financial statements unless these additional presentations furnish information not otherwise already available in the basic financial statements and the combining financial statements.

---

[47] NCGA Statement 1, paragraph 4.

[48] The notion of *functional basis combining* may be useful for this purpose. Using this notion, numerous individual *funds* that serve an identical purpose may be combined, for financial reporting purposes, into a single fund. See GFOA recommended practice on "Improving the Effectiveness of Fund Accounting" (2004).

[49] By definition, only legally separate entities can qualify as component units. See chapter 4.

Examples of situations where individual fund financial statements and schedules would be appropriate or necessary include the following:

- *Budgetary comparisons not required in connection with the basic financial statements.* Budgetary comparisons must be presented in connection with the basic financial statements for the general fund and any individual major special revenue funds with annual (or biennial) appropriated budgets.[50] For governments preparing CAFRs, budgetary comparisons also are required for any other individual governmental funds for which annual (or biennial) appropriated budgets have been adopted (nonmajor special revenue funds, capital projects funds, debt service funds, and permanent funds). Individual fund *schedules*[51] often are presented for this purpose in the financial section of the CAFR.[52]

- *Detailed budgetary comparisons for the general fund and major individual special revenue funds.* Budgetary comparisons must be presented in connection with the basic financial statements for the general fund and major individual special revenue funds. These particular budgetary comparisons need be presented only at the functional level of detail (i.e., the same level of detail used to present current expenditures in the statement of revenues, expenditures, and changes in fund balances), which often is not sufficiently detailed to demonstrate legal compliance. A CAFR, however, must include budgetary comparisons for *all* governmental funds with annual (or biennial) appropriated budgets, presented at a level of detail sufficient to demonstrate legal compliance. Accordingly, a second, more detailed budgetary comparison often must be presented for the general fund and major special revenue funds elsewhere in the financial section of the CAFR to meet this requirement.[53] (In exceptional cases, where it would be impractical to provide the detail needed to demonstrate compliance at the legal level of budgetary control, reference may be made to a separately issued budgetary report that demonstrates compliance at the legal level of control.)[54]

- *Comparative data.* Governments often wish to provide comparative data from the prior year for individual funds, especially in the case of enterprise funds. Typically, it is not feasible to format the basic and combining financial statements to present comparative data for individual funds. Accordingly, individual fund presentations in the financial section of the CAFR frequently are used for this purpose.

- *Greater detail.* The accounts used for combining presentations are necessarily somewhat generic because of the practical need to encompass a broad range of activities. Governments frequently desire more descriptive accounts, however, especially in the case of enterprise funds.

---

[50] As explained in chapter 10, these required budgetary comparisons might be presented either as basic governmental fund financial statements or as RSI.

[51] Except for budgetary comparisons included as part of the basic financial statements (as discussed in chapter 10), budgetary comparisons are properly referred to as *schedules* rather than as *statements*.

[52] NCGA Statement 1, paragraph 9c. The requirement to present the original budget in addition to the final amended budget applies only to the budgetary comparisons presented for the general fund and major special revenue funds in connection with the basic financial statements.

[53] The legal level of budgetary control is discussed in chapter 16. There is no requirement to present the original budget in this connection, only the final amended budget and actual amounts.

[54] NCGA Interpretation 10, *State and Local Government Budgetary Reporting*, paragraph 14.

Individual fund presentations within the financial section of the CAFR are a practical means of providing this additional detail.

Funds of discretely presented component units

Normally, no fund data are provided for discretely presented component units because it is presumed that financial statement users interested in such detailed information will turn to the separately issued financial statements of the component unit referenced in the notes to the financial statements. However, if a discretely presented component unit with multiple funds does not issue a separate, publicly available financial report with the needed fund data (general fund, other major individual governmental funds, major individual enterprise funds, fund type data for internal service funds and fiduciary funds) for each of the basic financial statements (including a statement of cash flows for proprietary funds), then this information must be presented within the financial section of the CAFR. Even then, there is no requirement to present information either on the individual nonmajor governmental and enterprise funds of discretely presented component units or on the individual internal service funds and fiduciary funds of such units.[55]

Formatting

A divider page should precede each of the separate combining statements and related individual fund statements and schedules. This divider page should be used to present a brief description of the nature and operations of each individual fund presented in the combining statements, except for those funds whose nature and operations are clearly evident from their name.

Sets of financial statements should always be presented together as a unit. Thus, a complete set of combining financial statements should be presented before any related individual fund statements and schedules are presented. Sets of individual fund financial statements should be sequenced in the same order in which the related columns appear in the combining statements. Exhibit 13-2 provides a diagram illustrating the order in which the contents of the CAFR's financial section might be presented.

As noted, the basic financial statements should always carry a reference to the notes to the financial statements. Such references, however, are *not* appropriate for combining and individual fund presentations that are covered by only an *in-relation-to* opinion from the independent auditor.

Governments sometimes wish to present supplementary information that they believe would be useful to financial statement users or whose presentation is otherwise mandated (for instance, general fund cash receipts and disbursements). Such information also should be situated in the financial section of the CAFR. Such supplementary presentations are properly described as *schedules* rather than as *statements*. Likewise, budgetary comparisons are properly described as schedules rather than as statements, except when they are included as part of the basic governmental fund financial statements.

---

[55] GASB Statement No. 14, paragraph 50; GASB, *Comprehensive Implementation Guide (2004)*, 7.371 and 7.373.

EXHIBIT 13-2
Order of presentation: Combining and individual fund presentations and supplementary information

Governmental funds	Combining financial statements	1) Separate column for *each individual nonmajor governmental fund*, regardless of fund type *or* 2) Separate column for *each governmental fund type* (except for the general fund) containing aggregated data for all individual nonmajor funds of that fund type or 3) *Combination* of the above (i.e., fund-type columns used only for fund types with numerous individual nonmajor funds)
	Subcombining financial statements	Separate column for *each individual nonmajor governmental fund of a fund type presented in the aggregate on the combining financial statements.* (Separate financial statements presented for each fund type presented in the aggregate in the combining financial statements.)
	Individual fund financial statements	1) Budgetary comparisons for – the general fund and *major* individual special revenue funds (if needed to demonstrate compliance at the legal level of budgetary control) – budgetary comparisons for *nonmajor* special revenue funds with annual appropriated budgets – budgetary comparisons for debt service funds with annual appropriated budgets – budgetary comparisons for capital projects funds with annual appropriated budgets – budgetary comparisons for permanent funds with annual appropriated budgets 2) Other individual fund statements (as needed)
	Supplementary information	As needed (e.g., schedule of cash receipts and disbursements for the general fund)
Proprietary funds	Combining financial statements	– Individual *nonmajor* enterprise funds – *All* individual internal service funds
	Individual fund financial statements	As needed (e.g., to provide comparative data or more detailed accounts)
	Supplementary information	As needed (e.g., schedules required by bond covenants)
Fiduciary funds	Combining financial statements	– All individual private-purpose trust funds – All individual pension (and other employee benefit) trust funds – All individual investment trust funds – All individual agency funds
	Individual fund financial statements	As needed (rare)
	Supplementary information	Combining statement of changes in assets and liabilities – all agency funds
Component units	Combining financial statements	All *nonmajor* discretely presented component units
	Individual component unit fund presentations	*All* discretely presented component units that use multiple funds and that do *not* issue separate, publicly available financial reports with fund information. (Information required only for major funds, nonmajor governmental funds in the aggregate, nonmajor enterprise funds in the aggregate, the internal service fund type, and the fiduciary fund types. No information required for individual nonmajor governmental and enterprise funds, or for individual internal service or fiduciary funds.)

STATISTICAL SECTION

Objectives

The statistical section of the CAFR is the chief source of information regarding a government's *economic condition*. All of the information presented in the statistical section is organized around five specific objectives:[56]

- *Provide information on financial trends.* Information is needed to help users understand and assess how a government's financial position has changed over time.
- *Provide information on revenue capacity.* Information is needed to help users understand and assess a government's ability to generate own-source revenues.
- *Provide information on debt capacity.* Information is needed to help users understand and assess a government's debt burden and its ability to issue additional debt.
- *Provide demographic and economic information.* Information is needed to help users understand the government's socioeconomic environment and to facilitate comparisons of financial statement information over time and among governments.
- *Provide operating information.* Information is needed to help users understand a government's operations and resources as well as to provide a context for understanding and assessing its economic condition.

Financial trend data

Information about net assets (ten years).[57] A government must present data on each of the three categories of net assets presented in the government-wide statement of net assets, taking care to distinguish governmental activities from business-type activities. A total for the primary government must also be presented.[58] Net assets restricted by enabling legislation should be displayed separately from other restricted assets.[59]

Information about changes in net assets (ten years).[60] A government must reproduce as trend data much of the information provided in the government-wide statement of activities, with these modifications:

- Net (expense) revenue need not be presented by function.
- Program revenues (except as described in the next bullet) may be reported by category (i.e., charges for services; operating grants and contributions; capital grants and contributions) without regard to function.
- The most significant items within the charges for services category of program revenue need to be reported individually by function (e.g., water and sewer).

The presentation must distinguish governmental activities from business-type activities, as well as provide totals for the primary government.[61]

---

[56] GASB Statement No. 44, *Economic Condition Reporting: The Statistical Section, an amendment of NCGA Statement 1*, paragraph 5.
[57] GASB Statement No. 44, paragraph 9.
[58] It is recommended that this information be presented starting with the fiscal year in which a government first implemented GASB Statement No. 34, although data are only required for periods beginning after June 15, 2005.
[59] GASB Exposure Draft of proposed statement on *Net Assets Restricted by Enabling Legislation, an amendment of GASB Statements No. 34 and No. 44*, paragraph 6.
[60] GASB Statement No. 44, paragraphs 10-11.

Information about fund balances (ten years).[62] A government should provide information about both reserved and unreserved fund balance. This information should be presented separately for 1) the general fund and 2) all other governmental funds in the aggregate. There is no requirement to present the components of reserved fund balance. Unreserved fund balance, however, must be reported by fund type.[63]

Information about changes in fund balances (ten years).[64] Governments must provide for governmental funds in the aggregate virtually all of the information found in the statement of revenues, expenditures, and changes in fund balances. While there is no requirement to report a separate line item for the excess of revenues over expenditures, the principal and interest portions of debt service expenditures must be reported separately. In addition, total debt service expenditures should be expressed as a ratio/percentage of total noncapital expenditures (a calculation that requires the removal from current expenditures of amounts that are capitalized on the accrual basis government-wide statement of net assets).[65]

Information on revenue capacity

The following schedules on revenue capacity should focus on the government's largest single own-source revenue (e.g., property taxes). In situations where one or more other own-source revenues are almost as significant, financial statement preparers are encouraged (but not required) to present information on those revenues as well.[66]

Information about the revenue base (ten years).[67] Governments must present each of the major components of their largest own source revenue(s), as well as the total direct rate applied to that base. For property taxes, the major components would likely be the different classes of real and personal property (presented using assessed values).[68] In the case of property taxes, moreover, there is also a specific requirement to present the total estimated actual value of taxable property (unless the amount is not reasonably estimable, in which case the circumstances would need to be explained).

Information about revenue rates (ten years).[69] This schedule complements the previous one by providing information on the various components of the total direct rate. Any restriction on a government's ability to raise its direct rates would need to be disclosed (e.g., referendum requirement). The schedule also must provide separate rate information for any overlapping governments (defined as governments sharing some common geographical area). The overlapping concept does not apply to state governments, either from their own perspective or from that of their underlying governments. Furthermore, regional governments are encouraged, rather than required, to present information on the overlapping rates of their underlying governments.

---

[61] It is recommended that this information be presented starting with the fiscal year in which a government first implemented GASB Statement No. 34, although data are only required for periods beginning after June 15, 2005.

[62] GASB Statement No. 44, paragraph 12a.

[63] It is recommended that the required information be presented on this basis for all ten years, not simply for periods beginning after June 15, 2005.

[64] GASB Statement No. 44, paragraph 12b.

[65] It is recommended that the required information be presented on this basis for all ten years, not simply for periods beginning after June 15, 2005.

[66] GASB Statement No. 44, paragraph 13, including footnote 6.

[67] GASB Statement No. 44, paragraphs 14-15.

[68] The components of water revenues, for example, might be types of customer.

[69] GASB Statement No. 44, paragraphs 16-18.

Information about principal revenue payers (current period and period nine years prior).[70] Governments must list their ten principal payers (or remitters) for their largest own-source revenue(s) (unless fewer than ten are needed to account for at least 50 percent of total payments or remittances). The amount of the revenue base attributable to each also needs to be presented and expressed as a percentage of the total revenue base (or the amount of actual taxes levied on each needs to be presented and expressed as a percentage of total taxes levied). If governments cannot legally disclose this information (e.g., some income taxes), they must present other appropriate information indicative of revenue concentration.[71]

Information about property tax levies and collections (ten years).[72] Governments for which property taxes are included as part of the three prior schedules must also disclose property tax levies and collections, as follows:

- amount of each year's levy;
- collections as of end of the levy year (both in dollars and as a percentage of the levy);
- collections in later years (in dollars); and
- total collections to date (both in dollars and as a percentage of the levy).

The information provided in each schedule concerning property taxes should reflect the "year for which levied" used for purposes of revenue recognition. In the case of overlapping governments with different fiscal years, their data should be based upon taxes payable by the taxpayers during the reporting government's "year for which levied."

Debt capacity information

Ratios of outstanding debt (ten years).[73] Governments should present each type of outstanding debt separately (e.g., general obligation bonds, revenue-backed bonds, loans, certificates of participation, capital leases), taking care to distinguish debt related to governmental activities from debt related to business-type activities. A total for the primary government must also be presented. The total outstanding debt burden then needs to be expressed as two ratios:

- total outstanding debt to personal income (or to some other economic base if information on personal income is either unobtainable or inappropriate for assessing a particular revenue base); and
- total debt per capita (or on a basis more relevant in the circumstances, such as per customer/ratepayer for utilities).

Ratios of general bonded debt (ten years).[74] The next required table focuses on that portion of a government's debt that will be financed, in whole or in part, by general government resources. Such general bonded debt needs to be presented both by type of debt and in total. If resources have been externally restricted for the repayment of the *principal* of that debt, the table should show those amounts as a deduction from general bond debt to arrive at net general bonded debt. General bonded debt (or net general bonded debt) then needs to be expressed as two ratios:

---

[70] GASB Statement No. 44, paragraphs 19-20.
[71] For example, personal income tax by income tax level.
[72] GASB Statement No. 44, paragraph 21.
[73] GASB Statement No. 44, paragraphs 23-24.
[74] GASB Statement No. 44, paragraphs 25-26.

- (net) general bonded debt to the estimated actual value of taxable property; and
- (net) general bonded debt per capita.

If the debt is not going to be repaid from property taxes, an appropriate alternative revenue base would need to be used instead for the ratio. A base other than population could be used if per capita information were irrelevant.

Information about direct and overlapping debt (current year).[75] Governments also need to present the combination of direct and overlapping debt related to governmental activities. The concept of overlapping governments, as discussed earlier, does not apply to state governments. Likewise, regional governments, and in this case counties as well, are encouraged rather than required to present such information. The essential components of the schedule are as follows:

- outstanding debt for each overlapping government;
- percentage of overlap for each such government (with an explanation of the method used to calculate the overlap);
- the government's proportionate share of each overlapping government's debt;
- total overlapping debt;
- total direct debt (from an earlier schedule); and
- total direct and overlapping debt.

Once again, if debt is not to be repaid from property taxes, an appropriate alternative revenue base should be used instead to calculate the percentage of overlap (e.g., share of taxable sales for sales taxes). If the needed revenue-base information is not available, or if no specific revenue base is associated with debt repayment, alternatives such as population or personal income may be used to calculate the percentage of overlap.

Information on debt limitations (most recent year for calculation, ten years for results).[76] Governments subject to a legal debt limit have to provide the information needed to calculate their legal debt margin (e.g., relevant revenue base; amount and explanation of limitation; applicable debt; reserves to be deducted; net applicable debt; legal debt margin) for the current year. They also must show the debt limit, total net applicable debt, and the legal debt margin (but not the calculation itself) for each of the preceding nine years. In addition, one of the two following ratios must be presented for all ten years as well:

- outstanding net debt/debt limit; or
- legal debt margin/debt limit.

Information about pledged-revenue coverage (ten years).[77] Governments with revenue-backed debt must present coverage information for each type of debt, along with a description of pledged revenues. The essential elements of this presentation are as follows:

- gross revenues;
- deductible operating expenses (if applicable);
- net available revenues;
- principal and interest requirements; and

---

[75] GASB Statement No. 44, paragraphs 27-28.
[76] GASB Statement No. 44, paragraph 29.
[77] GASB Statement No. 44, paragraph 30.

- coverage ratio.

The purpose of this presentation is to help users assess economic condition, not to demonstrate legal compliance. Therefore, the schedule should be presented as just described, even if the contractual coverage formula is different.

Demographic and economic information

Demographic and economic indicators (ten years).[78] At a minimum, governments are required to present the following specific demographic and economic indicators:

- population;
- total personal income (if not already presented in connection with debt ratios);
- per capita personal income; and
- unemployment rate.

If such data are not relevant, more relevant indicators should be presented in their place. Other items that could be considered for inclusion are median age, education level, and school enrollment.

Information on principal employers (current period and period nine years prior).[79] Governments must identify their ten largest employers (unless fewer than ten are needed to account for at least 50 percent of employment) and the number of employees of each. Likewise, each employer's percentage of total employment should also be presented.

Operating information

Operating indicators (ten years).[80] Governments are required to present the following three type of information at the same functional level used in the government-wide statement of activities:

- the number of government employees;
- indicators of the demand or level of service;[81] and
- indicators of the volume, usage, or nature of capital assets.[82]

Categories other than functions may be used if they are more appropriate for a given government.

Primary government focus

The focus of the statistical section, like that of the basic financial statements, should be the primary government rather than the financial reporting entity. Accordingly, the decision whether to include data from discretely presented component units in the statistical section should be made using the same guidelines used to determine whether note disclosures are required for discretely presented component units. All the same, the application of these guidelines may properly differ between the notes and the statistical section. That is, a discretely presented component unit that requires certain note disclosures may not have to be included in the statistical section, and vice versa.[83]

---

[78] GASB Statement No. 44, paragraphs 32-33.
[79] GASB Statement No. 44, paragraph 34.
[80] GASB Statement No. 44, paragraph 35.
[81] For example, the police function might report the number of physical arrests, parking violations, and traffic violations. (See GASB Statement No. 44, exhibit F-2.)
[82] For example, the police function might report the number of stations, zone offices, and patrol units. (See GASB Statement No. 44, Exhibit F-3.)
[83] GASB Statement No. 44, paragraph 4.

Narrative explanations[84] The schedules just described should be accompanied by appropriate narrative explanations. While "a certain minimal level of educational descriptive narrative likely cannot be avoided," explanatory material should be primarily analytical in character, as well as "consistent with the objective, fact-based approach used in MD&A."[85] Specific requirements for narrative explanations are as follows:

- *Describe the objectives of the different types of information contained in the statistical section.* A narrative should be provided to explain the goal of the statistical section in general, and of each of the five categories of information it contains in particular (i.e., financial trend data; revenue capacity data; debt capacity data; demographic and economic information; and operating information). This narrative could be located on the divider page that typically precedes the statistical section of the CAFR.

- *Explain basic but potentially unfamiliar concepts.* A government, for example, might wish to indicate on the face of the schedules that government-wide trend data are presented on the accrual basis of accounting, whereas governmental fund trend data are presented on the modified accrual basis of accounting, thereby avoiding the confusion that could otherwise arise as a result of comparing similar items reported in both places.

- *Explain how information provided elsewhere may help the reader to better appreciate the data presented in a given statistical table.* For example, a government reporting significant increases in property tax revenues may wish to refer the reader to the schedules that present assessed values and tax rates to help the reader better understand the underlying cause of the increase.

- *Explain atypical trends and anomalous data that users would not otherwise understand.* For example, a government might choose to explain why a particular account (e.g., intergovernmental revenues) at first declined, but later increased.

- *Describe the source of data not extracted from the financial statements.*

ADDITIONAL SECTIONS OF A CAFR

Governments are free to present other sections in their CAFR *in addition to* the three basic sections described. The most common examples of additional sections are listed below.

- *Investment section.* Investing is a major activity of pension/OPEB plans and governmental external investment pools. Thus it is common for pension/OPEB plans and governmental external investment pools that publish CAFRs to devote a separate section of the CAFR to investments.[86] Indeed, a separate investment section must be included for a pension/OPEB plan report or governmental external investment pool report to receive GFOA's Certificate of Achievement for Excellence in Financial Reporting. The investment section, when

---

[84] GASB Statement No. 44, paragraph 42.
[85] GASB Statement No. 44, paragraph 105.
[86] Detailed information on the recommended contents of the investment section of a CAFR for a pension plan is found in chapter 15.

included in a CAFR, typically is presented immediately following the financial section.

- *Actuarial section.* Defined benefit pension/OPEB plans rely heavily on the work of actuaries in establishing their funding plan. As a result, pension/OPEB plans commonly devote a separate section of their CAFR to the work of the actuaries.[87] Moreover, a separate actuarial section is required for a pension plan report to receive GFOA's Certificate of Achievement for Excellence in Financial Reporting. The actuarial section, when included in a CAFR, typically is presented immediately following the investment section.

- *Single Audit section.* Governments receiving any substantial amount of federal awards, either directly or through an intermediate level of government, are required to undergo a Single Audit.[88] The documentation that results from a federally mandated Single Audit includes specialized reports by the independent auditor concerning internal controls and compliance, audit findings and recommendations, and a schedule of federal expenditures and awards. Typically, governments include these Single Audit materials in a report that is issued separately from the CAFR. Alternatively, some governments elect to include this information in a separate section within the CAFR. If so, it is important that the inclusion of Single Audit documentation *not* be allowed to unduly delay the release of the CAFR. The Single Audit Section, when included in a CAFR, typically is presented following the statistical section.

USING THE CAFR TO MEET SEC REQUIREMENTS

SEC Rule 15c2-12 requires a legal undertaking on the part of governmental debt issuers to provide certain annual financial information on an ongoing basis. Rule 15c2-12 does not establish a standardized format for presenting this information. Rather, the appropriate means of meeting the periodic disclosure requirements is left to the determination of the governmental issuer.

GFOA has formally recognized the CAFR as an appropriate document for meeting the disclosure requirements of SEC Rule 15c2-12. In its legal undertaking, however, a government is advised to commit itself only to the periodic disclosure of specified annual financial information, as provided in the amendments to SEC Rule 15c2-12, rather than to the periodic issuance of a CAFR as such.[89]

PLACING THE CAFR ON THE GOVERNMENT'S WEB SITE

A CAFR can only fully achieve its objectives if it is readily available to all interested parties. Presentation of the CAFR prominently on the government's Web site offers an unparalleled means of providing easy access to the CAFR. Specific benefits include the following:

---

[87] Detailed information on the recommended contents of the actuarial section of a CAFR for a pension plan is found in chapter 15.

[88] The Single Audit is discussed in detail in chapter 19.

[89] See GFOA's recommended practice on "Using the Comprehensive Annual Financial Report to Meet SEC Requirements for Periodic Disclosure" (1996).

- *Increased awareness.* Many potential users of the information provided in the CAFR may be unaware of its existence. Presentation on the government's Web site is a practical means of ensuring that all those with a potential interest in the government's finances are able to profit from the information available in the CAFR.
- *Increased usage.* The difficulties inherent in obtaining any published document pose a significant barrier to usage by ordinary citizens. An additional barrier arises when a government must charge for the CAFR to recover the cost of printing or copying. Both barriers are eliminated when the CAFR is presented on the government's Web site.
- *Application of analytical tools.* The availability of the CAFR in electronic form makes it easy for users to employ computerized tools to find, extract, and analyze the data contained in this often lengthy document.
- *Avoidance of disclosure redundancy.* Much information of use to potential purchasers of a government's debt securities is already available in the CAFR. In particular, the statistical section is a rich source of data for investors and analysts. Consequently, the routine presentation of the CAFR on the government's Web site may help to avoid redundancy and assist in complying with federally mandated disclosure requirements.
- *Savings.* The length and detail typical of the CAFR often make it expensive to print. Electronic publication can help to reduce this cost.

Accordingly, GFOA recommends that every government publish its CAFR on its Web site. In doing so, it is recommended that:
- the electronic CAFR be identical to the printed version;
- the Web site prominently notify users that the information in the CAFR has not been updated for developments subsequent to the date of the independent auditor's report;
- the Web site clearly identify prior year CAFRs (if presented) as "dated information for historical reference only" and clearly segregate them from current information (a "library" or "archive" section of the Web site is advisable for this purpose); and
- The security of the Web site be evaluated to protect it from manipulation by external or unauthorized persons.[90]

14

Professional Recognition Programs

Since its founding in 1906, the Government Finance Officers Association (GFOA), known first as the Municipal Finance Officers Association (MFOA), has actively promoted improvements in all aspects of public-sector financial management. Important tools for fostering these improvements have been GFOA's professional recognition programs, which include the Certificate of Achievement for Excellence in Financial Reporting Program and the Popular Annual Financial Reporting Award Program. This chapter examines these two programs and the role they play in improving the quality of public-sector financial reporting.

CERTIFICATE OF ACHIEVEMENT FOR EXCELLENCE IN FINANCIAL REPORTING PROGRAM

From its very beginnings, GFOA has taken a leadership role in promoting improvements in accounting and financial reporting. MFOA took the lead in identifying and promulgating generally accepted accounting principles (GAAP) for local governments through its sponsorship of the National Committee on Municipal Accounting (NCMA), the National Committee on Governmental Accounting, and the National Council on Governmental Accounting (NCGA). Likewise, MFOA played a crucial role in establishing the Governmental Accounting Standards Board (GASB), which succeeded the NCGA in 1984.[1]

The Securities Acts of the 1930s endowed the Securities and Exchange Commission (SEC) with broad regulatory powers over financial reporting by private-sector businesses with publicly traded securities. While the SEC has used its regulatory power to promote GAAP compliance by publicly held companies, state and local governments are exempt from all but the anti-fraud provisions of that legislation. Thus, there has been no national regulatory force equivalent to the SEC to promote GAAP compliance in the

---

[1] Chapter 1 provides a full discussion of the development of public-sector GAAP.

public sector. As a result, compliance with GAAP in the public sector developed more gradually than in the private sector.

MFOA saw little practical benefit in identifying and promulgating GAAP if those standards would not, in fact, be followed in practice. Further, GAAP are designed to provide the *minimum* standards for financial reporting, and MFOA believed that governments should be encouraged to go beyond these minimum standards and prepare truly comprehensive annual financial reports (CAFRs).[2]

Thus in 1945, MFOA established the Certificate of Conformance Program to encourage and assist governments in preparing CAFRs of the highest quality in conformity with GAAP. In 1984, the program adopted the more descriptive title of the Certificate of Achievement for Excellence in Financial Reporting Program (Certificate of Achievement Program) to better reflect governments' high level of achievement in meeting the program's demanding requirements.

For some time, relatively few governments were able to participate in the program. Today, more than 3,200 governments of all types from throughout the United States submit their CAFRs to the Certificate of Achievement Program. Indeed, more than half of all cities/towns/villages/townships with populations in excess of 25,000 participate in the program, along with almost half of U.S. counties with populations in excess of 50,000. Further, more than 40 states submit their CAFRs to the program, and numerous special-purpose governments and public employee retirement systems also participate.

Objectives and benefits

The Certificate of Achievement Program has three key objectives:
- to *encourage* governments to prepare and publish an easily readable and understandable CAFR;
- to *assist* governments in meeting the first goal by providing educational materials, comments, and suggestions for improvements; and
- to *recognize* governments and individuals that have met the challenge of preparing and issuing a high-quality CAFR.

The Certificate of Achievement Program offers the following important benefits to participating governments:
- Obtaining the Certificate of Achievement is a significant accomplishment that reflects well on a government's financial management.
- Award-winning CAFRs provide much of the information needed for credit assessments. Moreover, receipt of the Certificate of Achievement can itself be a positive factor in credit assessments.
- The Certificate of Achievement Program requirements are designed to produce CAFRs that are clear and complete, and so better meet the needs of citizens, investors, and other potential users.

---

[2] This view is not unique to GFOA. NCGA Statement 1, *Governmental Accounting and Financial Reporting Principles*, states: "Every governmental unit should prepare and publish, as a matter of public record, a comprehensive annual financial report (CAFR) . . . " (paragraph 135). Likewise, the Governmental Accounting Standards Board (GASB) Statement No. 34, *Basic Financial Statements—and Management's Discussion and Analysis—for State and Local Governments*, paragraph 281, reaffirms in the context of the new governmental financial reporting model: "The requirements of this Statement do not alter the provision in . . . NCGA Statement 1 that states that governments should prepare and publish a CAFR."

Eligibility

To be eligible to participate in the Certificate of Achievement Program, a government's CAFR must first meet the specific eligibility requirements that follow.

Type of report

The report submitted to the program must be the published CAFR[3] of a state or local governmental entity, which includes special-purpose entities such as public employee retirement systems, public colleges and universities, government investment pools, stand-alone business-type activities, and school districts. Component units and departments are eligible to submit their CAFRs to the program, provided they meet certain requirements that follow.

Scope

To qualify as "comprehensive," the CAFR must include all funds and component units of the entity, in accordance with GAAP as established by the GASB.[4] A component unit that publishes a CAFR is eligible to submit that report to the program for review, provided it includes all of the component unit's own funds and (sub)component units. Furthermore, except for a blended component unit's general fund, the fund types used in a blended component unit's report must be the same as those used to account for its activities in the primary government's report. (A blended component unit's general fund is properly reclassified as a special revenue fund in the primary government's report).[5] For instance, a blended component unit may not use proprietary fund accounting in its separately issued report if its activities are reported in governmental funds in the primary government's report.

A department of a government that publishes a CAFR is eligible to submit its report to the program for review, provided the department is composed of one or more separate funds. Thus a department reported as a separate special revenue or enterprise fund is eligible to participate, but a department included as part of the general fund is ineligible. Once again, the fund type(s) used in the department's report must be consistent with the fund type(s) used in the government's report. Furthermore, the program recommends that departmental reports always be accompanied by management's discussion and analysis.[6]

Audit requirements

The financial section of the CAFR must include an independent auditor's report on the fair presentation of the financial statements. The auditor must have performed the audit in accordance with either generally accepted auditing standards (GAAS) or generally accepted government auditing standards (GAGAS)[7] as set forth in the Government Accountability Office's *Government Auditing Standards*.[8] Also, the scope of the independent auditor's opinion at least must encompass the fair presentation of the basic financial statements.[9]

In most cases, a qualified opinion or a disclaimer of opinion based on the inadequacy or unavailability of the government's accounting records will

---

[3] Publication includes documents that are made available electronically.
[4] See chapter 4.
[5] See chapter 4.
[6] GFOA recommended practice on "Voluntary Reporting of Management's Discussion and Analysis" (2004).
[7] Because GAGAS are set forth in the publication, *Government Auditing Standards* (GAS), they are sometimes referred to as GAS rather than GAGAS.
[8] A detailed discussion of both GAAS and GAGAS is found in chapter 19.
[9] That is, governmental activities, business-type activities, major governmental funds, major enterprise funds, and, in the aggregate, other funds/discretely presented component units.

render a report ineligible, as will the omission of a fund type, individual fund, or component unit from the scope of the auditor's opinion.

Other eligibility requirements

The application must be postmarked or e-mailed no later than six months after the end of the government's fiscal year. An extension of thirty days is available when justified by extenuating circumstances (such as personnel changes, illness, systems conversions). A government is not eligible to receive an extension in two consecutive years *for the same reason.*

If the government participated in the program in the preceding year, its submission package must include written responses to all of the prior year's comments and suggestions for improvement.

If the CAFR references a separately issued budgetary report to demonstrate budgetary compliance at the legal level of budgetary control,[10] it must submit one copy of that report as part of its submission package.

The CAFR of a public employee retirement system (PERS) must include the most recent actuarial certificate of opinion or a letter from the system's independent actuary.

Likewise, the CAFR of a PERS must include both an actuarial and an investment section in addition to the three basic sections required in any CAFR (introductory, financial, and statistical). Investment pools are required to present an investment section in addition to the three basic sections required in any CAFR.

Judging process

Once a CAFR has been determined eligible for submission, it is judged using one of several detailed checklists (general government, stand-alone business-type activities, pension and other postemployment benefit systems, school district, or cash and investment pool). These checklists incorporate all relevant GAAP as well as applicable program policies. Responsibility for judging the reports rests with GFOA's Special Review Committee (SRC) and GFOA's professional staff. The SRC is a pool of more than 600 active reviewers drawn from government, the public accounting profession, and academe. As a matter of policy, reports are never assigned to a reviewer from the same state as the report under review, nor to a reviewer from the same audit firm that audited the report. A Certificate of Achievement is awarded only when reviewers agree that a report has substantially met the program's criteria. Policy for the Certificate of Achievement Program is set by GFOA's Special Review Executive Committee (SREC), subject to approval by GFOA's Executive Board.

Awards

Award-winning governments, SRC reviewers, and SREC members are listed in the Certificate of Achievement Program's annual report, which is distributed to the GFOA's more than 15,500 U.S. members. First-time winners also receive special mention in GFOA's biweekly *Newsletter*. Award-winning governments receive a plaque acknowledging the award and are allowed to reproduce a copy of the Certificate of Achievement in the subsequent year's CAFR. The Certificate of Achievement also may be mentioned in reports other than the CAFR (such as offering statements), provided that approved language is used and the Certificate of Achievement itself is not reproduced.[11] Also, GFOA issues an Award for Financial

---

[10] See chapter 13.
[11] Consistent with this treatment, the Certificate of Achievement may be reproduced on a government's Web site, but only if the full CAFR is reproduced there as well.

Reporting Achievement to the individual(s) designated by the government as being most responsible for the government's success in preparing an award-winning report.

As its name indicates, the Certificate of Achievement for Excellence in Financial Reporting is designed to encourage and recognize excellence in *financial reporting.* That is, the program is concerned with how well a government tells its financial story rather than with the underlying story itself. Accordingly, the Certificate of Achievement should *not* be viewed as a barometer of a government's financial health. A government facing severe financial challenges may produce a high-quality financial report. Indeed, high quality financial reporting may be especially valuable when a government is facing serious financial difficulties.

The Certificate of Achievement Program's emphasis on *how* a government tells its financial story in no way reduces the need for the information presented in a CAFR to be reliable (thus the requirement for an independent audit in conformity with GAAS or GAGAS). However, because the Certificate of Achievement Program, like all other users of financial reports in the public and private sectors, must rely on the independent auditor's work for the reliability of the CAFR's data, the Certificate of Achievement cannot guarantee against "audit failure."

POPULAR ANNUAL FINANCIAL REPORTING AWARD PROGRAM

The CAFR, as its name implies, is intended to have a *comprehensive* scope. Furthermore, CAFRs normally present information at a high level of detail (for instance, information on each individual fund). Such scope and detail are necessary to meet the needs of decision makers and to demonstrate compliance with legal requirements to oversight bodies and other interested parties. Unfortunately, this same scope and detail can confuse or discourage those unfamiliar with public-sector accounting and financial reporting.

While GFOA strongly supports both GAAP financial reporting and the CAFR[12] the association also acknowledges a need to *supplement* (rather than replace) the traditional CAFR with simpler, "popular" reports designed to assist those who need or desire a less detailed overview of a government's financial activities.[13] In that spirit, GFOA has established a Popular Annual Financial Reporting (PAFR) Award Program to encourage and assist governments in preparing popular reports. The program has operated since 1991, and it now counts more than 100 governments as participants.

Objectives and benefits   The goals of the PAFR Program parallel those of the Certificate of Achievement Program:

- to *encourage* governments to prepare and publish a popular annual financial report that is appealing, understandable, and readily available to its intended audience;
- to *assist* governments in meeting the first goal by providing general guidelines on the essential characteristics of an effective PAFR; and

---

[12] GFOA recommended practice on "Governmental Accounting, Auditing, and Financial Reporting Practices" (1997).

[13] GFOA formally adopted this position in two separate recommended practices (1991 and 1996) that have since been amalgamated into the single recommended practice, "Preparing Popular Reports."

EXHIBIT 14-1
Criteria for PAFR reviews

Category	Criteria	Weight
Reader appeal	The report is short enough to easily maintain user interest	3.0%
	The format of the report is logical and easy to understand	3.0%
	The report's typography is easy to read	1.5%
	The report's typography is appealing to readers	1.5%
	The photographs, charts, graphics or other artwork enhance the report's appeal	1.0%
	Subtotal for reader appeal	**10.0%**
Understandability	The report avoids jargon and technical language that may not be immediately understandable to those without a financial or accounting background	5.0%
	The report makes good use of charts or graphs to help users better understand the financial data presented and to enhance the financial data presented	5.0%
	The report uses narrative to explain financial data and to highlight significant items	5.0%
	The report helps users to understand financial data in their proper context by providing appropriate information on past trends (e.g., comparative data)	5.0%
	The report minimizes the potential for misinterpreting the information presented (e.g., the data are consistent, statements are not misleading)	5.0%
	Subtotal for understandability	**25.0%**
Distribution	The number of reports distributed was appropriate for the target audience	3.0%
	The mode of distribution was appropriate for the target audience	4.5%
	Subtotal for distribution	**7.5%**
Other	The report was an especially notable achievement for a government of its type and size	1.5%
	The report was especially innovative or creative in form or content	1.5%
	If I were a user or potential user of the entity's services (e.g., citizen/taxpayer/pension plan participant) this report would be useful to me	1.5%
	If I were a member of a legislative or oversight body this report would be useful to me	1.5%
	This report would make the entity more attractive to interested parties (e.g., new businesses and citizens)	1.5%
	Subtotal for other	**7.5%**
Summary	A good popular report is more than the sum of its parts. This category is designed to allow the judges to evaluate whether the report is successful in achieving its goals overall	50.0%
	TOTAL	**100.0%**

- to *recognize* governments and individuals for meeting the challenge of preparing and issuing a high-quality PAFR.

The PAFR Program offers at least three important benefits to participating governments:

- Obtaining the PAFR award is a significant accomplishment that reflects well on a government's financial management.
- Award-winning PAFRs provide a practical demonstration of a government's commitment to increase the involvement of citizens and other interested parties in its activities.
- An award-winning PAFR may encourage interested parties to seek additional information directly from the CAFR, thereby increasing the audience for the CAFR.

Eligibility

To participate in the PAFR Program, a government must meet all of the following eligibility requirements:

Successful participation in the Certificate of Achievement Program

Popular reporting is no substitute for a CAFR prepared in conformity with GAAP. Accordingly, participation in the PAFR Program is limited to governments (including component units and departments) that submit their CAFR to the Certificate of Achievement Program.

Reference to the CAFR

It is important to emphasize the link between the PAFR and the CAFR. Also, the PAFR itself may create a demand from certain readers for more detailed financial data; so, GFOA requires that popular reports submitted to the PAFR Program advise readers of the availability of the CAFR.

Basis of presentation consistent with GAAP and disclosed

The financial data presented in the PAFR must be *derived* from the CAFR and *consistent* with GAAP. For example, information on governmental funds must be presented using the current financial resources measurement focus and the modified accrual basis of accounting.[14] Nonetheless, the typical PAFR is *not* expected to provide all of the detail and disclosure required for fair presentation in conformity with GAAP. Likewise, a PAFR need not encompass the entire financial reporting entity as defined by GAAP. To minimize the possibility for confusion, GFOA requires that popular reports submitted to the PAFR Program indicate whether they are presented in a manner consistent with GAAP and, if not, that they briefly disclose how their manner of presentation differs from GAAP (for example, they eliminate certain component units and funds).

Narrative or graphic analysis

Popular reports are expressly designed to meet the needs of those who may lack expertise in financial matters. Therefore, GFOA believes it is essential that some form of analysis accompany financial presentations within popular reports.[15] This analysis may take the form of narrative, graphics, or, ideally, a combination of both. The focus of such analysis should be items of potentially significant financial interest or concern.

Judging process

Once a report is judged eligible for submission to the PAFR Program, it is submitted to four judges. As a matter of policy, reports are neither assigned to a reviewer from the same state as the report under review, nor to a reviewer from the same audit firm that audited the CAFR. Each judge independently evaluates the report on the basis of four categories of criteria: 1) reader appeal (10 percent), 2) understandability (25 percent), 3) distribution methods (7.5 percent), and 4) other (such as creativity and notable achievement, 7.5 percent). The remaining 50 percent of the score is based on each judge assessing the overall quality and usefulness of the report, considering the four categories for judging. A PAFR must obtain a weighted average rating of at least 75 percent to qualify for the PAFR award. Exhibit 14-1 presents the specific components of the four basic categories of criteria for judging.

Awards

Award-winning governments and reviewers are recognized each year in a special insert included with GFOA's biweekly *Newsletter*. Award-winning governments also receive a plaque recognizing their achievement, and they are allowed to reproduce a copy of their award in the subsequent year's PAFR.

---

[14] See chapter 2.
[15] Indeed, GAAP require that management's discussion and analysis accompany the basic financial statements.

15

States and Certain Special-purpose Governments

This chapter examines some of the unique accounting and financial reporting challenges facing states and certain types of special-purpose governments. It also addresses situations where government-wide financial statements and fund financial statements can be combined into a single presentation.

STATES

Generally accepted accounting principles (GAAP) do not provide specialized accounting and financial reporting for states; however, specialized guidance is available on several types of transactions encountered solely or primarily at the state level.

Escheat property
States take custody of private property when its legal owner cannot be found or identified (for instance, estates without heirs and abandoned bank accounts). Such property is said to *escheat* (revert) to the state. Most often, the rightful owners of escheat property retain their legal claim to these assets in perpetuity. As a practical matter, however, most escheat assets are never reclaimed. States typically remit most escheat property to the general fund, where it is used to finance the government's regular operations. Usually, only a portion of such assets is retained to pay claims by property owners.

States may report escheat property directly in the fund to which it ultimately reverts (e.g., general fund). In that case, a liability must be recognized for any amounts expected eventually to be paid out to individuals or private organizations, regardless of the timing of the payments.

Some states prefer to account for escheat resources in a separate fund, in which case a private-purpose trust fund should be used. Consistent with the definition of a fiduciary fund, only that portion of escheat resources whose eventual payment to claimants is considered to be probable may be reported in a private-purpose trust fund.[1] Likewise, escheat resources not expected eventually to be paid to claimants should be reported directly as revenue of the general fund. Furthermore, no liability to eventual claimants should be reported in the fund, because the net assets of a trust fund, by definition, belong to the beneficiaries of the trust.

When escheat property is held on behalf of another government rather than on behalf of individuals or private organizations, an agency fund should be used rather than a private-purpose trust fund. Alternatively, an asset and liability could be reported in governmental or proprietary funds, avoiding altogether the need to report a separate fund.[2]

Food stamps

The federal government's food stamp program is designed to increase the food purchasing power of economically disadvantaged people. Electronic benefit transfer (EBT) systems allow program beneficiaries to directly charge their qualifying food purchases. Revenues and expenditures should be reported when the underlying transaction (the food purchase) occurs.[3]

Pass-through grants

Agency funds are used to account for those rare pass-through arrangements where a state functions as a pure cash conduit. To function as a pure cash conduit, a state must meet two criteria. First, the state must have no administrative involvement with the program. Examples of disqualifying administrative involvement include the monitoring of subrecipients for compliance with program-specific requirements; the determination of eligible subrecipients (even if using grantor-established criteria); and the ability to exercise discretion in how funds are allocated.

Second, the state may have no *direct* financial involvement with the grant program. Examples of direct financial involvement that would disqualify a grant from being reported in an agency fund include a requirement that the state finance some direct program costs (for example, through matching requirements), or state exposure to liability for disallowed costs.

These criteria do not address *indirect* financial involvement with pass-through grants because such involvement typically arises only in connection with administrative functions, which fall within the scope of the first criterion. As a practical matter, it is rare for a grant to qualify for the pure cash conduit classification based on the criteria described. [4] In situations where grants do *not* qualify under the pure cash conduit definition, states that provide pass-through resources to other governments should recognize revenue as soon as all eligibility requirements have been met, *even though amounts may not have yet been remitted to subrecipients.* In the interim, the associated purpose restriction (i.e., the obligation to remit the resources to subrecipients) should be reported as restricted net assets.[5]

---

[1] GASB, *Comprehensive Implementation Guide (2004)*, 7.272.
[2] GASB Statement No. 37, *Basic Financial Statements—and Management's Discussion and Analysis—for State and Local Governments: Omnibus,* paragraph 3 and GASB, *Comprehensive Implementation Guide (2004),* 7.272.
[3] GASB Statement No. 24, *Accounting and Financial Reporting for Certain Grants and Other Financial Assistance,* paragraph 6, especially footnote 4.
[4] GASB Statement No. 24, paragraph 5.
[5] GASB Statement No. 33, *Accounting and Financial Reporting for Nonexchange Transactions,* appendix D, example 9.

Special funding situations for pension and other postemployment benefits (OPEB)

A *special funding situation* for pension/OPEB benefits occurs when one government is legally required to make contributions to a pension/OPEB plan on behalf of the employees of one or more other governments. For example, a state may be obligated to contribute to a pension plan on behalf of school district employees. In such cases, the paying government is to treat the plan just like a plan offered to its own employees. If the government is the only contributor, the plan qualifies as a single-employer plan, even if employees of several entities participate.[6]

Special funding situations are just one example of *on-behalf benefit payments* (payments to third parties of *salaries or benefits* on behalf of the employees of another government). States should classify on-behalf benefit payments in the same way they classify similar cash payments (such as grant expenditures) to other governments.[7]

Unemployment compensation benefit plans

GAAP direct that state unemployment compensation benefit plans be accounted for in an enterprise fund.[8] Administrative costs associated with such programs, however, should be accounted for in the general fund or some other fund (if legally required).[9] Despite certain similarities, state unemployment compensation plans should *not* be treated as public-entity risk pools.[10]

Lotteries

State lotteries typically meet the criteria that mandate the use of enterprise fund accounting.[11] Two key accounting issues arise in connection with lotteries. First, annuity contracts often are purchased *in the name of individual lottery winners.* In that case, both the asset (annuity contract) and the related liability should be removed from the statement of position. If the government is still contingently liable in such situations, this contingency should be disclosed in the notes to the financial statements.[12] Second, lotteries sometimes involve games with prizes that accumulate over time. When such games are in progress at the end of the fiscal year, it is necessary to report a liability based on the estimated present value of the prizes that will eventually be awarded.[13] As a practical matter, prize costs normally are calculated as a percentage of ticket sales revenues.[14]

Debt-financed capital grants to other governments

States commonly issue debt to finance capital grants to other levels of government. Because the capital assets acquired with such debt are those of another entity, such debt should be included as part of the state's calculation of its own *unrestricted net assets.*[15]

---

[6] GASB Statement No. 27, *Accounting for Pensions by State and Local Governmental Employers*, paragraph 28 and GASB Statement No. 45, *Accounting and Financial Reporting by Employers for Postemployment Benefits Other Than Pensions*, paragraph 32.
[7] GASB Statement No. 24, paragraph 13.
[8] GASB Statement No. 34, *Basic Financial Statements—and Management's Discussion and Analysis—for State and Local Governments*, footnote 34.
[9] NCGA Interpretation 9, *Certain Fund Classifications and Balance Sheet Accounts*, paragraph 9. Also, *Comprehensive Implementation Guide (2004)*, 7.257.
[10] GASB, *Comprehensive Implementation Guide (2004)*, 7.256.
[11] GASB Statement No. 34, paragraph 67, and American Institute of Certified Public Accountants (AICPA), *State and Local Governments*, Section 12.103.
[12] AICPA, *State and Local Governments*, Section 12.105.
[13] AICPA, *State and Local Governments*, Section 12.106.
[14] AICPA, *State and Local Governments*, Section 12.104.
[15] GASB, *Comprehensive Implementation Guide (2004)*, 7.137.

Unrestricted fees and charges

GAAP require that charges for services be reported as program revenue. For state governments, many charges for services are not restricted to financing the function in which they are generated. Indeed, it is common for such amounts to be spent for some entirely unrelated purpose. All the same, these amounts still must be reported as program revenue of the function in which they are generated in the government-wide statement of activities. That is, restriction is considered only in determining whether *grants and contributions* should be classified as program revenue; restriction is *not* considered in determining whether *charges for services* should be so classified.[16]

Financing authorities

Financing authorities often function essentially as legal devices for the issuance of construction-related debt, with the authority having little if any actual involvement with either construction or debt service. Since the recipients of the debt proceeds are responsible for making subsequent debt service payments, the authority's debt liability essentially is offset by a corresponding receivable from the recipients of the proceeds. In practice, two different approaches are taken to preparing the financial statements of such authorities. One approach is to report both the asset and the liability on the authority's statement of position. The other approach is to report neither. In both cases, the operating statement would report revenues and expenses only in connection with administrative costs and payments received in excess of future debt service requirements.[17]

Tobacco settlement accounting

In 1998, most states arrived at a legal settlement with the nation's largest tobacco companies. Under the terms of the resulting master settlement agreement, the "settling governments" agreed to forego all current and future legal claims against the participating tobacco companies in return for a claim in perpetuity to a portion of future revenues from tobacco sales. The amount remitted each year by the tobacco companies is determined using a formula that relates directly to domestic shipments of cigarettes.

Rather than wait for future tobacco-related revenues to materialize, a number of governments have sought immediate access to at least some of these resources by issuing bonds secured by anticipated future collections. Typically, a legally separate financing authority is created for the express purpose of issuing this debt. The financing authority uses the bond proceeds it receives to "purchase" a portion of the settling government's claim to future tobacco settlement revenues. Amounts later remitted by the tobacco companies to the authority are then used to pay bondholders. Amounts collected by the authority in excess of debt service requirements and administrative costs ultimately belong to the settling government rather than to the authority.

A financing authority created to issue tobacco-related debt will be legally separate from the settling government that created it. Because it does not constitute a general-purpose government, nor have a board chosen by voters in a general election, such an authority would *not* qualify as a primary government in its own right. Rather, it would need to be considered as a potential component unit of the settling government.

---

[16] GASB Statement No. 37, paragraph 12; GASB, *Comprehensive Implementation Guide* (2004), 7.207; AICPA, *State and Local Governments*, Section 12.108.
[17] AICPA, *State and Local Governments*, Section 15.24.

A financing authority created in connection with the tobacco settlement normally will qualify as a component unit based on the two-pronged "financial accountability" criterion of GASB Statement No. 14, *The Financial Reporting Entity*. Specifically, the authority's board members typically would be appointed by the primary government (board appointment test) and the settling government would have a claim to tobacco-related revenues collected in excess of debt service requirements and administrative costs (financial benefit/burden test).

Once it has been determined that a legally separate entity qualifies as a component unit, a second issue is whether that unit should be blended (treated as an integral part of the primary government) or discretely presented (reported together with, but separate from, the primary government). Tobacco settlement-related financing authorities normally are likely to meet the "exclusive benefit" test for blending. Nonetheless, classification as a discretely presented component unit remains a possibility when the "exclusively, or almost exclusively" criterion is not met.

As already mentioned, the amounts paid by tobacco companies are calculated based upon domestic shipments of cigarettes. For that reason, it is not acceptable to recognize either a receivable or revenue for tobacco-related revenues until the underlying shipments have actually taken place. Conversely, a receivable and revenue would need to be recognized for payments related to shipments already made but not yet remitted.

Note that it would *not* be appropriate for the financing authority itself to recognize an asset resulting from its "purchase" of the settling government's rights to future tobacco revenues. Recognition of an asset for the purchase of these rights would violate generally accepted accounting principles (GAAP). Specifically, Accounting Principles Board Opinion No. 16, *Business Combinations*, precludes the recognition of an asset where none previously had been recognized solely on the basis of a transaction between entities under "common control."

The net effect of the guidance just described will be as follows:

- The issuance of tobacco-related debt will have an initial *positive* impact on the settling government and an initial *negative* impact on the financing authority, but *no overall impact* on the financial reporting entity.
- The financing authority will initially report a deficit that will diminish over time as tobacco-related revenues materialize and come to be recognized as revenue.
- The financial reporting entity will recognize tobacco-related revenues only as they materialize (i.e., when the tobacco is shipped).

In short, the issuance of bonds will in no way accelerate the recognition of tobacco-related revenues by the financial reporting entity, as illustrated in Exhibit 15-1.

SCHOOL DISTRICTS

Letter of transmittal

The basic contents of the letter of transmittal have already been discussed elsewhere.[18] Several considerations may be helpful in applying that general guidance to school districts.

---
[18] See chapter 13.

Exhibit 15-1
Net effect of tobacco settlement activities

	Primary government										Net effect on the primary government's operating statement
	Settling government			Financing authority (blended component unit)							
Event	Cash	Interfund receivable	Transfers in	Cash	Tobacco receivable	Interfund payable	Bonds payable	Revenue	Transfers out		
Issuance of bonds by tobacco authority				$100			($100)				$0
Recognition of liability to settling government		$100	($100)			($100)			$100		$0
Remittance of bond proceeds to settling government	$100	($100)		($100)		$100					$0
Shipments of cigarettes by tobacco companies					$10			($10)			($10)
Collections from tobacco companies				$10	($10)						$0
Payments to bondholders				($10)			$10				$0

It is a general recommendation that the letter of transmittal offer a profile of the government. In the case of school districts, that profile ought to include the following:

- description of the district (e.g., K-12, high school only, vocational education only);
- number of students;
- types of programs the district offers (general education, special education, vocational education);
- relationship of the district to other governments (e.g., independent district, component unit of county); and
- discussion of any charter schools, including their relationship to the district and how they are funded.[19]

It also is generally recommended that the letter of transmittal provide information useful in assessing the government's economic condition. Two specific items are of particular value in this regard for school districts: 1) projected enrollment and 2) the age of school buildings.

While it is appropriate to mention awards in a letter of transmittal, the awards thus mentioned ought to have some bearing on the school district's *financial management.* The inclusion of long lists of academic, professional, or extra-curricular awards should be avoided, especially as such lists tend to unduly lengthen the letter of transmittal, making it less attractive and accessible to potential readers.

Classification of shared revenues

School districts often benefit from property taxes raised by other governments on their behalf. Such shared revenues are *not* considered to be *taxes*

---

[19] A mission statement may also be included, but only if *brief.*

from the perspective of the benefiting school district. The same is true of sales taxes raised at the state level to fund education. Instead, such shared revenues are properly classified as either government-mandated or voluntary nonexchange transactions.

Unlike taxes, government-mandated and voluntary nonexchange transactions potentially qualify as program revenue, but only if they are restricted to a purpose narrower than just "education." If not, they should be reported as general revenue.[20]

Dedicated property taxes

Sometimes different portions of a school district's property tax levy will be devoted to specific purposes (e.g., debt retirement). In that case, the school district may wish to report a separate line for each within the *general revenues* category, although it is not required to do so.[21]

Revenue associated with multi-functional programs

School districts sometimes account for a single program in more than one functional category. Normally, multipurpose grants only qualify as program revenue if the amount to be spent on each function is specified.[22] This rule does *not* apply, however, to a single program grant that is accounted for in more than one function. Rather, single-program grants should always be treated as program revenue, even if a formula is needed to allocate that revenue among the various functions used to account for the single program.[23]

Tuition revenue

School districts sometimes accept students from other districts, who pay tuition for the education they receive from the school district. As a *charge for services*, tuition automatically qualifies as program revenue of the functional category that generates it (instructional), even though the amount billed may have been calculated with a view to recovering costs reported in other functional categories as well (administrative and support).[24]

Contributed services

GAAP require that governments report revenues and expenditures/ expense to reflect payments of salaries and benefits made on behalf of the government's employees for services rendered to the government.[25] GAAP also require that governments recognize the receipt of capital assets in connection with non-exchange transactions.[26] GAAP are silent, however, regarding the treatment of contributed *services* (e.g., volunteers).

In the absence of authoritative guidance on contributed services, school districts may wish to consider the treatment prescribed by Financial Accounting Standards Board (FASB) Statement No. 116, *Accounting for Contributions Received and Contributions Made,* which limits the recognition of revenue and expense in connection with contributed services to just those services that meet one or the other of the following criteria:
- the donated service creates or enhances nonfinancial assets (e.g., volunteer improvements to a capital asset); or

---

[20] GASB, *Comprehensive Implementation Guide (2004),* 7.191 and 7.187.
[21] GASB, *Comprehensive Implementation Guide (2004),* 7.212.
[22] GASB Statement No. 34, paragraph 50.
[23] GASB, *Comprehensive Implementation Guide (2004),* 7.185.
[24] GASB, *Comprehensive Implementation Guide (2004),* 7.210.
[25] GASB Statement No. 24, paragraph 8.
[26] GASB Statement No. 33, paragraph 5.

- the donated service requires specialized skills, and is provided by individuals possessing those skills, and would typically need to be purchased if not provided by donation (e.g., the services of accountants, architects, carpenters, doctors, electricians, lawyers, nurses, plumbers, teachers, and other professionals and craftsmen).[27]

Level of detail for expense/expenditures

GAAP require that expenditures be presented, at a minimum, at the functional level, although more detailed presentations are encouraged.[28] In the case of school districts, it would not be unusual for 90 percent of total expense to fall within a single functional category (instructional). Therefore, school districts may wish to consider presenting information on programs within functions (e.g., regular education, special education, vocational education).

Annualized payroll for shorter academic terms

Many school districts pay their teachers on a year-round basis, even though the academic term may be shorter (e.g., nine months). Since payroll is an exchange transaction, an expenditure/expense and a liability should be recognized as of the end of the academic term for any unpaid salaries earned during the most recently completed academic term.[29]

School lunch programs

Student lunch programs may be reported in either an enterprise fund or a governmental fund (special revenue fund). In either case, donated commodities are recognized in both the fund and government-wide financial statements as revenues when all the eligibility requirements are met (typically in the period received) and as expense/expenditure when consumed.[30]

Capital asset considerations

The rules discussed elsewhere in regard to accounting and financial reporting for capital assets[31] apply equally to school districts. In that regard, the following points should be emphasized:

- *Capital asset impairments.* School districts frequently convert school buildings to use for some other purpose (e.g., storage). Accordingly, school districts should be careful to recognize any resulting capital asset impairment (i.e., change in manner or duration of use).
- *Estimated useful lives of capital assets.* While school districts certainly should consider the experience of other school districts in estimating the useful lives of their own capital assets (standard life tables), they also need to consider whether their own particular circumstances require that adjustments be made to such standardized or average estimated useful lives.
- *Fully depreciated capital assets.* It is not appropriate for a school district to report significant amounts of fully depreciated capital assets. While reporting some fully depreciated capital assets may be inevitable, significant amounts indicate that the estimated useful lives used for depreciation need to be adjusted to reflect the school district's actual experience.

---

[27] FASB Statement 116, *Accounting for Contributions Received and Contributions Made*, paragraph 9.
[28] GASB Statement No. 34, paragraph 40.
[29] AICPA, *State and Local Governments*, Section 12.17.
[30] GASB, *Comprehensive Implementation Guide (2004)*, 7.446; AICPA, *State and Local Governments*, Section 12.19.
[31] See chapter 12.

Scholarships

It is common for school districts to operate privately funded scholarship programs for their students. In practice, the private-purpose trust fund commonly is used to account for such scholarship activity.

Student activity funds

There is considerable diversity in practice regarding the fund type used to account for student activity funds. While GAAP do not offer specific guidance, the following general guidelines should be followed in selecting a fund-type for this purpose:

- *Instructional activities should not be reported in fiduciary funds.* GAAP limit the use of fiduciary funds to accounting for resources that are not available to support any of the government's own programs.[32] Therefore, it would *not* be appropriate to classify student activity funds that support instructional activities as fiduciary funds.
- *Budgeted resources should not be reported in fiduciary funds.* Consistent with the principle just described, the inclusion of a given student activity fund in the school district's budget argues against reporting the activity in a fiduciary fund.
- *Agency funds should not be used for resources that qualify for fiduciary reporting (i.e., existence of a trust agreement) if there is a high degree of involvement by the school's administration.* Sometimes a school's administration exercises considerable discretion over the use of student activity funds. A high degree of management involvement is incompatible with the use of an agency fund.[33]
- *Agency funds should be used for resources that qualify for fiduciary reporting when administrative involvement is limited.* In most cases, student activity funds involve little more than the receipt, temporary investment, and remittance of resources to outside parties. The agency fund type is specifically designed for such purposes.[34] Perhaps it is for this reason that agency funds are the most common fund type encountered in practice in connection with student activity funds.[35]

It is entirely possible that related activities may be reported differently. Thus resources raised for band uniforms may be reported in a special revenue fund (as part of the music education program), while resources raised for a band field trip may be reported in an agency fund (funds raised and owned by the students participating in the trip).

Charter schools

Charter schools are legally separate from the school district in which they are located and operate with a considerable degree of independence. As a practical matter, charter schools typically do *not* meet the criteria for inclusion as a component unit of a school district because there normally is neither board appointment nor fiscal dependence.[36] All the same, charter schools sometimes are included as component units on the grounds that their exclusion would be potentially misleading.[37]

Foundations

As discussed elsewhere,[38] a legally separate tax-exempt organization may be included as a component unit because of the nature of its relationship to

---

[32] GASB Statement No. 34, paragraph 69.
[33] GASB Statement No. 34, paragraph 69.
[34] GASB Statement No. 34, paragraph 73.
[35] AICPA, *State and Local Governments*, Section 12.18.
[36] As explained in chapter 4, ongoing financial burden is *not* evidence of fiscal dependence.
[37] See chapter 4.

the primary government. Specifically, inclusion as a component unit is appropriate if *all three* of the following criteria are met:

- the resources of the organization entirely (or almost entirely) benefit the government;
- the government is entitled to or can otherwise access the organization's resources; and
- the resources of the organization are significant to the government.

Many legally separate, tax-exempt organizations associated with school districts meet the first two of these criteria. The third criterion, however, is more problematic. Some have argued that numerous small foundations should be classified as component units on the grounds that their aggregate effect is significant to the district. GAAP, however, expressly direct that the assessment of significance focus on each *individual organization* rather than on organizations in the aggregate.[39]

Statutorily required schedules

As explained elsewhere,[40] the required supplementary information (RSI) category may only be used for information so designated in the authoritative accounting literature. Therefore, statutorily required schedules may *not* be reported as RSI. Likewise, such schedules may not replace the combining and individual fund presentations normally required in the financial section of a comprehensive annual financial report (CAFR), but rather should be presented at the end of the relevant subsection (e.g., governmental funds) of the financial section of the CAFR.

Statistical section

GAAP establish the basic contents of the statistical section.[41] All the same, governments are free to include additional information consistent with the underlying objectives of that section (e.g., provide demographic and economic information, provide operating information).[42] In the case of school districts, it is recommended that the following specific items be included:

- cost per student (based on expense as reported in the government-wide statement of activities) and teacher/student ratio;
- percentage of free and reduced students in lunch program (income levels are a strong predictor of academic success and the basis for certain types of funding);
- list of schools/square footage/ capacity/ percentage of capacity used/ building age;[43] and
- teacher data (salary ranges, number of teachers in each range, average salary, education).

STAND-ALONE BUSINESS-TYPE ACTIVITIES

Some clarifications may be helpful in preparing the financial reports of stand-alone business-type activities.

---

[38] See chapter 4.
[39] GASB Statement No. 14, *The Financial Reporting Entity*, paragraph 40a3, as amended by GASB Statement No. 39, *Determining Whether Certain Organizations Are Component Units (an amendment of GASB Statement 14)*.
[40] See chapter 13.
[41] See chapter 13.
[42] GASB Statement No. 44, *Economic Condition Reporting: The Statistical Section (an amendment of NCGA Statement 1)*, paragraph 40.
[43] See GASB Statement No. 44, exhibit F-4.

Comparative data and trend data in management's discussion and analysis (MD&A) and statistical presentations

The minimum level of detail for comparative financial data presented in MD&A is set in terms of the accounts that appear in government-wide financial statements. Stand-alone business-type activities, however, do not present government-wide financial statements as such. Therefore, appropriate modifications should be made, as follows:

Requirement	Modification
total liabilities, distinguishing between long-term liabilities and other liabilities	total liabilities, distinguishing between current and noncurrent liabilities
program revenues, by major source	operating revenue, by major source
general revenues, by major source	nonoperating revenue, by major source
program expenses, at a minimum by function	expenses by function or natural classification, to be consistent with the basic financial statements[44]

Similar modifications would apply to the related ten-year financial trend data presented in the statistical section of the CAFR.

Furthermore, as explained elsewhere,[45] *three years* of data would need to be presented in MD&A for a stand-alone business-type activity that presented comparative financial statements.

Avoidance of a budgetary discussion in MD&A

The contents of MD&A are strictly limited to items specifically identified in the authoritative accounting and financial reporting literature.[46] Governments are required to discuss budgetary variances for the general fund *or its equivalent.*[47] In this case, the reference to a fund that would be equivalent to the general fund is intended to apply to some other *governmental* fund with an annual (or biennial) appropriated budget. A stand-alone business-type activity never qualifies in this regard, and so should never include a budgetary discussion in MD&A, *even if it does have a legally adopted annual budget.*

Discrete presentation for multi-fund business-type activities

Normally, multi-fund business-type activities do *not* report government-wide financial statements, but instead use a combining-style presentation with a total column. One option would be to report component units to the right of this total column on the combining-style presentation. Another option would be to create additional statements that combined the total column from the combining-style presentations with one or more columns for the discretely presented component units.[48]

Reference to primary government

As discussed elsewhere,[49] the separately issued report of a component unit should make clear its relationship to its primary government, both on the cover and title page, as well as in the notes to the financial statements. For example, the cover of a utility district might refer to "The City of XYZ Utility District: A Component Unit of the City of XYZ."

[44] GASB, *Comprehensive Implementation Guide (2004)*, 7.319.
[45] See chapter 13.
[46] See chapter 13.
[47] GASB Statement No. 34, paragraph 11e.
[48] GASB, *Comprehensive Implementation Guide (2004)*, 7.374.
[49] See chapter 13.

PENSION PLANS

The basic GAAP requirements for pension plan reporting are provided by GASB Statement No. 25, *Financial Reporting for Defined Benefit Pension Plans and Note Disclosures for Defined Contribution Plans.* In addition, the Government Finance Officers Association (GFOA) has established guidelines governing the presentation of CAFRs of public employee retirement systems (PERS).[50]

The CAFR of a PERS builds on the same basic structure used for CAFRs of state or local governments.[51] Special issues arise, however, in connection with the following features:
- financial statement presentation and note disclosure;
- RSI;
- supporting schedules;
- investment section;
- actuarial section;
- statistical section; and
- securities lending arrangements.

Financial statement presentation and note disclosure

A PERS may administer more than one pension plan. GAAP require that the PERS basic financial statements present information separately for each pension plan the PERS administers. This requirement can be met in one of two ways:
- *Separate columns.* For each pension plan, a PERS may present a separate column on the face of the statement of plan net assets and the statement of changes in plan net assets.
- *Combining statements.* A PERS may include combining statements *within the basic financial statements* to support the single column reported for pension trust funds on the face of the PERS' statement of plan net assets and statement of changes in plan net assets.[52]

A pension *plan* is an arrangement where all assets accumulated for the payment of benefits may be used to pay any beneficiary. If certain assets are legally restricted to the payment of certain beneficiaries, then there is more than one pension plan for financial reporting purposes.[53]

Statement of plan net assets

Pension plans and other fiduciary funds use the same two basic financial statements. Still, the authoritative guidance regarding the contents of these two statements is more detailed for pension plans than it is for other types of fiduciary funds.

All assets of a pension plan (such as cash and cash equivalents, receivables, investments, assets used in plan operations) should be reported by category in the statement of plan net assets. Receivables and investment

---

[50] A PERS is a special-purpose government that administers one or more defined benefit pension plans and, sometimes, other types of employee benefit plans, including defined contribution, deferred compensation, and postemployment healthcare plans.

[51] See chapter 13.

[52] GASB Statement No. 34, paragraph 140.

[53] It is possible to have separate actuarial valuations, or even separate *reserves, funds,* or *accounts,* and still be a single pension plan, provided all assets accumulated to pay benefits may legally be used to pay any beneficiary. Conversely, resource pooling for investment purposes does not mean there is a single pension plan if certain assets may only be used to pay certain beneficiaries. Agent multiple-employer plans, however, should always be treated as a single pension plan. (GASB Statement No. 25, paragraphs 15-16.)

balances should be further subdivided into their principal components. [54]
The pension plan should recognize a receivable for contributions when
due, but only if there is a statutory or legal requirement to make the contribution, or if the employer makes a formal commitment to contribute. [55] Brokerage commissions and other costs typically associated with the sale of
investments should be deducted from the fair value of investments, if
determinable. [56] Capital assets used in plan operations should be reported at
their historical cost and depreciated over their estimated useful life. [57]

The statement of plan net assets should report only accounting rather
than actuarial liabilities. Examples of such accounting liabilities are obligations for benefits and refunds due and payable to plan members and beneficiaries, as well as accrued investment and administrative expenses. [58]

Sometimes pension plans purchase *allocated insurance contracts,* annuity
contracts to benefit specific beneficiaries. Such contracts and related liabilities should *not* be reported on the pension plan's statement of plan net
assets. [59]

The difference between plan assets and plan liabilities is to be reported
as *net assets held in trust for pension benefits,* rather than divided into the three
categories normally used to classify *net assets.* This caption must be accompanied by a parenthetical reference to the schedule of funding progress. [60]

**Statement of changes in
plan net assets**

All changes in plan net assets that occurred during the period must be
reported in one of two categories: *additions* and *deductions.* [61] Additions to
plan net assets should be reported in the following categories: [62]
- contributions from employers;
- contributions from plan members (even if transmitted by the
employer);
- contributions from other sources (for instance, state contributions to a
school district plan); and
- net investment income:
  - net appreciation (depreciation) in investments reported at fair
value
  - interest income, dividend income, and other income not included
in net appreciation (depreciation)
  - less: total investment expense (for instance, investment management and custodial fees). [63]

Deductions to plan net assets should be reported in two separate categories:
- benefits and refunds paid to plan members and beneficiaries; [64] and
- total administrative expense (excluding investment-related expenses). [65]

---

[54] GASB Statement No. 25, paragraph 21.
[55] GASB Statement No. 25, paragraph 22.
[56] GASB Statement No. 25, footnote 7.
[57] GASB Statement No. 25, paragraph 25.
[58] GASB Statement No. 25, paragraph 26.
[59] GASB Statement No. 25, paragraphs 24 and 26.
[60] GASB Statement No. 25, paragraph 27.
[61] GASB Statement No. 25, paragraph 28.
[62] GASB Statement No. 25, paragraph 29.
[63] Investment expense should be reported separately unless it cannot readily be distinguished from investment income or administrative expense. Other elements of net investment income may be combined.
[64] Benefits paid do *not* include amounts paid by an insurance company pursuant to an allocated insurance contract. (GASB Statement No. 25, paragraph 31.)

Note that realized investment income may *not* be reported separately from unrealized investment income on the face of the statement of changes in plan net assets. Pension plans may disclose realized gains and losses, however, in the notes to the financial statements.[66] Also, note that investment-related expenses are to be treated as a reduction in the additions category of the statement of changes in plan net assets, not as a deduction.

Note disclosures

The following disclosures must be provided in the PERS report for defined benefit pension plans:[67]

- plan description
  - type of pension plan (such as "single-employer defined benefit plan") and the number of participating employers and other contributors
  - classes of employees covered and current membership, including the number of retirees and others currently receiving benefits, terminated employees entitled to receive benefits in the future, and current active plan members (A PERS should disclose if the plan is closed to new entrants.)
  - a brief description of benefit provisions and the authority for establishing or amending those provisions
- summary of significant accounting policies
  - basis of accounting (such as timing of recognition for contributions, benefits, and refunds)
  - method used to determine the fair value of investments
- contributions and reserves
  - authority for establishing or amending the obligation to make contributions
  - how contributions are determined (by statute, for instance) and how administrative costs are financed
  - required contribution rates for active members of the plan
  - terms of long-term contracts for contributions and the amount outstanding as of the plan's reporting date
  - balances in legally required reserves as of the plan's reporting date; also, the purpose and funded status of each reserve
  - (optional) designations[68] as of the plan's reporting date; also, the purpose and funded status of each designation
- concentrations of 5 percent or more of the plan's net investments in securities of a single organization (other than the U.S. government or securities explicitly guaranteed by the U.S. government).[69]

RSI

In addition to the two basic financial statements and various note disclosures, defined benefit pension plans also are required to provide two schedules of long-term actuarial data. Typically, these schedules are presented as RSI immediately following the notes to the financial statements.[70]

---

[65] GASB Statement No. 25, paragraph 30.
[66] GASB Statement No. 25, footnote 10.
[67] GASB Statement No. 25, paragraph 32.
[68] Reserves result from the actions of outside parties, while designations result from action of the plan's own governing body. Neither are reported on the face of the statement of plan net assets.
[69] This disclosure requirement, which is aimed at highlighting potentially inadequate diversification, does *not* apply to positions in pools or mutual funds. (GASB, *Comprehensive Implementation Guide (2004)*, 5.79.)
[70] GASB Statement No. 25, paragraph 33.

Schedule of funding progress	Defined benefit pension plans are required to present the following data as of the plan's reporting date for the past six consecutive fiscal years (plans with biennial valuations need not present duplicate information for the intervening years[71]):

- actuarial valuation date;
- actuarial value of plan assets;[72]
- actuarial accrued liability (calculated using the cost allocation method selected for funding purposes within the parameters established by GAAP);
- total unfunded actuarial liability (actuarial accrued liability less actuarial value of plan assets);
- funded ratio (actuarial value of assets as a percentage of the actuarial accrued liability);
- annual covered payroll; and
- ratio of the total unfunded actuarial liability to annual covered payroll.[73]

The schedule of funding progress need not be presented for pension plans that use the aggregate actuarial cost method (which does not identify or separately amortize unfunded actuarial liabilities).[74]

Schedule of employer contributions

The following data must be presented for defined benefit pension plans as of the plan's reporting date for the past six consecutive fiscal years:

- annual required contributions (in dollars) based on the parameters set by GAAP;[75] and
- percentage of annual required contributions recognized as contributions from employers in the plan's statement of changes in plan net assets.

When parties other than the employer or employees contribute to the plan, their contributions should be reported as well, and the schedule should be titled accordingly: "Schedule of contributions from employers *and other contributing entities*."[76]

Notes to the schedules of trend information

Notes should be attached to the schedules of RSI to address the following topics:

- actuarial cost method;
- method used to value assets;
- assumed inflation rate;
- assumed investment return;
- assumed projected salary increases;
- assumed postretirement benefit increases;
- amortization method (level dollar or level percentage of projected payroll);
- amortization period (equivalent single amortization period if multiple amortization periods are being used);
- selection of *open* or *closed* amortization approach;

---

[71] GASB Statement No. 25, footnote 26.

[72] This would be the valuation used for actuarial purposes, which usually is a smoothed average value, and thus would differ from the point-in-time fair value reported on the statement of plan net assets.

[73] GASB Statement No. 25, paragraph 37.

[74] GASB Statement No. 25, footnote 17.

[75] Contribution requirements may be presented on the basis of projected, budgeted, or actual payroll, provided the method used is employed consistently.

[76] GASB Statement No. 25, paragraph 38.

- if the aggregate method is used, a disclosure that the aggregate method does not identify or separately amortize unfunded actuarial liabilities (the method produces no measure of the unfunded actuarial liability); and
- factors that affect trends (such as changes in benefits, material changes in the size or composition of the plan's population, changes in actuarial methods or assumptions).[77]

Supporting schedules

GFOA recommends that the following supporting schedules also be included within the financial section of a PERS CAFR:

Schedule of administrative expenses

As discussed earlier, the statement of changes in plan net assets should report *administrative expenses* as a separate item. This amount should be supported by a schedule of administrative expenses. If the pension plan reports depreciable assets, depreciation expense should be reported on this schedule.

Schedule of investment expenses

The statement of changes in plan net assets reports investment expense as a reduction of investment income in the *additions* section of the statement. This amount should be supported by a schedule of investment expenses.

Schedule of payments to consultants

The final recommended supporting schedule is the schedule of payments to consultants. This schedule is used to provide information on fees paid to outside professionals other than investment advisors (such as actuaries, auditors, legal counsel, benefits consultants). While it is desirable to itemize amounts paid by individual or firm, this level of detail is not required.

Investment section

GFOA recommends that every CAFR of a PERS include a separate investment section in addition to the introductory, financial, and statistical sections required of all CAFRs.[78] The recommended contents of this section, described below, are:

- a report on investment activities;
- an outline of investment policies;
- investment results;
- asset allocation;
- a list of largest assets held;
- a schedule of fees and commissions; and
- an investment summary.

Report on investment activities

The investment section should begin with a report prepared by the investment consultant. If the retirement system does not engage the services of an investment consultant, the report on the investment section should be prepared by an individual with responsibility for overseeing the retirement system's investments (the chief investment officer, perhaps). One purpose of the report on investment activity is to reassure readers concerning the reliability of the information presented in the investment section of the CAFR. The report also should indicate the basis of presentation for the data reported in the investment section. Pension plans are strongly encouraged to present investment information to the greatest degree possible in conformance with the presentation standards of the Association for Investment

---

[77] GASB Statement No. 25, paragraph 40.

[78] This recommendation is a requirement for participants in GFOA's Certificate of Achievement for Excellence in Financial Reporting Program.

Management and Research. In addition, the report should discuss the retirement system's investment objectives and any other topics deemed relevant.

Outline of investment policies

The report should include a brief outline of the retirement system's investment policies. Issues of corporate governance and the use of proxies should be discussed as part of this outline, if relevant.

Investment results

A schedule of investment results should present the rate of return for each major category of investments and for the total portfolio for different periods. It is recommended that information on the rate of return be presented at least for the latest twelve months, along with annualized rates of return for the preceding three- and five-year periods. Additional information could be presented (for instance, rate of return each year for the past five years or annualized ten-year information). Moreover, rates of return should be matched with appropriate benchmark indices (such as Lehman Brothers, Salomon Brothers, Standard & Poors). Peer benchmarks also could be provided (for instance, other public funds, small capitalization managers, international benchmarks). Finally, the schedule of investment results should indicate, either in a narrative preface or in a footnote, the basis for the calculations (for example, time-weighted rate of return based on the market rate of return).

Asset allocation

The CAFR's investment section also should include information on asset allocation. The many different ways that such information could be presented include the following:

- asset allocation as of year-end presented in pie chart form;
- asset allocation as of year-end presented as several pie charts (for instance, representing total asset allocation, equity manager's asset allocation, fixed-income manager's asset allocation);
- an area graph showing changes in asset allocation over a given period;
- a percentage chart showing changes in asset allocation over a given period;
- a comparison of target and actual allocations (when a retirement system uses target allocations); and
- narrative description of asset allocation as of year-end and changes in asset allocation over a given period.

Also, information on prior asset allocation should be presented in any year there is a significant change in allocation. In addition to presenting information on asset allocation, preparers of CAFRs for retirement systems are advised to consider presenting other information that may be useful to readers in assessing risk.

List of largest assets held

It is not practical to include a list of the entire investment portfolio in the CAFR. It can be useful to readers, however, to present a list of the portfolio's largest holdings. Typically, such a presentation would include information on the 10 largest bond holdings and the ten largest stock holdings. Holdings should be reported in the aggregate by individual issue and should be ranked according to their relative dollar value. It is recommended that the list of largest assets inform readers that a complete list of the portfolio's holdings is available.

Schedule of fees and commissions

The fees portion of the schedule of fees and commissions should report fees (and optionally, basis points) by category, along with an indication of assets under management. The commissions portion of the schedule of fees and commissions may report the name of each firm receiving a commission, the number of shares traded, the total value of commissions, and the amount of commissions per share. Alternatively, information on commissions may be reported at some other level of detail or in the aggregate. The schedule also should fully disclose any commission recapture arrangements, directed payments to third parties, or similar arrangements.

Investment summary

The CAFR's investment section also should present an investment summary, reporting the fair value and percent of total fair value for each major type of investment.

Actuarial section

Under the GFOA guidelines, every PERS CAFR should contain an actuarial section in addition to the introductory, financial, investment, and statistical sections. The recommended contents of this section, described below, are:
- actuary's certification letter;
- summary of actuarial assumptions and methods;
- schedule of active member valuation data;
- schedule of retirants and beneficiaries added to and removed from rolls;
- solvency test;
- analysis of financial experience;
- independent actuarial review opinion (if available); and
- changes in plan provisions.

Actuary's certification letter

The actuary's certification letter should be addressed to the plan's administrative board and should be signed and dated by the actuary or actuaries having primary responsibility for the valuation. The certification letter should be on the actuary's letterhead, and the signature block should contain professional designations, as appropriate.[79] The letter should be specific regarding the following:
- the funding objective of the plan;
- if the funding objective is not currently being realized, a discussion of the progress being made toward achieving this objective;
- the frequency of the plan's actuarial valuations and the date of the most recent actuarial valuation;
- the extent to which the actuary a) relied on data provided by the plan's administrative staff with specific reference to data certified by the plan's auditor; and/or b) conducted an examination of the data for reasonableness;
- a list of the supporting schedules in the Actuarial Section that were prepared by the actuary;
- the extent of the actuary's responsibility or the responsibility of the actuary's firm for the trend data schedules presented in the financial section of the report;

---

[79] As noted later, if the actuary who prepared the certification letter is a member of the retirement system's staff, it is advisable to demonstrate independent review by having an actuary who is not a staff member periodically examine and comment on plan actuarial information.

- an indication that the assumptions and methods used for funding purposes meet the parameters set for financial reporting by GASB Statement No. 25 (if not, a description of the differences); and
- any other information which the actuary believes necessary or useful to fully and fairly disclose the actuarial condition of the plan (including references to supporting schedules deserving special attention).

Summary of actuarial assumptions and methods

This summary should state the assumptions and methods used in the most recent actuarial valuation, as follows (to conserve space, decrements can be reported for sample ages, such as every fifth year):

- Investment return rate;
- The method used to value plan assets for actuarial valuation purposes. If a value other than fair value is used, the actuary should explain the method;
- An indication whether the actuarial assumptions and methods shown in the supporting schedules were a) selected by the actuary, b) specified by the administrative board of the plan with or without the recommendation of the actuary, c) specified by state or local law, or d) other;
- The mortality table used for postretirement mortality [specify any sex differential];
- The assumed retirement age if a single age is used, or the probabilities of retirement for sample ages if a retirement pattern is used;
- The probabilities of withdrawal from active service [including death] before age and service requirements for sample ages;
- The pay increase assumption(s). If a single percentage is used, indicate that percentage. If a salary scale is used, show the assumed increase in salary for sample ages. In either case, indicate the portion, if any, of the assumed salary increase attributable to the effects of inflation on salaries;
- If applicable, the extent to which total active member payroll is expected to increase as a result of inflation (GAAP do not permit the use for financial reporting purposes of a growth rate assumption that reflects an increase in the number of active plan members. If, however, such an assumption is used for funding purposes, it should be disclosed);
- The actuarial method used, with specific reference to the treatment of actuarial gains and losses;
- If applicable, the extent to which benefits are expected to increase as a result of cost-of-living-type adjustments;
- The date(s) of adoption of the above items;
- If applicable, the date of the last study of the plan's actual experience. Actuarial assumptions are to be based on the plan's actual experience to the extent credible experience data are available. Indicate the date of the most recent experience study and which assumptions used for the most recent actuarial valuation were based on that study. If not based on such a study, indicate upon what basis assumptions were determined;
- Discuss recent changes in: 1) the nature of the plan, 2) actuarial assumptions, 3) actuarial method, or 4) the retained actuary or actuar-

ial firm. Include a brief description of the changes on the results of the valuation; and

- Any other specific assumptions that have a material impact on valuation results.

Schedule of active member valuation data

This schedule should present information on the number of active members, annual payroll for active members, annual average pay for active members, and the percentage increase in average pay for active members. Six years of data are required. If different classifications of employees (such as general, police, fire) are covered by the plan, it may be desirable to present this information for each classification. Multiple-employer plans should indicate the number of participating employers. If the amount reported as *annual payroll* on this schedule differs from that reported in the financial section of the report, the reason for the disparity should be disclosed.

Schedule of retirants and beneficiaries added to and removed from rolls

A schedule of retirants and beneficiaries added to and removed from the rolls should also be presented. This schedule should present data for six years. If different classifications of employees are covered by the plan (e.g., general, police, fire), it may be desirable to present information separately for each classification. The following format may be used:

Year ended	Added to rolls		Removed from rolls		Rolls end of year		% increase in annual allowances	Average annual allowances
	No.	Annual allow-ances	No.	Annual allow-ances	No.	Annual allow-ances		

Postretirement adjustments in benefits should be included in the annual allowances column under *added to rolls*.

Solvency test

A short-term solvency test is one means of checking a pension system's progress under its funding program. In a short-term solvency test, the actuarial value of the plan's present assets is compared with aggregate accrued liabilities classified into the following categories:

- liability for active member contributions on deposit;
- liability for future benefits to present retired lives; and
- liability for service already rendered by active members.

In a system that has been following the discipline of level percentage of payroll financing, the liability for active member contributions on deposit and the liability for future benefits to present retired lives will be fully covered by present assets (except in rare circumstances). In addition, the liability for service already rendered by active members will be partially covered by the remainder of present assets. Generally, if the system has been using level cost financing, the funded portion of this last liability will increase over time, although it is uncommon for it to be fully funded. Six years of data are required. The actuary should use footnotes to indicate years in which changes were made that affect the comparability of the numbers presented (for instance, changes in plan provisions, changes in actuarial assumptions, changes in funding methods).

In preparing this schedule, valuation assets should arbitrarily be allocated first to the liability for active member contributions on deposit, second to the liability for future benefits to present retired lives, and third to the liability for service already rendered by active members, regardless of the method used for asset allocation. The sum of these three liabilities equals the aggregate accrued liability of the plan.

Analysis of financial experience

An actuarial investigation reveals the difference between actual and assumed experience in the various risk areas. One of the more easily understood types of actuarial investigations is the gain/loss analysis of changes in accrued liabilities. While a gain/loss analysis requires considerable data processing and actuarial work, the significant results can be presented in a concise, one-page format. Such gain/loss knowledge is very helpful in understanding the financial condition of a retirement system and in adopting sound financial assumptions for the retirement system.

Independent actuarial review opinion (if available)

If the actuary who prepared the certification letter is a member of the retirement system's staff, an actuary who is not a staff member should periodically examine and comment on plan actuarial information. This step is advised to demonstrate independent review. When the review is complete, a statement from the reviewing actuary should be included in the report. Similarly, a retirement system that retains an independent actuary may periodically have an actuarial review or actuarial audit performed by someone other than the system's retained actuary. This is generally done to verify compliance with the retirement system's stated financial objectives. When this review is performed, an abbreviated version of the report from the reviewing firm should be included in the retirement system's CAFR.

Changes in plan provisions

If the plan has been amended since the last CAFR was issued, the actuary should describe the amendments and indicate whether they were considered in the most recent actuarial valuation.

Statistical section

The authoritative accounting literature offers specialized guidance on the following four statistical presentations that must be included in a PERS CAFR:
- schedule of changes in net assets;
- schedule of retired members by type of benefit;
- schedule of average benefit payments; and
- schedule of principal participating employers (if applicable).

Before reviewing that guidance, several observations are necessary:
- A CAFR of a PERS presents only one of the four schedules of financial trend data normally required of general-purpose governments. Since pension (and other employee benefit) trust funds report only one category of *net assets*, there is no need for a *schedule of net assets*. Likewise, the two remaining schedules of financial trend data ordinarily presented by general-purpose governments apply only to governmental funds.
- Required schedules concerning revenue capacity could be presented using investment income as the primary own-source revenue.
- No schedules concerning debt capacity generally are presented as a PERS normally does not issue long-term debt.
- The standard schedules of demographic and economic information normally are *not* presented, because information on population, total personal income, per capita personal income, and the unemployment rate ordinarily are irrelevant to a PERS. Conversely, demographic

information about the workforce and retirees (e.g., average age of current employee population) would be relevant to the underlying objective.

- A PERS should present the regularly required schedules of operating information (i.e., employees, operating indicators, and capital asset information) in addition to the three specialized types of operating information mentioned earlier (i.e., retired members by type of benefit, average benefit payments, and principal participating employers).

Schedule of changes in net assets (ten years)

This schedule should present separately for each pension plan ten years of trend data (extracted from the statement of changes in plan net assets)

Exhibit 15-2
Securities lending arrangements with cash collateral

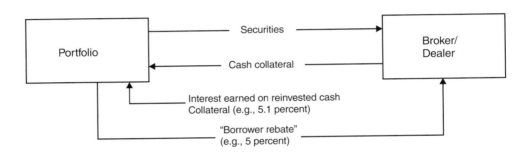

showing, at a minimum, *additions* by source, *deductions* by type, and *total changes in net assets*. Furthermore, deductions for benefits should be presented by type (e.g., age and service benefits, disability), as should deductions for refunds (e.g., death, separation). A separate schedule may be used, if needed, to provide the detail just described for benefits and refunds.[80]

Schedule of retired members by type of benefit (current year)

This schedule should present data about retired members by type of benefit for the current year. Numbers of retired members should be organized by ranges of benefit levels and by major plan features (e.g., normal retirement, disability retirement, beneficiary payment) or options.[81]

Schedule of average benefit payments (ten years)

This schedule should present the following information for ten years organized by years of credited service in five-year increments:
- average monthly benefit;
- average final average salary; and
- number of retired members.[82]

---

[80] GASB Statement No. 44, paragraph 10b.
[81] GASB Statement No. 44, paragraph 39a.
[82] GASB Statement No. 44, paragraph 39b.

Schedule of principal participating employers (current period and nine years prior)

In the case of multiple-employer plans, a schedule should present, for both the current year and the period nine years previous, a list of the ten principal participating employers (unless fewer are needed to cover half of total covered employees). This schedule should show each employer's number of covered employees and each employer's percentage of total covered employees.[83]

Securities lending arrangements

Pension plans frequently enter into securities lending arrangements, under which a pension plan "lends" selected investment securities from its portfolio to brokers and dealers to fill orders to clients. The pension plan's interest in the lent securities is secured either by collateral (cash or securities) or by a letter of credit until the same or similar securities are returned, according to the agreement. If cash is used as collateral for the agreement, the pension plan is obliged to rebate interest on the collateral to the broker or dealer at a rate specified by the agreement.

Exhibit 15-3
Securities lending arrangements backed by letters of credit or by securities that cannot be pledged or sold

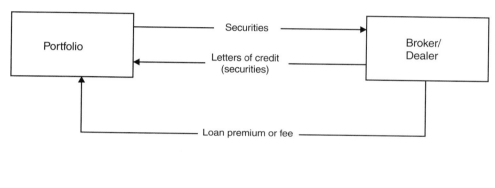

Pension plans enter into securities lending arrangements to increase their investment income. They accomplish this goal in one of two ways, depending on the structure of the particular securities lending arrangement in which they participate:

- *Reinvestment of collateral at a higher rate of return.* If a government receives cash collateral to secure its lent securities, it can increase its investment income by reinvesting the collateral at a higher rate of return than it is contractually obligated to rebate to the broker or dealer. The same method is used when the government receives securities as collateral that can be sold or pledged without a default by the broker or dealer (see Exhibit 15-2).
- *Loan premium or fee.* If a securities lending agreement is backed by a letter of credit, there is no collateral available for reinvestment to obtain additional investment income for the lending government. Instead, the broker or dealer agrees to pay a loan premium or fee to compensate the government for its assistance (see Exhibit 15-3).

Regardless of the type of securities lending agreement, the underlying or "lent" securities must continue to be reported on the lending pension plan's statement of net assets.[84] Further, in the case of securities lending agreements that are collateralized by cash or by securities that can be sold or pledged even without a default by the broker or dealer, these additional

---

[83] GASB Statement No. 44, paragraph 39c.
[84] GASB Statement No. 28, *Accounting and Financial Reporting for Securities Lending Transactions*, paragraph 5.

amounts (and subsequent reinvestments) must also be reported as assets in the statement of position, along the contractual liability to the counterparty.[85]

It was just noted in the case of securities lending arrangements secured by cash collateral that a pension plan produces income in such situations by reinvesting the collateral at a higher rate of interest than it is paying as a rebate to the party that provided the collateral. Pension plans participating in such transactions like to focus attention on the net difference between the rate of interest on the borrowing and the income generated by the reinvestment. GAAP, however, specifically prohibit the netting of these amounts.[86]

GFOA believes that assets, liabilities, income, and expenses related to securities lending arrangements should be reported in the financial statements in the manner that best reflects the true nature of these transactions, consistent with GAAP. Specifically, the GFOA formally recommends the following presentation of securities lending transactions on the statement of plan net assets and the statement of changes in plan net assets.[87]

- *Statement of plan net assets.* Cash received as collateral in connection with securities lending transactions should be reported separately from other cash and short-term investments. This treatment avoids creating the potentially misleading impression that a significant percentage of a portfolio's total assets may not be fully invested.
- *Statement of changes in plan net assets.* Securities lending income and related expenses (borrower rebates and management fees) should be reported together (but *not* netted) rather than divided between investment income and investment expense. For pension plans, income and expenses related to securities lending activities should be reported as a separate component of total net investment income, immediately following net income from all other types of investing activities on the statement of changes in plan net assets (see Exhibit 15-4).

OPEB PLANS

OPEB encompass all postemployment benefits provided apart from a pension plan, except for healthcare, which is always classified as OPEB.[88] Because of the close conceptual similarities between OPEB and pension benefits (i.e., both are forms of deferred employee compensation), the accounting and financial reporting for both is quite similar.

Benefits to be measured   Normally the terms of a defined benefit pension plan are more or less clear to participating employers and employees. OPEB, on the other hand, tend to be much less clearly defined in practice. For this reason, financial statement preparers seeking to gain an understanding of the terms of an OPEB plan need to go beyond the plan document and to focus instead on the *substantive plan*, which is defined as "the plan as understood by the participating employer(s) and plan members" as of the actuarial valuation date. The substantive plan, thus defined, would take into consideration both the plan

[85] GASB Statement No. 28, paragraph 6.
[86] GASB Statement No. 28, paragraph 8.
[87] See GFOA recommended practice on "Presenting Securities Lending Transactions in Financial Statements" (1998).
[88] GASB Statement No. 43, *Financial Reporting for Postemployment Benefit Plans Other Than Pension Plans*, paragraph 1.

Exhibit 15-4
Recommended presentation of securities lending arrangements in the statement of changes in plan net assets

XYZ Retirement System
Statement of Changes in Plan Net Assets
Year Ended June 30, 200X

Additions

Contributions:

State contributions	$137,555,388
Member purchase of service credit	726,527
State reimbursement of non-funded benefits	9,907,505
Employer contributions service transfers	135,598
Total contributions	$148,325,018

Investment income:
From investment activities

Net appreciation in fair value of investments	$333,040,768
Interest	67,808,592
Dividends	44,711,334
Real estate operating income, net	4,605,881
Venture capital income	9,045,261
	$459,211,836

Investment activity expenses:

Investment management fees	$(4,518,692)
Investment consulting fees	(150,000)
Investment custodial fees	(441,889)
Total investment expenses	(5,110,581)
Net income from investing activities	$454,101,255

From securities lending activities:

Securities lending income	$10,047,888
Securities lending expenses:	
Borrower rebates	(8,672,110)
Management fees	(399,472)
Total securities lending activities expenses	(9,071,582)
Net Income from securities lending activities	976,306
Total net investment income	$455,077,561
Miscellaneous income	9,152
Total additions	$603,411,731

Deductions

Benefits	$126,168,796
Service transfer payments	30,327
Administrative expense	3,229,541
Legal settlement expense	23,148,000
Total deductions	$152,576,664
Net increase	$450,835,067

Beginning of year	$2,794,632,453
End of year	$3,245,467,520

document and "other communications between the plan's trustees and administrators, employer(s), and plan members"[89] such as "amendments made and communicated to plan members *by the valuation date*" [emphasis added], as well as "the employer's historical pattern of allocating benefit

---

[89] GASB Statement No. 43, paragraph 124.

costs between the employer and plan members *up to that date*"[90] [emphasis added].

The substantive plan concept is intended to provide "an objective and reliable basis for the projection of benefits for financial reporting."[91] Thus, the focus is to be on events and trends that have actually occurred as of the actuarial valuation date. Expressly excluded from consideration are factors such as contemplated amendments to plan terms that have not yet been adopted, or adjustments that reflect a "general assumption that the plan terms probably will be amended in some way, not specifically predictable, in the future."[92]

Trusts and equivalent arrangements

Resources accumulated to pay pension benefits are routinely held in trust. The same cannot be said of assets accumulated to pay OPEB. The implications of this fact for accounting and financial reporting are significant. Thus, each of the following three situations must be treated differently:

- *Assets held in trust or equivalent arrangements.* To be accounted for in a pension (and other employee benefit) trust fund.
- *Assets of multiple-employer plans not held in trust or equivalent arrangements.* To be accounted for in an agency fund (any excess of plan assets over related liabilities in the aggregate would be reported as a liability to employers rather than as net assets of the plan, consistent with the fact that agency funds do not report equity).[93]
- *Assets of a single employer not held in trust or equivalent arrangements.* Such assets remain those of the employer and do not constitute an OPEB plan. Examples would include resources reported by employers as designated unreserved fund balance in the general fund, or as designated unreserved fund balance or unrestricted net assets in a separate governmental or proprietary fund established for this purpose.[94]

An OPEB plan that must be reported in an agency fund because it does not qualify as a trust or equivalent arrangement could not be treated as a cost-sharing plan by participating employers. Rather, employers would need to follow the authoritative guidance for participants in an agent multiple-employer plan.[95] The practical result is that employers in the situation just described would not be permitted to use their contractually required payments as the measure of pension cost (as is normally the case for participants in cost-sharing multiple-employer plans), but would instead have to calculate their annual required contribution (ARC) for that purpose.

Framework of financial reporting

When an OPEB plan qualifies as a trust or equivalent arrangement, it must present the same two basic financial statements required for any pension (and other employee benefit) trust fund: a *statement of plan net assets* and a *statement of changes in plan net assets.* In addition, as is true for most pension plans, these two basic financial statements must be supplemented by certain actuarial trend data presented as RSI: a schedule of funding progress and a schedule of employer contributions.[96]

---

[90] GASB Statement No. 43, paragraph 129.
[91] GASB Statement No. 43, paragraph 129.
[92] GASB Statement No. 43, paragraph 127.
[93] GASB Statement No. 43, paragraph 41a.
[94] GASB Statement No. 45, paragraph 13g and 141.
[95] GASB Statement No. 45, paragraph 22b.
[96] GASB Statement No. 43, paragraph 17.

The basic unit for financial reporting purposes is the OPEB plan.[97] Therefore, it is important to distinguish OPEB plans from the systems that administer them. An OPEB plan is an arrangement where all assets accumulated for the payment of benefits may be used to pay any beneficiary. If certain assets are legally restricted to the payment of certain beneficiaries, then there is more than one OPEB plan for financial reporting purposes. It is possible, of course, to have separate actuarial valuations, or even separate "reserves," "funds" or "accounts," and still be a single OPEB plan, provided that all assets accumulated to pay benefits may legally be used to pay any beneficiary. Conversely, the pooling of resources for investment purposes does not mean there is a single OPEB plan if certain assets may only be used to pay certain beneficiaries. Separate reporting and disclosure is required for each individual OPEB plan, even when multiple plans are managed by a single system. Combining statements and required schedules should be used to meet this requirement.[98]

Agent multiple-employer OPEB plans constitute an important exception to the rule just described. They are always treated as a single OPEB plan for financial reporting purposes, thus avoiding the need to present separate financial statements and schedules for each participating employer.[99]

Statement of plan net assets

Plan assets should be reported by category (e.g., cash and cash equivalents, receivables, investments, assets used in plan operations). Both receivables and investment balances should be further subdivided into their principal components.[100] For example, receivables might be classified by transaction type, source, or relative liquidity.

A receivable for employer contributions should be recognized only if there is a formal commitment by the employer to make the contribution, or a statutory or legal requirement to do so. For example, an appropriation by a contributing employer would be sufficient basis for reporting a receivable in the OPEB plan's statement of net assets, as would a consistent pattern of an employer making required contributions attributable to the preceding plan year subsequent to the plan's reporting date. Conversely, an employer's recognition of a liability for unfunded contributions would not, of itself, be enough to justify reporting a receivable on the OPEB plan's statement of net assets. Investments, which should be reported as of the trade date rather than as of the settlement date,[101] should be shown at their fair value.[102] Assets used in plan operations should be reported at their historical cost less accumulated depreciation or amortization.[103]

The statement of plan net assets should report only accounting (rather than actuarial) liabilities (e.g., benefits and refunds due, accrued investment and administrative expenses). The plan's actuarial accrued liability should not be reported.[104]

OPEB plans may purchase annuity contracts for the benefit of specific beneficiaries (i.e., "allocated insurance contracts"). Such contracts and re-

---

[97] GASB Statement No. 43, paragraph 13.
[98] GASB Statement No. 43, paragraph 14.
[99] GASB Statement No. 43, paragraph 13.
[100] GASB Statement No. 43, paragraph 19.
[101] GASB Statement No. 43, paragraph 18.
[102] GASB Statement No. 43, paragraph 22.
[103] GASB Statement No. 43, paragraph 23.
[104] GASB Statement No. 43, paragraph 24.

lated liabilities should not be reported on the OPEB plan's statement of plan net assets.[105]

The difference between plan assets and plan liabilities should be reported as *net assets held in trust for OPEB*.[106] Note that *OPEB plans do not have to provide a parenthetical reference to their statement of funding progress, as is the case for pension plans.*[107] The reason for this difference is that OPEB plans, unlike pension plans, must include the most recent year's data from the schedule of funding progress within the notes to the financial statements. Likewise, note disclosures for OPEB plans specifically address the significance of the information provided in the two schedules of RSI. In view of the prominence thus accorded information on funding progress, an additional parenthetical reference was considered to be unwarranted.[108]

Statement of changes in plan net assets

Changes in plan net assets should be reported as additions and deductions rather than as revenues and expenses. Additions are to be displayed in four separate categories:[109]

- contributions from employers;
- contributions from plan members (even if transmitted by the employer);
- contributions from other sources; and
- net investment income.

This last item, in turn, is subdivided into three categories, only the first two of which may be combined for financial reporting purposes:

- net appreciation (depreciation) in fair value;
- interest income, dividend income, and other income; and
- total investment expense (e.g., investment management and custodial fees).[110]

Note that investment-related expenses are treated as a reduction in the additions category rather than as a deduction.

Deductions to plan net assets should be reported in two separate categories: 1) benefits and refunds paid to plan members and beneficiaries and 2) total administrative expense.[111]

Note disclosures

OPEB plans present, in slightly modified form, virtually all of the note disclosures applicable to pension plans. At the same time, they expand these traditional pension disclosures in two significant ways. First, they include within the notes to the financial statements certain information that pension plans report as RSI or as part of the notes to RSI. Second, they make some disclosures specifically designed to educate financial statement users, who are presumed to be less familiar with OPEB plans than with pension plans.

Modified pension disclosures. The following disclosures for OPEB plans have been adopted, with minor modifications, from those traditionally required for pension plans:

- plan description[112]

---

[105] GASB Statement No. 43, paragraphs 22 and 24.
[106] GASB Statement No. 43, paragraph 25.
[107] GASB Statement No. 25, paragraph 27.
[108] GASB Statement No. 25, paragraph 96.
[109] GASB Statement No. 43, paragraph 27.
[110] GASB Statement No. 43, paragraph 27.
[111] GASB Statement No. 43, paragraph 28.
[112] GASB Statement No. 43, paragraph 30a.

- identification of the type of OPEB plan and the number of participating employers and other contributing entities
- classes of employees covered and current membership (including the number of retires and others currently receiving benefits, terminated employees entitled to receive benefits in the future, and current active plan members). If the plan is closed to new entrants, this fact also should be disclosed.
- brief description of benefit provisions and the authority for establishing or amending those provisions. *Note that this description should specifically address provisions or policies regarding automatic and ad hoc postretirement benefit increases.*
- summary of significant accounting policies[113]
  - basis of accounting (such as timing of recognition of contributions, benefits, and refunds)
  - method used to determine the fair value of investments
- contributions and reserves[114]
  - authority for establishing or amending the obligation to make contributions
  - how contributions are determined (e.g., statute) and how administrative costs are financed. *Also, legal or contractual maximum contribution rates should be disclosed.*
  - required contribution rates for active or retired plan members, expressed either as 1) a rate or amount per member or 2) as a percentage of covered payroll
  - terms of long-term contracts for contributions and the amount outstanding as of the plan's reporting date
  - balances in legally required reserves as of the plan's reporting date (designations may be disclosed as well)
  - purpose and funded status of each reserve or designation reported. (Note: reserves and designations are not presented on the face of the statement of plan net assets.)

Disclosures provided as RSI by pension plans. The following data from the most recent actuarial valuation should be disclosed in the notes to the financial statements:[115]
- actuarial valuation date;
- actuarial value of assets;
- actuarial accrued liability;
- total unfunded actuarial accrued liability (or excess);
- actuarial value of assets as a percentage of the actuarial accrued liability (funded ratio);
- annual covered payroll; and
- ratio of the unfunded actuarial liability to annual covered payroll.

Furthermore, virtually all of the information normally presented as part of the notes to RSI in a pension plan report would need to be presented as part of the notes to the financial statements of an OPEB plan. That information would include:[116]
- actuarial cost method;

---

[113] GASB Statement No. 43, paragraph 30b.
[114] GASB Statement No. 43, paragraph 30c.
[115] GASB Statement No. 43, paragraph 30d(1).
[116] GASB Statement No. 43, paragraph 30d(2)(e).

- method(s) used to determine the actuarial value of assets;
- assumption regarding the inflation rate;
- assumption regarding investment return (discount rate);
- method used to determine a blended rate for a partially funded plan (if applicable);
- assumption regarding projected salary increases if relevant to benefit levels;
- the assumption for the healthcare cost trend rate (for postemployment healthcare plans);
- amortization method (level dollar or level percentage of projected payroll); and
- amortization period (equivalent single amortization period, for plans that use multiple periods) for the most recent actuarial valuation and whether the period is closed or open.

If the various economic assumptions listed contemplate different rates for successive years (year-based or select and ultimate rates), the rates that should be disclosed are the initial and ultimate rates.[117]

Pension plans that use the aggregate actuarial cost method, as noted earlier, are exempted altogether from the requirement to present information on funding progress because that particular actuarial cost method does not provide the information needed to present a schedule of funding progress. OPEB plans, however, must disclose information on funding progress regardless of the actuarial cost method used. Accordingly, an OPEB plan that uses the aggregate actuarial cost method is directed to provide the missing information needed to prepare a schedule of funding progress based upon the entry age actuarial cost method. Likewise, the notes to the financial statements would need to disclose that because the aggregate actuarial cost method does not identify or separately amortize unfunded actuarial accrued liabilities, information about the plan's funded status and funding progress was prepared using the entry age actuarial cost method.[118]

Additional disclosures for OPEB plans. Finally, OPEB plans are required to make the following additional disclosures not required of pension plans:

- a discussion of the fact that actuarial valuations involve estimates of the value of reported amounts and assumptions about the probability of events far into the future, and that actuarially determined amounts are subject to continual revision as actual results are compared to past expectations and new estimates are made about the future;[119]
- a discussion of the fact that the required schedule of funding progress immediately following the notes to the financial statements presents multi-year trend information about whether the actuarial value of plan assets is increasing or decreasing over time relative to the actuarial accrued liability for benefits;[120]
- a discussion of the fact that calculations are based on the benefits provided under the terms of the substantive plan in effect at the time of each valuation and on the pattern of sharing of costs between the employer and plan members to that point;[121]

---

[117] GASB Statement No. 43, paragraph 30d(2)(e)iii.
[118] GASB Statement No. 43, paragraph 30d(2)(e)iv.
[119] GASB Statement No. 43, paragraph 30d(2)(a).
[120] GASB Statement No. 43, paragraph 30d(2)(b).

- a discussion of the fact that the projection of benefits for financial reporting purposes does not explicitly incorporate the potential effects of legal or contractual funding limitations on the pattern of cost sharing between the employer and plan members in the future (if applicable);
- a discussion of the fact that actuarial calculations reflect a long-term perspective;[122] and
- a discussion of the fact that that the actuarial methods and assumptions used include techniques that are designed to reduce short-term volatility in actuarial accrued liabilities and the actuarial value of assets (if applicable).[123]

Schedule of funding progress

The schedule of funding progress must present data for each of the three most recent actuarial valuations. When actuarial valuations are made every other year or every third year, data should be presented only for the valuation years. Thus, information from a biennial valuation, for instance, should *not* be duplicated for two years on the schedule to provide numbers for each year of the biennium.

The specific information to be included in this schedule was already examined as part of the discussion of the notes to the financial statements for OPEB plans. The cost method used to calculate the actuarial accrued liability should be identified on the face of the schedule since this information is not required to be presented in the notes to RSI (as is the case for pension plans).[124]

Schedule of employer contributions

The schedule of employer contributions, like the schedule of funding progress, must present data for each of the three most recent actuarial valuations. In the case of biennial or triennial valuations, data should be presented for each year of the biennium or triennium, because employer contributions may change from one year to the next. The schedule should present:

- annual required contributions (in dollars); and
- percentage of ARC recognized as *contributions from employers* in the plan's statement of changes in plan net assets.

When parties other than the employer or employees contribute to the plan, their contributions should be reported along with the employer's and the schedule should be titled accordingly (e.g., "schedule of contributions from the employers and other contributing entities").[125]

Notes to RSI

As indicated previously, virtually all of the notes to RSI found in a pension plan report are incorporated into the notes to the financial statements in an OPEB plan report. Nonetheless, notes to RSI may still be needed to disclose factors that significantly affect trends in the amounts reported in the schedule.[126]

---

[121] GASB Statement No. 43, paragraph 30d(2)(c).
[122] GASB Statement No. 43, paragraph 30d(2)(d).
[123] GASB Statement No. 43, paragraph 30d(2)(d).
[124] GASB Statement No. 43, paragraph 35.
[125] GASB Statement No. 43, paragraph 36.
[126] GASB Statement No. 43, paragraph 37.

GOVERNMENTAL EXTERNAL INVESTMENT POOLS

The GAAP requirements for government external investment pools can be found in GASB Statement No. 31, *Accounting and Financial Reporting for Certain Investments and for External Investment Pools.*

The basic financial statements for external investment pools are essentially the same as those used for pension trust funds and other fiduciary funds: that is, a statement of net assets and a statement of changes in net assets. GAAP, however, do not provide specific guidance concerning the level of detail to be presented in these two financial statements as they do for pension trust funds.

The rules that apply to investment valuation are somewhat different for governmental external investment pools than for entities other than pools:

- the general requirement to report investments at fair value applies to *all types of investments* of a governmental external investment pool, while that same requirement applies only to specific categories of investments for entities other than pools;[127]
- Securities and Exchange Commission (SEC) 2a7-like pools may report their investments at amortized cost rather than at fair value;[128] and
- other exceptions to fair value reporting for pools are limited to 1) *nonparticipating* investment contracts[129] and 2) short-term debt investments with remaining maturities of up to 90 days as of the date of the financial statements.[130]

Also, it is important to note that realized gains and losses *may* be reported separately from unrealized gains and losses on the face of the statement of changes in net assets in the *separately issued* financial statements of governmental external investment pools. In contrast, the separate reporting of realized and unrealized gains and losses is specifically *prohibited* for pension trust funds.[131]

GAAP set the following note disclosure requirements for the separately issued reports of governmental external investment pools:

- methods and assumptions used to estimate fair value;[132]
- application of the amortized cost option (ninety-day exception for short-term debt investments);[133]
- an explanation of realized and unrealized gains/losses (if separate amounts are presented on the face of the financial statements or disclosed in the notes to the financial statements);[134]
- description of regulatory oversight (including whether the pool is registered with the SEC as an investment company);[135]
- frequency and purpose of fair value determinations;[136]

---

[127] See chapter 12.
[128] GASB Statement No. 31, paragraph 16.
[129] By definition, nonparticipating investment contracts are unaffected by market (interest rate) changes. See chapter 12.
[130] GASB Statement No. 31, paragraph 16. Note that "for an investment that was originally purchased with a longer maturity, the investment's fair value on the day it becomes a short-term investment should be the basis for purposes of applying amortized cost."
[131] GASB Statement No. 31, paragraph 13.
[132] GASB Statement No. 31, paragraph 15a.
[133] GASB Statement No. 31, paragraph 15b.
[134] GASB Statement No. 31, paragraph 15.
[135] GASB Statement No. 31, paragraph 17a.
[136] GASB Statement No. 31, paragraph 17b.

- method used to determine participants' shares sold and redeemed and whether that method differs from the method used to report investments;[137]
- whether legally binding guarantees of share values were provided or obtained;[138]
- extent of involuntary participation in the pool;[139]
- summary of fair value, carrying amount (if different), number of shares or the principal amount, ranges of interest rates, and maturity dates for each major investment classification;[140] and
- if a distinction is made among different components of investment income (such as interest, dividends, net increase or decrease in fair value), the accounting policy for defining those components.[141]

PUBLIC-ENTITY RISK POOLS

The authoritative guidance for public-entity risk pools is provided by GASB Statement No. 10, *Accounting and Financial Reporting for Risk Financing and Related Insurance Issues.*[142] GAAP define a public-entity risk pool as a "cooperative group of governmental entities joining together to finance an exposure, liability, or risk." The types of risk covered by public-entity risk pools may include:

- property and liability;
- workers' compensation; and
- employee health care.[143]

There are conceptually four basic types of public-entity risk pools:

- *risk-sharing pools*—arrangements by which governments pool risks and funds and share in the cost of losses;
- *insurance-purchasing pools*—arrangements by which governments pool funds or resources to purchase commercial insurance products; also called a *risk-purchasing group*;
- *banking pools*—arrangements by which monies are made available on a loan basis for pool members in the event of loss; and
- *claims-servicing or account pools*—arrangements by which a pool manages separate accounts for each pool member, paying losses for each member from their respective accounts.[144]

In practice, a pool may combine elements of more than one of these basic types. For example, a single pool may function both as a banking and claims-servicing pool.

---

[137] GASB Statement No. 31, paragraph 17c.

[138] GASB Statement No. 31, paragraph 17d.

[139] GASB Statement No. 31, paragraph 17e.

[140] GASB Statement No. 31, paragraph 17f.

[141] GASB Statement No. 31, paragraph 17.

[142] This guidance was subsequently amended by GASB Statement No. 30, *Risk Financing Omnibus—An Amendment of GASB Statement No. 10*; and GASB Interpretation No. 4, *Accounting and Financial Reporting for Capitalization Contributions to Public Entity Risk Pools*. These amendments are reflected in the guidance described here.

[143] GASB Statement No. 10, paragraph 10. Although state unemployment compensation benefit plans share some common features with public-entity risk pools, they should *not* themselves be treated as public-entity risk pools. (GASB, *Comprehensive Implementation Guide (2004)*, 7.256.)

[144] GASB Statement No. 10, paragraph 13.

To the extent that pools function solely as banking or claims-servicing arrangements (the third and fourth types listed above), risk is not considered to be transferred from participants to the pool.[145]

The proper accounting and financial reporting for public-entity risk pools depends on whether participants in the pool are, in fact, able to transfer or share their risk.

Pools with the transfer or pooling of risk

The following guidance applies to pools where there is some transfer or pooling (sharing) of risk.

Fund type

The enterprise fund-type should be used to report the activities of public-entity risk pools, including those that involve the transfer or pooling of risk.[146]

Premiums

In most cases, protection from risk is provided to pool participants evenly over the contract period. Accordingly, premium revenue typically is recognized on an even basis over this same period. There are two exceptions, however:

- In some instances, the risk period may differ significantly from the contract period. In such cases, premium revenue should be recognized over the risk period rather than the contract period.
- Risk protection may vary over the contract period according to a predetermined schedule. In such situations, premium revenue should be recognized over the contract period in proportion to the risk protection provided.[147]

In some pooling arrangements, premiums may be subject to adjustment. In a retrospectively rated policy, for instance, the final amount of the premium is based on actual experience during the coverage period (sometimes subject to maximum and minimum limits). Similarly, in a reporting-form contract, the final premium on the contract is determined by applying a contract rate to the average value of property insured during the period.

When premiums are subject to adjustment, premium revenue recognition depends on whether the ultimate premium can be reasonably estimated. If the ultimate premium can be reasonably estimated, it should be recognized as revenue over the contract period, with appropriate revisions to reflect current experience. If the ultimate premium cannot be reasonably estimated, premium revenue may be recognized using either the cost recovery or deposit method.[148]

When a specific portion of premiums is identified for future catastrophe losses, that revenue should be recognized over the contract period. In addition, the resulting equity should be reported as "restricted" if it is contractually restricted for that specific purpose or legally restricted for that specific purpose by an organization or individual outside the financial reporting entity.[149]

Claim cost recognition

Pools should report a liability for claims costs when the underlying events occur (or in the case of *claims-made* policies, when the "triggering" events occur). Underlying events include incurred but not reported claims

---

[145] GASB Statement No. 10, paragraph 13.
[146] GASB Statement No. 10, paragraph 18.
[147] GASB Statement No. 10, paragraph 19.
[148] GASB Statement No. 10, paragraph 20.
[149] GASB Statement No. 10, paragraph 21.

(IBNRs) that are both probable and reasonably estimable. The liability for claims should be valued at the ultimate cost of settlement, using experience adjusted for current trends and other factors that could modify experience. Accordingly, inflation and societal and economic factors should be considered. Moreover, the liability should be reported net of anticipated recoveries (for example, salvage or subrogation).

Changes in estimates and adjustments to reflect actual payments are reflected in the pool's results of operations in the period they were made.[150]

Claims adjustment expenses

Claims adjustment expenses should be recognized at the same time as the liability for unpaid claims and should include both *allocated* and *unallocated* amounts. *Allocated* amounts are those either directly associated with specific claims paid or in the process of settlement (such as legal and adjusters' fees). *Unallocated* amounts are those that cannot be associated with specific claims but are still related either to claims paid or in the process of settlement (such as internal costs of the claims department).[151]

Discounting

As a general rule, GAAP neither mandate nor prohibit the discounting of claims liabilities. However, if the pool is involved in a structured settlement (contractual obligations to pay specific amounts on fixed or determinable dates), discounting would be required. When pools discount claims liabilities, they should select a discount rate that considers the pool's settlement rate and investment yield.[152]

Annuity contracts

In some cases, pools may choose to settle a claim by purchasing an annuity contract in the claimant's name. The pool should consider the related loss liability to be "defeased" and remove both the liability and the annuity contract from its statement of position.[153]

Acquisition costs and other costs

Costs that are primarily related to contracts issued or renewed during the period in which the costs are incurred (for instance, commissions) should be capitalized and recognized as expense in proportion to premium revenue. However, other costs that do not vary with and are not primarily related to acquisition of new and renewal contracts (such as general administration and policy maintenance) should be recognized as expenses of the period.[154]

Policyholder dividends

Policyholder dividends are based on the experience of the pool or of a class of policies within the pool, rather than on the experience of an individual participant or policyholder. From the participants' perspective, such dividends are considered a reduction in expenditure/expense. From the pool's perspective, however, they are *not* a reduction in revenue, even if pool participants use them to reduce premiums. Instead, the pool would accrue expense related to the dividend and continue to report as revenue the amount deducted from participants' premiums.[155] Note that the distribution to risk pool participants of earnings in excess of expectations is no more than a practical example of a policyholder dividend.[156]

---

[150] GASB Statement No. 10, paragraph 22.
[151] GASB Statement No. 10, paragraph 23.
[152] GASB Statement No. 10, paragraphs 24-25.
[153] GASB Statement No. 10, paragraph 26.
[154] GASB Statement No. 10, paragraphs 28-31.
[155] GASB Statement No. 10, paragraph 32.
[156] GASB, *Comprehensive Implementation Guide (2004)*, 3.16.

Experience refunds

Unlike policyholder dividends, experience refunds are based on the experience of individual policyholders or pool participants rather than on the experience of the pool or of a class of policies within the pool. GAAP provide that experience refunds should be treated as a reduction of revenue rather than as an expense.[157]

Premium deficiencies

GAAP indicate that a probable loss exists if there is a premium deficiency; that is, if total costs exceed unearned premiums. Premium deficiencies are determined by applying the following formula to each group of contracts.[158]

Unearned premiums
    Less: Expected claims costs (including IBNRs)
    Less: Expected claims adjustment expenses
    Less: Expected dividends
    <u>Less: Unamortized acquisition costs</u>
(Premium deficiency)[159]

If a premium deficiency exists, unamortized acquisition costs should be expensed in that period to the extent of the deficiency.[160] The groups of contracts used for purposes of determining a premium deficiency should be consistent with the pool's method of acquiring, servicing, and measuring revenue and expense on its contracts.[161]

For example, assume the following facts:

Unearned premiums	$ 85	
Less: Expected claims costs (including IBNRs)		60
Less: Expected claims adjustment expenses		5
Less: Expected dividends		18
<u>Less: Unamortized acquisition costs</u>		<u>5</u>
(Premium deficiency)	$ (3)	

This situation results in a $3 premium deficiency: $85 unearned premiums - $88 total costs = $3 premium deficiency. Accordingly, assuming that unamortized issuance costs previously had been reported at $5, the balance would be reduced to $2, and the reduction would be reflected as an increase in expenses of the period.

If the amount of the premium deficiency exceeds the balance of unamortized acquisition costs, the excess should be reported as a liability.[162] If no premium deficiency exists, the full amount of unamortized acquisition costs are charged to expense over the course of the contract term in proportion to premium revenue recognized.[163]

In addition, risk-sharing pools should report revenue and an assessments receivable to cover the deficiency if 1) the deficiency is reasonably estimable, 2) the pool has a legally enforceable claim, and 3) collectibility is both probable and reasonably estimable.[164]

Reinsurance

When a pool is reinsured for claims and adjustment expenses that have already been paid, the pool should report both an asset and a reduction of

---

[157] GASB Statement No. 10, paragraph 33.
[158] Pools are allowed to consider anticipated investment income in determining whether a premium deficiency exists. Pools should disclose whether they have used this option. (GASB Statement No. 10, footnote 6.)
[159] GASB Statement No. 10, paragraph 35, as amended.
[160] GASB Statement No. 10, paragraph 36, as amended.
[161] GASB Statement No. 10, paragraph 34.
[162] GASB Statement No. 10, paragraph 36, as amended.
[163] GASB Statement No. 10, paragraph 29.
[164] GASB Statement No. 10, paragraph 36, as amended.

expense. When a pool is reinsured for unpaid claims and adjustment expenses, the pool should report the reinsurance as a reduction to its claims liabilities rather than as an asset.

In addition, GAAP provide that the following should be netted:

- unearned premiums from ceded contracts and premiums paid but not yet earned by the reinsurer; and
- receivables and payables from the same reinsurers.

Moreover, GAAP also provide that pools may net the following in their statement of activities: [165]

- reinsurance premiums paid and earned premiums; and
- reinsurance recoveries and incurred claim costs. [166]

Sometimes a risk pool will transfer the risk for a portion of *existing* losses to another insurer (i.e., *retroactive* reinsurance). In the private sector, such a transaction would be treated in conformity with FASB Statement No. 113, *Accounting and Reporting for Reinsurance of Short-Duration and Long- Duration Contracts*. That is, reinsurance would be reported gross rather than net, and any gain on the transaction would be deferred and amortized. The treatment prescribed by FASB Statement No. 113, however, is irrelevant in the public sector because it contradicts applicable GASB guidance. The latter requires that reinsurance be reported net rather than gross and that any gain be reported in the period as either a component of claims expense or as a separate component of operating income or expense. [167]

Classification of investment income

Interest income may only be classified as *operating revenue* in an enterprise fund if an entity's primary purpose is investing. Therefore, public-entity risk pools should *not* classify interest income as operating revenue since their primary purpose is risk financing rather than investing. [168]

Capital distributions

When resources are distributed to pool participants upon dissolution of the pool, the pool should label the disbursements as *capital distributions* and report them as a separate item in the risk pool's operating statement, immediately following *income before other revenues, expenses, gains, losses, and transfers*. [169]

Disclosures

GAAP set a number of detailed disclosure requirements for public-entity risk pools. These disclosures can be summarized as follows: [170]

- a description of the risk transfer or pooling arrangement that includes the rights and responsibilities of the pool and pool participants and the number and types of entities participating;
- the basis for estimating claims liabilities with a statement that "the liabilities are based on the estimated ultimate cost of settling the claims, including the effects of inflation and other societal and economic factors;"
- information on acquisition costs (nature, method of amortizing, amount amortized during the period);

---

[165] As noted later, these amounts are *not* netted in the RSI that accompanies a public-entity risk pool's financial statements.
[166] GASB Statement No. 10, paragraph 37.
[167] GASB, *Comprehensive Implementation Guide (2004)*, 3.36.
[168] GASB, *Comprehensive Implementation Guide (2004)*, 7.329.
[169] GASB, *Comprehensive Implementation Guide (2004)*. 3.19.
[170] GASB Statement No. 10, paragraph 49.

- the face amount and carrying amount of any claims liabilities reported at present value, including the range of interest rates used to discount those liabilities;
- statement of whether investment income is considered in determining premium deficiencies;
- nature of excess insurance or reinsurance transactions and their significance to the pool's operations, including type of coverage and reinsurance premiums ceded, as well as estimated amounts that are recoverable from excess insurers and reinsurers *and* that reduce the liabilities as of the date of the statement of position for unpaid claims and claim adjustment expenses; and
- reconciliation of total claims liabilities for the current and prior fiscal year, in the following tabular format:
  – unpaid claims and claim adjustment expenses, beginning of year
  – incurred claims and claim adjustment expenses
  – payments
  – other (describe if material)
  – unpaid claims and claim adjustment expenses, end of year.

If annuity contracts are purchased in the name of claimants, and related liabilities have been removed from the statement of position, the aggregate outstanding amount of the defeased claims liabilities should be reported in the notes. This requirement does not apply, however, if annuity contract beneficiaries have signed an agreement releasing the government from further obligation, and the likelihood of further payments is remote. The notes also should provide information on the nature and amount of contingent losses. This disclosure normally is required when there is at least a reasonable possibility that a loss has been incurred, but the loss does not meet the criteria for accrual (the loss is not probable and measurable).

RSI

GAAP require that public-entity risk pools present certain RSI on revenue and claims development immediately after the notes to the financial statements. The specific RSI required can be summarized as follows:[171]

- A table displaying:
  1. Premium and investment revenues (past ten fiscal years), presented as follows:
     ¤ gross amounts earned
     ¤ amounts ceded (for example, reinsurance)
     ¤ net amounts earned
  2. Unallocated claim adjustment expenses and other costs (past 10 fiscal years)
  3. Incurred claims and allocated claim adjustment expenses as originally reported (past 10 fiscal years), presented as follows:[172]
     ¤ gross amounts incurred
     ¤ amounts ceded (for example, reinsurance)
     ¤ net incurred
  4. Cumulative payments related to item no. 3 at the end of each policy year
  5. Re-estimated ceded losses and expenses[173]

---

[171] GASB Statement No. 10, paragraph 50, as amended.
[172] For this purpose, GAAP allow use of either the policy year, the accident year (for occurrence-based policies), or the report year (for claims-made policies).

6. Re-estimated net incurred claims and claim adjustment expenses at the end of each year
7. The change between nos. 3 and 6
- Reconciliation of claims liabilities by type of contract, including an analysis of changes in liabilities for claims and claim adjustment expenses of the current fiscal year and the prior year, in the same tabular format prescribed for the note disclosure reconciliation described earlier.

Pools without the transfer or pooling of risk

As with pools involving the transfer or pooling of risk, public-entity risk pools that do not involve the transfer or pooling of risk are reported as enterprise funds. However, these pools do not use the insurance accounting just described for pools that do transfer or pool risk. Instead, pools not involving the transfer or pooling of risk should report claims-servicing revenue and administrative costs. Amounts collected or due from participants, and amounts paid or to be paid for settling claims, should be reported simply as a net asset or liability.[174]

Capitalization contributions

If it is probable that capitalization contributions will be returned to pool participants, the pool should report a liability to participants. If not, the pool should report a liability for "unearned premiums" and recognize premium revenue over the periods during which the pool is providing coverage. (These periods should be consistent with the period during which the contribution is factored into the pool's determination of premiums; if this period is not readily determinable, revenue should be reported over a period not to exceed 10 years.) If the pool does not transfer risk, the liability associated with capitalization contributions should be netted with other amounts that are collected or due from pool participants and that are paid or to be paid for settling claims.[175]

COMBINING GOVERNMENT-WIDE AND FUND FINANCIAL REPORTING FOR SPECIAL-PURPOSE GOVERNMENTS

A key feature of the governmental financial reporting model is its unique combination of government-wide and fund financial reporting. This combination of government-wide and fund financial reporting is designed to accomplish two goals: to provide *information using the economic resources measurement focus and the accrual basis of accounting* for functions reported in governmental funds, and to provide *net cost information by function* for governmental activities.

Once these objectives are understood, it is clear that there are two situations involving special-purpose governments where one or both of these objectives is superfluous, making it unnecessary to provide separate government-wide and fund financial statements:

- *Single-program governments.* One obstacle prevents a special-purpose government that uses only governmental funds from combining its fund financial statements and its government-wide financial statements into a single combining presentation simply by adding a recon-

---

[173] See previous note.
[174] GASB Statement No. 10, paragraph 51.
[175] GASB Interpretation No. 4, paragraphs 11-13.

ciling column.[176] That obstacle is the requirement that the government-wide statement of activity also present net cost information *by program* (or function), which does not lend itself to the combining presentation. This obstacle, however, does not exist for *single-program governments*. Therefore, single-program governments that use only governmental funds have the *option* to combine their fund financial statements and their government-wide financial statements into a single, combining presentation.[177]

- *Business-type entities.* There is no need to convert the data of entities that use enterprise fund accounting to the economic resources measurement focus and the accrual basis of accounting. Likewise, the requirement to report activities by *function* applies only to governmental *activities*.[178] Therefore, entities comprising one or more enterprise funds need not present both government-wide and fund financial statements.[179]

GAAP clarify that a government may *not* be considered a single-program government "if it budgets, manages, or accounts for its activities as multiple programs."[180] Thus, a typical school district would *not* be expected to qualify as a single-program government.[181] Examples of special-purpose governments that are likely to qualify as single-program governments include cemetery districts, levee districts, assessment districts, and drainage districts.[182]

Also, single-program governments are not required to use a combining presentation, even though they qualify to do so. For example, a single-program government may wish to present separate government-wide and fund financial statements so that it can vary the format used for its statement of activities.[183]

---

[176] That is, to convert the governmental fund data to the economic resources measurement focus and the accrual basis of accounting.
[177] GASB Statement No. 34, paragraph 136.
[178] Segment reporting replaces this requirement in the case of enterprise funds.
[179] GASB Statement No. 34, paragraph 138.
[180] GASB Statement No. 34, paragraph 137.
[181] It is very important to note that this definition of a program is much narrower than the definition of a function, even though the latter is the minimum level of detail required for the government-wide statement of activities. See GASB, *Comprehensive Implementation Guide (2004)*, 7.395.
[182] GASB Statement No. 34, paragraph 136.
[183] GASB Statement No. 34, paragraph 136.

16

Budgetary Integration and Reporting

While budgeting is an essential element of sound financial management in both the public and private sectors, budgeting plays a more prominent role in the public sector than in the private sector. As a result, accounting and financial reporting are much more closely linked with budgeting in the public sector than in the private. This chapter explores this important relationship and its practical implications for accounting and financial reporting.

THE ROLE OF THE BUDGET

State and local government budgets serve three essential purposes: 1) to set public policy, 2) to act as a legislative control on taxing and spending by the executive branch, and 3) to serve as a financial planning tool. The first two objectives are unique to the public sector.

The use of the budget to set public policy

A key characteristic of the American political system is the separation of powers among the executive, legislative, and judicial branches of government. Under this separation of powers arrangement, the legislative body (such as state legislature, county board, or city council) has the prerogative to establish public policy, which is then carried out or *executed* by the executive branch. The budget represents the practical embodiment of legislative policy setting in the form of specific funding decisions.

The use of the budget as a legislative control on taxing and spending by the executive branch

Each branch of government functions as a control on the exercise of power by the other two branches through a system of checks and balances. The need for checks and balances is perhaps greatest in the case of the executive branch, which controls the administrative apparatus of government. Accordingly, the legislative branch is entrusted with sole power to levy taxes and authorize spending, thereby wielding the "power of the purse." The legislative branch exercises this taxing and spending power through its approval of the annual (or biennial) operating budget. Should the executive branch violate the budget, it violates the *law,* and is subject to sanction by the judicial branch.

The use of the budget as a financial planning tool

Like any household, business, or nonprofit organization, a government must plan for its financial future to ensure that its inflows of resources will be adequate to meet its needs, both anticipated and unanticipated. This financial planning function underlies the entire process leading to approval of the annual (or biennial) operating budget of a state or local government.

TYPES OF BUDGETS AND THEIR USE

Budgets are classified in a number of ways, including:
- period of the budget (annual or biennial budgets versus project-length budgets);
- character of the budget (operating budgets versus capital budgets);
- degree of legal authority (appropriated budgets versus financial plans); and
- anticipated variability (flexible budgets versus fixed budgets).

The operating budget, which is the focal point of public-sector budgeting, is always adopted on either an annual or a biennial basis. Capital construction normally takes place over more than one fiscal period. Accordingly, capital budgets generally are adopted on a project-length basis.[1]

Virtually all budgets encountered in the public sector are *fixed* budgets, establishing a single spending cap that management may not exceed without special authorization. An alternative to the fixed budget is the *flexible* budget, which authorizes varying levels of spending depending on demand or revenues. A flexible budget is of greatest potential benefit to a government's enterprise funds, where it sometimes may be difficult to estimate the demand for services and, therefore, the level of spending needed to meet demand.

In almost all cases, an annual or biennial budget is legally adopted (*appropriated*) for the general fund. Annual appropriated budgets also are extremely common for special revenue funds. For two reasons, annual appropriated budgets are less common for debt service funds. In some cases, debt covenants already provide adequate control over balances and spending related to debt service funds, making an appropriated budget superfluous. In other cases, budgetary control over debt service funds is achieved indirectly through budgeting transfers in the general fund for debt service payments to be made in debt service funds. Capital projects funds commonly do *not* have annual appropriated budgets, but instead operate using project-length budgets.

In some cases, for control purposes, annual legal budgets also are adopted for proprietary funds. Frequently, however, proprietary fund budgets serve only as financial plans. Annual legal budgets are even less common for fiduciary funds, where other forms of control (such as trust agreements) typically are in place. In this regard, although permanent funds are a governmental fund type, they tend to operate more like fidu-

---

[1] Of course, all or a portion of a project-length budget may subsequently be incorporated into the operating budget, as in situations where a government is legally required to appropriate all spending on an annual or biennial basis, including spending on capital projects.

ciary funds unless there is a legal requirement to adopt an annual appropriated budget for *all governmental funds*.

BUDGETARY INTEGRATION

Because of the importance of budgeting in the public sector, it is essential that a government have a system of controls to ensure and demonstrate budgetary compliance. Such a system requires that management have access to timely information concerning both of the following:

- *The uncommitted balance of appropriations.* An appropriation creates the legal authority to spend or otherwise commit a government's resources. If managers are to avoid overspending or overcommitting the budget, they must be able to determine, on an ongoing basis, the remaining uncommitted balance of each appropriation.
- *Unrealized revenues.* Because most governments operate under a legal requirement to prepare a balanced budget, revenues often must be estimated. A typical example is sales tax receipts. If actual revenues fail to attain projected estimates, the *unrealized* revenues could result in a budgetary deficit. Therefore, managers need to monitor unrealized revenues, on an ongoing basis to determine whether spending reductions are needed to keep the budget in balance, even if spending remains within appropriations.[2]

When an accounting system is designed to automatically provide timely information concerning the uncommitted balance of appropriations and unrealized revenues, it is said to have *integrated* the budget.

Budgetary integration is a basic feature of the computer-based accounting systems used by most state and local governments. Before modern computer-based systems, budgetary integration was accomplished by means of a series of special journal entries. Although these journal entries are rarely made today, they still merit attention for the insight they provide into *how* budgetary integration is accomplished.

Unrealized revenues

Actual revenues, of course, are recorded as a credit balance in the accounting system. Accordingly, a practical way to generate information on the balance of unrealized revenues at any given moment is to record a *budgetary debit balance* equal to the amount of *estimated* revenues. The difference in the two accounts provides an automatic measure of unrealized revenues, as follows:

Sales Taxes		
Estimated Revenue	*Realized Revenue*	*Unrealized Revenues*
$2,650,000	($2,579,000)	$71,000

Encumbrances and uncommitted appropriations

Determining the uncommitted balance of appropriations is not so simple as determining unrealized revenues. It is not enough to simply compare budgeted appropriations against actual expenditures. To learn the true uncommitted balance of appropriations, a government also must consider any commitments it has made. Assume that a government issues a purchase order for supplies or signs a contract for services. No expenditure would be recognized until the ordered goods were received or the signed contract

---

[2] Care should be taken to avoid overlooking this important aspect of budgetary management.

was fulfilled. Nonetheless, it is clear that issuing a purchase order or signing a contract reduces the amount of resources available for other spending (that is, issuing a purchase order or signing a contract *commits* all or a portion of the appropriation).

An integrated budget uses *encumbrances* to keep track of commitments related to open purchase orders and executory (unfulfilled) contracts. That is, a *budgetary debit balance* (encumbrances) is reported for commitments, acting much like an expenditure for budgetary purposes. Actual expenditures and encumbrances can then be compared against the amount of authorized spending (*appropriations*) to determine the remaining uncommitted balance of appropriations. To effect this comparison, a *budgetary credit balance* is recorded for appropriations so that the juxtaposition of expenditures, encumbrances, and appropriations automatically produces the uncommitted balance of appropriations, as follows:

Police Safety Program

Appropriations	Expenditures	Encumbrances	Uncommitted Appropriation
($88,000)	$72,000	$6,500	($9,500)

While encumbrance accounting can be useful, it is not necessary for *all* types of commitments. For example, governments typically do *not* record encumbrances for routine outlays, such as salaries and wages.[3]

Basic budgetary journal entries

So far, three separate *budgetary* accounts have been described: 1) ESTIMATED REVENUES, 2) APPROPRIATIONS, and 3) ENCUMBRANCES.[4] The initial budget includes the first two items; encumbrances arise subsequently as appropriations are committed through purchase orders and contracts.[5]

Equal amounts of ESTIMATED REVENUES and APPROPRIATIONS might be expected in a balanced budget. In fact, these amounts often differ for a variety of reasons. The difference is reflected as BUDGETARY FUND BALANCE, which can be reported as either a *budgetary debit balance* or a *budgetary credit balance,* depending on a government's specific circumstances. Assume that a government estimates budgetary revenues of $27 million, but plans to authorize spending for only $25 million in a deliberate effort to increase fund balance levels as a cushion against budgetary shortfalls. In that case, the initial journal entry to record the budget would be as follows:

	DR	CR
ESTIMATED REVENUES	$ 27,000,000	
APPROPRIATIONS		$25,000,000
BUDGETARY FUND BALANCE		2,000,000
(To record the appropriated operating budget)		

Since the sole purpose of these budgetary accounts is to serve as a point of reference for actual revenues, expenditures, and encumbrances, these bud-

[3] Control over salaries and wages often is assured by means of positions controls maintained within a government's human resources system.
[4] Budgetary accounts exist only within the accounting system and do *not* play a role in external financial reporting (except for budgetary comparison statements). To emphasize this critical distinction between budgetary accounts and regular accounts, it has been customary to use ALL CAPS when referring to purely budgetary accounts. That practice has been retained throughout this publication.
[5] The appropriate handling of encumbrances carried over from one budget year to the next is treated later in this discussion.

getary accounts would remain unchanged throughout the year, except for budgetary amendments.

At the end of the budget period, there would be no further need for these budgetary accounts. Accordingly, the journal entry used initially to record the budget (adjusted for any subsequent amendments) would be reversed, as follows:

	DR	CR
APPROPRIATIONS	$ 25,000,000	
BUDGETARY FUND BALANCE	2,000,000	
ESTIMATED REVENUES		$27,000,000
(To close the appropriated operating budget)		

During the budget period, commitments resulting from purchase orders or contracts would be recorded as encumbrances as follows:

	DR	CR
ENCUMBRANCES	$ 5,770	
BUDGETARY FUND BALANCE RESERVED FOR ENCUMBRANCES		$ 5,770
(To record encumbrances for purchase orders issued)		

Once a purchase order is filled or a contract is fulfilled, the encumbrance would be removed and an expenditure would be reported in its place, as follows:

	DR	CR
BUDGETARY FUND BALANCE RESERVED FOR ENCUMBRANCES	$ 5,770	
ENCUMBRANCES		$ 5,770
(To liquidate encumbrances on purchase orders for goods received)		
Expenditures	$ 5,270	
Vouchers payable		$ 5,270
(To record the receipt of ordered supplies)		

As the example illustrates, the amount encumbered does not always agree with the amount eventually recorded as an expenditure. The reason for this disparity is that encumbrances sometimes are based on estimates. Naturally, once the expenditure related to an encumbrance has been incurred, the full amount of the encumbrance is removed because it no longer is needed as a placeholder for the anticipated expenditure.[6] Note also that the journal entry to liquidate encumbrances, like the journal entry to set up encumbrances, involves only BUDGETARY ACCOUNTS. The recognition of an expenditure and a related liability, on the other hand, involves the regular accounts used for external financial reporting.

Alternative approaches to the disposition of encumbrances outstanding at the end of the budget period

Reappropriate and reestablish prior-period encumbrances

In practice, two approaches can be taken to dispose of encumbrances that a government still intends to honor at the end of the budget period:
- reappropriate and reestablish prior-period encumbrances; and
- extend the budget period for encumbrances (use of a *lapse period*).

For most governments, encumbrances lapse at the end of the budget period and then are reappropriated automatically as part of the subsequent period's budget. In that case, governments typically would make three sep-

[6] Naturally, the full amount of the encumbrance would not be removed if only a partial shipment were received.

arate budgetary journal entries to mark the lapsing and subsequent reappropriation of encumbrances.

First, like any other budgetary account, the ENCUMBRANCES account must be closed at the end of the budget period.[7] Assume that $52,000 in encumbrances are still outstanding at the end of the budget period. The appropriate journal entry would be as follows:

	DR	CR
BUDGETARY FUND BALANCE RESERVED FOR ENCUMBRANCES	$ 52,000	
ENCUMBRANCES		$ 52,000
(To remove encumbrances outstanding at the end of the budget period)		

The government, as noted, intends to honor these encumbrances and so has reappropriated the necessary resources as part of the subsequent period's budget. This commitment of a portion of the subsequent period's APPROPRIATIONS must be recognized in the subsequent period by reversing the entry used to close the ENCUMBRANCES account at the end of the prior budget period, as follows:

	DR	CR
ENCUMBRANCES	$ 52,000	
BUDGETARY FUND BALANCE RESERVED FOR ENCUMBRANCES		$ 52,000
(To record the reappropriation of encumbrances from the prior budget period)		

The amount of *unreserved fund balance* in a governmental fund is intended to present current financial resources *available for appropriation* in the subsequent period's budget. Encumbered amounts necessarily meet this criterion whenever a government takes the reappropriation and reestablishment approach to encumbrances, since encumbered items are, in fact, reappropriated as part of the following year's budget. Accordingly, no amount of *fund balance* needs to be reserved for encumbrances, although the government may wish to designate a portion of *unreserved fund balance* to indicate that such amounts are not available for *new* spending, as follows:

	DR	CR
Unreserved, undesignated fund balance	$ 52,000	
Unreserved fund balance designated for encumbrances		$ 52,000
(To designate a portion of unreserved fund balance for encumbrances outstanding at fiscal year-end)		

This last journal entry involves the regular accounts used for financial reporting purposes rather than the specialized BUDGETARY ACCOUNTS discussed earlier. This entry would be reversed immediately following preparation of the financial statements.

Extend the budget period for encumbrances   Some governments do not immediately close their budget at the end of the budget period. Instead, the budget remains in force for some additional time, commonly referred to as a *lapse period*, to allow for liquidation of encumbrances in force as of the end of the budget period. Thus, a government with a December 31 fiscal year-end may provide for a three-month

---

[7] The ENCUMBRANCES account can no longer serve its intended purpose once the related APPROPRIATIONS account has been closed.

lapse period (through March 31) during which encumbrances in force as of the end of the prior budget period may continue to be liquidated *under the prior period's budget*. That is, governments taking this approach have two budgets operating simultaneously during the lapse period: the prior period's budget for expenditures related to the liquidation of previously encumbered items, and the current period's budget for all other expenditures.

Three practical observations are useful in applying this approach:
- expenditures incurred during the lapse period must be coded to indicate the budget period to which they are to be charged;[8]
- encumbrances themselves must be coded to indicate the budget period to which their eventual liquidation is to be charged; and
- the budgetary accounts are closed only at the end of the lapse period.

Because of these complications associated with the use of lapse periods, this approach to budgeting has become much less common in recent years.

If encumbrances are to be liquidated under the current period's budget—even if the liquidation occurs in the subsequent period—such amounts cannot be considered available for appropriation in the subsequent period's budget. Accordingly, GAAP require that fund balance be reserved for encumbrances outstanding at the end of the fiscal year whenever a government uses the lapse period approach, assuming that the government still intends to honor the encumbrances.[9] The appropriate journal entries for this purpose are as follows:

	DR	CR
Unreserved fund balance	$ 52,000	
Fund balance reserved for encumbrances		$ 52,000
(To designate a portion of unreserved fund balance for encumbrances outstanding at fiscal year-end)		

Once again, this last journal entry involves the regular accounts used for financial reporting purposes rather than the specialized BUDGETARY ACCOUNTS discussed earlier. Likewise, this entry would be reversed immediately following preparation of the financial statements.

Allotments

The appropriated budget is adopted on an annual (or biennial) basis. There is a certain degree of risk, however, in making an entire period's appropriation immediately available for spending. Accordingly, governments sometimes divide their appropriations into *allotments*. Thus, a total annual budgetary appropriation of $10 million, for example, may be divided into four quarterly allotments of $2.5 million. When an allotment system is used, actual expenditures and ENCUMBRANCES are compared against an ALLOTMENTS budgetary account, which represents the balance of the appropriation made available for spending thus far.

---

[8] This treatment has no effect on financial reporting under generally accepted accounting principles (GAAP), where expenditures are always reported in the period in which they are incurred, regardless of the budget to which they are charged.
[9] National Council on Governmental Accounting (NCGA) Statement 1, *Governmental Accounting and Financial Reporting Principles,* paragraph 91 (4).

BUDGETARY REPORTING

The authoritative accounting and financial reporting literature requires the presentation of budgetary comparisons in two specific instances:

- *Budgetary reporting in connection with the basic financial statements.* Budget-to-actual comparisons are required in connection with the basic financial statements for the general fund and any major individual special revenue funds for which annual (or biennial) budgets are legally adopted.[10] These comparisons normally may be presented either as one of the basic financial statements for governmental funds or as required supplementary information (RSI).[11] In that case, the Government Finance Officers Association (GFOA) recommends that these budgetary comparisons be presented as part of the basic governmental fund financial statements.[12] The one exception is situations where the framework used for budgeting is incompatible with the fund structure used for financial reporting (irreconcilable perspective differences), in which case the budgetary comparison must be presented as RSI in a manner consistent with the framework used for budgeting.[13] An example would be a situation where a government adopts a program-based budget that does not rely on a fund structure. Conversely, this exception is *not* intended to apply to minor perspective differences that are easily resolved by means of a simple reconciliation (e.g., debt service payments budgeted in the general fund but reported in a debt service fund under generally accepted accounting principles (GAAP) in the financial statements).

- *Budgetary reporting in connection with the comprehensive annual financial report (CAFR).* Budget-to-actual comparisons must be presented *at the legal level of budgetary control* within the CAFR for *all* individual governmental funds with legally adopted annual budgets (including capital projects funds, debt service funds, permanent funds, and *nonmajor* special revenue funds).[14] If the budgetary comparisons presented for the general fund and major individual special revenue funds in connection with the basic financial statements and RSI meet this requirement, no additional presentation need be made for these funds elsewhere within the CAFR. If the comparisons do *not* meet this requirement, a presentation that is sufficiently detailed to demonstrate compliance at the legal level of budgetary control must be presented for these funds also within the CAFR.

---

[10] Sometimes a given fund will be classified in one manner for financial reporting purposes and in another manner for budgetary purposes. Budgetary reporting requirements apply based solely upon how a fund is classified for financial reporting purposes. Thus, no budgetary comparison should be presented in the basic financial statements (or as required supplementary information) for a budgetary special revenue fund that is classified as an enterprise fund for financial reporting purposes. (Governmental Accounting Standards Board (GASB), *Comprehensive Implementation Guide (2004)*, 7.380.)

[11] GASB Statement No. 34, *Basic Financial Statements—and Management's Discussion and Analysis—for State and Local Governments*, paragraph 130.

[12] GFOA recommended practice on "Presenting Budget to Actual Comparisons Within the Basic Financial Statements" (2000).

[13] GASB Statement No. 34, paragraph 130, as amended by GASB Statement No. 41, *Budgetary Comparison Schedules—Perspective Differences (an amendment of GASB Statement No. 34)*, paragraph 3.

[14] NCGA Statement 1, paragraph 155 and NCGA Interpretation 10, *State and Local Government Budgetary Reporting*, paragraph 14.

The requirements for the budgetary comparison that must be presented in connection with the basic financial statements and RSI are discussed in detail elsewhere.[15] It should be noted that *there is no requirement to present the original budget for other budgetary comparisons presented within the CAFR* (although it may be presented voluntarily to anticipate potential questions that might otherwise arise); nor is there a requirement to reconcile the budgetary data in these other budgetary comparisons with GAAP if the basis of budgeting is different.

There is no requirement to present budgetary comparisons for proprietary funds with legally adopted annual budgets. In practice, however, it is quite common for such presentations to be included within the CAFR.

Legal level of budgetary control

Normally, there are various levels of detail in an appropriated budget. Consider the following possible levels of detail:

Fund level:	General fund
Function level:	Public safety
Department level:	Fire department
Activity level:	Fire prevention
Object level:	Personal services—salaries and wages
Subobject level:	Regular employees

Although budgets normally are prepared at all of these levels of detail, management frequently retains some latitude in using appropriated resources. For example, management may not legally be able to move resources from one department to another, but it may still be able to reallocate resources from one activity to another within a single department. The lowest level at which a government's management may not reallocate resources without special approval is known as the *legal level of budgetary control*. This legal level can vary greatly from one government to another. For some governments, the legal level of control is as high as the fund or function level; for others, it may be as low as the object level or even lower.

Often there are practical difficulties in attempting to demonstrate compliance at the legal level of budgetary control in individual fund budgetary comparisons. Following are some common examples:

• *Different sources of legal control.* A state may mandate that all local governments within its jurisdiction exercise budgetary control at a minimum specified legal level of control (for example, the fund level). At the same time, local governments within the state may retain the right to impose an even lower level of legal control on their own initiative (perhaps the activity level). In such cases, the individual fund budgetary comparisons must demonstrate both levels of legal control.

• *Different legal levels of control within a single government.* Governments often make one or more specific exceptions to their normal legal level of budgetary control. For example, a government that otherwise controls expenditures by fund may elect to control certain specified expenditures at the object level—for instance, personal services. The individual fund budgetary comparison must provide information at the more detailed level, at least for the specified expenditures. In this example, the individual fund budgetary comparison must, at a minimum, report separate lines for "personal services" and "other expen-

---
[15] See the discussion of the basic financial statements for governmental funds found in chapter 10.

ditures." Also, in many cases, there is a limit on the amounts that may be transferred at a given level (for example, no more than 10 percent of expenditures by object), so the legal level of control would effectively be that level.

- *Cross-cutting legal levels of control.* In some situations, governments budget both by fund and across funds. For example, various portions of a single department may be accounted for in different funds, and management may be precluded from overspending either by fund or by department. In such cases, a separate departmental budgetary presentation (e.g., note disclosure or subsection schedule) may be needed to supplement the individual fund presentations to meet the requirement of demonstrating compliance at the legal level of budgetary control.
- *Unofficial budgets.* It is not always a simple matter to change the appropriated budget once it is approved. In at least one state, some local governments adopt both an official "appropriated budget" and an unofficial "operating budget." The operating budget is actually used for planning and control purposes. The appropriated budget is used simply as a fallback device to avoid the need for formal budgetary amendments. Because a key goal of budgetary reporting is to demonstrate legal compliance, the appropriated budget (which alone has the force of law) normally should be used for purposes of budgetary reporting. Nonetheless, because compliance with the lower spending levels of the operating budget would automatically signify compliance with the higher spending levels of the appropriated budget, the operating budget may be presented *in situations where no overspending of the operating budget has occurred.*

In certain extreme cases, the legal level of budgetary control may be so detailed that it is not practical to demonstrate compliance within the CAFR itself. In such cases, a separate budgetary report may be issued to demonstrate compliance at the legal level of budgetary control, provided the CAFR contains a reference to the existence of this separately issued report.[16] This reference to a separately issued budgetary report, however, does *not* eliminate the need to present budgetary comparisons within the CAFR for all individual governmental funds with legally adopted annual budgets. Rather, the level of detail for individual fund budgetary comparisons simply need not exceed the level associated with the basic financial statements (that is, expenditures by function).[17]

Often there are significant differences between GAAP and the basis of budgeting. In the case of budgetary comparisons presented in connection with the basic financial statements, a reconciliation between the two is required.[18] As mentioned, there is no similar requirement for budgetary comparisons presented elsewhere within the CAFR. However, whenever the basis of budgeting differs from GAAP, this disparity should be clearly indicated on the title of the individual fund budgetary comparisons.

Exhibit 16-1 summarizes the budgetary reporting requirements just described.

---

[16] This separately issued budgetary report must provide *all* of the information that otherwise would have been presented in the CAFR (e.g., same fund structure, fund names, subtotals, and totals).
[17] NCGA Interpretation 10, paragraph 14.
[18] See chapter 10.

Exhibit 16-1
Budgetary reporting requirements

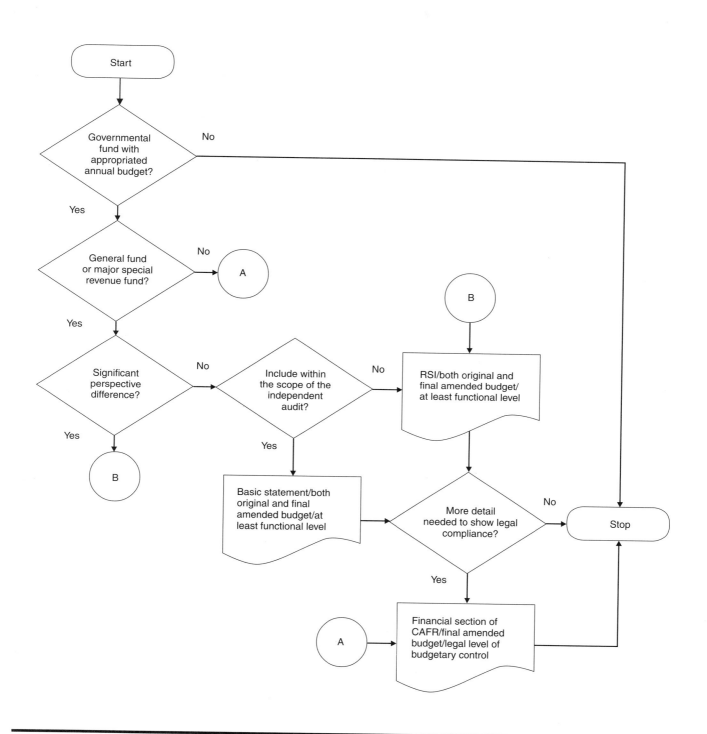

17

Performance Measurement

In recent years, interest in performance measurement in the public sector has increased markedly. This chapter examines the current state of performance measurement for state and local governments and explores the relationship of performance measurement to budgeting and financial reporting.

BACKGROUND

Private-sector businesses, despite the vast range of goods and services they provide, share a common goal—profit. Since profit is a *financial* concept, it is only logical that those interested in evaluating the performance of a business have turned principally to the *financial* statements. The primary objective of governments, on the other hand, is to provide services. Service quality, of course, unlike profit, is not inherently a financial concept. Consequently, financial statements have not played the same role in assessing performance in the public sector as they have in the private sector.

The absence of an integral tie between financial reporting and performance measurement in the public sector does not mean that performance measurement is somehow less important for state and local governments than it is for private-sector businesses. To the contrary, because there is no profit motive, there is almost universal agreement on the value and need for performance measurement in the public sector. Rather, the key issue has been how, in practical terms, to best realize the full promise of performance measurement for state and local governments.

PERFORMANCE MEASUREMENT AND BUDGETING

In 1995, the Government Finance Officers Association (GFOA) joined seven other state and local government organizations to form the National Advisory Council on State and Local Budgeting (NACSLB).[1] The council's goal was to create a comprehensive framework for public-sector budgeting that state and local governments could use as an ideal against which to measure and

improve the quality of their own budget practices. The NACSLB determined that a comprehensive budget framework should do all of the following:
- incorporate a long-term perspective;
- establish links to broad organizational goals;
- focus budget decisions on results and outcomes;
- involve and promote effective communication with stakeholders;[2] and
- provide incentives to government management and employees.

Performance measurement is essential if budget decisions are to focus on results and outcomes. Consequently, the following is one of the council's four basic principles of public-sector budgeting:

Evaluate performance and make adjustments. Program and financial performance should be continually evaluated, and adjustments [should be] made, to encourage progress toward achieving goals.

In 1998, the GFOA formally adopted as its own the recommendations of the NACSLB,[3] reinforcing the GFOA's previous specific recommendations on performance measurement, which were themselves refined and reissued in 2002.[4] These recommendations address: 1) the basic characteristics of sound performance measures; 2) minimal guidelines for the initial incorporation of performance measures into the budget process; and 3) advice on the direction in which performance measurement should develop.

Basic characteristics of sound performance measures

The GFOA believes that performance measures are an important component of long-term strategic planning and decision making and should be linked to governmental budgeting. At a minimum, performance measures should:
- be based on program goals and objectives that tie to a statement of program mission or purpose;
- measure program outcomes;
- provide for resource allocation comparisons over time;
- measure efficiency and effectiveness for continuous improvement;
- be verifiable, understandable, and timely;
- be consistent throughout the strategic plan, budget, accounting and reporting systems to the extent practical;
- be consistent over time;
- be reported internally and externally;
- be monitored and used in managerial decision-making processes;
- be limited to a number and degree of complexity that can provide an efficient and meaningful way to assess the effectiveness and efficiency of key programs; and

[1] Those seven organizations are the Association of School Business Officials, the Council of State Governments, the International City/County Management Association, the National Association of Counties, the National Conference of State Legislatures, the National League of Cities, and the U.S. Conference of Mayors.
[2] In the public sector, *stakeholders* include citizens, customers, elected officials, management, employees, businesses, other governments, and the media.
[3] GFOA recommended practice on "Recommended Budget Practices of the National Advisory Council on State and Local Budgeting (NACSLB)" (1998).
[4] GFOA recommended practice on "Performance Management: Using Performance Measurement for Decision Making" (2002).

- be designed in such a way to motivate staff at all levels to contribute toward organizational improvement.

Minimal guidelines for the initial incorporation of performance measures into the budget process

The GFOA encourages all governments to utilize performance measures as an integral part of the budget process. Over time performance measures should be used to report on the outputs and outcomes of each program and should be related to each department's mission, goals, and objectives. Governments in the early stages of incorporating performance measures into their budget process should strive to:

- develop a mission statement for the government and its service delivery units by evaluating the needs of the community;
- develop its service delivery units in terms of programs;
- identify goals, short- and long-term, that contribute to the attainment of the mission;
- identify program goals and objectives that are specific in timeframe and measurable to accomplish goals;
- identify and track performance measures for a manageable number of services within programs;
- identify program inputs in the budgeting process that address the amount of resources allocated to each program;
- identify program outputs in the budgeting process that address the amount of service units produced;
- identify program efficiencies in the budgeting process that address the cost of providing a unit of service;
- identify the program outcomes in the budgeting process that address the extent to which the goals of the program have been accomplished;
- take steps to ensure that the entire organization is receptive to evaluating performance;
- integrate performance measures into the budget, which, at a minimum, should present goals and input, output, efficiency, and outcome measures by program; and
- calculate costs and document changes that occur as a direct result of the performance management program in order to review the effectiveness of the performance management program.

Advice on the direction in which performance measurement should develop

As governments gain experience with performance measures, the GFOA encourages them to develop more detailed information and use a variety of measures to report on program outcomes. These measures should be linked to the goals of the programs and the missions and priorities of the organization. In the GFOA's view, governments should:

- ensure that the benefits of establishing and using performance measures exceed the resources required to establish performance measures;
- develop multiyear series of efficiency indicators to measure the efficiency of service delivery within programs;
- develop multiyear series of quality or outcome indicators to measure the effectiveness of service delivery within programs;
- develop a mechanism to cost government services;
- analyze the implications of using particular measures for decision making and accountability;
- use customer or resident satisfaction surveys;

- adopt common definitions of key efficiency and effectiveness performance measures to allow intergovernmental comparisons;
- develop, measure, and monitor more detailed information within programs;
- develop common or improved approaches to utilizing financial and non-financial performance measures in making and evaluating decisions;
- use community condition measures to assess resident needs that may not be addressed by current programs;
- develop and periodically review supportable targets for each performance measure;
- evaluate the data to use in long-term resource allocation and budget decisions for continuous improvement; and
- utilize performance information in resource allocation decisions and report on efficiency and effectiveness and on the extent to which program goals have been accomplished.

Performance measurement cannot function in a vacuum. Consequently, GFOA urges governments to create a climate that is receptive to performance measurement; that is, one in which "stakeholders at all levels ..embrace the concept of continuous improvement and are willing to be measured against objective expectations."

PERFORMANCE MEASUREMENT AND FINANCIAL REPORTING

Some have argued that readers of state and local government financial statements cannot properly assess a government's *financial* accountability unless they first know whether a government has obtained sufficient value for resources expended. This concern led the Governmental Accounting Standards Board (GASB) to explore the possibility of expanding general-purpose external financial reporting to include performance measures, which the GASB refers to as "service efforts and accomplishments" (SEA) reporting.

GASB project background   In 1985, the GASB passed a resolution encouraging state and local governments to experiment with the measuring and reporting of SEA data. In 1987, the GASB's concern for SEA reporting was reflected in the following objective contained in GASB Concepts Statement No. 1, *Objectives of Financial Reporting*:

> *Financial reporting should provide information to assist users in assessing the service efforts, costs, and accomplishments of the governmental entity.* This information, when combined with information from other sources, helps users assess the economy, efficiency, and effectiveness of government and may help form a basis for voting or funding decisions. The information should be based on objective criteria to aid interperiod analysis within an entity and comparisons among similar entities.[5]

---

[5] GASB Concepts Statement No. 1, *Objectives of Financial Reporting*, paragraph 77c.

That same year, the GASB undertook a comprehensive research project to explore the current state of SEA measurement and reporting. That project has led to the issuance of a number of reports in a series entitled, *Service Efforts and Accomplishments Reporting: Its Time Has Come.*[6]

The results of the GASB's research on the current status of SEA measurement and reporting led the standards board in 1989 to pass a second resolution further encouraging SEA experimentation and reporting. Finally, in 1994, the GASB issued Concepts Statement No. 2, *Service Efforts and Accomplishments Reporting*, which formally committed the board in theory to expanding the scope of financial reporting to encompass SEA.

Levels of accountability

Traditionally, financial reporting for state and local governments has focused on demonstrating a government's "probity and legality" in handling public funds.[7] The GASB believes this focus should be significantly broadened. Specifically, the GASB believes that general-purpose external financial reporting should help users to assess a government's "performance accountability" (efficiency and economy) and its "program accountability" (effectiveness). At the same time, the GASB has formally rejected any role in general-purpose external financial reporting for measures of "policy accountability" (justification of the selection of one among several possible options).

The example of a sanitation department illustrates the GASB position. Current general-purpose external financial reporting typically would report only the amount spent on sanitation, and how that amount compared with the original and the final amended budget. The GASB believes that ideally, general-purpose external financial reporting should eventually be expanded to also address the efficiency, economy, and effectiveness of sanitation services. Conversely, the GASB does *not* believe it would be appropriate that general-purpose external financial reporting attempt to demonstrate whether more funds should be spent for sanitation rather than for other competing public needs, such as education or recreation, for instance.

Categories of SEA measures

The GASB has identified three categories of SEA measures and believes that all three ideally should be included within the scope of general-purpose external financial reporting:

- *Measures of efforts* can take the form of *financial* or *nonfinancial* information. The amount spent per pupil per year is an example of a financial measure of effort. Nonfinancial measures of effort could include the number of personnel assigned to a task (such as the number of police officers on patrol duty) or similar measures.
- *Measures of accomplishment* can be divided into *output* and *outcome* measures. *Output* measures tend to focus on the *quantity* of a service provided (for example, the number of tons of garbage removed), while *outcome* measures emphasize the *results* achieved by providing

---

[6] The overview report in this series covers 12 service areas: elementary and secondary education; police; fire; public health; hospitals; public assistance; public transit; highway maintenance; economic development; sanitation; water and wastewater; and colleges and universities. Eight of these are also the subjects of more detailed individual reports in this same series.
[7] GASB Concepts Statement No. 2 defines "probity and legality accountability" as being concerned with "spending funds in accordance with the approved budget or being in compliance with laws and regulations" (paragraph 21).

a service (for example, number of miles of road maintained at a certain level).

- *Measures that relate efforts to accomplishments.* Measures of *efficiency* relate service efforts to outputs (cost per ton of garbage removed, for instance). *Cost-outcome* measures relate service efforts to results (cost per mile of road maintained at a predetermined level, for example).

SEA indicators easily could be misunderstood if certain environmental factors are not adequately explained to users. For example, test scores for secondary schools could be affected by a variety of economic and social factors. Similarly, roads subject to particularly heavy truck traffic might result in higher maintenance costs than roads devoted exclusively to passenger vehicles. Therefore, SEA indicators must be accompanied by appropriate explanatory data.

Objectives and characteristics of SEA data

The main objective of SEA reporting is to provide information useful in assessing the government's performance. The GASB believes, therefore, that while all categories of SEA data should be presented, the major focus should be on measures of accomplishments (outputs and outcomes) and measures that relate efforts to accomplishments (efficiency measures and cost-outcome measures).

The GASB believes that SEA data must possess the following essential characteristics of accounting data if they are to be part of general-purpose external financial reporting: understandability, reliability, relevance, timeliness, consistency, and comparability.[8] Several observations may be useful regarding the specific application of these characteristics to SEA data:

- Understandability requires that SEA reporting be concise and comprehensive.
- Understandability also requires that SEA data be accompanied by explanatory information on factors within and outside of the government's control.
- Comparability requires that SEA reporting be placed within an appropriate frame of reference (for example, comparisons with prior periods, comparisons with government-established targets, comparisons of similar units within the government, comparisons with other comparable entities).
- Reliability requires that SEA data be derived from systems that produce controlled and verifiable data. Specifically, such systems should be "subjected to analysis similar to that used for financial information systems."[9]

Developing SEA standards

The GASB acknowledges that further experimentation is needed before it will be able to mandate the reporting of specific SEA indicators. The GASB also recognizes that it must rely heavily on the expertise of professionals in the relevant disciplines to create sets of SEA measures that could serve as a starting point for the GASB's own standard-setting activity.

In addition, SEA data must meet the cost/benefit test. Factors to be considered in this assessment for a specific SEA measure include:

---

[8] See chapter 9 for a discussion of each of these characteristics.
[9] The level of reliability here would probably be similar to that mandated for required supplementary information. Note that the nonfinancial nature of some of the data poses special challenges in this regard.

Exhibit 17-1
GASB suggested criteria for effective communication of performance information

The External Report on Performance Information

The external report on performance information should provide a basis for understanding the extent to which an organization has accomplished its mission, goals, and objectives in the context of potential significant decision-making or accountability implications.

Criterion	Description
Purpose and scope	The purpose and scope of the report should be stated clearly. The statement of scope should include information about the completeness of the report in its coverage of key, major, or critical programs and services.
Statement of major goals and objectives	The report should clearly state the major goals and objectives of the organization and the source of those goals and objectives.
Involvement in establishing goals and objectives	The report should include a discussion of the involvement of citizens, elected officials, management, and employees in the process of establishing goals and objectives for the organization.
Multiple levels of reporting	Performance information should be presented at different levels (layers) of reporting. The relationship between levels of available performance information should be clearly communicated and should include how the user can find information at the different levels reported.
Analysis of results and challenges	The report should include an executive or management analysis that objectively discusses the major results for the reporting period as well as the identified challenges facing the organization in achieving its mission, goals, and objectives.
Focus on key measures	The report should focus on key measures of performance that provide a basis for assessing the results for key, major, or critical programs and services; and major goals and objectives of the organization. An external performance report should be concise, yet comprehensive in its coverage of performance.
Reliable information	The report should contain information that readers can use to assess the reliability of reported performance information.

What Performance Information to Report

The performance information reported should assist in communicating the extent to which the organization and its programs, services, and strategies have contributed to achieving goals and objectives

Criterion	Description
Relevant measures of results	Reported performance measures should be relevant to what the organization has agreed to try to accomplish and, where possible, should be linked to its mission, goals, and objectives as set forth in a strategic plan, budget, or other source.
Resources used and efficiency	Reported performance information should include information about resources used or costs of programs and services. It also could report performance information relating cost to outputs or outcomes (efficiency measures).
Citizen and customer perceptions	Citizen and customer perceptions of the quality and results of major and critical programs and services should be reported when appropriate.
Comparisons for assessing performance	Reported performance information should include comparative information for assessing performance, such as to other periods, established targets, or other internal and external sources.
Factors affecting results	The report should include a discussion or identified external and internal factors that have had a significant effect on performance and will help provide a context for understanding the organization's performance.
Aggregation and disaggregation of information	Reported performance information should be aggregated or disaggregated based on the needs and interests of intended users.
Consistency	Reported performance measures should be consistent from period to period; however, if performance measures or the measurement methodology used is significantly changed, that change and the reason(s) for the change should be noted.

Communication of Performance Information

A reasonably informed, interested user should be able to learn about the availability of reports on performance and should be able to access, understand, and use reported performance information.

Criterion	Description
Easy to find, access, and understand	The availability of an external report on performance and how to obtain that report should be widely communicated through channels appropriate for the organization and intended users. Performance information should be communicated through a variety of mediums and methods suitable to the intended users.
Regular and timely reporting	Performance information should be reported on a regular basis (usually annually). The reported information should be made available as soon after the end of the reporting period as possible.

- the measure's value in assessing accomplishments;
- the extent to which the measure has gained general acceptance;
- the measure's understandability to citizen and oversight groups; and
- the relative benefits of other, less costly, measures.

When and if the GASB believes these preliminary conditions are met, the board could take one of several different approaches to mandating SEA reporting. One possibility would be to require the presentation of SEA measures for all major services, but to refrain initially from mandating any *specific* SEA measures. A second approach would be to establish a minimum set of specific SEA measures for certain common major services, but to keep the reporting of SEA measures for other activities on a voluntary basis. A third alternative would be for the GASB to establish a minimum set of specific SEA indicators for certain common activities, but to require the presentation of unspecified SEA indicators for other major services.

Still another alternative being considered by the GASB is to provide SEA criteria for those who wish to use them. A possible first step in this direction was the release in 2003 of a special report on *Reporting Performance Information: Suggested Criteria for Effective Communication.* That report offered sixteen criteria for those desiring guidance on how to report performance information effectively (see exhibit 17-1).

At least two other issues also would need to be addressed before the GASB could begin mandating the reporting of SEA data: the frequency of SEA reporting, and *where* SEA data should be reported. The frequency could be either annual or cyclical,[10] while the data could be reported as required supplementary information, in the statistical section of the comprehensive annual financial report, or in a separate SEA report. The GASB has indicated that it is most likely to choose the last option for placement.

SUMMARY

There is virtually universal agreement on the value and need for performance measurement for state and local governments. The GFOA, consistent with the recommendations of the NACSLB, strongly supports the increased use of performance measurement in the context of budgeting rather than as part of financial reporting. The GASB, for its part, sees a role for performance measurement as part of a much-expanded general-purpose external financial reporting. Common to both positions is commitment to the increased use of performance measurement in the public sector.

[10] For example, only triennial condition assessments are required for governments that elect to use the modified approach for infrastructure reporting.

18

The Internal Control Framework

An accounting system is designed to assemble, analyze, classify, record, and report financial data. In performing these functions, an accounting system also must maintain adequate control over a government's assets. Like any information system, an accounting system is only as reliable as the underlying data it processes. A government's internal control framework must provide assurance that the accounting system and its underlying data are reliable. This chapter examines the internal control framework as it relates specifically to accounting and financial reporting.

THE SCOPE OF INTERNAL CONTROL

The management of any entity—government, business, or nonprofit organization—is charged with providing the leadership needed for the entity to achieve its purpose. Moreover, management is not free simply to act in any way it chooses to achieve the entity's goals. Rather, management's options and actions are circumscribed by constraints and expectations, both implicit and explicit. Management's responsibilities may be summarized as follows:

- *Effectiveness.* Ultimately, management's success must be judged on the basis of whether the entity is achieving its objectives.
- *Efficiency.* Because there are legitimate and conflicting demands for scarce resources, management is expected to make optimal use of the resources placed under its control. Naturally, an activity can only be truly efficient if it is first effective.
- *Compliance.* Management does not have unlimited authority over the resources under its control. Rather, management's control over resources normally is limited by policy, law, or regulation, particularly in the public sector. A condition of management's stewardship of resources is that it strictly comply with all such restrictions.
- *Reporting.* Managers must be accountable to those who have provided the resources they manage. An essential part of meeting this responsi-

bility is the regular preparation of financial reports for the benefit of interested parties.[1]

Naturally, the fulfillment of these important responsibilities cannot be left to chance. Management must create a *framework of internal control* to ensure that it will meet its responsibilities. Thus, internal control, by its very nature, is *management-oriented*.

The scope of internal control is necessarily broad, encompassing all management activities, both programmatic and financial. This discussion, however, focuses solely on internal control as it relates directly to accounting and financial reporting.

ELEMENTS OF A COMPREHENSIVE FRAMEWORK OF INTERNAL CONTROL

The greatest challenge to effective internal control is ensuring that the control framework established by management is *comprehensive*—that is, broad enough to fully achieve its intended purpose. It is generally recognized[2] that any truly comprehensive framework of internal control must possess five essential elements. The framework must:

- provide a favorable *control environment*;
- provide for the *continuing assessment of risk*;
- provide for the design, implementation, and maintenance of effective *control-related policies and procedures*;
- provide for the effective *communication* of information; and
- provide for ongoing *monitoring* of the effectiveness of control-related policies and procedures, as well as the resolution of any potential problems identified.

The control environment

Internal control does not operate in a vacuum. *Control environment* describes what is commonly referred to in the private sector as an entity's "corporate culture." It is impossible to exaggerate the importance of this environment to the effectiveness of internal control. When management believes that internal control is important to achieving its goals, and it communicates that view to employees at all levels, internal control is likely to function well. Conversely, if management views internal control as unrelated to achieving its objectives, or as an obstacle to that purpose, this attitude almost certainly will be communicated to staff at all levels, despite official statements or policies to the contrary. It is difficult or impossible for even the best-designed internal control framework to function effectively in such an environment.

The key element in a favorable control environment is management's attitude, as demonstrated through its actions. Management must lead by example, creating a "tone at the top" that sets the standard for the entire organization. A favorable control environment also requires that management throughout the organization communicate the importance of internal control to staff at all levels. To be truly effective, such guidance must be

---

[1] Reports on performance measurement also have a role to play in this regard (see chapter 17).

[2] A key document in this regard is *Internal Control—Integrated Framework* (1992). Commonly referred to simply as the "COSO Report," this two-volume document is a report issued by the Committee of Sponsoring Organizations (COSO) of the National Commission on Fraudulent Financial Reporting ("Treadway Commission").

communicated in a practical way and reviewed periodically. In particular, managers at the highest levels must regularly communicate the importance of internal control to lower-level managers, who are in the best position to ensure that control-related policies and procedures are actually followed on a day-to-day basis. Finally, there must be swift and appropriate disciplinary action for employees who violate standards of conduct. Failure to take appropriate disciplinary action inevitably weakens the perception that management is committed to internal control.

Management also can improve the quality of the control environment by establishing an internal audit function. Internal auditors typically play an active role in monitoring the effectiveness of control-related policies and procedures, thereby contributing significantly to improving the quality of the overall control environment.[3]

Risk assessment

Governments operate in a constantly changing environment. As the environment changes, so too do the risks that a government must face. Yesterday's policies and procedures may be inadequate to meet today's challenges. *On an ongoing basis,* management must attempt to identify and assess potential risks that could prevent management from fully meeting its responsibilities. Such risks can arise from inside as well as outside the government. Management should strive to identify potential internal and external risks as soon as possible to have adequate opportunity for crafting an effective and efficient response.

If top management alone is involved in assessing risk, there is a good possibility for missing many specific risks that face individual programs and activities. Conversely, if a government's ongoing risk assessment is confined to lower-level managers operating on an activity-by-activity basis, it is possible that more generalized risks may be overlooked. Effective risk assessment, then, must include both macro and micro components and necessarily involves managers at all levels.

Risks generally arise either as a result of changes in the government's operating environment or as a result of *inherent* risk.

- *Changes in the government's operating environment.* By nature, change always creates a certain degree of risk. Management must assess every significant change a government undergoes or anticipates, looking for potential related risks. In particular, common experience has identified certain types of changes as requiring particular attention from management. Examples include changes in personnel (especially in sensitive positions), changes in information systems and technology, rapid growth, the introduction of new programs and services, and structural changes.
- *Inherent risk.* Other factors, sometimes known collectively as *inherent risk*, also can indicate that special management attention may be warranted. Examples of factors involving a degree of inherent risk include administrative complexity, a high volume of cash receipts,

---

[3] See the Government Finance Officers Association's (GFOA) recommended practice on "Establishment of an Internal Audit Function" (1997). The document recommends, among other things, that "every government should consider the feasibility of establishing a formal internal audit function because such a function can play an important role in helping management to maintain a comprehensive framework of internal control." Internal auditing is addressed in chapter 19.

the existence of direct third-party beneficiaries, a history of prior problems, and previous unresponsiveness to identified problems.

The goal of risk assessment is to enable management to prevent or minimize harm. To achieve this goal, management must take prompt action to address any significant potential risks identified through the risk-assessment process.

Effective control-related policies and procedures

The third essential component of any truly comprehensive framework of internal control is the design, implementation, and maintenance of specific, control-related policies and procedures. Such control-related policies and procedures are essential to ensuring the integrity of the data processed by the accounting system and included in financial reports, both internal and external. The key categories of control-related policies and procedures for accounting and financial reporting are as follows:

- *Authorization.* Only specified individuals should be able to initiate a transaction, such as purchase requisitions and check requests.
- *Properly designed records.* Accounting records must be properly designed. For example, documents should be sequentially numbered to ensure that *all* documents are accounted for. Likewise, automatic duplicates should be provided for any documents furnished to parties outside the government (copies of receipts, for instance).
- *Security of assets and records (including backup and disaster recovery).* Security must be maintained over a government's assets and records to minimize the danger of loss or misuse. Thus, individuals should have access to assets or records based on the specific needs of their positions, and assets and records should be protected against physical harm. Likewise, management should provide for the regular backup of computer records. A disaster recovery plan should be in place to ensure continued timely processing of transactions in the event of unforeseen circumstances (for example, natural disasters) that might adversely affect the accounting system's regular operation. At a minimum, a government's policies and procedures for computer disaster recovery should:
  - formally assign disaster recovery coordinators for each agency or department to form a disaster recovery team;
  - require the creation and preservation of back-up data;
  - provide for alternative processing of data following a disaster;
  - provide detailed instructions for restoring disk files; and
  - establish guidelines for the immediate aftermath of a disaster.

  Likewise, it is recommended that:
  - a copy of the government's formal computer disaster recovery policies and procedures be kept off-site to ensure its availability in the event of a disaster;
  - a government periodically test its computer disaster recovery plan and take immediate action to remedy deficiencies identified by that testing (it is essential that such testing encompass restoration as well as processing of the government's data); and
  - a government satisfy itself concerning the adequacy of disaster recovery plans for outsourced services.[4]

---

[4] See GFOA recommended practice on "Computer Disaster Recovery Planning" (1999).

- *Segregation of incompatible duties.* Duties are said to be "incompatible" from an internal control perspective if they allow a single individual to commit an irregularity and then conceal it. Incompatible duties should be *segregated*—ideally among different departments, or at least among individuals within the same department in very small governments—so that different departments or individuals can serve as a check on one another. In practice, three types of functions are commonly considered to be mutually incompatible: 1) authorization of transactions, 2) record-keeping, and 3) custody of assets. Ideally, then, no one individual should be able to *authorize* a transaction, *record* the transaction in the accounting records, and maintain *custody* of the assets resulting from the transaction.
- *Periodic reconciliations.* It is important that related accounting records be compared periodically. For example, the amount of cash reported in the accounting records should be reconciled to the cash balances reported on the bank statement. Likewise, the balances reported in general ledger control accounts (such as accounts payable—control) should be reconciled to related amounts reported in subsidiary ledgers (such as total balances in individual payable accounts). Moreover, data entry in computer systems should incorporate built-in *edit checks* to ensure that all items are entered properly (reasonableness checks).
- *Periodic verifications.* Accounting records are good only to the extent that they faithfully reflect underlying facts. Thus, management should periodically compare data contained in the accounting records to what those data purport to represent. For example, management should periodically undertake a physical inventory of its fixed assets, compare the results of that inventory to the accounting records, and make appropriate adjustments to those records.[5] Likewise, balances of receivables and payables should occasionally be confirmed directly with taxpayers, customers, and suppliers.
- *Analytical review.* This is the process of attempting to determine the reasonableness of financial data by comparing their behavior with other financial and nonfinancial data. From another perspective, analytical review attempts to compare what is reported to what might reasonably be expected. Analytical review is particularly important because it is often the only practical means of determining if data in the financial statements are complete.[6]

Communication

Communication is the fourth essential element of a comprehensive framework of internal control. To emphasize its importance, communication usually is treated as a separate element in its own right. As a practical matter, however, communication really is a *pervasive characteristic* that must permeate all elements of the internal control framework if the framework is to function effectively.

---

[5] See GFOA recommended practice on "The Need for Periodic Inventories of Tangible Capital Assets" (2001). The document indicates that every state or local government should "perform a physical inventory of its tangible capital assets, either simultaneously or on a rotating basis, so that all of a government's tangible capital assets are physically accounted for at least once every five years."
[6] It is easier to determine that something ought *not* to be in the financial statements than it is to determine if something is missing.

For internal control to function properly, it is essential that there be clear lines of communication throughout the organization. Top-level management must be able to communicate its directives to management and staff at all levels. Conversely, it is equally important that staff at all levels be able to communicate upward to management. Indeed, non-managerial employees at all levels often are in a unique position to identify many potential risks that management should address. Moreover, some means must be provided for staff to "communicate around" managers who may be involved in improper conduct. Lateral communication also is important, particularly regarding the finance function, since its work directly affects all government functions and departments.

In addition, it is very important that governments maintain open lines of communication with appropriate outside parties. For example, good communication with suppliers and contractors can help to deter or detect inappropriate purchasing and bidding practices.

Communication can take various forms, from policy memos and formally documented procedures, to highly informal oral updates. Likewise, good communication combines regularly scheduled exchanges of information (for example, monthly staff meetings) with special efforts (such as task forces).

One method of communication that is particularly effective for internal control over accounting and financial reporting is the comprehensive formal documentation of finance-related policies and procedures. A well-designed and properly maintained system for documenting finance-related policies and procedures enhances both accountability and consistency. Traditionally, such documentation has taken the form of a policies and procedures manual. Thanks to advances in technology, other even more effective methods are now also available for this purpose. Finance-related policies and procedures should be promulgated by an appropriate level of management to emphasize their importance and authority. The documentation of finance-related policies and procedures should be updated periodically according to a predetermined schedule. Changes in policies and procedures that occur between these periodic reviews should be updated in the documentation promptly as they occur. A specific employee should be assigned the duty of overseeing this process. Management is responsible for ensuring that this duty is performed consistently. The documentation of finance-related policies and procedures should be readily available to all employees who need it. It should delineate the authority and responsibility of all employees, especially the authority to authorize transactions and the responsibility for the safekeeping of assets and records. Likewise, the documentation of finance-related policies and procedures should indicate which employees are to perform which procedures. Procedures should be described as they are actually intended to be performed rather than in some idealized form. Also, the documentation of finance-related policies and procedures should explain the design and purpose of control-related procedures to increase employee understanding of and support for controls.[7]

Monitoring

The fifth essential element of a comprehensive framework of internal control is monitoring. It is essential that management continuously monitor

---

[7] GFOA recommended practice on "Documentation of Accounting Policies and Procedures" (2002).

control-related policies and procedures to ensure that they are continuing to function properly. Management must also verify that policies and procedures have, in fact, been updated to adequately address new challenges (e.g., changes in technology) identified as the result of the government's ongoing risk-assessment process. Likewise, management must monitor potential problems disclosed by internal control to ensure that such situations are corrected or otherwise resolved on a timely basis.

It also is important that management carefully monitor the resolution of audit findings resulting from internal audits and from the independent audit of the government's financial statements. Management is primarily responsible for ensuring that weaknesses, once identified, are promptly and effectively corrected.

RESPONSIBILITY FOR INTERNAL CONTROL

Since internal control is essentially management-oriented, management, both financial and programmatic (*not* the internal or external auditors), is primarily responsible for the effectiveness of internal control, just as it is accountable for all other aspects of its performance. Furthermore, a basic principle of good management is that authority and responsibility should not be separated. Therefore, since management alone is in a position to establish and maintain internal control, management also must be held primarily accountable for the proper functioning of the internal control framework.[8]

An entity's governing board oversees management's performance; so while management is *primarily* responsible for internal control, the governing board is *ultimately* responsible for ensuring that management fulfills its duty in this regard. The governing board's oversight role is particularly important because of management's ability to override controls.[9]

Audit professionals—the independent auditors of the entity's financial statements and members of the entity's internal audit staff—can play a valuable role in *helping* management and the board to fulfill their respective responsibilities for internal control. Nevertheless, auditors cannot themselves assume either primary or ultimate responsibility for internal control.[10]

---

[8] GFOA takes the position that financial managers are ethically obligated to assume responsibility for internal control in its recommended practice on "Enhancing Management Involvement with Internal Controls" (2004):

> GFOA's *Code of Professional Ethics* requires of finance officers as part of their responsibility as public officials, to "exercise prudence and integrity in the management of funds in their custody and in all financial transactions." GFOA's *Code of Professional Ethics* also requires of finance officers in connection with the issuance and management of information that they "not knowingly sign, subscribe to, or permit the issuance of any statement or report which contains any misstatement or which omits any material fact." Both provisions presume the existence of a sound framework of internal control:
> - Prudence in the management of public funds requires that there be adequate control procedures in place to protect those funds.
> - A sound framework of internal control is necessary to afford a reasonable basis for finance officers to assert that the information they provide can be relied upon.

[9] "Ultimately, it is the responsibility of appropriate elected officials to ensure that the managers who report to them fulfill their responsibility for implementing and maintaining a sound and comprehensive framework of internal control." GFOA recommended practice on "Enhancing Management Involvement with Internal Control" (2004).

[10] "While a government's independent auditors and similar outside parties often can provide valuable assistance to management in meeting its internal-control-related responsibilities, their contribution can never be a substitute for management's direct and informed involvement with internal

Independent auditors must gain an understanding of the entity's internal control framework as part of the process of assessing *audit risk*. Accordingly, management has sometimes reached the understandable but mistaken conclusion that the independent audit of the financial statements is sufficient to ensure that the internal control framework is adequately designed and functioning properly. In fact, however, the purpose and scope of the independent auditor's assessment of internal control is quite limited.

The objective of the independent audit is to assure potential users of financial statements that they can reasonably rely on those statements to be free from errors that could change the users' overall assessment of the entity's finances. A properly designed and conducted financial statement audit should uncover all internal control weaknesses (auditors call them *material weaknesses*) that could have such a major impact on financial reporting. However, while most internal control weaknesses are important to management, they are not significant enough to potentially affect a user's overall assessment of the entity's finances. So there is no assurance that all immaterial weaknesses will be uncovered, even in a thorough and well-conducted financial statement audit. Thus, the independent auditor's assessment of internal control should *not* be viewed as a substitute for management's own ongoing monitoring of the effectiveness of its control-related policies and procedures.

Financial managers must, of course, obtain the information and training needed to meaningfully take responsibility for internal control. In particular, they should obtain a sound understanding of the essential components of a comprehensive framework of internal control. They also should ensure that all employees responsible in any way for internal control receive the information and training they need to fulfill their particular responsibilities.[11]

INHERENT LIMITATIONS OF INTERNAL CONTROL

The cost of internal control, of course, should never exceed related benefits. Thus, a key limitation on internal control is that cost considerations will prevent management from ever installing a "perfect" system. Instead, management will deliberately and properly choose to run certain risks because the cost of preventing such risks cannot be justified.

A second important limitation of internal control is that control-related policies and procedures are potentially subject to management override. That is, if management has the power to establish a control-related policy or procedure, management probably has the ability to override that same policy or procedure.

The risk of collusion is a third limitation of internal control. Often, control-related policies and procedures are designed so that one employee functions as a check on another employee's work (segregation of incompatible duties). In such cases, there is always the risk that employees who are

control." GFOA recommended practice on "Enhancing Management Involvement with Internal Control" (2004).
[11] GFOA recommended practice on "Enhancing Management Involvement with Internal Control" (2004).

supposed to serve as a check on one another may instead work together to circumvent control.

EVALUATING CONTROL-RELATED POLICIES AND PROCEDURES

The importance of monitoring the ongoing effectiveness of control-related policies and procedures was identified earlier as an essential element of a comprehensive framework of internal control. Such monitoring takes the practical form of a *periodic evaluation of internal control,* which is necessary for two reasons:

- Changes in a government's circumstances can render inadequate or obsolete some control-related policies and procedures that once were satisfactory.
- Control-related policies and procedures have a natural tendency to deteriorate over time unless management properly maintains them.

Accordingly, governments must evaluate their control-related policies and procedures periodically to determine that they:

- have been *properly designed* to achieve what they are intended to achieve;
- have been *implemented* as designed;
- are *still functioning* as designed; and
- are *still adequate* in light of the government's current circumstances (taking into account the results of the government's ongoing risk-assessment process).[12]

Identifying control cycles   It is easy for management to be daunted by the sheer volume and complexity of control-related policies and procedures over accounting and financial reporting. The first step in evaluating these policies and procedures is to know where to start. The best place to begin is by subdividing them into manageable groupings of similar or related activities, commonly referred to as *control cycles.* For example, billings lead to the creation of receivables and subsequent cash collections, so the policies and procedures related to these three processes are naturally interconnected.

There are two key advantages in using control cycles to evaluate control-related policies and procedures. Using control cycles: 1) promotes *efficiency* by avoiding the duplication that can result when a single policy or procedure benefits multiple related activities; and 2) highlights the natural links that exist among policies and procedures, thereby improving the *effectiveness* of the evaluation process.

There is no single "right" way to subdivide control-related policies and procedures into control cycles, but it is essential that related activities and controls be dealt with together. In practice, control cycles typically focus on flows of resources (for example, revenue or cash receipts cycle, expenditure or cash disbursements cycle) or asset management (such as treasury or cash management cycle, capital assets cycle).

Performing a vulnerability assessment   Typically, the sheer volume of control-related policies and procedures makes it impractical for a government to simultaneously perform a thor-

---

[12] GFOA recommended practice on "Enhancing Management Involvement with Internal Control" (2004).

ough evaluation of all of them. Consequently, governments must set priorities in an internal control evaluation. For this purpose, a *vulnerability assessment* is a common tool for logically establishing priorities among control cycles.

A vulnerability assessment functions on the premise that governments should evaluate high-risk control cycles before low-risk control cycles. A control cycle's degree of risk can be assessed based on two questions:

- If a control failure were to occur, how significant would the potential effect be?
- How likely is it that a control failure will occur?

The answer to the first question often is determined on the basis of management's assessment of the *inherent risk* connected with a particular control cycle. The answer to the second question typically is based on management's assessment of the quality of the *control environment*.

Once management has assessed inherent risk and the quality of the control environment, it can logically prioritize its efforts. For example, management clearly should begin by evaluating control cycles that have both a high level of inherent risk and an unfavorable control environment. Conversely, control cycles involving little inherent risk and a favorable control environment would be a much lower priority. Other situations fall between these extremes.

Documenting how transactions and events are processed

After management has completed its vulnerability assessment to determine where to begin the task of evaluating control-related policies and procedures, the next step is to document how transactions and events are supposed to be handled. Typically, this documentation takes the form of a narrative memorandum describing how various transactions and events are processed. In some cases, this memorandum is further developed into a flow chart, which visually represents how transactions and events are processed.

The purpose of documenting the flow of transactions and events is to provide management with a practical tool for identifying potential risks and weaknesses as well as compensating controls. To be effective for this purpose, the documentation must clearly disclose 1) *who* is performing each step of each process, 2) *what* is involved in each step of each process, and 3) any *resulting documentation* (e.g., purchase order, receiving report).

Identifying potential risks

After documenting the flow of transactions and events, management's next step in the evaluation process is to identify the specific risks associated with the control cycle under review. The following questions are often useful in helping to identify potential risks involving accounting and financial reporting:

- How do we know that all recorded assets and liabilities actually exist?
- How do we know that all recorded assets and liabilities are really those *of the government* rather than of some other entity? (For instance, is a copy machine the government's own property or merely rental equipment?)
- How do we know that all recorded transactions and events actually took place?
- How do we know that nothing has been omitted (such as missing invoices)?

- Have all items been properly classified (for example, listed in the correct account, fund, and period)?
- Have all assets and liabilities been valued properly?
- Are assets reasonably protected against the danger of loss or misuse?

Identifying compensating controls

Once a government has made an inventory of a control cycle's potential risks, it should make a similar inventory of all control-related policies and procedures that are in place for that same control cycle. These two inventories should then be compared to identify the specific internal control policies and procedures designed to compensate for each identified risk. As a rule, *there should be at least one compensating control for each identified risk*. If not, immediate corrective action should be taken, unless the cost of the missing control(s) is considered to outweigh the potential benefit.

Evaluating the design of compensating controls

Because a control-related policy or procedure is *intended* to accomplish a particular purpose does *not* mean it succeeds in doing so. The first step in evaluating the adequacy of control-related policies and procedures is to evaluate the effectiveness of their *design*. Management must determine whether each compensating control is designed so that it could reasonably be expected to accomplish its intended purpose if it were properly implemented and maintained. If not, it would be of little use to test whether the control was implemented and remains operational.

Normally, when a control's design is determined to be inadequate, management changes the design so that the control can function effectively; however, there are exceptions to this rule. In some situations, other controls may already be in place to provide the needed assurance. In other cases, management may determine that the benefits of a redesigned control do not justify the costs. In such instances, management may choose to eliminate rather than redesign the inadequate control.

Testing compensating controls

The best-designed internal control policies and procedures are of little value if they are not actually followed in practice. Once a government determines that a control-related policy or procedure is well designed, it should next perform tests to determine whether that policy or procedure has been properly implemented and remains operational. If testing shows that a control is *not* operational, the appropriate response depends on the specific circumstances, described below.

- *Redundant controls.* Sometimes a control is not operational because some other control is accomplishing the same purpose, and the government's personnel are relying on the alternative control. In that case, the preferred control should be used and the unnecessary control eliminated.
- *Inefficient controls.* Sometimes a control is not operational because the costs of the control clearly exceed the benefits. In that case, the government should replace the inefficient control with a more efficient control, or eliminate the control altogether.
- *Lapsed controls.* Sometimes, there is no good reason why a control is not operating as designed, as it appears both well designed and cost-efficient. In that case, steps must be taken to reactivate the lapsed control. Management also may wish to schedule future similar tests of that control to ensure that corrective action, in fact, was taken.

EXHIBIT 18-1

The process for evaluating control-related policies and procedures for accounting and financial reporting

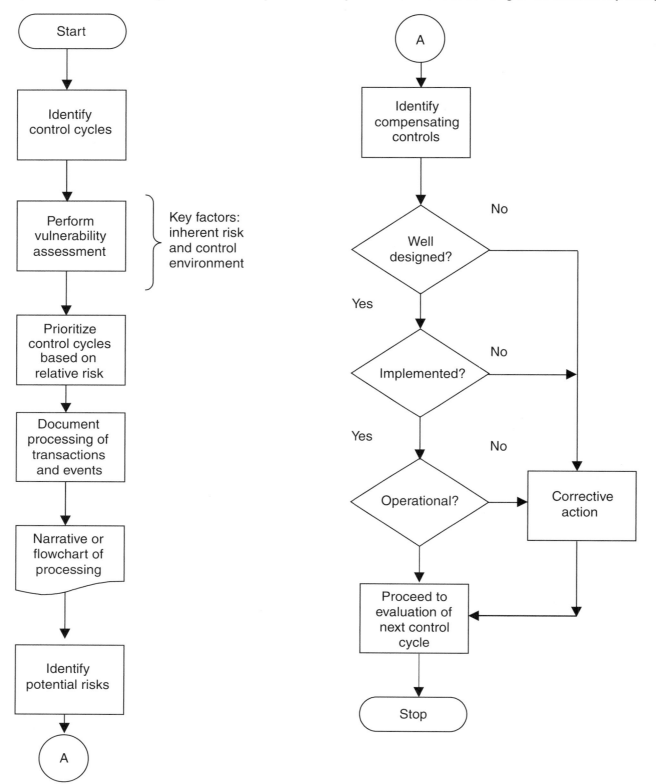

Exhibit 18-1 illustrates the process for evaluating control-related policies and procedures for accounting and financial reporting.

INTERNAL CONTROL AND FRAUD PREVENTION

Auditors have identified three conditions that generally are present when fraud occurs:
- incentive/pressure;
- opportunity; and
- attitude/rationalization.[13]

It is important to emphasize the special role played by *opportunity*. No matter how great the incentive or pressure to commit fraud, fraud simply cannot occur without opportunity. Conversely, opportunity, *by itself,* produces the incentive needed to commit fraud. Therefore, opportunity not only *permits* fraud to occur, but actually *promotes* fraud by creating a potential trap for otherwise honest individuals.

Individual control-related policies and procedures can be divided between those that are designed to *prevent* the occurrence of errors and irregularities and those that are designed to *detect* errors and irregularities after they have occurred. Controls involving periodic verifications and analytical review fall into the second category. However, controls designed to *detect* errors and irregularities also can be highly effective in *preventing* their occurrence, as the prospect of prompt detection and exposure can be a powerful disincentive to fraud. Thus, educating employees at all levels about the purpose and operation of control-related policies and procedures can help to minimize irregularities.

SUMMARY

All managers share certain basic responsibilities, which include: 1) achieving the entity's purpose (effectiveness); 2) making optimal use of scarce resources (efficiency); 3) observing restrictions on the use of resources (compliance); and 4) periodically demonstrating accountability for the stewardship of resources placed in their care (reporting). Internal control comprises the tools management uses to ensure that it fulfills these important responsibilities.

A comprehensive framework of internal control must possess five essential elements. It must: 1) provide a favorable *control environment*; 2) provide for the *continuing assessment of risk*; 3) provide for the design, implementation, and maintenance of effective *control-related policies and procedures*; 4) provide for the effective *communication* of information; and 5) provide for the ongoing *monitoring* of the effectiveness of control-related policies and procedures, as well as the resolution of potential problems identified by controls.

Internal control involves *management* tools designed to help *management* meet its responsibilities and achieve its objectives. Accordingly, management (*not* the internal or external auditors) is primarily responsible for the effectiveness of internal control, just as it is accountable for all other aspects

---

[13] American Institute of Certified Public Accountants, *Professional Standards*, AU 316.33.

of its performance. An entity's governing board oversees management's performance. So while management is *primarily* responsible for internal control, the governing board is *ultimately* responsible for ensuring that management fulfills its duty. Auditing professionals can play a valuable role in *helping* management and the board to fulfill their respective responsibilities for internal control. Nevertheless, auditors cannot assume ultimate responsibility for internal control.

There are inherent limitations associated with internal control. Specifically, cost considerations prevent management from ever installing a perfect system; internal control is potentially subject to management override; and the risk of collusion exists.

Changes in a government's circumstances can render once satisfactory control-related policies and procedures inadequate or obsolete. Also, controls have a natural tendency to deteriorate over time unless management properly maintains them. Accordingly, governments must periodically evaluate control-related policies and procedures to determine whether they have been properly designed and implemented and are still adequate and functioning.

The key steps in this evaluation process involve 1) identifying control cycles, 2) conducting a vulnerability assessment, 3) documenting the control cycle to be evaluated, 4) identifying potential risks and compensating controls, 5) evaluating the design of compensating controls, and 6) testing compensating controls.

A sound internal control framework is a government's primary defense against fraud. An inadequate internal control framework permits and actually encourages fraud. Controls designed to *detect* fraud may be useful in *preventing* fraud, because the threat of prompt detection can function as a powerful deterrent.

19

Auditing in the Public Sector

Auditing plays an especially important role in the public sector because accountability and legal compliance are critically important to state and local governments. This chapter examines the different types of audits, auditors, and auditing standards encountered in connection with state and local governments.

TYPES OF AUDITS AND AUDITORS

Auditing is broadly defined as *the systematic review or examination of the assertions or actions of a third party to evaluate conformance to some norm or benchmark*. In the public sector, audits generally are classified in one of two categories:

- *Financial audits* are designed to assure the reliability of financial reports.[1]
- *Performance audits* are conducted to establish whether government programs and activities are meeting stated goals and objectives, and to determine if governments are performing duties in the most economic and efficient manner possible (in the private sector, the term *operational audit* commonly describes audits performed for this purpose).

The basic criterion for classifying auditors is the nature of their relationship to the entity under audit. *Independent* or *external auditors* work primarily for the benefit of outside parties (typically users of the government's external financial reports). They must be fully independent, both in fact and appearance, of the entities they audit.[2] The primary role of *internal auditors*, on the

---

[1] Auditors use special *attestation standards* when engaged to provide assurance regarding finance-related matters outside the scope of financial statement auditing (e.g., grant compliance). These same attestation standards also can be used, as discussed later, by auditors engaged to conduct performance audits.

[2] Auditors performing engagements in conformity with *Government Auditing Standards* (discussed later in this chapter) must be free of any personal, external, or organizational impairments to their independence (*Government Auditing Standards*, Section 3.03).

other hand, is to assist management to achieve its control and operational objectives. As employees of the entity under audit, internal auditors are expected to maintain a high degree of independence/objectivity, but not so great as that required of external auditors.

External and internal auditors play complementary roles. Most commonly, external auditors are encountered in connection with the annual independent audit of a government's financial statements, as described in the next section on financial audits.

The public sector typically draws external auditors from one of two sources: firms of certified public accountants (as in the private sector) or government audit agencies (such as the office of the state auditor).

FINANCIAL AUDITS

The objective of a financial audit, as defined, is to provide users of financial reports with reasonable assurance from an independent source that the reports are reliable.

Auditing standards for financial audits

Like other professionals, auditors must have criteria by which to guide and judge the quality of their performance. For state and local governments, there are two closely linked sets of standards that fulfill this function.

The basic guidelines for financial audits in the public and the private sectors are provided by *generally accepted auditing standards* (GAAS). There are ten basic generally accepted auditing standards, which are traditionally grouped into three categories: *general standards*, *standards of field work,* and *standards of reporting.* Those basic standards have been set forth and developed in a series of *Statements of Auditing Standards* (SASs) issued by the Auditing Standards Board of the American Institute of Certified Public Accountants (AICPA).[3]

In the public sector, there is a second set of guidelines that commonly govern financial audits. These standards are set by the Comptroller General of the United States and are found in the Government Accountability Office's (GAO) publication, *Government Auditing Standards*, commonly referred to as the *Yellow Book*. The terms *generally accepted government auditing standards* (GAGAS) or *government auditing standards* (GAS) are commonly used to describe these GAO or "Yellow Book" standards.

The basic framework of GAGAS, like that of GAAS, distinguishes three categories of standards—general standards, standards of fieldwork, and standards of reporting—around which individual standards are organized. Moreover, in the matter of the fieldwork and reporting standards, GAGAS expressly adopt and build on GAAS. Thus, GAGAS incorporate all of the GAAS standards of fieldwork (unless specifically excluded) and *supplement* those standards with *additional* GAGAS standards of fieldwork. In the same way, GAGAS incorporate all of the GAAS standards of reporting (unless specifically excluded) and *supplement* those standards with *additional* GAGAS standards of reporting.[4] On the other hand, the general standards of GAGAS, while broadly patterned on GAAS guidance, do *not* incorporate the GAAS general standards.

[3] In the private sector, the Public Company Accounting Oversight Board has ultimate jurisdiction over audits of publicly traded companies pursuant to the Sarbanes-Oxley Act of 2002.
[4] *Government Auditing Standards,* Section 1.09.

All audits performed in conformity with *federal* audit requirements (e.g., Single Audits) must be conducted in accordance with GAGAS. Likewise, a number of states have voluntarily mandated the use of GAGAS standards for state and local government financial audits, even in the absence of a federal requirement to employ GAGAS. Absent such a requirement, financial audits of state and local governments, like those of private-sector businesses and nonprofit organizations, are performed in conformity with GAAS. Because GAAS and GAGAS are closely linked, all auditors engaged in public-sector auditing must thoroughly understand both sets of standards.

Key financial audit concepts

Regardless of whether GAAS or GAGAS are used, the goal of a financial statement audit is to provide users of a set of financial statements with reasonable assurance from an independent source that the information presented in those statements is reliable. Auditors use a variety of means to obtain the evidence they need to provide such assurance. Auditors *inspect* relevant documentation; *observe* employee performance; *inquire* concerning policies, procedures, transactions, and events; *confirm* balances and transactions with outside parties; and *perform analytical procedures* to determine the reasonableness of transactions and balances.[5]

Reasonable assurance

The goal of the auditor is to obtain *reasonable*—not absolute— assurance that the financial statements are fairly presented. Accordingly, auditors typically do not attempt to individually examine every transaction or event affecting a government's finances. Instead, they make extensive use of *sampling* to provide the evidence they need. Similarly, the concept of reasonable assurance means that auditors do not attempt to ensure that all data contained in financial statements are 100 percent accurate; rather, they seek to affirm that the financial statements are free from *material* misstatement.[6]

Materiality

All potential misstatements are not equally important. Accordingly, given the objective of *reasonable assurance* just described, an auditor is primarily concerned with those potential misstatements that could have a *material* (important or significant) impact on how a financial statement user evaluates an entity's finances. In making a judgment regarding the materiality of a potential misstatement, an auditor must consider its *quantitative* and *qualitative* aspects.[7]

In the private sector, *quantitative materiality* normally is assessed in relation to the financial statements taken as a whole. Auditors traditionally have taken a very different approach, however, in assessing quantitative materiality for state and local governments with their unique blend of fund accounting and government-wide financial reporting:

- In the government-wide financial statements, quantitative materiality should be assessed separately for *governmental activities* and *business-type activities*.
- In the fund financial statements, quantitative materiality should be assessed separately for each major governmental and enterprise fund.[8]

---

[5] AICPA *Professional Standards*, AU150.02 (third standard of field work).
[6] AICPA *Professional Standards*, AU230.10-13.
[7] AICPA *Professional Standards*, AU 312.10-11.
[8] Governmental Accounting Standards Board (GASB) Statement No. 34, *Basic Financial Statements—and Management's Discussion and Analysis—for State and Local Governments*, provides specific criteria for identifying situations where a given governmental fund or enterprise fund must be reported as a major

- Auditors enjoy considerable latitude in assessing quantitative materiality for nonmajor governmental and enterprise funds, internal service
funds, and fiduciary funds.[9]

A reconciliation often is presented on the face of the basic fund financial
statements to tie totals reported in those statements to corresponding
amounts reported in the government-wide financial statements. Quantitative materiality for the various items in this reconciliation is assessed based
upon the related column (*governmental activities* or *business-type activities*) in
the government-wide financial statements.[10]

Size is not the only factor considered in assessing materiality. Auditors
may also consider an item to be *qualitatively material*. For example, a relatively small potential misstatement that had the practical effect of converting a deficit to a surplus typically is considered material, despite its size,
because of the importance that many financial statement users attach to a
deficit of *any* size. Likewise, a potential misstatement that had the practical
effect of changing the direction of trend data typically is considered material, regardless of size. Similarly, many financial statement users consider
potential misstatements involving legal violations to be qualitatively material by their very nature. Examples include violations of the legally adopted
budget and violations of bond covenants.[11]

Audit scope   In the private sector, the independent auditor's report offers a *single opinion*
on the fair presentation of the basic financial statements, *taken as a whole*. In
the public sector, the independent auditor's report on the basic financial
statements offers *separate opinions* on a series of *opinion units*. These opinion
units are *governmental activities*, *business-type activities*, each major governmental fund, each major enterprise fund, and, in the aggregate, nonmajor
funds and discretely presented component units.[12]

As discussed elsewhere,[13] governments are encouraged to produce a
comprehensive annual financial report (CAFR), which typically will
include combining and individual fund financial statements. In that case,
the scope of the independent audit must be framed in one of two ways:

- *Exclude combining and individual fund financial statements from the scope
of the audit.* The auditor can decline to audit the combining and individual fund financial statements as such, offering instead only the
assurance that, *based solely on the audit of the basic financial statements,*
the combining and individual fund financial statements are fairly presented *in relation to* the basic financial statements, *taken as a whole.* In

---

fund (i.e., the 5 percent and 10 percent tests). Governments also may voluntarily elect to report as major
funds governmental funds and enterprise funds that do not meet these criteria. Any fund selected for
voluntary major fund reporting is subject to all of the requirements normally applicable to major funds.
Thus, if a given fund is voluntarily reported as a major fund, quantitative materiality would need to be
assessed separately for that fund, just as it would for any other major fund. (GASB, *Comprehensive Implementation Guide (2004)*, 7.8.)

[9] GASB, *Comprehensive Implementation Guide (2004)*, 7.6, and AICPA, *State and Local Governments*, Section
4.23.

[10] GASB, *Comprehensive Implementation Guide (2004)*, 7.7.

[11] AICPA, *Professional Standards*, AU 9312.4.17.

[12] Normally 1) all other funds in the aggregate and 2) discretely presented component units in the aggregate are treated as separate opinion units. They may be combined into a single opinion unit, however, if
either is not quantitatively or qualitatively material to the primary government, in which case the combined opinion unit is known as "aggregate discretely presented component unit and remaining fund
information." (AICPA, *State and Local Governments*, 4.25.)

[13] See chapter 13.

that case, the auditor is commonly said to be offering an "in-relation-to opinion."

- *Include combining and individual fund financial statements within the
  scope of the audit.* The auditor can treat each individual fund as an
  opinion unit in its own right. In that case, the auditor would need to
  assess materiality separately for each individual fund, which typically requires audit work beyond what would otherwise be necessary
  for a simple audit of the basic financial statements.

The Government Finance Officers Association (GFOA) makes the following recommendation on establishing the scope of the independent audit for
a CAFR:

> The scope of the independent audit should encompass not only the
> fair presentation of the basic financial statements, but also the fair
> presentation of the financial statements of individual funds. The cost
> of extending full audit coverage to the financial statements of
> individual funds can be justified by the additional degree of assurance
> provided. Nevertheless, the selection of the appropriate scope of the
> independent audit ultimately remains a matter of professional
> judgment. Accordingly, those responsible for securing independent
> audits should make their decision concerning the appropriate scope of
> the audit engagement based upon their particular government's
> specific needs and circumstances, consistent with applicable legal
> requirements.[14]

By definition, required supplemental information (RSI) falls outside the
scope of the financial statement audit. Nonetheless, GAAS have established
certain limited procedures that ordinarily must be performed by the independent auditor in connection with RSI.[15]

First, the independent auditor must ask management about the methods it used to prepare RSI. These inquiries should specifically address 1)
whether RSI is presented in conformity with authoritative standards, 2)
whether (and why) there have been any changes in measurement from
prior periods, and 3) significant assumptions or interpretations underlying
the measurement and presentation of RSI.

Second, the independent auditor must compare RSI with 1) the information gained from the inquiries described above, 2) the information in the
audited financial statements, and 3) any other knowledge obtained in the
course of the financial statement audit. The independent auditor also is
directed to consider requesting that management address RSI as part of the
management representation letter.

Finally, in the absence of any other specific requirements, the independent auditor should make additional inquiries if there is reason to believe
that RSI may not be measured or presented in conformity with authoritative standards.

Because RSI is *not* part of the basic financial statements, the absence of
RSI or a deficiency in its presentation does *not* affect the auditor's ultimate
opinion on the fair presentation of those statements. Nonetheless, an auditor must amend the standard auditor's report to indicate if 1) RSI has been

---

[14] GFOA recommended practice on "Audit Procurement" (1996).
[15] These procedures are outlined in AICPA's *Professional Standards*, AU 558.07.

EXHIBIT 19-1
Audit scope for the comprehensive annual financial report

Specific component of the financial section of a CAFR	Audit scope	
	Basic financial statements only	Basic, combining and individual fund, and component unit financial statements
Basic financial statements	Audited	Audited
Required supplementary information	Unaudited, but subject to certain limited procedures by the auditor	Unaudited, but subject to certain limited procedures by the auditor
Combining, individual fund, and component unit financial statements	In-relation-to audit coverage	Audited
Supplementary information	In-relation-to audit coverage	In-relation-to audit coverage
Introductory and statistical sections of the CAFR	Unaudited	Unaudited

omitted, 2) the measurement or presentation of RSI depart from authoritative standards, 3) the auditor is unable to perform the limited procedures just described, or 4) the auditor is unable to remove substantial doubts regarding whether RSI meets the measurement and presentation requirements of GAAP.

Like RSI, the contents of the CAFR's introductory and statistical sections also fall outside the scope of the independent audit of the financial statements; however, the auditor is *not* required to perform certain limited procedures in regard to either section. Nonetheless, as is generally the case for unaudited material accompanying audited financial statements, the auditor is expected to read the introductory and statistical sections of the CAFR to ensure that they do not contain information that is inconsistent with the audited financial statements. The independent auditor's report normally need not mention either the introductory or the statistical section of the CAFR. However, if the CAFR is considered an "auditor-submitted document," the auditor must explicitly state that both sections are unaudited.

The scope of the independent audit of the financial statements is illustrated in Exhibit 19-1.

Reportable conditions and material weaknesses

Auditors typically perform extensive tests of a government's internal control as part of the effort to obtain evidence to support an opinion on the fair presentation of the financial statements. While performing these tests, auditors may become aware of significant deficiencies in internal control. Auditors refer to such deficiencies as *reportable conditions*.[16] Under GAAS, auditors are responsible for notifying management of such matters.

Some reportable conditions are more serious than others. Specifically, some reportable conditions are of such magnitude that they could potentially result in a material misstatement of the financial statements. Reportable conditions of this type are known as *material weaknesses*.[17] By definition, all material weaknesses are reportable conditions, while a reportable condition need not be a material weakness.

---

[16] AICPA, *Professional Standards*, AU 325.02.
[17] AICPA, *Professional Standards*, AU 325.15.

Financial statements as management's representations

For practical reasons, the independent auditor often plays a role in preparing the financial statements (e.g., formatting, accruals).[18]   Nonetheless, regardless of the assistance provided by the independent auditor, the financial statements always remain management's responsibility. That is, financial statements are management's representations concerning the government's finances, and management cannot transfer its responsibility for its own representations to a third party.[19]

The Single Audit

State and local governments frequently receive substantial federal financial assistance, which often is provided by several different grantor agencies. At one time, state and local governments were subject to the separate audit requirements of each individual grantor. As a result, a state or local government sometimes found itself forced to undergo several audits related to the federal financial assistance it had received for a single period. Such multiple audits often resulted in a wasteful duplication of effort, with different audit teams examining and reexamining the same internal control framework. Moreover, such audits were subject to a bewildering array of conflicting audit guidance provided by different grantor agencies. The federal response to remedy this situation was the Single Audit Act of 1984, which was further strengthened by the Single Audit Act Amendments of 1996.[20]

Under the Single Audit Act, the multiple grant audits of the past were replaced by a single audit specifically designed to meet the needs of *all* federal grantor agencies. Individual grantors still retain the right to have additional audit work performed; however, any additional audit work must be paid for by the grantor and must build on the Single Audit.

The provisions of the Single Audit Act apply to all governments that expend $500,000 or more per fiscal year in federal awards.[21] *Expenditures* include expenditure/expense transactions associated with grants, cost reimbursement contracts, cooperative agreements and direct appropriations, as well as amounts disbursed to subrecipients (pass-through grants), the use of loan proceeds under loan and loan-guarantee programs, the receipt of property, the receipt of surplus property, the receipt or use of program income, the distribution or consumption of food commodities, the disbursement of amounts entitling an entity to an interest subsidy, and insurance (during the award period).[22]

Normally, audits performed in accordance with the Single Audit Act encompass the entire government. However, governments subject to the Single Audit Act have the *option* of obtaining a series of audits conducted for just those organizational units (for example, departments or agencies) that expended or administered federal awards during the fiscal period under audit.[23] Further, in certain circumstances, governments with only a single federal program have the option of procuring a program-specific audit.[24]

Like all federal audits, Single Audits must be performed in accordance with GAGAS. In addition, Single Audits are subject to the requirements of

---

[18] The issue of what types of services independent auditors can perform without compromising their independence is discussed at length later in this chapter.
[19] The situation somewhat parallels taxpayers' inability to transfer ultimate responsibility for their tax returns to a paid tax preparer.
[20] All subsequent references in this chapter to the "Single Audit Act" refer to the act as amended in 1996.
[21] The Office of Management and Budget is authorized to *raise* this threshold in the future without congressional action.
[22] AICPA, *Government Auditing Standards and Circular A-133 Audits*, Section 2.13.

EXHIBIT 19-2
Identification of "Type A" programs for single audits*

Total federal awards expended	Criteria for "Type A" program
Less than or equal to $100 million	Greater of $300,000 or 3% of federal awards
Greater than $100 million and less than or equal to $10 billion	Greater of $3 million or 0.3% (0.003) of federal awards
Greater than $10 billion	Greater than $30 million or 0.15% (0.0015) of federal awards

*The existence of a large loan or loan guarantee program could significantly decrease the number of federal programs that would otherwise be included in the Type A category. In such situations, the loan or loan guarantee program should *not* be considered as part of total federal awards for purposes of applying these thresholds, although the loan or loan guarantee program would itself still be treated as a Type A Program.

the Office of Management and Budget's (OMB) Circular A-133, *Audits of States, Local Governments, and Non-Profit Organizations.*[25] The circular places special testing and reporting responsibilities on auditors dealing with federal awards.

First, an auditor performing a Single Audit needs to determine if the mandated supplementary schedule of expenditures of federal awards prepared by the government is fairly presented in relation to the government's financial statements.[26] The auditor then must test internal control and compliance for federal awards programs. As a practical matter, auditors cannot devote the same level of attention to all of a government's various federal award programs. Therefore, Single Audits focus on *major* federal award programs. Auditors take the following approach to identifying such major programs.

- *Identification of "Type A" and "Type B" programs.* The first step in identifying major programs is to inventory all federal programs, classifying each as a "Type A" or a "Type B" program using the criteria set forth in Exhibit 19-2. By definition, all programs that do not qualify as "Type A" programs are classified as "Type B" programs.[27]
- *Identification of low-risk "Type A" programs.* The second step in identifying major programs is to assess each "Type A" program to identify those that are *low-risk*. Generally, to qualify as low-risk, a "Type A" program 1) must have been audited as a major program within the last two years and 2) must have no audit findings.[28] By definition, all "Type A" programs that are *not* low-risk automatically qualify as *major* programs.

---

[23] Separate financial statements are required for each organizational unit so audited. Typically, the materiality level for separate financial statements will be *lower* (more demanding) than for entity-wide financial statements. (AICPA, *Government Auditing Standards and Circular A-133 Audits*, Section 3.32.)

[24] In a program-specific audit, the auditor focuses solely on the federal award program. Such audits may be subject to detailed guidance provided in separate federal agency audit guides. (AICPA, *Government Auditing Standards and Circular A-133 Audits*, Section 2.02.)

[25] AICPA, *Government Auditing Standards and Circular A-133 Audits*, Section 1.12.

[26] AICPA, *Government Auditing Standards and Circular A-133 Audits*, Section 1.08. This schedule need not be presented on the same basis of accounting as the financial statements; however, if a different basis of accounting is utilized, the amounts in the schedule must be reconcilable to the underlying financial statements.

[27] AICPA, *Government Auditing Standards and Circular A-133 Audits*, Section 7.05.

[28] AICPA, *Government Auditing Standards and Circular A-133 Audits*, Section 7.11. As discussed later, audit findings are used to communicate internal control weaknesses or instances of noncompliance with laws or regulations.

- *Assessment of risk for "Type B" programs.* If one or more "Type A" programs is identified as low-risk, the auditor must assess risk for "Type B" programs, using either of the following approaches:[29]
  - *Assessment of risk for all "Type B" programs.* One option is for the auditor to complete a risk assessment for *all* "Type B" programs, then to classify as major programs *half* of the "Type B" programs identified as high-risk (with the number of "Type B" programs so classified capped at the number of low-risk "Type A" programs).
  - *Assessment of risk for only some "Type B" programs.* The other option is for the auditor to undertake a risk assessment of "Type B" programs *until* a number of high-risk "Type B" programs are identified equal to the number of low-risk "Type A" programs, then to classify the high-risk "Type B" programs so identified as major.

In addition to the major programs identified in the previous steps, programs must also be considered major if they are formally designated as major by a federal grantor agency.[30]

The Single Audit Act requires that at least half of all federal program awards expended be audited as major programs. Therefore, if major programs as identified above fail to account for at least half of all federal program awards expended, then additional programs (either low-risk "Type A" programs or "Type B" programs at any level of risk) must be reclassified as major to ensure the 50 percent coverage.[31]

For each major program, the auditor must gain an understanding of internal control over compliance and then test those controls. In addition, the auditor must render an opinion on whether the government complied with laws, regulations, and provisions of contracts or grant agreements that could have a direct and material effect on each major federal program.[32]

Moreover, in rendering an opinion on compliance for a major program, the auditor must consider materiality separately for each of the following categories of compliance requirements: activities allowed or unallowed, allowable costs/cost principles, cash management, Davis-Bacon Act, eligibility, equipment and real property management, matching/level of effort/earmarking, period of availability of federal funds, procurement and suspension and debarment, program income, real property acquisition and relocation assistance, reporting, subrecipient monitoring, and special tests and provisions.[33]

Materiality also must be considered in connection with any individual objective for a major program contained in the OMB's *Compliance Supplement.*[34]

The auditor's report reflecting these special Single Audit responsibilities is discussed later in this chapter.

Reporting the results of financial audits

In the public sector, there are three commonly encountered auditor's reports:

[29] AICPA, *Government Auditing Standards and Circular A-133 Audits,* Section 7.15.
[30] AICPA, *Government Auditing Standards and Circular A-133 Audits,* Section 7.13.
[31] The threshold for award coverage is reduced to 25 percent for governments determined to be low-risk auditees. (AICPA, *Government Auditing Standards and Circular A-133 Audits,* Section 7.24.)
[32] AICPA, *Government Auditing Standards and Circular A-133 Audits,* Section 1.30-1.32.
[33] AICPA, *Government Auditing Standards and Circular A-133 Audits,* Section 6.22.
[34] AICPA, *Government Auditing Standards and Circular A-133 Audits,* Section 3.44.

- the auditor's report on the fair presentation of the financial statements;
- the auditor's report on compliance and internal control over financial reporting based on an audit of the financial statements; and
- the auditor's report on compliance and internal control over compliance applicable to each major federal award program.

The auditor prepares the first of these reports in an ordinary financial statement audit conducted in accordance with GAAS, the first two reports in a GAGAS engagement, and all three reports in a Single Audit engagement. Moreover, in a Single Audit, the auditor's report on the fair presentation of the financial statements typically is expanded to include an opinion on the fair presentation of the supplementary schedule of expenditures of federal awards in relation to the audited financial statements.[35]

Ideally, all of the auditor's reports should be issued together. In practice, however, it is common for Yellow Book and Single Audit reports to be issued separate from the auditor's report on the fair presentation of the financial statements. If the Yellow Book report is issued separate from the auditor's report on the fair presentation of the financial statements, the auditor's report on the fair presentation of the financial statements should make explicit reference to the availability of the separate Yellow Book report.[36]

All auditors' reports related to a GAGAS engagement must refer to those standards if they are to be submitted pursuant to federal requirements.[37]

Also, auditors have special reporting responsibilities relating to indications of fraud and illegal acts. Such reporting sometimes is accomplished separately from the auditor's reports just described.[38]

The auditor's report on the financial statements

The auditor's report on the financial statements provides the auditor's opinion (or disclaimer of an opinion) on whether the financial statements are fairly presented. Typically, the report has three paragraphs. The first paragraph sets out the scope of the audit and defines management's and the auditor's differing responsibilities (management is responsible for the financial statements, the auditor is responsible for determining if those statements are fairly presented). The second paragraph provides general information concerning the audit standards followed, as well as the nature and limitations of a financial audit. The third or "opinion" paragraph sets forth the auditor's considered assessment of whether the financial statements are fairly presented in all material respects in accordance with GAAP.[39]

The auditor's report on the fair presentation of the financial statements may contain a fourth or even additional paragraphs. These later paragraphs

---

[35] When materials related to the Single Audit are issued separate from the financial statements, the auditor's report on the fair presentation of the schedule of expenditures of federal awards is included as part of this separate package.

[36] *Government Auditing Standards*, Section 5.11. This requirement applies only when the auditor's report on the fair presentation of the financial statements refers to GAGAS, as is required for auditor's reports attached to financial statements submitted to the federal government pursuant to federal audit requirements.

[37] *Government Auditing Standards*, Section 5.06. This reference may be direct or indirect. A direct reference would refer to the audit as having been conducted "in accordance with generally accepted government auditing standards." An indirect reference would refer to the audit as having been conducted "in accordance with generally accepted auditing standards and *Government Auditing Standards*, issued by the Comptroller General of the United States."

[38] *Government Auditing Standards*, Section 5.25.

[39] AICPA, *Professional Standards*, AU 508.08.

may provide additional information that may need to be disclosed to clarify the circumstances surrounding the auditor's opinion (for example, doubts regarding the government's viability as a "going concern"). Also, a special paragraph sometimes may be inserted immediately preceding the opinion paragraph to explain any circumstances that may have precluded the auditor from issuing an unqualified opinion.[40]

An *unqualified* or "clean" opinion is issued when the auditor can state, without reservation, that the financial statements are fairly presented in all material respects in conformity with GAAP.[41]

A *qualified* opinion is issued when the auditor expresses reservations about the fair presentation of the financial statements in conformity with GAAP. A common reason that auditors qualify their opinions on financial statements is that the government's underlying records may not be sufficient to support some of the data contained in the financial statements. In that case, the auditor qualifies the opinion by stating that the financial statements are fairly presented *except for* the insufficiently supported data in question. Inconsistent application of accounting principles from one year to the next is another situation that can lead to a qualified opinion.[42]

As mentioned, auditors sometimes do not have all of the underlying documentation needed to support an unqualified opinion on the fair presentation of the financial statements. Beyond a certain point, the amounts in question may be so material as to make it impossible to render any opinion on all or a significant portion of the financial statements. In that case, the auditor issues a report that *disclaims an opinion* on all or a portion of the financial statements.[43]

An *adverse* opinion is issued when the auditor states that the financial statements are *not* fairly presented in conformity with GAAP (or some other comprehensive basis of accounting).[44] For example, a government's failure to accompany the government-wide financial statements with required fund financial statements would result in an adverse opinion, as would presentation of the basic fund financial statements without the required government-wide financial statements.[45] Likewise, a government's failure to report general infrastructure assets in the government-wide financial statements, if material, would result in an adverse opinion.[46]

The auditor's report on compliance and internal control over financial reporting

In a GAGAS audit, auditors are required to report on internal control tested as part of the financial statement audit, listing any reportable conditions that came to light as a result of internal control testing.[47] In addition, this report must distinguish reportable conditions that are also material weaknesses from those that are not.[48] The report does *not* offer the auditor's opin-

[40] AICPA, *Professional Standards*, AU 508.11-508.19.
[41] AICPA, *Professional Standards*, AU 508.10. Technically, the auditor also may issue an unqualified opinion in accordance with an "other comprehensive basis of accounting" instead of GAAP. In that case, the auditor's opinion must explain that this basis of accounting was not in conformity with GAAP.
[42] AICPA, *Professional Standards*, AU 508.10.
[43] AICPA, *Professional Standards*, AU 508.10.
[44] AICPA, *Professional Standards*, AU 508.10.
[45] AICPA, *State and Local Governments*, Section 14.10.
[46] AICPA, *State and Local Governments*, Section 14.24.
[47] *Government Auditing Standards*, Section 5.12. An auditor is precluded from making the statement that no reportable conditions were found. (AICPA, *Professional Standards*, AU 325.17.)
[48] *Government Auditing Standards*, Section 5.14.

ion on the overall design and operation of the government's internal control framework.

In a GAGAS audit, auditors are also obliged to report on compliance with applicable laws and regulations. This report does *not* offer an opinion on whether the government complied with applicable laws and regulations. Instead, the report only lists significant instances of noncompliance discovered in the course of the financial statement audit.[49]

As a practical matter, the report on compliance and internal control over financial reporting often refers readers to a separate set of findings for information on specific reportable conditions and specific instances of noncompliance revealed in the course of the financial audit.[50]

The auditor's report on compliance and internal control over compliance applicable to each major federal award program

In a Single Audit, auditors are required to report on their tests of internal control over compliance for major federal award programs, describing test scope and results.[51] In addition, the auditor is required to express an opinion (or a disclaimer of opinion) on whether the government complied with laws, regulations, and provisions of contracts or grant agreements that could have a direct and material effect on each major federal award program.[52]

The report on compliance and internal control over compliance applicable to each major federal award program often refers readers to a separate set of findings for information on specific control weaknesses and instances of noncompliance disclosed by the audit.[53]

Findings

When audits are conducted in accordance with GAGAS, reportable conditions and instances of noncompliance with applicable laws and regulations are presented in a special format known as an *audit finding*. Ideally, a finding is composed of the following four elements:[54]
- *condition*–the internal control weakness or instance of noncompliance identified by the auditor;
- *criterion/criteria*—the basis for determining that a condition is an internal control weakness or an instance of noncompliance;
- *cause*—explanation of why the weakness or instance of noncompliance occurred; and
- *effect*—the negative result attributable to the condition.

Findings often are accompanied by a specific recommendation for action and by management's response.[55]

Findings related to the GAGAS report on internal control and compliance over financial reporting must be presented separate from findings associated with internal control and compliance over major federal award programs.[56] Also, governments subject to a Single Audit are required to prepare a schedule of prior audit findings that presents the status of corrective action on audit findings from previous years.[57]

Questioned costs

When an expenditure under a federal grant does not meet all of the grantor's requirements, the recipient may have to refund the amount to the

[49] *Government Auditing Standards*, Section 5.08.
[50] *Government Auditing Standards*, Section 5.08.
[51] AICPA, *Government Auditing Standards and Circular A-133 Audits*, Section 10.15.
[52] AICPA, *Government Auditing Standards and Circular A-133 Audits*, Section 6.52.
[53] AICPA, *Government Auditing Standards and Circular A-133 Audits*, Section 10.03.
[54] *Government Auditing Standards*, Section 5.15.
[55] *Government Auditing Standards*, Section 5.26.
[56] AICPA, *Government Auditing Standards and Circular A-133 Audits*, Section 10.55-10.56.
[57] AICPA, *Government Auditing Standards and Circular A-133 Audits*, Section 2.21.

federal government. Amounts that the auditor determines may be subject to refund to the grantor are known as *questioned costs*.[58]

There are two kinds of questioned costs. A *known* questioned cost is a specific amount that has been identified as a result of audit testing. A *likely* questioned cost reflects the auditor's estimation of unknown questioned costs based on questioned costs actually identified.[59] The Single Audit Act requires that known questioned costs for major programs in excess of $10,000 be reported.[60] Likewise, known questioned costs for major programs of less than $10,000 must also be reported if the total of known *and likely* questioned costs is estimated to exceed $10,000.[61] Finally, known questioned costs of more than $10,000 connected with *nonmajor* federal award programs also must be reported.[62]

While not all findings result in questioned costs, all questioned costs are connected with findings. Questioned costs are typically reported in a *schedule of findings and questioned costs*. Also, if a questioned cost is, in fact, ultimately rejected by the grantor, it is then referred to as a *disallowed cost*.[63]

The auditor's letter to management

Auditors are required to communicate all reportable conditions.[64] In GAGAS audits, including Single Audits, this communication takes the form of the auditor's reports on internal control and compliance and the accompanying schedule of findings and questioned costs. For government audits not subject to Yellow Book standards, reportable conditions are communicated to management in a separate *management letter*.

In some circumstances, however, an auditor may choose to issue a management letter even in connection with a GAGAS audit. In that case, the management letter normally is restricted to items considered too immaterial for inclusion in the findings and recommendations accompanying the reports on internal control and compliance. If such a management letter is issued in conjunction with a Yellow Book audit, it must be mentioned in the auditor's reports on compliance and internal control.[65]

Reporting package for Single Audits

Governments subject to the Single Audit are required to submit a reporting package to the Federal Audit Clearing House that includes the government's financial statements, the government's supplementary schedule of expenditures of federal awards, the auditor's reports, a summary schedule of prior audit findings, and a corrective action plan.[66]

This package is accompanied by a special data collection form summarizing the information contained in the reporting package. The independent auditor must complete certain sections of this form. Special care must be taken to ensure that the data collection form fully complies with OMB requirements.[67]

---

[58] AICPA, *Government Auditing Standards and Circular A-133 Audits*, Sections 2.21 and 6.54.
[59] AICPA, *Government Auditing Standards and Circular A-133 Audits*, Section 6.55.
[60] This $10,000 reporting threshold applies to questioned costs for each major compliance requirement/objective of each major federal program.
[61] Auditors are *not* required to disclose the total of known and likely questioned costs.
[62] AICPA, *Government Auditing Standards and Circular A-133 Audits*, Section 6.58.
[63] AICPA, *Government Auditing Standards and Circular A-133 Audits*, Section 6.56.
[64] AICPA, *Professional Standards*, AU 325.09.
[65] *Government Auditing Standards*, Section 5.16. The auditor's letter to management described here should be distinguished from the management *representation* letter. Management addresses the representation letter to the auditor and in it accepts formal responsibility for the completeness of the data contained in the financial statements.
[66] *Government Auditing Standards and Circular A-133 Audits*, Section 2.24.
[67] *Government Auditing Standards and Circular A-133 Audits*, Section 2.25.

Obtaining a financial audit

Sometimes selection of the independent auditor is the legal responsibility of some higher level of government (for example, some municipalities are required to be audited by the office of the state auditor). More often, selection of the independent auditor is ultimately the responsibility of a government's own legislative body. In this case, the responsibility for selecting an independent auditor often is assigned to a task force or committee of the legislative body, such as the finance committee. Ideally, however, the task should be assigned to an *audit committee*. In any case, those charged with selection responsibility usually are expected to return to the full legislative body with a formal recommendation for approval.

The process for selecting the independent auditor

The quality of auditors, like that of other professionals, can vary substantially from one practitioner to another. Some audit firms perform high-quality audits of state and local governments, while others lack the specialized experience and expertise needed to successfully complete such engagements. It is important that governments carefully select their auditors to ensure that they obtain the high-quality audit they need.

One GAO study indicated a strong correlation between the quality of a government's audit procurement process and the quality of the audit it receives.[68] To avoid a substandard audit, a government's audit procurement process should exhibit four specific characteristics:

- *Openness and competition.* An open and competitive audit procurement process is likely to encourage greater participation by high-quality audit firms.
- *Preparation of a comprehensive request for proposals (RFP).* A sound RFP should obtain from proposers all information needed to evaluate their technical qualifications to perform the audit. The RFP also should provide proposers with a detailed description of the government, its specific audit needs, and the government's audit procurement process.[69]
- *Focus on auditor qualifications.* The principal factor in selecting an auditor should be the auditor's technical qualifications. While fees are an important consideration, they cannot be allowed to dominate the auditor selection process. A poor-quality audit is never economical.
- *Preparation of a written agreement.* It is essential that the government enter into a written agreement with the auditor that outlines the rights and responsibilities of both parties. Such contracts may incorporate the terms of the RFP by reference. Governments should *not* rely solely on the engagement letter furnished by their auditors.

A government's responsibility for the independent audit does not end with selecting a qualified auditor and preparing an adequate audit contract. The government also must monitor the auditor's success in meeting deadlines, as well as assess the auditor's overall performance at the end of each year's audit.

Consulting (nonaudit services)

In practice, auditors often provide other services to their clients in conjunction with financial statement audits. To avoid any potential conflict of interest, the independence standard of the Yellow Book provides specific

---

[68] GAO, *CPA Audit Quality: A Framework for Procuring Audit Services* (August 1987).
[69] A model RFP for auditing services is available on diskette from GFOA.

guidance on the types of *nonaudit services* that may be performed by independent auditors. The Yellow Book's guidance can be summarized in the form of two *overarching principles:*

- auditors should not perform management functions or make management decisions; and
- auditors should not audit their own work or provide non-audit services in situations where the amounts or services involved are significant/material to the subject matter of the audit. [70]

Any nonaudit service that violates either or both of these principles would constitute an impairment to the auditor's independence.

The following contrasting examples may be useful for gaining an understanding of the practical application of these two overarching principles:

- the auditor *may* prepare draft financial statements based on management's chart of accounts and trial balance *but may not* maintain the basic financial records or post transactions (whether coded or uncoded) to the entity's financial records or to other records that subsequently provide data to the entity's financial records;[71]
- the auditor *may* draft the notes to the financial statements, *but may not* produce the information disclosed in the notes;[72]
- the auditor *may* maintain depreciation schedules, *but may not* determine the method of depreciation, the rate of depreciation, or the estimated salvage value;[73]
- the auditor *may* compute amounts for payroll, *but may not* maintain or approve time records [Furthermore, if the auditor processed the entire payroll and payroll is considered to be material to the audit, the auditor's independence would be impaired];[74]
- the auditor *may* review evaluations or appraisals of capital assets, *but may not* perform such appraisals or evaluations;[75]
- the auditor *may* calculate pension liabilities, *but may not* select the underlying assumptions or provide the underlying data;[76] and
- the auditor *may* provide information useful to management in assessing the qualifications of job applicants based upon interviews or a review of applications, *but may not* recommend a single individual for a single position, or conduct an executive search or a recruiting program for the client.[77]

In the critical matter of the accounting system itself, auditors *may* provide *advice* on system design, system installation, and system security, provided that management does not rely primarily upon this advice for determining (1) whether to implement a new system, (2) the adequacy of the new system's design, (3) the adequacy of major design changes to an existing system, or (4) the adequacy of the system to comply with regulatory or other requirements. Auditors may *not*, however, actually design, develop, or install the audited entity's accounting system, nor may they operate or supervise the operation of the system.[78]

---

[70] *Government Auditing Standards*, Section 3.13.
[71] *Government Auditing Standards*, Section 3.18a.
[72] *Government Auditing Standards*, Section 3.18a.
[73] *Government Auditing Standards*, Section 3.18a.
[74] *Government Auditing Standards*, Section 3.18b.
[75] *Government Auditing Standards*, Section 3.18c.
[76] *Government Auditing Standards*, Section 3.18c.
[77] *Government Auditing Standards*, Section 3.18f.

Auditors remain free, of course, to provide nonaudit services of the type traditionally offered on a routine basis to audit clients (e.g., advice on internal control and implementing audit recommendations). Similarly auditors are free to answer their clients' technical questions, offer training, or provide tools and methodologies to their clients (e.g., best practice guides, benchmarking studies, internal control assessment methodologies).[79]

To limit the potential for misunderstandings, the Yellow Book requires that a number of safeguards be in place whenever auditors offer nonroutine nonaudit services. These safeguards aim at ensuring and documenting that all parties involved with nonaudit services understand both the nature and effect of those services as well as their respective responsibilities. *These safeguards also expressly preclude personnel who perform nonaudit services from performing related audit work.* Likewise, the safeguards require that auditors perform at least the same level of audit work that would have been necessary had the nonaudit services been performed by another unrelated party.[80]

The independence standard just described technically applies only to audits performed in accordance with GAGAS (which includes all Single Audits). GFOA, however, recommends that governments not subject to GAGAS contractually require of their auditors that they conform to the Yellow Book's independence standard. Also, GFOA recommends that nonaudit services be approved in advance by the audit committee and that the audit committee explore the possibility of alternative service providers.[81]

Length of the audit contract

Auditors are required to gain and document an understanding of a government's internal control framework as part of the audit planning process for the independent audit of the financial statements. Understandably, this process is especially costly in the first year of an audit engagement, because the auditors are becoming acquainted with and documenting the internal control framework for the first time. A multi-year audit contract has the advantage of allowing auditors to recover these and similar start-up costs (such as the cost of responding to the RFP) over a longer period of time, and so can lead to lower overall audit costs. Also, multi-year audit contracts can help to create needed continuity in the audit process. GFOA recommends that governmental entities enter into multi-year agreements of at least five years in duration when obtaining the services of independent auditors. Such multi-year agreements can take a variety of forms (including a series of single-year contracts), consistent with applicable legal requirements.[82]

Auditor rotation

There has been considerable debate on whether it is opportune to mandate the rotation of audit firms. GFOA takes the position that it is important to balance theoretical and practical considerations in this regard:

> Ideally, auditor independence would be enhanced by a policy requiring that the independent auditor be replaced at the end of the audit contract, as is often the case in the private sector. Unfortunately, the frequent lack of competition among audit firms fully qualified to perform public-sector audits could make a policy of mandatory

---

[78] *Government Auditing Standards*, Section 3.18e.
[79] *Government Auditing Standards*, Section 3.15.
[80] *Government Auditing Standards*, Section 3.17.
[81] GFOA recommended practice on "Audit Procurement" (2002).
[82] GFOA recommended practice on "Audit Procurement" (2002).

auditor rotation counterproductive. In such cases, it is recommended that a governmental entity actively seek the participation of all qualified firms, including the current auditors, assuming that the past performance of the current auditors has proven satisfactory. Except in cases where a multiyear agreement has taken the form of a series of single-year contracts, a contractual provision for the automatic renewal of the audit contract (e.g., an automatic second term for the auditor upon satisfactory performance) is inconsistent with this recommendation.[83]

Audit committees

The independent auditor of a state or local government's financial statements must be independent in fact and appearance. A properly constituted audit committee helps to enhance the auditor's real and perceived independence of management by providing a direct link between the auditor and the governing board.

An important advantage of an audit committee is that it helps to facilitate communication between management (and its internal auditors), the auditors, and the governing board. An audit committee is useful, too, in helping to focus and document the government's process for managing the financial statement audit.

In recent years, the importance of audit committees has become better recognized in both the public and private sectors. Indeed, GAAS require that auditors be certain that the audit committee (or its equivalent[84]) is informed of various important matters related to the financial statement audit.[85]

The audit committee should act in an advisory capacity to the governing body. Management and the governing board remain ultimately responsible for the fair presentation of the financial statements and for obtaining and monitoring the financial statement audit.

GFOA recommends that every government establish an audit committee or its equivalent. This committee should be formally established by charter, enabling resolution, or other appropriate legal means.

The members of the audit committee collectively should possess the expertise and experience in accounting, auditing, and financial reporting needed to understand and resolve issues raised by the independent audit of the financial statements. When necessary or otherwise desirable, members of the audit committee should be selected from outside the government to provide needed expertise and experience.[86] A majority of audit committee members should be selected from outside of management, and the committee should include at least one representative each from the executive and legislative branches of the government. An audit committee should be small enough to operate efficiently, yet large enough to ensure that its members possess all skills necessary to realize the committee's objectives. As a rule, no less than five and no more than seven members should comprise an audit committee. Members of the audit committee should be educated regarding both the role of the audit committee and their personal

[83] GFOA recommended practice on "Audit Procurement" (2002).

[84] In the public sector, a city council or a legislative standing committee would be good examples of an equivalent body in the absence of a formal audit committee. (AICPA, *Professional Standards*, AU 801.22, footnote 16.)

[85] AICPA, *Professional Standards*, AU 380.

[86] Note that in the private sector, all members of the audit committee are members of the board of directors.

responsibility as members, including their duty to exercise an appropriate degree of professional skepticism.

The audit committee's primary responsibility should be to oversee the financial reporting and disclosure process, including all aspects of the independent audit, from the selection of the auditor to the resolution of audit findings. The audit committee should have access to the reports of any internal auditors, as well as access to any annual internal audit work plans.[87] The audit committee should present to the governing board and management an annual written report of how the committee has discharged its duties and met its responsibilities. It is further recommended that this report be made public.[88]

PERFORMANCE AUDITING

Performance audits form the second basic category of audits encountered in the public sector. The goal of a performance audit is to establish whether government programs and activities are meeting their stated goals and objectives, and to determine if governments are performing their duties in the most economic and efficient manner possible.

Performance auditing and financial auditing share many goals and techniques, yet there are some crucial differences between the two audit types. First, the scope of the typical financial audit encompasses all transactions and activities affecting a government's financial statements. In contrast, performance audits typically are much more narrowly focused, often on a single program, department, or activity.

Second, financial statement audits enjoy the benefit of widely accepted criteria (GAAP) that define *fair presentation*. Because there are no such widely accepted standards of efficient or effective performance, an important part of the performance auditor's task is to develop persuasive criteria of efficiency and effectiveness to apply to each audit engagement.

A third difference between audit types is that the financial auditor's role is limited to rendering an opinion on the financial report, which is a *management* document. On the other hand, the entire report connected with a performance audit (except for management's response) is an *auditor* document.

The Yellow Book allows two different approaches to performance auditing. One approach is to follow the specialized standards on performance auditing provided in the Yellow Book. The other approach is to follow the AICPA's attestation standards, as expanded and modified by the Yellow Book. This latter approach is designed to minimize the need for those with a financial auditing background to learn a completely new set of standards to conduct performance audits.

INTERNAL AUDITING

The goal of the internal auditor is to help management function more efficiently and effectively. In doing so, the internal auditor typically plays a vital role in helping management to establish and maintain a comprehen-

---

[87] Such information is useful in helping the audit committee to monitor management's exercise of responsibility for the design, implementation, and maintenance of a comprehensive framework of internal control (see chapter 18).
[88] GFOA recommended practice on "Establishment of an Audit Committee" (2002).

sive framework of internal control.[89] Indeed, internal auditors actually function as an integral part of the internal control framework, serving as a secondary level of control to ensure that a government's control-related policies and procedures remain relevant and operational.

The role of the internal auditor differs substantially from that of the independent auditor of the government's financial statements. Internal auditors work directly for the entities they audit. While a significant degree of independence is required for the internal audit function to be effective, it is not the same degree of independence required of the independent auditor of the financial statements. Also, the primary focus of the independent auditor of the financial statements is on the fair presentation of a particular set of financial statements. The focus of internal auditors often extends to much broader managerial concerns, such as performance auditing.

The internal auditor may help the work of the independent auditor of the financial statements in two ways. First, the independent auditor of the financial statements may be able to rely on the internal auditor's work to limit the amount of study and testing that would otherwise be necessary to form an opinion on the fair presentation of the financial statements. Second, the internal auditor may, under the supervision of the independent auditor of the financial statements, help to perform portions of the financial statement audit. For example, internal auditors may assist in the annual physical inventory of supplies or in preparing confirmation requests.

Several factors can help to maximize the benefits of collaboration between internal and external auditors. First, external auditors may be in a better position to rely on the work of their internal audit colleagues if they are informed of the internal auditor's annual work plan and kept abreast of progress made to date on that plan. Second, if the independent auditor of the financial statements plans to use the services of internal auditors in conducting portions of the financial statement audit, there should be a clear, prior understanding concerning the amount of staff time and the level of internal audit staff to be devoted to that effort, as well as the types of tasks that are appropriate. This understanding should be incorporated into the audit contract.

The GFOA urges every government to consider the feasibility of establishing a formal internal audit function. As a rule, a formal internal audit function is particularly valuable for activities involving a high degree of risk (for instance, complex accounting systems, contracts with outside parties, a rapidly changing environment). The internal audit function should be established formally by charter, enabling resolution, or other appropriate legal means.

It is recommended that internal auditors of state and local governments conduct their work in accordance with Yellow Book professional standards relevant to internal auditing. These standards direct, for example, that internal auditors "report the results of their audits and be accountable to the head or deputy head of the government entity and should be organizationally located outside the staff or line management function of the unit under audit."[90]

---

[89] The internal control framework is the subject of chapter 18.

[90] Internal auditors in the public sector also may wish to consider *Standards for the Professional Practice of Internal Auditing*, published by the Institute of Internal Auditors (commonly known as the "Red Book"). Note that the Red Book standards are not always consistent with those found in the Yellow Book.

At a minimum, the head of the internal audit function should possess a college degree and appropriate relevant experience. It is highly desirable that the head of the internal audit function hold some appropriate professional certification, perhaps as a certified internal auditor, certified public accountant, or certified information systems auditor. All reports of internal auditors, as well as the annual internal audit work plan, should be made available to the government's audit committee or its equivalent.[91]

SUMMARY

In general, public-sector audits are classified as financial audits or performance audits. Financial audits are designed to assure users of financial reports that those reports are reliable. Performance audits are conducted to establish whether government programs and activities are meeting their stated goals and objectives, and to determine if governments are performing their duties in the most economic and efficient manner possible.

GAAS provide the fundamental standards for financial audits in the public and private sectors. In the public sector, there is also a second set of standards known as GAGAS, which expressly adopt and build upon the fieldwork and reporting standards of GAAS. All audits performed in conformity with *federal* audit requirements must be conducted in accordance with GAGAS.

The goal of the financial auditor is to obtain *reasonable*—not absolute—assurance that the financial statements are fairly presented. The concept of reasonable assurance means that auditors attempt to ensure that the financial statements are free from *material* misstatement. In making a judgment regarding the materiality of a potential misstatement, an auditor must consider its *quantitative* and *qualitative* aspects.

In the public sector, the independent auditor's report focuses on various opinion units, rather than on the basic financial statements taken as a whole. In rendering an opinion on the financial information contained in a CAFR, the auditor can offer either an "in-relation-to opinion" on combining and individual fund statements, or treat each individual fund as an opinion unit in its own right. This latter approach, while recommended, typically requires more audit work than would otherwise be necessary for a simple audit of the basic financial statements. By definition, RSI need not be audited, although it still is subject to certain limited procedures on the part of the independent auditor. The introductory and statistical sections of the CAFR are unaudited and are *not* subject to even the limited procedures required in the case of RSI.

As auditors perform extensive tests of a government's internal control, they may become aware of significant deficiencies. Such deficiencies are called *reportable conditions* because GAAS require that auditors make management aware of them.

Under the Single Audit Act, one audit is conducted to meet the needs of *all* federal grantor agencies. The provisions of the Single Audit Act apply to all governments that expend $500,000 or more per fiscal year in federal awards. Like all federal audits, Single Audits must be performed in accor-

---

[91] GFOA recommended practice on "Establishment of an Internal Audit Function" (1997).

dance with GAGAS. In addition, Single Audits are subject to the requirements of OMB Circular A-133.

In the public sector, there are three types of commonly issued auditor's reports: 1) the auditor's report on the fair presentation of the financial statements; 2) the auditor's report on compliance and internal control over financial reporting based on an audit of the financial statements; and 3) the auditor's report on compliance and internal controls over compliance applicable to each major federal award program. The auditor prepares only the first of these reports in an ordinary financial statement audit conducted in accordance with GAAS. The auditor is responsible for the first two reports in a GAGAS engagement, and all three reports in a Single Audit engagement.

When audits are conducted in accordance with GAGAS, reportable conditions and instances of noncompliance with applicable laws and regulations are presented in a special format known as an *audit finding*. Findings often are accompanied by a specific recommendation for action and by management's response.

Sometimes the selection of the independent auditor is the legal responsibility of some higher level of government (for instance, some municipalities are required to be audited by the office of the state auditor). More often, selection of the independent auditor is ultimately the responsibility of a government's own legislative body.

Four specific qualities should characterize a government's audit procurement process: 1) openness and competition, 2) preparation of a comprehensive RFP, 3) focus on auditor qualifications, and 4) preparation of a written agreement.

GFOA recommends that governmental entities enter into multi-year agreements of at least five years duration when obtaining the services of independent auditors. GFOA believes that practical considerations can make the mandatory rotation of audit firms undesirable.

A properly constituted audit committee helps to enhance the financial statement auditor's real and perceived independence by providing a direct link between the auditor and the governing board. GFOA recommends that every government establish an audit committee or its equivalent.

Performance auditing and financial auditing share many goals and techniques, yet there are some crucial differences between the two audit types. The Yellow Book sets the authoritative standards for performance auditing.

The goal of the internal auditor is to help management function more efficiently and effectively. In doing so, the internal auditor typically plays a vital role in helping management to establish and maintain a comprehensive framework of internal control. While a significant degree of independence is required for the internal audit function to be effective, it is not the same degree of independence required of the independent auditor of the financial statements. GFOA urges every government to consider the feasibility of establishing a formal internal audit function.

A

Illustrative Journal Entries

RELATIONSHIP OF APPENDICES

The first four appendices illustrate the preparation of a comprehensive annual financial report (CAFR) prepared in conformity with Governmental Accounting Standards Board Statement No. 34, *Basic Financial Statements—and Management's Discussion and Analysis—for State and Local Governments* and the requirements of the Government Finance Officers Association's Certificate of Achievement for Excellence in Financial Reporting Program.

- **Illustrative Journal Entries (appendix A).** This appendix illustrates the different types of journal entries used to collect data in the government's fund-based accounting system.
- **Illustrative Trial Balances (appendix B).** This appendix provides 1) a trial balance as of the beginning of the current fiscal year, 2) a preclosing trial balance, and 3) a trial balance as of the end of the current fiscal year for each of the funds for which illustrative journal entries are provided in appendix A.
- **Illustrative Conversion Worksheet (appendix C).** This appendix illustrates how the data reported in governmental funds and internal service funds are converted and consolidated for presentation as *governmental activities* in the government-wide financial statements.
- **Illustrative CAFR (appendix D).** This appendix offers a complete illustrative CAFR. The numbers in this illustrative CAFR are supported by the journal entries, trial balances, and conversion worksheet provided in appendices A, B, and C.

ILLUSTRATIVE JOURNAL ENTRIES

This appendix provides sample journal entries to support the fund financial statements presented in the illustrative CAFR in appendix D. With one exception, a complete set of journal entries is furnished to illustrate the appropriate accounting and financial reporting for each fund type. No sample journal entries have been provided for the special revenue fund type because all of the transactions reported in those funds essentially duplicate transactions already illustrated in connection with the general fund. In cases where there is more than one individual fund of a given fund type, sample journal entries are provided for only one of the individual funds. The sample journal entries are presented by fund type in the following order:

- general fund
- debt service funds
- capital projects funds
- permanent funds
- enterprise funds
- internal service funds
- pension (and other employee benefit) trust funds

Journal entries have been numbered sequentially throughout this appendix for journal entries of all fund types. Also, amounts throughout are expressed in thousands. ALL CAPS are used to indicate budgetary accounts used to effect budgetary integration.

GENERAL FUND

Reversal of the prior fiscal year's designation for encumbrances

As a matter of law, all of the government's appropriations lapse at the end of the fiscal year including those related to encumbrances; encumbered amounts must be reappropriated as part of the following year's budget if they are to remain in force. Therefore, at the end of the prior fiscal year the government designated a portion of unreserved fund balance to reflect its intent to reappropriate encumbered items as part of the current year's budget. (If appropriations for encumbered items had *not* legally lapsed at the end of the prior fiscal year, fund balance would have been reserved rather than designated). The need to designate (or reserve) a portion of fund balance for encumbrances disappears with the start of each new fiscal year, at which time the entry made for that purpose at the close of the prior fiscal year needs to be reversed, as follows:

		DR	CR
1.	Fund balance—unreserved, designated for encumbrances	$ 211	
	Fund balance—unreserved, undesignated		$ 211
	(To reverse prior-year encumbrance designations)		

Integration of the original appropriated budget

The following journal entry illustrates the integration of the $37,128 original annual appropriated budget for the current fiscal year into the government's accounts.

		DR	CR
2.	ESTIMATED REVENUES—PROPERTY TAXES	$ 14,007	
	ESTIMATED REVENUES—SALES TAXES	5,900	
	ESTIMATED REVENUES—FRANCHISE TAXES	4,312	
	ESTIMATED REVENUES—LICENSES AND PERMITS	1,827	
	ESTIMATED REVENUES—INTERGOVERNMENTAL	5,661	
	ESTIMATED REVENUES—CHARGES FOR SERVICES	2,101	
	ESTIMATED REVENUES—FINES	810	
	ESTIMATED REVENUES—INVESTMENT EARNINGS	555	
	ESTIMATED REVENUES—MISCELLANEOUS	345	
	ESTIMATED OTHER FINANCING SOURCES—TRANSFERS IN	1,576	
	ESTIMATED OTHER FINANCING SOURCES—CAPITAL LEASES	34	
	APPROPRIATIONS—GENERAL GOVERNMENT—COUNCIL		$ 110
	APPROPRIATIONS—GENERAL GOVERNMENT—COMMISSIONS		86
	APPROPRIATIONS—GENERAL GOVERNMENT—MANAGER		490
	APPROPRIATIONS—GENERAL GOVERNMENT—ATTORNEY		380
	APPROPRIATIONS—GENERAL GOVERNMENT—CLERK		275
	APPROPRIATIONS—GENERAL GOVERNMENT—PERSONNEL		356
	APPROPRIATIONS—GENERAL GOVERNMENT—FINANCE AND ADMINISTRATION		904
	APPROPRIATIONS—GENERAL GOVERNMENT—OTHER—UNCLASSIFIED		2,389
	APPROPRIATIONS—PUBLIC SAFETY—POLICE		6,488
	APPROPRIATIONS—PUBLIC SAFETY—FIRE		6,025
	APPROPRIATIONS—PUBLIC SAFETY—INSPECTION		1,092

	DR	CR
APPROPRIATIONS—HIGHWAYS AND STREETS— MAINTENANCE		$ 3,012
APPROPRIATIONS—HIGHWAYS AND STREETS— ENGINEERING		814
APPROPRIATIONS—SANITATION		3,848
APPROPRIATIONS—CULTURE AND RECREATION		5,950
APPROPRIATIONS—OTHER FINANCING USES— TRANSFERS OUT		4,760
BUDGETARY FUND BALANCE		149
(To record the annual appropriated budget)		

Property tax levy

The government levies $14,097 of property taxes during the current fiscal year to provide resources for budgetary expenditures. Payment of the taxes is due before the end of the current fiscal year. Prior experience indicates that approximately 0.1 percent of the property tax levy should be classified as uncollectible. As a practical matter, the entire collectible amount is intially recorded in the accounting system as *revenues*. At the end of the current fiscal year, the unavailable portion of these revenues will be reclassified as *deferred revenue* for financial reporting purposes (journal entry 59). Note that total revenues are reported net of uncollectible amounts.

	DR	CR
3. Taxes receivable—property taxes	$ 14,097	
Allowance for uncollectible taxes—property taxes		$ 14
Revenues—property taxes		14,083
(To record property tax levy)		

Payments in lieu of taxes

In addition to property taxes levied on property owners, the government also assesses the water and sewer fund a payment in lieu of property taxes equivalent to the value of the services that fund receives from the government as a property owner in its own right. The current fiscal year's assessment to the water and sewer fund is $345. The water and sewer fund, in turn, makes a payment of $473 in the current fiscal year, which represents payment in full for the balance due for services provided in the previous fiscal year (i.e., $193) and partial payment of the current fiscal year's assessment (i.e., $280).

	DR	CR
4. Due from other funds—water and sewer fund	$ 345	
Revenues—miscellaneous—payments in lieu of taxes		$ 345
(To record assessments for payments in lieu of taxes from the water and sewer fund)		

	DR	CR
5. Cash	$ 473	
Due from other funds—water and sewer fund		$ 473
(To record receipt of payments in lieu of taxes)		

A state mental health facility is located in the government's taxing jurisdiction. State statutes prohibit the assessment of local property taxes on state institutions. The state, however, does remit to the government annually a payment in lieu of taxes equivalent to the cost of the services that the government provides to the facility. The government bills the state $20 for payments in lieu of taxes in the current fiscal year and is promptly paid.

		DR	CR
6.	Intergovernmental receivable—state	$ 20	
	Revenues—miscellaneous—payments in lieu of taxes		$ 20
	(To record assessments for payments in lieu of taxes from the state for the mental health facility)		

		DR	CR
7.	Cash	$ 20	
	Intergovernmental receivable—state		$ 20
	(To record receipt of payment in lieu of taxes from the state)		

Donation

The government's recreation program received an anonymous restricted donation of $145 to be used to partially fund a new recreational program for the elderly.

		DR	CR
8.	Cash	$ 145	
	Revenues—miscellaneous—contributions		$ 145
	(To record receipt of restricted cash contribution)		

Encumbrances

The government uses an encumbrance accounting system and during the year records $9,613 of encumbrances on purchase orders and contracts in the current fiscal year. This amount includes the $211 in encumbrances carried forward from the prior fiscal year (journal entry 1).

		DR	CR
9.	ENCUMBRANCES—GENERAL GOVERNMENT—COUNCIL	$ 18	
	ENCUMBRANCES—GENERAL GOVERNMENT—COMMISSIONS	30	
	ENCUMBRANCES—GENERAL GOVERNMENT—MANAGER	191	
	ENCUMBRANCES—GENERAL GOVERNMENT—ATTORNEY	219	
	ENCUMBRANCES—GENERAL GOVERNMENT—CLERK	71	
	ENCUMBRANCES—GENERAL GOVERNMENT—PERSONNEL	139	
	ENCUMBRANCES—GENERAL GOVERNMENT—FINANCE AND ADMINISTRATION	237	
	ENCUMBRANCES—GENERAL GOVERNMENT—OTHER—UNCLASSIFIED	1,222	
	ENCUMBRANCES—PUBLIC SAFETY—POLICE	1,789	
	ENCUMBRANCES—PUBLIC SAFETY—FIRE	1,054	
	ENCUMBRANCES—PUBLIC SAFETY—INSPECTION	233	
	ENCUMBRANCES—HIGHWAYS AND STREETS—MAINTENANCE	1,272	
	ENCUMBRANCES—HIGHWAYS AND STREETS—ENGINEERING	207	
	ENCUMBRANCES—SANITATION	1,590	
	ENCUMBRANCES—CULTURE AND RECREATION	1,341	
	BUDGETARY FUND BALANCE—RESERVED FOR ENCUMBRANCES		$ 9,613
	(To record encumbrances for purchase orders and contracts)		

Property tax collections

The government collects $14,000 of the current fiscal year's property tax levy during the year.

		DR	CR
10.	Cash	$ 14,000	
	Taxes receivable—property taxes		$ 14,000
	(To record collection of current year's property taxes)		

The government also collects $70 of delinquent property taxes and related interest, penalties, and liens receivable. The entire amount of delinquent taxes, interest, penalties, and tax liens remitted had been accrued and deferred previously.

		DR	CR
11.	Cash	$ 70	
	Taxes receivable—property taxes		$ 65
	Interest and penalties receivable—property taxes		3
	Tax liens receivable—property taxes		2
	(To record collection of property-tax related receivables)		

		DR	CR
12.	Deferred revenue—taxes receivable—property taxes	$ 65	
	Deferred revenue—interest and penalties receivable— property taxes	3	
	Deferred revenue—tax liens receivable—property taxes	2	
	Revenues—property taxes		$ 70
	(To recognize revenue from the collection of property taxes, interest, penalties and liens)		

Interest and penalties – property taxes

Interest and penalty charges begin immediately after property taxes are deemed to be delinquent. The penalty and interest rates are established by state statute. The amounts are treated as deferred revenue because they are not considered to be available to liquidate liabilities of the current period. The total amount of deferred revenue for interest and penalties is recorded net of uncollectible amounts.

		DR	CR
13.	Interest and penalties receivable—property taxes	$ 14	
	Allowance for uncollectible interest and penalties— property taxes		$ 2
	Deferred revenue—interest and penalties receivable— property taxes		12
	(To record interest and penalties on delinquent property taxes)		

When delinquent property taxes are not paid within a specified period as established by statute, a lien attaches to the property. The property is then subject to sale for the delinquent taxes. During the year, the government places a lien on property for $10 of uncollected taxes, interest, and penalties. The attachment of the lien requires a reclassification of related receivables, uncollectibles, and deferred revenues.

		DR	CR
14.	Tax liens receivable—property taxes	$ 10	
	Taxes receivable—property taxes		$ 8
	Interest and penalties receivable—property taxes		2
	(To record property tax liens)		

		DR	CR
15.	Deferred revenue—taxes receivable—property taxes	$ 6	
	Deferred revenue—interest and penalties receivable— property taxes	2	
	Deferred revenue—tax liens receivable—property taxes		$ 8
	(To reclassify deferred revenues related to property tax liens)		

		DR	CR
16.	Allowance for uncollectible taxes—property taxes	$ 2	
	Allowance for uncollectible tax liens—property taxes		$ 2
	(To reclassify allowance accounts related to property tax liens)		

User charges

The government provides various services that are financed in part by user charges (e.g., garbage collection, recreation programs). Total billings for the current fiscal year amounted to $2,300, of which $2,292 is collected during the year. In addition, $25 of the prior fiscal year's outstanding balance is collected.

		DR	CR
17.	Accounts receivable	$ 2,276	
	Due from other funds—fleet management fund	8	
	Due from other funds—management information systems fund	16	
	Revenues—charges for services		$ 2,300
	(To record user-charge billings)		

		DR	CR
18.	Cash	$ 2,317	
	Accounts receivable		$ 2,263
	Due from other funds—management information systems fund		16
	Due from other funds—transportation fund		38
	(To record collection of user charges)		

Sales taxes

The government levies a 1 percent sales tax that is collected by merchants and forwarded to the state. The state distributes the taxes to the government approximately one month after collection as part of its normal processing cycle. The government receives $6,612 in payments from the state during the current fiscal year, including $800 from sales of the prior fiscal year that were accrued by the government as revenue at that time.

		DR	CR
19.	Cash	$ 800	
	Taxes receivable—sales taxes		$ 800
	(To record collection of December 2014 sales tax receipts)		

		DR	CR
20.	Cash	$ 5,812	
	Revenues—sales taxes		$ 5,812
	(To record the receipt of the current year's sales taxes)		

Transfer to special revenue fund

The government transfers $63 from the general fund to the Community Development Block Grant (CDBG) Revitalization Project special revenue fund for the government's share of costs toward the federally subsidized project.

		DR	CR
21.	Other financing uses—transfers out— CDBG Revitalization Project Fund	$ 63	
	Cash		$ 63
	(To record transfer to special revenue fund)		

Sale of capital assets

During the current fiscal year, the government sells for $5 capital assets that originally had cost $42. As capital assets, the sold items were not reported in the general fund. Had the amounts been deemed immaterial, the government may have elected to report the proceeds of the sale as *other revenues*.

		DR	CR
22.	Cash	$ 5	
	Other financing sources—sales of general capital assets		$ 5
	(To record proceeds from the sale of general capital assets)		

Reimbursement

During the current fiscal year, the general fund receives a $3 reimbursement for current-year expenditures properly applicable to the fleet management internal service fund.

		DR	CR
23.	Cash	$ 3	
	Expenditures—general government—other— Unclassified		$ 3
	(To record reimbursement from the fleet management fund)		

Interest payments received

Thanks to its revenue collection cycle, the government is able to maintain a significant investment portfolio during much of the fiscal year. In the current fiscal year, the government receives interest payments of $531. Of this amount, $48 represents the payment of interest accrued during the prior fiscal year, but not recognized as revenue at that time because it was not yet considered to be available.

		DR	CR
24.	Cash	$ 531	
	Interest receivable—investments		$ 48
	Revenues—investment earnings		483
	(To record interest receipts for the year)		

		DR	CR
25.	Deferred revenue—interest receivable—investments	$ 48	
	Revenues—investment earnings		$ 48
	(To recognize interest revenue that had been deferred in the prior year)		

Accrued interest receivable

As of the end of the current fiscal year, the government has earned $92 in interest on its investments. This entire amount is considered to be available and therefore is recognized as revenue of the current fiscal year.

		DR	CR
26.	Interest receivable—investments	$ 92	
	Revenues—investment earnings		$ 92
	(To record interest accrued at year end)		

Transfer from enterpise fund

The general fund receives a transfer from the government's electric enterprise fund.

		DR	CR
27.	Cash	$ 1,576	
	Other financing sources—transfers in—electric fund		$ 1,576
	(To record receipt of transfer from the electric fund)		

Receipts from grants and shared revenues

During the current fiscal year, the general fund receives $5,928 in receipts from grants and shared revenues. Of this amount, $3,323 is received in connection with the county's shared-revenue program, $127 of which was recognized as revenue in the prior fiscal year.

		DR	CR
28.	Cash	$ 3,323	
	Intergovernmental receivable—county		$ 127
	Revenues—intergovernmental		3,196
	(To record county revenue sharing receipts)		

Receipts also include $150 from the federal government as reimbursement for expenditures incurred during the prior fiscal year and recognized as revenue at that time.

		DR	CR
29.	Cash	$ 150	
	Intergovernmental receivable—federal		$ 150
	(To record receipt of federal grant monies related to eligible grant expenditures incurred in the prior year)		

The balance of the receipts represents a drawdown of $2,455 associated with various federal grants. These drawdowns are made as soon as the government either has established an encumbrance or paid salaries and benefits related to one of its federal grants. Of this amount, $2,359 is recognized as revenue in connection with reimbursement grants that are not subject to matching requirements.

		DR	CR
30.	Cash	$ 2,455	
	Unearned revenue—federal government		$ 2,455
	(To recognize cash received from federal government grant drawdowns)		

		DR	CR
31.	Unearned revenue—federal government	$ 2,359	
	Revenues—intergovernmental		$ 2,359
	(To recognize revenue based on eligible federal grant-related expenditures)		

Miscellaneous collections

Revenues not previously susceptible to accrual are received from several sources. Amounts collected during the current fiscal year total $7,142.

		DR	CR
32.	Cash	$ 7,142	
	Revenues—franchise taxes		$ 4,293
	Revenues—licenses and permits		2,041
	Revenues—fines		808
	(To record receipt of franchise taxes, license and permit fees, and fines)		

The government receives a delayed shared-revenue payment of $215 from the county soon after the close of the current fiscal year. The amount was not recognized previously as a receivable.

		DR	CR
33.	Intergovernmental receivable—county	$ 215	
	Revenues—intergovernmental		$ 215
	(To record delayed shared-revenue payment)		

Sales tax accrual

The government obtains reports from the state that provide information on sales tax remittances subsequent to the close of the current fiscal year that relate to sales of the current fiscal year. These amounts are considered to be available.

		DR	CR
34.	Taxes receivable—sales tax	$ 830	
	Revenues—sales taxes		$ 830
	(To accrue current year sales taxes collected by the state)		

Liquidation of encumbrances

The government receives $7,675 in billings during the current fiscal year for expenditures related to $8,017 of encumbrances. The full amount of the encumbrances must be removed from the accounts, even though the related expenditures were less than anticipated at the time the encumbrances were established.

		DR	CR
35.	BUDGETARY FUND BALANCE—RESERVED FOR ENCUMBRANCES	$ 8,017	
	ENCUMBRANCES—GENERAL GOVERNMENT—COUNCIL		$ 16
	ENCUMBRANCES—GENERAL GOVERNMENT—COMMISSIONS		27
	ENCUMBRANCES—GENERAL GOVERNMENT—MANAGER		173
	ENCUMBRANCES—GENERAL GOVERNMENT—ATTORNEY		216
	ENCUMBRANCES—GENERAL GOVERNMENT—CLERK		57
	ENCUMBRANCES—GENERAL GOVERNMENT—PERSONNEL		130
	ENCUMBRANCES—GENERAL GOVERNMENT—FINANCE AND ADMINISTRATION		205
	ENCUMBRANCES—GENERAL GOVERNMENT—OTHER—UNCLASSIFIED		1,092
	ENCUMBRANCES—PUBLIC SAFETY—POLICE		1,264
	ENCUMBRANCES—PUBLIC SAFETY—FIRE		763
	ENCUMBRANCES—PUBLIC SAFETY—INSPECTION		199
	ENCUMBRANCES—HIGHWAYS AND STREETS—MAINTENANCE		1,073
	ENCUMBRANCES—HIGHWAYS AND STREETS—ENGINEERING		157
	ENCUMBRANCES—SANITATION		1,558
	ENCUMBRANCES—CULTURE AND RECREATION		1,087
	(To cancel encumbrances related to billings for goods and services received)		

	DR	CR
36. Expenditures—general government—council	$ 12	
Expenditures—general government—commissions	22	
Expenditures—general government—manager	169	
Expenditures—general government—attorney	214	
Expenditures—general government—clerk	47	
Expenditures—general government—personnel	111	
Expenditures—general government—finance and administration	200	
Expenditures—general government—other—unclassified	956	
Expenditures—public safety—police	1,253	
Expenditures—public safety—fire	750	
Expenditures—public safety—inspection	193	
Expenditures—highways and streets—maintenance	1,071	
Expenditures—highways and streets—engineering	150	
Expenditures—sanitation	1,490	
Expenditures—culture and recreation	1,037	
Accounts payable		$ 4,824
Contracts payable		1,363
Due to other funds—water and sewer fund		175
Due to other funds—fleet management fund		872
Due to other funds—management information systems fund		441
(To record billings for goods and services received except for materials and supplies inventories)		

During the current fiscal year, the government also purchases $863 of inventories related to $950 of encumbrances.

	DR	CR
37. BUDGETARY FUND BALANCE—RESERVED FOR ENCUMBRANCES	$ 950	
ENCUMBRANCES—GENERAL GOVERNMENT—COUNCIL		$ 2
ENCUMBRANCES—GENERAL GOVERNMENT—COMMISSIONS		3
ENCUMBRANCES—GENERAL GOVERNMENT—MANAGER		8
ENCUMBRANCES—GENERAL GOVERNMENT—ATTORNEY		3
ENCUMBRANCES—GENERAL GOVERNMENT—CLERK		14
ENCUMBRANCES—GENERAL GOVERNMENT—PERSONNEL		9
ENCUMBRANCES—GENERAL GOVERNMENT—FINANCE AND ADMINISTRATION		32
ENCUMBRANCES—GENERAL GOVERNMENT—OTHER—UNCLASSIFIED		35
ENCUMBRANCES—PUBLIC SAFETY—POLICE		144
ENCUMBRANCES—PUBLIC SAFETY—FIRE		191
ENCUMBRANCES—PUBLIC SAFETY—INSPECTION		14
ENCUMBRANCES—HIGHWAYS AND STREETS—MAINTENANCE		159
ENCUMBRANCES—HIGHWAYS AND STREETS—ENGINEERING		50
ENCUMBRANCES—SANITATION		32
ENCUMBRANCES—CULTURE AND RECREATION		254
(To cancel encumbrances related to materials and supplies inventories received)		

		DR	CR
38.	Inventories	$ 863	
	Accounts payable		$ 863
	(To record billings for materials and supplies inventories received)		

Consumption of inventories

The government accounts for its materials and supplies inventories on a consumption basis. The government determines that it has consumed $861 in inventories during the current fiscal year.

		DR	CR
39.	Expenditures—general government—council	$ 2	
	Expenditures—general government—commissions	3	
	Expenditures—general government—manager	8	
	Expenditures—general government—attorney	3	
	Expenditures—general government—clerk	14	
	Expenditures—general government—personnel	7	
	Expenditures—general government—finance and administration	25	
	Expenditures—general government—other—unclassified	30	
	Expenditures—public safety—police	134	
	Expenditures—public safety—fire	151	
	Expenditures—public safety—inspection	14	
	Expenditures—highways and streets—maintenance	145	
	Expenditures—highways and streets—engineering	47	
	Expenditures—sanitation	30	
	Expenditures—culture and recreation	248	
	Inventories		$ 861
	(To record consumption of materials and supplies inventories during the year)		

Accrual of accounts payable

In addition to encumbered billings, the government also records accounts payable totaling $22,369 for unencumbered transactions (i.e., primary payroll).

		DR	CR
40.	Expenditures—general government—council	$ 78	
	Expenditures—general government—commissions	39	
	Expenditures—general government—manager	328	
	Expenditures—general government—attorney	170	
	Expenditures—general government—clerk	189	
	Expenditures—general government—personnel	186	
	Expenditures—general government—finance and administration	655	
	Expenditures—general government—other—unclassified	779	
	Expenditures—public safety—police	4,827	
	Expenditures—public safety—fire	5,130	
	Expenditures—public safety—inspection	846	
	Expenditures—highways and streets—maintenance	1,723	
	Expenditures—highways and streets—engineering	599	
	Expenditures—sanitation	2,206	
	Expenditures—culture and recreation	4,614	
	Accounts payable		$ 18,702
	Due to other funds—public safety pension system fund		1,780
	Intergovernmental payable—state		1,887
	(To record salaries and other unencumbered benefit liabilities)		

Liquidation of liabilities

Outstanding liabilities of $30,932 are paid during the current fiscal year.

		DR	CR

41. Accounts payable — $ 24,352
Contracts payable — 1,447
Due to other funds—water and sewer fund — 159
Due to other funds—fleet management fund — 825
Due to other funds—management information systems fund — 482
Due to other funds—public safety pension system fund — 1,780
Intergovernmental payable—state — 1,887
    Cash — $ 30,932
(To record payment of liabilities incurred during the year)

Transfers to capital projects fund

During the year, the government agrees to participate in a special assessment street construction project in newly developed areas at an estimated cost of $1,200 before change orders. The government makes $1,025 in payments to the capital projects fund during the current fiscal year in partial fulfillment of this commitment.

	DR	CR

42. Other financing uses—transfers out—housing development street construction fund — $ 1,200
    Due to other funds—housing development street construction fund — $ 1,200
(To record the government's portion of special assessment project)

43. Due to other funds—housing development street construction fund — $ 1,025
    Cash — $ 1,025
(To record partial payment of project construction costs)

As part of the special assessment construction project agreement, the government also committed to provide additional resources in the event of a shortfall due to a bond discount. The special assessment bonds are sold at a $10 discount; therefore, the government is obligated to transfer an amount equal to the discount to the capital projects fund. Furthermore, the government agreed to pay the special assessment bond issuance costs of $150 from general fund resources. The assumption of this liability also requires a $150 transfer of expenditure authority.

44. Other financing uses—transfers out—housing development street construction fund — $ 10
    Due to other funds—housing development street construction fund — $ 10
(To record government commitment to provide additional resources)

45. APPROPRIATIONS—GENERAL GOVERNMENT—OTHER—UNCLASSIFIED — $ 150
    APPROPRIATIONS—DEBT SERVICE—OTHER—BOND ISSUANCE COSTS — $ 150
(To record budget transfer)

	DR	CR
46. Expenditures—debt service—other—bond issuance costs	$ 150	
Due to other funds—housing development street construction fund		$ 150
(To record amount due to housing development street construction fund for reimbursement of bond issuance costs)		

Transfer to debt service fund

During the current fiscal year, the general fund transfers $3,327 to the debt service fund for the retirement of general obligation debt.

	DR	CR
47. Other financing uses—transfers out—debt service fund	$ 3,327	
Cash		$ 3,327
(To record transfers to debt service fund for the retirement of debt)		

Capital lease

During the year, the government entered into a capital lease agreement to acquire police communications equipment worth $140. The lease agreement calls for an initial down payment of $15. Originally, $296 had been encumbered for the purchase of this equipment. An additional $30 had been encumbered for the anticipated down payment. Regular scheduled lease payments begin only the subsequent fiscal year. It is the government's practice to classify down payments on capital leases as debt service expenditures rather than as current expenditures of the benefitting function(s).

	DR	CR
48. BUDGETARY FUND BALANCE—RESERVED FOR ENCUMBRANCES	$ 326	
ENCUMBRANCES—PUBLIC SAFETY—POLICE		$ 326
(To cancel encumbrances related to capital lease acquisition)		

	DR	CR
49. Expenditures—public safety—police	$ 140	
Other financing sources—capital leases		$ 140
(To record capital lease acquisition)		

	DR	CR
50. Expenditures—debt service—principal	$ 15	
Cash		$ 15
(To record capital lease down payment)		

Asset forfeitures

The government's police department is active in undercover drug operations and routinely seizes drug-related cash. As permitted by federal law, the government retains 75 percent of all seized funds for use in drug-related law enforcement (as required by law). During the current fiscal year, the government seized $100 of illegal drug funds, 75 percent of which were retained by the government.

	DR	CR
51. Cash	$ 75	
Revenues—miscellaneous—drug forfeitures		$ 75
(To record receipt of seized funds)		

Reimbursement from component unit

The general fund bills the School District, a discretely presented component unit, $12 for a utility bill of the School District initially paid as a matter of convenience by the government's finance and administration department.

	DR	CR
52. Due from component unit—School District	$ 12	
Expenditures—general government—finance and administration		$ 12
(To record government's billing of component unit for a reimbursement)		

Subsidy to component unit

The general fund provides $25 to support the operations of the School District, a discretely presented component unit.

	DR	CR
53. Expenditures—general government—other—unclassified	$ 25	
Cash		$ 25
(To record general support provided to component unit)		

Purchase of investments

The government purchases an additional $865 of investments during the current fiscal year.

	DR	CR
54. Investments	$ 865	
Cash		$ 865
(To record purchase of additional investments)		

Interfund loan

In addition to an original advance of $50 that has not yet been repaid, the general fund advances $20 to the management information systems fund and $40 to the fleet management fund.

	DR	CR
55. Advance to other funds—management information systems fund	$ 20	
Advance to other funds—fleet management fund	40	
Cash		$ 60
(To record advances to the management information systems and fleet management funds)		

Reservation of fund balance for advances

An additional portion of fund balance is reserved to indicate that advances do not represent available financial resources. The additional amount needed is calculated as follows:

Advances outstanding at beginning of year	$ 50
Additional advances (journal entry 55)	60
Subtotal of advances	$ 110
Less: amounts reclassified as current (journal entry 58)	(32)
Total amount of advances outstanding at end of year	$ 78
Less: reserved fund balance at beginning of year	(50)
Additional amount of reserved fund balance needed	$ 28

	DR	CR
56. Fund balance—unreserved, undesignated	$ 28	
Fund balance—reserved for advances		$ 28
(To reclassify fund balance for outstanding advances)		

Transfer to internal service fund

The general fund also provides the fleet management internal service fund with a working capital contribution of $45 in its start-up period.

	DR	CR
57. Other financing uses—transfers out—fleet management fund	$ 45	
Cash		$ 45
(To record start-up transfer to the fleet management fund)		

Reclassification of current portion of advances

At year end, the government classifies the portion of advances expected to be repaid in the following year. The amount is calculated based on a repayment schedule.

	DR	CR
58. Due from other funds—management information systems fund	$ 24	
Due from other funds—fleet management fund	8	
Advance to other funds—management information systems fund		$ 24
Advance to other funds—fleet management fund		8
(To reclassify current portions of long-term loans to other funds)		

Deferral of unavailable property tax revenues

The government, as a matter of convenience, recorded the full amount of collectible property taxes as *revenues* at the time of the levy (journal entry 3). As a practical matter, the government reclassifies all amounts still uncollected at year end as *deferred revenue* ($14,083 revenues [journal entry 3] less $14,000 collections [journal entry 10] = $83). A separate journal entry will be made to recognize a portion of this amount as revenue for amounts received during the availability period at the start of the subsequent fiscal year.

	DR	CR
59. Revenues—property taxes	$ 83	
Deferred revenue—taxes receivable—property taxes		$ 83
(To adjust deferred revenue for property taxes receivable not meeting revenue recognition criteria)		

During the 60-day availability period immediately following the end of the current fiscal year, $63 in property taxes are collected by the government. This previously deferred amount is now recognized as revenue.

	DR	CR
60. Deferred revenue—taxes receivable—property taxes	$ 63	
Revenues—property taxes		$ 63
(To recognize revenue for taxes received within 60 days of the year end)		

Appreciation in the fair value of investments

At the end of the current fiscal year, the fair value of the government's investments had increased by $150.

	DR	CR
61. Investments	$ 150	
Revenues—investment earnings		$ 150
(To record increase in the fair value of investments)		

Budgetary amendments

In addition to the transfer of budgetary authority discussed earlier (journal entry 45), the government adopted several other budgetary amendments during the current fiscal year.

		DR	CR
62.	ESTIMATED REVENUES—SALES TAXES	$ 600	
	ESTIMATED REVENUES—LICENSES AND PERMITS	125	
	ESTIMATED REVENUES—INTERGOVERNMENTAL	75	
	ESTIMATED REVENUES—CHARGES FOR SERVICES	107	
	ESTIMATED REVENUES—INVESTMENT EARNINGS	170	
	BUDGETARY FUND BALANCE	20	
	APPROPRIATIONS—GENERAL GOVERNMENT—OTHER—UNCLASSIFIED		$ 17
	APPROPRIATIONS—PUBLIC SAFETY—POLICE		825
	APPROPRIATIONS—PUBLIC SAFETY—FIRE		115
	APPROPRIATIONS—HIGHWAYS AND STREETS—MAINTENANCE		140
	(To record budgetary amendments)		

Closing of budgetary accounts

At the end of the current fiscal year, all budgetary accounts are closed. (Compare this journal entry with journal entry 2, as modified by journal entries 45 and 62.)

		DR	CR
63.	APPROPRIATIONS—GENERAL GOVERNMENT—COUNCIL	$ 110	
	APPROPRIATIONS—GENERAL GOVERNMENT—COMMISSIONS	86	
	APPROPRIATIONS—GENERAL GOVERNMENT—MANAGER	490	
	APPROPRIATIONS—GENERAL GOVERNMENT—ATTORNEY	380	
	APPROPRIATIONS—GENERAL GOVERNMENT—CLERK	275	
	APPROPRIATIONS—GENERAL GOVERNMENT—PERSONNEL	356	
	APPROPRIATIONS—GENERAL GOVERNMENT—FINANCE AND ADMINISTRATION	904	
	APPROPRIATIONS—GENERAL GOVERNMENT—OTHER—UNCLASSIFIED	2,256	
	APPROPRIATIONS—PUBLIC SAFETY—POLICE	7,313	
	APPROPRIATIONS—PUBLIC SAFETY—FIRE	6,140	
	APPROPRIATIONS—PUBLIC SAFETY—INSPECTION	1,092	
	APPROPRIATIONS—HIGHWAYS AND STREETS—MAINTENANCE	3,152	
	APPROPRIATIONS—HIGHWAYS AND STREETS—ENGINEERING	814	
	APPROPRIATIONS—SANITATION	3,848	
	APPROPRIATIONS—CULTURE AND RECREATION	5,950	
	APPROPRIATIONS—DEBT SERVICE—BOND ISSUANCE COSTS	150	
	APPROPRIATIONS—OTHER FINANCING USES—TRANSFERS OUT	4,760	
	BUDGETARY FUND BALANCE	129	
	ESTIMATED REVENUES—PROPERTY TAXES		$ 14,007
	ESTIMATED REVENUES—SALES TAXES		6,500
	ESTIMATED REVENUES—FRANCHISE TAXES		4,312
	ESTIMATED REVENUES—LICENSES AND PERMITS		1,952
	ESTIMATED REVENUES—INTERGOVERNMENTAL		5,736
	ESTIMATED REVENUES—CHARGES FOR SERVICES		2,208
	ESTIMATED REVENUES—FINES		810
	ESTIMATED REVENUES—INVESTMENT EARNINGS		725
	ESTIMATED REVENUES—MISCELLANEOUS		345

	DR	CR
ESTIMATED OTHER FINANCING SOURCES—CAPITAL LEASES		$ 34
ESTIMATED OTHER FINANCING SOURCES—TRANSFERS IN		1,576
(To close budgetary accounts)		

The closing of budgetary accounts applies as well to outstanding encumbrances at the end of the current fiscal year of $320.

		DR	CR
64.	BUDGETARY FUND BALANCE—RESERVED FOR ENCUMBRANCES	$ 320	
	ENCUMBRANCES—GENERAL GOVERNMENT—MANAGER		$ 10
	ENCUMBRANCES—GENERAL GOVERNMENT—OTHER—UNCLASSIFIED		95
	ENCUMBRANCES—PUBLIC SAFETY—POLICE		55
	ENCUMBRANCES—PUBLIC SAFETY—FIRE		100
	ENCUMBRANCES—PUBLIC SAFETY—INSPECTION		20
	ENCUMBRANCES—HIGHWAYS AND STREETS—MAINTENANCE		40
	(To cancel encumbrances at year end for outstanding purchase orders and contracts)		

Designation of fund balance for encumbrances

The government intends to honor $320 of encumbered contracts and purchase orders outstanding at the end of the current year. As noted earlier, all encumbrances legally lapse at the end of each fiscal year. Therefore, the government chooses to designate a portion of unreserved fund balance to reflect its intent to reappropriate encumbered items as part of the following year's budget.

		DR	CR
65.	Fund balance—unreserved, undesignated	$ 320	
	Fund balance—unreserved, designated for encumbrances		$ 320
	(To reclassify fund balance for purchase orders and contracts expected to be honored in the following year)		

Closing of temporary accounts

The government closes its temporary accounts for the general fund at the close of the current fiscal year.

		DR	CR
66.	Revenues—property taxes	$ 14,133	
	Revenues—sales taxes	6,642	
	Revenues—franchise taxes	4,293	
	Revenues—licenses and permits	2,041	
	Revenues—intergovernmental	5,770	
	Revenues—charges for services	2,300	
	Revenues—fines	808	
	Revenues—investment earnings	773	
	Revenues—miscellaneous—contributions	145	
	Revenues—miscellaneous—payments in lieu of taxes	365	
	Revenues—drug forfeitures	75	
	Other financing sources—sales of general capital assets	5	
	Other financing sources—capital leases	140	
	Other financing sources—transfers in—electric fund	1,576	

	DR	CR
Expenditures—general government—council		$ 92
Expenditures—general government—commissions		64
Expenditures—general government—manager		505
Expenditures—general government—attorney		387
Expenditures—general government—clerk		250
Expenditures—general government—personnel		304
Expenditures—general government—finance and administration		868
Expenditures—general government—other—unclassified		1,787
Expenditures—public safety—police		6,354
Expenditures—public safety—fire		6,031
Expenditures—public safety—inspection		1,053
Expenditures—highways and streets—maintenance		2,939
Expenditures—highways and streets—engineering		796
Expenditures—sanitation		3,726
Expenditures—culture and recreation		5,899
Expenditures—debt service—principal		15
Expenditures—debt service—bond issuance costs		150
Other financing uses—transfers out—debt service fund		3,327
Other financing uses—transfers out—housing development street construction fund		1,210
Other financing uses—transfers out—CDBG revitalization project fund		63
Other financing uses—transfers out—fleet management fund		45
Fund balance—unreserved, undesignated		2,981
Fund balance—reserved for senior recreation program		145
Fund balance—reserved for drug enforcement		75
(To close operating statement accounts)		

DEBT SERVICE FUND

Integration of the appropriated budget

The following journal entry illustrates the integration of the $5,690 annual appropriated budget for the current fiscal year into the government's accounts.

		DR	CR
67.	ESTIMATED REVENUES—PROPERTY TAXES	$ 1,500	
	ESTIMATED REVENUES—SPECIAL ASSESSMENTS	470	
	ESTIMATED REVENUES—INVESTMENT EARNINGS	220	
	ESTIMATED OTHER FINANCING SOURCES— TRANSFERS IN	3,500	
	APPROPRIATIONS—DEBT SERVICE—PRINCIPAL		$ 2,060
	APPROPRIATIONS—DEBT SERVICE—INTEREST		2,950
	BUDGETARY FUND BALANCE		680
	(To record the annual appropriated budget)		

Property tax levy

The government levies $1,595 of property taxes during the current fiscal year to provide resources for budgetary expenditures. Payment of the taxes is due before the end of the current fiscal year. As a practical matter, the entire amount is intially recorded in the accounting system as *revenues*. At the end of the current fiscal year, the unavailable portion of these revenues will be reclassified as *deferred revenue* for financial reporting purposes (journal entry 88).

		DR	CR
68.	Taxes receivable—property taxes	$ 1,595	
	Revenues—property taxes		$ 1,595
	(To record property tax levy)		

Special assessment levy

The government approves a special assessment levy of $4,700 in the current fiscal year to repay special assessment debt. Interest accrues on outstanding balances assessed to property owners at the rate of 8 percent. The government does not consider special assessments to be available until collected.

		DR	CR
69.	Special assessments receivable	$ 4,700	
	Deferred revenue—special assessments		$ 4,700
	(To record special assessment levy)		

Advance refunding

The government determines during the year that a $3,000 advance refunding of general obligation bonds (refunded bonds) can be achieved with a $3,315 payment into an escrow account. The advance refunding will result in a $105 economic gain (i.e., the difference between the present value of the debt service stream on the refunded bonds and the present value of the debt service stream on the refunding bonds, adjusted for additional cash paid). Resources for the advance refunding are obtained through the sale of $3,365 in general obligation bonds (refunding bonds) and the use of $15 in other debt service fund resources. Issuance costs associated with the refunding bonds amount to $65. The advance refunding is approved by the governing body through the adoption of a $3,365 supplemental appropriation and a $15 budget transfer.

		DR	CR
70.	ESTIMATED OTHER FINANCING SOURCES—		
	REFUNDING BONDS ISSUED	$ 3,365	
	APPROPRIATIONS—OTHER FINANCING USES—		
	PAYMENT TO REFUNDED BOND ESCROW		
	AGENT		$ 3,300
	APPROPRIATIONS—DEBT SERVICE—OTHER—		
	REFUNDING BOND ISSUANCE COSTS		65
	(To record budget amendment related to advance refunding)		

		DR	CR
71.	APPROPRIATIONS—DEBT SERVICE—PRINCIPAL	$ 6	
	APPROPRIATIONS—DEBT SERVICE—INTEREST	9	
	APPROPRIATIONS—DEBT SERVICE—OTHER—		
	ADVANCE REFUNDING ESCROW		$ 15
	(To record transfer of appropriated budget related to advance refunding)		

		DR	CR
72.	Cash	$ 3,300	
	Expenditures—debt service—other—refunding bond issuance costs	65	
	Other financing sources—refunding bonds issued		$ 3,365
	(To record refunding bond issuance and related costs)		

The government remits $3,315 to the refunded bond escrow agent from refunding bond proceeds ($3,300) and other debt service fund resources ($15).

		DR	CR
73.	Expenditures—debt service—other—advance refunding Escrow	$ 15	
	Other financing uses—payment to refunded bond escrow agent	3,300	
	Cash		$ 3,315
	(To record payment to refunded bond escrow agent)		

Special assessment collections

The government collects the $658 first installment of the special assessment levy from property owners. Of this amount, $188 represents 6 months interest at 8 percent on the outstanding assessment balance prior to the first installment ($4,700).

		DR	CR
74.	Cash	$ 658	
	Special assessments receivable		$ 470
	Revenues—investment earnings		188
	(To record annual collection of special assessment levy)		

		DR	CR
75.	Deferred revenue—special assessments	$ 470	
	Revenues—special assessments		$ 470
	(To recognize revenues associated with special assessment collections)		

Purchase of investments

The government invests $1,500 of the property tax revenues and $1,500 of collections and/or transfers related to special assessments.

		DR	CR
76.	Investments	$ 3,000	
	Cash		$ 3,000
	(To record purchase of investments)		

Maturing investments

Investments of property tax revenues mature. Proceeds of $1,557 include $62 of interest.

		DR	CR
77.	Cash	$ 1,557	
	Investments		$ 1,495
	Revenues—investment earnings		62
	(To record proceeds including interest revenue from matured investments)		

Transfer from general fund

The government's debt service fund receives a $3,327 transfer from the general fund (journal entry 47) for the retirement of general obligation debt.

		DR	CR
78.	Cash	$ 3,327	
	Other financing sources—transfers in—general fund		$ 3,327
	(To record transfer from the general fund for debt service payment)		

Transfer from capital projects fund

The government receives $846 from the housing development street construction capital projects fund (journal entry 107) to establish a subaccount for the payment of special assessment debt. Debt service payments are scheduled to begin in the following year.

		DR	CR
79.	Cash	$ 846	
	Other financing sources—transfers in—housing development street construction fund		$ 846
	(To record transfer of debt service reserve from the housing development street construction fund)		

Debt service payments

The government remits to its fiscal agent semiannual bond interest payments of $1,450. The entire amount is paid by the fiscal agent to bondholders.

		DR	CR
80.	Cash with fiscal agent	$ 1,450	
	Cash		$ 1,450
	(To record transmittal of cash to fiscal agent for payment of semiannual bond interest)		

		DR	CR
81.	Expenditures—debt service—interest	$ 1,450	
	Matured interest payable		$ 1,450
	(To record expenditures for semiannual bond interest)		

		DR	CR
82.	Matured interest payable	$ 1,450	
	Cash with fiscal agent		$ 1,450
	(To record payments to bondholders by fiscal agent)		

The government also remits to its fiscal agent annual bond principal payments of $2,030 and semiannual interest payments of $1,478. Of the $3,508 remitted, $3,500 ($2,025 principal and $1,475 interest) was paid to bondholders by the escrow agent.

		DR	CR
83.	Cash with fiscal agent	$ 3,508	
	Cash		$ 3,508
	(To record transmittal of cash to fiscal agent for payment of annual bond principal and semiannual bond interest)		

		DR	CR
84.	Expenditures—debt service—principal	$ 2,030	
	Expenditures—debt service—interest	1,478	
	Matured bonds payable		$ 2,030
	Matured interest payable		1,478
	(To record expenditures for annual bond principal and semiannual bond interest)		

		DR	CR
85.	Matured bonds payable	$ 2,025	
	Matured interest payable	1,475	
	Cash with fiscal agent		$ 3,500
	(To record payments to bondholders by fiscal agent)		

Property tax collections

The government collects $1,585 of the current fiscal year's property tax levy before year end.

		DR	CR
86.	Cash	$ 1,585	
	Taxes receivable—property taxes		$ 1,585
	(To record collection of current year's property taxes)		

Accrual of interest on investments

At year fiscal year end, $30 of interest is accrued on outstanding investments.

		DR	CR
87.	Interest receivable—investments	$ 30	
	Revenues—investment earnings		$ 30
	(To record accrued interest revenue)		

Deferral of unavailable property tax revenues

The government determines that $10 of the property tax revenues recognized during the year (journal entry 68) are not available, and therefore must be reclassified as deferred revenue.

		DR	CR
88.	Revenues—property taxes	$ 10	
	Deferred revenue—taxes receivable—property taxes		$ 10
	(To adjust deferred revenue at year end)		

Appreciation in the fair value of investments

At the end of the current fiscal year, the fair value of the government's investments had increased by $42.

		DR	CR
89.	Investments	$ 42	
	Revenue—investment earnings		$ 42
	(To record increase in fair value of investments)		

Closing of budgetary accounts

At the end of the current fiscal year, all budgetary accounts are closed. (Compare this journal entry with journal entry 67, as modified by journal entries 70 and 71.)

		DR	CR
90.	APPROPRIATIONS—DEBT SERVICE—PRINCIPAL	$ 2,054	
	APPROPRIATIONS—DEBT SERVICE—INTEREST	2,941	
	APPROPRIATIONS—DEBT SERVICE—OTHER— ADVANCE REFUNDING ESCROW	15	
	APPROPRIATIONS—DEBT SERVICE—OTHER— REFUNDING BOND ISSUANCE COSTS	65	
	APPROPRIATIONS—OTHER FINANCING USES— PAYMENT TO REFUNDED BOND ESCROW AGENT	3,300	
	BUDGETARY FUND BALANCE	680	
	ESTIMATED REVENUES—PROPERTY TAXES		$ 1,500
	ESTIMATED REVENUES—SPECIAL ASSESSMENTS		470
	ESTIMATED REVENUES—INVESTMENT EARNINGS		220
	ESTIMATED OTHER FINANCING SOURCES— REFUNDING BONDS ISSUED		3,365
	ESTIMATED OTHER FINANCING SOURCES— TRANSFERS IN		3,500
	(To close budgetary accounts)		

Closing of temporary accounts

The government closes its temporary accounts for the debt service fund at the close of the current fiscal year.

		DR	CR
91.	Revenues—property taxes	$ 1,585	
	Revenues—special assessments	470	
	Revenues—investment earnings	322	
	Other financing sources—transfers in—general fund	3,327	
	Other financing sources—transfers in—housing development street construction fund	846	
	Other financing sources—refunding bonds issued	3,365	
	Expenditures—debt service—principal		$ 2,030
	Expenditures—debt service—interest		2,928

	DR	CR
Expenditures—debt service—other—advance refunding escrow		$ 15
Expenditures—debt service—other—refunding bond issuance costs		65
Other financing uses—payment to refunded bond escrow agent		3,300
Fund balance—reserved for debt service		1,577
(To close operating statement accounts at year end)		

CAPITAL PROJECTS FUND

The government establishes a new capital projects fund to account for road construction in portions of the government's service area with newly developed housing. The construction will take place over the current fiscal year and the subsequent fiscal year. All amounts are presented in thousands.

Projected sources of funds:

Special assessment debt		$ 4,700
State grant		248
General fund		1,200
Total sources of funds		$ 6,148

Projected uses of funds:

Appropriation for special assessments:		
Contract	$ 3,815	
Projected change orders	39	
Operating transfer to establish mandatory "reserve"	846	
		$ 4,700
Appropriation for public purpose portion of project:		
Contract	$ 1,146	
Projected change orders	12	
Other costs (to be borne directly by government)	290	
		1,448
Total uses of funds		$ 6,148

Issuance costs on the special assessment debt will be paid by the general fund (journal entry 46). Also, the general fund will be responsible for transferring an amount equal to any proceeds shortfall if the special assessment debt is issued at a discount (journal entry 44). If the issuance of the special assessment debt results in a premium, that amount will be transferred to the debt service fund. The state grant is expenditure-driven, with one half of the total amount to be advanced at the beginning of each of the two fiscal years of the project. Both contracts contain retainage provisions allowing the government to withhold payment of up to 5 percent of progress billings until the project is completed satisfactorily. The special assessment debt issue calls for even, annual payments of principal and semiannual payments of interest at 8 percent over 10 years, and requires that a "reserve" be established in the debt service fund equal to the following year's total payments of principal and interest.

Integration of the appropriated budget

The following journal entry illustrates the integration of the $6,148 project-length budget into the government's accounts.

		DR	CR
92.	ESTIMATED REVENUES—INTERGOVERNMENTAL—STATE	$ 248	
	ESTIMATED OTHER FINANCING SOURCES—TRANSFERS IN—GENERAL FUND	1,200	
	ESTIMATED OTHER FINANCING SOURCES—SPECIAL ASSESSMENT BONDS ISSUED	4,700	
	APPROPRIATIONS—CAPITAL OUTLAY—HIGHWAYS AND STREETS		$ 1,448
	APPROPRIATIONS—CAPITAL OUTLAY—SPECIAL ASSESSMENTS		3,854
	APPROPRIATIONS—OTHER FINANCING USES—TRANSFERS OUT—DEBT SERVICE FUND		846

(To record the project budget)

Advance from state

The government receives an advance of $124 from the state to cover the state's portion of project expenditures for the first year of the project. The state's participation is in the form of a reimbursement grant. Therefore, revenue can be recognized only as expenditures are incurred in conformity with the grant agreement.

		DR	CR
93.	Cash	$ 124	
	Deferred revenue—intergovernmental—state		$ 124

(To record the state portion of project costs)

Transfer from general fund

An interfund receivable of $1,200 is established in the capital projects fund for the general fund's portion of the project costs (journal entry 42).

		DR	CR
94.	Due from other funds—general fund	$ 1,200	
	Other financing sources—transfers in—general fund		$ 1,200

(To record the general fund's portion of project costs)

The capital projects fund receives $1,025 as partial payment from the general fund for its portion of project costs (journal entry 43).

		DR	CR
95.	Cash	$ 1,025	
	Due from other funds—general fund		$ 1,025

(To record collection of part of the amount receivable from the general fund)

Issuance of special assessment debt

The government issues special assessment debt with a face value of $4,700. The government receives bond proceeds of $4,540 (i.e., net of a $160 discount). Of this discount, $150 represents issuance costs withheld by the underwriters. The remaining discount ($10) arises from the fact that the stated rate of interest on the special assessment bonds is less than the market rate of interest for similar securities at the time of issuance. The general fund has agreed to reimburse all issuance costs arising in connection with the special assessment bonds (journal entry 46).

		DR	CR
96.	Cash	$ 4,540	
	Due from other funds—general fund	150	
	Other financing uses—discount on special assessment bonds issued	10	
	Other financing sources—special assessment bonds issued		$ 4,700
	(To record the issuance of special assessment bonds)		

The government records the general fund's obligation to make up the $10 discount resulting from the disparity between the stated rate of interest on the special assessment bonds and the market rate of interest for similar securities at the time of issuance (journal entry 44).

		DR	CR
97.	Due from other funds—general fund	$ 10	
	Other financing sources—transfers in—general fund		$ 10
	(To record the general fund's commitment to make up the difference between the face value of the special assessment bonds and their present value)		

Encumbrances

The government records $5,161 of encumbrances on purchase orders issued and contracts approved.

		DR	CR
98.	ENCUMBRANCES—CAPITAL OUTLAY—HIGHWAYS AND STREETS—CONTRACTS	$ 1,146	
	ENCUMBRANCES—CAPITAL OUTLAY—HIGHWAYS AND STREETS—PURCHASE ORDERS	253	
	ENCUMBRANCES—CAPITAL OUTLAY—SPECIAL ASSESSMENTS	3,762	
	BUDGETARY FUND BALANCE—RESERVED FOR ENCUMBRANCES		$ 5,161
	(To record encumbrances for purchase orders and contracts)		

Purchase of investments

The government determines that it can invest $3,839 of the cash in the capital projects fund and still meet its cash needs for the immediate future.

		DR	CR
99.	Investments	$ 3,839	
	Cash		$ 3,839
	(To record the purchase of investments)		

Sale of investments

The capital projects fund sells $2,004 of investments. The sales price of $2,149 includes $145 of interest accrued during the current fiscal year.

		DR	CR
100.	Cash	$ 2,149	
	Investments		$ 2,004
	Revenues—investment earnings		145
	(To record the sale of investments)		

Change order

The government agrees to a change-order request from the contractor that will raise by $15 the contract amount related to the special assessment project.

		DR	CR
101.	ENCUMBRANCES—CAPITAL OUTLAY—SPECIAL ASSESSMENTS	$ 15	
	BUDGETARY FUND BALANCE—RESERVED FOR ENCUMBRANCES		$ 15
	(To record change order to a special-assessment related contract)		

Progress billings and payment

The government receives progress billings of $2,979 ($2,225 related to the special assessment contract and $754 related to the contract for the general public benefit portion of the project). These amounts had been encumbered. The government also receives invoices for goods and services totaling $251, which had been encumbered at the purchase order amount of $253. Of the $2,979 of progress billings, $149 is to be withheld as retainage pending the successful completion of the project.

		DR	CR
102.	BUDGETARY FUND BALANCE—RESERVED FOR ENCUMBRANCES	$ 3,232	
	ENCUMBRANCES—CAPITAL OUTLAY—HIGHWAYS AND STREETS—CONTRACTS		$ 754
	ENCUMBRANCES—CAPITAL OUTLAY—HIGHWAYS AND STREETS—PURCHASE ORDERS		253
	ENCUMBRANCES—CAPITAL OUTLAY—SPECIAL ASSESSMENTS		2,225
	(To cancel encumbrances related to progress billings and invoices for goods and services received)		

		DR	CR
103.	Expenditures—capital outlay—highways and streets	$ 1,005	
	Expenditures—capital outlay—special assessments	2,225	
	Contracts payable—highways and streets		$ 716
	Contracts payable—special assessments		2,114
	Accounts payable—highways and streets		251
	Retainage payable—highways and streets		38
	Retainage payable—special assessments		111
	(To record progress billings and invoices for goods and services received)		

The government pays the $2,830 due on contracts payable.

		DR	CR
104.	Contracts payable—highways and streets	$ 716	
	Contracts payable—special assessments	2,114	
	Cash		$ 2,830
	(To record the payment of progress billings less retainage)		

Accrued interest receivable

The government accrues interest of $64 on its capital projects fund investments at year end.

		DR	CR
105.	Interest receivable—investments	$ 64	
	Revenues—investment earnings		$ 64
	(To record the year-end accrual of interest on investments)		

Revenue recognition for reimbursement grant

The government recognizes that it has earned the $124 advanced by the state because qualified expenditures have been incurred and matching requirements have been met.

		DR	CR
106.	Deferred revenue—intergovernmental—state	$ 124	
	Revenues—intergovernmental—state		$ 124
	(To recognize revenue for expenditure-driven grant from the state)		

Transfer to debt service fund

The government transfers to a "reserve" established in the debt service fund (journal entry 78) an amount equal to the following year's principal and interest requirements for special assessment debt.

		DR	CR
107.	Other financing uses—transfers out—debt service fund	$ 846	
	Cash		$ 846
	(To record transfer to debt service fund to establish mandatory "reserve" of one year's principal and interest)		

Appreciation in the fair value of investments

At the end of the current fiscal year, the fair value of the government's investments had increased by $64.

		DR	CR
108.	Investments	$ 64	
	Revenues—investment earnings		$ 64
	(To record increase in the fair value of investments)		

Closing of temporary accounts

The government closes its temporary accounts for the capital projects fund at the close of the current fiscal year.

		DR	CR
109.	Revenues—intergovernmental—state	$ 124	
	Revenues—investment earnings	273	
	Other financing sources—transfers in—general fund	1,210	
	Other financing sources—special assessment bonds issued	4,700	
	Expenditures—capital outlay—highways and streets		$ 1,005
	Expenditures—capital outlay—special assessments		2,225
	Other financing uses—transfers out—debt service fund		846
	Other financing uses—discount on special assessment bonds issued		10
	Fund balance—unreserved, undesignated		2,221
	(To close operating statement accounts)		

Closing of budgetary accounts

At the end of the current fiscal year, all budgetary accounts are closed. (Compare this journal entry with journal entry 92.) Because this is a project-length budget, the amounts to be integrated as the budget of the following fiscal period will be the unused balances in each of these accounts (i.e., unexpended appropriations and unrealized estimated revenues).

		DR	CR
110.	APPROPRIATIONS—CAPITAL OUTLAY—HIGHWAYS AND STREETS	$ 1,448	
	APPROPRIATIONS—CAPITAL OUTLAY—SPECIAL ASSESSMENTS	3,854	
	APPROPRIATIONS—OTHER FINANCING USES—TRANSFERS OUT—DEBT SERVICE FUND	846	

	DR	CR
ESTIMATED REVENUES—		
INTERGOVERNMENTAL—STATE		$ 248
ESTIMATED OTHER FINANCING SOURCES—		
TRANSFERS IN—GENERAL FUND		1,200
ESTIMATED OTHER FINANCING SOURCES—		
SPECIAL ASSESSMENT BONDS ISSUED		4,700
(To close budgetary accounts)		

The closing of budgetary accounts applies as well to outstanding encumbrances at the end of the current fiscal year of $1,944.

		DR	CR
111.	BUDGETARY FUND BALANCE—RESERVED FOR		
	ENCUMBRANCES	$ 1,944	
	ENCUMBRANCES—CAPITAL OUTLAY—		
	HIGHWAYS AND STREETS—CONTRACTS		$ 392
	ENCUMBRANCES—CAPITAL OUTLAY—		
	SPECIAL ASSESSMENTS		1,552
	(To cancel encumbrances at year end for outstanding purchase orders and contracts)		

Reservation of fund balances for encumbrances

The government intends to honor the contracts and purchase orders related to the $1,944 of encumbrances outstanding at the end of the current fiscal year. Accordingly, a portion of fund balance is reserved to indicate that this amount is not available for new spending. This journal entry will be reversed immediately at the start of the subsequent fiscal year.

		DR	CR
112.	Fund balance—unreserved, undesignated	$ 1,944	
	Fund balance—reserved for encumbrances		$ 1,944
	(To establish a reserve for actual encumbrances open at year end)		

PERMANENT FUND

Sale of investments

Investments are sold for $1,788. The government treats the full amount received from the sale of the investments as a reduction in the *investments* account, without regard for the value at which the specific underlying investments had been reported (i.e., their fair value as of the end of the prior fiscal year). Any difference between this value and the actual sales price will be reflected automatically in the change in the fair value of investments reported at the end of the current fiscal year (journal entry 118).

		DR	CR
113.	Cash	$ 1,788	
	Investments		$ 1,788
	(To record sale of investments)		

Accrued interest receivable

Interest earned on investments, but not yet received, totaled $41.

		DR	CR
114.	Interest receivable—investments	$ 41	
	Revenues—investment earnings		$ 41
	(To record accrued interest on investments)		

Accounts payable

Various services are provided by outside vendors and invoices are received totaling $13.

	DR	CR
115. Expenditures—culture and recreation	$ 13	
Accounts payable		$ 13
(To record billings for goods and services received)		

Outstanding accounts payable of $18 were paid.

	DR	CR
116. Accounts payable	$ 18	
Cash		$ 18
(To record payment of outstanding payables)		

Purchase of investments

Excess cash of $1,555 is placed in short-term investments.

	DR	CR
117. Investments	$ 1,555	
Cash		$ 1,555
(To record purchase of short-term investments)		

Appreciation in the fair value of investments

The fair value of investments during the current fiscal year increased by $192.

	DR	CR
118. Investments	$ 192	
Revenues—investment earnings		$ 192
(To record increase in the fair value of investments)		

Closing of temporary accounts

The government closes its temporary accounts for the permanent fund at the close of the current fiscal year.

	DR	CR
119. Revenues—investment earnings	$ 233	
Expenditures—culture and recreation		$ 13
Fund balance—unreserved, undesignated		220
(To close operating statement accounts at year end)		

ENTERPRISE FUND

Billings for services

The authority issues bills for services totaling $14,046 during the current fiscal year. Water sales amounted to $8,699 and sewer charges equaled $5,347. Approximately 1 percent of the billings are expected to be uncollectible. Note that revenues are reported net of uncollectibles.

	DR	CR
120. Accounts receivable	$ 13,842	
Due from other funds—general fund	202	
Due from other funds—fleet management fund	2	
Allowance for uncollectible accounts receivable		$ 138
Operating revenues—water sales		8,614
Operating revenues—sewer charges		5,294
(To record billings for water sales and sewer charges		
and related allowance for uncollectible amounts)		

Operating grant

The authority received a one-time operating grant from the Federal Regional Commission.

	DR	CR
121. Cash	$ 350	
Nonoperating revenue—intergovernmental		$ 350
(To record receipt of operating grant)		

Tap fees

During the current fiscal year the authority connects various customers and developers to water and sewer lines. Billings for these services amount to $5,815, which exceeds actual connection costs by $4,294. State law requires this excess amount to be used for capital purposes.

	DR	CR
122. Accounts receivable	$ 5,815	
Operating revenues—tap fees		$ 1,521
Capital contributions—customers		208
Capital contributions—developers		4,086
(To record charges for tap fees)		

Collection of accounts receivable

The authority collects $20,195 of outstanding accounts receivable during the current fiscal year, including a portion of accounts receivable outstanding at the beginning of the current fiscal year.

	DR	CR
123. Cash	$ 20,195	
Accounts receivable		$ 19,991
Due from other funds—general fund		204
(To record the collection of outstanding amounts)		

Write-off of uncollectible accounts receivable

The authority writes off $10 of accounts receivable for which allowances had been previously established.

	DR	CR
124. Allowance for uncollectible accounts receivable	$ 10	
Accounts receivable		$ 10
(To write off uncollectible accounts receivable)		

Customer deposits

During the year, the authority collects $250 of deposits from new customers.

	DR	CR
125. Restricted assets—customer deposits	$ 250	
Customer deposits payable—restricted assets		$ 250
(To record collection of new customer deposits)		

Purchase of capital assets

The authority acquires $374 of machinery and equipment during the year.

	DR	CR
126. Machinery and equipment	$ 374	
Accounts payable		$ 374
(To record purchase of capital assets)		

Purchase of investments

The authority purchases investments of $7,288 with cash generated from operations and contributions.

		DR	CR
127.	Investments	$ 7,288	
	Cash		$ 7,288
	(To record purchase of investments)		

Capital lease

The authority enters into a capital lease agreement for the acquisition of wastewater trucks. The net present value of the future minimum lease payments is $119. The lessor requires a 5 percent down payment. During the current fiscal year, the authority remits $17 (including $5 of interest) in capital lease payments. Payments are due every six months.

		DR	CR
128.	Machinery and equipment	$ 119	
	Cash		$ 6
	Capital leases payable		113
	(To record acquisition of trucks under capital lease agreements and related down payments)		

		DR	CR
129.	Capital leases payable	$ 12	
	Nonoperating expenses—interest	5	
	Cash		$ 17
	(To record capital lease payments)		

Payroll and benefits

Payroll vouchers totaling $3,162 are generated for the current fiscal year, including $477 of pension contributions due to the statewide retirement system. In addition, a $15 increase in accumulated compensated absences, based on salary rates in effect at the end of the current fiscal year, was authorized to be carried over into the following fiscal year.

		DR	CR
130.	Operating expenses—costs of sales and services	$ 2,037	
	Operating expenses—administration	1,140	
	Accounts payable		$ 2,685
	Compensated absences payable		15
	Intergovernmental payable—state		477
	(To record payroll and benefits)		

Inventory

The authority purchases $1,497 of consumable materials and supplies for its stock of inventory. During the current fiscal year, the government uses $1,650 of its inventory stock.

		DR	CR
131.	Inventories	$ 1,497	
	Accounts payable		$ 1,497
	(To record purchase of inventories)		

		DR	CR
132.	Operating expenses—costs of sales and services	$ 1,650	
	Inventories		$ 1,650
	(To record consumption of inventories)		

Purchase of goods and services

The authority purchases $5,084 of various goods and services during the normal course of operations, including $659 of services from other funds.

	DR	CR
133. Operating expenses—costs of sales and services	$ 3,087	
Operating expenses—administration	1,997	
Accounts payable		$ 4,425
Due to other funds—general fund		345
Due to other funds—fleet management fund		264
Due to other funds—management information systems fund		50
(To record operating expenses incurred)		

Issuance of revenue bonds

The authority issues $34,600 of revenue bonds. The bonds are sold at a discount. Issuance costs of $150 were incurred with the sale.

	DR	CR
134. Cash	$ 34,150	
Deferred charge—revenue bond issuance costs	150	
Unamortized discounts on bonds—revenue bonds	300	
Revenue bonds payable		$ 34,600
(To record sale of revenue bonds and related discount and issuance costs)		

The cash received from the issuance of the revenue bonds is allocated to various restricted asset accounts in accordance with the provisions of the bond indenture.

	DR	CR
135. Restricted assets—revenue bond construction account	$ 28,200	
Restricted assets—revenue bond operations and maintenance account	200	
Restricted assets—revenue bond current debt service account	3,500	
Restricted assets—revenue bond future debt service account	700	
Restricted assets—revenue bond renewal and replacement account	1,550	
Cash		$ 34,150
(To record allocation of revenue bond proceeds to restricted Accounts)		

Current refunding

The authority decides to free itself from certain restrictive bond covenants by entering into a current refunding transaction that will extinguish existing debt of $8,580 in the form of revenue bonds. General obligation refunding bonds will be issued for this purpose at par with a face value of $8,500. Issuance costs, which are withheld from the refunding bond proceeds, amount to $77. The general obligation refunding bonds are expected to be repaid with the water and sewer authority's resources and therefore are reported as a fund liability.

	DR	CR
136. Cash	$ 8,423	
Deferred charge—general obligation bond issuance costs	77	
General obligation bonds payable		$ 8,500
(To record sale of general obligation bonds for current refunding)		

The $8,580 extinguishment of revenue bonds lifts the restrictions on amounts held in the revenue bond renewal and replacement account ($1,165) associated with those bonds.

	DR	CR
137. Cash	$ 1,165	
Restricted assets—revenue bond renewal and replacement account		$ 1,165
(To reclassify assets no longer restricted by a bond covenant)		

The authority extinguishes $8,580 of revenue bonds and $448 of related accrued interest with the proceeds of the refunding bonds. The current portion of the revenue bonds outstanding ($530) is not part of the extinguishment but is repaid with restricted assets on hand. Remaining assets in restricted debt service accounts are applied to the extinguishment of the revenue bonds. At the date of the refunding, issuance costs of $103 related to the extinguished debt remain unamortized. The reacquisition price exceeded the net carrying amount of the old debt by $871. This difference is to be amortized over the life of the refunding bonds (which is shorter than the life of the refunded debt). As disclosed in the notes to the financial statements, the transaction resulted in an economic gain of $265 and a reduction of $460 in future debt service payments.

	DR	CR
138. Revenue bonds payable—restricted assets	$ 530	
Accrued interest payable—restricted assets	448	
Revenue bonds payable	8,580	
Unamortized charge—refunding bonds	871	
Cash		$ 8,423
Restricted assets—revenue bond current debt service account		1,380
Restricted assets—revenue bond future debt service account		523
Deferred charge—revenue bond issuance costs		103
(To record extinguishment of revenue bonds)		

Construction

The authority undertakes a two-phase construction project with $28,200 of proceeds from the sale of revenue bonds. Progress billings of $10,738 are received. Of this amount, $536 is to be withheld, in accordance with the provisions of the contracts, until both phases of the project are completed satisfactorily.

	DR	CR
139. Construction in progress	$ 10,738	
Contracts payable		$ 10,202
Retainage payable		536
(To record construction in progress billings)		

	DR	CR
140. Construction in progress	$ 978	
Nonoperating expense—interest		$ 978
(To record capitalization of net interest expense related to tax-exempt revenue bonds)		

The contractor completes the $7,828 first phase of the construction project.

		DR		CR	
141.	Buildings and system	$	7,828		
	Construction in progress			$	7,828
	(To record completion of first phase of the construction project)				

The authority pays $20,317 of outstanding liabilities; $10,202 of the payments are related to the capital construction project.

		DR		CR	
142.	Accounts payable	$	8,848		
	Contracts payable		10,202		
	Due to other funds—general fund		473		
	Due to other funds—fleet management fund		247		
	Due to other funds—management information systems fund		59		
	Intergovernmental payable—state		488		
	Cash			$	10,115
	Restricted assets—revenue bond construction account				10,202
	(To record payment of liabilities incurred during the year)				

Interest payments received

Interest of $1,347 is collected on investments during the current fiscal year. The amount collected includes $316 of interest receivable at the end of the prior fiscal year and $609 related to restricted asset accounts.

		DR		CR	
143.	Cash	$	738		
	Restricted assets—customer deposits		59		
	Restricted assets—revenue bond construction account		324		
	Restricted assets—revenue bond operations and maintenance account		43		
	Restricted assets—revenue bond current debt service account		112		
	Restricted assets—revenue bond future debt service account		22		
	Restricted assets—revenue bond renewal and replacement account		49		
	Customer deposits payable—restricted assets			$	59
	Nonoperating revenues—investment earnings				972
	Interest receivable—investments				316
	(To record collection of interest on investments)				

Return of customer deposits

During the year, the authority returns $17 of deposits to customers who have moved away from the service area.

		DR		CR	
144.	Customer deposits payable—restricted assets	$	17		
	Restricted assets—customer deposits			$	17
	(To record return of customer deposits)				

Sale of capital assets

Capital assets with a book value of $15 ($35 cost less $20 accumulated depreciation) are to be replaced as part of a modernization project. The assets are sold by the government for $5.

	DR	CR
145. Cash	$ 5	
Accumulated depreciation—machinery and equipment	20	
Nonoperating expenses—loss on sale of capital assets	10	
Machinery and equipment		$ 35
(To record sale of capital assets)		

Debt service payments

The authority remits to its fiscal agent semiannual revenue and general obligation bond interest payments of $1,857. The entire amount is paid by the fiscal agent to bondholders.

	DR	CR
146. Cash with fiscal agent	$ 1,857	
Restricted assets—revenue bond current debt service Account		$ 557
Cash		1,300
(To record transmittal of cash to fiscal agent for payment of semiannual revenue and general obligation bond interest)		

	DR	CR
147. Nonoperating expenses—interest	$ 757	
Accrued interest payable	1,100	
Matured general obligation bond interest payable		$ 1,300
Matured revenue bond interest payable		557
(To recognize semiannual revenue and general obligation bond interest)		

	DR	CR
148. Matured general obligation bond interest payable	$ 1,300	
Matured revenue bond interest payable	557	
Cash with fiscal agent		$ 1,857
(To record interest payment to bondholders by fiscal agent)		

The authority also remits to its fiscal agent a bond principal payment of $1,360 for general obligation bonds. Revenue bond principal and interest payments are not due until the following year. The semiannual interest payment totaled $1,249 for the general obligation bonds. The fiscal agent pays $2,486 to the bondholders. A total of $123 remains unpaid at the end of the current fiscal year.

	DR	CR
149. Cash with fiscal agent	$ 2,609	
Cash		$ 2,609
(To record transmittal of cash to fiscal agent for payment of annual principal and semiannual interest for general obligation bonds)		

	DR	CR
150. Nonoperating expenses—interest	$ 1,249	
Matured general obligation bond interest payable		$ 1,249
(To record accrual of general obligation interest due)		

	DR	CR
151. General obligation bonds payable—current	$ 1,360	
Matured general obligation bonds payable		$ 1,360
(To record maturation of general obligation bonds)		

	DR	CR
152. Matured general obligation bonds payable	$ 1,292	
Matured general obligation bond interest payable	1,194	
Cash with fiscal agent		$ 2,486
(To record payment to bondholders by fiscal agent)		

Accrual of interest on investments

At year end, the authority accrues $833 of interest on outstanding investments, including $424 for investments held in restricted assets accounts.

	DR	CR
153. Interest receivable—investments	$ 409	
Restricted assets—customer deposits	52	
Restricted assets—revenue bond construction account	220	
Restricted assets—revenue bond operations and maintenance account	28	
Restricted assets—revenue bond current debt service account	76	
Restricted assets—revenue bond future debt service account	15	
Restricted assets—revenue bond renewal and replacement account	33	
Customer deposits payable—restricted assets		$ 52
Nonoperating revenues—investment earnings		781
(To accrue interest income at year end)		

Billings for services

The authority determines that $528 of water sales and $324 of sewer charges have not been billed as of the end of the current fiscal year. Approximately 10 percent of the unbilled amounts are expected to be uncollectible.

	DR	CR
154. Accounts receivable	$ 852	
Operating revenues—water sales		$ 475
Operating revenues—sewer charges		292
Allowance for uncollectible accounts receivable		85
(To record unbilled accounts at year end and related allowance for uncollectible amounts)		

Replenishment of restricted account

The authority moves $575 to the revenue bond current debt service restricted account for the subsequent fiscal year's revenue bond principal and interest payments, as required by the bond indenture.

	DR	CR
155. Restricted assets—revenue bond current debt service account	$ 575	
Cash		$ 575
(To reclassify cash to restricted assets account)		

Reclassification of debt outstanding

At the end of the current fiscal year, the authority adjusts bond-related accounts to reclassify current principal portions of general obligation bonds payable ($1,480) and revenue bonds payable ($1,484).

	DR	CR
156. General obligation bonds payable	$ 1,480	
Revenue bonds payable	1,484	
General obligation bonds payable—current		$ 1,480
Revenue bonds payable—restricted assets		1,484
(To reclassify current portion of general obligation and revenue bonds payable)		

At year end, the authority reclassifies the $23 current portion of capital leases payable.

	DR	CR
157. Capital leases payable	$ 23	
Capital leases payable—current		$ 23
(To reclassify current portion of capital leases payable)		

Accrual of interest expense

At the end of the current fiscal year, the authority accrues interest expense on outstanding general obligation ($1,045) and revenue ($1,331) bonds.

	DR	CR
158. Nonoperating expenses—interest	$ 2,376	
Accrued interest payable		$ 1,045
Accrued interest payable—restricted assets		1,331
(To accrue interest expense on general obligation and		
revenue bonds at year end)		

Accrual of depreciation expense

The authority determines that depreciation expense for the year is $2,436 (i.e., buildings and system, $512; improvements other than buildings, $154; and machinery and equipment, $1,770).

	DR	CR
159. Operating expenses—depreciation	$ 2,436	
Accumulated depreciation—buildings and system		$ 512
Accumulated depreciation—improvements other than		
buildings		154
Accumulated depreciation—machinery and equipment		1,770
(To record depreciation expense)		

Amortization of bond-related deferred charges

At the end of the current fiscal year, the authority amortizes a portion of deferred charges related to bond issuance costs. The amortization amounts to $25.

	DR	CR
160. Nonoperating expenses—issuance costs	$ 25	
Deferred charge—general obligation bond issuance		
costs		$ 20
Deferred charge—revenue bond issuance costs		5
(To record amortization of bond issuance costs)		

At the end of the current fiscal year, the authority amortizes a portion of bond discounts. The amortization amounts to $12.

	DR	CR
161. Nonoperating expenses—interest	$ 12	
Unamortized bond discount—revenue bonds		$ 12
(To record amortization of bond discount)		

At the end of the current fiscal year, the authority also amortizes a portion of the $871 difference between the reacquisition price of refunded revenue bonds and their net carrying amount at the time of the refunding (journal entry 138). The amortization period is 20 years. The government has elected to use the straight-line method to record amortization, although any systematic and rational method is permitted (e.g., effective interest rate method, proportionate-to-stated-interest-requirements method). Amortization for the five-month period falling within the current fiscal year amounts to $18.

		DR	CR
162.	Nonoperating expenses—interest	$ 18	
	Unamortized charge—refunding bonds		$ 18
	(To record amortization of difference between the reacquisition price and the net carrying amount of the old debt)		

Appreciation in the fair value of investments

At the end of the current fiscal year, the fair value of investments had increased by $1,397.

		DR	CR
163.	Investments	$ 1,397	
	Nonoperating revenue—investment earnings		$ 1,397
	(To record increase in the fair value of investments)		

Closing of temporary accounts

The government closes its temporary accounts for the enterprise fund at the close of the current fiscal year.

		DR	CR
164.	Operating revenues—water sales	$ 9,089	
	Operating revenues—sewer charges	5,586	
	Operating revenues—tap fees	1,521	
	Nonoperating revenue—intergovernmental	350	
	Nonoperating revenues—investment earnings	3,150	
	Capital contributions—customers	208	
	Capital contributions—developers	4,086	
	Operating expenses—costs of sales and services		$ 6,774
	Operating expenses—administration		3,137
	Operating expenses—depreciation		2,436
	Nonoperating expenses—interest		3,439
	Nonoperating expenses—bond issuance costs		25
	Nonoperating expenses—loss on sale of fixed assets		10
	Net assets—unrestricted		8,169
	(To close operating accounts at year end)		

Reclassification of the components of net assets

At the close of the current fiscal year, the government reclassifies the various components of net assets.

		DR	CR
165.	Net assets—restricted for debt service	$ 3,011	
	Net assets—invested in capital assets, net of related debt		$ 1,580
	Net assets—unrestricted		1,431
	(To reclassify net assets)		

INTERNAL SERVICE FUND

Establishment of fund and initial capitalization

A new fleet management internal service fund is being established to account for the cost of operating a maintenance facility and providing vehicles for use by the government's various departments. Previously, this activity was reported in the general fund. The general fund provides $85 of working capital to this internal service fund. Of this amount, $40 is scheduled to be repaid in equal annual installments over a five-year period (i.e., $8 per year). The remaining $45 is considered to be a contribution, which will not be repaid. The amount to be repaid is reported as an advance payable, and the balance is reported as a transfer in.

		DR	CR
166.	Cash	$ 85	
	Advance from other funds—general fund		$ 40
	Transfer in		45
	(To record advance and contribution from general fund)		

The general government contributes capital assets with a book value of $2,160 (vehicles and tools: $4,166 cost - $2,089 accumulated depreciation = $2,077; garage: $87 cost - $4 accumulated depreciation = $83; $2,077 + $83 = $2,160) to a new internal service fund. The internal service fund records the receipt of these contributed capital assets as a *capital contribution*. (There is no corresponding journal entry in any other fund because the assets contributed, as general government capital assets, were not reported in any fund, but only in the government-wide financial statements.)

		DR	CR
167.	Buildings	$ 87	
	Machinery and equipment	4,166	
	Accumulated depreciation—buildings		$ 4
	Accumulated depreciation—machinery and equipment		2,089
	Capital contributions		2,160
	(To record contribution of general capital assets)		

Billing for services

Billings for services totaling $1,264 are issued; $128 is sent to outside governments receiving the services; $872 to the general fund, and $264 to the water and sewer enterprise fund.

		DR	CR
168.	Intergovernmental receivable	$ 128	
	Due from other funds—general fund	872	
	Due from other funds—water and sewer fund	264	
	Operating revenues—charges for services		$ 1,264
	(To record billings)		

Collections

Cash of $825 is received on account from the general fund, $247 from the water and sewer fund, and $124 from other governments.

		DR	CR
169.	Cash	$ 1,196	
	Intergovernmental receivable		$ 124
	Due from other funds—general fund		825
	Due from other funds—water and sewer fund		247
	(To record cash receipts for services rendered)		

Purchase and consumption of inventory

Consumable materials and supplies costing $153 are purchased and delivered. Inventories valued at $130 are withdrawn from stock and used.

		DR	CR
170.	Inventories	$ 153	
	Accounts payable		$ 153
	(To record purchase of inventories)		

		DR	CR
171.	Operating expenses—costs of services	$ 130	
	Inventories		$ 130
	(To record inventories withdrawn and used)		

Payroll and benefits

Payroll vouchers totaling $533 are generated for the current fiscal year, including $47 of pension contributions due to the statewide retirement system. In addition, a $5 increase in accumulated compensated absences, based on salary rates in effect at the end of the current fiscal year, was authorized to be carried over into the following fiscal year.

		DR	CR
172.	Operating expenses—costs of services	$ 561	
	Operating expenses—administration	24	
	Accounts payable		$ 533
	Compensated absences payable		5
	Intergovernmental payable—state		47
	(To record payroll and benefits)		

Purchase of capital assets with trade-in

Vehicles are purchased for $572 (fair market value of $663 less trade-in allowance of $91). The traded-in vehicles originally cost $452 and had a book value of $48.

		DR	CR
173.	Machinery and equipment	$ 620	
	Accumulated depreciation—machinery and equipment	404	
	Accounts payable		$ 572
	Machinery and equipment		452
	(To record acquisition of vehicles and disposal of traded-in vehicles)		

Purchase of goods and services

Various goods and services totaling $81 are received from outside vendors.

		DR	CR
174.	Operating expenses—costs of services	$ 81	
	Accounts payable		$ 81
	(To record operating expenses on account)		

Purchase and sale of investments

Excess cash of $48 is placed in short-term investments that are reported at cost.

		DR	CR
175.	Investments	$ 48	
	Cash		$ 48
	(To record purchase of short-term investments)		

Short-term investments with a cost of $31 are sold prior to the end of the current fiscal year. The proceeds of $35 include $4 of interest earned during the year.

		DR	CR
176.	Cash	$ 35	
	Investments		$ 31
	Nonoperating revenues—investment earnings		4
	(To record sale of investment and interest revenue earned)		

Reimbursement to general fund

A reimbursement of $3 for expenditures paid from the general fund is made by the fleet management internal service fund (journal entry 23).

	DR	CR
177. Operating expenses—costs of services	$ 3	
Cash		$ 3
(To record reimbursement to general fund)		

Interfund services used

A $2 billing is received from the water and sewer fund and an $8 billing is received from the general fund for various administrative services.

	DR	CR
178. Operating expenses—costs of services	$ 2	
Operating expenses—administration	8	
Due to other funds—general fund		$ 8
Due to other funds—water and sewer fund		2
(To record interfund billings)		

Payments of liabilities

Outstanding liabilities of $1,159 are paid.

	DR	CR
179. Accounts payable	$ 1,112	
Intergovernmental payable—state	47	
Cash		$ 1,159
(To record payment of liabilities incurred during the year)		

Insurance

A $76 two-year insurance policy is acquired. One-half of the insurance premium expires and is charged to operations.

	DR	CR
180. Prepaid items	$ 76	
Cash		$ 76
(To record prepaid insurance)		

	DR	CR
181. Operating expenses—administration	$ 38	
Prepaid items		$ 38
(To adjust prepaid items at year end)		

Accrued interest receivable

Interest of $2 is earned on investments, but has not been received at year end.

	DR	CR
182. Interest receivable—investments	$ 2	
Nonoperating revenues—investment earnings		$ 2
(To record accrued interest on investments)		

Accrued depreciation expense

Depreciation expense for the year totals $419 (i.e., building, $4; and machinery and equipment, $415).

	DR	CR
183. Operating expenses—depreciation	$ 419	
Accumulated depreciation—buildings		$ 4
Accumulated depreciation—machinery and equipment		415
(To record depreciation expense)		

Reclassification of liabilities outstanding

Twenty percent of the advance due to the general fund is reclassified as current.

		DR		CR	
184.	Advance from other funds—general fund	$	8		
	Due to other funds—general fund			$	8
	(To reclassify current portion of long-term loan from general fund)				

Closing of temporary accounts

The government closes its temporary accounts for the internal service fund at the close of the current fiscal year.

		DR		CR	
185.	Operating revenues—charges for services	$	1,264		
	Nonoperating revenues—investment earnings		6		
	Capital contributions		2,160		
	Transfer in		45		
	Operating expenses—costs of services			$	777
	Operating expenses—administration				70
	Operating expenses—depreciation				419
	Net assets—unrestricted				2,209
	(To close operating statement accounts)				

Reclassification of the components of net assets

At the close of the current fiscal year, the government reclassifies the various components of net assets.

		DR		CR	
186.	Net assets—unrestricted	$	2,313		
	Net assets—invested in capital assets			$	2,313
	(To reclassify net assets)				

PENSION (AND OTHER EMPLOYEE BENEFIT) TRUST FUND

Sale of investments

Investments of $1,788 are sold during the current fiscal year. The sales price includes $138 of accrued interest that was earned as of the date of sale.

		DR		CR	
187.	Cash	$	1,788		
	Investments			$	1,650
	Additions—investment earnings—interest				138
	(To record sale of investments and interest revenue earned)				

Receipt of interest

Interest of $115 accrued on investments was received.

		DR		CR	
188.	Cash	$	115		
	Interest receivable—investments			$	115
	(To record receipt of interest)				

Interest earned and received in cash during the current fiscal year totaled $370.

		DR		CR	
189.	Cash	$	370		
	Additions—investment earnings—interest			$	370
	(To record interest earnings)				

Accrued interest receivable

Interest earned on investments, but not yet received, totaled $341.

		DR	CR
190.	Interest receivable—investments	$ 341	
	Additions—investment earnings—interest		$ 341
	(To record accrued interest on investments)		

Contributions

Employer contributions of $1,496, along with $284 in employee contributions withheld from payroll, are received from the general fund (journal entries 40 and 41).

		DR	CR
191.	Cash	$ 1,780	
	Additions—member contributions		$ 284
	Additions—employer contributions		1,496
	(To record receipt of employer and employee contributions)		

Purchase of investments

Investments of $2,700 are purchased at par value.

		DR	CR
192.	Investments	$ 2,700	
	Cash		$ 2,700
	(To record purchase of investments)		

Investments of $670 are purchased with accrued interest of $2.

		DR	CR
193.	Investments	$ 670	
	Interest receivable—investments	2	
	Cash		$ 672
	(To record the purchase of investments with accrued interest)		

Benefit payments

Benefits of $455 are paid to retired employees.

		DR	CR
194.	Deductions—benefits	$ 455	
	Cash		$ 455
	(To record payment of benefits)		

Refunds

Refunds of $15 are paid to terminated employees.

		DR	CR
195.	Deductions—refunds	$ 15	
	Cash		$ 15
	(To record payment of refunds to terminated employees)		

Administrative costs

Administrative costs of $160 were incurred during the current fiscal year. Of this amount, $158 was paid.

		DR	CR
196.	Deductions—administrative expenses	$ 160	
	Accounts payable		$ 160
	(To record administrative expenses incurred)		

		DR	CR
197.	Accounts payable	$ 158	
	Cash		$ 158
	(To record payment of administrative expenses)		

Fees

The government paid its investment advisor $75 for services provided during the year. (Although recorded as a deduction, investment expenses are presented as a reduction of additions—investment earnings in the statement of changes in plan net assets.)

		DR	CR
198.	Deductions—investment expense	$ 75	
	Cash		$ 75
	(To record payment of investment advisor expense)		

Appreciation in the fair value of investments

At the end of the current fiscal year, the fair value of the investments had increased by $398.

		DR	CR
199.	Investments	$ 398	
	Additions—investment earnings—net increase (decrease) in the fair value of investments		$ 398
	(To record increase in the fair value of investments)		

Closing of temporary accounts

The government closes its temporary accounts for the pension trust fund at the close of the current fiscal year.

		DR	CR
200.	Additions—investment earnings—interest	$ 849	
	Additions—investment earnings—net increase (decrease) in the fair value of investments	398	
	Additions—member contributions	284	
	Additions—employer contributions	1,496	
	Deductions—benefits		$ 455
	Deductions—refunds		15
	Deductions—administrative expenses		160
	Deductions—investment expense		75
	Net assets held in trust for pension benefits		2,322
	(To close temporary accounts at year end)		

B

Illustrative Trial Balances

The first four appendices illustrate the preparation of a comprehensive annual financial report (CAFR) prepared in conformity with Governmental Accounting Standards Board Statement No. 34, *Basic Financial Statements—and Management's Discussion and Analysis—for State and Local Governments* and the requirements of the Government Finance Officers Association's Certificate of Achievement for Excellence in Financial Reporting Program.

- **Illustrative Journal Entries (appendix A).** This appendix illustrates the different types of journal entries used to collect data in the government's fund-based accounting system.
- **Illustrative Trial Balances (appendix B).** This appendix provides 1) a trial balance as of the beginning of the current fiscal year, 2) a preclosing trial balance, and 3) a trial balance as of the end of the current fiscal year for each of the funds for which illustrative journal entries are provided in appendix A.
- **Illustrative Conversion Worksheet (appendix C).** This appendix illustrates how the data reported in governmental funds and internal service funds are converted and consolidated for presentation as *governmental activities* in the government-wide financial statements.
- **Illustrative CAFR (appendix D).** This appendix offers a complete illustrative CAFR. The numbers in this illustrative CAFR are supported by the journal entries, trial balances, and conversion worksheet provided in appendices A, B, and C.

Matrix of illustrative trial balances

Name of fund	Initial trial balance	Preclosing trial balance	Final trial balance
General fund	Page 465	Page 466	Page 468
Debt service fund	Page 469	Page 470	Page 471
Capital projects fund	Not presented (new fund)	Page 472	Page 473
Permanent fund	Page 474	Page 475	Page 476
Enterprise fund	Page 477	Page 478	Page 480
Internal service fund	Not presented (new fund)	Page 481	Page 482
Pension (and other employee benefit) trust fund	Page 483	Page 484	Page 485

Name of Government
GENERAL FUND
TRIAL BALANCE
January 1, 2015
(amounts expressed in thousands)

	DR	CR
Cash	$ 557	
Investments	1,226	
Interest receivable—investments	48	
Taxes receivable—property taxes	90	
Allowance for uncollectible taxes—property taxes		$ 16
Interest and penalties receivable—property taxes	5	
Allowance for uncollectible interest and penalties—property taxes		1
Tax liens receivable—property taxes	25	
Allowance for uncollectible tax liens—property taxes		6
Taxes receivable—sales taxes	800	
Accounts receivable	61	
Allowance for uncollectible accounts receivable		2
Intergovernmental receivable—federal	150	
Intergovernmental receivable—county	127	
Due from other funds—water and sewer fund	193	
Due from other funds—transportation fund	38	
Inventories	37	
Advance to other funds—management information systems fund	50	
Accounts payable		1075
Contracts payable		151
Due to other funds—water and sewer fund		21
Due to other funds—management information systems fund		98
Deferred revenue—interest receivable—investments		48
Deferred revenue—taxes receivable—property taxes		75
Deferred revenue—interest and penalties receivable—property taxes		3
Deferred revenue—tax liens receivable—property taxes		19
Unearned revenue—federal government		85
Fund balance—reserved for advances		50
Fund balance—unreserved, designated for encumbrances		211
Fund balance—unreserved, undesignated		1,546
	$ 3,407	$ 3,407

Name of Government
GENERAL FUND
PRECLOSING TRIAL BALANCE
December 31, 2015
(amounts expressed in thousands)

	DR	CR
Cash	$ 3,097	
Investments	2,241	
Interest receivable—investments	92	
Taxes receivable—property taxes	114	
Allowance for uncollectible taxes—property taxes		$ 28
Interest and penalties receivable—property taxes	14	
Allowance for uncollectible interest and penalties—property taxes		3
Tax liens receivable—property taxes	33	
Allowance for uncollectible tax liens—property taxes		8
Taxes receivable—sales taxes	830	
Accounts receivable	74	
Allowance for uncollectible accounts receivable		2
Intergovernmental receivable—county	215	
Due from other funds—water and sewer fund	65	
Due from other funds—fleet management fund	16	
Due from other funds—management information systems fund	24	
Due from component unit—school district	12	
Inventories	39	
Advance to other funds—fleet management fund	32	
Advance to other funds—management information systems fund	46	
Accounts payable		1,112
Contracts payable		67
Due to other funds—housing development street construction fund		335
Due to other funds—water and sewer fund		37
Due to other funds—fleet management fund		47
Due to other funds—management information systems fund		57
Deferred revenue—taxes receivable—property taxes		24
Deferred revenue—interest and penalties receivable—property taxes		10
Deferred revenue—tax liens receivable—property taxes		25
Unearned revenue—federal government		181
Fund balance—reserved for advances		78
Fund balance—unreserved, undesignated		1,729
ESTIMATED REVENUES—PROPERTY TAXES	14,007	
ESTIMATED REVENUES—SALES TAXES	6,500	
ESTIMATED REVENUES—FRANCHISE TAXES	4,312	
ESTIMATED REVENUES—LICENSES AND PERMITS	1,952	
ESTIMATED REVENUES—INTERGOVERNMENTAL	5,736	
ESTIMATED REVENUES—CHARGES FOR SERVICES	2,208	
ESTIMATED REVENUES—FINES	810	
ESTIMATED REVENUES—INVESTMENT EARNINGS	725	
ESTIMATED REVENUES—MISCELLANEOUS	345	
Revenues—property taxes		14,133
Revenues—sales taxes		6,642
Revenues—franchise taxes		4,293
Revenues—licenses and permits		2,041
Revenues—intergovernmental		5,770
Revenues—charges for services		2,300
Revenues—fines		808
Revenues—investment earnings		773
Revenues—miscellaneous—contributions		145
Revenues—miscellaneous—payments in lieu of taxes		365
Revenues—miscellaneous—drug forfeitures		75

	DR	CR
ESTIMATED OTHER FINANCING SOURCES— TRANSFERS IN	$ 1,576	
ESTIMATED OTHER FINANCING SOURCES—CAPITAL LEASES	34	
Other financing sources—transfer in—electric fund		$ 1,576
Other financing sources—sales of general capital assets		5
Other financing sources—capital leases		140
APPROPRIATIONS—GENERAL GOVERNMENT—COUNCIL		110
APPROPRIATIONS—GENERAL GOVERNMENT—COMMISSIONS		86
APPROPRIATIONS—GENERAL GOVERNMENT—MANAGER		490
APPROPRIATIONS—GENERAL GOVERNMENT—ATTORNEY		380
APPROPRIATIONS—GENERAL GOVERNMENT—CLERK		275
APPROPRIATIONS—GENERAL GOVERNMENT—PERSONNEL		356
APPROPRIATIONS—GENERAL GOVERNMENT—FINANCE AND ADMINISTRATION		904
APPROPRIATIONS—GENERAL GOVERNMENT—OTHER— UNCLASSIFIED		2,256
APPROPRIATIONS—PUBLIC SAFETY—POLICE		7,313
APPROPRIATIONS—PUBLIC SAFETY—FIRE		6,140
APPROPRIATIONS—PUBLIC SAFETY—INSPECTION		1,092
APPROPRIATIONS—HIGHWAYS AND STREETS—MAINTENANCE		3,152
APPROPRIATIONS—HIGHWAYS AND STREETS—ENGINEERING		814
APPROPRIATIONS—SANITATION		3,848
APPROPRIATIONS—CULTURE AND RECREATION		5,950
APPROPRIATIONS—DEBT SERVICE—OTHER—BOND ISSUANCE COSTS		150
ENCUMBRANCES—GENERAL GOVERNMENT—MANAGER	10	
ENCUMBRANCES—GENERAL GOVERNMENT—OTHER—UNCLASSIFIED	95	
ENCUMBRANCES—PUBLIC SAFETY—POLICE	55	
ENCUMBRANCES—PUBLIC SAFETY—FIRE	100	
ENCUMBRANCES—PUBLIC SAFETY—INSPECTION	20	
ENCUMBRANCES—HIGHWAYS AND STREETS—MAINTENANCE	40	
Expenditures—general government—council	92	
Expenditures—general government—commissions	64	
Expenditures—general government—manager	505	
Expenditures—general government—attorney	387	
Expenditures—general government—clerk	250	
Expenditures—general government—personnel	304	
Expenditures—general government—finance and administration	868	
Expenditures—general government—other—unclassified	1,787	
Expenditures—public safety—police	6,354	
Expenditures—public safety—fire	6,031	
Expenditures—public safety—inspection	1,053	
Expenditures—highways and streets—maintenance	2,939	
Expenditures—highways and streets—engineering	796	
Expenditures—sanitation	3,726	
Expenditures—culture and recreation	5,899	
Expenditures—debt service—principal	15	
Expenditures—debt service—other—bond issuance costs	150	
APPROPRIATIONS—OTHER FINANCING USES—TRANSFERS OUT		4,760
Other financing uses—transfers out—debt service fund	3,327	
Other financing uses—transfers out—housing development street construction fund	1,210	
Other financing uses—transfers out—CDBG Revitalization Project Fund	63	
Other financing uses—transfers out—fleet management fund	45	
BUDGETARY FUND BALANCE—RESERVED FOR ENCUMBRANCES		320
BUDGETARY FUND BALANCE		129
	$ 81,344	$ 81,344

Name of Government
GENERAL FUND
TRIAL BALANCE
December 31, 2015
(amounts expressed in thousands)

	DR	CR
Cash	$ 3,097	
Investments	2,241	
Interest receivable—investments	92	
Taxes receivable—property taxes	114	
Allowance for uncollectible taxes—property taxes		$ 28
Interest and penalties receivable—property taxes	14	
Allowance for uncollectible interest and penalties—property taxes		3
Tax liens receivable—property taxes	33	
Allowance for uncollectible tax liens—property taxes		8
Taxes receivable—sales tax	830	
Accounts receivable	74	
Allowance for uncollectible accounts receivable		2
Intergovernmental receivable—county	215	
Due from other funds—water and sewer fund	65	
Due from other funds—fleet management fund	16	
Due from other funds—management information systems fund	24	
Due from component unit—school district	12	
Inventories	39	
Advance to other funds—fleet management fund	32	
Advance to other funds—management information systems fund	46	
Accounts payable		1,112
Contracts payable		67
Due to other funds—housing development street construction fund		335
Due to other funds—water and sewer fund		37
Due to other funds—fleet management fund		47
Due to other funds—management information systems fund		57
Deferred revenue—taxes receivable—property taxes		24
Deferred revenue—interest and penalties—property taxes		10
Deferred revenue—tax liens receivable—property taxes		25
Unearned revenue—federal government		181
Fund balance—reserved for senior recreation program		145
Fund balance—reserved for drug enforcement		75
Fund balance—reserved for advances		78
Fund balance—unreserved, designated for encumbrances		320
Fund balance—unreserved, undesignated		4,390
	$ 6,944	$ 6,944

Name of Government
DEBT SERVICE FUND
TRIAL BALANCE
January 1, 2015
(amounts expressed in thousands)

	DR	CR
Cash	$ 2	
Investments	8	
Fund balance—reserved for debt service		$ 10
	$ 10	$ 10

Name of Government
DEBT SERVICE FUND
PRECLOSING TRIAL BALANCE
December 31, 2015
(amounts expressed in thousands)

	DR	CR
Cash	$ 2	
Cash with fiscal agent	8	
Investments	1,555	
Interest receivable—investments	30	
Taxes receivable—property taxes	10	
Special assessments receivable	4,230	
Matured bonds payable		$ 5
Matured interest payable		3
Deferred revenue—taxes receivable—property taxes		10
Deferred revenue—special assessments		4,230
Fund balance—reserved for debt service		10
ESTIMATED REVENUES—PROPERTY TAXES	1,500	
ESTIMATED REVENUES—SPECIAL ASSESSMENTS	470	
ESTIMATED REVENUES—INVESTMENT EARNINGS	220	
Revenues—property taxes		1,585
Revenues—special assessments		470
Revenues—investment earnings		322
ESTIMATED OTHER FINANCING SOURCES—REFUNDING BONDS ISSUED	3,365	
ESTIMATED OTHER FINANCING SOURCES—TRANSFERS IN	3,500	
Other financing sources—transfers in—general fund		3,327
Other financing sources—transfers in—housing development street construction fund		846
Other financing sources—refunding bonds issued		3,365
APPROPRIATIONS—DEBT SERVICE—PRINCIPAL		2,054
APPROPRIATIONS—DEBT SERVICE—INTEREST		2,941
APPROPRIATIONS—DEBT SERVICE—OTHER—ADVANCE REFUNDING ESCROW		15
APPROPRIATIONS—DEBT SERVICE—OTHER—REFUNDING BONDS ISSUANCE COSTS		65
Expenditures—debt service—principal	2,030	
Expenditures—debt service—interest	2,928	
Expenditures—debt service—other—advance refunding escrow	15	
Expenditures—debt service—other—refunding bond issuance costs	65	
APPROPRIATIONS—OTHER FINANCING USES—PAYMENT TO REFUNDED BOND ESCROW AGENT		3,300
Other financing uses—payment to refunded bond escrow agent	3,300	
BUDGETARY FUND BALANCE		680
	$ 23,228	$ 23,228

Name of Government
DEBT SERVICE FUND
TRIAL BALANCE
December 31, 2015
(amounts expressed in thousands)

	DR	CR
Cash	$ 2	
Cash with fiscal agent	8	
Investments	1,555	
Interest receivable—investments	30	
Taxes receivable—property taxes	10	
Special assessments receivable	4,230	
Matured bonds payable		$ 5
Matured interest payable		3
Deferred revenue—taxes receivable—property taxes		10
Deferred revenue—special assessments		4,230
Fund balance—reserved for debt service		1,587
	$ 5,835	$ 5,835

Name of Government
HOUSING DEVELOPMENT STREET CONSTRUCTION CAPITAL PROJECTS FUND
PRECLOSING TRIAL BALANCE
December 31, 2015
(amounts expressed in thousands)

	DR	CR
Cash	$ 323	
Investments	1,899	
Interest receivable—investments	64	
Due from other funds—general fund	335	
Accounts payable—highways and streets		$ 251
Retainage payable—highways and streets		38
Retainage payable—special assessments		111
ESTIMATED REVENUES—INTERGOVERNMENTAL—STATE	248	
Revenues—intergovernmental—state		124
Revenues—investment earnings		273
APPROPRIATIONS—CAPITAL OUTLAY—HIGHWAYS AND STREETS		1,448
APPROPRIATIONS—CAPITAL OUTLAY—SPECIAL ASSESSMENTS		3,854
ENCUMBRANCES—CAPITAL OUTLAY—HIGHWAYS AND STREETS—CONTRACTS	392	
ENCUMBRANCES—CAPITAL OUTLAY—SPECIAL ASSESSMENTS	1,552	
Expenditures—capital outlay—highways and streets	1,005	
Expenditures—capital outlay—special assessments	2,225	
ESTIMATED OTHER FINANCING SOURCES—SPECIAL ASSESSMENT BONDS ISSUED	4,700	
ESTIMATED OTHER FINANCING SOURCES—TRANSFERS In—GENERAL FUND	1,200	
Other financing sources—special assessment bonds issued		4,700
Other financing sources—transfers in—general fund		1,210
APPROPRIATIONS—OTHER FINANCING USES—TRANSFERS OUT—DEBT SERVICE FUND		846
Other financing uses—transfers out—debt service fund	846	
Other financing uses—discount on special assessment bonds issued	10	
BUDGETARY FUND BALANCE—RESERVED FOR ENCUMBRANCES		1,944
	$ 14,799	$ 14,799

Name of Government
HOUSING DEVELOPMENT STREET CONSTRUCTION CAPITAL PROJECTS FUND
TRIAL BALANCE
December 31, 2015
(amounts expressed in thousands)

	DR	CR
Cash	$ 323	
Investments	1,899	
Interest receivable—investments	64	
Due from other funds—general fund	335	
Accounts payable—highways and streets		$ 251
Retainage payable—highways and streets		38
Retainage payable—special assessments		111
Fund balance—reserved for encumbrances		1,944
Fund balance—unreserved, undesignated		277
	$2,621	$ 2,621

Name of Government
PERPETUAL CARE PERMANENT FUND
TRIAL BALANCE
January 1, 2015
(amounts expressed in thousands)

	DR	CR
Cash	$ 16	
Investments	1,848	
Interest receivable—investments	41	
Accounts payable		$ 18
Fund balance—reserved for perpetual care		1,102
Fund balance—unreserved, undesignated		785
	$ 1,905	$ 1,905

Name of Government
PERPETUAL CARE PERMANENT FUND
PRECLOSING TRIAL BALANCE
December 31, 2015
(amounts expressed in thousands)

	DR	CR
Cash	$ 231	
Investments	1,807	
Interest receivable—investments	82	
Accounts payable		$ 13
Fund balance—reserved for perpetual care		1,102
Fund balance—unreserved, undesignated		785
Revenues—investment earnings		233
Expenditures—culture and recreation	13	
	$ 2,133	$ 2,133

Name of Government
PERPETUAL CARE PERMANENT FUND
TRIAL BALANCE
December 31, 2015
(amounts expressed in thousands)

	DR	CR
Cash	$ 231	
Investments	1,807	
Interest receivable—investments	82	
Accounts payable		$ 13
Fund balance—reserved for perpetual care		1,102
Fund balance—unreserved, undesignated		1,005
	$2,120	$ 2,120

Name of Government
WATER AND SEWER AUTHORITY ENTERPRISE FUND
TRIAL BALANCE
January 1, 2015
(amounts expressed in thousands)

	DR	CR
Cash	$ 823	
Investments	7,322	
Interest receivable—investments	316	
Accounts receivable	2,585	
Allowance for uncollectible accounts receivable		$ 259
Due from other funds—general fund	39	
Inventories	461	
Restricted assets—customer deposits	1,199	
Restricted assets—revenue bond operations and maintenance account	1,023	
Restricted assets—revenue bond current debt service account	1,380	
Restricted assets—revenue bond future debt service account	523	
Restricted assets—revenue bond renewal and replacement account	1,165	
Deferred charge—general obligation bond issuance costs	366	
Deferred charge—revenue bond issuance costs	103	
Land	604	
Buildings and system	13,100	
Accumulated depreciation—buildings and system		1,964
Improvements other than buildings	1,250	
Accumulated depreciation—improvements other than buildings		188
Machinery and equipment	103,825	
Accumulated depreciation—machinery and equipment		12,973
Accounts payable		1,104
Compensated absences payable		359
Accrued interest payable		1,100
Intergovernmental payable—state		11
Due to other funds—general fund		193
Due to other funds—management information systems fund		14
General obligation bonds payable—current		1,360
Customer deposits payable—restricted assets		1,199
Revenue bonds payable—restricted assets		530
Accrued interest payable—restricted assets		448
General obligation bonds payable		23,798
Revenue bonds payable		8,580
Net assets—invested in capital assets, net of related debt		69,386
Net assets—restricted for debt service		3,643
Net assets—unrestricted		8,975
	$ 136,084	$ 136,084

Name of Government
WATER AND SEWER AUTHORITY ENTERPRISE FUND
PRECLOSING TRIAL BALANCE
December 31, 2015
(amounts expressed in thousands)

	DR	CR
Cash	$ 1,366	
Cash with fiscal agent	123	
Investments	16,007	
Interest receivable—investments	409	
Accounts receivable	3,093	
Allowance for uncollectible accounts receivable		$ 472
Due from other funds—general fund	37	
Due from other funds—fleet management fund	2	
Inventories	308	
Restricted assets—customer deposits	1,543	
Restricted assets—revenue bond operations and maintenance account	1,294	
Restricted assets—revenue bond construction account	18,542	
Restricted assets—revenue bond current debt service account	3,706	
Restricted assets—revenue bond future debt service account	737	
Restricted assets—revenue bond renewal and replacement account	1,632	
Deferred charge—general obligation bond issuance costs	423	
Deferred charge—revenue bond issuance costs	145	
Land	604	
Buildings and system	20,928	
Accumulated depreciation—buildings and system		2,476
Improvements other than buildings	1,250	
Accumulated depreciation—improvements other than buildings		342
Machinery and equipment	104,283	
Accumulated depreciation—machinery and equipment		14,723
Construction in progress	3,888	
Accounts payable		1,237
Compensated absences payable		374
Matured bonds payable		68
Matured interest payable		55
Accrued interest payable		1,045
Retainage payable		536
Due to other funds—general fund		65
Due to other funds—fleet management fund		17
Due to other funds—management information systems fund		5
General obligation bonds payable—current		1,480
Capital leases payable—current		23
Customer deposits payable—restricted assets		1,543
Revenue bonds payable—restricted assets		1,484
Accrued interest payable—restricted assets		1,331
General obligation bonds payable		30,818
Revenue bonds payable		33,116
Unamortized discounts on bonds—revenue bonds	288	
Unamortized charge—refunding bonds	853	
Capital leases payable		78
Net assets—invested in capital assets, net of related debt		69,386
Net assets—restricted for debt service		3,643
Net assets—unrestricted		8,975
Operating revenues—water sales		9,089
Operating revenues—sewer charges		5,586
Operating revenues—tap fees		1,521
Operating expenses—costs of sales and services	6,774	
Operating expenses—administration	3,137	
Operating expenses—depreciation	2,436	

	DR	CR
Nonoperating revenues—intergovernmental		$ 350
Nonoperating revenues—investment earnings		3,150
Nonoperating expenses—interest	$ 3,439	
Nonoperating expenses—bond issuance costs	25	
Nonoperating expenses—loss on sale of fixed assets	10	
Capital contributions—customers		208
Capital contributions—developers		4,086
	$ 197,282	$ 197,282

Name of Government
WATER AND SEWER AUTHORITY ENTERPRISE FUND
TRIAL BALANCE
December 31, 2015
(amounts expressed in thousands)

	DR	CR
Cash	$ 1,366	
Cash with fiscal agent	123	
Investments	16,007	
Interest receivable—investments	409	
Accounts receivable	3,093	
Allowance for uncollectible accounts receivable		$ 472
Due from other funds—general fund	37	
Due from other funds—fleet management fund	2	
Inventories	308	
Restricted assets—customer deposits	1,543	
Restricted assets—revenue bond operations and maintenance account	1,294	
Restricted assets—revenue bond construction account	18,542	
Restricted assets—revenue bond current debt service account	3,706	
Restricted assets—revenue bond future debt service account	737	
Restricted assets—revenue bond renewal and replacement account	1,632	
Deferred charge—general obligation bond issuance costs	423	
Deferred charge—revenue bond issuance costs	145	
Land	604	
Buildings and system	20,928	
Accumulated depreciation—buildings and system		2,476
Improvements other than buildings	1,250	
Accumulated depreciation—improvements other than buildings		342
Machinery and equipment	104,283	
Accumulated depreciation—machinery and equipment		14,723
Construction in progress	3,888	
Accounts payable		1,237
Compensated absences payable		374
Matured bonds payable		68
Matured interest payable		55
Accrued interest payable		1,045
Retainage payable		536
Due to other funds—general fund		65
Due to other funds—fleet management fund		17
Due to other funds—management information systems fund		5
General obligation bonds payable—current		1,480
Capital leases payable—current		23
Customer deposits payable—restricted assets		1,543
Revenue bonds payable—restricted assets		1,484
Accrued interest payable—restricted assets		1,331
General obligation bonds payable		30,818
Revenue bonds payable		33,116
Unamoritized discounts on bonds—revenue bonds	288	
Unamortized charge—refunding bonds	853	
Capital leases payable		78
Net assets—invested in capital assets, net of related debt		70,966
Net assets—restricted for debt service		632
Net assets—unrestricted		18,575
	$ 181,461	$ 181,461

Name of Government
FLEET MANAGEMENT INTERNAL SERVICE FUND
PRECLOSING TRIAL BALANCE
December 31, 2015
(amounts expressed in thousands)

	DR	CR
Cash	$ 30	
Investments	17	
Interest receivable—investments	2	
Intergovernmental receivable	4	
Due from other funds—general fund	47	
Due from other funds—water and sewer fund	17	
Inventories	23	
Prepaid items	38	
Buildings	87	
Accumulated depreciation—buildings		$ 8
Machinery and equipment	4,334	
Accumulated depreciation—machinery and equipment		2,100
Accounts payable		227
Compensated absences payable		5
Due to other funds—general fund		16
Due to other funds—water and sewer fund		2
Advance from other funds—general fund		32
Operating revenues—charges for services		1,264
Operating expenses—costs of services	777	
Operating expenses—administration	70	
Operating expenses—depreciation	419	
Nonoperating revenues—investment earnings		6
Capital contributions		2,160
Transfer in		45
	$ 5,865	$ 5,865

Name of Government
FLEET MANAGEMENT INTERNAL SERVICE FUND
TRIAL BALANCE
December 31, 2015
(amounts expressed in thousands)

	DR	CR
Cash	$ 30	
Investments	17	
Interest receivable—investments	2	
Intergovernmental receivable	4	
Due from other funds—general fund	47	
Due from other funds—water and sewer fund	17	
Inventories	23	
Prepaid items	38	
Buildings	87	
Accumulated depreciation—buildings		$ 8
Machinery and equipment	4,334	
Accumulated depreciation—machinery and equipment		2,100
Accounts payable		227
Compensated absences payable		5
Due to other funds—general fund		16
Due to other funds—water and sewer fund		2
Advance from other funds—general fund		32
Net assets—invested in capital assets		2,313
Net assets—unrestricted	104	
	$ 4,703	$ 4,703

Name of Government
PUBLIC SAFETY EMPLOYEES PENSION TRUST FUND
TRIAL BALANCE
January 1, 2015
(amounts expressed in thousands)

	DR	CR
Cash	$ 55	
Investments	12,615	
Interest receivable—investments	118	
Accounts payable		$ 16
Net assets held in trust for pension benefits		12,772
	$ 12,788	$ 12,788

Name of Government
PUBLIC SAFETY EMPLOYEES PENSION TRUST FUND
PRECLOSING TRIAL BALANCE
December 31, 2015
(amounts expressed in thousands)

	DR	CR
Cash	$ 33	
Investments	14,733	
Interest receivable—investments	346	
Accounts payable		$ 18
Net assets held in trust for pension benefits		12,772
Additions—investment earnings—interest		849
Additions—investment earnings—net increase (decrease) in the fair value of investments		398
Additions—member contributions		284
Additions—employer contributions		1,496
Deductions—benefits	455	
Deductions—refunds	15	
Deductions—administrative expenses	160	
Deductions—investment expense	75	
	$ 15,817	$ 15,817

Name of Government
PUBLIC SAFETY EMPLOYEES PENSION TRUST FUND
TRIAL BALANCE
December 31, 2015
(amounts expressed in thousands)

	DR	CR
Cash	$ 33	
Investments	14,733	
Interest receivable—investments	346	
Accounts payable		$ 18
Net assets held in trust for pension benefits		15,094
	$ 15,112	$ 15,112

C

Illustrative Conversion Worksheet

RELATIONSHIP OF APPENDICES

The first four appendices illustrate the preparation of a comprehensive annual financial report (CAFR) prepared in conformity with Governmental Accounting Standards Board Statement No. 34, *Basic Financial Statements— and Management's Discussion and Analysis—for State and Local Governments* and the requirements of the Government Finance Officers Association's Certificate of Achievement for Excellence in Financial Reporting Program.

- **Illustrative Journal Entries (appendix A).** This appendix illustrates the different types of journal entries used to collect data in the government's fund-based accounting system.
- **Illustrative Trial Balances (appendix B).** This appendix provides 1) a trial balance as of the beginning of the current fiscal year, 2) a preclosing trial balance, and 3) a trial balance as of the end of the current fiscal year for each of the funds for which illustrative journal entries are provided in appendix A.
- **Illustrative Conversion Worksheet (appendix C).** This appendix illustrates how the data reported in governmental funds and internal service funds are converted and consolidated for presentation as *governmental activities* in the government-wide financial statements.
- **Illustrative CAFR (appendix D).** This appendix offers a complete illustrative CAFR. The numbers in this illustrative CAFR are supported by the journal entries, trial balances, and conversion worksheet provided in appendices A, B, and C.

WORKSHEET TO CONVERT FROM GOVERNMENTAL FUNDS TO GOVERNMENTAL ACTIVITIES

As many as four types of adjustments may be necessary before the data reported in governmental funds is ready to be incorporated into the government-wide financial statements:

- Data must be converted from the current financial resources measurement focus and the modified accrual basis of accounting to the economic resources measurement focus and the accrual basis of accounting;
- The effects of interfund activity within the primary government (including internal service funds) must be eliminated (except for *interfund services provided and used* between functions);
- Any allocation of indirect costs to individual functions in the fund financial statements must be reversed; and
- Any direct costs included as part of *general government* expenditures in the fund financial statements must be allocated to the appropriate function.

In regard to these various adjustments, please note the following:

- A fund's closing balances at the end of one year must be its opening balances at the start of the next. The adjustments necessary to prepare the government-wide financial statements are purely worksheet in character and in no way affect what is reported in the fund financial statements.
- Assets and liabilities related to governmental activities, but *not* reported in governmental funds (e.g., general government capital assets, long-term debt), must be tracked separately. *ALL CAPS BOLD ITALICS* are used in this appendix to signal these accounts. The difference between these particular *ASSETS* and *LIABILITIES* is labeled *NET ASSETS* (which should *not* be confused with *net assets–governmental activities* of which it is but one component, as explained below).
- The amounts used in the worksheet for *ASSETS* and *LIABILITIES* of the general government are the *post-closing balances* as of the end of the *prior* fiscal year. In contrast, the balances used for the governmental funds are taken from the *preclosing trial balance* of the *current* fiscal year. The reason for this difference is that conversion adjustments for the latter will almost always automatically incorporate changes in the former during the current fiscal year.
- As a matter of convenience, conversion adjustments that affect amounts reported in prior years are treated as an adjustment to the *fund balance* account on the worksheet (whose adjusted balance is one of the components of the amount eventually reported as *net assets–governmental activities*, as explained below).
- As a matter of convenience, expenses that do not qualify as *expenditures* are reported in the related *expenditure* account all the same (rather than in a separate *expense* account), because once all the conversion adjustments have been made, the amount reported in what were originally *expenditure* accounts will, in fact, represent *expense*.
- The amount ultimately reported as *net assets–governmental activities* in the government-wide statement of net assets is calculated by combin-

ing the adjusted balances of both 1) *fund balance* and 2) **NET ASSETS**, and then adding 3) the net increase/decrease in net assets for the period. It is only once this total has been calculated that accounts should be analyzed to calculate the relative portions to be classified as *invested in capital assets, net of related debt, restricted,* and *unrestricted.*

MEASUREMENT FOCUS AND BASIS OF ACCOUNTING CONVERSION: FROM GOVERNMENTAL FUNDS TO GOVERNMENTAL ACTIVITIES[1]

Capital outlays

Action needed: Remove expenditures incurred for the acquisition or construction of capital assets and report instead a capital asset for the items thus acquired on the statement of net assets.

Adjustments:

(a) — Convert capital outlay from functional activities to capital assets

	DR	CR
LAND	$ 558	
MACHINERY	1,035	
Expenditures — general government		$ 475
Expenditures — public safety		648
Expenditures — highways and streets		165
Expenditures — sanitation		1
Expenditures — culture and recreation		304

Not all capital assets are constructed or purchased in a capital projects fund or reported in a separate "capital outlays" line in some other governmental fund. Therefore, capital outlays that were included as part of current expenditures in the various functional categories in the governmental fund statement of revenues, expenditures, and changes in fund balances need to be reported instead as capital assets in the government-wide statement of net assets.

(b) — Convert capital outlay from capital projects fund to capital assets

	DR	CR
CONSTRUCTION IN PROGRESS — INFRASTRUCTURE	$ 3,785	
Capital outlay		$ 3,785

Some capital acquisition is specifically designated as "capital outlay" in the governmental fund statement of revenues, expenditures, and changes in fund balances. Once again, such amounts need to be reported instead as capital assets in the government-wide statement of net assets.

(c) — Convert capital lease expenditure to capital assets

	DR	CR
MACHINERY	$ 140	
Expenditures — public safety		$ 140

Generally accepted accounting principles (GAAP) require that a capital lease be reflected in a governmental fund by an expenditure equal to the present value of the minimum lease payments. This amount should be reported instead as a capital asset in the government-wide statement of net assets.

---

[1] The order of presentation followed here is that described in Exhibit 8-2 (see pages 130-131).

Debt service principal payments

Action needed: Remove debt service principal payments and treat the amount paid as a reduction of the balance of the related liability.

Adjustments:

(d) — Convert debt principal payments to liability reduction

	DR	CR
GENERAL OBLIGATION DEBT	$ 2,030	
Debt service — principal — general obligation debt		$ 2,030

Debt service principal payments normally are reported separately in the governmental fund statement of revenues, expenditures, and changes in fund balances. This expenditure should be removed and replaced by a corresponding reduction in the related liability reported in the government-wide statement of net assets.

(e) — Convert lease down payment to reduction of lease liability

	DR	CR
CAPITAL LEASES	$ 15	
Debt service — principal — capital leases		$ 15

The same treatment just described for regular debt service payments on bonds and notes also applies to the principal portion of payments on capital leases.

Eliminate other financing sources/uses and expenditures related to the issuance of debt

Action needed: The issuance of debt needs to be reflected on the government-wide statement of net assets rather than in the government-wide statement of activities.

Adjustments:

(f) — Convert debt issuance from temporary to permanent accounts

	DR	CR
DEFERRED CHARGE — ISSUANCE COSTS	$ 150	
Other financing sources — special assessment bonds issued	4,700	
DISCOUNT — SPECIAL ASSESSMENT DEBT	10	
SPECIAL ASSESSMENT DEBT		$ 4,700
Debt service — bond issuance costs		150
Other financing uses — discount — special assessment debt		10

Governmental funds report the issuance of debt as an other financing source in the governmental fund statement of revenues, expenditures, and changes in fund balances. Likewise, discounts on debt are treated as an other financing use and issuance costs (including underwriter's discounts) are treated as an expenditure in that same statement. In contrast, all of these amounts should appear on the government-wide statement of net assets as a liability (debt payable), a contra-liability (discount), and a deferred charge (unamortized issuance costs).

(g) — Convert capital lease from temporary to permanent accounts

	DR	CR
Other financing sources — capital lease	$ 140	
CAPITAL LEASES		$ 140

GAAP require that a capital lease be reflected in a governmental fund as an other financing source in the amount of the net present value of the minimum lease payments. This amount should be reported as a liability in the government-wide statement of net assets.

(h) — Convert refunding from temporary to permanent accounts

	DR	CR
DEFERRED CHARGE — ISSUANCE COSTS	$ 65	
DEFERRED CHARGE — REFUNDING	315	
GENERAL OBLIGATION DEBT	3,000	
Other financing sources — refunding bonds issued	3,365	
GENERAL OBLIGATION DEBT		$ 3,365
Debt service — bond issuance costs		65
Debt service — advance refunding escrow		15
Other financing uses — payment to refunded bond escrow agent		3,300

A refunding transaction essentially combines the issuance of new debt (see item (f) above) and the repayment of existing debt (see item (d) above). The key difference is that the disparity between the net carrying value of the refunded debt and its reacquisition price is treated as a deferred charge (this amount is reported as a deduction from or an addition to the new debt liability) in the government-wide statement of net assets and subsequently amortized over the life of the refunding or refunded debt, whichever is shorter.

Donations of capital assets

Action needed: Donations of capital assets typically are *not* reported in governmental funds. Such donations must be reported, however, in both of the government-wide financial statements.

Adjustment:

(i) — Donation of capital assets

	DR	CR
MACHINERY	$ 13	
Investment earnings and miscellaneous		$ 13

Sales of capital assets

Action needed: Sales and other disposals of capital assets must be reported in the government-wide statement of net assets. Gains on such disposals should be reported as general revenues. Losses should *not* be reported as direct expenses of specific functions, but should instead be included as part of the general government function. If such amounts are insignificant, a practical alternative is simply to adjust the current year's depreciation expense for these items.

Adjustments:

(j) — Sale of machinery and equipment

	DR	CR
ACCUMULATED DEPRECIATION — MACHINERY	$ 39	
Other financing source — proceeds of sale of capital assets	5	
MACHINERY		$ 42
Gain — sale of capital assets		2

Governmental funds typically report whatever proceeds they receive in connection with the disposal of capital assets as a *special item* or an *other financing source* (if material) or an *other revenue* (if immaterial). This amount must be removed and replaced by an adjustment to the appropriate capital asset and accumulated depreciation accounts. Any disparity should be reported as a gain or loss in the government-wide statement of activities as discussed above.

(k) — Trade-in of machinery

	DR	CR
MACHINERY	$ 17	
ACCUMULATED DEPRECIATION — MACHINERY	9	
MACHINERY		$ 14
Expenditures — general government		12

A trade-in transaction is similar to the acquisition of a capital asset (see items (a) and (b) above). That is, the expenditure needs to be removed and reported instead as part of the cost of the newly acquired asset in the government-wide statement of net assets. Any gain or loss on the trade-in should be reported in the government-wide statement of activities as discussed above.

(l) — Scrapping of fully depreciated machinery

	DR	CR
ACCUMULATED DEPRECIATION — MACHINERY	$ 8	
MACHINERY		$ 8

Neither capital assets nor related accumulated depreciation are reported in the governmental fund balance sheet, whereas both are reported in the government-wide statement of net assets. Accordingly, the scrapping of a fully depreciated capital asset would need to be reflected in the government-wide financial statements, although it would not have an effect on the governmental fund financial statements.

Eliminate revenues related to prior periods

Action needed: Remove governmental fund revenues that relate to prior periods.

Adjustments:

(m) — Eliminate property tax revenue related to prior years

	DR	CR
Deferred revenue	$ 27	
Revenues — taxes	70	
Fund balance		$ 97

Governmental funds may not report revenues until they are *available*. The government-wide statement of activities, however, is *not* subject to this availability criterion. Therefore, amounts related to prior periods that first became available as revenue in the governmental funds during the current period must be removed and reflected instead as an adjustment to government-wide net assets (i.e., because they had been recognized as revenue in an earlier period). Likewise ongoing deferred revenue balances *from prior periods* must be reclassified as net assets in this same way.

(n) — Eliminate interest revenue related to prior year

	DR	CR
Revenues — investment earnings and miscellaneous	$ 48	
Fund balance		$ 48

Accrued interest is only recognized in governmental funds to the extent that it is considered to be available. Accordingly, interest revenue of the current period *earned in prior periods* must be removed and reported instead as an adjustment to government-wide net assets (i.e., because the interest had been previously recognized in the period in which earned).

Eliminate expenditures related to prior periods

Action needed: Some governmental fund expenditures reflect payments related to prior periods (e.g., claims and judgments). Such amounts should *not* be included in the government-wide statement of activities as they relate to prior periods.

Adjustment:

(o) — Eliminate expenditures related to prior years

	DR	CR
ACCRUED INTEREST PAYABLE	$ 632	
COMPENSATED ABSENCES	646	
Expenditures — general government		$ 90
Expenditures — public safety		278
Expenditures — highways and streets		78
Expenditures — sanitation		78
Expenditures — culture and recreation		122
Debt service — interest		632

Governmental funds typically recognize interest expenditures in the period in which payment is made rather than in the period in which it accrues. Such amounts must be removed from expenditures and be reported instead as a reduction of the accrued liability for interest payable at year end (see item (q) following). Likewise, expenditures related to compensated absences earned in prior years must be reported instead as a reduction in the liability for compensated absences.

Earned but unavailable revenues

Action needed: Revenues of the current year should be recognized in the government-wide statement of net assets regardless of whether they are available.

Adjustment:

(p) — Add earned but unavailable revenue

	DR	CR
Deferred revenue	$ 4,272	
Revenues — taxes		$ 42
Revenues — special assessments		4,230

Deferred revenue *related to the current period* should be reclassified as revenue. (See item (m) above for the appropriate handling of deferred revenues related to prior periods.)

Liabilities not normally liquidated with current financial resources

Action needed: Expenses need to be accrued in connection with liabilities incurred during the period, but not normally expected to be liquidated with current available financial resources (i.e., accrued interest, compensated absences, claims and judgments, special termination benefits, landfill closure and postclosure care costs, operating leases with scheduled rent increases, and the government's net pension obligation as an employer).

Adjustments:

(q) — Liabilities not normally liquidated with current financial resources

	DR	CR
Expenditures — general government	$ 340	
Expenditures — public safety	368	
Expenditures — highways and streets	103	
Expenditures — sanitation	103	
Expenditures — culture and recreation	163	
Debt service — interest	683	
ACCRUED INTEREST PAYABLE		$ 683
COMPENSATED ABSENCES		857
CLAIMS AND JUDGMENTS		220

Regular year-end accruals are required for all liabilities, regardless of whether they are expected to be liquidated with current available financial resources. Accordingly, an increase in the appropriate expenditure/expense line item and corresponding liability account is required.

Depreciation expense

Action needed: Depreciation expense must be reported in connection with all of a government's depreciable capital assets.

Adjustment:

(r) — Depreciation expense

	DR	CR
Expenditures — general government	$ 232	
Expenditures — public safety	94	
Expenditures — highways and streets	501	
Expenditures — sanitation	29	
Expenditures — culture and recreation	347	
ACCUMULATED DEPRECIATION — BUILDINGS		$ 12
ACCUMULATED DEPRECIATION — IMPROVEMENTS		163
ACCUMULATED DEPRECIATION — MACHINERY		549
ACCUMULATED DEPRECIATION — INFRASTRUCTURE		479

The appropriate expenditure/expense line must be increased to reflect depreciation, with a corresponding adjustment to the related contra-asset account for accumulated depreciation.

Amortization

Action needed: Premiums, discounts, and deferred charges need to be amortized in the government-wide statement of activities.

Adjustment:

(s) — Amortization

	DR	CR
Expenditures — general government	$ 15	
Debt service — interest	33	
DEFERRED CHARGES — ISSUANCE COSTS		$ 15
DISCOUNT— SPECIAL ASSESSMENT DEBT		1
DEFERRED CHARGE — REFUNDING		32

The appropriate expenditure/expense line must be adjusted for the effect of the amortization of premiums, discounts, and deferred charges. Likewise, the premium, discount, or deferred charge accounts (or contra-account) must themselves be adjusted.

CONSOLIDATION OF INTERNAL SERVICE FUNDS

Incorporation of assets and liabilities of internal service funds

Action needed: Internal service funds that primarily serve governmental funds must be incorporated with those funds as part of governmental activities for purposes of government-wide financial reporting. Since internal service funds inherently involve a high degree of duplication, consolidation is required.

Adjustment:

(t) – Allocate permanent accounts of internal service funds

	DR	CR
Cash and cash equivalents	$ 94	
Investments	50	
Receivables (net)	6	
Due from other funds	126	
Inventories	23	
Prepaids	38	
BUILDINGS	87	
MACHINERY	5,283	
ACCUMULATED DEPRECIATION — BUILDINGS		$ 8
ACCUMULATED DEPRECIATION — MACHINERY		2,458
Accounts payable		242
Due to other funds		42
Advances from other funds		78
COMPENSATED ABSENCES		28
Fund balance		2,851

The assets and liabilities of internal service funds that primarily serve governmental funds need to be included with those of the governmental funds themselves for purposes of government-wide financial reporting. The difference between internal service fund assets and liabilities is treated as an adjustment to the net assets account.

Direct incorporation of amounts not to be consolidated

Action needed: There is no need to consolidate revenues and expenses of internal service funds that relate to services provided to parties outside the primary government. Likewise, items that cannot properly be classified as part of net program expense (e.g., interest revenue/expense) must be excluded from consolidation to avoid being included in functional expense indirectly as a result of the "look-back adjustment." Such amounts should be incorporated directly into the government-wide statement of activities.

Adjustment:

(u) — Direct incorporation of revenues and expenses that are not subject to consolidation

	DR	CR
Fund balance	$ 13	
Expenditures — general government	123	
Revenues — charges for service		$ 128
Revenues — investment earnings and miscellaneous		8

Interest revenue, as well as revenues earned and expenses incurred in connection with providing services to customers *outside the primary government* need to be included as part of the revenues and expenses of the primary government. Consolidation of these amounts is unnecessary as they do *not* involve duplication.

Elimination of internal service funds' profit generated by customers within the primary government

Action needed: Any current period net profit or loss in an internal service fund resulting from interfund activity within the primary government needs to be removed from governmental activities in the government-wide statement of activities.

Adjustments:

(v) — Current period "look-back" adjustment ("crossover") to eliminate profit reported in internal service fund

	DR	CR
Fund balance	$ 56	
Due to other funds		$ 9
Expenditures — general government		20
Expenditures — public safety		11
Expenditures — highways and streets		3
Expenditures — sanitation		6
Expenditures — culture and recreation		7

The premise of consolidation is that internal service funds operate on a pure break-even basis. Accordingly, a profit in an internal service fund represents an over-billing that needs to be eliminated from the government-wide statement of activities by an adjustment to the amounts reported as functional expenses.

(w) — Net "crossover" from prior years

	DR	CR
Fund balance	$ 84	
Due to other funds		$ 84

The beginning balances of the government-wide statement of net assets include the effect of prior period adjustments made to record internal balances resulting from "lookback" adjustments made to the business-type activities column. Accordingly, an adjustment is necessary to beginning net assets for the cumulative total (i.e., the net amount) of all such previous "crossover" adjustments (in this particular case, the entire amount is the result of the "look-back" adjustment of the previous year).

ADDITIONAL CONSOLIDATION

Elimination of transfers within governmental activities

Action needed: Transfers within funds incorporated as part of governmental activities need to be removed from the government-wide statement of activities.

Adjustments:

(x) — Removal of transfers to internal service fund

	DR	CR
ACCUMULATED DEPRECIATION — BUILDINGS	$ 4	
ACCUMULATED DEPRECIATION — MACHINERY	2,089	
Fund balance	2,205	
BUILDINGS		$ 87
MACHINERY		4,166
Transfers out		45

A capital contribution of capital assets related to governmental funds (book value of $2,160) to the internal service funds must be removed for purposes of government-wide financial reporting. Also, a transfer of financial resources of $45 from governmental funds to the internal service funds must be removed for purposes of government-wide financial reporting. [Note: As explained at the beginning of this appendix, general government accounts are needed to track assets and liabilities that are not otherwise accounted for in the funds. In the case of a transfer of general government capital assets to an internal service fund, general government accounts for these capital assets are no longer necessary because the required information will henceforth be maintained in the records of the internal service fund receiving the capital assets. Accordingly, the changes to the general government accounts shown in this adjustment would be made to the general ledger accounts, even though consolidating adjustments normally are confined to the worksheet.]

(y) — Consolidation to arrive at net transfers between governmental and business-type activities

	DR	CR
Transfers in	$ 5,446	
Transfers out		$ 5,446

Transfers were made during the year between various governmental funds and between governmental funds and enterprise funds. Such amounts must be consolidated within governmental activities so that only the net amount of transfers from or to business-type activities are reported for purposes of government-wide financial reporting.

Elimination of interfund balances

Action needed: All interfund balances within governmental activities must be eliminated.

Adjustments:

(z) — Elimination of balances between individual governmental funds

	DR	CR
Due to other funds	$ 335	
Due from other funds		$ 335

As a result of interfund activity, balances remained outstanding between certain governmental funds at year end. Such amounts must be eliminated for purposes of government-wide financial reporting.

(aa) — Consolidation to arrive at net internal balances between governmental and business-type activities

	DR	CR
Advances from other funds	$ 78	
Due to other funds	276	
Internal balances		$ 45
Advances to other funds		78
Due from other funds		231

ACCOUNTS RELATED TO GOVERNMENTAL ACTIVITIES

ASSETS	Trial Balance DR	Trial Balance CR	Adjustments DR	Adjustments CR	Total	Statement of Activities DR	Statement of Activities CR	Statement of Net Assets DR	Statement of Net Assets CR
Cash and cash equivalents	$3,872		(t) $94		$3,966			$3,966	
Investments	$9,121		(t) $50		$9,171			$9,171	
Receivables (net)	$5,749		(t) $6		$5,755			$5,755	
Due from other funds	$440		(t) $126	(z) -$335; (aa) -$231					
Due from component unit	$12				$12			$12	
Internal balances				(aa) -$45	-$45				-$45
Inventories	$39		(t) $23		$62			$62	
Prepaids			(t) $38		$38			$38	
Advances to other funds	$78			(aa) -$78					
Restricted assets — cash and cash equivalents	$4				$4			$4	
Restricted assets — receivables	$315				$315			$315	
DEFERRED CHARGES - ISSUANCE COSTS			(f) $150; (h) $65	(s) -$15	$200			$200	
LAND	$38,775		(a) $558		$39,333			$39,333	
BUILDINGS	$7,875		(t) $87	(x) -$87	$7,875			$7,875	
ACCUMULATED DEPRECIATION ON BUILDINGS		-$1,968	(x) $4	(r) -$12; (t) -$8	-$1,984				-$1,984
IMPROVEMENTS	$4,604				$4,604			$4,604	
ACCUMULATED DEPRECIATION ON IMPROVEMENTS		-$1,335		(r) -$163	-$1,498				-$1,498
MACHINERY	$8,123		(a) $1,035; (c) $140; (i) $13; (k) $17; (t) $5,283	(j) -$42; (k) -$14; (l) -$8; (x) -$4,166	$10,381			$10,381	
ACCUMULATED DEPRECIATION ON MACHINERY		-$2,355	(j) $39; (k) $9; (l) $8; (x) $2,089	(r) -$549; (t) -$2,458	-$3,217				-$3,217
INFRASTRUCTURE	$28,500				$28,500			$28,500	
ACCUMULATED DEPRECIATION ON INFRASTRUCTURE		-$4,560		(r) -$479	-$5,039				-$5,039
CONSTRUCTION IN PROGRESS — INFRASTRUCTURE			(b) $3,785		$3,785			$3,785	
LIABILITIES									
Accounts payable		-$2,198		(t) -$242	-$2,440				-$2,440
Contracts and retainage payable		-$227			-$227				-$227
Due to other funds		-$476	(z) $335; (aa) $276	(t) -$42; (v) -$9; (w) -$84					
Advances from other funds			(aa) $78	(t) -$78					
Matured bonds payable		-$5			-$5				-$5

ACCOUNTS RELATED TO GOVERNMENTAL ACTIVITIES, cont.

	Trial Balance		Adjustments		Total	Statement of Activities		Statememt of Net Assets	
	DR	CR	DR	CR		DR	CR	DR	CR
LIABILITIES, cont.									
Matured interest payable		-$3			-$3				-$3
Deferred revenue		-$4,299	(m) $27 (p) $4,272						
Unearned revenue		-$181			-$181				-$181
Liabilities payable from restricted assets		-$18			-$18				-$18
ACCRUED INTEREST PAYABLE		-$632	(o) $632	(q) -$683	-$683				-$683
COMPENSATED ABSENCES		-$1,811	(o) $646	(q) -$857 (t) -$28	-$2,050				-$2,050
CLAIMS AND JUDGMENTS				(q) -$220	-$220				-$220
GENERAL OBLIGATION DEBT		-$37,455	(d) $2,030 (h) $3,000	(h) -$3,365	-$35,790				-$35,790
SPECIAL ASSESSMENT DEBT				(f) -$4,700	-$4,700				-$4,700
DISCOUNT ON SPECIAL ASSESSMENT DEBT			(f) $10	(s) -$1	$9			$9	
DEFERRED CHARGE —REFUNDING			(h) $315	(s) -$32	$283			$283	
CAPITAL LEASES			(e) $15	(g) -$140	-$125				-$125
FUND BALANCE/NET ASSETS									
Fund balance — governmental funds		-$5,038	(u) $13 (v) $56 (w) $84 (x) $2,205	(m) -$97 (n) -$48 (t) -$2,851	-$5,670				-$5,676
NET ASSETS		-$37,761			-$37,761				-$37,761*
REVENUES/GAINS									
Taxes		-$28,181	(m) $70	(p) -$42	-$28,153		-$28,153		
Fees, licenses, and permits		-$2,041			-$2,041		-$2,041		
Intergovernmental		-$6,661			-$6,661		-$6,661		
Charges for services		-$2,300		(u) -$128	-$2,428		-$2,428		
Fines		-$808			-$808		-$808		
Special assessments		-$470		(p) -$4,230	-$4,700		-$4,700		
Investment earnings and miscellaneous		-$2,128	(n) $48	(i) -$13 (u) -$8	-$2,101		-$2,101		
Payments in lieu of taxes		-$365			-$365		-$365		
Gain — sale of capital assets				(j) -$2	-$2		-$2		
EXPENDITURES/ EXPENSES AND LOSSES									
Current:									
General government	$4,257		(q) $340 (r) $232 (s) $15 (u) $123	(a) -$475 (k) -$12 (o) -$90 (v) -$20	$4,364	$4,370			

*This number needs to be adjusted in the general ledger to reflect the difference between general government asset and liability accounts at the end of the period (*not* including assets and liabilities reported in internal service funds).

ACCOUNTS RELATED TO GOVERNMENTAL ACTIVITIES, cont.

EXPENDITURES/EXPENSES AND LOSSES	Trial Balance DR	Trial Balance CR	Adjustments DR		Adjustments CR		Total	Statement of Activities DR	Statement of Activities CR	Statement of Net Assets DR	Statement of Net Assets CR
Public safety	$13,438		(q)	$368	(a)	-$648	$12,823	$12,823			
			(r)	$94	(c)	-$140					
					(o)	-$278					
					(v)	-$11					
Highways and streets	$4,477		(q)	$103	(a)	-$165	$4,835	$4,835			
			(r)	$501	(o)	-$78					
					(v)	-$3					
Sanitation	$3,726		(q)	$103	(a)	-$1	$3,773	$3,773			
			(r)	$29	(o)	-$78					
					(v)	-$6					
Economic and physical development	$401						$401	$401			
Culture and recreation	$6,913		(q)	$163	(a)	-$304	$6,990	$6,990			
			(r)	$347	(o)	-$122					
					(v)	-$7					
Capital outlay:											
Capital outlay	$3,785				(b)	-$3,785					
Debt service:											
Debt service — principal	$2,045				(d)	-$2,030					
					(e)	-$15					
Debt service — interest	$2,928		(q)	$683	(o)	-$632	$3,012	$3,012			
			(s)	$33							
Debt service — bond issuance costs	$215				(f)	-$150					
					(h)	-$65					
Debt service — advance refunding escrow	$15				(h)	-$15					
OTHER FINANCING SOURCES/USES											
Transfers in		-$7,022	(y)	$5,446			-$1,576		-$1,576		
Transfers out	$5,491				(x)	-$45					
					(y)	-$5,446					
Special assessment bonds issued		-$4,700	(f)	$4,700							
Discount on special assessment debt	$10				(f)	-$10					
Refunding bonds issued		-$3,365	(h)	$3,365							
Payment to refunded bond escrow agent	$3,300				(h)	-$3,300					
Capital leases		-$140	(g)	$140							
Proceeds of sale of capital assets		-$5	(j)	$5							
SUBTOTAL	$158,508	-$158,508		$44,521		-$44,521	$0	$36,204	-$48,835	$114,293	-$101,662
INCREASE IN NET ASSETS								$12,631			-$12,631
TOTAL	$158,508	-$158,508		$44,521		-$44,521	$0	$48,835	-$48,835	$114,293	-$114,293

CONVERSION AND ANNUAL ACCRUALS

(a) Convert capital outlay from functional activities to capital assets
(b) Convert capital outlay from capital projects fund to capital assets
(c) Convert capital lease expenditure to capital assets
(d) Convert debt principal payments to liability reduction
(e) Convert lease down payment to reduction of lease liability
(f) Convert debt issuance from temporary to permanent accounts
(g) Convert capital lease from temporary to permanent accounts
(h) Convert refunding from temporary to permanent accounts
(i) Donation of capital assets
(j) Sale of machinery and equipment
(k) Trade-in of machinery
(l) Scrapping of fully depreciated machinery
(m) Eliminate property tax revenue related to prior years
(n) Eliminate interest revenue related to prior year
(o) Eliminate expenditures related to prior years
(p) Add earned but unavailable revenue
(q) Expenses not normally liquidated with current financial resources
(r) Depreciation expense
(s) Amortization

CONSOLIDATION

(t) Allocate permanent accounts of internal service funds
(u) Inclusion of revenues and expenses not subject to consolidation
(v) "Crossover" from current year's "look-back" adjustment
(w) Net "crossover" from prior year's "look-back"
(x) Removal of transfers to internal service fund
(y) Consolidation to arrive at net transfers between governmental and business-type activities
(z) Elimination of balances between individual governmental funds
(aa) Consolidation to arrive at net internal balances between governmental and business-type activities

D

Illustrative Comprehensive Annual Financial Report

RELATIONSHIP OF APPENDICES

The first four appendices illustrate the preparation of a comprehensive annual financial report (CAFR) prepared in conformity with Governmental Accounting Standards Board Statement No. 34, *Basic Financial Statements—and Management's Discussion and Analysis—for State and Local Governments* and the requirements of the Government Finance Officers Association's Certificate of Achievement for Excellence in Financial Reporting Program.

- **Illustrative Journal Entries (appendix A).** This appendix illustrates the different types of journal entries used to collect data in the government's fund-based accounting system.
- **Illustrative Trial Balances (appendix B).** This appendix provides 1) a trial balance as of the beginning of the current fiscal year, 2) a preclosing trial balance, and 3) a trial balance as of the end of the current fiscal year for each of the funds for which illustrative journal entries are provided in appendix A.
- **Illustrative Conversion Worksheet (appendix C).** This appendix illustrates how the data reported in governmental funds and internal service funds are converted and consolidated for presentation as *governmental activities* in the government-wide financial statements.
- **Illustrative CAFR (appendix D).** This appendix offers a complete illustrative CAFR. The numbers in this illustrative CAFR are supported by the journal entries, trial balances, and conversion worksheet provided in appendices A, B, and C.

NAME OF GOVERNMENT
Comprehensive Annual Financial Report
For the fiscal year ended
December 31, 2015

Prepared by:

Department of Finance and Administration

Name of Government
Comprehensive Annual Financial Report
For the Fiscal Year Ended December 31, 2015

TABLE OF CONTENTS

INTRODUCTORY SECTION

LETTERHEAD OF GOVERNMENT

April 30, 2016

To the Honorable Mayor, Members of the Governing Council, and Citizens of the NAME OF GOVERNMENT:

State law requires that every general-purpose local government publish within six months of the close of each fiscal year a complete set of audited financial statements. This report is published to fulfill that requirement for the fiscal year ended December 31, 2015.

Management assumes full responsibility for the completeness and reliability of the information contained in this report, based upon a comprehensive framework of internal control that it has established for this purpose. Because the cost of internal control should not exceed anticipated benefits, the objective is to provide reasonable, rather than absolute, assurance that the financial statements are free of any material misstatements.

West, Lee, Roberts & Co., Certified Public Accountants, have issued an unqualified ("clean") opinion on the NAME OF GOVERNMENT'S financial statements for the year ended December 31, 2015. The independent auditor's report is located at the front of the financial section of this report.

Management's discussion and analysis (MD&A) immediately follows the independent auditor's report and provides a narrative introduction, overview, and analysis of the basic financial statements. MD&A complement this letter of transmittal and should be read in conjunction with it.

Profile of the Government

The NAME OF GOVERNMENT, incorporated in 1853, is located in the western part of the state, which is considered to be one of the top growth areas in both the state and the country. It currently occupies 17 square miles and serves a population of 61,434. The NAME OF GOVERNMENT is empowered to levy a property tax on both real and personal property located within its boundaries. It also is empowered by state statute to extend its corporate limits by annexation, which it has done from time to time.

The NAME OF GOVERNMENT has operated under the council-manager form of government since 1913, having been the first in the state to adopt this form of government. Policy-making and legislative authority are vested in a governing council (Council) consisting of the mayor and eight other members, all

3

elected on a non-partisan basis. The Council appoints the government's manager, who in turn appoints the heads of the various departments. Council members serve four-year terms, with four members elected every two years. The mayor is elected for a two-year term. The mayor and two council members are elected at large; the remaining Council members are elected by district.

The NAME OF GOVERNMENT provides a full range of services, including police and fire protection; the construction and maintenance of highways, streets and other infrastructure; and recreational and cultural activities. Certain sanitation services are provided through a legally separate Water and Sewer Authority, which functions, in essence, as a department of the NAME OF GOVERNMENT and therefore has been included as an integral part of the NAME OF GOVERNMENT'S financial statements. The NAME OF GOVERNMENT also is financially accountable for a legally separate school district and a legally separate cable television operation, both of which are reported separately within the NAME OF GOVERNMENT'S financial statements. Additional information on all three of these legally separate entities can be found in the notes to the financial statements (See Note I.A).

The Council is required to adopt a final budget by no later than the close of the fiscal year. This annual budget serves as the foundation for the NAME OF GOVERNMENT'S financial planning and control. The budget is prepared by fund, function (e.g., public safety), and department (e.g., police). Department heads may transfer resources within a department as they see fit. Transfers between departments, however, need special approval from the governing council.

Local economy

Major industries located within the government's boundaries or in close proximity include manufacturers of computer hardware, computer software, electrical controls, and automobile components, as well as several financial institutions and insurance companies. The state also is a significant economic presence thanks to a major mental health facility that provides employment to more than 1,000 healthcare professionals and staff.

Because of its location in a region with a varied economic base, unemployment is relatively stable. During the past ten years, the unemployment rate rose from an initial low of 4.1 percent (2006) to a decade high of 8.4 percent (2012), only to descend once more to the current rate of 5.4 percent. Unemployment is expected either to remain stable or decrease still further in the near term for two reasons. First, it is estimated that jobs in the regional economy will increase by 2 or 3 percent annually for each of the next several years, which would roughly equal average population growth over the past decade (2.6 percent). Second, a major, nationally known furniture manufacturer is contemplating opening a new facility nearby that would employ as many as 1,200 individuals, many of whom would likely be recruited locally.

As the result of a variety of revitalization efforts undertaken over the past decade, the occupancy rate for the central business district has increased from 85 percent (2006) to its current 97 percent level, with no significant decline anticipated in the foreseeable future.

During the past ten years, the government's expenses related to public safety and parks and recreation have increased not only in amount, but also as a percentage of total expenses (a ten-year increase of 7.1 percent and 3.4 percent, respectively). In the case of public safety, much of the increase reflects a regional trend that has seen the salaries and benefits of police and firefighters growing at a much faster rate than those of other categories of public-sector employees. The growth in parks and recreation expenses reflects an increase in the number of sponsored programs and events.

During this same ten-year period, charges for services, while continuing to increase in amount, have actually decreased as a percentage of total revenue (a ten-year decrease of 19.3 percent). The reason for this relative decline is the relative increase in expenses related to services that are *not* supported by fees and charges (e.g., public safety); thus, as taxes have increased to support these services, so has the proportion of total revenue generated by taxes.

Long-term financial planning

Unreserved, undesignated fund balance in the general fund (11.7 percent of total general fund revenues) falls within the policy guidelines set by the Council for budgetary and planning purposes (i.e., between 5 and 15 percent of total general fund revenues). Following its recent review of the NAME OF GOVERNMENT's strategic plan, the Council now plans to raise the target to between 15 and 25 percent of total general fund revenues so as to reduce the amount that will need to be borrowed to finance future construction.

Also as part of the strategic plan, the Council envisions developing a new park along the Green River to provide river access for residents and tourists. Eventually, the project could include the development of a riverside walk, the construction of picnic facilities, restaurant and shopping complexes, and boat access ramps. In addition to initial construction costs (estimated at between $4 million and $6 million), the NAME OF GOVERNMENT would likely incur significant additional operating costs to staff, operate, and maintain the new facilities.

Relevant financial policies

The state supreme court recently held that the state must compensate local governments for the cost of retroactive compliance with the Local Wetlands Protection Act of 2005. It is the NAME OF GOVERNMENT's policy that "onetime" resource inflows *not* be used for operating purposes. Accordingly, the Council plans to designate the amount it eventually receives from the state for the acquisition of new park land.

Major initiatives

It is expected that both the state and federal governments will enact new regulations on water quality that could take effect as early as December 2019. The Water and Sewer Authority is developing plans for a substantial upgrade of the water filtration plant, which had its last upgrade in 2009. The project would encompass the expansion of holding tanks for finished water storage and the replacement of the original filtration equipment. The overall cost of the project would probably exceed $12 million and would be financed by the issuance of revenue bonds.

The next transportation-related project is expected to be the replacement of the Veterans Memorial Bridge over the Green River. Three quarters of the expected $1 million total cost would be financed with Federal highway funds. The government tentatively plans to begin soliciting bids in early 2016, pending federal approval for the final plans. If construction does begin in early 2016, the bridge would probably be completed sometime in late 2018.

Awards and Acknowledgements

The Government Finance Officers Association (GFOA) awarded a Certificate of Achievement for Excellence in Financial Reporting to the NAME OF GOVERNMENT for its comprehensive annual financial report (CAFR) for the fiscal year ended December 31, 2014. This was the twentieth consecutive year that the government has received this prestigious award. In order to be awarded a Certificate of Achievement, the government had to publish an easily readable and efficiently organized CAFR that satisfied both generally accepted accounting principles and applicable legal requirements.

A Certificate of Achievement is valid for a period of one year only. We believe that our current CAFR continues to meet the Certificate of Achievement Program's requirements and we are submitting it to the GFOA to determine its eligibility for another certificate.

In addition, the government also received the GFOA's Distinguished Budget Presentation Award for its annual budget document dated December 18, 2014. In order to qualify for the Distinguished Budget Presentation Award, the government's budget document had to be judged proficient as a policy document, a financial plan, an operations guide, and a communications device.

The preparation of this report would not have been possible without the efficient and dedicated service of the entire staff of the finance and administration department. We wish to express our appreciation to all members of the department who assisted and contributed to the preparation of this report. Credit also must be given to the mayor and the governing council for their unfailing support for maintaining the highest standards of professionalism in the management of the NAME OF GOVERNMENT'S finances.

Respectfully submitted,

Lorraine M. Desmarais
Manager

Susan L. Wakefield
Finance Director

Certificate of Achievement for Excellence in Financial Reporting

Presented to

Name of Government

For its Comprehensive Annual
Financial Report
for the Fiscal Year Ended
December 31, 2014

A Certificate of Achievement for Excellence in Financial
Reporting is presented by the Government Finance Officers
Association of the United States and Canada to
government units and public employee retirement
systems whose comprehensive annual financial
reports (CAFRs) achieve the highest
standards in government accounting
and financial reporting.

President

Executive Director

Name of Government Organizational Chart

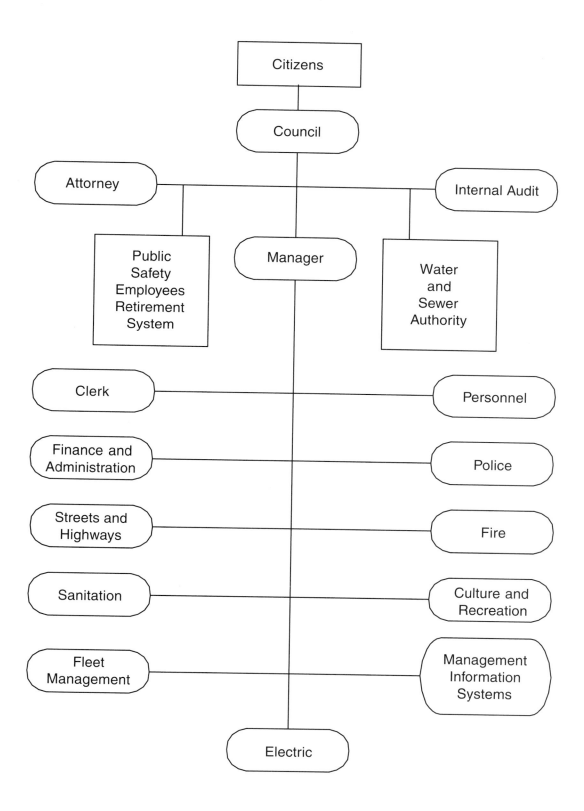

Name of Government
List of Elected and Appointed Officials
December 31, 2015

Elected Officials

Mayor	Barbara J. McCown
Council Member – Ward 1	Marc Christian
Council Member – Ward 2	Brittain A. Neal
Council Member – Ward 3	Paul Édouard
Council Member – Ward 4	Wilma J. Gouge
Council Member – Ward 5	Gregory Joseph
Council Member – Ward 6	Marie Desmarais
Council Member – At large	Hannah Lee
Council Member – At large	Nathan Scott

Appointed Officials

Manager	Lorraine M. Desmarais
Assistant Manager	Josephine Paquette
Attorney	James M. Falconer
Clerk	Lynn Nguyen
Culture and Recreation Director	John D. Fishbein
Electric Manager	Julius G. Howard III
Finance Director	Susan L. Wakefield
Fire Chief	James A. Phillips
Fleet Management Director	Delores Smith
Internal Audit Director	Bonnie Ashman
Management Information Systems Director	Kathleen Schultz
Personnel Director	Zhikuan Hu
Police Chief	Asia Roberson
Sanitation Director	Krisztina Mihaly
Streets and Highways Director	Carole Colin
Public Safety Employees Retirement System President	Richard M. Stefanovich
Water and Sewer Authority Chair	Qun Wang

FINANCIAL SECTION

OFFICIAL LETTERHEAD OF THE INDEPENDENT AUDITOR

INDEPENDENT AUDITOR'S REPORT

We have audited the accompanying financial statements of the governmental activities, the business-type activities, each major fund, and the aggregate remaining fund information of the NAME OF GOVERNMENT, as of and for the year ended December 31, 2015, which collectively comprise the NAME OF GOVERNMENT'S basic financial statements as listed in the table of contents. We also have audited the financial statements of each of the NAME OF GOVERNMENT'S nonmajor governmental and internal service funds presented in the accompanying combining and individual fund financial statements and schedules as of and for the year ended December 31, 2015, as listed in the table of contents. These financial statements are the responsibility of the NAME OF GOVERNMENT'S management. Our responsibility is to express opinions on these financial statements based on our audit. We did not audit the financial statements of the School District and Cable Television discretely presented component units, which represent 100 percent of the assets, net assets, and revenues of the aggregate discretely presented component units. Those financial statements were audited by other auditors whose reports thereon have been furnished to us, and our opinion, insofar as it relates to the amounts included for the aggregate discretely presented component units is based on the report of the other auditors.

We conducted our audit in accordance with auditing standards generally accepted in the United States of America and the standards applicable to financial audits contained in *Government Auditing Standards,* issued by the Comptroller General of the United States. Those standards require that we plan and perform the audit to obtain reasonable assurance about whether the financial statements are free of material misstatement. An audit includes examining, on a test basis, evidence supporting the amounts and disclosures in the financial statements. An audit also includes assessing the accounting principles used and significant estimates made by management, as well as evaluating the overall financial statement presentation. We believe that our audit and the report of other auditors provide a reasonable basis for our opinions.

In our opinion, based on our audit and the report of other auditors, the financial statements referred to above present fairly, in all material respects, the respective financial position of the governmental activities, the business-type activities, the aggregate discretely presented component units, each major fund, and the aggregate remaining fund information of the NAME OF GOVERNMENT, as of December 31, 2015, and the respective changes in financial position and cash flows, where applicable, thereof and the budgetary comparison for the general fund for the year then ended in conformity with accounting principles generally accepted in the United States of America. In addition, in our opinion, the financial statements referred to above present fairly, in all material respects, the respective financial position of each nonmajor governmental, and internal service fund of the NAME OF GOVERNMENT, as of December 31, 2015, and the respective changes in financial position and cash flows, where applicable, thereof and the budgetary comparison for the debt service, transportation special revenue, parks maintenance special revenue, CDBG revitalization project special revenue, housing development street construction capital projects, and street construction capital projects funds for the years then ended in conformity with accounting principles generally accepted in the United States of America.

In accordance with *Government Auditing Standards,* we have also issued a report dated April 15, 2016, on our consideration of the NAME OF GOVERNMENT'S internal control over financial reporting and our tests of its compliance with certain provisions of laws, regulations, contracts and grants. That report is an integral part of an audit performed in accordance with *Government Auditing Standards* and should be read in conjunction with this report in considering the results of our audit.

Management's discussion and analysis and the schedules of funding progress for the Public Safety Employees Retirement System and the Public Safety Employees Other Postemployment Benefits Plan on pages 15 through 28 and page 78 are not a required part of the basic financial statements but are supplementary information required by accounting principles generally accepted in the United States of America. We have applied certain limited procedures, which consisted principally of inquiries of management regarding the methods of measurement and presentation of the required supplementary information. However, we did not audit the information and express no opinion on it.

The introductory section and statistical section have not been subjected to the auditing procedures applied in the audit of the basic financial statements and, accordingly, we express no opinion on them.

West, Lee, Roberts & Company
Certified Public Accountants

April 15, 2016

Management's Discussion and Analysis

As management of the NAME OF GOVERNMENT, we offer readers of the NAME OF GOVERNMENT'S financial statements this narrative overview and analysis of the financial activities of the NAME OF GOVERNMENT for the fiscal year ended December 31, 2015. We encourage readers to consider the information presented here in conjunction with additional information that we have furnished in our letter of transmittal, which can be found on pages 3-7 of this report. All amounts, unless otherwise indicated, are expressed in thousands of dollars.

Financial Highlights

- The assets of the NAME OF GOVERNMENT exceeded its liabilities at the close of the most recent fiscal year by $158,319 (*net assets*). Of this amount, $28,566 (*unrestricted net assets*) may be used to meet the government's ongoing obligations to citizens and creditors.
- The government's total net assets increased by $22,479. Approximately one third of this increase is attributable to a one-time infusion of resources from tap fees and special assessments.
- As of the close of the current fiscal year, the NAME OF GOVERNMENT'S governmental funds reported combined ending fund balances of $12,223, an increase of $7,185 in comparison with the prior year. Approximately half of this total amount, $6,606, is *available for spending* at the government's discretion (*unreserved, undesignated fund balance*).
- At the end of the current fiscal year, unreserved, undesignated fund balance for the general fund was $4,390, or 14 percent of total general fund expenditures.
- The NAME OF GOVERNMENT'S total debt increased by $35,665 (50 percent) during the current fiscal year. The key factor in this increase was the issuance of $34,600 in revenue bonds for the Water and Sewer Authority.

Overview of the Financial Statements

This discussion and analysis are intended to serve as an introduction to the NAME OF GOVERNMENT'S basic financial statements. The NAME OF GOVERNMENT'S basic financial statements comprise three components: 1) government-wide financial statements, 2) fund financial statements, and 3) notes to the financial statements. This report also contains other supplementary information in addition to the basic financial statements themselves.

Government-wide financial statements. The *government-wide financial statements* are designed to provide readers with a broad overview of the NAME OF GOVERNMENT'S finances, in a manner similar to a private-sector business.

The *statement of net assets* presents information on all of the NAME OF GOVERNMENT'S assets and liabilities, with the difference between the two reported as *net assets*. Over time, increases or decreases in net assets may serve as a useful indicator of whether the financial position of the NAME OF GOVERNMENT is improving or deteriorating.

The *statement of activities* presents information showing how the government's net assets changed during the most recent fiscal year. All changes in net assets are reported as soon as the underlying event giving rise to the change occurs, *regardless of the timing of related cash flows*. Thus, revenues and expenses are reported in this statement for some items that will only result in cash flows in future fiscal periods (e.g., uncollected taxes and earned but unused vacation leave).

Both of the government-wide financial statements distinguish functions of the NAME OF GOVERNMENT that are principally supported by taxes and intergovernmental revenues (*governmental activities*) from other functions that are intended to recover all or a significant portion of their costs through user fees and charges (*business-type activities*). The governmental activities of the NAME OF GOVERNMENT include general government, public safety, highways and streets, sanitation, economic development, and culture and recreation. The business-type activities of the NAME OF GOVERNMENT include a Water and Sewer Authority and an electric distribution operation.

The government-wide financial statements include not only the NAME OF GOVERNMENT itself (known as the *primary government*), but also a legally separate school district and a legally separate cable television station for which the NAME OF GOVERNMENT is financially accountable. Financial information for these *component units* is reported separately from the financial information presented for the primary government itself. The Water and Sewer Authority, although also legally separate, functions for all practical purposes as a department of the NAME OF GOVERNMENT, and therefore has been included as an integral part of the primary government.

The government-wide financial statements can be found on pages 30-31 of this report.

Fund financial statements. A *fund* is a grouping of related accounts that is used to maintain control over resources that have been segregated for specific activities or objectives. The NAME OF GOVERNMENT, like other state and local governments, uses fund accounting to ensure and demonstrate compliance with finance-related legal requirements. All of the funds of the NAME OF GOVERNMENT can be divided into three categories: governmental funds, proprietary funds, and fiduciary funds.

Governmental funds. *Governmental funds* are used to account for essentially the same functions reported as *governmental activities* in the government-wide financial statements. However, unlike the government-wide financial statements, governmental fund financial statements focus on *near-term inflows and outflows of spendable resources*, as well as on *balances of spendable resources* available at the end of the fiscal year. Such information may be useful in evaluating a government's near-term financing requirements.

Because the focus of governmental funds is narrower than that of the government-wide financial statements, it is useful to compare the information presented for *governmental funds* with similar information presented for *governmental activities* in the government-wide financial statements. By doing so, readers may better understand the long-term impact of the government's near-term financing decisions. Both the governmental fund balance sheet and the governmental fund statement of revenues, expenditures, and changes in fund balances provide a reconciliation to facilitate this comparison between *governmental funds* and *governmental activities*.

The NAME OF GOVERNMENT maintains eight individual governmental funds. Information is presented separately in the governmental fund balance sheet and in the governmental fund statement of revenues, expenditures, and changes in fund balances for the general fund and the debt service fund, both of which are considered to be major funds. Data from the other six governmental funds are combined into a single, aggregated presentation. Individual fund data for each of these nonmajor governmental funds is provided in the form of *combining statements* elsewhere in this report.

The NAME OF GOVERNMENT adopts an annual appropriated budget for its general fund. A budgetary comparison statement has been provided for the general fund to demonstrate compliance with this budget.

The basic governmental fund financial statements can be found on pages 32-35 of this report.

Proprietary funds. The NAME OF GOVERNMENT maintains two different types of proprietary funds. *Enterprise funds* are used to report the same functions presented as *business-type activities* in the government-wide financial statements. The NAME OF GOVERNMENT uses enterprise funds to account for its Water and Sewer Authority and for its electric distribution operation. *Internal service funds* are an accounting device used to accumulate and allocate costs internally among the NAME OF GOVERNMENT'S various functions. The NAME OF GOVERNMENT uses internal service funds to account for its fleet of vehicles and for its management information systems. Because both of these services predominantly benefit governmental rather than business-type functions, they have been included within *governmental activities* in the government-wide financial statements.

Proprietary funds provide the same type of information as the government-wide financial statements, only in more detail. The proprietary fund financial statements provide separate information for the Water and Sewer Authority and for the electric distribution operation, both of which are considered to be major funds of the NAME OF GOVERNMENT. Conversely, both internal service funds are combined into a single, aggregated presentation in the proprietary fund financial statements. Individual fund data for the internal service funds is provided in the form of *combining statements* elsewhere in this report.

The basic proprietary fund financial statements can be found on pages 36-41 of this report.

Fiduciary funds. Fiduciary funds are used to account for resources held for the benefit of parties outside the government. Fiduciary funds are *not* reflected in the government-wide financial statement because the resources of those funds are *not* available to support the NAME OF GOVERNMENT'S own programs. The accounting used for fiduciary funds is much like that used for proprietary funds.

The basic fiduciary fund financial statements can be found on pages 42-43 of this report.

Notes to the financial statements. The notes provide additional information that is essential to a full understanding of the data provided in the government-wide and fund financial statements. The notes to the financial statements can be found on pages 45-77 of this report.

Other information. In addition to the basic financial statements and accompanying notes, this report also presents certain *required supplementary information* concerning the NAME OF GOVERNMENT'S progress in funding its obligation to provide pension benefits to its employees. Required supplementary information can be found on page 78 of this report.

The combining statements referred to earlier in connection with nonmajor governmental funds and internal service funds are presented immediately following the required supplementary information on pensions. Combining and individual fund statements and schedules can be found on pages 80-92 of this report.

Government-wide Financial Analysis

As noted earlier, net assets may serve over time as a useful indicator of a government's financial position. In the case of the NAME OF GOVERNMENT, assets exceeded liabilities by $158,319 at the close of the most recent fiscal year.

By far the largest portion of the NAME OF GOVERNMENT'S net assets (76 percent) reflects its investment in capital assets (e.g., land, buildings, machinery, and equipment), less any related debt used to acquire those assets that is still outstanding. The NAME OF GOVERNMENT uses these capital assets to provide services to citizens; consequently, these assets are *not* available for future spending. Although the NAME OF GOVERNMENT'S investment in its capital assets is reported net of related debt, it should be noted that the resources needed to repay this debt must be provided from other sources, since the capital assets themselves cannot be used to liquidate these liabilities.

NAME OF GOVERNMENT'S Net Assets

	Governmental activities		Business-type activities		Total	
	2015	2014	2015	2014	2015	2014
Current and other assets	$ 19,478	$ 6,807	$ 57,203	$ 23,974	$ 76,681	$ 30,781
Capital assets	82,740	78,267	118,429	108,497	201,169	186,764
Total assets	102,218	85,074	175,632	132,471	277,850	217,545
Long-term liabilities outstanding	42,593	39,284	66,248	34,646	108,841	73,930
Other liabilities	3,557	2,353	7,133	5,422	10,690	7,775
Total liabilities	46,150	41,637	73,381	40,068	119,531	81,705
Net assets:						
Invested in capital assets, net of related debt	45,092	34,817	75,983	74,229	121,075	109,046
Restricted	8,046	6,528	632	3,113	8,678	9,641
Unrestricted	2,930	2,092	25,636	15,061	28,566	17,153
Total net assets	$ 56,068	$43,437	$102,251	$ 92,403	$158,319	$135,840

An additional portion of the NAME OF GOVERNMENT'S net assets (5 percent) represents resources that are subject to external restrictions on how they may be used. The remaining balance of *unrestricted net assets* ($28,566) may be used to meet the government's ongoing obligations to citizens and creditors.

At the end of the current fiscal year, the NAME OF GOVERNMENT is able to report positive balances in all three categories of net assets, both for the government as a whole, as well as for its separate governmental and business-type activities. The same situation held true for the prior fiscal year.

There was a decrease of $2,481 in restricted net assets reported in connection with the NAME OF GOVERNMENT'S business-type activities. Almost half of this decrease ($1,165) resulted from the removal of restrictions on certain assets associated with revenue bonds that were refunded during the current fiscal year.

The government's net assets increased by $22,479 during the current fiscal year. About one third of this increase represents the degree to which increases in ongoing revenues have outstripped similar increases in ongoing expenses. Approximately another third is attributable to a one-time infusion of resources from tap fees and special assessments. The remainder of this growth largely reflects rate increases, increases in operating grants, and investment earnings.

Governmental activities. Governmental activities increased the NAME OF GOV-ERNMENT'S net assets by $12,631, thereby accounting for 56 percent of the total growth in the net assets of the NAME OF GOVERNMENT. Key elements of this increase are as follows:

NAME OF GOVERNMENT'S Changes in Net Assets

	Governmental activities		Business-type activities		Total	
	2015	2014	2015	2014	2015	2014
Revenues:						
Program revenues:						
Charges for services	$ 5,642	$ 5,473	$ 31,446	$ 28,197	$ 37,088	$ 33,670
Operating grants and contributions	3,399	2,648	396	172	3,795	2,820
Capital grants and contributions	5,166	688	4,294	—	9,460	688
General revenues:						
Property taxes	15,690	13,886	—	—	15,690	13,886
Other taxes	12,463	10,385	—	—	12,463	10,385
Grants and contributions not restricted to specific programs	3,411	3,284	—	—	3,411	3,284
Other	1,488	1,397	3,673	2,357	5,161	3,754
Total revenues	47,259	37,761	39,809	30,726	87,068	68,487
Expenses:						
General government	4,370	3,988	—	—	4,370	3,988
Public safety	12,823	12,400	—	—	12,823	12,400
Highways/streets	4,835	3,972	—	—	4,835	3,972
Sanitation	3,773	3,404	—	—	3,773	3,404
Economic development	401	28	—	—	401	28
Culture and recreation	6,990	6,772	—	—	6,990	6,772
Interest on long-term debt	3,012	2,615	—	—	3,012	2,615
Water	—	—	9,968	8,924	9,968	8,924
Sewer	—	—	5,848	4,804	5,848	4,804
Electric	—	—	12,569	12,781	12,569	12,781
Total expenses	36,204	33,179	28,385	26,509	64,589	59,688
Increase in net assets before transfers	11,055	4,582	11,424	4,217	22,479	8,799
Transfers	1,576	—	-1,576	—	—	—
Increase in net assets	12,631	4,582	9,848	4,217	22,479	8,799
Net assets – 1/1/15	43,437	38,855	92,403	88,186	135,840	127,041
Net assets—12/31/15	$56,068	$43,437	$102,251	$92,403	$158,319	$135,840

- Property taxes increased by $1,804 (13 percent) during the year. Most of this increase is the product of a restricted tax levy for debt service that totaled $1,585.
- Operating grants for governmental activities increased by $751, mostly as a result of an aggressive grant application strategy undertaken by the NAME OF GOVERNMENT during the current fiscal year. The new grant awards furnished resources to support three of the NAME OF GOVERNMENT'S functions: public safety, highways and streets, and culture and recreation.

Expenses and Program Revenues – Governmental Activities

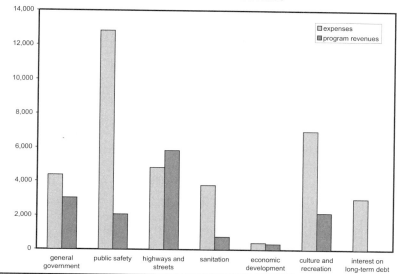

Revenues by Source – Governmental Activities

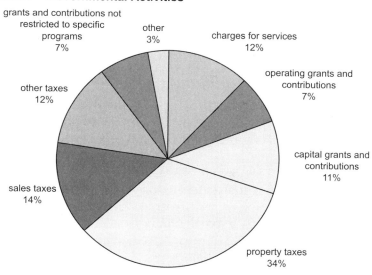

For the most part, increases in expenses closely paralleled inflation and growth in the demand for services. One noteworthy exception, however, was the NAME OF GOVERNMENT'S highways and streets function. In that instance, the growth in expenses of $863 (22 percent) reflects the cost of additional road repairs necessitated by an unusually harsh winter (including a severe ice storm). Also, some of the various grants discussed earlier were used to undertake maintenance projects that had been delayed in the past because of inadequate funding.

Business-type activities. Business-type activities increased the NAME OF GOVERNMENT'S net assets by $9,848, accounting for 44 percent of the total growth in the government's net assets. Key elements of this increase are as follows.

- Charges for services for business-type activities increased by 11.5 percent. The Water and Sewer Authority accounts for a significant portion of this increase, which resulted from the approval of a 15 percent rate increase designed primarily to provide additional resources to meet debt service requirements. Revenues also increased as a result of a modest increase in demand. Together, these factors account for the $3,109 increase in charges for services for the Water and Sewer Authority. The remaining $140 increase is attributable to modest growth in the electrical distribution operation's customer base, which resulted from a combination of the addition of new customers and increased usage on the part of several of the largest current customers.
- The Water and Sewer Authority received a one-time $350 operating grant from the Federal Regional Commission.
- Capital contributions emerged as a major revenue source for the Water and Sewer Authority during the current fiscal year, producing $4,294 in revenue. This increase is the direct result of legislation passed by the state legislature last year establishing mandatory tap fees. These tap fees, which are set significantly in excess of actual connection costs, must be used for capital purposes.
- Investment earnings increased by $1,316 for business-type activities because of an overall increase in the size of the investment portfolio (due, in part, to the temporary investment of debt proceeds), as well as a strong market.

Financial Analysis of the Government's Funds

As noted earlier, the NAME OF GOVERNMENT uses fund accounting to ensure and demonstrate compliance with finance-related legal requirements.

Governmental funds. The focus of the NAME OF GOVERNMENT'S *governmental funds* is to provide information on near-term inflows, outflows, and balances of *spendable* resources. Such information is useful in assessing the NAME OF GOVERNMENT'S financing requirements. In particular, *unreserved fund balance* may serve as a useful measure of a government's net resources available for spending at the end of the fiscal year.

Expenses and Program Revenues – Business-type Activities

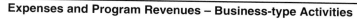

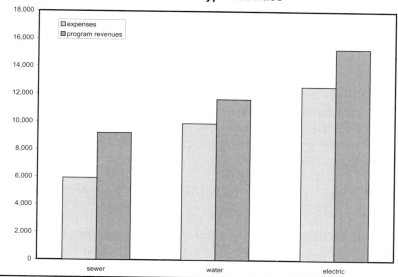

Revenues by Source – Business-type Activities

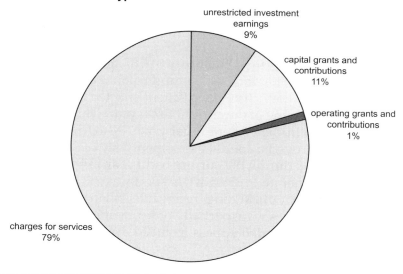

As of the end of the current fiscal year, the NAME OF GOVERNMENT'S governmental funds reported combined ending fund balances of $12,223, an increase of $7,185 in comparison with the prior year. Approximately half of this total amount ($6,606) constitutes *unreserved, undesignated fund balance,* which is available for spending at the government's discretion. The remainder of fund balance is *reserved or designated* to indicate that it is not available for new spending because it has already been committed 1) to liquidate contracts and purchase orders of the prior period ($2,630), 2) to pay debt service ($1,587), 3) to generate income to pay for the perpetual care of the municipal cemetery ($1,102), or 4) for a variety of other restricted purposes ($298).

The general fund is the chief operating fund of the NAME OF GOVERNMENT. At the end of the current fiscal year, unreserved, undesignated fund balance of the general fund was $4,390, while total fund balance reached $5,008. As a measure of the general fund's liquidity, it may be useful to compare both unreserved fund balance and total fund balance to total fund expenditures. Unreserved, undesignated fund balance represents 14 percent of total general fund expenditures, while total fund balance represents 16 percent of that same amount.

The fund balance of the NAME OF GOVERNMENT'S general fund increased by $3,201 during the current fiscal year. Key factors in this growth are as follows:

- An increase in the local sales tax rate (one quarter of one cent) increased tax revenues by $1,389.
- Intergovernmental revenues of the general fund increased significantly as well, by $1,301, as a result of an increase in state shared revenues. However, $900 of this increase simply replaces local tax revenues that were lost when the state recently abolished the inventory tax on small businesses.
- The general fund received for the first time a transfer from the electric fund. This transfer of $1,576 was used to forestall the need for a property tax increase.

The debt service fund has a total fund balance of $1,587, all of which is reserved for the payment of debt service. The net increase in fund balance during the current year in the debt service fund was $1,577. The government enacted a dedicated property tax for debt service at the beginning of the current fiscal year. This new property tax produced revenues of $1,585 in the current fiscal year. Also, during the current fiscal year the government approved a special assessment levy of $4,700 to repay the special assessment debt issued during the current fiscal year. The first installment of the special assessment levy generated $658 ($470 in special assessment revenues and $188 in interest earning on the outstanding receivable balance) from property owners.These new revenue sources were partially offset by increases of $1,063 in interest expenditures because of new indebtedness incurred during the year.

Proprietary funds. The NAME OF GOVERNMENT'S proprietary funds provide the same type of information found in the government-wide financial statements, but in more detail.

Unrestricted net assets of the Water and Sewer Authority at the end of the year amounted to $18,575, and those for the electric distribution operation amounted to $6,968. The total growth in net assets for both funds was $8,169 and $1,670, respectively. Other factors concerning the finances of these two funds have already been addressed in the discussion of the NAME OF GOVERNMENT'S business-type activities.

General Fund Budgetary Highlights

During the year there was a $1,097 increase in appropriations between the original and final amended budget. Following are the main components of the increase:

- $825 supplemental appropriation to the police department in anticipation of several additional patrol officer positions and the implementation of new programs in high crime areas of the government;
- $115 supplemental appropriation to the fire department for the expansion of the government's fire safety and prevention citizen workshop program; and
- $140 supplemental appropriation for highway maintenance for repairs necessary because of road damage from a severe ice storm.

The increase was possible because of additional anticipated revenues. Those revenues included an upturn in sales tax collections ($600), an increase in revenues from licenses and permits ($125), an increase in various user charges ($107), an increase in intergovernmental revenues available to fund the new crime prevention programs ($75), and greater investment returns resulting from positive market conditions ($170).

Capital Asset and Debt Administration

Capital assets. The NAME OF GOVERNMENT'S investment in capital assets for its governmental and business-type activities as of December 31, 2015, amounts to $201,169 (net of accumulated depreciation). This investment in capital assets includes land, buildings and system, improvements, machinery and equipment, park facilities, roads, highways, and bridges. The total increase in the NAME OF GOVERNMENT'S investment in capital assets for the current fiscal year was 8 percent (a 6 percent increase for governmental activities and a 9 percent increase for business-type activities).

Major capital asset events during the current fiscal year included the following:

- Construction began on the additional wastewater treatment facilities for the Water and Sewer Authority; construction in progress as of the close of the fiscal year had reached $3,888.
- A variety of street construction projects in new residential developments and widening and expansion projects for existing streets and bridges began; construction in progress as of the end of the current fiscal year had reached $3,785.
- Through the power of eminent domain, land was acquired for eventual use as rights of way at a cost $558.
- Various building and system additions and improvements were completed in the Water and Sewer Authority at a cost of $7,828.

NAME OF GOVERNMENT'S Capital Assets
(net of depreciation)

	Governmental activities		Business-type activities		Total	
	2015	2014	2015	2014	2015	2014
Land	$39,333	$38,775	$ 1,055	$ 1,055	$ 40,388	$ 39,830
Buildings and system	5,891	5,903	22,482	15,048	28,373	20,951
Improvements other than buildings	3,106	3,269	908	1,062	4,014	4,331
Machinery and equipment	7,164	6,380	90,096	91,332	97,260	97,712
Infrastructure	23,461	23,940	—	—	23,461	23,940
Construction in progress	3,785	—	3,888	—	7,673	—
Total	$82,740	$78,267	$118,429	$108,497	$201,169	$186,764

Additional information on the NAME OF GOVERNMENT'S capital assets can be found in note IV.C on pages 59-62 of this report.

Long-term debt. At the end of the current fiscal year, the NAME OF GOVERNMENT had total bonded debt outstanding of $107,388. Of this amount, $68,088 comprises debt backed by the full faith and credit of the government and $4,700 is special assessment debt for which the government is liable in the event of default by the property owners subject to the assessment. The remainder of the NAME OF GOVERNMENT'S debt represents bonds secured solely by specified revenue sources (i.e., revenue bonds).

NAME OF GOVERNMENT'S Outstanding Debt
General Obligation and Revenue Bonds

	Governmental activities		Business-type activities		Total	
	2015	2014	2015	2014	2015	2014
General obligation bonds	$35,790	$37,455	$32,298	$25,158	$ 68,088	$62,613
Special assessment debt with governmental commitment	4,700	—	—	—	4,700	—
Revenue bonds	—	—	34,600	9,110	34,600	9,110
Total	$40,490	$37,455	$66,898	$34,268	$107,388	$71,723

The NAME OF GOVERNMENT'S total debt increased by $35,665 (50 percent) during the current fiscal year. The key factor in this increase was a $34,600 revenue bond issuance for the NAME OF GOVERNMENT'S Water and Sewer Authority. The government also issued $4,700 in special assessment bonds to finance street construction in new residential developments.

During the current fiscal year, the government refinanced some of its existing debt to take advantage of favorable interest rates.

- The NAME OF GOVERNMENT issued general obligation bonds to refinance previously outstanding special revenue bonds of the water and sewer function. The result is expected to be a decrease in future debt service payments of $460.
- The NAME OF GOVERNMENT also entered into a general obligation bond refinancing that is expected to decrease future debt service payments by $182.

The NAME OF GOVERNMENT and its Water and Sewer Authority both maintain a "AA" rating from Standard & Poor's and Fitch Ratings and a "Aa" rating from Moody's Investors Service for general obligation debt. The revenue bonds of the Water and Sewer Authority have been rated "A" by all three of these rating agencies.

State statutes limit the amount of general obligation debt a governmental entity may issue to 10 percent of its total assessed valuation. The current debt limitation for the NAME OF GOVERNMENT is $408,974, which is significantly in excess of the NAME OF GOVERNMENT'S outstanding general obligation debt.

In January 2016, the NAME OF GOVERNMENT issued $5,000 of revenue bonds to finance an upgrade of the electric distribution system. This is the first indebtedness incurred by the electric distribution operation in 11 years. No debt was outstanding for the electric distribution operation prior to this debt issue.

Additional information on the NAME OF GOVERNMENT'S long-term debt can be found in note IV.F on pages 65-68 of this report.

Economic Factors and Next Year's Budgets and Rates

- The unemployment rate for the NAME OF GOVERNMENT is currently 5.4 percent, which is a decrease from a rate of 6.1 percent a year ago. This compares favorably to the state's average unemployment rate of 6.6 percent and the national average rate of 6.9 percent.
- The occupancy rate of the government's central business district has remained at 97 percent for the past three years.
- Inflationary trends in the region compare favorably to national indices.

All of these factors were considered in preparing the NAME OF GOVERNMENT'S budget for the 2016 fiscal year.

During the current fiscal year, unreserved, undesignated fund balance in the general fund increased to $4,390. The NAME OF GOVERNMENT has appropriated $750 of this amount for spending in the 2016 fiscal year budget. It is intended that this use of available fund balance will avoid the need to raise taxes or charges during the 2016 fiscal year. It also is intended to obviate the need for the transfer of additional resources to the general fund from the electric distribution operation, as occurred during the 2015 fiscal year.

Both the Water and Sewer Authority's rates and the electric distribution operation's rates were increased for the 2016 budget year. The water and sewer rates were increased by an average of 2 percent for all customers, while the average increase in the electric rates was 1.5 percent. While the water and sewer rates affected both residential and industrial consumers by approximately the same percentage, the electric rate increase applied only to industrial customers. These rate increases were necessary to finance debt service on the new debt issued during the current fiscal year by the Water and Sewer Authority and for the debt subsequently issued by the electric distribution operation in 2016.

Requests for Information

This financial report is designed to provide a general overview of the NAME OF GOVERNMENT'S finances for all those with an interest in the government's finances. Questions concerning any of the information provided in this report or requests for additional financial information should be addressed to the Office of the Finance Director, 2516 West Walnut Street, NAME OF GOVERNMENT, STATE, ZIP CODE.

BASIC FINANCIAL STATEMENTS

Name of Government
Statement of Net Assets
December 31, 2015
(amounts expressed in thousands)

	Primary Government			Component Units	
	Governmental Activities	Business-type Activities	Total	School District	Cable Television
ASSETS					
Cash and cash equivalents	$ 3,966	$ 5,742	$ 9,708	$ 156	$ 3,128
Investments	8,069	17,802	25,871	110	5,344
Receivables (net of allowance for uncollectibles)	5,755	4,459	10,214	1,781	1,576
Due from component unit	12	—	12	—	—
Internal balances	(45)	45	—	—	—
Inventories	62	945	1,007	10	6
Prepaids	38	—	38	—	—
Deferred charges	200	568	768	—	—
Restricted assets:					
Temporarily restricted:					
Cash and cash equivalents	4	8,799	8,803	—	193
Investments	—	18,843	18,843	—	—
Intergovernmental receivable	315	—	315	—	—
Permanently restricted:					
Investments	1,102	—	1,102	—	—
Capital assets not being depreciated:					
Land	39,333	1,055	40,388	961	96
Construction in progress	3,785	3,888	7,673	—	—
Capital assets net of accumulated depreciation:					
Buildings and system	5,891	22,482	28,373	9,865	4,762
Improvements other than buildings	3,106	908	4,014	2,058	240
Machinery and equipment	7,164	90,096	97,260	2,383	350
Infrastructure	23,461	—	23,461	—	—
Total assets	102,218	175,632	277,850	17,324	15,695
LIABILITIES					
Accounts payable and other current liabilities	2,685	4,634	7,319	39	1,343
Matured bonds and interest payable	8	123	131	—	—
Accrued interest payable	683	2,376	3,059	—	—
Due to primary government	—	—	—	12	—
Unearned revenue	181	—	181	—	—
Noncurrent liabilities:					
Due within one year	3,177	3,147	6,324	—	—
Due in more than one year	39,416	63,101	102,517	—	—
Total liabilities	46,150	73,381	119,531	51	1,343
NET ASSETS					
Invested in capital assets, net of related debt	45,092	75,983	121,075	15,267	5,448
Restricted for:					
Highways and streets	950	—	950	—	—
Culture and recreation	466	—	466	—	—
Debt service	4,298	632	4,930	—	—
Perpetual care:					
Expendable	1,005		1,005		
Nonexpendable	1,102		1,102		
Other purposes	225	—	225	—	—
Unrestricted	2,930	25,636	28,566	2,006	8,904
Total net assets	$ 56,068	$102,251	$158,319	$ 17,273	$ 14,352

The notes to the financial statements are an integral part of this statement.

Name of Government
Statement of Activities
For the Year Ended December 31, 2015
(amounts expressed in thousands)

Functions/Programs	Expenses	Program Revenues: Charges for Services	Program Revenues: Operating Grants and Contributions	Program Revenues: Capital Grants and Contributions	Primary Government: Governmental Activities	Primary Government: Business-type Activities	Primary Government: Total	Component Units: School District	Component Units: Cable Television
Primary government:									
Governmental activities:									
General government	$ 4,370	$ 3,033	$ —	$ —	$ (1,337)		$ (1,337)		
Public safety	12,823	808	1,255	13	(10,747)		(10,747)		
Highways and streets	4,835	—	689	5,153	1,007		1,007		
Sanitation	3,773	743	—	—	(3,030)		(3,030)		
Economic development	401	—	338	—	(63)		(63)		
Culture and recreation	6,990	1,058	1,117	—	(4,815)		(4,815)		
Interest on long-term debt	3,012	—	—	—	(3,012)		(3,012)		
Total governmental activities	36,204	5,642	3,399	5,166	(21,997)		(21,997)		
Business-type activities:									
Water	9,888	9,698	228	1,718	—	1,756	1,756		
Sewer	5,928	6,498	122	2,576	—	3,268	3,268		
Electric	12,569	15,250	46	—	—	2,727	2,727		
Total business-type activities	28,385	31,446	396	4,294		7,751	7,751		
Total primary government	$ 64,589	$ 37,088	$ 3,795	$ 9,460	(21,997)	7,751	(14,246)		
Component units:									
School district	$ 29,450	$ 407	$ 6,898	$ —				$ (22,145)	
Cable television	15,824	16,265	—	—					441
Total component units	$ 45,274	$ 16,672	$ 6,898	$ —				(22,145)	441
General revenues:									
Property taxes					15,690	—	15,690	—	—
Sales taxes					6,642	—	6,642	—	—
Franchise taxes					4,293	—	4,293	—	—
Motor fuel taxes					729	—	729	—	—
Alcoholic beverage taxes					799	—	799	—	—
Grants and contributions not restricted to specific programs					3,411		3,411		
Unrestricted investment earnings					1,486	3,673	5,159	19,887	659
Gain on sale of capital assets					2		2		
Transfers					1,576	(1,576)	—	—	—
Total general revenues and transfers					34,628	2,097	36,725	19,887	659
Change in net assets					12,631	9,848	22,479	(2,258)	1,100
Net assets - beginning					43,437	92,403	135,840	19,531	13,252
Net assets - ending					$ 56,068	$ 102,251	$ 158,319	$ 17,273	$ 14,352

The notes to the financial statements are an integral part of this statement.

Name of Government
Balance Sheet
Governmental Funds
December 31, 2015
(amounts expressed in thousands)

	General	Debt Service	Other Governmental Funds	Total Governmental Funds
ASSETS				
Cash and cash equivalents	$ 3,097	$ 2	$ 765	$ 3,864
Cash with fiscal agent	—	8	—	8
Investments	2,241	1,555	5,325	9,121
Receivables (net of allowance for uncollectibles)	1,331	4,270	148	5,749
Due from other funds	105	—	335	440
Due from component unit	12	—	—	12
Inventories	39	—	—	39
Advances to other funds	78	—	—	78
Cash – restricted	—	—	4	4
Intergovernmental receivable – restricted	—	—	315	315
Total assets	$ 6,903	$ 5,835	$ 6,892	$ 19,630
LIABILITIES AND FUND BALANCES				
Liabilities:				
Accounts payable	1,112	—	1,086	2,198
Contracts payable	67	—	—	67
Retainage payable		—	160	160
Due to other funds	476	—	—	476
Matured bonds payable	—	5	—	5
Matured interest payable	—	3	—	3
Deferred revenue	59	4,240	—	4,299
Unearned revenue	181			181
Liabilities payable from restricted assets	—	—	18	18
Total liabilities	1,895	4,248	1,264	7,407
Fund balances:				
Reserved for:				
Encumbrances	—	—	1,949	1,949
Senior citizens program	145	—	—	145
Drug enforcement	75	—	—	75
Advances	78	—	—	78
Debt service	—	1,587	—	1,587
Perpetual care	—	—	1,102	1,102
Unreserved, designated for, reported in:				
Encumbrances	320	—	—	320
Special revenue funds	—	—	361	361
Unreserved, undesignated reported in:				
General fund	4,390	—	—	4,390
Special revenue funds	—	—	1,055	1,055
Capital projects funds	—	—	156	156
Permanent fund	—	—	1,005	1,005
Total fund balances	5,008	1,587	5,628	12,223
Total liabilities and fund balances	$ 6,903	$ 5,835	$ 6,892	

Amounts reported for governmental activities in the statement of net assets are different because:

Capital assets used in governmental activities are not financial resources and, therefore, are not reported in the funds.	79,836
Other long-term assets are not available to pay for current-period expenditures and, therefore, are deferred in the funds.	4,299
Internal service funds are used by management to charge the costs of fleet management and management information systems to individual funds. The assets and liabilities of the internal service funds are included in governmental activities in the statement of net assets.	2,758
Long-term liabilities, including bonds payable, are not due and payable in the current period and therefore are not reported in the funds.	(43,048)
Net assets of governmental activities	$ 56,068

The notes to the financial statements are an integral part of this statement.

Name of Government
Statement of Revenues, Expenditures, and Changes in Fund Balances
Governmental Funds
For the Year Ended December 31, 2015
(amounts expressed in thousands)

	General	Debt Service	Other Governmental Funds	Total Governmental Funds
REVENUES				
Taxes:				
Property	$ 14,133	$ 1,585	$ —	$ 15,718
Sales	6,642	—	—	6,642
Franchise	4,293	—	—	4,293
Motor Fuel	—	—	729	729
Alcoholic beverage	—	—	799	799
Licenses and permits	2,041	—	—	2,041
Intergovernmental	5,770	—	891	6,661
Charges for services	2,300	—	—	2,300
Fines	808	—	—	808
Special assessments	—	470	—	470
Investment earnings	773	322	664	1,759
Contributions and donations	145	—	149	294
Payments in lieu of taxes	365	—	—	365
Drug forfeitures	75	—	—	75
Total revenues	37,345	2,377	3,232	42,954
EXPENDITURES				
Current:				
General government	4,257	—	—	4,257
Public safety	13,438	—	—	13,438
Highways and streets	3,735	—	742	4,477
Sanitation	3,726	—	—	3,726
Economic and physical development	—	—	401	401
Culture and recreation	5,899	—	1,014	6,913
Debt service:				
Principal	15	2,030	—	2,045
Interest	—	2,928	—	2,928
Bond issuance costs	150	65	—	215
Advance refunding escrow	—	15	—	15
Capital outlay:				
Highways and streets	—	—	1,560	1,560
Special assessment	—	—	2,225	2,225
Total expenditures	31,220	5,038	5,942	42,200
Excess (deficiency) of revenues over (under) expenditures	6,125	(2,661)	(2,710)	754
OTHER FINANCING SOURCES (USES)				
Transfers in	1,576	4,173	1,273	7,022
Transfers out	(4,645)	—	(846)	(5,491)
Refunding bonds issued	—	3,365	—	3,365
Special assessment bonds issued	—	—	4,700	4,700
Discount on special assessment debt	—	—	(10)	(10)
Payment to refunded bond escrow agent	—	(3,300)	—	(3,300)
Capital leases	140	—	—	140
Sale of capital assets	5	—	—	5
Total other financing sources and uses	(2,924)	4,238	5,117	6,431
Net change in fund balances	3,201	1,577	2,407	7,185
Fund balances — beginning	1,807	10	3,221	5,038
Fund balances — ending	$ 5,008	$ 1,587	$ 5,628	$ 12,223

The notes to the financial statements are an integral part of this statement.

Name of Government
Reconciliation of the Statement of Revenues,
Expenditures, and Changes in Fund Balances of Governmental Funds
To the Statement of Activities
For the Year Ended December 31, 2015
(amounts expressed in thousands)

Amounts reported for governmental activities in the statement of activities (page 31) are different because:

Net change in fund balances—total governmental funds (page 33)	$ 7,185
Governmental funds report capital outlays as expenditures. However, in the statement of activities the cost of those assets is allocated over their estimated useful lives and reported as depreciation expense. This is the amount by which capital outlays exceeded depreciation in the current period.	4,330
The net effect of various miscellaneous transactions involving capital assets (i.e., sales, trade-ins, and donations) is to increase net assets.	7
Revenues in the statement of activities that do not provide current financial resources are not reported as revenues in the funds.	4,154
The issuance of long-term debt (e.g., bonds, leases) provides current financial resources to governmental funds, while the repayment of the principal of long-term debt consumes the current financial resources of governmental funds. Neither transaction, however, has any effect on net assets. Also, governmental funds report the effect of issuance costs, premiums, discounts, and similar items when debt is first issued, whereas these amounts are deferred and amortized in the statement of activities. This amount is the net effect of these differences in the treatment of long-term debt and related items.	(2,620)
Some expenses reported in the statement of activities do not require the use of current financial resources and, therefore, are not reported as expenditures in governmental funds.	(530)
Internal service funds are used by management to charge the costs of fleet management and management information systems to individual funds. The net revenue of certain activities of internal service funds is reported with governmental activities.	105
Change in net assets of governmental activities (page 31)	$ 12,631

The notes to the financial statements are an integral part of this statement.

Name of Government
General Fund
Statement of Revenues, Expenditures, and Changes in Fund Balances - Budget and Actual
For the Year Ended December 31, 2015
(amounts expressed in thousands)

	Budgeted Amounts			
	Original	Final	Actual Amounts	Variance with Final Budget
REVENUES				
Taxes:				
Property	$ 14,007	$ 14,007	$ 14,133	$ 126
Sales	5,900	6,500	6,642	142
Franchise	4,312	4,312	4,293	(19)
Licenses and permits	1,827	1,952	2,041	89
Intergovernmental	5,661	5,736	5,770	34
Charges for services	2,101	2,208	2,300	92
Fines	810	810	808	(2)
Investment earnings	555	725	773	48
Contributions and donations	—	—	145	145
Payments in lieu of taxes	345	345	365	20
Drug forfeitures	—	—	75	75
Total revenues	35,518	36,595	37,345	750
EXPENDITURES				
Current:				
General government:				
Council	110	110	92	18
Commissions	86	86	64	22
Manager	490	490	505	(15)
Attorney	380	380	387	(7)
Clerk	275	275	250	25
Personnel	356	356	304	52
Finance and administration	904	904	868	36
Other – unclassified	2,389	2,256	1,787	469
Total general government	4,990	4,857	4,257	600
Public safety:				
Police	6,488	7,313	6,354	959
Fire	6,025	6,140	6,031	109
Inspection	1,092	1,092	1,053	39
Total public safety	13,605	14,545	13,438	1,107
Highways and streets:				
Engineering	814	814	796	18
Maintenance	3,012	3,152	2,939	213
Total highways and streets	3,826	3,966	3,735	231
Sanitation	3,848	3,848	3,726	122
Culture and recreation	5,950	5,950	5,899	51
Debt service:				
Principal	—	—	15	(15)
Bond issuance costs	—	150	150	—
Total debt service	—	150	165	(15)
Total expenditures	32,219	33,316	31,220	2,096
Excess of revenues over expenditures	3,299	3,279	6,125	2,846
OTHER FINANCING SOURCES (USES)				
Transfers in	1,576	1,576	1,576	—
Transfers out	(4,760)	(4,760)	(4,645)	115
Capital leases	—	—	140	140
Sale of capital assets	34	34	5	(29)
Total other financing sources and uses	(3,150)	(3,150)	(2,924)	226
Net change in fund balances	149	129	3,201	3,072
Fund balances – beginning	1,807	1,807	1,807	—
Fund balances – ending	$ 1,956	$ 1,936	$ 5,008	$ 3,072

The notes to the financial statements are an integral part of this statement.

Name of Government
Statement of Net Assets
Proprietary Funds
December 31, 2015
(amounts expressed in thousands)

	Business-type Activities–Enterprise Funds					Governmental Activities– Internal Service Funds
	Water and Sewer Authority Current Year	Water and Sewer Authority Prior Year	Electric Current Year	Electric Prior Year	Totals Current Year	
ASSETS						
Current assets:						
Cash and cash equivalents	$ 1,366	$ 823	$ 4,253	$ 3,298	$ 5,619	$ 94
Cash with fiscal agent	123	—	—	—	123	—
Investments	16,007	7,322	1,795	1,557	17,802	50
Restricted cash, cash equivalents and investments:						
Customer deposits	1,543	1,199	188	176	1,731	—
Revenue bond covenant accounts	2,815	978	—	—	2,815	—
Interest receivable	409	316	51	119	460	2
Accounts receivable (net of allowance for uncollectibles)	2,621	2,326	1,378	1,225	3,999	126
Due from other funds	39	39	—	—	39	4
Intergovernmental receivable	—	—	—	—	—	23
Inventories	308	461	637	469	945	—
Prepaid items	—	—	—	—	—	38
Total current assets	25,231	13,464	8,302	6,844	33,533	337
Noncurrent assets:						
Restricted cash, cash equivalents, and investments:						
Revenue bond covenant accounts	23,096	3,113	—	—	23,096	—
Deferred charges	568	469	—	—	568	—
Capital assets:						
Land	604	604	451	451	1,055	—
Buildings and system	20,928	13,100	7,043	6,717	27,971	87
Improvements other than buildings	1,250	1,250	—	—	1,250	—
Machinery and equipment	104,283	103,825	1,094	936	105,377	5,283
Construction in progress	3,888	—	—	—	3,888	—
Less accumulated depreciation	(17,541)	(15,125)	(3,571)	(3,261)	(21,112)	(2,466)
Total capital assets (net of accumulated depreciation)	113,412	103,654	5,017	4,843	118,429	2,904
Total noncurrent assets	137,076	107,236	5,017	4,843	142,093	2,904
Total assets	162,307	120,700	13,319	11,687	175,626	3,241

Business-type Activities–Enterprise Funds

	Water and Sewer Authority Current Year	Water and Sewer Authority Prior Year	Electric Current Year	Electric Prior Year	Totals Current Year	Governmental Activities– Internal Service Funds
LIABILITIES						
Current liabilities:						
Accounts payable	1,237	1,104	1,130	1,177	2,367	242
Due to other funds	87	207	—	—	87	42
Compensated absences	154	136	6	7	160	9
Retainage payable	536	—	—	—	536	—
Customer deposits payable	1,543	1,199	188	176	1,731	—
Intergovernmental payable	—	11	—	—	—	—
Matured bonds payable	68	—	—	—	68	—
Matured interest payable	55	—	—	—	55	—
Accrued interest payable	2,376	1,548	—	—	2,376	—
General obligation bonds - current	1,480	1,360	—	—	1,480	—
Capital leases payable - current	23	—	—	—	23	—
Revenue bonds payable - current	1,484	530	—	—	1,484	—
Total current liabilities	9,043	6,095	1,324	1,360	10,367	293
Noncurrent liabilities:						
Compensated absences	220	223	10	12	230	19
General obligation bonds payable (net of unamortized discounts)	30,818	23,798	—	—	30,818	—
Revenue bonds payable (net of unamortized discounts and deferred amount on refunding)	31,975	8,580	—	—	31,975	—
Capital leases payable	78	—	—	—	78	—
Advances from other funds	—	—	—	—	—	78
Total noncurrent liabilities	63,091	32,601	10	12	63,101	97
Total liabilities	72,134	38,696	1,334	1,372	73,468	390
NET ASSETS						
Invested in capital assets, net of related debt	70,966	69,386	5,017	4,843	75,983	2,904
Restricted for debt service	632	3,643	—	—	632	—
Unrestricted	18,575	8,975	6,968	5,472	25,543	(53)
Total net assets	$ 90,173	$ 82,004	$ 11,985	$ 10,315	102,158	$ 2,851

Adjustment to reflect the consolidation of internal service fund activities related to enterprise funds. 93

Net assets of business-type activities $ 102,251

The notes to the financial statements are an integral part of this statement.

37

Name of Government
Statement of Revenues, Expenses, and Changes in Fund Net Assets
Proprietary Funds
For the Year Ended December 31, 2015
(amounts expressed in thousands)

	Business-type Activities—Enterprise Funds					Governmental Activities—Internal Service Funds
	Water and Sewer Authority Current Year	Water and Sewer Authority Prior Year	Electric Current Year	Electric Prior Year	Totals	
Operating revenues:						
Charges for sales and services:						
Water sales	$ 9,089	$ 7,588	$ —	—	$ 9,089	$ —
Sewer charges pledged as security for revenue bonds	5,586	4,344	—	—	5,586	—
Tap fees pledged as security for revenue bonds	912	693			912	
Tap fees – unpledged	609	462			609	
Electric sales	—	—	15,250	15,110	15,250	—
Other services						1,857
Total operating revenues	16,196	13,087	15,250	15,110	31,446	1,857
Operating expenses:						
Costs of sales and services	6,774	5,886	10,772	10,993	17,546	1,151
Administration	3,137	2,824	1,483	1,518	4,620	134
Depreciation	2,436	2,290	318	307	2,754	511
Total operating expenses	12,347	11,000	12,573	12,818	24,920	1,796
Operating income	3,849	2,087	2,677	2,292	6,526	61
Nonoperating revenues (expenses):						
Intergovernmental	350	—	46	172	396	—
Investment earnings	3,150	1,884	523	473	3,673	8
Interest expense	(3,439)	(2,765)	—	—	(3,439)	—
Bond issuance costs	(25)	(10)	—	—	(25)	—
Loss on sale of capital assets	(10)	—	—	—	(10)	—
Total nonoperating revenue (expenses)	26	(891)	569	645	595	8
Income before contributions and transfers	3,875	1,196	3,246	2,937	7,121	69
Capital contributions - tap fees and other	4,294	—	—	—	4,294	2,160
Transfers in	—	—	—	—	—	45
Transfers out	—	—	(1,576)	—	(1,576)	—
Change in net assets	8,169	1,196	1,670	2,937	9,839	2,274
Total net assets – beginning	82,004	80,808	10,315	7,378		577
Total net assets – ending	$ 90,173	$ 82,004	$ 11,985	$ 10,315		$ 2,851

Adjustment to reflect the consolidation of internal service fund activities related to enterprise funds.   9

Change in net assets of business-type activities (page 31) $ 9,848

The notes to the financial statements are an integral part of this statement.

38

This page is intentionally left blank.

Name of Government
Statement of Cash Flows
Proprietary Funds
For the Year Ended December 31, 2015
(amounts expressed in thousands)

	Business-type Activities—Enterprise Funds					Governmental Activities—Internal Service Funds
	Water and Sewer Authority Current Year	Water and Sewer Authority Prior Year	Electric	Electric Prior Year	Totals	
CASH FLOWS FROM OPERATING ACTIVITIES						
Receipts from customers and users	$ 15,947	$ 13,100	$ 15,097	$ 14,264	$ 31,044	$ 767
Receipts from interfund services provided	204	—	—	—	204	1,072
Payments to suppliers	(6,191)	(6,062)	(10,558)	(10,002)	(16,749)	(1,056)
Payments to employees	(3,162)	(2,599)	(1,903)	(1,739)	(5,065)	(116)
Payments for interfund services used	(779)	—	—	—	(779)	—
Net cash provided by operating activities	6,019	4,439	2,636	2,523	8,655	667
CASH FLOWS FROM NONCAPITAL FINANCING ACTIVITIES						
Transfer from other funds	—	—	—	—	—	45
Transfer to other funds	—	—	(1,576)	—	(1,576)	—
Advances from other funds	—	—	—	—	—	60
Subsidy from federal grant	350	—	46	172	396	—
Net cash provided (used) by noncapital financing activities	350	—	(1,530)	172	(1,180)	105
CASH FLOWS FROM CAPITAL AND RELATED FINANCING ACTIVITIES						
Proceeds from capital debt	42,573	—	—	—	42,573	—
Capital contributions	4,294	6,744	—	—	4,294	—
Purchases of capital assets	—	—	(494)	(1,637)	(494)	(639)
Acquisition and construction of capital assets	(10,202)	(1,885)	—	—	(10,202)	—
Principal paid on capital debt	(11,182)	(2,887)	—	—	(11,182)	—
Interest paid on capital debt	(3,504)	—	—	—	(3,504)	—
Capital lease down payment	(6)	—	—	—	(6)	—
Proceeds from sales of capital assets	5	—	—	—	5	—
Net cash provided (used) by capital and related financing activities	21,978	1,972	(494)	(1,637)	21,484	(639)
CASH FLOWS FROM INVESTING ACTIVITIES						
Proceeds from sales and maturities of investments	1,568	710	2,038	2,277	3,606	31
Purchase of investments	(23,860)	(7,435)	(2,276)	(2,461)	(26,136)	(81)
Interest and dividends received	1,347	1,815	593	501	1,940	6
Net cash provided (used) by investing activities	(20,945)	(4,910)	355	317	(20,590)	(44)
Net increase in cash and cash equivalents	7,402	1,501	967	1,375	8,369	89

Cash and cash equivalents, January 1 (including $1,875 and $176, for the authority and electric funds, respectively, reported in restricted accounts)	2,698	1,197	3,474	2,099	6,172	5
Cash and cash equivalents, December 31 (including $8,611 and $188 for the authority and electric funds, respectively, reported in restricted accounts)	$ 10,100	$ 2,698	$ 4,441	$ 3,474	$ 14,541	$ 94

Reconciliation of operating income to net cash provided (used) by operating activities:

Operating income	$ 3,849	$ 2,087	$ 2,677	$ 2,292	$ 6,526	$ 61
Adjustments to reconcile operating income to net cash provided (used) by operating activities:						
Depreciation expense	2,436	2,290	318	307	2,754	511
(Increase) decrease in accounts receivable	(508)	(59)	(153)	19	(661)	—
(Increase) in intergovernmental receivables	—	(11)	—	—	—	—
(Increase) in due from other funds	—	—	—	—	—	(4)
Increase in allowance for uncollectible accounts	213	110	(168)	(83)	—	(14)
(Increase) decrease in inventories	153	(47)	12	20	213	(23)
(Increase) in prepaid items	—	—	(47)	(33)	(15)	(38)
Increase in customer deposits	233	64	—	—	245	—
Increase (decrease) in accounts payable	133	(1)	(3)	1	86	154
(Increase) in amounts payable related to equipment purchases	(374)	—	—	—	(374)	—
Increase (decrease) in compensated absences payable	15	(3)	—	—	12	10
Increase (decrease) in intergovernmental payables	(11)	4	—	—	(11)	—
Increase (decrease) in due to other funds	(120)	5	—	—	(120)	10
Total adjustments	2,170	2,352	(41)	231	2,129	606
Net cash provided by operating activities	$ 6,019	$ 4,439	$ 2,636	$ 2,523	$ 8,655	$ 667

Noncash investing, capital, and financing activities:

Borrowing under capital lease	101	—	—	—	—	—
Contributions of capital assets from government	—	—	—	—	—	—
Purchase of equipment on account	374	—	—	—	2,160	—
Increase in fair value of investments	1,397	793	—	—	—	48
Capital asset trade-ins	—	—	—	—	—	—

The notes to the financial statements are an integral part of this statement.

Name of Government
Statement of Fiduciary Net Assets
Fiduciary Funds
December 31, 2015
(amounts expressed in thousands)

	Public Safety Employees RetirementI System Pension Trust Fund
ASSETS	
Cash and cash equivalents	$ 33
Interest receivable	346
Investments, at fair value:	
U.S. Government securities	12,624
Corporate bonds	2,109
Total investments	14,733
Total assets	15,112
LIABILITIES	
Accounts payable	18
Total liabilities	18
NET ASSETS	
Held in trust for pension benefits and other purposes	$ 15,094

The notes to the financial statements are an integral part of this statement.

Name of Government
Statement of Changes in Fiduciary Net Assets
Fiduciary Funds
For the Year Ended December 31, 2015
(amounts expressed in thousands)

	Public Safety Employees Retirement System Pension Trust Fund
ADDITIONS	
Contributions:	
Employer	$ 1,496
Plan members	284
Private donations	—
Total contributions	1,780
Investment earnings:	
Interest	849
Net increase in the fair value of investments	398
Total investment earnings	1,247
Less investment expense	75
Net investment earnings	1,172
Total additions	2,952
DEDUCTIONS	
Benefits	455
Refunds of contributions	15
Administrative expenses	160
Educational outreach	—
Total deductions	630
Change in net assets	2,322
Net assets – beginning	12,772
Net assets – ending	$ 15,094

The notes to the financial statements are an integral part of this statement.

This page is intentionally left blank.

NAME OF GOVERNMENT
Notes to the Financial Statements
December 31, 2015
(amounts expressed in thousands)

I. Summary of significant accounting policies

A. Reporting entity

The NAME OF GOVERNMENT (government) is a municipal corporation governed by an elected mayor and eight-member council. The accompanying financial statements present the government and its component units, entities for which the government is considered to be financially accountable. Blended component units, although legally separate entities, are, in substance, part of the government's operations. Each discretely presented component unit is reported in a separate column in the government-wide financial statements (see note below for description) to emphasize that it is legally separate from the government.

Blended component unit. The Water and Sewer Authority (Authority) serves all the citizens of the government and is governed by a board comprised of the government's elected council. The rates for user charges and bond issuance authorizations are approved by the government's council and the legal liability for the general obligation portion of the Authority's debt remains with the government. The Authority is reported as an enterprise fund.

Discretely presented component units. The School District (District) is responsible for elementary and secondary education within the government's jurisdiction. The members of the District's governing board are elected by the voters. However, the government is financially accountable for the District because the government's council approves the District's budget, levies taxes (if necessary), and must approve any debt issuances.

Cable Television (CATV) is responsible for providing cable services to the county region that includes the government's jurisdiction. It is managed by a six-member board appointed by the government's council. The government issued bonds in previous years (fully matured as of December 31, 2015) to provide capital for the construction of the system. The government is liable for any operating deficits (to date, CATV has not experienced any operating deficits) and would be secondarily liable for any debt issuances of CATV (currently, there is no debt outstanding).

Complete financial statements for each of the individual component units may be obtained at the entity's administrative offices.

CATV   School District
1110 Neal Street   22662 Wakefield Boulevard
Government City   Government City

Water and Sewer Authority
1102 Cottonwood Drive
Government City

B. Government-wide and fund financial statements

The government-wide financial statements (i.e., the statement of net assets and the statement of changes in net assets) report information on all of the nonfiduciary activities of the primary government and its component units. *Governmental activities*, which normally are supported by taxes and intergovernmental revenues, are reported separately from *business-type activities*, which rely to a significant extent on fees and charges for support. Likewise, the *primary government* is reported separately from certain legally separate *component units* for which the primary government is financially accountable.

The statement of activities demonstrates the degree to which the direct expenses of a given function or segment are offset by program revenues. *Direct expenses* are those that are clearly identifiable with a specific function or segment. *Program revenues* include 1) charges to customers or applicants who purchase, use, or directly benefit from goods, services, or privileges provided by a given function or segment and 2) grants and contributions that are restricted to meeting the operational or capital requirements of a particular function or segment. Taxes and other items not properly included among program revenues are reported instead as *general revenues*.

Separate financial statements are provided for governmental funds, proprietary funds, and fiduciary funds, even though the latter are excluded from the government-wide financial statements. Major individual governmental funds and major individual enterprise funds are reported as separate columns in the fund financial statements.

C. Measurement focus, basis of accounting, and financial statement presentation

The government-wide financial statements are reported using the *economic resources measurement focus* and the *accrual basis of accounting*, as are the proprietary fund and fiduciary fund financial statements. Revenues are recorded when earned and expenses are recorded when a liability is incurred, regardless of the timing of related cash flows. Property taxes are recognized as revenues in the year for which they are levied. Grants and similar items are recognized as revenue as soon as all eligibility requirements imposed by the provider have been met.

Governmental fund financial statements are reported using the *current financial resources measurement focus* and the *modified accrual basis of accounting*. Revenues are recognized as soon as they are both measurable and available. Revenues are considered to be *available* when they are collectible within the current period or soon enough thereafter to pay liabilities of the current period. For this purpose, the government considers revenues to be available if they are collected within 60 days of the end of the current fiscal period. Expenditures generally are recorded when a liability is incurred, as under accrual accounting. However, debt service expenditures, as well as expenditures related to compensated absences and claims and judgments, are recorded only when payment is due.

Property taxes, sales taxes, franchise taxes, licenses, and interest associated with the current fiscal period are all considered to be susceptible to accrual and so have been recognized as revenues of the current fiscal period. Only the portion of special assessments receivable due within the current fiscal period is considered to be susceptible to accrual as revenue of the current period. All other revenue items are considered to be measurable and available only when cash is received by the government.

The government reports the following major governmental funds:

The *general fund* is the government's primary operating fund. It accounts for all financial resources of the general government, except those required to be accounted for in another fund.

The *debt service fund* accounts for the resources accumulated and payments made for principal and interest on long-term general obligation debt of governmental funds.

The government reports the following major proprietary funds:

The *water and sewer authority fund* accounts for the activities of the Authority, a blended component unit of the government. The Authority operates the sewage treatment plant, sewage pumping stations and collection systems, and the water distribution system.

The *electric fund* accounts for the activities of the government's electric distribution operations.

Additionally, the government reports the following fund types:

Internal service funds account for data processing and fleet management services provided to other departments or agencies of the government, or to other governments, on a cost reimbursement basis.

The *pension trust fund* accounts for the activities of the Public Safety Employees Retirement System, which accumulates resources for pension benefit payments to qualified public safety employees.

Private-sector standards of accounting and financial reporting issued prior to December 1, 1989, generally are followed in both the government-wide and proprietary fund financial statements to the extent that those standards do not conflict with or contradict guidance of the Governmental Accounting Standards Board. Governments also have the *option* of following subsequent private-sector guidance for their business-type activities and enterprise funds, subject to this same limitation. The government has elected not to follow subsequent private-sector guidance.

As a general rule the effect of interfund activity has been eliminated from the government-wide financial statements. Exceptions to this general rule are payments-in-lieu of taxes where the amounts are reasonably equivalent in value to the interfund services provided and other charges between the government's water and sewer function and various other functions of the government. Elimination of these charges would distort the direct costs and program revenues reported for the various functions concerned.

Amounts reported as *program revenues* include 1) charges to customers or applicants for goods, services, or privileges provided, 2) operating grants and contributions, and 3) capital grants and contributions, including special assessments. Internally dedicated resources are reported as *general revenues* rather than as program revenues. Likewise, general revenues include all taxes.

Proprietary funds distinguish *operating* revenues and expenses from *nonoperating* items. Operating revenues and expenses generally result from providing services and producing and delivering goods in connection with a proprietary fund's principal ongoing operations. The principal operating revenues of the Authority enterprise fund, of the electric enterprise fund, and of the government's internal service funds are charges to customers for sales and services. The Authority also recognizes as operating revenue the portion of tap fees intended to recover the cost of connecting new customers to the system. Operating expenses for enterprise funds and internal service funds include the cost of sales and services, administrative expenses, and depreciation on capital assets. All revenues and expenses not meeting this definition are reported as nonoperating revenues and expenses.

When both restricted and unrestricted resources are available for use, it is the government's policy to use restricted resources first, then unrestricted resources as they are needed.

D. Assets, liabilities, and net assets or equity

1. Deposits and investments

The government's cash and cash equivalents are considered to be cash on hand, demand deposits, and short-term investments with original maturities of three months or less from the date of acquisition.

State statutes authorize the government and the District to invest in obligations of the U.S. Treasury, commercial paper, corporate bonds, repurchase agreements, and the State Treasurer's Investment Pool.

The CATV is authorized by its governing board to invest in obligations of the U.S. Treasury, commercial paper, and mutual funds.

Investments for the government, as well as for its component units, are reported at fair value. The State Treasurer's Investment Pool operates in accordance with appropriate state laws and regulations. The reported value of the pool is the same as the fair value of the pool shares.

2. Receivables and payables

Activity between funds that are representative of lending/borrowing arrangements outstanding at the end of the fiscal year are referred to as either "due to/from other funds" (i.e., the current portion of interfund loans) or "advances to/from other funds" (i.e., the non-current portion of interfund loans). All other outstanding balances between funds are reported as "due to/from other funds." Any residual balances outstanding between the governmental activities and business-type activities are reported in the government-wide financial statements as "internal balances."

Advances between funds, as reported in the fund financial statements, are offset by a fund balance reserve account in applicable governmental funds to indicate that they are not available for appropriation and are not expendable available financial resources.

All trade and property tax receivables, including those for CATV, are shown net of an allowance for uncollectibles. Trade accounts receivable in excess of 180 days comprise the trade accounts receivable allowance for uncollectibles, including those for CATV. The property tax receivable allowance is equal to 4 percent of outstanding property taxes at December 31, 2015.

Property taxes are levied as of January 1 on property values assessed as of the same date. The tax levy is divided into two billings: the first billing (mailed on February 1) is an estimate of the current year's levy based on the prior year's taxes; the sec-

49

ond billing (mailed on August 1) reflects adjustments to the current year's actual levy. The billings are considered past due 60 days after the respective tax billing date, at which time the applicable property is subject to lien, and penalties and interest are assessed.

3. Inventories and prepaid items

All inventories are valued at cost using the first-in/first-out (FIFO) method. Inventories of governmental funds are recorded as expenditures when consumed rather than when purchased.

Certain payments to vendors reflect costs applicable to future accounting periods and are recorded as prepaid items in both government-wide and fund financial statements.

4. Restricted assets

Certain proceeds of the Authority's enterprise fund revenue bonds, as well as certain resources set aside for their repayment, are classified as restricted assets on the balance sheet because they are maintained in separate bank accounts and their use is limited by applicable bond covenants. The "revenue bond operations and maintenance" account is used to report resources set aside to subsidize potential deficiencies from the Authority's operation that could adversely affect debt service payments. The "revenue bond construction" account is used to report those proceeds of revenue bond issuances that are restricted for use in construction. The "revenue bond current debt service" account is used to segregate resources accumulated for debt service payments over the next twelve months. The "revenue bond future debt service" account is used to report resources set aside to make up potential future deficiencies in the revenue bond current debt service account. The "revenue bond renewal and replacement" account is used to report resources set aside to meet unexpected contingencies or to fund asset renewals and replacements.

5. Capital assets

Capital assets, which include property, plant, equipment, and infrastructure assets (e.g., roads, bridges, sidewalks, and similar items), are reported in the applicable governmental or business-type activities columns in the government-wide financial statements. Capital assets, other than infrastructure assets, are defined by the government as assets with an initial, individual cost of more than $5,000 (amount not rounded) and an estimated useful life in excess of two years. The government reports infrastructure assets on a network and subsystem basis. Accordingly, the amounts spent for the construction or acquisition of infrastructure assets are capitalized and reported in the government-wide financial statements regardless of their amount.

In the case of the initial capitalization of general infrastructure assets (i.e., those reported by governmental activities) the government chose to include all such items regardless of their acquisition date or amount. The government was able to estimate the historical cost for the initial reporting of these assets through backtrending (i.e., estimating the current replacement cost of the infrastructure to be capitalized and using an appropriate price-level index to deflate the cost to the acquisition year or estimated acquisition year). As the government constructs or acquires additional capital assets each period, including infrastructure assets, they are capitalized and reported at historical cost. The reported value excludes normal maintenance and repairs which are essentially amounts spent in relation to capital assets that do not increase the capacity or efficiency of the item or extend its useful life beyond the original estimate. In the case of donations the government values these capital assets at the estimated fair value of the item at the date of its donation.

Interest incurred during the construction phase of capital assets of business-type activities is included as part of the capitalized value of the assets constructed. The total interest expense incurred by the Authority during the current fiscal year was $4,417. Of this amount, $978 was included as part of the cost of capital assets under construction in connection with wastewater treatment facilities construction projects.

Property, plant, and equipment of the primary government, as well as the component units, is depreciated using the straight line method over the following estimated useful lives:

Assets	Years
Buildings	50
Building improvements	20
Public domain infrastructure	50
System infrastructure	30
Vehicles	5
Office equipment	5
Computer equipment	5

6. Compensated absences

It is the government's policy to permit employees to accumulate earned but unused vacation and sick pay benefits. There is no liability for unpaid accumulated sick leave since the government does not have a policy to pay any amounts when employees separate from service with the government. All vacation pay is accrued when incurred in the government-wide, proprietary, and fiduciary fund financial statements. A liability for these amounts is reported in governmental funds only if they have matured, for example, as a result of employee resignations and retirements.

7. Long-term obligations

In the government-wide financial statements, and proprietary fund types in the fund financial statements, long-term debt and other long-term obligations are reported as liabilities in the applicable governmental activities, business-type activities, or proprietary fund type statement of net assets. Bond premiums and discounts, as well as issuance costs, are deferred and amortized over the life of the bonds using the effective interest method. Bonds payable are reported net of the applicable bond premium or discount. Bond issuance costs are reported as deferred charges and amortized over the term of the related debt.

In the fund financial statements, governmental fund types recognize bond premiums and discounts, as well as bond issuance costs, during the current period. The face amount of debt issued is reported as other financing sources. Premiums received on debt issuances are reported as other financing sources while discounts on debt issuances are reported as other financing uses. Issuance costs, whether or not withheld from the actual debt proceeds received, are reported as debt service expenditures.

8. Fund equity

In the fund financial statements, governmental funds report reservations of fund balance for amounts that are not available for appropriation or are legally restricted by outside parties for use for a specific purpose. Designations of fund balance represent tentative management plans that are subject to change.

9. Comparative data/reclassifications

Comparative total data for the prior year have been presented only for individual enterprise funds in the fund financial statements in order to provide an understanding of the changes in the financial position and operations of these funds. Also, certain amounts presented in the prior year data have been reclassified in order to be consistent with the current year's presentation.

II. Reconciliation of government-wide and fund financial statements

A. Explanation of certain differences between the governmental fund balance sheet and the government-wide statement of net assets

The governmental fund balance sheet includes a reconciliation between *fund balance – total governmental funds* and *net assets – governmental activities* as reported in the government-wide statement of net assets. One element of that reconciliation explains that "long-term liabilities, including bonds payable, are not due and payable in the current period and therefore are not reported in the funds." The details of this $43,048 difference are as follows:

Bonds payable	$40,490
Less: Deferred charge on refunding (to be amortized as interest expense)	(283)
Less: Deferred charge for issuance costs (to be amortized over life of debt)	(200)
Less: Issuance discount (to be amortized as interest expense)	(9)
Accrued interest payable	683
Capital leases payable	125
Claims and judgments	220
Compensated absences	2,022
Net adjustment to reduce *fund balance – total governmental funds* to arrive at *net assets – governmental activities*	$43,048

Another element of that reconciliation explains that "Internal service funds are used by management to charge the costs of fleet management and management information systems to individual funds. The assets and liabilities of the internal service funds are included in governmental activities in the statement of net assets." The details of this $2,758 difference are as follows:

Net assets of the internal service funds	$2,851
Less: Internal payable representing charges in excess of cost to business-type activities – prior years	(84)
Less: Internal payable representing charges in excess of cost to business-type activities – current year	(9)
Net adjustment to increase *fund balance – total governmental funds* to arrive at *net assets – governmental activities*	$2,758

B. Explanation of certain differences between the governmental fund statement of revenues, expenditures, and changes in fund balances and the government-wide statement of activities

The governmental fund statement of revenues, expenditures, and changes in fund balances includes a reconciliation between *net changes in fund balances – total governmental funds* and *changes in net assets of governmental activities* as reported in the government-wide statement of activities. One element of that reconciliation explains that "Governmental funds report capital outlays as expenditures. However, in the statement of activities the cost of those assets is allocated over their estimated useful lives and reported as depreciation expense." The details of this $4,330 difference are as follows:

Capital outlay	$5,533
Depreciation expense	(1,203)

Net adjustment to increase *net changes in fund balances – total governmental funds* to arrive at *changes in net assets of governmental activities* $4,330

Another element of that reconciliation states that "The net effect of various miscellaneous transactions involving capital assets (i.e., sales, trade-ins, and donations) is to increase net assets." The details of this $7 difference are as follows:

In the statement of activities, only the *gain* on the sale of capital assets is reported. However, in the governmental funds, the proceeds from the sale increase financial resources. Thus, the change in net assets differs from the change in fund balance by the cost of the capital assets sold.   (3)

Donations of capital assets increase net assets in the statement of activities, but do not appear in the governmental funds because they are not financial resources.   13

The statement of activities reports *losses* arising from the trade-in of existing capital assets to acquire new capital assets. Conversely, governmental funds do not report any gain or loss on a trade-in of capital assets.   (3)

Net adjustment to increase *net changes in fund balances – total governmental funds* to arrive at *changes in net assets of governmental activities* $7

Another element of that reconciliation states that "the issuance of long-term debt (e.g., bonds, leases) provides current financial resources to governmental funds, while the repayment of the principal of long-term debt consumes the current financial resources of governmental funds. Neither transaction, however, has any effect on net assets. Also, governmental funds report the effect of issuance costs, premiums, discounts, and similar items when debt is first issued, whereas these amounts are deferred and amortized in the statement of activities." The details of this $2,620 difference are as follows:

Debt issued or incurred:	
Capital lease financing	$ 140
Issuance of general obligation bonds	3,365
Issuance of special assessment debt	4,700
Less discounts	(225)

Principal repayments:

General obligation debt	(2,030)
Down payment on capital lease	(15)
Payment to escrow agent for refunding	(3,315)

Net adjustment to decrease *net changes in fund balances – total* governmental funds to arrive at *changes in net assets of governmental activities*   <u>$2,620</u>

Another element of that reconciliation states that "Some expenses reported in the statement of activities do not require the use of current financial resources and therefore are not reported as expenditures in governmental funds." The details of this $530 difference are as follows:

Compensated absences	$211
Claims and judgments	220
Accrued interest	51
Amortization of deferred charge on refunding	32
Amortization of issuance costs	15
Amortization of bond discounts	1

Net adjustment to decrease *net changes in fund balances – total* *governmental funds* to arrive at *changes in net assets of* *governmental activities*   <u>$530</u>

Another element of that reconciliation states that "Internal service funds are used by management to charge the costs of fleet management and management information systems to individual funds. The net revenue of certain activities of internal service funds is reported with governmental activities." The details of this $105 difference are as follows:

Change in net assets of the internal service funds	$2,274
Less: Contribution of capital assets previously reported by governmental activities	(2,160)
Less: Profit from charges to business-type activities	(9)

Net adjustment to increase *net changes in fund balances - total* *governmental funds* to arrive at *changes in net assets of* *governmental activities*   <u>$ 105</u>

C. Explanation of certain differences between the proprietary fund statement of net assets and the government-wide statement of net assets

The proprietary fund statement of net assests includes a reconciliation between *net assets - total enterprise funds* and *net assets of business-type activities* as reported in the government-wide statement of net assets. The description of the sole element of that reconciliation is "Adjustment to reflect the consolidation of internal service fund activities related to enterprise funds." The details of this $93 difference are as follows:

Internal receivable representing charges in excess of cost to business-type activities – prior years	$84
Internal receivable representing charges in excess of cost to business-type activities – current year	9
Net adjustment to increase *net assets – total enterprise funds* to arrive at *net assets – business-type activities*	$93

III. Stewardship, compliance, and accountability

A. Budgetary information

Annual budgets are adopted on a basis consistent with generally accepted accounting principles for all governmental funds except the CDBG Revitalization Project special revenue fund and the capital projects funds, which adopt project-length budgets, and the permanent fund, which is not budgeted. All annual appropriations lapse at fiscal year end.

The appropriated budget is prepared by fund, function, and department. The government's department heads may make transfers of appropriations within a department. Transfers of appropriations between departments require the approval of the council. The legal level of budgetary control (i.e., the level at which expenditures may not legally exceed appropriations) is the department level. The council made several supplemental budgetary appropriations throughout the year, including a $3,365 increase in the debt service fund budget related to the advance refunding. The supplemental budgetary appropriations made in the general fund were not material.

Encumbrance accounting is employed in governmental funds. Encumbrances (e.g., purchase orders, contracts) outstanding at year end are reported as reservations of fund balances and do not constitute expenditures or liabilities because the commitments will be reappropriated and honored during the subsequent year.

B. Excess of expenditures over appropriations

For the year ended December 31, 2015, expenditures exceeded appropriations in the manager and attorney departments (the legal level of budgetary control) of the general fund by $15 and $7, respectively, and in the culture and recreation department of the Parks Maintenance special revenue fund by $6. These overexpenditures were funded by greater than anticipated revenues in the case of the general fund and by available fund balance in the case of the Parks Maintenance special revenue fund.

C. Deficit fund equity

The Street Construction capital projects fund had a deficit fund balance of $121 as of December 31, 2015. The fund incurred expenditures that are currently not part of the original costs approved by the Federal Highway Administration. If the Federal Highway Administration does not approve the costs to be added to the project requests for reimbursement, the government plans to transfer funds from the electric fund to cover the expenditures.

IV. Detailed notes on all funds

A. Deposits and investments

As of December 31, 2015, the government had the following investments:

Investment Type	Fair Value	Weighted Average Maturity (Years)
U.S. Treasuries	$41,416	0.35
Commercial paper	13,511	0.52
Repurchase agreements	4,374	0.02
State Treasurer's investment pool	2,814	0.55
Corporate bonds	2,109	1.46
Total fair value	$64,224	
Portfolio weighted average maturity		0.41

Interest rate risk. In accordance with its investment policy, the government manages its exposure to declines in fair values by limiting the weighted average maturity of its investment portfolio to less than ten months.

Credit risk. State law limits investments in commercial paper and corporate bonds to the top two ratings issued by nationally recognized statistical rating organizations (NRSROs). It is the government's policy to limit its investments in these investment types to the top rating issued by NRSROs. As of December 31, 2015, the government's investment in the State Treasurer's investment pool was rated AAAm by Standard & Poor's and Aaa by Moody's Investors Service. The government's investments in commercial paper were rated A1 by Standard & Poor's, F-1 by Fitch Ratings, and P-1 by Moody's Investors Service. The government's investments in corporate bonds were rated AAA by Standard & Poor's and Fitch Ratings, and Aaa by Moody's Investors Service.

Concentration of credit risk. The government's investment policy does not allow for an investment in any one issuer that is in excess of five percent of the government's total investments.

Custodial credit risk - deposits. In the case of deposits, this is the risk that in the event of a bank failure, the government's deposits may not be returned to it. Neither the government nor the CATV, a discretely presented component unit, has a deposit policy for custodial credit risk. As of December 31, 2015, $1,382 of the government's bank balance of $17,226 was exposed to custodial credit risk because it was uninsured and collateralized with securities held by the pledging financial institution's trust department or agent, but not in the government's name. As of the same date the CATV had exposure to custodial credit risk because $251 of the CATV's bank balance of $3,606 was uninsured and collateralized with securities held by the pledging financial institution's trust department or agent, but not in the CATV's name.

Custodial credit risk - investments. For an investment, this is the risk that, in the event of the failure of the counterparty, the government will not be able to recover the value of its investments or collateral securities that are in the possession of an outside party. Of the investment in corporate bonds of $2,109 the government has a custodial credit risk exposure of $998 because the related securities are uninsured, unregistered and held by the government's brokerage firm which is also the counterparty for these particular securities. The government's investment policy limits the amount of securities that can be held by counterparties to no more than $2 million.

B. Receivables

Receivables as of year end for the government's individual major funds and nonmajor, internal service, and fiduciary funds in the aggregate, including the applicable allowances for uncollectible accounts, are as follows:

	General	Debt Service	Water and Sewer Authority	Electric	Nonmajor Governmental Funds	Internal Service Funds	Pension Trust Fund	Total
Receivables:								
Interest	$ 92	$ 30	$ 409	$ 51	$148	$ 2	$ 346	$ 1,078
Taxes	991	10	—	—	—	—	—	1,001
Accounts	74	—	3,093	1,510	—	—	—	4,677
Special assessments	—	4,230	—	—	—	—	—	4,230
Intergovernmental	215	—	—	—	—	4	—	219
Intergovernmental-Restricted	—	—	—	—	315	—	—	315
Gross receivables	1,372	4,270	3,502	1,561	463	6	346	11,520
Less: allowance for uncollectibles	(41)	—	(472)	(132)	—	—	—	(645)
Net total receivables	$1,331	$4,270	$3,030	$1,429	$463	$ 6	$ 346	$10,875

The only receivables not expected to be collected within one year are $3,760 of special assessment receivables reported in the debt service fund.

Revenues of the Water and Sewer Authority are reported net of uncollectible amounts. Total uncollectible amounts related to revenues of the current period are as follows:

Uncollectibles related to water sales	$138
Uncollectibles related to sewer charges	85
Total uncollectibles of the current fiscal year	$223

Governmental funds report *deferred revenue* in connection with receivables for revenues that are not considered to be available to liquidate liabilities of the current period. Governmental funds also defer revenue recognition in connection with resources that have been received, but not yet earned. At the end of the current fiscal year, the various components of *deferred revenue* and *unearned revenue* reported in the governmental funds were as follows:

	Unavailable	Unearned
Delinquent property taxes receivable (general fund)	$ 59	
Delinquent property taxes receivable (debt service fund)	10	
Special assessments not yet due (debt service fund)	4,230	
Grant drawdowns prior to meeting all eligibility requirements		$181
Total deferred/unearned revenue for governmental funds	$4,299	$181

C. Capital assets

Capital asset activity for the year ended December 31, 2015 was as follows:

Primary Government

	Beginning Balance	Increases	Decreases	Ending Balance
Governmental activities:				
Capital assets, not being depreciated:				
Land	$38,775	$ 558	—	$39,333
Construction in progress		3,785	—	3,785
Total capital assets, not being depreciated	38,775	4,343	—	43,118
Capital assets, being depreciated:				
Buildings	7,875	—	—	7,875
Improvements other than buildings	4,604	—	—	4,604
Machinery and equipment	9,005	1,440	(64)	10,381
Infrastructure	28,500	—	—	28,500
Total capital assets being depreciated	49,984	1,440	(64)	51,360
Less accumulated depreciation for:				
Buildings	(1,972)	(12)	—	(1,984)
Improvements other than buildings	(1,335)	(163)	—	(1,498)

	Beginning Balance	Increases	Decreases	Ending Balance
Machinery and equipment	(2,625)	(648)	56	(3,217)
Infrastructure	(4,560)	(479)	—	(5,039)
Total accumulated depreciation	(10,492)	(1,302)	56	(11,738)
Total capital assets, being depreciated, net	39,492	138	(8)	39,622
Governmental activities capital assets, net	$ 78,267	$ 4,481	$ (8)	$82,740

Business-type activities:

	Beginning Balance	Increases	Decreases	Ending Balance
Capital assets, not being depreciated:				
Land	$ 1,055		—	$ 1,055
Construction in progress		$11,716	$(7,828)	3,888
Total capital assets, not being depreciated	1,055	11,716	(7,828)	4,943
Capital assets, being depreciated:				
Buildings and system	19,817	8,164	(10)	27,971
Improvements other than buildings	1,250			1,250
Machinery and equipment	104,761	651	(35)	105,377
Total capital assets, being depreciated	125,828	8,815	(45)	134,598
Less accumulated depreciation for:				
Buildings and system	(4,769)	(728)	8	(5,489)
Improvements other than buildings	(188)	(154)		(342)
Machinery and equipment	(13,429)	(1,872)	20	(15,281)
Total accumulated depreciation	(18,386)	(2,754)	28	(21,112)
Total capital assets, being depreciated, net	107,442	6,061	(17)	113,486
Business-type activities capital assets, net	$108,497	$17,777	$(7,845)	$118,429

Depreciation expense was charged to functions/programs of the primary government as follows:

Governmental activities:	
General government	$ 232
Public safety	94
Highways and streets, including depreciation of general infrastructure assets	501
Sanitation	29
Culture and recreation	347
Capital assets held by the government's internal service funds are charged to the various functions based on their usage of the assets	99
Total depreciation expense – governmental activities	$1,302

Business-type activities:

Water	$1,461
Sewer	975
Electric	318
Total depreciation expense – business-type activities	$2,754

Construction commitments

The government has active construction projects as of December 31, 2015. The projects include street construction in areas with newly developed housing, widening and construction of existing streets and bridges, and the construction of additional wastewater treatment facilities. At year end the government's commitments with contractors are as follows:

Project	Spent-to-Date	Remaining Commitment
Residential street construction—special assessments	$2,225	$1,552
Residential street construction—public purpose portion	754	392
Road and bridge expansion	633	129
Wastewater treatment facilities	3,623	3,612
Total	$7,235	$5,685

The special assessment portion of the commitment for residential street construction is being financed by special assessment bonds that will be repaid by the benefiting property owners. The public-purpose portion of this same project is being funded by the transfer of existing resources from the general fund. The commitment for road and bridge expansion is being financed entirely from grants from the Federal Highway Administration. The commitment for wastewater treatment facilities is being financed by revenue bonds secured by sewer revenues.

Discretely presented component units

Activity for the District for the year ended December 31, 2015, was as follows:

	Beginning Balance	Increases	Decreases	Ending Balance
Capital assets, not being depreciated:				
Land	$ 961	—	—	$ 961
Capital assets, being depreciated:				
Buildings	14,093	—	—	14,093
Improvements other than buildings	1,960	$ 765	—	2,725
Machinery and equipment	2,466	951	$(196)	3,221
Totals, capital assets being depreciated	18,519	1,716	(196)	20,039
Less accumulated depreciation for:				
Buildings	(3,382)	(846)	—	(4,228)

Improvements other than buildings	(549)	(118)	—	(667)
Machinery and equipment	(690)	(148)	—	(838)
Total accumulated depreciation	(4,621)	(1,112)	—	(5,733)
Total capital assets, being depreciated, net	13,898	604	(196)	14,306
District capital assets, net	$14,859	$ 604	$(196)	$15,267

Activity for the CATV for the year ended December 31, 2015, was as follows:

	Beginning Balance	Increases	Decreases	Ending Balance
Capital assets, not being depreciated:				
Land	$ 96	—	—	$ 96
Capital assets, being depreciated:				
Buildings and system	7,463	$ 147	—	7,610
Improvements other than buildings	410	—	—	410
Machinery and equipment	401	98	—	499
Totals, capital assets being depreciated	8,274	245	—	8,519
Less accumulated depreciation for:				
Buildings and system	(2,159)	(689)	—	(2,848)
Improvements other than buildings	(125)	(45)	—	(170)
Machinery and equipment	(107)	(42)	—	(149)
Total accumulated depreciation	(2,391)	(776)	—	(3,167)
Total capital assets, being depreciated, net	5,883	(531)	—	5,352
CATV capital assets, net	$5,979	$(531)	—	$5,448

D. Interfund receivables, payables, and transfers

The composition of interfund balances as of December 31, 2015, is as follows:

Due to/from other funds:

Receivable Fund	Payable Fund	Amount
General	Water and sewer	$ 65
	Fleet management*	16
	Management information systems*	24
Water and sewer	General	37
	Fleet management*	2
Fleet management*	General	47
	Water and sewer	17
Management information systems*	General	57
	Water and sewer	5
Nonmajor governmental fund	General	$335
Total		$605

*Internal service funds

The outstanding balances between funds result mainly from the time lag between the dates that (1) interfund goods and services are provided or reimbursable expenditures occur, (2) transactions are recorded in the accounting system, and (3) payments between funds are made. These balances also include the amount of working capital loans made to internal service funds that the general fund expects to collect in the subsequent year.

Advances from/to other funds:

Receivable Fund	Payable Fund	Amount
General	Fleet management*	$ 32
	Management information systems*	46
Total		$ 78

*Internal service funds

The amounts payable to the general fund relate to working capital loans made to the internal service funds upon their creation. None of the balance is scheduled to be collected in the subsequent year.

Interfund transfers:

	Transfer In:				
Transfer out:	General Fund	Debt Service Fund	Nonmajor Governmental	Internal Service Funds	Total
General fund	—	$3,327	$1,273	$ 45	$4,645
Nonmajor governmental funds		846	—	—	846
Electric enterprise fund	$1,576	—	—	—	1,576
Total	$1,576	$4,173	$1,273	$ 45	$7,067

Transfers are used to 1) move revenues from the fund with collection authorization to the debt service fund as debt service principal and interest payments become due, 2) move restricted amounts from borrowings to the debt service fund to establish mandatory reserve accounts, 3) move unrestricted general fund revenues to finance various programs that the government must account for in other funds in accordance with budgetary authorizations, including amounts provided as subsidies or matching funds for various grant programs.

In the year ended December 31, 2015, the government made the following one-time transfers:

A transfer for the first time of $1,576 from the electric enterprise fund to the general fund to forestall the need for a property tax increase; and

A transfer of $1,200 from the general fund to the housing development street construction capital projects fund to fulfill the general fund's commitment to participate in a special assessment project to construct streets in the government's new housing development.

E. Leases

Operating Leases

The government leases building and office facilities and other equipment under noncancelable operating leases. Total costs for such leases were $123 for the year ended December 31, 2015. The future minimum lease payments for these leases are as follows:

Year Ending Dec. 31	Amount
2016	$123
2017	123
2018	123
2019	63
2020	63
2021-2025	252
Total	$747

Capital Leases

The government has entered into a lease agreement as lessee for financing the acquisition of police communications equipment with a down payment of $15. The government also has financed the acquisition of certain trucks for its Water and Sewer Authority by means of leases with a down payment of $6. These lease agreements qualify as capital leases for accounting purposes and, therefore, have been recorded at the present value of their future minimum lease payments as of the inception date.

The assets acquired through capital leases are as follows:

	Governmental Activities	Water and Sewer Authority
Asset:		
Machinery and equipment	$140	$125
Less: Accumulated depreciation	(14)	(24)
Total	$126	$101

The future minimum lease obligations and the net present value of these minimum lease payments as of December 31, 2015, were as follows:

Year Ending Dec. 31	Governmental Activities	Water and Sewer Authority
2016	$ 49	$ 40
2017	49	40
2018	48	39
Total minimum lease payments	146	119
Less: amount representing interest	(21)	(18)
Present value of minimum lease payments	$125	$101

F. Long-term debt

General Obligation Bonds

The government issues general obligation bonds to provide funds for the acquisition and construction of major capital facilities. General obligation bonds have been issued for both governmental and business-type activities. The original amount of general obligation bonds issued in prior years was $70,600. During the year, general obligation bonds totaling $11,865 were issued to refund both general obligation and revenue bonds.

General obligation bonds are direct obligations and pledge the full faith and credit of the government. These bonds generally are issued as 20-year serial bonds with equal amounts of principal maturing each year. General obligation bonds currently outstanding are as follows:

Purpose	Interest Rates	Amount
Governmental activities	6.0 - 7.5%	$32,425
Governmental activities — refunding	6.9%	3,365
Business-type activities	6.0 - 7.5%	22,231
Business-type activities — refunding	6.9%	10,067
		$68,088

Annual debt service requirements to maturity for general obligation bonds are as follows:

Year Ending	Governmental Activities		Business-type Activities	
December 31	Principal	Interest	Principal	Interest
2016	$ 2,227	$ 1,979	$ 1,480	$ 2,597
2017	2,175	1,913	1,561	2,401
2018	2,133	1,840	1,635	2,210
2019	2,088	1,767	1,723	2,007
2020	2,042	1,697	1,947	1,665
2021-2025	9,897	6,928	11,682	8,332
2026-2030	9,523	6,133	9,011	5,532
2031-2035	5,705	2,660	3,259	1,547
Total	$35,790	$24,917	$32,298	$26,291

The government also issued $4,700 of special assessment debt in 2015 to provide funds for the construction of streets in new residential developments. These bonds will be repaid from amounts levied against the property owners benefited by this construction. In the event that a deficiency exists because of unpaid or delinquent special assessments at the time a debt service payment is due, the government must provide resources to cover the deficiency until other resources, for example, foreclosure proceeds, are received. The bonds have a stated rate of interest of 6.5 percent and are payable in equal installments of principal over the next 10 years.

Annual debt service requirements to maturity for special assessment bonds are as follows:

Year Ending	Governmental Activities	
December 31	Principal	Interest
2016	$ 470	$ 376
2017	470	268
2018	470	238
2019	470	203
2020	470	172
2021-2025	2,350	423
Total	$4,700	$1,680

Revenue bonds

The government also issues bonds where the government pledges income derived from the acquired or constructed assets to pay debt service. No amounts outstanding at the end of the current fiscal year related to bonds issued in prior years. During the year $34,600 of revenue bonds were issued to finance construction projects to both expand existing wastewater treatment facilities and construct additional facilities. Revenue bonds outstanding at year end are as follows:

Purpose	Interest Rates	Amount
Wastewater treatment — Water and Sewer Authority	6.75 - 8.0%	$34,600

Revenue bond debt service requirements to maturity are as follows:

Year Ending December 31	Principal	Interest
2016	$ 1,484	$ 2,377
2017	1,501	2,265
2018	1,596	2,074
2019	1,637	1,937
2020	1,701	1,777
2021-2025	9,355	8,201
2026-2030	9,051	7,910
2031-2035	8,275	6,840
Total	$34,600	$33,381

Advance and current refundings

The government issued $3,365 of general obligation refunding bonds to provide resources to purchase U.S. Government State and Local Government Series securities that were placed in an irrevocable trust for the purpose of generating resources for all future debt service payments of $3,000 of general obligation bonds. As a result, the refunded bonds are considered to be defeased and the liability has been removed from the governmental activities column of the statement of net assets. The reacquisition price exceeded the net carrying amount of the old debt by $315. This amount is being netted against the new debt and amortized over the remaining life of the refunded debt, which is shorter than the life of the new debt issued. This advance refunding was undertaken to reduce total debt service payments over the next 20 years by $182 and resulted in an economic gain of $105.

In addition, the government issued $8,500 of general obligation bonds for a current refunding of $8,580 of revenue bonds of the Water and Sewer Authority. The refunding was undertaken to remove restrictive bond covenants associated with the revenue bonds and to reduce total future debt service payments. The reacquisition price exceeded the net carrying amount of the old debt by $871. This amount is being netted against the new debt and amortized over the new debt's life, which is shorter than the refunded debt. The transaction also resulted in an economic gain of $265 and a reduction of $460 in future debt service payments.

Changes in long-term liabilities

Long-term liability activity for the year ended December 31, 2015, was as follows:

	Beginning Balance	Additions	Reductions	Ending Balance	Due Within One Year
Governmental activities:					
Bonds payable:					
General obligation bonds	$37,455	$ 3,365	$ (5,030)	$35,790	$2,227
Special assessment debt with government commitment	—	4,700	—	4,700	470
Less deferred amounts:					
For issuance discounts	—	(10)	1	(9)	—
On refunding	—	(315)	32	(283)	—
Total bonds payable	37,455	7,740	(4,997)	40,198	2,697
Capital leases	—	140	(15)	125	35
Claims and judgments	—	220	—	220	220
Compensated absences	1,829	867	(646)	2,050	225
Governmental activity Long-term liabilities	$39,284	$ 8,967	$ (5,658)	$42,593	$3,177
Business-type activities:					
Bonds payable:					
General obligation bonds	$25,158	$ 8,500	$ (1,360)	$32,298	$1,480
Revenue bonds	9,110	34,600	(9,110)	34,600	1,484
Less deferred amounts:					
For issuance discounts	—	(300)	12	(288)	—
On refunding	—	(871)	18	(853)	—
Total bonds payable	34,268	41,929	(10,440)	65,757	2,964
Capital leases	—	113	(12)	101	23
Compensated absences	378	146	(134)	390	160
Business-type activity Long-term liabilities	$34,646	$42,188	$(10,586)	$66,248	$3,147

Internal service funds predominantly serve the governmental funds. Accordingly, long-term liabilities for them are included as part of the above totals for governmental activities. At year end $28 of internal service funds compensated absences are included in the above amounts. Also, for the governmental activities, claims and judgments and compensated absences are generally liquidated by the general fund.

G. Segment information

The government issued revenue bonds to finance its sewer department, which operates the government's sewage treatment plant, sewage pumping stations, and collection systems. Both the water and sewer departments are accounted for in a single fund (i.e., the Authority). However, investors in the revenue bonds rely solely on the revenue generated by the individual activities for repayment. Summary financial information for the sewer department is presented below.

CONDENSED STATEMENT OF NET ASSETS

Assets:	
Current assets	$ 9,377
Due from other funds	15
Restricted assets	26,661
Capital assets	68,047
Total assets	104,100
Liabilities:	
Current liabilities	1,123
Due to other funds	33
Current liabilities payable from restricted assets	3,565
Noncurrent liabilities	32,053
Total liabilities	36,774
Net assets:	
Invested in capital assets, net of related debt	57,309
Restricted	632
Unrestricted	9,385
Total net assets	$ 67,326

CONDENSED STATEMENT OF REVENUES, EXPENSES, AND CHANGES IN NET ASSETS

Sewer charges (pledged against bonds)	$ 6,498
Depreciation expense	(1,461)
Other operating expenses	(3,469)
Operating income	1,568
Nonoperating revenues (expenses):	
Investment earnings	1,102
Intergovernmental	122
Interest expense	(920)
Capital contributions	2,576
Change in net assets	4,448
Beginning net assets	62,878
Ending net assets	$67,326

CONDENSED STATEMENT OF CASH FLOWS

Net cash provided (used) by:	
Operating activities	$ 2,106
Noncapital financing activities	122
Capital and related financing activities	23,936
Investing activities	(19,354)
Net increase (decrease)	6,810
Beginning cash and cash equivalents	1,604
Ending cash and cash equivalents	$ 8,414

H. Restricted assets

The balances of the restricted asset accounts in the enterprise funds are as follows:

Customer deposits — Authority	$ 1,543
Customer deposits — electric fund	188
Revenue bond operations and maintenance account	1,294
Revenue bond construction account	18,542
Revenue bond current debt service account	3,706
Revenue bond future debt service account	737
Revenue bond renewal and replacement account	1,632
Total restricted assets	$27,642

V. Other information

A. Risk management

The government is exposed to various risks of loss related to torts; theft of, damage to, and destruction of assets; errors and omissions; and natural disasters for which the government carries commercial insurance. The government established a limited risk management program for workers' compensation in 2014. Premiums are paid into the general fund by all other funds and are available to pay claims, claim reserves, and administrative costs of the program. These interfund premiums are used to reduce the amount of claims expenditure reported in the general fund. As of December 31, 2015, such interfund premiums did not exceed reimbursable expenditures.

Liabilities of the fund are reported when it is probable that a loss has occurred and the amount of the loss can be reasonably estimated. Liabilities include an amount for claims that have been incurred but not reported (IBNRs). The result of the process to estimate the claims liability is not an exact amount as it depends on many complex factors, such as inflation, changes in legal doctrines, and damage awards. Accordingly, claims are reevaluated periodically to consider the effects of inflation, recent claim settlement trends (including frequency and amount of pay-outs), and other economic and social factors. The estimate of the claims liability also includes amounts for incremental claim adjustment expenses related to specific claims and other claim adjustment expenses regardless of whether allocated to specific claims. Estimated recoveries, for example from salvage or subrogation, are another component of the claims liability estimate. An excess coverage insurance policy covers individual claims in excess of $50. Settlements have not exceeded coverages for each of the past three fiscal years. Changes in the balances of claims liabilities during the past two years are as follows:

	Year ended 12/31/15	Year ended 12/31/14
Unpaid claims, beginning of fiscal year	$ —	$ —
Incurred claims (including IBNRs)	220	98
Claim payments	=	(98)
Unpaid claims, end of fiscal year	$220	$ =

B. Related party transaction

The government's electric enterprise has entered into a management consulting contract with a regional executive training group. The training group is owned and operated by a member of the government's governing council. The contract is for a six-month management evaluation study and has a set fee of $75. As of the year end, the government had remitted a 20 percent down payment. The remainder of the contract ($60) is due and payable after services are completed.

C. Subsequent events

On January 18, 2016, the government issued $5,000 of revenue bonds to finance an upgrade of the government's electric distribution system. The interest rate on the bonds range from 6.15 - 7.75 percent and the maturity date is January 18, 2030.

On January 30, 2016, a former government employee filed a lawsuit against the government alleging wrongful termination related to illness. The plaintiff is seeking damages of $2 million. It is the preliminary assessment of the government's counsel that the accusations are without merit. In management's opinion, the ultimate liability of the suit, if any, would not a have a material effect on the financial statements.

On January 31, 2016, the receiving station of CATV was severely damaged by fire. The facility was covered by fire insurance. Preliminary damage estimates range between $1,050 and $1,450. Ninety-five percent of the loss will be covered by insurance. The remaining five percent of the loss will be absorbed by CATV. Currently, there are no plans to request financial assistance from the primary government.

D. Contingent liabilities

Amounts received or receivable from grant agencies are subject to audit and adjustment by grantor agencies, principally the federal government. Any disallowed claims, including amounts already collected, may constitute a liability of the applicable funds. The amount, if any, of expenditures that may be disallowed by the grantor cannot be determined at this time, although the government expects such amounts, if any, to be immaterial.

The government is a defendant in various lawsuits. Although the outcome of these lawsuits is not presently determinable, in the opinion of the government's counsel the resolution of these matters will not have a material adverse effect on the financial condition of the government.

E. Jointly governed organization

The government, in conjunction with 19 other governmental entities that provide distribution of electric services, created the Government Power Authority (GPA). The GPA generates power that is purchased and distributed by the 20 governmental entities that operate electric distribution systems. The GPA's board is comprised of one member from each participating entity. Except for minimum purchase requirements, no participant has any obligation, entitlement, or residual interest. The government's purchases of power for the year ended December 31, 2015, were $10,772.

F. Other postemployment benefits

The government provides other postemployment benefits (OPEB) for all of its public safety employees through an agent multiple-employer, defined benefit OPEB plan and participates in the Statewide Local Government OPEB Plan (SLGOP), a cost-sharing multiple-employer defined benefit plan, that covers all of the government's general employees and the Water and Sewer Authority's employees.

Public Safety Employees OPEB Plan (PSEOP)

Plan Description. The government's PSEOP provides health and dental benefits to eligible retired police and fire employees and their beneficiaries. PSEOP is affiliated with the Municipal Retired Public Safety Employees OPEB Plan (MRPSOP), an agent multiple-employer defined benefit postemployment healthcare plan, administered by the State Pension Board through the Statewide Local Government Retirement System (SLGRS). State statutes assign the authority to establish and amend the benefit provisions of the plans that participate in MRPSOP to the respective employer governments. The State issues a publicly available financial report that includes financial statements and required supplementary information for MRPSOP. The report may be obtained by writing to SLGRS, 204 Caraway Lane, State Capital City.

Funding Policy. The contribution requirements of plan members and the government are established and may be amended by the State Pension Board. PSEOP members receiving benefits contribute $75 per month for retiree-only coverage and $150 per month for retiree and spouse coverage to age 65, and $40 and $80 per month, respectively, thereafter. The government is required to contribute at a rate that is based on an actuarial valuation that is prepared in accordance within certain parameters. The current rate is 13.75 percent of annual covered payroll.

Annual OPEB Cost. For 2015, the government's annual OPEB cost of $782 for PSEOP was equal to the required contribution. The government's annual OPEB cost, the percentage of annual OPEB cost contributed to the plan, and the net OPEB obligation for 2015 and the two preceding years were as follows:

Fiscal Year Ended	Annual OPEB Cost	Percentage of Annual OPEB Cost Contributed	Net OPEB Obligation
12/31/13	$733	100%	$0
12/31/14	757	100%	0
12/31/15	782	100%	0

Funded Status and Funding Progress. The funded status of the plan as of January 1, 2015, was as follows:

Actuarial accrued liability (AAL)	$10,190
Actuarial value of plan assets	7,898
Unfunded actuarial accrued liability (UAAL)	$ 2,292
Funded ratio (actuarial value of plan assets/AAL)	77.5%
Covered payroll (active plan members)	$5,684
UAAL as a percentage of covered payroll	40.3%

Actuarial valuations of an ongoing plan involve estimates of the value of reported amounts and assumptions about the probability of occurrence of events far into the future. Examples include assumptions about future employment, mortality, and the healthcare cost trend. Amounts determined regarding the funded status of the plan and the annual required contributions of the employer are subject to continual revision as actual results are compared with past expectations and new estimates are made about the future. The schedule of funding progress, presented as required supplementary information following the notes to the financial statements, presents multiyear trend information that shows whether the actuarial value of plan assets is increasing or decreasing over time relative to the actuarial accrued liabilities for benefits.

Actuarial Methods and Assumptions. Projections of benefits for financial reporting purposes are based on the substantive plan (the plan as understood by the employer and plan members) and include the types of benefits provided at the time of each valuation and the historical pattern of sharing of benefit costs between the employer and plan members to that point. The actuarial methods and assumptions used include techniques that are designed to reduce short-term volatility in actuarial accrued liabilities and the actuarial value of assets, consistent with the long-term perspective of the calculations.

In the January 1, 2015, actuarial valuation, the entry age actuarial cost method was used. The actuarial assumptions included a 7.5 percent investment rate of return (net of administrative expenses) and an annual healthcare cost trend rate of 12 percent initially, reduced by decrements to an ultimate rate of 5 percent after ten years. Both rates include a 4.5 percent inflation assumption. The actuarial value of PSEOP assets was determined using techniques that spread the effects of short-term volatility in the market value of investments over a five-year period. PSEOP's unfunded actuarial accrued liability is being amortized as a level percentage of projected payroll on a closed basis. The remaining amortization period at December 31, 2015 was twenty-two years.

Statewide Local Government OPEB Plan (SLGOP)

Plan Description. The government contributes to the SLGOP, a cost-sharing multiple-employer defined benefit postemployment healthcare plan administered by the State Pension Board through the Statewide Local Government Retirement System (SLGRS). SLGOP provides medical and dental benefits to retired employees. State statutes assign the authority to establish and amend benefit provisions to the State Pension Board. The State issues a publicly available financial report that includes financial statements and required supplementary information for the SLGOP. The report may be obtained by writing to SLGRS, 204 Caraway Lane, State Capital City.

Funding Policy. State statutes provide that contribution requirements of the plan members and the participating employers are established and may be amended by the State Pension Board. Plan members or beneficiaries receiving benefits contribute $65 per month for retiree-only coverage and $135 for retiree and spouse coverage to age 65, and $35 and $75 per month, respectively, thereafter.

Participating governments are contractually required to contribute at a rate assessed each year by SLGRS, currently 8.75 percent of annual covered payroll. The State Pension Board sets the employer contribution rate based on an actuarial valuation prepared in accordance with certain parameters. The government's contributions to SLGOP for the years ended December 31, 2015, 2014, and 2013, were $1,066, $1,035, and $974, respectively, which equaled the required contributions each year.

G. Employee retirement systems and pension plans

Pension plans – primary government

The government maintains a single-employer, defined benefit pension plan that covers all of its public safety employees; participates in the statewide local government retirement system, a cost-sharing multiple-employer defined benefit public employee pension plan that covers all of the government's general employees and the Water and Sewer Authority's employees; and maintains a defined contribution plan for all full-time sworn police officers.

Public Safety Employees Retirement System (PSERS)

Plan description. The government administers the PSERS, a single-employer, defined benefit pension plan in which all full-time police and fire employees of the government participate. PSERS provides retirement, disability, and death benefits to plan members and their beneficiaries. The government has authorized the PSERS board to establish and amend all plan provisions. The PSERS issues a publicly available financial report that includes the applicable financial statements and required supplementary information. The report may be obtained at the government's offices.

Summary of significant accounting policies – basis of accounting and valuation of investments. The financial statements of PSERS are prepared using the accrual basis of accounting. Plan member contributions are recognized in the period in which the contributions are due. The government's contributions are recognized when due and a formal commitment to provide the contributions has been made. Benefits and refunds are recognized when due and payable in accordance with the terms of the plan. All plan investments are reported at fair value. Securities traded on a national exchange are valued at the last reported sales price on the government's balance sheet date. Securities without an established market are reported at estimated fair value.

Funding policy. The contribution requirements of plan members and the government are established and may be amended by the PSERS board. Plan members are required to contribute 5.0 percent of their annual covered salary. The government is required to contribute at an actuarially determined rate; the current rate is 26.3 percent of annual covered payroll.

Annual pension cost. For 2015, the government's annual pension cost of $1,496 for PSERS was equal to the government's required and actual contributions. The required contribution was determined as part of the January 1, 2015, actuarial valuation using the entry age normal actuarial cost method. The actuarial assumptions included (a) 7.5 percent investment rate of return (net of administrative expenses), (b) projected salary increases due to inflation of 4.5 percent per year, compounded annually, and (c) projected salary increases due to seniority/merit raises of 3.0 percent per year, compounded annually. The actuarial value of assets was determined using techniques that smooth the effects of short-term volatility in the market value of investments over a five-year period. PSERS' unfunded actuarial accrued liability is being amortized as a level percentage of projected payroll on a closed basis. The remaining amortization period at December 31, 2015, was 17 years.

Three-Year Trend Information for PSERS

Fiscal Year Ending	Annual Pension Cost (APC)	Percentage of APC Contributed	Net Pension Obligation
12/31/13	$1,402	100%	$0
12/31/14	1,447	100%	$0
12/31/15	1,496	100%	$0

Statewide Local Government Retirement System (SLGRS)

Plan description. The government participates in the SLGRS, a cost-sharing, multiple-employer defined benefit pension plan administered by the State Pension Board. SLGRS provides retirement, disability, and death benefits to plan members and their beneficiaries. State statutes authorize the State to establish and amend all plan provisions. The State issues a publicly available financial report that includes the applicable financial statements and required supplementary information for SLGRS. The report may be obtained by writing to SLGRS, 204 Caraway Lane, State Capital City.

Funding policy. The contribution requirements of the plan members and the government are established and may be amended by the State. Plan members are required to contribute 4.7 percent of their annual covered salary. The government is required to contribute at an actuarially determined rate; the current rate is 10.8 percent of covered payroll. The government's contributions to SLGRS for the years ending December 31, 2015, 2014, 2013 were $ 1,316, $1,277, and $1,202, respectively, and were equal to the required contributions for each year.

Law Enforcement Supplemental Retirement Plan (LESRP)

Plan description and funding requirements. The LESRP is a defined contribution pension plan established and administered by the State to provide retirement benefits for all full-time sworn police officers employed by local governments. At December 31, 2015, there were 139 plan members from the government. Plan members are allowed to make voluntary contributions to the plan. State statutes required the government to contribute 4 percent of the annual covered payroll of plan participants. Plan provisions and contribution requirements are established by state statute and may be amended by the State. Total contributions for the year ended December 31, 2015, were $10 by the employees and $152 by the government.

Pension plan - discretely presented component unit

Statewide Educator's Retirement System (SERS)

Plan description. The District participates in the SERS, a cost-sharing, multiple-employer, defined benefit pension plan administered by the State. SERS provides retirement, disability, and death benefits to plan members and their beneficiaries. The State is authorized by statute to establish and amend all plan provisions. The State issues a publicly available financial report that includes the applicable financial statements and required supplementary information for SERS. The report may be obtained by writing to SERS, 204 Caraway Lane, State Capital City.

Funding policy. The contribution requirements of the plan members and the District are established and may be amended by the State. Plan members are required to contribute 6.0 percent of their annual covered salary. The government is required to contribute at an actuarially determined rate; the current rate is 9.3 percent of covered payroll. The government's contributions to SERS for the years ending December 31, 2015, 2014, and 2013 were $1,219, $1,195, and $1,104 respectively, and were equal to the required contributions for each year.

Required Supplementary Information

Public Safety Employees Retirement System
Schedule of Funding Progress

Actuarial Valuation Date	Actuarial Value of Assets (a)	Actuarial Accrued Liability (AAL)- Entry Age (b)	Unfunded AAL (UAAL) (b-a)	Funded Ratio (a/b)	Covered Payroll (c)	UAAL as a Percentage of Covered Payroll [(b-a)/c]
01/01/13	$13,006	$13,999	$993	92.9%	$5,079	19.6%
01/01/14	13,887	14,725	838	94.3	5,359	15.6
01/01/15	14,530	15,007	477	96.8	5,684	8.4

Public Safety Employees Other Postemployment Benefits Plan
Schedule of Funding Progress

Actuarial Valuation Date	Actuarial Value of Assets (a)	Actuarial Accrued Liability (AAL)- Entry Age (b)	Unfunded AAL (UAAL) (b-a)	Funded Ratio (a/b)	Covered Payroll (c)	UAAL as a Percentage of Covered Payroll [(b-a)/c]
12/31/13	$5,300	$ 8,819	$3,519	60.1%	$5,079	69.3%
12/31/14	6,322	9,187	2,865	68.8	5,359	53.5
12/31/15	7,898	10,190	2,292	77.5	5,684	40.3

Nonmajor Governmental Funds

Special Revenue Funds

Special revenue funds are used to account for specific revenues that are legally restricted to expenditure for particular purposes.

Transportation Fund – This fund is used to account for the government's local option motor fuel tax revenues and special state grants that are restricted to the maintenance of state highways within the government's boundaries.

Parks Maintenance Fund – This fund is used to account for private donations and alcoholic beverage tax revenues that are specifically restricted to the maintenance of the government's parks.

CDBG Revitalization Project Fund – This fund is used to account for the community development block grant that is funding the revitalization project for substandard housing within the government.

Capital Projects Funds

Capital projects funds are used to account for the acquisition and construction of major capital facilities other than those financed by proprietary funds and trust funds.

Housing Development Street Construction Fund – This fund is used to account for the construction of roads in new housing developments within the government's geographic area. Special assessments, governmental resources, and state grant revenues will finance this two-year project.

Street Construction Fund – This fund is used to account for the construction and expansion of roads and bridges. The Federal Highway Administration is completely financing this two-year project.

Permanent Fund

Permanent funds are used to report resources that are legally restricted to the extent that only earnings, not principal, may be used for purposes that support the reporting government's programs.

Perpetual Care Permanent Fund – This fund is used to account for principal trust amounts received and related interest income. The interest portion of the trust can be used to maintain the community cemetery.

Name of Government
Combining Balance Sheet
Nonmajor Governmental Funds
December 31, 2015
(amounts expressed in thousands)

	Special Revenue				Capital Projects			Permanent Fund	Total Nonmajor Governmental Funds
	Transportation	Parks Maintenance	CDBG Revitalization	Total	Housing Development Street Construction	Street Construction	Total	Perpetual Care	
ASSETS									
Cash and cash equivalents	$ 65	$ 146	—	$ 211	$ 323	—	$ 323	$ 231	$ 765
Investments	1,216	403	—	1,619	1,899	—	1,899	1,807	5,325
Interest receivable	1	1	—	2	64	—	64	82	148
Due from other funds	—	—	—	—	335	—	335	—	335
Cash – restricted	—	—	4	4	—	—	—	—	4
Intergovernmental receivable – restricted	—	—	19	19	—	296	296	—	315
Total assets	$ 1,282	$ 550	$ 23	$ 1,855	$ 2,621	$ 296	$ 2,917	$ 2,120	$ 6,892
LIABILITIES									
Accounts payable	332	84	—	416	251	406	657	13	1,086
Retainage payable	—	—	—	—	149	11	160	—	160
Liabilities payable from restricted assets	—	—	18	18	—	—	—	—	18
Total liabilities	332	84	18	434	400	417	817	13	1,264
FUND BALANCES									
Reserved for encumbrances	$ —	$ —	5	$ 5	$ 1,944	—	$ 1,944	$ —	$ 1,949
Reserved for perpetual care	—	—	—	—	—	—	—	1,102	1,102
Unreserved, designated for encumbrances	353	8	—	361	—	—	—	—	361
Unreserved, undesignated	597	458	—	1,055	277	(121)	156	1,005	2,216
Total fund balances	950	466	5	1,421	2,221	(121)	2,100	2,107	5,628
Total liabilities and fund balances	$ 1,282	$ 550	$ 23	$ 1,855	$ 2,621	$ 296	$ 2,917	$ 2,120	$ 6,892

The notes to the financial statements are an integral part of this statement.

Name of Government
Combining Statement of Revenues, Expenditures, and Changes in Fund Balances
Nonmajor Governmental Funds
For the Year Ended December 31, 2015
(amounts expressed in thousands)

	Special Revenue				Capital Projects			Permanent Fund	Total Nonmajor Governmental Funds
	Transportation	Parks Maintenance	CDBG Revitalization	Total	Housing Development Street Construction	Street Construction	Total	Perpetual Care	
REVENUES									
Motor fuel tax	$ 729	$ —	$ —	$ 729	$ —	$ —	$ —	$ —	$ 729
Alcoholic beverage tax	—	799	—	799	—	—	—	—	799
Intergovernmental	100	—	338	438	124	329	453	—	891
Investment earnings	119	39	—	158	273	—	273	233	664
Donations	—	149	—	149	—	—	—	—	149
Total revenues	948	987	338	2,273	397	329	726	233	3,232
EXPENDITURES									
Current:									
Highways and streets	742	—	—	742	—	—	—	—	742
Economic and physical development	—	—	401	401	—	—	—	—	401
Culture and recreation	—	1,001	—	1,001	—	—	—	13	1,014
Capital outlay:									
Highways and streets	—	—	—	—	1,005	555	1,560	—	1,560
Special assessments	—	—	—	—	2,225	—	2,225	—	2,225
Total expenditures	742	1,001	401	2,144	3,230	555	3,785	13	5,942
Excess (deficiency) of revenues over (under) expenditures	206	(14)	(63)	129	(2,833)	(226)	(3,059)	220	(2,710)
OTHER FINANCING SOURCES (USES)									
Transfers in:									
General fund	—	—	63	63	1,210	—	1,210	—	1,273
Transfers out:									
Debt service fund	—	—	—	—	(846)	—	(846)	—	(846)
Special assessment bonds issued	—	—	—	—	4,700	—	4,700	—	4,700
Discount on special assessment debt	—	—	—	—	(10)	—	(10)	—	(10)
Total other financing sources and (uses)	—	—	63	63	5,054	—	5,054	—	5,117
Net change in fund balances	206	(14)	—	192	2,221	(226)	1,995	220	2,407
Fund balances – beginning	744	480	5	1,229	—	105	105	1,887	3,221
Fund balances – ending	$ 950	$ 466	$ 5	$ 1,421	$ 2,221	$ (121)	$ 2,100	$ 2,107	$ 5,628

The notes to the financial statements are an integral part of this statement.

Name of Government
Debt Service Fund
Schedule of Revenues, Expenditures, and Changes in Fund Balances - Budget and Actual
For the Year Ended December 31, 2015
(amounts expressed in thousands)

	Final Budgeted Amounts	Actual Amounts	Variance with Final Budget
REVENUES			
Property taxes	$ 1,500	$ 1,585	$ 85
Special assessments	470	470	—
Investment earnings	220	322	102
Total revenues	2,190	2,377	187
EXPENDITURES			
Debt service:			
Principal	2,054	2,030	24
Interest	2,941	2,928	13
Refunding bond issuance costs	65	65	—
Advance refunding escrow	15	15	—
Total expenditures	5,075	5,038	37
Deficiency of revenues under expenditures	(2,885)	(2,661)	224
OTHER FINANCING SOURCES (USES)			
Transfers in	3,500	4,173	673
Refunding bonds issued	3,365	3,365	—
Payment to refunded bond escrow agent	(3,300)	(3,300)	—
Total other financing sources and uses	3,565	4,238	673
Net change in fund balances	680	1,577	897
Fund balances – beginning	10	10	—
Fund balances – ending	$ 690	$ 1,587	$ 897

Name of Government
Transportation Special Revenue Fund
Schedule of Revenues, Expenditures, and Changes in Fund Balances - Budget and Actual
For the Year Ended December 31, 2015
(amounts expressed in thousands)

	Final Budgeted Amounts	Actual Amounts	Variance with Final Budget
REVENUES			
Motor fuel tax	$ 625	$ 729	$ 104
Intergovernmental	100	100	—
Investment earnings	42	119	77
Total revenues	767	948	181
EXPENDITURES			
Current:			
Highways and streets	1,437	742	695
Excess (deficiency) of revenues over (under) expenditures	(670)	206	876
Fund balances – beginning	744	744	—
Fund balances – ending	$ 74	$ 950	$ 876

Name of Government
Parks Maintenance Special Revenue Fund
Schedule of Revenues, Expenditures, and Changes in Fund Balances – Budget and Actual
For the Year Ended December 31, 2015
(amounts expressed in thousands)

	Final Budgeted Amounts	Actual Amounts	Variance with Final Budget
REVENUES			
Alcoholic beverage tax	$ 682	$ 799	$ 117
Investment earnings	31	39	8
Donations	23	149	126
Total revenues	736	987	251
EXPENDITURES			
Current:			
Culture and recreation	995	1,001	(6)
Deficiency of revenues under expenditures	(259)	(14)	245
Fund balances – beginning	480	480	—
Fund balances – ending	$ 221	$ 466	$ 245

Name of Government
CDBG Revitalization Project Special Revenue Fund
Schedule of Revenues, Expenditures, and Changes in Fund Balances – Budget and Actual
From Inception and for the Year Ended December 31, 2015
(amounts expressed in thousands)

	Prior Years	Current Year	Total to Date	Project Authorization
REVENUES:				
Intergovernmental – Community Development Block Grant	$ 28	$ 338	$ 366	$ 600
EXPENDITURES:				
Economic and physical development:				
Administration	20	14	34	90
Clearance activities	—	—	—	1
Housing rehabilitation	1	217	218	393
Street improvements	7	131	138	145
Drainage improvements	—	39	39	39
Total expenditures	28	401	429	668
Deficiency of revenues under expenditures	—	(63)	(63)	(68)
Other Financing Sources:				
Transfers in	5	63	68	68
Net change in fund balances	$ 5	—	$ 5	$ —
Fund balances – beginning		5		
Fund balances – ending		$ 5		

Name of Government
Housing Development Street Construction Capital Projects Fund
Schedule of Revenues, Expenditures, and Changes in Fund Balance – Budget and Actual
From Inception and for the Year Ended December 31, 2015
(amounts expressed in thousands)

	Prior Years	Current Year	Total to Date	Project Authorization
REVENUES				
Intergovernmental – State grant	$ —	$ 124	$ 124	$ 248
Investment earnings	—	273	273	—
Total revenues	—	397	397	248
EXPENDITURES				
Capital outlay:				
Highways and streets	—	1,005	—	1,448
Special assessments	—	2,225	2,225	3,854
Total expenditures	—	3,230	3,230	5,302
Deficiency of revenues under expenditures	—	(2,833)	(2,833)	(5,054)
OTHER FINANCING SOURCES (USES)				
Transfers in	—	1,210	1,210	1,200
Transfers out	—	(846)	(846)	(846)
Special assessment bonds issued	—	4,700	4,700	4,700
Discount on special assessment debt	—	(10)	(10)	—
Total other financing sources (uses)	—	5,054	5,054	5,054
Net change in fund balances	$ —	2,221	2,221	$ —
Fund balances – beginning		—		
Fund balances – ending		$ 2,221		

Name of Government
Street Construction Capital Projects Fund
Schedule of Revenues, Expenditures, and Changes in Fund Balances – Budget and Actual
From Inception and for the Year Ended December 31, 2015
(amounts expressed in thousands)

	Prior Years	Current Year	Total to Date	Project Authorization
REVENUES				
Intergovernmental - Federal Highway Administration Grant	$ 688	$ 329	$ 1,017	$ 1,267
EXPENDITURES				
Capital outlay:				
Highways and streets:				
Widening	416	89	505	505
Construction	167	466	633	762
Total expenditures	583	555	1,138	1,267
Excess (deficiency) of revenues over (under) expenditures	$ 105	$ (226)	(121)	$ —
Fund balances – beginning		105		
Fund balances – ending		(121)		

This page is intentionally left blank.

Internal Service Funds

Internal service funds are used to account for the financing of goods or services provided by one department or agency to other departments or agencies of the government and to other government units, on a cost reimbursement basis.

Fleet Management Fund — This fund is used to account for the rental of motor vehicles to other departments and related costs.

Management Information Systems Fund — This fund is used to account for the accumulation and allocation of costs associated with electronic data processing.

Name of Government
Internal Service Funds
Combining Statement of Net Assets
December 31, 2015
(amounts expressed in thousands)

	Fleet Management	Management Information Systems	Total
ASSETS			
Current assets:			
Cash and cash equivalents	$ 30	$ 64	$ 94
Investments	17	33	50
Interest receivable	2	—	2
Due from other funds	64	62	126
Intergovernmental receivable	4	—	4
Inventories	23	—	23
Prepaid items	38	—	38
Total current assets	178	159	337
Noncurrent assets:			
Capital assets:			
Buildings	87	—	87
Machinery and equipment	4,334	949	5,283
Less accumulated depreciation	(2,108)	(358)	(2,466)
Total capital assets (net of accumulated depreciation)	2,313	591	2,904
Total assets	2,491	750	3,241
LIABILITIES			
Current liabilities:			
Accounts payable	227	15	242
Due to other funds	18	24	42
Compensated absences	2	7	9
Total current liabilities	247	46	293
Noncurrent liabilities:			
Compensated absences	3	16	19
Advances from other funds	32	46	78
Total noncurrent liabilities	35	62	97
Total liabilities	282	108	390
NET ASSETS			
Invested in capital assets	2,313	591	2,904
Unrestricted	(104)	51	(53)
Total net assets	$ 2,209	$ 642	$ 2,851

The notes to the financial statements are an integral part of this statement.

Name of Government
Internal Service Funds
Combining Statement of Revenues, Expenses, and Changes in Fund Net Assets
For the Year Ended December 31, 2015
(amounts expressed in thousands)

	Fleet Management	Management Information Systems	Total
Operating revenues:			
Charges for sales and services	$ 1,264	$ 593	$ 1,857
Total operating revenues	1,264	593	1,857
Operating expenses:			
Costs of sales and services	777	374	1,151
Administration	70	64	134
Depreciation	419	92	511
Total operating expenses	1,266	530	1,796
Operating income (loss)	(2)	63	61
Nonoperating revenues (expenses):			
Investment earnings	6	2	8
Income before contributions and transfers	4	65	69
Capital contributions	2,160	—	2,160
Transfers in	45	—	45
Change in net assets	2,209	65	2,274
Total net assets - beginning	—	577	577
Total net assets - ending	$ 2,209	$ 642	$ 2,851

The notes to the financial statements are an integral part of this statement.

Name of Government
Internal Service Funds
Combining Statement of Cash Flows
For the Year Ended December 31, 2015
(amounts expressed in thousands)

	Fleet Management	Management Information Systems	Total
CASH FLOWS FROM OPERATING ACTIVITIES			
Receipts from customers and users	$ 124	$ 643	$ 767
Receipts from interfund services provided	1,072	—	1,072
Payments to suppliers	(606)	(450)	(1,056)
Payments to employees	(60)	(56)	(116)
Net cash provided by operating activities	530	137	667
CASH FLOWS FROM NONCAPITAL FINANCING ACTIVITIES			
Transfers from other funds	45	—	45
Advance from other funds	40	20	60
Net cash provided by noncapital and related financing activities	85	20	105
CASH FLOWS FROM CAPITAL AND RELATED FINANCING ACTIVITIES			
Purchases of capital assets	(572)	(67)	(639)
Net cash used by capital and related financing activities	(572)	(67)	(639)
CASH FLOWS FROM INVESTING ACTIVITIES			
Proceeds from sales and maturities of investments	31	—	31
Purchase of investments	(48)	(33)	(81)
Interest and dividends received	4	2	6
Net cash used by investing activities	(13)	(31)	(44)
Net increase in cash and cash equivalents	30	59	89
Cash and cash equivalents – January 1	—	5	5
Cash and cash equivalents – December 31	$ 30	$ 64	$ 94
Reconciliation of operating income to net cash provided (used) by operating activities:			
Operating income (loss)	$ (2)	$ 63	$ 61
Adjustments to reconcile operating income to net cash provided (used) by operating activities:			
Depreciation expense	419	92	511
(Increase) in intergovernmental receivable	(4)	—	(4)
(Increase) decrease in due from other funds	(64)	50	(14)
(Increase) in inventories	(23)	—	(23)
(Increase) in prepaid items	(38)	—	(38)
Increase (decrease) in accounts payable	227	(73)	154
Increase in compensated absences payable	5	5	10
Increase in due to other funds	10	—	10
Total adjustments	532	74	606
Net cash provided by operating activities	$ 530	$ 137	$ 667
Noncash investing, capital, and financing activities:			
Contributions of capital assets from government	2,160	—	
Capital asset trade-ins	48	—	

The notes to the financial statements are an integral part of this statement.

STATISTICAL SECTION

This part of the Name of Government's comprehensive annual financial report presents detailed information as a context for understanding what the information in the financial statements, note disclosures, and required supplementary information says about the government's overall financial health.

Contents   **Page**

Financial Trends   95

These schedules contain trend information to help the reader understand how the government's financial performance and well-being have changed over time.

Revenue Capacity   102

These schedules contain information to help the reader assess the government's most significant local revenue source, the property tax.

Debt Capacity   106

These schedules present information to help the reader assess the affordability of the government's current levels of outstanding debt and the government's ability to issue additional debt in the future.

Demographic and Economic Information   111

These schedules offer demographic and economic indicators to help the reader understand the environment within which the government's financial activities take place.

Operating Information   113

These schedules contain service and infrastructure data to help the reader understand how the information in the government's financial report relates to the services the government provides and the activities it performs.

Sources: Unless otherwise noted, the information in these schedules is derived from the comprehensive annual financial reports for the relevant year.

This page is intentionally left blank.

Name of Government
Net Assets by Component
Last Ten Fiscal Years
(accrual basis of accounting)
(amounts expressed in thousands)

	Fiscal Year									
	2006	2007	2008	2009	2010	2011	2012	2013	2014	2015
Governmental activities										
Invested in capital assets, net of related debt	$26,666	$27,896	$28,588	$29,567	$30,789	$31,067	$32,048	$33,892	$34,817	$45,092
Restricted	3,456	2,144	1,987	2,108	4,736	4,322	3,874	4,345	6,528	8,046
Unrestricted	1,772	1,555	924	1,004	764	2,324	1,655	618	2,092	2,930
Total governmental activities net assets	$31,894	$31,595	$31,499	$32,679	$36,289	$37,713	$37,577	$38,855	$43,437	$56,068
Business-type activities										
Invested in capital assets, net of related debt	$54,367	$55,768	$60,783	$65,783	$69,784	$71,111	$71,777	$72,898	$74,229	$75,983
Restricted	763	1,547	322	127	312	657	1,247	5,789	3,113	632
Unrestricted	6,114	5,007	3,869	2,868	3,739	6,914	10,083	9,499	15,061	25,636
Total business-type activities net assets	$61,244	$62,322	$64,974	$68,778	$73,835	$78,682	$83,107	$88,186	$92,403	$102,251
Primary government										
Invested in capital assets, net of related debt	$81,033	$83,664	$89,371	$95,350	$100,573	$102,178	$103,825	$106,790	$109,046	$121,075
Restricted	4,219	3,691	2,309	2,235	5,048	4,979	5,121	10,134	9,641	8,678
Unrestricted	7,886	6,562	4,793	3,872	4,503	9,238	11,738	10,117	17,153	28,566
Total primary government net assets	$93,138	$93,917	$96,473	$101,457	$110,124	$116,395	$120,684	$127,041	$135,840	$158,319

Name of Government
Changes in Net Assets
Last Ten Fiscal Years
(accrual basis of accounting)
(amounts expressed in thousands)

					Fiscal Year					
	2006	2007	2008	2009	2010	2011	2012	2013	2014	2015
Expenses										
Governmental activities:										
General government	$ 3,075	$ 3,170	$ 3,302	$ 3,513	$ 3,603	$ 3,753	$ 3,869	$ 3,908	$ 3,988	$ 4,370
Public safety	4,852	5,217	5,733	6,232	7,082	8,852	9,622	9,920	12,400[1]	12,823
Highways and streets	2,812	2,866	3,106	3,263	3,355	3,766	3,863	3,899	3,972	4,835
Sanitation	2,139	2,252	2,346	2,666	2,640	3,106	3,256	3,339	3,404	3,773
Economic development	15	15	28	165	44	226	35	27	28	401
Culture and recreation	2,815	3,027	3,121	3,392	3,609	4,101	4,825	5,079	6,772[2]	6,990
Interest on long-term debt	2,108	2,296	2,365	2,367	2,533	2,409	2,423	2,566	2,615	3,012
Total governmental activities expenses	17,816	18,843	20,001	21,598	22,866	26,213	27,893	28,738	33,179	36,204
Business-type activities:										
Water	6,943	7,121	7,266	7,569	7,763	7,921	8,251	8,506	8,924	9,968
Sewer	3,365	3,561	3,671	3,905	4,005	4,087	4,213	4,435	4,804	5,848
Electric	9,776	10,027	10,128	10,335	10,766	11,576	11,934	12,562	12,781	12,569
Total business-type activities expenses	20,084	20,709	21,065	21,809	22,534	23,584	24,398	25,503	26,509	28,385
Total primary government expenses	$37,900	$39,552	$41,066	$43,407	$45,400	$49,797	$52,291	$54,241	$59,688	$64,589
Program Revenues										
Governmental activities:										
Charges for services:										
General government	$ 1,950	$ 2,053	$ 2,144	$ 2,253	$ 2,379	$ 2,531	$ 2,664	$ 2,822	$ 2,791	$ 3,033
Culture and recreation	686	722	755	793	837	890	937	993	1,095	1,058
Other activities	975	1,026	1,072	1,126	1,189	1,265	1,332	1,411	1,587	1,551
Operating grants and contributions	1,858	1,914	1,843	2,011	1,994	2,089	1,851	1,892	2,648	3,399
Capital grants and contributions	544	600	610	463	607	506	500	533	688	5,166
Total governmental activities program revenues	6,013	6,315	6,424	6,646	7,006	7,281	7,284	7,651	8,809	14,207
Business-type activities:										
Charges for services:										
Water	6,056	6,374	6,661	6,997	7,388	7,860	8,274	8,764	7,852	9,698
Sewer	4,102	4,318	4,512	4,740	5,005	5,324	5,605	5,937	5,235	6,498
Electric	9,376	9,870	10,314	10,833	11,441	12,171	12,810	13,571	15,110	15,250
Operating grants and contributions	140	236	160	223	150	207	229	164	172	396
Capital grants and contributions	-	-	-	-	-	-	-	-	-	4,294
Total business-type activities program revenues	19,674	20,798	21,647	22,793	23,984	25,562	26,918	28,436	28,369	36,136
Total primary government program revenues	$25,687	$27,113	$28,071	$29,439	$30,990	$32,843	$34,202	$36,087	$37,178	$50,343

Fiscal Year

	2006	2007	2008	2009	2010	2011	2012	2013	2014	2015
Net (expense)/revenue										
Governmental activities	$(11,803)	$(12,528)	$(13,577)	$(14,952)	$(15,860)	$(18,932)	$(20,609)	$(21,087)	$(24,370)	$(21,997)
Business-type activities	(410)	89	582	984	1,450	1,978	2,520	2,933	1,860	7,751
Total primary government net expense	$(12,213)	$(12,439)	$(12,995)	$(13,968)	$(14,410)	$(16,954)	$(18,089)	$(18,154)	$(22,510)	$(14,246)
General Revenues and Other Changes in Net Assets										
Governmental activities:										
Taxes										
Property taxes	$ 6,864	$ 7,635	$ 8,072	$ 8,792	$10,249	$10,826	$11,022	$11,454	$13,886	$15,690
Sales taxes	1,752	2,047	2,216	2,437	2,713	3,242	3,629	4,294	5,253	6,642
Franchise taxes	1,446	1,231	1,379	1,773	2,215	2,727	2,804	3,446	4,126	4,293
Motor fuel taxes	-	-	-	-	-	-	-	-	355	729
Alcoholic beverage taxes	-	-	-	-	-	-	-	-	651	799
Unrestricted grants and contributions	895	906	833	1,975	2,166	2,137	2,233	2,007	3,284	3,411
Investment earnings	250	404	974	1,152	2,119	1,413	778	1,156	1,392	1,48
Miscellaneous	9	6	7	3	8	11	7	8	5	2
Transfers	-	-	-	-	-	-	-	-	-	1,576
Total governmental activities	11,216	12,229	13,481	16,132	19,470	20,356	20,473	22,365	28,952	34,628
Business-type activities:										
Investment earnings	508	989	2,070	2,820	3,607	2,869	1,905	2,146	2,357	3,673
Transfers	-	-	-	-	-	-	-	-	-	(1,576)
Total business-type activities	508	989	2,070	2,820	3,607	2,869	1,905	2,146	2,357	2,097
Total primary government	$11,724	$13,218	$15,551	$18,952	$23,077	$23,225	$22,378	$24,511	$31,309	$36,725
Change in Net Assets										
Governmental activities	$ (587)	$ (299)	$ (96)	$ 1,180	$ 3,610	$ 1,424	$ (136)	$ 1,278	$ 4,582	$12,631
Business-type activities	98	1,078	2,652	3,804	5,057	4,847	4,425	5,079	4,217	9,848
Total primary government	$ (489)	$ 779	$ 2,556	$ 4,984	$ 8,667	$ 6,271	$ 4,289	$ 6,357	$ 8,799	$22,479

[1] The increase from the prior period was caused by a substantial increase in the salaries and benefits paid to police and firefighters as a result of a new labor contract.

[2] The increase from the prior period was caused by an increase in sponsored programs and events to meet citizen demands.

Name of Government
Governmental Activities Tax Revenues By Source
Last Ten Fiscal Years
(accrual basis of accounting)
(amounts expressed in thousands)

Fiscal Year	Property Tax	Sales Tax	Franchise Tax	Motor Fuel Tax	Alcoholic Beverage Tax	Total
2006	$6,864	$1,752	$1,446	$ —	$ —	$10,062
2007	7,635	2,047	1,231	—	—	10,913
2008	8,072	2,216	1,379	—	—	11,667
2009	8,792	2,437	1,773	—	—	13,002
2010	10,249	2,713	2,215	—	—	15,177
2011	10,826	3,242	2,727	—	—	16,795
2012	11,022	3,629	2,804	—	—	17,455
2013	11,454	4,294	3,446	—	—	19,194
2014	13,886	5,253	4,126	355[1]	651[1]	24,271
2015	15,690	6,642	4,293	729	799	28,153

[1] First year of tax

Name of Government
Fund Balances of Governmental Funds
Last Ten Fiscal Years
(modified accrual basis of accounting)
(amounts expressed in thousands)

					Fiscal Year					
	2006	2007	2008	2009	2010	2011	2012	2013	2014	2015
General fund										
Reserved	$ 125	$ 100	$ 75	$ 50	$ 25	-	$ 100	$ 75	$ 50	$ 298
Unreserved	615	1,162	1,602	2,498	4,026	$3,066	1,404	5	1,757	4,710
Total general fund	$ 740	$1,262	$1,677	$2,548	$4,051	$3,066	$1,504	$ 80	$1,807	$5,008[1]
All other governmental funds										
Reserved	$1,102	$1,102	$1,102	$1,102	$8,272[2]	$1,102	$1,102	$1,652	$1,217	$4,638[1]
Unreserved, reported in:										
Special revenue funds	-	517	746	719	665	692	731	792	1,229	1,416
Capital projects funds	-	-	-	-	-	-	-	-	-	156
Permanent funds	58	125	212	304	406	513	622	736	785	1,005
Total all other governmental funds	$1,160	$1,744	$2,060	$2,125	$9,343	$2,307	$2,455	$3,180	$3,231	$7,215

[1] The increase in total fund balance of the general fund and the reserved fund balance of the debt service fund in 2015 is explained in Management's Discussion and Analysis.

[2] The increase in reserved fund balance in this period was due to unspent bond proceeds from an issuance during the period for capital projects.

Name of Government
Changes in Fund Balances of Governmental Funds
Last Ten Fiscal Years
(modified accrual basis of accounting)
(amounts expressed in thousands)

	Fiscal Year									
	2006	2007	2008	2009	2010	2011	2012	2013	2014	2015
Revenues										
Taxes	$10,072	$10,957	$11,702	$12,976	$15,207	$16,879	$17,472	$19,175	$24,271	$28,181
Licenses and permits	658	957	1,043	1,018	1,359	1,105	1,461	1,759	1,820	2,041
Intergovernmental	3,424	3,409	3,743	4,861	4,731	4,834	5,683	5,887	5,185	6,661
Charges for services	580	879	918	1,316	1,642	1,745	2,483	1,996	2,335	2,300
Fines	169	177	212	185	182	306	331	358	521	808
Investment earnings	377	559	882	1,098	1,258	1,567	929	1,355	1,613	1,759
Special assessments	519	756	260	335	411	159	506	253	-	470
Miscellaneous	1	571	348	119	109	-	-	11	553	734
Total revenues	15,800	18,265	19,108	21,908	24,899	26,595	28,865	30,794	36,298	42,954
Expenditures										
General government	3,047	3,226	3,423	3,835	4,189	4,130	4,250	4,872	3,844	4,257
Public safety	5,051	5,724	6,060	7,006	7,975	10,070	11,183	11,931	13,150	13,438
Highways and streets	1,444	1,499	1,548	1,850	2,214	2,653	2,856	3,051	3,389	4,477
Sanitation	1,597	1,790	1,843	2,228	2,309	3,092	3,151	3,240	3,404	3,726
Economic and physical development	-	-	-	-	-	-	-	-	28	401
Culture and recreation	2,085	2,314	2,610	3,232	3,797	4,428	5,234	5,643	6,787	6,913
Capital outlay	-	-	-	-	5,195	7,170	-	750	583	3,785
Debt service										
Principal	845	994	1,165	1,232	1,283	1,355	1,565	1,380	1,470	2,045
Interest	1,795	1,737	1,728	1,679	1,598	1,718	2,047	1,951	1,865	2,928
Other charges	-	-	-	-	-	-	-	-	-	230
Total expenditures	15,864	17,284	18,377	21,062	28,560	34,616	30,286	32,818	34,520	42,200
Excess of revenues over (under) expenditures	(64)	981	731	846	(3,661)	(8,021)	(1,421)	(2,024)	1,778	754

Fiscal Year

	2006	2007	2008	2009	2010	2011	2012	2013	2014	2015
Other financing sources (uses)										
Transfers in	2,640	2,731	2,893	2,911	2,881	3,073	3,612	3,331	3,340	7,022
Transfers out	(2,640)	(2,731)	(2,893)	(2,911)	(2,881)	(3,073)	(3,612)	(3,331)	(3,340)	(5,491)
Refunding bonds issued	-	-	-	-	-	-	-	-	-	3,365
Bonds issued	-	-	-	-	12,440	-	-	1,300	-	4,700
Premium on bonds issssued	-	-	-	-	-	-	-	25	-	-
Discount on bonds issued	-	-	-	-	(75)	-	-	-	-	(10)
Payments to refunded bond escrow agent	-	-	-	-	-	-	-	-	-	(3,300)
Capital leases	-	125	-	90	-	-	-	-	-	140
Sale of capital assets	12	-	-	-	17	-	7	-	-	5
Total other financing sources (uses)	12	125	-	90	12,382	-	7	1,325	-	6,431
Net change in fund balances	$ (52)	$ 1,106	$ 731	$ 936	$ 8,721	$ (8,021)	$ (1,414)	$ (699)	$ 1,778	$ 7,185
Debt service as a percentage of noncapital expenditures	17.3%	16.4%	16.4%	14.4%	12.8%	11.7%	12.4%	10.8%	10.2%	14.1%

Name of Government
General Governmental Tax Revenues By Source
Last Ten Fiscal Years
(modified accrual basis of accounting)
(amounts expressed in thousands)

Fiscal Year	Property Tax	Sales Tax	Franchise Tax	Motor Fuel Tax	Alcoholic Beverage Tax	Total
2006	$ 6,874	$1,752	$1,446	$ —	$ —	$10,072
2007	7,679	2,047	1,231	—	—	10,957
2008	8,107	2,216	1,379	—	—	11,702
2009	8,766	2,437	1,773	—	—	12,976
2010	10,279	2,713	2,215	—	—	15,207
2011	10,910	3,242	2,727	—	—	16,879
2012	11,039	3,629	2,804	—	—	17,472
2013	11,435	4,294	3,446	—	—	19,175
2014	13,886	5,253	4,126	355[1]	651[1]	24,271
2015	15,718	6,642	4,293	729	799	28,181

[1] First year of tax

Name of Government
Assessed Value and Estimated Actual Value of Taxable Property
Last Ten Fiscal Years
(in thousands of dollars)

| Fiscal Year Ended December 31 | Real Property | | Personal Property | | Less: Tax Exempt Real Property | Total Taxable Assessed Value | Total Direct Tax Rate | Estimated Actual Taxable Value | Assessed Value[1] as a Percentage of Actual Value |
	Residential Property	Commercial Property	Motor Vehicles	Other					
2006	$ 396,333	$ 325,454	$ 73,357	$ 5,522	$ 18,189	$ 782,477	$8.785	$1,098,710	72.87%
2007	416,655	361,993	81,677	7,102	24,443	842,984	9.109	1,181,012	73.45%
2008	469,914	419,737	95,133	9,409	26,223	967,970	8.375	1,314,038	75.66%
2009	525,326	543,714	95,261	10,585	41,812	1,133,074	7.736	1,555,841	75.51%
2010	894,903	798,243	159,101	17,678	23,907	1,846,018	5.568	2,415,116	77.43%
2011	868,456	1,252,316	173,331	19,259	260,537[2]	2,052,825	5.315	3,253,242	71.11%
2012	892,422	1,845,910	228,287	22,578	496,559	2,492,638	4.429	4,289,957	69.68%
2013	985,483	2,008,996	251,356	31,066	528,607	2,748,294	4.161	4,624,733	70.86%
2014	1,243,854	2,331,467	343,601	33,982	556,446	3,396,458	4.088	5,206,921	75.92%
2015	1,294,147	2,388,684	370,287	36,622	569,311	3,520,429	4.465	5,324,823	76.81%

Source: County Board of Equalization and Assessment.

Note: Property in the county is reassessed annually. The county assesses property at approximately 75 percent of actual value for all types of real and personal property. Estimated actual value is calculated by dividing assessed value by those percentages. Tax rates are per $1,000 of assessed value.

[1] Includes tax-exempt property.

[2] Homestead exemption was increased to $25,000 per household.

Name of Government
Property Tax Rates
Direct and Overlapping[1] Governments
Last Ten Fiscal Years

Fiscal Year	Name of Government			Overlapping Rates							
				County			School District				
	Operating Millage	Debt Service Millage	Total City Millage	Operating Millage	Debt Service Millage	Total County Millage	Operating Millage	Debt Service Millage	Total School Millage	Special Districts	Total Direct & Overlapping Rates
2006	5.411	3.374	8.785	6.382	.133	6.515	9.000	.970	9.970	2.519	27.789
2007	6.869	2.240	9.109	6.264	.114	6.378	8.930	.820	9.750	2.260	27.497
2008	5.384	2.991	8.375	6.136	.335	6.471	8.000	.300	8.300	2.174	25.320
2009	5.167	2.569	7.736	6.568	.371	6.939	6.750	.270	7.020	1.995	23.690
2010	4.007	1.561	5.568	6.891	.432	7.323	8.404	.226	8.630	2.790	24.311
2011	3.817	1.498	5.315	4.653	.284	4.937	6.796	.123	6.919	2.288	19.459
2012	2.979	1.450	4.429	3.979	.203	4.182	6.031	.102	6.133	1.736	16.480
2013	2.950	1.211	4.161	3.827	.422	4.249	6.825	.108	6.933	1.637	16.980
2014	3.102	.986	4.088	3.835	.349	4.184	7.172	—[2]	7.172	1.826	17.270
2015	3.028	1.437[3]	4.465	4.195	.332	4.527	7.228	—[2]	7.228	1.838	18.058

Source: County Board of Equalization and Assessment.

[1] Overlapping rates are those of local and county governments that apply to property owners within the Name of Government. Not all overlapping rates apply to all Name of Government property owners (e.g., the rates for special districts apply only to the proportion of the government's property owners whose property is located within the geographic boundaries of the special district.

[2] School district retired its debt on 12/31/13.

[3] A portion of the property taxes are reported as revenues in the debt service fund beginning in 2015.

103

Name of Government
Principal Property Taxpayers
December 31, 2015
(amounts expressed in thousands)

Taxpayer	2015			2006		
	Taxable Assessed Value	Rank	Percentage of Total Taxable Assessed Value	Taxable Assessed Value	Rank	Percentage of Total Taxable Assessed Value
XYZ Corporation	$ 325,197	1	9.2%	$ 78,976	2	10.1%
Beatle Corporation	300,339	2	8.5	91,065	1	11.6
Southwest Mutual Corporation	164,692	3	4.7	32,675	3	4.2
1st Interstate Bank of Name of Government	131,233	4	3.7	27,598	5	3.5
Spark Electric	83,753	5	2.4	-		-
ABC Development	82,811	6	2.4	-		-
Name of State Gas Company	73,945	7	2.1	19,044	6	2.4
PAW Parts, Inc.	57,612	8	1.6	-		-
EFG Development	44,623	9	1.3	-		-
Who Corporation	41,179	10	1.2	-		-
Tarmac Corporation	-		-	29,673	4	3.8
Carr Development	-		-	12,820	7	1.6
Peel Manufacturing Corporation			-	11,222	8	1.4
Ozali Films Corporation	-		-	9,443	9	1.2
Fye Construction Company	-		-	8,026	10	1.0
Totals	$ 1,305,384		37.1%	$ 320,542		40.8%

Source: County Board of Equalization and Assessment

Name of Government
Property Tax Levies and Collections
Last Ten Fiscal Years
(amounts expressed in thousands)

Fiscal Year Ended December 31	Total Tax Levy for Fiscal Year	Collected within the Fiscal Year of the Levy		Collections in Subsequent Years	Total Collections to Date	
		Amount	Percentage of Levy		Amount	Percentage of Levy
2006	$ 6,881	$ 6,841	99.4%	$ 22	$ 6,863	99.7%
2007	7,717	7,632	98.9	41	7,673	99.4
2008	8,162	8,089	99.1	65	8,154	99.9
2009	8,825	8,754	99.2	71	8,825	100.0
2010	10,400	10,264	98.7	104	10,368	99.7
2011	11,158	10,901	97.7	82	10,983	98.4
2012	11,567	11,012	95.2	75	11,087	95.9
2013	11,439	11,405	99.7	34	11,439	100.0
2014	12,823	12,733	99.3	90	12,823	100.0
2015	15,692	15,585	99.3	—	15,657	99.8

Name of Government
Ratios of Outstanding Debt by Type
Last Ten Fiscal Years
(amounts expressed in thousands, except per capita amount)

| Fiscal Year | Governmental Activities | | | Business-Type Activities | | | Total Primary Government | Percentage of Personal Income[1] | Per Capita[1] |
	General Obligation Bonds	Special Assessment Bonds	Capital Leases	Sewer Bonds	General Obligation Bonds	Capital Leases			
2006	$30,274	$ -	$ -	$10,747	$ -	$ -	$ 41,021	10.56%	$ 861
2007	29,280	-	125	10,593	-	-	39,998	8.96%	808
2008	28,140	-	100	10,427	-	-	38,667	6.95%	748
2009	26,933	-	165	10,247	-	-	37,345	5.59%	663
2010	38,145	-	110	10,053	28,990	-	77,298	10.87%	1,409
2011	36,845	-	55	9,843	28,038	-	74,781	9.75%	1,310
2012	35,335	-	-	9,617	27,078	-	72,030	9.54%	1,280
2013	38,925	-	-	9,373	26,118	-	74,416	9.41%	1,321
2014	37,455	-	-	9,110	25,158	-	71,723	8.27%	1,205
2015	35,790	4,700	125	34,600	32,298	101	107,614	11.52%	1,752

Note: Details regarding the city's outstanding debt can be found in the notes to the financial statements.
[1] See the Schedule of Demographic and Economic Statistics on page 111 for personal income and population data.

Name of Government
Ratios of General Bonded Debt Outstanding
Last Ten Fiscal Years
(amounts expressed in thousands, except per capita amount)

Fiscal Year	General Obligation Bonds	Less: Amounts Available in Debt Service Fund	Total	Percentage of Estimated Actual Taxable Value[1] of Property	Per Capita[2]
2006	$30,274	$ 484	$29,790	2.71%	$625
2007	29,280	549	$28,731	2.43%	581
2008	28,140	699	$27,441	2.09%	531
2009	26,933	525	$26,408	1.70%	469
2010	38,145	525	$37,620	1.56%	686
2011	36,845	846	$35,999	1.11%	630
2012	35,335	257	$35,078	0.82%	624
2013	38,925	9	$38,916	0.84%	691
2014	37,455	10	$37,445	0.72%	629
2015	35,790	1,587	$34,203	0.64%	557

Note: Details regarding the city's outstanding debt can be found in the notes to the financial statements.

[1] See the Schedule of Assessed Value and Estimated Actual Value of Taxable Property on page 102 for property value data.
[2] Population data can be found in the Schedule of Demographic and Economic Statistics on page 111.

Name of Government
Direct and Overlapping Governmental Activities Debt
As of December 31, 2015
(amounts expressed in thousands)

Governmental Unit	Debt Outstanding	Estimated Percentage Applicable[1]	Estimated Share of Overlapping Debt
Debt repaid with property taxes: County	$72,240	13.80%	$ 9,969
Subtotal, overlapping debt			9,969
Name of Government direct debt			40,615
Total direct and overlapping debt			$ 50,584

Sources: Assessed value data used to estimate applicable percentages provided by the County Board of Equalization and Assessment. Debt outstanding data provided by the county.

Note: Overlapping governments are those that coincide, at least in part, with the geographic boundaries of the city. This schedule estimates the portion of the outstanding debt of those overlapping governments that is borne by the residents and businesses of the Name of Government. This process recognizes that, when considering the government's ability to issue and repay long-term debt, the entire debt burden borne by the residents and businesses should be taken into account. However, this does not imply that every taxpayer is a resident, and therefore responsible for repaying the debt, of each overlapping government.

[1] The percentage of overlapping debt applicable is estimated using taxable assessed property values. Applicable percentages were estimated by determining the portion of the county's taxable assessed value that is within the government's boundaries and dividing it by the county's total taxable assessed value.

Name of Government
Legal Debt Margin Information
Last Ten Fiscal Years
(amounts expressed in thousands)

	Fiscal Year									
	2006	2007	2008	2009	2010	2011	2012	2013	2014	2015
Debt limit	$80,067	$86,743	$99,419	$117,489	$186,992	$231,336	$298,920	$327,690	$395,290	$408,974
Total net debt applicable to limit	29,790	28,731	27,541	26,408	66,610	64,037	62,156	65,034	62,603	66,501
Legal debt margin	$50,277	$58,012	$71,878	$91,081	$120,382	$167,299	$236,764	$262,656	$332,687	$342,473
Total net debt applicable to the limit as a percentage of debt limit	37.21%	33.12%	27.70%	22.48%	35.62%	27.68%	20.79%	19.85%	15.84%	16.26%

Legal Debt Margin Calculation for Fiscal Year 2015

Assessed value	$3,520,429
Add back: exempt real property	$ 569,311
Total assessed value	$4,089,740
Debt limit (10% of total assessed value)	408,974
Debt applicable to limit:	
General obligation bonds	68,088
Less: Amount set aside for repayment of general obligation debt	(1,587)
Total net debt applicable to limit	66,501
Legal debt margin	$ 342,473

Note: Under state finance law, the Name of Government's outstanding general obligation debt should not exceed 10 percent of total assessed property value. By law, the general obligation debt subject to the limitation may be offset by amounts set aside for repaying general obligation bonds.

Name of Government
Pledged-Revenue Coverage
Last Ten Fiscal Years
(amounts expressed in thousands)

| | Sewer Revenue Bonds | | | | | | Special Assessment Bonds | | | |
Fiscal Year	Sewer Charges and Other	Less: Operating Expenses	Net Available Revenue	Debt Service Principal	Interest	Coverage	Special Assessment Collections	Debt Service Principal	Interest	Coverage
2006	$1,772	$ 863	$ 909	$ 154	$ 840	0.91	$ -	$ -	$ -	-
2007	1,915	961	954	166	828	0.96	-	-	-	-
2008	2,282	1,252	1,030	180	814	1.04	-	-	-	-
2009	2,756	1,588	1,168	194	800	1.18	-	-	-	-
2010	3,797	1,844	1,953	210	784	1.96	-	-	-	-
2011	4,113	2,171	1,942	226	768	1.95	-	-	-	-
2012	4,318	2,429	1,889	244	750	1.90	-	-	-	-
2013	4,911	2,428	2,483	263	731	2.50	-	-	-	-
2014	4,966	3,049	1,917	285	709	1.93	-	-	-	-
2015	6,810	3,469	3,341	1,484	2,377	0.87	658	-¹	188	3.50

Note: Details regarding the government's outstanding debt can be found in the notes to the financial statements. Sewer charges and other includes investment earnings but not tap fees. Operating expenses do not include interest or depreciation.

¹ No principal payments were scheduled in this the period in which the debt was issued.

Name of Government
Demographic and Economic Statistics
Last Ten Fiscal Years

Fiscal Year	Population[1]	Personal Income (amounts expressed in thousands)	Per Capita Personal income[2]	Median Age[3]	Education Level in Years of Formal Schooling[4]	School Enrollment[4]	Unemployment Rate[2]
2006	47,663	$388,310	$ 8,147	27.7	14.9	9,590	4.1%
2007	49,481	446,319	9,020	27.9	14.9	8,790	4.1
2008	51,662	556,245	10,767	28.1	15.0	8,220	3.2
2009	56,343	688,341	11,862	28.3	15.1	7,683	5.5
2010	54,874	711,002	12,957	28.5	15.3	7,093	5.9
2011	57,100	767,196	13,436	28.7	15.4	6,813	7.7
2012	56,252	754,677	13,416	28.9	15.5	7,146	8.4
2013	56,340	790,619	14,033	29.1	15.7	6,991	7.3
2014	59,534	866,994	14,563	29.3	15.8	6,723	6.1
2015	61,434	934,165	15,206	29.5	15.9	6,703	5.4

Data sources

[1] Bureau of the Census/County Regional Planning Commission

[2] State Department of Labor

[3] State Department of Commerce

[4] School District

Note: Population, median age, and education level information are based on surveys conducted during the last quarter of the calendar year. Personal income information is a total for the year. Unemployment rate information is an adjusted yearly average. School enrollment is based on the census at the start of the school year.

Name of Government
Principal Employers
Current Year and Nine Years Ago

Employer	2015			2006		
	Employees	Rank	Percentage of Total City Employment	Employees	Rank	Percentage of Total City Employment
Beatle Corporation	1,550	1	3.26%	1,100	1	3.38%
State Mental Health Facility	1,039	2	2.19%	750	2	2.31%
Southwest Mutual Corporation	810	3	1.71%	450	3	1.38%
XYZ Corporation	650	4	1.37%	390	4	1.20%
Name of Government	472	5	0.99%	372	5	1.14%
1st Interstate Bank of Name of Government	315	6	0.66%	235	6	0.72%
Name of State Gas Company	275	7	0.58%	225	7	0.69%
PAW Parts, Inc.	180	8	0.38%	—		—
Spark Electric	120	9	0.25%	—		—
Who Corporation	115	10	0.24%	—		—
Tarmac Corporation	—		—	175	8	0.54%
Peel Manufacturing Corporation	—		—	125	9	0.38%
Ozali Films Corporation	—		—	75	10	0.23%
Total	5,526		11.63%	3,897		11.97%

Source: State Department of Commerce.

Name of Government
Full-time Equivalent City Government Employees by Function
Last Ten Fiscal Years

	Full-time Equivalent Employees as of December 31									
Function	2006	2007	2008	2009	2010	2011	2012	2013	2014	2015
General government	64	64	65	66	66	67	68	68	71	72
Public safety										
Police										
Officers	40	41	43	44	45	46	47	48	49	52
Civilians	18	18	19	19	20	20	20	21	21	22
Fire										
Firefighters and officers	36	38	39	40	41	42	43	46	47	48
Civilians	14	14	15	15	15	16	16	17	17	17
Highways and streets										
Engineering	15	15	16	17	18	21	22	23	24	25
Maintenance	10	10	10	10	10	11	11	12	12	12
Sanitation	17	17	18	18	18	18	18	18	20	22
Culture and recreation	47	49	48	49	50	49	49	49	49	50
Water[1]	35	37	39	41	42	43	47	49	51	52
Sewer	24	26	26	26	26	27	29	30	31	32
Electric	52	54	55	56	58	61	62	64	66	68
Total	372	383	393	401	409	421	432	445	458	472

Source: Government Budget Office.

[1] The government has added additional water staff in recent years in connection with several infrastructure improvement initiatives.

Name of Government
Operating Indicators by Function
Last Ten Fiscal Years

Function	Fiscal Year									
	2006	2007	2008	2009	2010	2011	2012	2013	2014	2015
Police										
Physical arrests	2,577	2,630	2,683	2,738	2,794	2,851	2,909	2,969	3,029	3,091
Parking violations	21,602	22,042	22,492	22,951	23,420	23,898	24,385	24,883	25,391	25,909
Traffic violations	7,983	8,146	8,312	8,482	8,655	8,832	9,012	9,196	9,384	9,575
Fire										
Number of calls answered	859	876	894	912	931	950	969	989	1,009	1,030
Inspections	3,960	4,041	4,124	4,208	4,294	4,381	4,471	4,562	4,655	4,750
Highways and streets										
Street resurfacing (miles)	25.7	26.0	26.2	26.5	26.8	27.1	27.3	27.6	27.9	28.2
Potholes repaired	898	906	913	921	928	988	996	1,003	1,011	1,019
Sanitation										
Refuse collected (tons/ day)	215.6	218.8	222.2	225.6	229.0	203.6	204.6	205.6	206.7	207.7
Recyclables collected (tons/day)[1]	27.7	28.2	28.8	29.4	30.0	60.0	62.5	65.1	67.8	70.6
Culture and recreation										
Athletic field permits issued	770	786	802	819	835	852	870	887	906	924
Community center admissions	5,373	5,482	5,594	5,708	5,825	5,944	6,065	6,189	6,315	6,444
Water										
New connections	146	142	144	145	147	148	150	151	153	154
Water mains breaks	9	9	4	7	12	10	6	5	10	14
Average daily consumption (thousands of gallons)	3,905	3,985	4,066	4,149	4,234	4,320	4,409	4,499	4,590	4,684
Wastewater										
Average daily sewage treatment (thousands of gallons)	2,696	2,751	2,807	2,864	2,922	2,982	3,043	3,105	3,168	3,233

Sources: Various government departments.

Note: Indicators are not available for the general government function.

[1] The Department of Sanitation implemented a recycling initiative in 2011.

Name of Government
Capital Asset Statistics by Function
Last Ten Fiscal Years

Function	Fiscal Year									
	2006	2007	2008	2009	2010	2011	2012	2013	2014	2015
Public safety										
Police:										
Stations	1	1	1	1	1	1	1	1	1	1
Patrol units	24	24	24	25	26	26	25	28	32	33
Fire stations	2	2	2	2	3	3	3	3	3	3
Sanitation										
Collection trucks	5	5	5	5	5	6	6	7	7	7
Highways and streets										
Streets (miles)	179.3	182.9	186.6	190.5	194.3	198.3	202.4	206.5	210.7	215.0
Streetlights	2,835	2,893	2,952	3,012	3,073	3,136	3,200	3,265	3,332	3,400
Traffic signals	62	64	65	66	68	69	71	72	74	75
Culture and recreation										
Parks acreage	600	600	600	600	600	600	625	625	625	625
Parks	23	23	23	23	23	23	25	25	25	25
Swimming pools	38	38	38	38	39	30	39	39	39	4
Tennis courts	25	25	30	30	35	35	35	40	45	45
Community centers	4	4	4	5	5	5	5	5	5	5
Water										
Water mains (miles)	170.9	174.4	178.0	181.6	185.3	189.1	192.9	196.9	200.9	205.0
Fire hydrants	1,051	1,061	1,072	1,083	1,094	1,105	1,116	1,127	1,139	1,150
Maximum daily capacity (thousands of gallons)	5,500	5,500	5,500	5,500	5,500	5,500	5,500	5,571	5,571	5,571
Sewer										
Sanitary sewers (miles)	187.6	191.4	195.3	199.3	203.4	207.5	211.8	216.1	220.5	225.0
Storm sewers (miles)	170.9	174.4	178.0	181.6	185.3	189.1	192.9	196.9	200.9	205.0
Maximum daily treatment capacity (thousands of gallons)	3,200	3,200	3,200	3,200	3,200	3,200	3,200	3,716	3,716	3,716
Electric										
Number of distribution stations	2	2	3	3	3	3	3	3	3	3
Miles of service lines	207.6	211.8	216.2	220.6	225.1	229.7	234.4	239.1	244.0	249.0

Sources: Various city departments.

Note: No capital asset indicators are available for the general government function.

E

Illustrative Accounts, Classifications, and Descriptions

PRELIMINARY NOTE

It is a basic principle of governmental accounting and financial reporting that "a common terminology and classification should be used consistently throughout the budget, the accounts, and the financial reports of each fund."[1] The first step toward fully realizing this principle is to establish a chart of accounts with appropriate descriptions of each account.

Governments typically maintain their accounting system on a fund basis. The accounting system is thus automatically able to provide the fund-based data needed to prepare the separate governmental fund, proprietary fund, and fiduciary fund financial statements required by generally accepted accounting principles (GAAP). GAAP also require that governments prepare government-wide financial statements to accompany the fund financial statements. These government-wide financial statements consolidate all of the information reported in a government's governmental and proprietary funds.

Governmental funds use the current financial resources measurement focus and the modified accrual basis of accounting, whereas proprietary funds use the economic resources measurement focus and the accrual basis of accounting. Naturally, a consolidated government-wide presentation needs to be presented using a single measurement focus and basis of accounting. Therefore, the data reported in a government's various governmental funds must first be converted to the economic resources measurement focus and the accrual basis of accounting before they can be consolidated with the data for a government's proprietary activities. The details of this conversion are described in chapter 8 and illustrated in appendix C.

---

[1] National Council on Governmental Accounting, Statement 1, *Governmental Accounting and Financial Reporting Principles*, principle 11.

The process of converting governmental fund data is complicated by the fact that the underlying fund data must remain intact to permit the continued reporting of governmental fund financial statements in subsequent periods. That is, governmental fund data cannot be altered in the process of conversion. Accordingly, governments typically use a worksheet to make the adjustments needed to convert governmental fund data to the economic resources measurement focus and the accrual basis of accounting for inclusion in the government-wide financial statements.

Not all assets and liabilities related to *governmental activities* are reported in governmental funds (e.g., capital assets and long-term debt). Accordingly, the additional data needed for government-wide financial reporting must be maintained separately in the accounting system. As a practical matter, the government-wide financial statements function essentially in the same manner as a proprietary fund. Therefore, it generally is not necessary to invent special accounts for this purpose. Instead, needed data can be maintained in the same accounts used for proprietary funds, only with special coding to indicate that these particular balances relate to the government-wide financial statements rather than to an enterprise fund or an internal service fund. The net difference between general government asset and liability account balances may be recorded in a separate *net assets—general government* account to keep the general ledger in balance.

NOTES ON THE ILLUSTRATIVE MATERIAL

This appendix is divided into two sections. The first section provides a summary of account classifications. The second section furnishes definitions of each of the account classifications presented in the first section.

Accounts are numbered consecutively as follows:

100 - Assets
200 - Liabilities and accounts reflecting the difference between assets and liabilities
300 - Revenues and other financing sources
400 - Expenditures and other financing uses

This numbering system is intended primarily to facilitate reference to individual accounts in the illustrative material. With appropriate modifications, however, it could also serve as the basis for a coding system for a government's accounting system. In this latter case, adjustments may be needed to make the coding system consistent with the budget.

The account titles presented in the first section are not exhaustive, but are typical of the types of accounts used by general-purpose local governments. Additional accounts may be needed to provide other types of information useful for managerial purposes.

This chart of accounts generally is limited to accounts used for accounting and financial reporting purposes. It does not include budgetary accounts employed for purposes of budgetary integration (see chapter 16 for a discussion of budgetary accounts).

Many state governments have established a uniform chart of accounts for local governments. Naturally, such a chart of accounts should be used if mandated. Often the use of a uniform state-mandated chart of accounts is connected with the completion of prescribed forms that must be submitted by local governments to a designated state oversight department. If a state-mandated uniform chart of accounts is inconsistent with GAAP, appropriate adjustments should be made in preparing general-purpose external financial reports.

FUND CLASSIFICATIONS

Governments typically maintain their accounting system on a fund basis. Governments also maintain additional data on general government assets and liabilities, as explained earlier, for purposes of government-wide financial reporting. Accordingly, special coding is necessary to indicate the portion of each account balance related to a given fund or to governmental activities in general, as follows:

1	Governmental funds
1.1	General fund
1.2	Special revenue funds
1.3	Capital projects funds
1.4	Debt service funds
1.5	Permanent funds
1.6	Governmental activities (government-wide financial reporting)
2	Proprietary funds
2.1	Enterprise funds
2.2	Internal service funds
3	Fiduciary funds
3.1	Pension (and other employee benefit) trust funds
3.2	Investment trust funds
3.3	Private-purpose trust funds
3.4	Agency funds

A description of each of these items is provided later in this appendix.

CLASSIFICATIONS – STATEMENTS OF POSITION

A summary of the accounts typically used for the various statements of position follows. Most of these accounts are visible in the illustrative financial statements presented in appendix D. Detailed descriptions of each account are provided later in this appendix. Valuation accounts and similar "contra accounts" (e.g., allowance for doubtful accounts, accumulated depreciation, premiums, and discounts) are reported together with the asset or liability account to which they pertain.

The account coding of individual items often will not exactly match the detail presented in a government's published financial statements. Such differences arise as part of the process of summarizing or grouping accounts or portions of accounts for financial reporting purposes. Likewise, certain details needed for financial reporting purposes (e.g., current balance versus noncurrent balance of liabilities, restricted cash and investments versus unrestricted cash and investments) typically are obtained through an analysis of the accounts at year end rather than through the maintenance of separate accounts. Analysis also is needed to classify appropriate portions of *net assets—governmental activities* as *invested in capital assets, net of related debt*; *restricted*; and *unrestricted*.

Code   *Classification*

Assets

101.   Cash (including cash equivalents)
101.1   Petty cash
102.   Cash with fiscal agent
103.   Investments—current
104.   Interest receivable—investments
105.   Taxes receivable—current
105.1   Allowance for uncollectible current taxes (credit)
107.   Taxes receivable—delinquent
107.1   Allowance for uncollectible delinquent taxes (credit)
109.   Interest and penalties receivable—taxes
109.1   Allowance for uncollectible interest and penalties (credit)
111.   Tax liens receivable
111.1   Allowance for uncollectible tax liens (credit)
115.   Accounts receivable
115.1   Allowance for uncollectible accounts receivable (credit)
117.   Unbilled accounts receivable
117.1   Allowance for uncollectible unbilled accounts receivable (credit)
121.   Special assessments receivable—current
121.1   Allowance for uncollectible current special assessments (credit)
122.   Special assessments receivable—noncurrent
122.1   Allowance for uncollectible noncurrent special assessments (credit)
123.   Special assessments receivable—delinquent
123.1   Allowance for uncollectible delinquent special assessments (credit)
124.   Special assessment liens receivable
124.1   Allowance for uncollectible special assessment liens (credit)
125.   Interest receivable—special assessments
125.1   Allowance for uncollectible special assessment interest (credit)
126.   Intergovernmental receivable
127.   Taxes levied for other governments
128.   Notes receivable
128.1   Allowance for uncollectible notes (credit)
129.   Loans receivable
129.1   Allowance for uncollectible loans (credit)
130.   Due from other funds—_____ fund
132.   Due from component unit
136.   Rent receivable
136.1   Allowance for uncollectible rent (credit)
141.   Inventories—materials and supplies
142.   Inventories—stores for resale
143.   Prepaid items
149.   Deferred charges
151.   Investments—noncurrent
151.1   Unamortized premiums—investments
151.2   Unamortized discounts—investments (credit)
152.   Advance to other funds—_____ fund
153.   Investments—joint venture
161.   Land
162.   Infrastructure
162.1   Accumulated depreciation—infrastructure (credit)
163.   Buildings
163.1   Accumulated depreciation—buildings (credit)
164.   Improvements other than buildings

164.1   Accumulated depreciation—improvements other than buildings (credit)
165.   Machinery and equipment
165.1   Accumulated depreciation—machinery and equipment (credit)
166.   Construction in progress
170   Other assets

Liabilities, Fund Balances, and Net Assets

201.   Vouchers payable
202.   Accounts payable
203.   Compensated absences payable
204.   Claims and judgments payable
205.   Contracts payable
206.   Retainage payable
207.   Intergovernmental payable
208.   Due to other funds—_____ fund
210.   Due to component unit
212.   Matured bonds payable
213.   Matured interest payable
214.   Accrued interest payable
222.   Deferred revenue—unavailable
223.   Deferred revenue—unearned
224.   Notes payable—current
225.   Bonds payable—current
225.1   General obligation bonds payable
225.2   Special assessment debt with government commitment
225.3   Revenue bonds payable
225.4   Other bonds payable
226.   Capital leases payable—current
227.   Other current liabilities
228.   Customer deposits
230.   Advance from other funds—_____fund
231.   Bonds payable—noncurrent
231.1   General obligation bonds payable
231.2   Special assessment debt with government commitment
231.3   Revenue bonds payable
231.4   Other bonds payable
232.   Unamortized premiums on bonds
233.   Unamortized discounts on bonds (debit)
234.   Unamortized charge—refunding bonds
235.   Notes payable—noncurrent
237.   Capital leases payable—noncurrent
238.   Net pension obligation
239.   Other noncurrent liabilities
241.   Fund balance—reserved for debt service
242.   Fund balance—reserved for endowments
244.   Fund balance—reserved for encumbrances
245.   Fund balance—reserved for inventories
246.   Fund balance—reserved for prepaid items
247.   Fund balance—reserved for noncurrent loans receivable
248.   Fund balance—reserved for advance to other funds
249.   Fund balance—reserved for capital assets held for resale
250.   Fund balance—reserved for _____
253.   Fund balance—unreserved
253.1   Fund balance—unreserved, designated for _____
253.2   Fund balance—unreserved—undesignated
261.   Net assets, invested in capital assets, net of related debt
262.   Net assets, restricted for _____
262.1   Net assets restricted for _____—permanent restriction
262.2   Net assets restricted for _____—temporary restriction

263. Net assets, held in trust for pension benefits
264. Net assets, held in trust for pool participants
265. Net assets, held in trust for other purposes
266. Net assets, unrestricted
267. Net assets—general government

REVENUES AND OTHER FINANCING SOURCES CLASSIFICATION

A summary of the *revenue* and *other financing source* accounts typically used in preparing the governmental fund statement of revenues, expenditures, and changes in fund balances is presented below. Most of these accounts are visible in the illustrative financial statements presented in appendix D. Detailed descriptions of each account are provided later in this appendix.

GAAP require that *program revenues* be distinguished from *general revenues* in the government-wide statement of activities. Furthermore, GAAP require that *program revenues* be classified as either 1) charges for services, 2) operating grants and contributions, or 3) capital grants and contributions. A government may use analysis to obtain the necessary information, or it may use special coding similar to that described earlier for funds:

1   General revenue
2   Program revenue – charges for services
3   Program revenue – operating grants and contributions
4   Program revenue – capital grants and contributions

Likewise, analysis or coding would be needed to associate program revenues with the appropriate function or program. Illustrative *function, program, and activity* classifications are provided later as part of the discussion of *expenditures and other financing uses.*

Code	Classification
311.	General property taxes
311.1	Real property
311.2	Personal property
311.21	Tangible personal
311.22	Intangible personal
312.	Property taxes on other than assessed valuation
313.	General sales and use taxes
314.	Selective sales and use taxes
314.1	Motor fuel
314.2	Tobacco products
314.3	Alcoholic beverages
315.	Income taxes
315.1	Individual
315.2	Corporate
315.3	Unincorporated business
316.	Gross receipts business taxes
316.1	Privately owned public utility
316.2	Publicly owned public utility
316.3	Insurance companies
316.4	Amusements
317.	Death and gift taxes
318.	Other taxes
318.1	Severance taxes
318.2	Franchise taxes
319.	Penalties and interest on delinquent taxes

319.1	General property taxes
319.11	Real property
319.12	Personal property
319.2	Property taxes on other than assessed valuation
319.3	General sales and use taxes
319.4	Selective sales and use taxes
319.5	Income taxes
319.6	Gross receipts business taxes
319.7	Death and gift taxes
320.	Licenses and permits
321.	Business licenses and permits
321.1	Alcoholic beverages
321.2	Health
321.3	Police and protective
321.4	Corporate
321.5	Public utilities
321.6	Professional and occupational
321.7	Amusements
322.	Nonbusiness licenses and permits
322.1	Building structures and equipment
322.2	Motor vehicles
322.3	Motor vehicle operators
322.4	Hunting and fishing
322.5	Marriage licenses
322.6	Animal licenses
330.	Intergovernmental revenues
331.	Federal government grants
331.1	Operating—categorical
331.11	Direct
331.12	Indirect
331.2	Operating—noncategorical
331.21	Direct
331.22	Indirect
331.3	Capital
331.31	Direct
331.32	Indirect
333.	Federal government payments in lieu of taxes
334.	State government grants
334.1	Operating—categorical
334.2	Operating—noncategorical
334.3	Capital
335.	State government shared revenues
335.1	Property taxes
335.2	Income taxes
335.21	Individual income taxes
335.22	Corporate income taxes
335.3	General sales and use taxes
335.4	Motor vehicle fuel taxes
335.5	Motor vehicle licenses
335.6	Tobacco taxes
335.7	Alcoholic beverage taxes
335.8	Death and gift taxes
335.9	Gross receipts business taxes
336.	State government payments in lieu of taxes
337.	Local government unit (specify unit) grants
338.	Local government unit (specify unit) shared revenues
339.	Local government unit (specify unit) payments in lieu of taxes
340.	Charges for services
341.	General government
341.1	Court costs, fees, and charges

341.2	Recording of legal instruments
341.3	Zoning and subdivision fees
341.4	Printing and duplicating services
342.	Public safety
342.1	Special police services
342.2	Special fire protection services
342.3	Correctional fees
342.4	Protective inspection fees
344.	Sanitation
344.1	Sewerage charges
344.2	Street sanitation charges
344.3	Refuse collection charges
345.	Health
345.1	Vital statistics
345.2	Health and inspection fees
345.3	Hospital fees
345.4	Clinic fees
345.5	Animal control and shelter fees
346.	Welfare
346.1	Institutional charges
347.	Culture-recreation
347.1	Golf fees
347.2	Swimming pool fees
347.3	Playground fees
347.4	Park and recreation concessions
347.5	Auditorium use fees
347.6	Library use fees (not fines)
347.7	Zoo charges
351.	Fines
351.1	Court
351.2	Library
352.	Forfeits
355.	Special assessments
355.1	Capital improvement
355.2	Service
361.	Investment earnings
361.1	Interest revenues
361.2	Dividends
361.3	Net increase (decrease) in the fair value of investments
362.	Rents and royalties
363.	Escheats
364.	Contributions and donations from private sources
365.	Contributions from property owners—special assessments
370.	Special assessment financing
390.	Other financing sources
391.	Interfund transfers in—_____ fund
392.	Proceeds of general capital asset dispositions
392.1	Sale of general capital assets
392.2	Compensation for loss of general capital assets
393.	General long-term debt issued
393.1	General obligation bonds issued
393.2	Special assessment bonds issued
393.3	Special assessment debt with government commitment issued
393.4	Other bonds issued
393.5	Refunding bonds issued
393.6	Premiums on bonds sold
393.7	Capital leases
395.	Special items— _____
396.	Extraordinary items—_____
397.	Capital contributions

EXPENDITURES AND OTHER FINANCING USES CLASSIFICATION

A summary of the *expenditure* and *other financing use* accounts typically used in preparing the governmental fund statement of revenues, expenditures, and changes in fund balances is presented below. Most of these accounts are visible in the illustrative financial statements presented in appendix D. Detailed descriptions of each account are provided later in this appendix.

Expenditure information is used for a variety of different purposes (e.g., internal evaluation, external financial reporting, and intergovernmental comparisons). Accordingly, it is important to apply a multi-faceted classification system to expenditures so that the appropriate information is available, as needed. The major elements of the expenditure classification system typically are as follows:

- *Character.* Classification based upon the fiscal period presumed to benefit from an expenditure. In practice, four character classifications are commonly used:
  - *Current expenditures.* These are expenditures that benefit the current fiscal period.
  - *Capital outlay expenditures.* These are expenditures that benefit both the current and future fiscal periods.
  - *Debt service expenditures.* These are expenditures that benefit prior periods, as well as the current and future fiscal periods.
  - *Intergovernmental.* These are expenditures that represent the transfer of resources to another government.
- *Function or program.* Classification based upon the overall purpose or objective of an expenditure.
  - *Functions.* Functions are group-related activities aimed at accomplishing a major service or regulatory responsibility.
  - *Programs.* Programs include group activities, operations, or organizational units directed to attaining specific purposes or objectives. Sometimes governments use program classifications and sub-classifications in addition to or instead of functional classifications (e.g., program budgeting)
- *Activity.* A specific and distinguishable service performed by one or more organizational components of a government to accomplish a function for which the government is responsible. The activity classification is particularly significant because of its usefulness in isolating data needed to evaluate the economy and efficiency of operations (e.g., expenditures per unit of activity).

In addition to the types of classification just described, it also is essential to classify expenditures by *organizational unit* and by *object class* (i.e., type of goods or services obtained).

Classification by organizational unit is important because a single organizational unit may be responsible for several activities or programs. Conversely, a single activity or program may be the responsibility of more than one organizational unit.

Classification by object also is important. Nonetheless, excessively detailed object classifications should be avoided. As a practical matter, relatively few object classifications typically are needed given the emphasis placed on organizational units, functions (or programs), and activities.

FUNCTION, PROGRAM, AND ACTIVITY CLASSIFICATION

Code   *Classification*

410.   **General government**
411.   Legislative
411.1   Governing body
411.2   Legislative committees and special bodies
411.3   Ordinances and proceedings
411.4   Clerk of council
412.   Judicial
412.1   Criminal courts
412.2   Grand jury
412.3   Public defender
412.4   Civil courts
412.41   Chancery court
412.42   Small claims court
412.43   Civil court
412.44   Domestic relations court
412.5   Law library
413.   Executive
413.1   Mayor
413.2   Chief executive
413.3   Boards and commissions
414.   Elections
415.   Financial administration
415.1   Finance
415.11   General supervision
415.12   Accounting
415.13   Independent audit
415.14   Budget
415.15   Tax administration
415.16   Treasury
415.17   Licensing
415.18   Purchasing
415.19   Debt administration
415.21   Internal audit
415.3   Law
415.4   Recording and reporting
415.5   Personnel administration
419.   Other—unclassified
419.1   Planning and zoning
419.2   Data processing
419.3   Research and investigation
419.4   General government buildings and plant
420.   **Public safety**
421.   Police
421.1   Police administration
421.2   Crime control and investigation
421.21   Criminal investigation
421.22   Vice control
421.23   Patrol
421.24   Records and identification
421.25   Youth investigation and control
421.26   Custody of prisoners

421.27   Custody of property
421.28   Crime laboratory
421.3   Traffic control
421.31   Motor vehicle inspection and regulation
421.4   Police training
421.5   Support service
421.51   Communications services
421.52   Automotive services
421.53   Ambulance services
421.54   Medical services
421.6   Special detail services
421.7   Police stations and buildings
422.   Fire
422.1   Fire administration
422.2   Fire fighting
422.3   Fire prevention
422.4   Fire training
422.5   Fire communications
422.6   Fire repair services
422.7   Medical services
422.8   Fire stations and buildings
423.   Corrections
423.1   Correctional administration
423.2   Adult correctional institutions
423.3   Juvenile correctional institutions
423.4   Delinquents in other institutions
423.5   Adult probation and parole
423.6   Juvenile probation and parole
424.   Protective inspection
424.1   Protective inspection administration
424.2   Building inspection
424.3   Plumbing inspection
424.4   Electrical inspection
424.5   Gas inspection
424.6   Air conditioning inspection
424.7   Boiler inspection
424.8   Elevator inspection
424.9   Weights and measures
429.   Other protection
429.1   Civil defense
429.2   Militia and armories
429.3   Traffic engineering
429.4   Examination of licensed occupations
429.5   Public scales
429.6   Flood control
431.   **Highways and streets**
431.21   Paved streets
431.22   Unpaved streets
431.23   Alleys
431.24   Sidewalks and crosswalks
431.25   Snow and ice removal
431.3   Bridges, viaducts, and grade separations
431.4   Tunnels
431.5   Storm drainage
431.6   Street lighting
432.   **Sanitation**
432.1   Sanitary administration
432.2   Street cleaning
432.3   Waste collection
432.4   Waste disposal

432.5		Sewage collection and disposal
432.51		Sanitary sewer construction
432.52		Sanitary sewer maintenance
432.53		Sanitary sewer cleaning
432.54		New sewer services
432.55		Sewer lift stations
432.56		Sewage treatment plants
432.6		Weed control
440.		**Health and welfare**
441.		Health
441.1		Public health administration
441.2		Vital statistics
441.3		Regulation and inspection
441.31		Food and drugs
441.32		Milk and dairy products
441.33		Other sanitary inspection
441.4		Communicable disease control
441.41		Tuberculosis
441.42		Socially transmitted diseases
441.43		Rabies and animal control
441.44		Other communicable diseases
441.5		Maternal and child health services
441.51		Maternal and preschool
441.52		School
441.6		Adult health services
441.7		Health centers and general clinics
441.8		Laboratory
444.		Welfare
441.1		Welfare administration
444.2		Institutional care
444.3		Direct assistance
444.31		General assistance
444.32		Old-age assistance
444.33		Aid to dependent children
444.34		Aid to the blind
444.35		Aid to the disabled
444.36		Other direct assistance
444.4		Intergovernmental welfare payments
444.41		General assistance
444.42		Old-age assistance
444.43		Aid to dependent children
444.44		Aid to the blind
444.45		Aid to the disabled
444.46		Other welfare assistance
444.5		Vendor welfare payments
444.51		Vendor medical payments
444.52		Other vendor payments
450.		**Culture—recreation**
451.		Recreation
451.1		Culture-recreation administration
451.2		Participant recreation
451.21		Supervision
451.22		Recreation centers
451.23		Playgrounds
451.24		Swimming pools
451.25		Golf courses
451.26		Tennis courts
451.27		Other recreational facilities
451.3		Spectator recreation
451.31		Botanical gardens

451.32	Museums
451.33	Art galleries
451.34	Zoos
451.4	Special recreational facilities
452.	Parks
452.1	Supervision
452.2	Park areas
452.3	Parkways and boulevards
452.4	Forestry and nursery
452.5	Park policing
452.6	Park lighting
455.	Libraries
455.1	Library administration
455.2	Circulation
455.3	Catalog
455.4	Reference
455.5	Order
455.6	Periodicals
455.7	Extension
455.8	Special collections
455.9	Branch libraries
461.	**Conservation**
461.1	Water resources
461.2	Agricultural resources
461.3	Forest resources
461.4	Mineral resources
461.5	Fish and game resources
463.	**Urban redevelopment and housing**
463.1	Urban redevelopment and housing administration
463.2	Urban redevelopment
463.21	Redevelopment administration
463.22	Conservation projects
463.23	Rehabilitation projects
463.24	Clearance projects
463.25	Relocation
463.3	Public housing
463.4	Other urban redevelopment
465.	**Economic development and assistance**
465.1	Economic development and assistance administration
465.2	Economic development
465.3	Employment security
466.	**Economic opportunity**
466.1	Job corps
466.11	Men's urban training centers
466.12	Women's urban training centers
466.13	Rural conservation centers
466.14	Youth camps
466.2	Youth work-training programs
466.21	In-school projects
466.22	Out-of-school projects
466.3	Community action programs
466.31	Preschool readiness instruction
466.32	Study centers
466.33	Day-care centers
466.34	Remedial instruction for elementary school students
466.35	Family health education
466.36	Other projects
466.4	Adult basic education
466.5	Assistance to migrant agricultural workers and families
466.6	Work experience programs for needy persons

470.   **Debt service**
471.1   Bond principal
471.2   Other debt principal
472.1   Interest—bonds
472.2   Interest—other debt
475.   Fiscal agent's fees
476.   Issuance costs
477.   Advance refunding escrow
480.   **Intergovernmental expenditures**
490.   **Other financing uses**
491.   Interfund transfers out—_____ fund
492.   Payment to refunded bond escrow agent
493.   Discount on bonds issued
495.   **Special items—_____**
496.   **Extraordinary items—_____**

CHARACTER AND OBJECT CLASSIFICATION

Code   *Classification*

100.   Personal services—salaries and wages
110.   Regular employees
120.   Temporary employees
130.   Overtime
200.   Personal services—employee benefits
210.   Group insurance
220.   Social security contributions
230.   Retirement contributions
240.   Tuition reimbursements
250.   Unemployment compensation
260.   Workers' compensation
290.   Other employee benefits
300.   Purchased professional and technical services
310.   Official/administrative
320.   Professional
330.   Other professional
340.   Technical
400.   Purchased-property services
410.   Utility services
411.   Water/sewerage
420.   Cleaning services
421.   Disposal
422.   Snow plowing
423.   Custodial
424.   Lawn care
430.   Repair and maintenance services
440.   Rentals
441.   Rental of land and buildings
442.   Rental of equipment and vehicles
450.   Construction services
500.   Other purchased services
520.   Insurance, other than employee benefits
530.   Communications
540.   Advertising
550.   Printing and binding
580.   Travel
600.   Supplies
610.   General supplies
620.   Energy

621.   Natural gas
622.   Electricity
623.   Bottled gas
624.   Oil
625.   Coal
626.   Gasoline
630.   Food
640.   Books and periodicals
700. Property
710.   Land
720.   Buildings
730.   Improvements other than buildings
740.   Machinery and equipment
741.   Machinery
742.   Vehicles
743.   Furniture and fixtures
800. Other objects

FUND CLASSIFICATION DESCRIPTIONS

Code   *Description*

1   **Governmental funds**—The funds through which most government functions typically are financed.

1.1   **General fund.** Accounts for all financial resources except those required to be accounted for in another fund.

1.2   **Special revenue funds.** Account for the proceeds of specific revenue sources (other than those for major capital projects) that are restricted legally to expenditure for specified purposes.

1.3   **Debt service funds.** Account for the accumulation of resources for, and the retirement of, general long-term debt principal and interest.

1.4   **Capital projects funds.** Account for financial resources to be used for the acquisition or construction of major capital facilities (other than those financed by proprietary funds and trust funds).

1.5   **Permanent funds.** Account for resources that are legally restricted to the extent that only earnings, and not principal, may be used for purposes that support the reporting government's programs (i.e., for the benefit of the government or its citizenry).

1.6   **Governmental activities (government-wide financial reporting).** Account for balances related to governmental funds that are only reported in the government-wide statement of net assets.

2.   **Proprietary funds**—Account for a government's business-type activities (activities supported at least in part by fees or charges).

2.1   **Enterprise funds.** Account for activities for which a fee is charged to external users for goods or services.

2.2   **Internal service funds.** Account for the financing of goods or services provided by one fund, department, or agency to other funds, departments, or agencies of the financial reporting entity, or to other governments, on a cost-reimbursement basis.

3. **Fiduciary funds**—The funds used to account for assets held by the government as trustee or agent and that cannot be used to support the government's own programs.

3.1 **Pension (and other employee benefit) trust funds.** Account for assets of defined benefit pension plans, defined contribution plans, other postemployment benefit plans, or other employee benefit plans held by a government in a trustee capacity.

3.2 **Investment trust funds.** Account for the external portion of investment pools (including individual investment accounts) reported by the sponsoring government.

3.3 **Private-purpose trust funds.** Account for trust arrangements, including those for escheat property, where principal and income benefit individuals, private organizations, or other governments.

3.4 **Agency funds.** Account for assets held by a government in a purely custodial capacity.

CLASSIFICATION DESCRIPTIONS — STATEMENTS OF POSITION

Code   Description

A.   ASSETS

101.   **Cash (including cash equivalents).** Currency, coins, checks, money orders, and bankers' drafts on hand or on deposit with an official or agent designated as custodian of cash or demand deposits with financial institutions. Cash equivalents are short-term highly liquid investments including Treasury bills, commercial paper, and money market funds. This account includes certain securities (e.g., Treasury bills) that are classified as investments in the notes to the financial statements to disclose credit and market risks.

101.1   **Petty cash.** Currency and coins set aside to make change or pay small obligations when the issuance of a formal voucher or check is not cost-effective.

102.   **Cash with fiscal agent.** Deposits with fiscal agents, such as commercial banks, typically for the payment of bonds and interest.

103.   **Investments—current.** Securities that are expected to be held for less than one year and that generate revenue in the form of interest or dividends. This account includes certain items (e.g., most certificates of deposit) that are classified as deposits in the notes to the financial statements to disclose custodial credit risk.

104.   **Interest receivable—investments.** The amount of interest receivable on all investments.

105.   **Taxes receivable—current.** The uncollected portion of taxes that a government has levied, that are due within one year and that are not yet considered delinquent.

105.1   **Allowance for uncollectible current taxes** (credit). That portion of current taxes receivable estimated not to be collectible. The balance in this account is reported as a deduction from **taxes receivable—current** to indicate net current taxes receivable.

107.   **Taxes receivable—delinquent.** Taxes remaining unpaid on and after the date on which a penalty for nonpayment attaches. Delinquent taxes receivable are classified as such until paid, abated, canceled, or converted into tax liens.

107.1   **Allowance for uncollectible delinquent taxes** (credit). That portion of delinquent taxes receivable estimated not to be collectible. The balance in this account is reported as a deduction from **taxes receivable—delinquent** to indicate net delinquent taxes receivable.

109.   **Interest and penalties receivable—taxes.** The uncollected portion of interest and penalties receivable on taxes.

109.1   **Allowance for uncollectible interest and penalties** (credit). That portion of interest and penalties receivable on taxes estimated not to be collectible. The balance in this account is reported as a deduction from **interest and penalties receivable—taxes** to indicate net interest and penalties receivable—taxes.

111.   **Tax liens receivable.** Legal claims against property that have been exercised because of nonpayment of delinquent taxes, interest, and penalties. Amounts accumulated in this account include delinquent taxes, interest, and penalties receivable thereon and costs of converting delinquent taxes into tax liens.

111.1   **Allowance for uncollectible tax liens** (credit). That portion of tax liens receivable estimated not to be collectible. The balance in this account is reported as a deduction from **tax liens receivable** to indicate net tax liens receivable.

115.   **Accounts receivable.** Amounts owed on open accounts from private individuals or organizations for goods and services furnished by a government (excluding amounts due from other funds or intergovernmental receivables). Although taxes and special assessments receivable could be considered forms of accounts receivable, they should be recorded and reported separately in **taxes receivable** and **special assessments receivable** accounts.

115.1   **Allowance for uncollectible accounts receivable** (credit). That portion of accounts receivable estimated not to be collectible. The balance in this account is reported as a deduction from **accounts receivable** to indicate net accounts receivable.

117.   **Unbilled accounts receivable.** The estimated amount of accounts receivable for goods and services rendered but not yet billed to customers.

117.1   **Allowance for uncollectible unbilled accounts receivable** (credit). That portion of unbilled accounts receivable estimated not to be collectible. The balance in this account is reported as a deduction from **unbilled accounts receivable** to indicate net unbilled accounts receivable.

121.   **Special assessments receivable—current.** The uncollected portion of special assessments a government unit has levied. This account represents amounts due within one year and not yet considered delinquent.

121.1   **Allowance for uncollectible current special assessments** (credit). That portion of current special assessments receivable estimated not to be collectible. The balance in this account is reported as a deduction from **special assessments receivable—current** to indicate net current special assessments receivable.

122.   **Special assessments receivable—noncurrent.** Special assessments that have been levied but that are not due within one year.

122.1   **Allowance for uncollectible noncurrent special assessments** (credit). That portion of noncurrent special assessments receivable estimated not to be collectible. The balance is reported as a deduction from **special assess-**

ments receivable—noncurrent to indicate net noncurrent special assessments receivable.

123.   **Special assessments receivable—delinquent.** Special assessments remaining unpaid on and after the date to which a penalty for nonpayment is attached.

123.1   **Allowance for uncollectible delinquent special assessments** (credit). That portion of delinquent special assessments receivable estimated not to be collectible. The balance in this account is reported as a deduction from **special assessments receivable—delinquent** to indicate net delinquent special assessments receivable.

124.   **Special assessment liens receivable.** Legal claims that have been exercised against property because of nonpayment of delinquent special assessments, interest, and penalties. Amounts accumulated in this account include delinquent special assessments, interest, and penalties receivable thereon and costs of converting delinquent special assessments into special assessment liens.

124.1   **Allowance for uncollectible special assessment liens** (credit). That portion of special assessment liens receivable estimated not to be collectible. The balance in this account is reported as a deduction from **special assessment liens receivable** to indicate net special assessment liens receivable.

125.   **Interest receivable—special assessments.** The uncollected portion of interest receivable due on unpaid installments of special assessments.

125.1   **Allowance for uncollectible special assessment interest** (credit). That portion of special assessment interest estimated not to be collectible. The balance in the account is reported as a deduction from **interest receivable—special assessments** to indicate net special assessment interest.

126.   **Intergovernmental receivable.** Amounts due the reporting government from another government. These amounts may represent intergovernmental grants, entitlements, or shared revenues or may represent taxes collected for the reporting government by an intermediary collecting government, loans, and charges for goods or services rendered by the reporting government for another government.

127.   **Taxes levied for other governments.** Taxes receivable that have been levied for other governments and that are to be collected and distributed to those governments by the reporting government.

128.   **Notes receivable.** An unconditional written promise, signed by the maker, to pay a certain sum on demand or at a fixed or determinable future time either to the bearer or to the order of a person designated therein.

128.1   **Allowance for uncollectible notes** (credit). That portion of notes receivable estimated not to be collectible. The balance in this account is reported as a deduction from **notes receivable** to indicate net notes receivable.

129.   **Loans receivable.** Amounts that have been loaned to individuals or organizations external to a government, including notes taken as security for such loans. Loans to other funds and governments should be recorded and reported separately.

129.1   **Allowance for uncollectible loans** (credit). That portion of loans receivable estimated not to be collectible. The balance in this account is reported as a deduction from **loans receivable** to indicate net loans receivable.

130.   **Due from other funds** (specify fund). Amounts owed for goods and services rendered to a particular fund by another fund in the government reporting entity or for interfund loans that are due within one year.

132.   **Due from component unit.** Amounts owed by a discretely presented component unit to a primary government as a result of goods or services provided or loans made to the discretely presented component unit.

136.   **Rent receivable.** Amounts due to the government pursuant to operating leases and rental agreements.

136.1   **Allowance for uncollectible rent** (credit). That portion of rent estimated not to be collectible. The balance in this account is reported as a deduction from rent receivable to indicate net rent receivable.

141.   **Inventories—materials and supplies.** Materials and supplies on hand for future consumption.

142.   **Inventories—stores for resale.** Goods held for resale rather than for use in operations.

143.   **Prepaid items.** Charges entered in the accounts for benefits not yet received. Prepaid items (e.g., prepaid rent and unexpired insurance premiums) differ from deferred charges in that they are spread over a shorter period of time than deferred charges and are regularly recurring costs of operation.

149.   **Deferred charges.** Nonregularly recurring, noncapital costs of operations that benefit future periods. These costs include those incurred in connection with the issuance of fund debt (e.g., underwriting and legal fees). Although bond discounts can be classified as deferred charges, discounts are reported in account 233.

151.   **Investments—noncurrent.** Securities and real estate that are held for more than one year and that generate revenue in the form of interest, dividends, rentals, or operating lease payments. This account does not include real estate used in government operations. This account includes certain items (e.g., most certificates of deposit) that are classified as deposits in the notes to the financial statements to disclose custodial credit risk.

151.1   **Unamortized premiums—investments.** The unamortized portion of the excess of the amount paid for securities over their face value (excluding accrued interest).

151.2   **Unamortized discounts—investments** (credit). The unamortized portion of the excess of the face value of securities over the amount paid for them (excluding accrued interest).

152.   **Advance to other funds** (specify fund). Amounts that are owed, other than charges for goods and services rendered, to a particular fund by another fund in the government reporting entity and that are not due within one year.

153.   **Investments—joint venture.** Investments and subsequent allocations of earnings or losses for joint ventures where the government has an equity interest.

161.   **Land.** Land purchased or otherwise acquired by the government. This account includes costs incurred in preparing land for use (e.g., razing of structures).

162.   **Infrastructure.** Tangible property that is normally both stationary in nature and can be preserved for a significantly greater number of years than other types of tangible property (e.g., roads, bridges, tunnels, drainage systems, water and sewer systems, dams, and lighting systems).

162.1   **Accumulated depreciation—infrastructure** (credit). The accumulation of systematic and rational allocations of the estimated cost of using infrastructure, on a historical cost basis, over the useful lives of the infrastructure. This account is not used for any networks or subsystems of infrastructure that are reported using the modified approach.

163.   **Buildings.** Permanent structures purchased or otherwise acquired by the government and improvements thereon. This account includes costs incurred in the acquisition of buildings (e.g., broker's fees).

163.1   **Accumulated depreciation—buildings** (credit). The accumulation of systematic and rational allocations of the estimated cost of using buildings, on a historical cost basis, over the useful lives of the buildings.

164.   **Improvements other than buildings.** Permanent improvements, other than buildings, that add value to land (e.g., fences, landscaping, parking lots, and retaining walls).

164.1   **Accumulated depreciation—improvements other than buildings** (credit). The accumulation of systematic and rational allocations of the estimated cost of using improvements, on a historical cost basis, over the useful lives of the improvements.

165.   **Machinery and equipment.** Tangible property of a more or less permanent nature, other than land or buildings and improvements thereon (e.g., machinery, tools, trucks, and furnishings). This account includes costs incurred in the acquisition of machinery and equipment (e.g., transportation costs).

165.1   **Accumulated depreciation—machinery and equipment** (credit). The accumulation of systematic and rational allocations of the estimated cost of using machinery and equipment, on a historical cost basis, over the useful lives of the machinery and equipment.

166.   **Construction in progress.** The cost of construction undertaken but not yet completed.

170.   **Other assets.** Intangible assets and other assets not previously classified. Appropriately descriptive account titles should be used for these items.

B.   LIABILITIES, FUND BALANCES, AND NET ASSETS

201.   **Vouchers payable.** Liabilities for goods and services evidenced by vouchers that have been pre-audited and approved for payment but that have not been paid. This account can include salaries and wages and related payroll taxes payable.

202.   **Accounts payable.** A short-term liability account reflecting amounts owed to private persons or organizations for goods and services received by a government.

203.   **Compensated absences payable.** Amounts owed to employees for unpaid vacation and sick leave liabilities.

204.   **Claims and judgments payable.** Amounts owed as the result of administrative or court decisions, including workers' compensation, unemployment, improper arrests, property damage, and condemnation awards.

205.   **Contracts payable.** Amounts due on contracts for goods or services furnished to a government.

206.   **Retainage payable.** Amounts due on construction contracts. Such amounts represent a percentage of the total contract price that is not paid pending final inspection, the lapse of a specified time, or both.

207. **Intergovernmental payable.** Amounts owed by the government reporting entity to another government.

208. **Due to other funds** (specify fund). Amounts owed for goods and services rendered by a particular fund to another fund in the government reporting entity or for interfund loans that are due within one year.

210. **Due to component unit.** Amounts owed by a primary government to a discretely presented component unit as a result of goods or services provided or loans made by the discretely presented component unit.

212. **Matured bonds payable.** Unpaid bonds that have reached or passed their maturity date.

213. **Matured interest payable.** Unpaid interest on bonds that have reached or passed their maturity date.

214. **Accrued interest payable.** Interest costs related to the current period and prior periods, but not due until a later date.

222. **Deferred revenue—unavailable.** Amounts under the modified accrual basis of accounting for which asset recognition criteria have been met, but for which revenue recognition criteria have not yet been met because such amounts are measurable but not available for expenditure.

223. **Deferred revenue—unearned.** Amounts under the accrual and modified accrual basis of accounting for which asset recognition criteria have been met, but for which revenue recognition criteria have not yet been met because such amounts have not yet been earned.

224. **Notes payable—current.** The face value of notes generally due within one year, including tax anticipation and revenue anticipation notes payable.

225. **Bonds payable-current.** The face value of bonds due within one year, except for deep-discount bonds (e.g., zero-coupon). The accreted value of deep-discount bonds due within one year should be presented in this account.

225.1 **General obligation bonds payable.** The face value of general obligation bonds due within one year.

225.2 **Special assessment debt with government commitment.** The face value of special assessment bonds due within one year when the government is secondarily obligated for the repayment of the bonds.

225.3 **Revenue bonds payable.** The face value of revenue bonds due within one year.

225.4 **Other bonds payable.** The face value of bonds due within one year to be repaid from specific governmental fund revenues.

226. **Capital leases payable—current.** Current portion of the discounted present value of total future stipulated payments on lease agreements that were capitalized.

227. **Other current liabilities.** Appropriately descriptive account titles should be used for such items.

228. **Customer deposits.** Liability for deposits made by customers as a prerequisite to receiving the goods or services the government provides.

230. **Advance from other funds** (specify funds). Amounts that are owed, other than charges for goods and services rendered, by a particular fund to an-

other fund in the government reporting entity and that are not due within one year.

231.   **Bonds payable—noncurrent.** The face value of bonds not due within one year, except for deep-discount bonds (e.g., zero-coupon). The accreted value of deep discount bonds not due within one year should be presented in this account.

231.1   **General obligation bonds payable.** The face value of general obligation bonds not due within one year.

231.2   **Special assessment debt with government commitment.** The face value of special assessment bonds not due within one year when the government is obligated in some manner for repayment of the bonds.

231.3   **Revenue bonds payable.** The face value of revenue bonds not due within one year.

231.4   **Other bonds payable.** The face value of bonds that are not due within one year and that are to be repaid from specific governmental fund revenues.

232.   **Unamortized premiums on bonds.** The unamortized portion of the excess of bond proceeds over their face value (excluding accrued interest and issuance costs).

233.   **Unamortized discounts on bonds** (debit). The unamortized portion of the excess of the face value of bonds over the amount received from their sale (excluding accrued interest and issuance costs).

234.   **Unamortized charge—refunding bonds.** The unamortized portion of the difference between the reacquisition price and the net carrying amount of debt that has been refunded in either an advance refunding or current refunding transaction. This account is added to or deducted from the related debt reported on the balance sheet.

235.   **Notes payable—noncurrent.** The face value of notes not due within one year.

237.   **Capital leases payable—noncurrent.** Noncurrent portion of the discounted present value of total future stipulated payments on lease agreements that are capitalized.

238.   **Net pension obligation.** The cumulative difference between annual pension cost and the employer contributions to a pension plan.

239.   **Other noncurrent liabilities.** Appropriately descriptive account titles should be used for these items.

241.   **Fund balance—reserved for debt service.** Segregation of a portion of fund balance for resources legally restricted to the payment of general long-term debt principal and interest maturing in future years.

242.   **Fund balance—reserved for endowments.** Account used to indicate that permanent trust fund balance amounts are legally restricted to endowment purposes.

244.   **Fund balance—reserved for encumbrances.** Segregation of a portion of fund balance for commitments related to unperformed contracts.

245.   **Fund balance—reserved for inventories.** Segregation of a portion of a fund balance to indicate, using the purchases method for budgetary purposes, that inventories do not represent expendable available financial resources.

246. **Fund balance—reserved for prepaid items.** Segregation of a portion of fund balance to indicate that prepaid items do not represent expendable available financial resources.

247. **Fund balance—reserved for noncurrent loans receivable.** Segregation of a portion of fund balance to indicate that noncurrent portions of loans receivable do not represent expendable available financial resources.

248. **Fund balance—reserved for advance to other funds.** Segregation of a portion of a fund balance to indicate that advances to other funds do not represent expendable available financial resources.

249. **Fund balance—reserved for capital assets held for resale.** Segregation of a portion of fund balance to indicate that capital assets held for resale do not represent expendable available financial resources.

250. **Fund balance—reserved for _____.**

253. **Fund balance—unreserved.** The excess of the assets of a governmental fund over its liabilities and reserved fund balance accounts.

253.1 **Fund balance—unreserved, designated** (specify designation). Segregation of a portion of fund balance to indicate tentative plans for future financial resource use, such as general contingencies or equipment replacement. These designations reflect tentative managerial plans or intent and should be clearly distinguished from reserves.

253.2 **Fund balance—unreserved, undesignated.** Portion of fund balance representing expendable available financial resources.

261. **Net assets, invested in capital assets, net of related debt.** The component of the difference between assets and liabilities of proprietary funds that consists of capital assets less both accumulated depreciation and the outstanding balance of debt (e.g., bonds, mortgages, notes) that is directly attributable to the acquisition, construction, or improvement of those assets.

262. **Net assets, restricted for _____.** The component of the difference between assets and liabilities of proprietary funds that consists of assets with constraints placed on their use by either external parties (e.g., creditors or grantors) or through constitutional provisions or enabling legislation.

262.1 **Net assets, restricted for _____—permanent restriction** are net assets that may never be spent (e.g., endowments).

262.2 **Net assets, restricted for _____—temporary restriction** are net assets that may be spent at some time, either in the present or future.

263. **Net assets, held in trust for pension benefits.** The difference between the assets and liabilities of pension plans reported by the employer or sponsor government in a pension trust fund.

264. **Net assets, held in trust for pool participants.** The difference between the assets and liabilities of external investment pools reported by the sponsor government in an investment trust fund.

265. **Net assets, held in trust for other purposes.** The difference between the assets and liabilities of fiduciary funds, other than pension trust funds or investment trust funds.

266. **Net assets, unrestricted.** The difference between the assets and liabilities of proprietary funds that is not reported as **net assets, invested in capital assets, net of related debt** or **restricted net assets**.

267.   **Net assets—general government.** The difference between general government asset and liability accounts.

REVENUES AND OTHER FINANCING SOURCES CLASSIFICATION DESCRIPTIONS

Code   *Description*

311.   **General property taxes** are ad valorem taxes levied on an assessed valuation of real and/or personal property. The distinguishing characteristics of general property taxes are that the revenues are (1) derived from taxes, (2) levied by the government reporting entity, and (3) assessed on the general property. From this group are eliminated (1) all nontax revenue, (2) all taxes levied by another level of government, such as a county or state or the federal government, even when they are distributed to another government, and (3) all taxes levied by the government reporting entity upon subjects or bases other than general property.
311.1   **Real property**
311.2   **Personal property**
   311.21   **Tangible personal**
   311.22   **Intangible personal**

312.   **Property taxes on other than assessed valuation** are direct taxes (1) assessed and levied on a valuation other than the general assessed valuation usually applied in the case of privately owned real property or (2) calculated at a specified rate per unit. Examples include taxes on a corporation's property levied upon the basis of the amount of corporate stock, corporate indebtedness or some basis other than an assessed valuation applied to all the corporation's property; taxes on banks and savings and loan associations levied in proportion to a certain specified portion of deposits; taxes on life insurance corporations assessed upon the basis of the valuation of their policies and all specific taxes on property, such as taxes on land at a specified amount per acre and taxes on animals at a specified amount per head.

313.   **General sales and use taxes** are imposed upon the sale or consumption of goods and/or services, generally with few or limited exemptions. An example of a general sales tax is a tax on the retail price of all goods sold within a taxing jurisdiction, with the exception of food purchased for consumption off the premises.

314.   **Selective sales and use taxes** are imposed upon the sale or consumption of selected goods or services.
314.1   **Motor fuel**
314.2   **Tobacco products**
314.3   **Alcoholic beverages**

315.   **Income taxes** are measured by net income (i.e., by gross income less certain deductions permitted by law).
315.1   **Individual**
315.2   **Corporate**
315.3   **Unincorporated business** (when business income is taxed separately from individual income)

316.   **Gross receipts business taxes** are levied in proportion to gross receipts on business activities of all or designated types of businesses.
316.1   **Privately owned public utility**
316.2   **Publicly owned public utility**
316.3   **Insurance companies**

316.4 **Amusements**

317. **Death and gift taxes** are imposed upon the transfer of property at death or gifts made in contemplation of death.

318. **Other taxes**
    318.1 **Severance taxes** are imposed on the privilege of removing designated natural resources from land or water. They are based upon the value and/or amount of resources removed or sold.
    318.2 **Franchise taxes** are imposed on the privilege of using public property for private purposes.

319. **Penalties and interest on delinquent taxes** are amounts assessed as penalties for the payment of taxes after their due date, and the interest charged on delinquent taxes from their due date to the date of actual payment. Separate accounts should be used for penalties and interest on each type of tax.
    319.1 **General property taxes**
        319.11 **Real property**
        319.12 **Personal property**
    319.2 **Property taxes on other than assessed valuation**
    319.3 **General sales and use taxes**
    319.4 **Selective sales and use taxes**
    319.5 **Income taxes**
    319.6 **Gross receipts business taxes**
    319.7 **Death and gift taxes**

320. **Licenses and permits** generally are segregated into business and nonbusiness categories.

321. **Business licenses and permits** are revenues from businesses and occupations that must be licensed before doing business within the government's jurisdiction.
    321.1 **Alcoholic beverages**
    321.2 **Health**
    321.3 **Police and protective**
    321.4 **Corporate**
    321.5 **Public utilities**
    321.6 **Professional and occupational**
    321.7 **Amusements**

322. **Nonbusiness licenses and permits** are revenues from all nonbusiness licenses and permits levied according to the benefits presumably conferred by the license or permit.
    322.1 **Building structures and equipment**
    322.2 **Motor vehicles**
    322.3 **Motor vehicle operators**
    322.4 **Hunting and fishing**
    322.5 **Marriage licenses**
    322.6 **Animal licenses**

330. **Intergovernmental revenues** are revenues from other governments in the form of operating grants, entitlements, shared revenues, or payments in lieu of taxes.

   An operating grant is a contribution or gift of cash or other assets from another government to be used or expended for a specified purpose, activity, or facility. Capital grants are restricted by the grantor for the acquisition and/or construction of capital assets. A grant may be received either directly from the granting government or indirectly as a pass-through from another government.

An entitlement is the amount of payment to which a government is entitled pursuant to an allocation formula contained in applicable statutes. A shared revenue is a revenue levied by one government but shared on a predetermined basis, often in proportion to the amount collected at the local level, with another government or class of governments.

Payments in lieu of taxes are payments made from general revenues by one government to another in lieu of taxes it would have to pay, had its property or other tax base been subject to taxation by the recipient government on the same basis as privately owned property or other tax base.

331.   **Federal government grants**
    331.1   **Operating—categorical**
        331.11 **Direct**
        331.12 **Indirect**
    331.2   **Operating—noncategorical**
        331.21 **Direct**
        331.22 **Indirect**
    331.3   **Capital**
        331.31 **Direct**
        331.32 **Indirect**

333.   **Federal government payments in lieu of taxes**

334.   **State government grants**
    334.1   **Operating—categorical**
    334.2   **Operating—noncategorical**
    334.3   **Capital**

335.   **State government shared revenues**
    335.1   **Property taxes**
    335.2   **Income taxes**
        335.21 **Individual income taxes**
        335.22 **Corporate income taxes**
    335.3   **General sales and use taxes**
    335.4   **Motor vehicle fuel taxes**
    335.5   **Motor vehicle licenses**
    335.6   **Tobacco taxes**
    335.7   **Alcoholic beverage taxes**
    335.8   **Death and gift taxes**
    335.9   **Gross receipts business taxes**

336.   **State government payments in lieu of taxes**

337.   **Local government unit** (specify unit) **grants**

338.   **Local government unit** (specify unit) **shared revenues**

339.   **Local government unit** (specify unit) **payments in lieu of taxes**

340.   **Charges for services** are charges for current services exclusive of revenues of proprietary funds.

341.   **General government**
    341.1   **Court costs, fees, and charges**
    341.2   **Recording of legal instruments**
    341.3   **Zoning and subdivision fees**
    341.4   **Printing and duplicating services**

342.   **Public safety**
    342.1   **Special police services**

342.2   Special fire protection services
342.3   Correctional fees
342.4   Protective inspection fees

344.   Sanitation
344.1   Sewerage charges
344.2   Street sanitation charges
344.3   Refuse collection charges

345.   Health
345.1   Vital statistics
345.2   Health and inspection fees
345.3   Hospital fees
345.4   Clinic fees
345.5   Animal control and shelter fees

346.   Welfare
346.1   Institutional charges

347.   Culture-recreation
347.1   Golf fees
347.2   Swimming pool fees
347.3   Playground fees
347.4   Park and recreation concessions
347.5   Auditorium use fees
347.6   Library use fees (not fines)
347.7   Zoo charges

351.   **Fines** include monies derived from fines and penalties imposed for the commission of statutory offenses, violation of lawful administrative rules and regulations, and for the neglect of official duty.
351.1   Court
351.2   Library

352.   **Forfeits** include monies derived from confiscating deposits held as performance guarantees.

355.   **Special assessments** are amounts levied against certain properties to defray all or part of the cost of a specific capital improvement or service deemed to benefit primarily those properties.
355.1   Capital improvement
355.2   Service

361.   **Investment earnings** are compensation for the use of financial resources over a period of time.
361.1   Interest revenues
361.2   Dividends
361.3   Net increase (decrease) in the fair value of investments

362.   **Rents and royalties** are financial resources derived from the use by others of the government's tangible and intangible assets.

363.   **Escheats** are the uncompensated acquisition of private property abandoned or otherwise alienated by its owners.

364.   **Contributions and donations from private sources** are financial resources provided by private contributors.

365.   **Contributions from property owners—special assessments** are resources provided by the issuance of special assessment debt for which the government is not obligated in any manner.

390.   **Other financing sources**

391.   **Interfund transfers in** (specify fund) are financial inflows from other funds of the government reporting entity that are not classified as interfund services provided and used, reimbursements or loans.

392.   **Proceeds of general capital asset dispositions** are financial inflows provided from the disposition of general capital assets.
    392.1   **Sales of general capital assets**
    392.2   **Compensation for loss of general capital assets**

393.   **General long-term debt issued** is the face amount of general long-term debt, which is often different from the financial resources provided because of discounts and premiums resulting from market conditions or bond issuance costs (e.g., underwriting or legal fees). In the case of capital leases, however, it is the net present value of the minimum lease payments.
    393.1   **General obligation bonds issued**
    393.2   **Special assessment bonds issued**
    393.3   **Special assessment debt with government commitment issued**
    393.4   **Other bonds issued**
    393.5   **Refunding bonds issued**
    393.6   **Premiums on bonds sold**
    393.7   **Capital leases**

395.   **Special items** result from significant transactions or other events within the control of management that are either unusual in nature or infrequent in occurrence.

396.   **Extraordinary items** are transactions or other events that are both unusual in nature and infrequent in occurrence.

397.   **Capital contributions** are contributions to permanent or term endowments, including those reported in permanent funds.

EXPENDITURES AND OTHER FINANCING USES CLASSIFICATION DESCRIPTIONS

Code   *Description*

410.   **General government** is charged with all expenditures for the legislative and judicial branches of a government. It also is charged with expenditures made by the chief executive officer and other top-level auxiliary and staff agencies in the administrative branch of the government. The accounts are subdivided into three groups: legislative, judicial, and executive.

FUNCTION, PROGRAM, AND ACTIVITY CLASSIFICATION

411.   **Legislative** is charged with expenditures of a governing body in the performance of its primary duties and subsidiary activities. A decision whether a given item should be charged to a legislative account is based on whether the item is a direct or an indirect cost. Direct costs are charged to legislative accounts. Indirect costs are charged to another account, usually a staff agency account (e.g., public safety—police).

411.1   **Governing body** is charged with the direct expenditures of the governing body. Direct expenditures, which include salaries and travel costs, represent expenditures incurred by members themselves or by a committee of the governing body. Indirect expenditures represent expenditures incurred for the governing body by a staff agency or official.

If the governing body is composed partly or wholly of administrative officials (e.g., the commissioner under the commission form of government), their salaries are charged to the departments they direct. (See 413.3 below.) If additional compensation is specifically provided in return for services as members of such body, their regular salaries are charged as explained above, and the remainder is charged to this account (411.1). The salaries of citizen members of such bodies also are charged to this account.

Expenditures of commissions or bodies acting in both a legislative and an executive capacity are classified as executive if their legislative function is incidental and subordinate to the executive function. The most common example of a dual capacity is encountered under the commission form of government. Expenditures of boards composed of exofficio members performing predominantly executive functions are charged to the respective functions headed by the board members.

411.2   **Legislative committees and special bodies** is charged with expenditures of regular committees of the governing body, special investigating committees, boards, or representatives responsible solely to the governing body. Costs of an investigation preliminary to the purchase of equipment or properties for a specific department should be included as a cost of the purchase.

411.3   **Ordinances and proceedings** is charged with expenditures for printing and advertising ordinances and for printing the proceedings of the governing body.

411.4   **Clerk of council** is charged with expenditures for the office of clerk of council. Where other officials (city clerk) also perform the duty of the clerk of council in addition to their regular duties, their expenditures are usually charged to account 415.4. Although it may not be practicable to allocate their expenditures to accounts other than 415.4, whenever possible these expenditures should be apportioned to 411.4 and 415.4 in proportion to the time required for each office.

412.   **Judicial** includes accounts for recording expenditures for judicial activities of the government.

412.1   **Criminal courts** is charged with expenditures for judicial activities involving criminal cases. When several courts try criminal cases, expenditures should be classified further by each court.

412.2   **Grand jury** is charged with expenditures for grand jury hearings and includes compensation of jurors, witness fees, investigation costs, and clerical costs.

412.3   **Public defender** is charged with expenditures for the office of public defender. If the public defender is attached to and a part of the law office, it may not be possible to segregate expenditures related to the activities performed as public defender. In such a case, the expenditure should be included in account 415.3.

412.4   **Civil courts** is charged with expenditures for judicial activities involving civil cases. When several courts try civil cases, expenditures should be classified by each court, such as **chancery court** (412.41), **small claims court** (412.42), **civil court** (412.43), and **domestic relations court** (412.44).

412.5   **Law library** is charged with all expenditures for acquiring and maintaining a law library.

413.   **Executive** includes accounts for recording expenditures of general executive officers and boards of the government.

413.1   **Mayor** is charged with expenditures for salaries and other costs of the mayor and employees connected with his or her office in the mayor-council form of government. Expenditures of a mayor under the council-manager form of government are charged to account 411.1 (governing body), and those for a mayor under the commission form are charged to the functions the mayor directs.

413.2   **Chief executive** is charged with expenditures of the government's chief executive and the employees connected with his or her office. This account title may be changed to indicate the chief executive's specific title, such as **manager** or **administrator**.

413.3   **Boards and commissions** is charged with expenditures of elected commissioners under the commission form of government and expenditures of other boards and commissions acting primarily in executive capacities to the extent that such expenditures cannot be allocated to the functions the commissioners or board members direct. Expenditures of elected commissioners who are also executive officers should be charged to the functions they direct to reflect the complete cost of each function of government. When a commissioner directs the finance function, the expenditures of his or her office should be charged to account 415.

Expenditures of a commissioner of utilities should not be charged to an account in the general fund, but to the proper accounts of the government's utility funds. When a commissioner directs two or more departments, the expenditures of that office should be allocated to the functions under the commissioner's direction.

414.   **Elections** includes accounts for recording direct expenditures for registering voters and holding general, primary and special elections. Salaries of the officials and police performing election duties recurrently and incidentally as part of their broader duties are not charged to elections but to their respective departmental activities. The salaries of election deputies, judges, tellers, hired watchers or inspectors, special clerks, and special police are chargeable to this account.

415.   **Financial administration** includes accounts for recording expenditures of central staff agencies performing financial management functions for the government.

415.1   **Finance** includes individual accounts for each of the following types of financial activities: **general supervision** (415.11), **accounting** (415.12), **independent audit** (415.13), **budget** (415.14), **tax administration** (415.15), **treasury** (415.16), **licensing** (415.17), **purchasing** (415.18), **debt administration** (415.19), and in**ternal audit** (415.21), if not performed in an independent role.

415.3   **Law** includes accounts for recording expenditures for legal services required by a government in the discharge of its functions and activities. Included are the costs of the attorney or other attorneys who render legal advice to the governing body or administrative agencies of the government, who draft laws, ordinances, or administrative regulations for it and its constituent agencies and who serve as counsel in lawsuits to which the government is a party.

415.4   **Recording and reporting** includes accounts for recording expenditures of those staff agencies whose main activity is the preparation and recording of government documents, records, proceedings, and papers. These include the recording of deeds, mortgages, and similar legal documents; and general public reports of the government. The clerical, stenographic, and filing costs of individual offices and agencies are not charged to these accounts, but to appropriate accounts elsewhere on the basis of functions and activities performed by such agencies.

415.5 **Personnel administration** includes accounts that record expenditures of the agency or agencies performing central personnel and related services for the entire government. Such services include general supervision of personnel management, classification of positions, recruitment, placement (transfers, promotions, demotions), service ratings, attendance, certification of payrolls, separations, fringe benefits, and retirement systems.

419.   **Other—unclassified**
419.1 **Planning and zoning**
419.2 **Data processing**
419.3 **Research and investigation**
419.4 **General government buildings and plant**

420.   **Public safety**, a major function of government, has as its objective the protection of persons and property. The major subfunctions under public safety are police protection, fire protection, protective inspection, and correction.

421.   **Police** includes accounts for recording expenditures incurred by the police department in the administration of various law enforcement activities.

421.1 **Police administration** is charged with all expenditures incurred by the chief of police and assistant chiefs in supervising the activities of the police department. In addition to directing departmental personnel and budgetary responsibilities, this supervision may include long-range planning, research into problems of criminal activity and law enforcement, and investigatory and intelligence activities that disclose the integrity and effectiveness of the department's administrative activities and that provide information on known criminals and organized crime.

421.2 **Crime control and investigation**

421.21 **Criminal investigation** is charged with expenditures made by detectives in investigating criminal activities, detecting and arresting criminal offenders, obtaining evidence for prosecution of criminal cases, filing cases, returning fugitive felons from other jurisdictions, testifying in court cases, locating missing persons, and recovering lost or stolen property. If a separate organizational unit handles youth and juvenile delinquency problems, its expenditures should not be recorded in this account, but should be recorded in account 421.25.

421.22 **Vice control** is charged with expenditures arising out of activities to suppress vice. These include investigation and procurement of evidence necessary for prosecution in gambling, prostitution, narcotics, and related cases and for regulation of vice-related businesses.

421.23 **Patrol** is charged with all expenditures for uniformed police patrol of assigned districts and such related police activities as investigating law violations of all kinds, arresting law violators, checking premises for illegal entry, checking open doors and windows, making reports of traffic accidents and other law violations, including suspected criminal activity.

421.24 **Records and identification** is charged with expenditures connected with the maintenance of the records of all police incidents and criminals, such as fingerprints, photographs, and case histories.

421.25 **Youth investigation and control** is charged with expenditures arising out of investigations of complaints against juveniles; programs to control juvenile delinquency; law violations involving accessories, accomplices, or contributors to the delinquency of minors; programs for self-education, rehabilitation and job placement for reformed youths; and location of missing juveniles.

421.26 **Custody of prisoners** is charged with all expenditures for the temporary detention and custody of offenders. Such expenditures include costs of operating a jail and caring for prisoners, pending conviction or permanent disposition of their cases. Maintaining prisoners serving sentences in penal institutions should not be charged to this account, but should be charged to appropriate corrections accounts (423).

421.27 **Custody of property** is charged with expenditures required in caring for property belonging to prisoners, lost and found properties, and stolen and recovered properties.

421.28 **Crime laboratory** is charged with all expenditures for laboratory examinations and analyses of physical evidence involved in law enforcement.

421.3 **Traffic control** is charged with expenditures arising out of controlling traffic, enforcing traffic laws, operating radar units, investigating traffic accidents, checking parking meter violations, issuing tickets for such violations, patrolling streets, and issuing tickets for moving violations.

421.31 **Motor vehicle inspection and regulation** is charged with expenditures for examining and licensing motor vehicles and motor vehicle operators.

421.4 **Police training** is charged with expenditures for training police officers. This training may include formal basic training for recruits, in-service training for commissioned police officers, and maintenance of training facilities.

421.5 **Support service**

421.51 **Communications services** is charged with all expenditures for providing and maintaining police communications, including receipt of calls for police assistance, dispatch of police units, and maintenance of police communications equipment.

421.52 **Automotive services** is charged with all expenditures for maintaining and servicing police vehicles, towing for police and confiscated vehicles, and equipping police vehicles with special equipment.

421.53 **Ambulance services** is charged with expenditures for emergency ambulance services provided directly by the police department or provided as a contracted service by the government.

421.54 **Medical services** is charged with expenditures for rendering first aid to civilians and for medical examinations, treatment and hospital care of prisoners and policemen, either directly by the government or as a contracted service.

421.6 **Special detail services** is charged with expenditures for police personnel exercising police functions outside of regular police assignments. This account includes special services for which the government receives compensation from private sources or other governments.

421.7 **Police stations and buildings** is charged with expenditures for police stations and buildings other than the general municipal building. If buildings are rented, rental payments are charged to this account.

422. **Fire** includes accounts for recording the expenditures incurred by the fire department in preventing and fighting fires.

    422.1 **Fire administration** is charged with expenditures of the fire chief and immediate assistants in supervising all the activities of the fire department. These activities include general administration of all official policies, budgetary and personnel administration, and long-range planning and research.

    422.2 **Fire fighting** is charged with expenditures for extinguishing fires and for providing such special services as building and fire-hydrant inspections, and assistance to persons and property during a disaster.

    422.3 **Fire prevention** is charged with expenditures for such fire prevention activities as inspection of fire hazards, investigation of the causes of fires, investigation and prosecution of persons involved in incendiary fires, fire prevention education, control of inflammable materials, and enforcement of fire prevention ordinances.

    422.4 **Fire training** is charged with all expenditures for training firefighters either in the department or by educational institutions outside the government. This account is also charged with maintenance of special training facilities.

    422.5 **Fire communications** is charged with expenditures for the acquisition, operation, and maintenance of fire alarm systems and other communication systems used by the fire department in preventing and fighting fires. It also is charged with the maintenance of current coverage maps and assignment schedules for fire apparatus and with the maintenance of records showing the locations of and changes in fire hydrants and sprinkler systems.

    422.6 **Fire repair services** is charged with all expenditures for repair of fire apparatus and equipment and for conducting regular equipment tests.

    422.7 **Medical services** is charged with all expenditures for the medical examination, treatment, and care of sick or injured firefighters.

    422.8 **Fire stations and buildings** is charged with expenditures for fire stations and buildings other than the general municipal building. If buildings are rented, rental payments are charged to this account.

423. **Corrections** includes accounts for recording expenditures for confinement of law violators and for probation and parole activities involved in their rehabilitation.

    423.1 **Correctional administration** is charged with expenditures of any officer, board, or commission having top-level responsibility for correctional activities. Expenditures for supervision of individual institutions are charged to the appropriate institution.

    423.2 **Adult correctional institutions** is charged with expenditures for the construction, operation, and maintenance of such correctional institutions as prisons, jails, prison factories, and prison farms. A separate subsidiary account should be established for each institution operated by the government.

    423.3 **Juvenile correctional institutions** is charged with expenditures for the construction, operation, and maintenance of correctional institutions for the punishment and rehabilitation of juvenile offenders. Such institutions include jails, detention homes, and reformatories. When a government maintains more than one institution of this kind, separate accounts should be established for each institution.

    423.4 **Delinquents in other institutions** is charged with expenditures for offenders confined in correctional institutions of other government jurisdictions, including jails, prisons, detention homes, reformatories, and foster homes. These expenditures include payments for transporting delinquents to and from such institutions. If both adult and youth offenders are cared for in this manner, this account should be divided into two separate accounts, one for youth and one for adults.

423.5   **Adult probation and parole** is charged with expenditures incurred in the supervision of adult offenders who are paroled or placed on probation.

423.6   **Juvenile probation and parole** is charged with expenditures incurred in the supervision of juvenile offenders who are paroled or placed on probation.

424.   **Protective inspection** includes accounts for recording expenditures incurred in making protective inspections, except those related to health and fire and those definitively assigned to other functions.

424.1   **Protective inspection administration** is charged with expenditures for the centralized administration of two or more inspection services.

424.2   **Building inspection** is charged with expenditures incurred in the examination of building plans, inspection of building construction, inspection of existing buildings for structural defects and compliance with minimum housing standards, and issuance of building permits.

424.3   **Plumbing inspection** is charged with expenditures incurred in the examination of plumbing plans, inspection of plumbing installations, and issuance of building permits.

424.4   **Electrical inspection** is charged with expenditures incurred in the examination of electrical plans, inspection of electrical installations, and issuance of electrical permits.

424.5   **Gas inspection** is charged with expenditures incurred in the examination of gas installations and fittings and issuance of gas permits.

424.6   **Air conditioning inspection** is charged with expenditures incurred in the examination of plans for air conditioning installations, inspection of such installations, and issuance of permits.

424.7   **Boiler inspection** is charged with expenditures for examining the plans for and the installation and operation of boilers, pressure tanks, steam engines, and similar devices.

424.8   **Elevator inspection** is charged with expenditures for examining the plans for and the installation and operation of elevators, dumb waiters, and escalators.

424.9   **Weights and measures** is charged with expenditures for determining the accuracy of devices used for weighing and measuring physical objects, checking such devices periodically, investigating complaints, and prosecuting violators.

429.   **Other protection** includes accounts for protection activities that are not strictly a part of the foregoing major account groupings.

429.1   **Civil defense** is charged with expenditures for the preparation of survival plans to be used in the event of war or natural disaster, for the administration of training programs for protection and survival, and for the provision and inspection of shelters, shelter supplies, and other civil defense installations and equipment.

429.2   **Militia and armories** is charged with expenditures for the construction and maintenance of armories, support of militias, and construction and maintenance of related facilities.

429.3   **Traffic engineering** is charged with expenditures for investigations relating to the design and location of traffic control devices and for the installation and maintenance of such traffic control and parking devices as traffic signals, street and curb markings, street signs, and parking meters.

429.4   **Examination of licensed occupations** is charged with the expenditures of boards and other administrative personnel who examine and license individuals to practice certain professions and vocations.

429.5 **Public scales** is charged with all expenditures incurred in the provision and maintenance of public scales.

429.6 **Flood control** is charged with expenditures for walls, levees, and other devices that protect persons and property from surface water damage.

431. **Highways and streets** includes accounts for recording expenditures for roadways and walkways, according to the type of facility involved. Roadways and walkways in parks are not charged to this account, but to appropriate accounts under the function of **culture-recreation** (450).

431.21 **Paved streets** is charged with expenditures for construction, maintenance and repair of street surfaces, curbs, and gutters on streets paved with concrete, asphalt, or brick.

431.22 **Unpaved streets** is charged with expenditures incurred for construction, maintenance, and repair of unpaved streets, including scraping, grading, graveling, dragging, cindering, and oiling.

431.23 **Alleys** is charged with expenditures for the construction, maintenance, and repair of alleys.

431.24 **Sidewalks and crosswalks** is charged with expenditures for the construction, maintenance, and repair of sidewalks, crosswalks, steps, and stairs.

431.25 **Snow and ice removal** is charged with expenditures for removing snow and ice and for sanding or salting streets, alleys, bridges, and sidewalks.

431.3 **Bridges, viaducts, and grade separations** is charged with expenditures for the construction, maintenance, and repair of bridges (stationary and movable), viaducts, grade separations, trestles, and railroad crossings.

431.4 **Tunnels** is charged with expenditures for the construction, maintenance and repair of tunnels, including payments to other government jurisdictions for the joint construction and maintenance of tunnels.

431.5 **Storm drainage** is charged with expenditures for the construction, maintenance, and repair of storm drainage inlets and collection and disposal systems.

431.6 **Street lighting** is charged with expenditures for street lighting fixtures and for lighting all streets, alleys, bridges, subways and tunnels, except those located in parks.

432. **Sanitation**, a major function of government, includes all activities involved in the removal and disposal of sewage and other types of waste.

432.1 **Sanitary administration** is charged with all expenditures for the general administrative direction of sanitation activities.

432.2 **Street cleaning** is charged with expenditures for sweeping and washing streets, flushing gutters and underpasses, and collecting and disposing of debris from streets and public roadways.

432.3 **Waste collection** is charged with expenditures for collecting garbage and other refuse and delivering it to the place of disposal.

432.4 **Waste disposal** is charged with expenditures for disposing of garbage and other refuse. When several methods of disposal are used, such as sanitary landfill and incineration, appropriate accounts should be set up for each disposal facility.

432.5 **Sewage collection and disposal** includes accounts for recording expenditures incurred in the collection and disposal of sewage.

432.51 **Sanitary sewer construction** is charged with expenditures for the construction of new sanitary sewer lines.

432.52 **Sanitary sewer maintenance** is charged with expenditures for repair, reconstruction, and maintenance of sanitary sewer lines.

432.53 **Sanitary sewer cleaning** is charged with expenditures for routine cleaning of sanitary sewer lines.

432.54 **New sewer services** is charged with expenditures for installing new sanitary sewer lines, clearing emergency stoppages in sanitary sewer service lateral lines, and making taps for service laterals installed by plumbers.

432.55 **Sewer lift stations** is charged with expenditures for construction and operation of lift stations that pump sewage over geographical elevations prior to disposition into gravity-flow sewer lines.

432.56 **Sewage treatment plants** is charged with expenditures for the construction and operation of plants that treat and dispose of sewage.

432.6 **Weed control** is charged with expenditures for cutting and removing weeds from private property when the property owners will not and from government property such as parkways, alleys, and easements.

440. **Health and welfare**

441. **Health**, a major function of government, includes all activities involved in the conservation and improvement of public health.

441.1 **Public health administration** is charged with expenditures for the general administration of public health activities.

441.2 **Vital statistics** is charged with expenditures for preparing and maintaining vital records of births, deaths, adoptions, marriages, and divorces; preparing reports and statistical analyses of such data and issuing certified copies of birth certificates, death certificates, and other records, as permitted and required by law.

441.3 **Regulation and inspection** includes expenditure accounts for various inspection and regulatory activities essential to the conservation and improvement of public health.

441.31 **Food and drugs** is charged with expenditures for regulation and inspection of food and drugs. Pertinent activities include licensing; inspection of food stores, factories, markets, and restaurants; laboratory tests of food and drugs; examination and licensing of food handlers; meat inspection; inspection of meat markets; and enforcement of pure food and drug laws and ordinances.

441.32 **Milk and dairy products** is charged with expenditures incurred in the inspection and regulation of milk, dairy products, dairies, dairy cattle, dairy establishments, and dairy delivery facilities.

441.33 **Other sanitary inspection** is charged with expenditures incurred in health inspection and regulatory activities other than those related to milk, food, and drugs. Examples of such activities include inspection of barber and beauty shops, hotels, motels, and tourist and trailer parks; inspection of nursing homes and children's institutions; mosquito, fly, and other insect inspections; inspections of government-owned and private premises for other types of health hazards; air pollution and radiological inspections; and inspection of refuse, water, and sewage facilities. If several of these activities are performed by a single government, separate accounts should be set up for each activity.

441.4 **Communicable disease control** includes accounts for expenditures incurred in the prevention and treatment (except hospitalization) of certain defined communicable diseases.

441.41 **Tuberculosis** is charged with expenditures incurred for the prevention and treatment (except hospitalization) of tuberculosis.

441.42 **Socially transmitted diseases** is charged with expenditures incurred for the prevention and treatment (except hospitalization) of socially transmitted diseases.

441.43 **Rabies and animal control** is charged with expenditures incurred for the prevention and treatment (except for hospitalization) of rabies.

441.44 **Other communicable diseases** is charged with expenditures incurred for the prevention and treatment (except hospitalization) of all communicable diseases other than tuberculosis, socially transmitted diseases, and rabies. Covered activities include vaccination and immunization against diseases, quarantine and disinfection, extermination of rodents, mosquitos and flies, and operation of clinics and dispensaries.

441.5 **Maternal and child health services** includes accounts for expenditures incurred for various maternal and child health services (except communicable diseases).

441.51 **Maternal and preschool** is charged with all expenditures for child hygiene, except in schools. Pertinent activities include operation of prenatal clinics, nursing visits to expectant mothers, supervision and medicine, operation of preschool clinics, and home visits to children by nurses.

441.52 **School** is charged with expenditures for health and hygiene activities in public and private schools. These activities include medical examination of school children and treatment by health officers, dental examination of school children and treatment by health officers, operation of school clinics, school nursing, nutrition nursing, psychological and psychiatric examinations, and treatment of school children.

441.6 **Adult health services** is charged with expenditures for health services for adults other than those rendered in connection with communicable diseases. These services include educational programs aimed at prevention and control of chronic diseases and accidents.

441.7 **Health centers and general clinics** is charged with expenditures for health centers and general clinics furnishing two or more types of clinical services. If the clinic is maintained exclusively for one service, such as tuberculosis, the expenditures should be charged to the appropriate activity account under **communicable disease control**. Dispensaries operated in connection with clinics should be considered as part of the clinic.

441.8 **Laboratory** is charged with expenditures for laboratory tests essential to the maintenance of public health. These tests include serologic tests for syphilis; bacteriological analysis of water, milk and milk products, and food products; chemical analysis of milk and dairy products; and bacteriological analysis for tuberculosis and other diseases.

444. **Welfare**, a major function of government, includes all activities designed to provide public assistance and institutional care for individuals economically unable to provide essential needs for themselves.

444.1 **Welfare administration** is charged with expenditures for the general administration of all public welfare activities.

444.2   **Institutional care** is charged with expenditures for the construction and operation of welfare institutions maintained by the government for the care of the indigent. Separate activity accounts should be set up for each type of institution, such as homes for the aged and orphanages.

444.3   **Direct assistance** is charged with expenditures, in cash or in kind, made directly to eligible welfare recipients by the government. If there are several categories of assistance programs, expenditures should be classified under one or more of the following categories.

444.31   **General assistance** is charged with expenditures to families or individuals who meet specified eligibility criteria and who are not classified under one of the other welfare programs. General assistance refers to such forms of welfare as home relief and general emergency relief.

444.32   **Old-age assistance** is charged with expenditures made by the government to persons older than a specified age.

444.33   **Aid to dependent children** is charged with expenditures for the care and support of needy dependent children, including payments made to parents, guardians, and foster parents.

444.34   **Aid to the blind** is charged with expenditures made by the government to persons judged legally blind.

444.35   **Aid to the disabled** is charged with expenditures made by the government to persons judged legally disabled.

444.36   **Other direct assistance** is charged with expenditures to needy persons other than those classified under the foregoing categories. If several additional classes of persons are welfare recipients, separate activity accounts should be established for each class.

444.4   **Intergovernmental welfare payments** is charged with expenditures made by the government to another government for welfare programs administered by it. Such expenditures should be classified under one of the following categories:

444.41   **General assistance**
444.42   **Old-age assistance**
444.43   **Aid to dependent children**
444.44   **Aid to the blind**
444.45   **Aid to the disabled**
444.46   **Other welfare assistance**

444.5   **Vendor welfare payments** is charged with expenditures made directly to private individuals and organizations who furnish authorized care, commodities, and services to welfare recipients.

444.51   **Vendor medical payments** is charged with expenditures to private individuals and organizations for medical assistance for the aged under federal and/or state programs and for medical assistance payments under general assistance, aid to the blind, and other programs.

444.52   **Other vendor payments** is charged with expenditures made to vendors of care, commodities and services for welfare recipients other than those for medical services. Examples include legal services, burial services, rent, food, and clothing. If more than one class of vendor payments exists, separate accounts should be established for each class.

450.   **Culture-recreation**, a major function of government, includes all cultural and recreational activities maintained for the benefit of residents and visitors.

451.   **Recreation**

451.1   **Culture-recreation administration** is charged with expenditures for the general administration of all cultural and recreational activities and facilities.

451.2   **Participant recreation** is charged with expenditures for recreational facilities and activities in which direct participation is the primary attribute. Examples include organized athletics, individual participant sports such as golf, indoor and outdoor games of various kinds, and dancing.

451.21   **Supervision** is charged with expenditures for supervision of two or more recreational activities classified under **participant recreation.**

451.22   **Recreation centers** is charged with expenditures for the construction, maintenance, and operation of multipurpose recreation centers, which contain a full compliment of recreational facilities such as gymnasiums, athletic fields, craft rooms, and swimming pools.

451.23   **Playgrounds** is charged with expenditures for the construction, maintenance, and operation of neighborhood playgrounds.

451.24   **Swimming pools** is charged with expenditures for the construction, maintenance, and operation of swimming pools. If more than one pool is maintained, a separate account should be established for each one. If a government operates other types of swimming facilities outside of those in recreation centers, such as a public beach, this account classification may be expanded to include them.

451.25   **Golf courses** is charged with expenditures for the construction, maintenance, and operation of golf courses and related facilities. A separate account should be established for each golf course.

451.26   **Tennis courts** is charged with expenditures for the construction, maintenance, and operation of tennis courts and related facilities.

451.27   **Other recreational facilities** is charged with expenditures for all other participant recreational facilities and areas other than those listed in the foregoing accounts. A separate account should be provided for each type of facility or area.

451.3   **Spectator recreation** is charged with expenditures for cultural and scientific recreational activities benefitting the public as spectators. These expenditures should be charged to one of the following accounts.

451.31   **Botanical gardens**

451.32   **Museums**

451.33   **Art galleries**

451.34   **Zoos**

451.4   **Special recreational facilities** is charged with expenditures for special recreational facilities not included in the foregoing accounts and maintained as separate recreational facilities. Examples include auditoriums, stadiums, camping areas, and marinas. When more than one type of special facility is maintained, a separate account should be established for each one.

452.   **Parks** is charged with expenditures for public parks, public squares, and similar ornamental areas. Excluded from this account classification are grounds surrounding public buildings, land encompassed in other recreational facilities such as zoos and incidental landscaping, and maintenance of areas elsewhere classified under recreation.

452.1 **Supervision** is charged with expenditures for supervising two or more park activities or facilities.

452.2 **Park areas** is charged with all expenditures for acquiring, operating, and maintaining park areas and related facilities. These include land used for a park: planting and care of park lawns, trees, shrubs and flowers; park roads, walks and paths; park waterways; and park structures and equipment. When more than one park is operated, a separate account should be established for each park.

452.3 **Parkways and boulevards** is charged with expenditures for landscaped areas with traffic lanes running through or adjacent to them. These parkways and boulevards are constructed primarily for beautification and recreation and must be distinguished from so-called boulevards routinely maintained by the street or highway department.

452.4 **Forestry and nursery** is charged with expenditures for growing trees and other plants and transplanting them along streets, in parks, in parkways, or other public areas. Other activities whose expenditures should be included in this account include removal and disposal of undesirable trees and other plants, supervision of tree trimming on public property, and granting of permits to plant trees in parks and other public areas.

452.5 **Park policing** is charged with expenditures for special policing in parks, whether under the direction of the police department or special park police.

452.6 **Park lighting** is charged with expenditures for lighting parks, whenever such expenditures can be separated from the cost of street lighting.

455. **Libraries**

455.1 **Library administration** is charged with expenditures for general administration of the library or the library system when more than one library is maintained.

455.2 **Circulation** is charged with expenditures incurred in the circulation of library books, periodicals, and other materials. Circulation activities include the registration of borrowers, maintenance of loan records, notification to borrowers of delinquencies, collection of fines for overdue or lost books, assistance to library patrons in the use of the card catalog, and provision of information about library circulation policies, resources and schedules.

455.3 **Catalog** is charged with expenditures incurred in the classification and cataloging of library materials, the preparation and filing of catalog cards and other acquisition records, and the processing and distribution of cataloged materials to various library divisions and/or branch libraries.

455.4 **Reference** is charged with expenditures for all reference services. These services include maintaining special files of clippings and pamphlets to supplement books and periodicals, answering reference questions, assisting library patrons in their search for information and the use of indexes and finding aids, processing interlibrary loans, and supervising rare book collections.

455.5 **Order** is charged with expenditures incurred in ordering books and periodicals, checking materials upon receipt, processing gift materials, and forwarding materials to the catalog division for further processing.

455.6 **Periodicals** is charged with expenditures incurred in ordering, receiving, and maintaining magazines and periodicals; maintaining records of periodical holdings; and furnishing information and assistance to library patrons in the use of periodicals.

455.7 **Extension** is charged with expenditures incurred in the selection, maintenance and circulation of books and other library materials from bookmobiles.

455.8 **Special collections** is charged with expenditures made for special collections or clientele sections within the library. Examples of such special collections are children's and young adults' divisions, art, music, science and technology, local history and culture, and newspapers. When more than one special collection of this type is maintained, a separate account should be established for each one.

455.9 **Branch libraries** is charged with expenditures for the construction, maintenance and operation of branch libraries located away from the central library or library headquarters of a library system.

461. **Conservation**, a major function of government, includes activities designed to conserve and develop such natural resources as water, soil, forests, and minerals. Expenditures for conservation should be classified according to the specific type of resource.

461.1 **Water resources**

461.2 **Agricultural resources** (including soil conservation)

461.3 **Forest resources**

461.4 **Mineral resources**

461.5 **Fish and game resources**

463. **Urban redevelopment and housing**, a major function of government, is concerned with the planning and provision of adequate housing and the redevelopment of substandard and blighted physical facilities in urban areas.

463.1 **Urban redevelopment and housing administration** is charged with expenditures for general administration of all urban redevelopment and housing activities when these are combined under a single administrative head.

463.2 **Urban redevelopment** is charged with expenditures for activities involved in the government's conservation, rehabilitation, and clearance of designated portions of urban areas. It also is charged with expenditures involved in the relocation of individuals, families, and businesses from clearance areas to new neighborhoods.

463.21 **Redevelopment administration** is charged with expenditures for planning and administering all redevelopment activities and projects carried out by the government.

463.22 **Conservation projects** is charged with expenditures for conservation of existing neighborhood structures and facilities to prolong their usable life and to prevent subsequent deterioration and blight. If more than one project of this type is carried on, a separate account should be established for each project.

463.23 **Rehabilitation projects** is charged with expenditures for renovation of deteriorated neighborhoods that still are capable of renovation without total clearance and complete redevelopment. If more than one project of this type is carried on, a separate account should be established for each project.

463.24 **Clearance projects** is charged with expenditures for complete demolition, clearance, and redevelopment. If more than one project of this type is carried on, a separate account should be established for each project.

463.25 **Relocation** is charged with expenditures incurred in the relocation and rehousing of persons displaced by redevelopment projects.

463.3 **Public housing** is charged with expenditures for the acquisition, furnishing, maintenance, and operation of the government's public housing for low-income persons. When more than one project of this type is carried on, a separate account should be established for each project.

463.4 **Other urban redevelopment** is charged with expenditures for urban redevelopment and housing projects not included under the foregoing accounts. Included are all intergovernmental expenditures for urban redevelopment and housing activities administered by other governments.

465. **Economic development and assistance** is a function whose activities are directed toward economically developing the area encompassed by the government and providing assistance to and opportunity for economically disadvantaged persons and businesses.

465.1 **Economic development and assistance administration** is charged with expenditures for the general supervision and administration of all development and assistance activities performed by the government.

465.2 **Economic development** is charged with expenditures made to foster economic growth and development of the area over which the government exercises jurisdiction. These development activities include economic and industrial surveys, financial assistance to new industries and businesses, acquisition of industrial sites, contact activities of industrial development agencies, and promotional advertising.

465.3 **Employment security** is charged with expenditures for the administration of unemployment compensation programs, public employment offices, and related activities.

466. **Economic opportunity** is charged with expenditures for various programs designed to eliminate or ameliorate poverty and its causes. Expenditures should be classified according to the specific type of program and/or project and in accordance with current federal grants made for such programs.

466.1 **Job corps**
466.11 **Men's urban training centers**
466.12 **Women's urban training centers**
466.13 **Rural conservation centers**
466.14 **Youth camps**
466.2 **Youth work-training programs**
466.21 **In-school projects**
466.22 **Out-of-school projects**
466.3 **Community action programs**
466.31 **Preschool readiness instruction**
466.32 **Study centers**
466.33 **Day-care centers**
466.34 **Remedial instruction for elementary school students**
466.35 **Family health education**
466.36 **Other projects**
466.4 **Adult basic education**
466.5 **Assistance to migrant agricultural workers and families**
466.6 **Work experience programs for needy persons**

470. **Debt service** includes interest and principal payments on general long-term debt.

471.1 **Bond principal** is charged with expenditures for periodic principal maturities of general obligation bonds.

471.2 **Other debt principal** is charged with payment of principal on general long-term debt other than bonds.

472.1 **Interest—bonds** is charged with periodic interest payments on general obligation bonds.

472.2 **Interest—other debt** is charged with interest payments on general long-term debt other than bonds.

475. **Fiscal agent's fees** is charged with payments made to financial institutions for services rendered in paying interest and redeeming debt at maturity.

476. **Issuance costs** is charged with payments to bond underwriters, legal fees, and other costs associated with bond issuance.

477. **Advance refunding escrow** is charged with payments made to an escrow agent from sources other than refunding debt proceeds.

480. **Intergovernmental expenditures** includes expenditures made by one level or unit of government to another government in support of government activities administered by the recipient unit. Excluded from this classification are matching employer contributions by a government to a pension or retirement system administered by another government. Such contributions should be allocated to the specific functions in which employees are compensated.

490. **Other financing uses** include financial outflows classified separately from expenditures.

491. **Interfund transfers out** (specify fund) are financial outflows to other funds of the government reporting entity that are not classified as interfund services provided and used, reimbursements, or loans.

492. **Payments to refunded bond escrow agent** are payments to an escrow agent from advance refunding debt proceeds that are to be placed in irrevocable trust.

493. **Discount on bonds issued**. The excess of the face value of bonds over the amount received from their sale (excluding accrued interest and issuance costs).

495. **Special items** result from significant transactions or other events within the control of management that are either unusual in nature or infrequent in occurrence.

496. **Extraordinary items** are transactions or other events that are both unusual in nature and infrequent in occurrence.

Object Classifications. This classification is used to describe the service or commodity obtained as the result of a specific expenditure. There are eight major object categories, each of which is further subdivided. The following are definitions of the object classes and selected subobject categories:

Code   *Description*

100. **Personal services—salaries and wages**. Amounts paid to both permanent and temporary government employees, including personnel substituting for those in permanent positions. This category includes gross salary for personal services rendered while on the payroll of the government. The third position in this number series has not been used so that a job classification code can be inserted by the government if desired.
    110. **Regular employees.** Full-time, part-time, and prorated portions of the costs for work performed by employees of the government.

120.   **Temporary employees.** Full-time, part-time, and prorated portions of the costs for work performed by employees of the government who are hired on a temporary or substitute basis.

130.   **Overtime.** Amounts paid to employees of the government in either temporary or permanent positions for work performed in addition to the normal work period for which the employee is compensated.

200.   **Personal services—employee benefits.** Amounts paid by the government on behalf of employees; these amounts are not included in the gross salary, but are in addition to that amount. Such payments are fringe benefit payments and, although not paid directly to employees, are part of the cost of personal services. The third position in this number series has not been used so that a job classification code can be inserted by the government if desired.

210.   **Group insurance.** Employer's share of any insurance plan.

220.   **Social security contributions.** Employer's share of social security paid by the government.

230.   **Retirement contributions.** Employer's share of any state or local employee retirement system paid by the government, including the amount paid for employees assigned to federal programs.

240.   **Tuition reimbursements.** Amounts reimbursed by the government to any employee qualifying for tuition reimbursement, based upon government policy.

250.   **Unemployment compensation.** Amounts paid by the government to provide unemployment compensation for its employees. These charges may be distributed to functions in accordance with the budget.

260.   **Workers' compensation.** Amounts paid by the government to provide workers' compensation insurance for its employees. These charges may be distributed to functions in accordance with the budget.

290.   **Other employee benefits.** Employee benefits other than those classified above. Government may establish subcodes locally for various accrued amounts, such as unused compensated absences. Such amounts may be distributed to the functions according to the employee's assignment.

300.   **Purchased professional and technical services.** Services that by their nature can be performed only by persons or firms with specialized skills and knowledge. Although a product may or may not result from the transaction, the primary reason for the purchase is the service provided. Included are the services of architects, engineers, auditors, dentists, physicians, lawyers, and consultants. A separate account should be established for each type of service provided to the government.

310.   **Official/administrative.** Services in support of the government's various policy-making and managerial activities. These services include management consulting activities directed toward general governance or business and financial management of the government, school management support activities, election, and tax-assessing and collecting services.

320.   **Professional.** Services supporting the instructional program and its administration. These services include curriculum improvement services, counseling and guidance services, library and media support, and contracted instructional services.

330.   **Other professional.** Professional services, other than educational, supporting the operation of the government. These professionals include physicians, lawyers, architects, auditors, therapists, systems analysts and planners.

340.   **Technical.** Services to the government that are not regarded as professional but that require basic scientific knowledge, manual skills,

or both. These services include data processing, purchasing and warehousing, and graphic arts.

400. **Purchased property services.** Services purchased to operate, repair, maintain and rent property owned or used by the government. These services are performed by persons other than government employees. Although a product may or may not result from the transaction, the primary reason for the purchase is the service provided.

    410. **Utility services.** Expenditures for utility services, other than energy services, supplied by public or private organizations. Telephone and telegraph are classified under object 530.

        411. **Water/sewerage.** Expenditures for water/sewage utility services from a private or public utility company.

    420. **Cleaning services.** Services purchased to clean buildings (apart from services provided by government employees).

        421. **Disposal.** Expenditures for garbage pickup and handling not provided by government personnel.

        422. **Snow plowing.** Expenditures for snow removal not provided by government personnel.

        423. **Custodial.** Expenditures to an outside contractor for custodial services.

        424. **Lawn care.** Expenditures for lawn and grounds upkeep, minor landscaping and nursery service not provided by government personnel.

    430. **Repair and maintenance services.** Expenditures for repair and maintenance services not provided directly by government personnel. These expenditures include contracts and agreements covering the upkeep of buildings and equipment. Costs for renovating and remodeling are not included here, but are classified under object 450.

    440. **Rentals.** Costs for renting or leasing land, buildings, equipment, and vehicles.

        441. **Rental of land and buildings.** Expenditures for leasing or renting land and buildings for both temporary and long-range use by the government.

        442. **Rental of equipment and vehicles.** Expenditures for leasing or renting equipment or vehicles for both temporary and long-range use by the government. These expenditures include bus and other vehicle rental when operated by a local capital lease arrangements and other rental agreements.

    450. **Construction services.** Includes amounts for constructing, renovating, and remodeling paid to contractors.

500. **Other purchased services.** Amounts paid for services rendered by organizations or personnel not on the payroll of the government (separate from professional and technical services or property services). Although a product may or may not result from the transaction, the primary reason for the purchase is the service provided.

    520. **Insurance other than employee benefits.** Expenditures for all types of insurance coverage, including property, liability and fidelity. Insurance for group health is not charged here, but is recorded underobject 210.

    530. **Communications.** Services provided by persons or businesses to assist in transmitting and receiving messages or information. This category includes telephone and telegraph services.

    540. **Advertising.** Expenditures for announcements in professional publications, newspapers or broadcasts over radio and television. These expenditures include advertising for such purposes as personnel recruitment, legal ads, new and used equipment, and sale of

property. Costs for professional advertising or public relations services are not recorded here, but are charged to object 330.

550. **Printing and binding.** Expenditures for job printing and binding, usually according to specifications of the government. This category includes designing and printing forms and posters, as well as printing and binding government publications. Preprinted standard forms are not charged here, but are recorded under object 610.

580. **Travel.** Expenditures for transportation, meals, hotel, and other expenses associated with staff travel for the government. Payments for per diem in lieu of reimbursements for subsistence (room and board) also are charged here.

600. **Supplies.** Amounts paid for items that are consumed or deteriorated through use or that lose their identity through fabrication or incorporation into different or more complex units or substances.

610. **General supplies.** Expenditures for all supplies (other than those listed below) for the operation of a government, including freight.

620. **Energy.** Expenditures for energy, including gas, oil, coal, gasoline, and services received from public or private utility companies.

621. **Natural gas.** Expenditures for gas utility services from a public or private utility company.

622. **Electricity.** Expenditures for electric utility services from a private or public utility company.

623. **Bottled gas.** Expenditures for bottled gas, such as propane gas received in tanks.

624. **Oil.** Expenditures for bulk oil normally used for heating.

625. **Coal.** Expenditures for raw coal normally used for heating.

626. **Gasoline.** Expenditures for gasoline purchased in bulk or periodically from a gasoline service station.

630. **Food.** Expenditures for food used in the school food service program. Food used in instructional programs is charged under object 610.

640. **Books and periodicals.** Expenditures for books, textbooks, and periodicals available for general use, including reference books. These expenditures include the cost of workbooks, textbook binding or repairs, as well as textbooks that are purchased to be resold or rented.

700. **Property.** Expenditures for acquiring capital assets, including land or existing buildings, improvements of grounds, initial equipment, additional equipment, and replacement of equipment.

710. **Land.** Expenditures for the purchase of land.

720. **Buildings.** Expenditures for acquiring existing buildings. These expenditures include the principal amount of capital lease payments resulting in the acquisition of buildings, except payments to building authorities or similar agencies. Expenditures for the contracted construction of buildings, for major permanent structural alterations, and for the initial or additional installation of heating and ventilating systems, fire protection systems, and other service systems in existing buildings are recorded under object 450. Buildings constructed and alterations performed by the government's own staff are charged to objects 100, 200, 610, and 730, as appropriate.

730. **Improvements other than buildings.** Expenditures for acquiring improvements not associated with buildings. These improvements include fences and retaining walls. Not included here, but generally charged to objects 450 or 340 as appropriate, are expenditures for improving sites and adjacent ways after acquisition by the government.

740.   **Machinery and equipment.** Expenditures for the initial, additional and replacement items of equipment such as machinery, furniture and fixtures, and vehicles.

    741.   **Machinery.** Expenditures for equipment usually composed of a complex combination of parts (excluding vehicles). Examples are lathes, drill presses, and printing presses.

    742.   **Vehicles.** Expenditures for equipment used to transport persons or objects. Examples include automobiles, trucks, and buses.

    743.   **Furniture and fixtures.** Expenditures for furniture and fixtures including office furniture and building fixtures.

800.   **Other objects.** Amounts paid for goods and services not previously classified.

F
Glossary

The following glossary provides definitions of the various specialized terms used in this publication. Whenever a definition is taken from or otherwise based upon an authoritative pronouncement, a reference to that standard is provided in brackets. The following abbreviations are used throughout this glossary:

AICPA	American Institute of Certified Public Accountants
FASB	Financial Accounting Standards Board
GAAP	Generally accepted accounting principles
GAAS	Generally accepted auditing standards
GAGAS	Generally accepted government auditing standards
GASB	Governmental Accounting Standards Board
IGAS	Interpretation of Governmental Accounting Standards
NCGA	National Council on Governmental Accounting
Q&A	Comprehensive Implementation Guide
SAS	Statement on Auditing Standards
SEC	Securities and Exchange Commission
SGAC	Statement of Governmental Accounting Concepts
SGAS	Statement of Governmental Accounting Standards
TB	Technical Bulletin

Accountability. Term used by the GASB to describe a government's duty to justify the raising and spending of public resources. The GASB has identified accountability as the "paramount objective" of financial reporting "from which all other objectives must flow." [SGAC 1]

Accounting Principles Board (APB). Authoritative private-sector standard-setting body that preceded the FASB. The APB issued guidance in the form of *Opinions*.

Accounting Standards Executive Committee (AcSEC). AICPA committee authorized to issue *Practice Bulletins*.

Accrual basis of accounting. Method of accounting that recognizes the financial effect of transactions, events, and interfund activities when they occur, regardless of the timing of related cash flows.

Acquisition costs. Term used by the GASB in connection with public-entity risk pools to describe costs that vary with and are primarily related to the acquisition of new and renewal contracts. [SGAS 10]

Activity. Specific and distinguishable service performed by one or more organizational components of a government to accomplish a function for which the government is responsible (e.g., *police* is an activity within the *public safety* function).

Actuarial accrued liability. Term used in connection with defined benefit pension and other postemployment benefit plans to describe that portion of the present value of benefits promised to employees that will *not* be provided through future normal cost. [SGAS 25 and SGAS 43]

Actuarial assumptions. Term used in connection with defined benefit pension and other postemployment benefit plans to describe assumptions that an actuary must make as to the occurrence of future events affecting benefit costs (e.g., mortality). [SGAS 25 and SGAS 43]

Actuarial cost method. Term used in connection with defined benefit pension and other postemployment benefit plans to describe a procedure used by an actuary to determine the actuarial present value of plan benefits and expenses and then allocate that value to specific periods. [SGAS 25 and SGAS 43]

Actuarial section. One of five required sections of a comprehensive annual financial report of a public employee retirement system.

Actuarial value of assets. Term used in connection with defined benefit pension and other postemployment benefit plans. The value assigned to plan assets for actuarial purposes. Because this value often represents an average over time, and because the valuation date may be different from the reporting date, the actuarial value of assets may differ from the amount reported in the financial statements as of the end of the fiscal period. [SGAS 25 and SGAS 43]

Additions. Term used to describe increases in the net assets of fiduciary funds.

Advance refunding. Transaction in which new debt is issued to refinance existing debt (old debt), but the proceeds must be placed in escrow pending call date or maturity (i.e., refunding in advance of redemption). [SGAS 7]

Adverse opinion. Independent auditor's opinion that financial statements are *not* fairly presented.

Agency funds. One of four types of fiduciary funds. Agency funds are used to report resources held by the reporting government in a purely custodial capacity (assets equal liabilities). Agency funds typically involve only the receipt, temporary investment, and remittance of fiduciary resources to individuals, private organizations, or other governments. [SGAS 34]

Agent multiple-employer defined benefit pension/other postemployment benefits plan. Group of single-employer plans with pooled administrative and investment functions, but separate actuarial valuations and contribution rates. [SGAS 27 and SGAS 45]

Allocated claims adjustment expenses. Term used in connection with risk financing activities to describe expenses associated directly with specific claims paid or in the process of settlement, such as legal and adjusters' fees. [SGAS 10]

Allotment. Portion of an annual or biennial appropriation allocated to an interim period.

Analytical review. Term used by auditors to describe the process of attempting to determine the reasonableness of financial data by comparing their behavior with other financial and nonfinancial data.

Annual covered payroll. Term used in connection with defined benefit pension and other postemployment benefit plans to describe all elements of annual compensation paid to active employees on which contributions to a plan are based. [SGAS 27]

Annual required contribution (ARC). Term used in connection with defined benefit pension and other postemployment benefit plans to describe the amount an employer must contribute in a given year. [SGAS 27 and SGAS 45]

Appropriated budget. Expenditure authority created by the appropriation bills or ordinances that are signed into law and related estimated revenues. The appropriated budget would include all reserves, transfers, allocations, supplemental appropriations, and other legally authorized legislative and executive changes. [NCGA Interpretation 10]

Arbitrage. In government finance, the reinvestment of the proceeds of tax-exempt securities in materially higher yielding taxable securities.

Assessed valuation. Valuation set upon real estate or other property by a government as a basis for levying taxes.

Asset allocation. Term used in connection with pension and other postemployment benefit plans to describe the process of determining which types of investments are to be included and the percentages that they are to comprise in an overall investment portfolio.

Audit committee. Group of individuals assigned specific responsibility for addressing issues related to the independent audit of the financial statements on behalf of the entity under audit.

Audit Guides. Series of AICPA publications that enjoy potential "level 2" status on the hierarchy of authoritative sources of GAAP (some publications in the series are titled Audit and Accounting Guides). In the public sector, the most important such publication is *State and Local Governments*.

Audit scope. In the context of a financial statement audit, the coverage provided by the independent auditor's opinion. For example, required supplementary information normally is not included within the scope of a financial statement audit (i.e., the independent auditor does not offer an opinion on its fair presentation).

Auditor rotation. Policy that a government periodically replace the independent auditor of its financial statements.

Auditor's report on internal control and compliance over financial reporting. Report issued in conjunction with a financial audit performed in accordance with GAGAS. The independent auditor reports on internal control weaknesses and instances of noncompliance discovered in connection with the financial audit, but does *not* offer an opinion on internal control or compliance.

Availability criterion. Requirement under the modified accrual basis of accounting that revenues be recognized only when they are collected or collectible within the current period or soon enough thereafter to be used to pay liabilities of the current period. [NCGA Statement 1]

Availability period. Designated period immediately following the close of the fiscal year by the end of which cash must be collected for related revenue to be recognized in accordance with the availability criterion of modified accrual accounting.

Bank holding company. Company that controls one or more banks and may own subsidiaries with operations closely related to banking. [TB 97-1]

Bank investment contract. Separate account at a financial institution that functions like a guaranteed investment contract.

Bankers' acceptances. Short-term, noninterest-bearing notes sold at a discount and redeemed by the accepting banks at maturity for face value. Bankers' acceptances generally are created based on a letter of credit issued in a foreign trade transaction. [SGAS 31]

Banking pool. Risk-financing arrangement by which monies are loaned to pool members in the event of a loss. [SGAS 10]

Basic financial statements. Minimum combination of financial statements and note disclosures required for fair presentation in conformity with GAAP.

Basis differences. Differences that arise when the basis of budgeting differs from the basis of accounting prescribed by GAAP for a given fund type. [NCGA Interpretation 10]

Basis of accounting. Timing of recognition for financial reporting purposes (i.e., when the effects of transactions or events should be recognized in financial statements). [SGAS 11]

Basis of budgeting. Method used to determine when revenues and expenditures are recognized for budgetary purposes.

Basis risk. Risk that arises when different indexes are used in connection with a derivative.

Betterment. Addition made to, or change made in, a capital asset, other than maintenance, to prolong its life or to increase its efficiency or capacity. The cost of the addition or change is added to the book value of the asset. The term *improvement* is preferred.

Blending. Presentation of the data of a component unit as though it were one or more fund(s) of the primary government. [SGAS 14]

Blue Book. Term commonly used to designate the Government Finance Officers Association's publication *Governmental Accounting, Auditing, and Financial Reporting.*

Bond anticipation note. Short-term, interest-bearing note issued by a government in anticipation of bond proceeds to be received at a later date. The note is retired from proceeds of the bonds to which it is related.

Book-entry system. System that eliminates the need for physically transferring bearer-form paper or registering securities by using a central depository facility. [SGAS 3]

Budgetary accounts. Special accounts used to achieve budgetary integration that are not reported in the financial statements. By convention, ALL CAPS commonly are used to designate budgetary accounts. The most common budgetary accounts are ESTIMATED REVENUES, APPROPRIATIONS, BUDGETARY FUND BALANCE, and ENCUMBRANCES.

Budgetary Guidelines. Recommendations on budgeting issued by the National Advisory Council on State and Local Budgeting (NACSLB). The NACSLB's Budgetary Guidelines are chiefly of interest to accountants because of the emphasis they place on performance measurement in the context of the budgetary process.

Budgetary integration. Use of budgetary accounts to record the operating budget in the general ledger to facilitate control over revenues and expenditures during the year.

Budgetary journal entries. Journal entries involving budgetary accounts. Budgetary journal entries arise in connection with budgetary integration.

Budgetary reporting. As used by accountants, requirement to present budget-to-actual comparisons in connection with general purpose external financial reporting. Budgetary reporting is required in connection with the basic financial statements for both the general fund and individual major special revenue funds with annual (or biennial) appropriated budgets. Budgetary reporting also is required within the comprehensive annual financial report to demonstrate compliance at the legal level of control for all governmental funds with annual (or biennial) appropriated budgets.

Business-type activities. One of two classes of activities reported in the government-wide financial statements. Business-type activities are financed in whole or in part by fees charged to external parties for goods or services. These activities are usually reported in enterprise funds. [SGAS 34]

Call option. Contract giving the buyer (owner) the right, but not the obligation, to purchase from (call option) the seller (writer) of the contract a fixed number of items (such as shares of equity securities) at a fixed or determinable "strike" price on a given date or at any time on or before a given date. [SGAS 31]

Capital and related financing activities. Term used in connection with cash flows reporting. Capital and related financing activities include (a) acquiring and disposing of capital assets used in providing services or producing goods, (b) borrowing money for acquiring, constructing, or improving capital assets and repaying the amounts borrowed, including interest, and (c) paying for capital assets obtained from vendors on credit. [SGAS 9]

Capital assets. Land, improvements to land, easements, buildings, building improvements, vehicles, machinery, equipment, works of art and historical treasures, infrastructure, and all other tangible or intangible assets that are used in operations and that have initial useful lives extending beyond a single reporting period. [SGAS 34]

Capital projects fund. Fund type used to account for financial resources to be used for the acquisition or construction of major capital facilities (other than those financed by proprietary funds and trust funds). [NCGA Statement 1]

Capitalization contribution. Contribution to a public-entity risk pool to meet initial or ongoing capital minimums established by statute, regulation, or the pooling agreement itself. Capitalization contributions generally take the form of cash. [IGAS 4]

Capitalization threshold. Dollar value at which a government elects to capitalize tangible or intangible assets that are used in operations and that have initial useful lives extending beyond a single reporting period. Generally, capitalization thresholds are applied to individual items rather than groups of items unless the result would be to exclude items that would clearly be material to the financial statements in the aggregate.

Capping. Term used in connection with municipal solid-waste landfills to describe the cost of final cover expected to be applied near or after the date that the landfill stops accepting solid waste. [SGAS 18]

Cash. In the context of cash flows reporting, not only currency on hand, but also demand deposits with banks or other financial institutions. Cash also includes deposits in other kinds of accounts or cash management pools that have the general characteristics of demand deposit accounts in that the governmental enterprise may deposit additional cash at any time and also effectively may withdraw cash at any time without prior notice or penalty. [SGAS 9]

Cash basis of accounting. Basis of accounting that recognizes transactions or events when related cash amounts are received or disbursed.

Cash equivalent. In the context of cash flows reporting, short-term, highly liquid investments that are both (a) readily convertible to known amounts of cash and (b) so near their maturity that they present insignificant risk of changes in value because of changes in interest rates. Generally, only investments with original maturities of three months or less meet this definition. For this purpose "original maturity" means maturity as of the date the investment is acquired. [SGAS 9]

Ceded premiums/claims costs. Premiums paid to a public-entity risk pool and claims costs that are transferred to another enterprise in connection with a reinsurance arrangement. [SGAS 10]

Certificate of Achievement for Excellence in Financial Reporting Program. Program sponsored by the Government Finance Officers Association to encourage and assist state and local governments to prepare high-quality comprehensive annual financial reports. The program has been in continuous operation since 1946. The program originally was known as the Certificate of Conformance Program.

Character classification. Classification of expenditures according to the periods they are presumed to benefit. The four character groupings are (a) current operating expenditures, presumed to benefit the current fiscal period; (b) debt service expenditures, presumed to benefit prior fiscal periods as well as current and future periods; (c) capital outlay expenditures, presumed to benefit the current and future fiscal periods, and (d) intergovernmental expenditures, when one government transfers resources to another. [NCGA Statement 1]

Claims-made policy. In connection with public-entity risk pools, a type of policy that covers losses from claims asserted (reported or filed) against the policyholder during the policy period, regardless of whether the liability-imposing events occurred during the current or any previous period in which the policyholder was insured under the claims-made contract or other specified period before the policy period (the policy retroactive date). [SGAS 10]

Claims-servicing pool. Public-entity risk pool that manages separate accounts for each pool member from which the losses of that member are paid. Also referred to as an "account pool." [SGAS 10]

Classified presentation. Separate reporting of the current and noncurrent portions of assets and liabilities to permit the calculation of working capital. A classified presentation is required for the proprietary fund statement of net assets.

Closed amortization period. Term used in connection with the unfunded actuarial accrued liability associated with defined benefit pension and other postemployment benefit plans. A specific number of years that is counted from one date and, therefore, declines to zero with the passage of time. For example, if the amortization period is initially 30 years on a closed basis, 29 years remain after the first year, 28 years after the second year, and so forth [SGAS 25 and SGAS 43]

Closed-end mutual fund. SEC-registered investment company that issues a limited number of shares to investors that are then traded as an equity security on a stock exchange. [SGAS 31]

Collateral. In the context of deposits with financial institutions, security pledged by a financial institution to a governmental entity for its deposit. [SGAS 3]

Collateral pool. A single financial institution collateral pool is a group of securities pledged by a single financial institution against all the public deposits it holds. A multiple financial institution collateral pool is a group of securities pledged by various financial institutions to provide common collateral for their deposits of public funds. In such a collateral pool, the assets of the pool and the power to make additional assessments against the members of the pool, if necessary, insure there will be no loss of public funds because of the default of a member. [SGAS 3]

Combining financial statements. Financial statements that report separate columns for individual funds or component units. Combining financial statements normally are required in a comprehensive annual financial report to support each column in the basic financial statements that aggregates information from more than one fund or component unit.

Commercial paper. Unsecured short-term promissory note issued by corporations, with maturities ranging from 2 to 270 days.

Committee on Accounting Procedure (CAP). Authoritative private-sector standard-setting body that preceded the Accounting Principles Board and the FASB. The CAP issued guidance in the form of *Accounting Research Bulletins*.

Commodities programs. Distribution of surplus agricultural products as a form of assistance, often in connection with school lunch programs.

Comparability. Principle according to which differences between financial reports should reflect substantive differences in the underlying transactions or the governmental structure rather than the selection of different alternatives in accounting procedures or practices. [SGAC 1]

Comparative data. Information from prior fiscal periods provided to enhance the analysis of financial data of the current fiscal period.

Comparative financial statements. Financial statements providing all of the information required by GAAP for two or more fiscal periods.

Compliance Supplement. Term used in connection with Single Audits. A publication of the U.S. Office of Management and Budget outlining compliance requirements for federal awards programs. The publication is designed to assist independent auditors performing Single Audits.

Component unit. Legally separate organization for which the elected officials of the primary government are financially accountable. In addition, component units can be other organizations for which the nature and significance of their relationship with a primary government are such that exclusion would cause the reporting entity's financial statements to be misleading or incomplete. [SGAS 14]

Composite depreciation methods. Depreciation methods applied to groups of assets rather than to individual assets.

Comprehensive annual financial report (CAFR). Financial report that contains, at a minimum, three sections: 1) introductory, 2) financial, and 3) statistical, and whose financial section provides information on each individual fund and component unit.

Comprehensive framework of internal control. Structure of internal control that provides for (a) a favorable control environment, (b) the continuing assessment of risk, (c) the design, implementation, and maintenance of effective control-related policies and procedures, (d) the effective communication of information, and (e) the ongoing monitoring of the effectiveness of control-related policies and procedures as well as the resolution of potential problems identified by controls.

Condensed financial statements. Abbreviated financial statements sometimes required by GAAP to be presented within the notes to the financial statements in connection with component units, external investment pools, and segments. In addition, GAAP prescribe the presentation of condensed financial information for the prior fiscal year as part of management's discussion and analysis.

Conduit debt. Certain limited-obligation revenue bonds, certificates of participation, or similar debt instruments issued by a state or local governmental entity for the express purpose of providing capital financing for a specific third party that is not a part of the issuer's financial reporting entity. Although conduit debt obligations bear the name of the governmental issuer, the issuer has no obligation for such debt beyond the resources provided by a lease or loan with the third party on whose behalf they are issued. [IGAS 2]

Connection fees. Fees charged to join or to extend an existing utility system. Often referred to as *tap fees* or *system development fees*.

Consistency. Notion that once an accounting principle or reporting method is adopted, it will be used for all similar transactions and events. [SGAC 1]

Control cycle. Term used in connection with the evaluation of internal control to describe a series of logically connected transactions/processes and associated control-related policies and procedures.

COSO. Organization that published *Internal Control: An Integrated Framework* (i.e., the Committee of Sponsoring Organizations of the Treadway Commission on Fraudulent Financial Reporting).

Cost-reimbursement basis. Setting of charges so that costs are systematically recovered on a break-even basis over time.

Cost-sharing multiple-employer defined benefit pension/other post-employment benefit plan. Plan in which a single actuarial valuation and contribution rate apply to all participating employers. [SGAS 25 and SGAS 43]

Counterparty. Another party in a deposit or investment transaction. [SGAS 3]

Coverage ratio. Ratio of pledged revenues to related debt service payments. [SGAS 44]

Covered group. Term used in connection with pension and other post-employment benefit plans to describe plan members included in an actuarial valuation. [SGAS 45]

Credit risk. Risk that an issuer or other counterparty to an investment will not fulfill its obligations. [SGAS 40]

Crossover refunding. Type of advance refunding in which the escrow established with the proceeds of the refunding bonds only begins to secure repayment of the refunded debt at some designated future time, known as the "crossover date."

Current costs. In connection with municipal solid-waste landfills, the amount that would be paid if all equipment, facilities, and services included in the estimate of closure and postclosure care costs were acquired during the current period. [SGAS 18]

Current financial resources measurement focus. Measurement focus where the aim of a set of financial statements is to report the near-term (current) inflows, outflows, and balances of expendable financial resources. The current financial resources measurement focus is unique to accounting and financial reporting for state and local governments and is used solely for reporting the financial position and results of operations of governmental funds.

Current refunding. Refunding transaction in which the proceeds of the refunding debt are applied immediately to redeem the debt to be refunded. This situation differs from an advance refunding, where the proceeds of the refunding bonds are placed in escrow pending the call date or maturity of the debt to be refunded.

Custodial credit risk. Risk that a government will not be able (a) to recover deposits if the depository financial institution fails or (b) to recover the value of investment or collateral securities that are in the possession of an outside party if the counterparty to the investment or deposit transaction fails. [Q&A]

Debt service fund. Governmental fund type used to account for the accumulation of resources for, and the payment of, general long-term debt principal and interest. [NCGA Statement 1]

Deductions. Term used to describe decrease in the net assets of a fiduciary fund.

Defeasance. In financial reporting, the netting of outstanding liabilities and related assets on the statement of position. Defeased debt is no longer reported as a liability on the face of the statement of position. Most refundings result in the defeasance of the refunded debt. Defeasance also is sometimes encountered in conjunction with annuity contracts purchased in connection with lottery prizes and settlements of claims and judgments.

Deferred revenue. Resource inflows that do not yet meet the criteria for revenue recognition. Unearned amounts are always reported as deferred revenue. In governmental funds, earned amounts also are reported as deferred revenue until they are available to liquidate liabilities of the current period.

Defined benefit other postemployment benefit plan. Plan having terms that specify the amount of benefits to be provided at or after separation from employment. The benefits may be specified in dollars (for example, a flat dollar payment or an amount based on one or more factors such as age, years of service, and compensation), or as a type or level of coverage (for example, prescription drugs or a percentage of healthcare insurance premiums). [SGAS 43]

Defined benefit pension plan. Pension plan having terms that specify the amount of pension benefits to be provided at a future date or after a certain period of time; the amount specified usually is a function of one or more factors such as age, years of service, and compensation. [SGAS 25]

Defined contribution pension/other postemployment benefit plan. Pension or OPEB plan having terms that (a) provide an individual account for each plan member and (b) specify how contributions to an active plan member's account are to be determined, rather than the income or other benefits the member or his or her beneficiaries are to receive at or after separation from employment. Those benefits will depend only on the amounts contributed to the member's account, earnings on investments of those contributions, and forfeitures of contributions made for other members that may be allocated to the member's account. [SGAS 25 and SGAS 43]

Deflated depreciated replacement cost. Method of measuring a capital asset impairment resulting from a change in the manner or duration of use of the asset. The method compares the book value of the asset with what would have been the book value of a different asset acquired at the same time for use in current circumstances (e.g., the book value of a school building constructed ten years ago, but now used as warehouse space, versus what would have been the value of equivalent warehouse space constructed ten years ago). [SGAS 42]

Demand bonds. Long-term debt issuances with demand ("put") provisions that require the issuer to repurchase the bonds upon notice from the bondholder at a price equal to the principal plus accrued interest. To assure its ability to redeem the bonds, issuers of demand bonds frequently enter into short-term standby liquidity agreements and long-term "take out" agreements. [IGAS 1]

Derivative. Financial instrument 1) whose value derives from the application of some variable ("underlying") to a contractually determined amount ("notional amount") or from the association of an underlying with a payment provision, 2) that involves little or no initial net investment, and 3) that allows for net settlement. [TB 2003-1]

Derived tax revenues. Nonexchange revenues that result from assessments imposed on exchange transactions (for example, income taxes, sales taxes, and other assessments on earnings or consumption). [SGAS 33]

Designated unreserved fund balance. Management's intended use of available expendable financial resources in governmental funds reflecting actual plans approved by the government's senior management. Expressed another way, designations reflect a government's self-imposed limitations on the use of otherwise available expendable financial resources in governmental funds.

Developer fees. Fees charged to developers to cover, in whole or in part, the anticipated cost of improvements that will be necessary as a result of development (e.g., parks, sidewalks).

Direct costing. Use of actual source data (e.g., invoices) to establish the historical cost of a capital asset.

Direct debt. Debt of the government preparing statistical information, in contrast to debt of other, overlapping governments. [SGAS 44]

Direct expense. Expense that is specifically associated with a service, program, or department and, thus, is clearly identifiable to a particular function. [SGAS 34]

Direct rate. Amount or percentage applied to a unit of a specific revenue base by the government preparing statistical information (e.g., a property tax rate of $1 per $1,000 of assessed property value; a sales tax rate of 5 percent of a retail sale; a water charge of a certain amount per 100 gallons of water used). [SGAS 44]

Disallowed costs. Claims for grantor resources that have been rejected by the grantor.

Discrete presentation. Method of reporting financial data of component units separately from financial data of the primary government. [SGAS 14]

Discussion memorandum. Due-process document issued by the GASB soliciting comments from interested parties on various aspects of a technical issue that is the subject of research by the board.

Due process. Procedures followed by the GASB to ensure that the views of all interested parties are solicited and considered prior to issuing an authoritative pronouncement. At a minimum, due process requires that all statements and interpretations be preceded by an exposure draft.

Duration. In the context of investment disclosure, a measure of a debt investment's exposure to fair value changes arising from changing interest rates based upon the present value of cash flows, weighted for those cash flows as a percentage of the investment's full price. [SGAS 40]

Early recognition option. Option to recognize an expenditure in the current period in a debt service fund for principal and interest payments due early in the subsequent period.

Economic resources measurement focus. Measurement focus where the aim of a set of financial statements is to report all inflows, outflows, and balances affecting or reflecting an entity's net assets. The economic resources measurement focus is used for proprietary and trust funds, as well as for government-wide financial reporting. It also is used by business enterprises and nonprofit organizations in the private sector.

Effectiveness. Term used by auditors to describe the degree to which an entity, program, or procedure is successful at achieving its goals and objectives.

Efficiency. Term used by auditors to describe the degree to which an entity, program, or procedure is successful at achieving its goals and objectives with the least use of scarce resources.

Eligibility requirements. Term used in connection with government-mandated and voluntary nonexchange transactions to describe conditions established by the provider of resources (e.g., qualifying characteristics of recipients, time requirements, allowable costs, other contingencies). [SGAS 33]

Embedded option. Provision or term in a financial instrument that allows one party to change the timing or amount of one or more cash flows associated with that instrument (e.g., prepayment options on asset-backed securities). [SGAS 40]

Emerging issues task force. Group established under the auspices of an authoritative standard-setting body and authorized to publish consensus positions on technical issues not specifically addressed by that body. The GASB has not established an emerging issues task force, although it is empowered to do so.

Employer contributions. Term used in the context of pension and other postemployment benefits to describe contributions actually made by the employer in relation to the annual required contribution (ARC) of the employer. (Only amounts paid to trustees and outside parties qualify.) [SGAS 43]

Encumbrances. Commitments related to unperformed (executory) contracts for goods or services. For financial reporting purposes, encumbrance accounting is restricted to governmental funds. [NCGA Statement 1]

Enterprise fund. Proprietary fund type used to report an activity for which a fee is charged to external users for goods or services. [SGAS 34]

Entity differences. Difference between the basis of budgeting and GAAP arising because 1) the appropriated budget includes organizations, programs, activities, or functions that are not within the financial reporting entity as defined by GAAP or 2) the appropriated budget excludes organizations program, activities, or functions that are part of the financial reporting entity. [NCGA Interpretation 10]

Equivalent single amortization period. Term used in the context of pension and other postemployment benefit plans. The weighted average of all amortization periods used when components of the total unfunded actuarial accrued liability are separately amortized and the average is calculated. [SGAS 25 and SGAS 43]

Escheat. Reversion of private property to a governmental entity in the absence of legal claimants or heirs. The laws of many governmental entities provide that a rightful owner or heir can reclaim escheat property in perpetuity. [SGAS 21]

Estimated actual value of taxable property. Fair value of taxable real or personal property or a surrogate measure of fair value if actual fair value information is not available. In practice, fair value is often referred to as *market value.* The estimated actual value of taxable property may be determined in a variety of manners, such as through a system that tracks changes in market values by monitoring property sales or by dividing the assessed value of property by an assumed assessment percentage. [SGAS 44]

Ethics Rule 202. Ethics rule established by the AICPA that places upon auditors the burden of proof for justifying any material departures from the guidance found on levels 2, 3, or 4 of the GAAP hierarchy.

Ethics Rule 203. Ethics rule established by the AICPA that makes it an ethical violation for an auditor to state that financial statements are "fairly presented in conformity with GAAP" if those statements materially violate standards issued by the FASB, the GASB, or the Federal Accounting Standards Advisory Board. A special exception applies when unusual circumstances would make the application of an authoritative standard misleading.

Exchange transactions. Transactions in which each party receives and gives up essentially equal values. [SGAS 33]

Exchange-like transactions. Transactions in which there is an identifiable exchange between the reporting government and another party, but the values exchanged may not be quite equal or the direct benefits of the exchange may not be exclusively for the parties to the exchange. Examples include certain fees for regulatory or professional licenses and permits, certain tap fees, certain developer contributions, certain grants and donations, and other transactions that, regardless of the label applied to them, are based on an exchange of similar but not equal values. [SGAS 33]

Expenditure-driven grants. Government-mandated or voluntary non-exchange transactions in which expenditure is the prime factor for determining eligibility. Also referred to as *reimbursement grants*.

Expenditures. Under the current financial resources measurement focus, decreases in net financial resources not properly classified as *other financing uses*.

Explicit measurable equity interest. Asset resulting from a stipulation in a joint venture agreement that the participants have a present or future claim to the net resources of the joint venture and setting forth the method to determine the participants' shares of the joint venture's net resources. [SGAS 14]

Exposure draft. Due-process document issued by the GASB soliciting comments from interested parties on a proposed authoritative pronouncement.

External auditors. Independent auditors, typically engaged to conduct the audit of a government's financial statements.

Fair value. In the context of investment valuation, the amount at which a financial instrument could be exchanged in a current transaction between willing parties, other than in a forced or liquidation sale. [SGAS 31]

Federal Accounting Standards Advisory Board (FASAB). Authoritative standard-setting body responsible for establishing GAAP for the federal government.

Fiduciary funds. Funds used to report assets held in a trustee or agency capacity for others and which therefore cannot be used to support the government's own programs. The fiduciary fund category includes pension (and other employee benefit) trust funds, investment trust funds, private-purpose trust funds, and agency funds. [SGAS 34]

Final amended budget. Original budget adjusted by all reserves, transfers, allocations, supplemental appropriations, and other legally authorized legislative and executive changes applicable to the fiscal year, whenever signed into law or otherwise legally authorized. [SGAS 34]

Financial accountability. Relationship warranting the inclusion of a legally separate organization in the reporting entity of another government. [SGAS 14]

Financial Accounting Foundation (FAF). Nonprofit organization responsible for overseeing the operations of both the GASB and the FASB.

Financial Accounting Standards Advisory Council (FASAC). Advisory group that assists the FASB. The FASAC includes representatives of all of the FASB's major constituents.

Financial Accounting Standards Board (FASB). Authoritative accounting and financial reporting standard-setting body for business enterprises and nonprofit organizations. The FASB is the direct successor to the Committee on Accounting Procedure and the Accounting Principles Board.

Financial audits. Audits designed to provide independent assurance of the fair presentation of financial information.

Financial reporting entity. Primary government, organizations for which the primary government is financially accountable, and other organizations for which the nature and significance of their relationship with the primary government are such that exclusion would cause the reporting entity's financial statements to be misleading or incomplete. The nucleus of a financial reporting entity usually is a primary government. However, a governmental organization other than a primary government (such as a component unit, a joint venture, a jointly governed organization, or other stand-alone government) serves as the nucleus for its own reporting entity when it issues separate financial statements. [SGAS 14]

Financial resources. Resources that are or will become available for spending. Financial resources include cash and resources ordinarily expected to be converted to cash (e.g., receivables, investments). Financial resources also may include inventories and prepaids (because they obviate the need to expend current available financial resources).

Financial section. One of the three basic sections of a comprehensive annual financial report. The financial section is used to present the independent auditor's report on the financial statements; management's discussion and analysis; the basic financial statements (including the notes to the financial statements); required supplementary information; combining statements, individual fund statements and schedules; and supplementary information, as needed.

Finding. Term used in connection with public-sector auditing. Published communication of an internal control weaknesses or instance of noncompliance in connection with an audit conducted in accordance with GAGAS.

Fiscal accountability. Responsibility of governments to justify that their actions in the current period have complied with public decisions concerning the raising and spending of public moneys in the short term (usually one budgetary cycle or one year). [SGAS 34]

Fiscal dependence. Situation requiring the inclusion of a legally separate entity as a component unit within the financial reporting entity because the governing board of the primary government may *arbitrarily* override the financial decisions of the legally separate entity regarding (a) its budget, (b) the levying of taxes or the setting of rates or charges, or (c) the issuance of bonded debt.

Fiscal funding clause. Term used in connection with capital leases. A clause in a lease agreement that generally provides that the lease is cancelable if the legislature or other funding authority does not appropriate the funds necessary for the government unit to fulfill its obligations under the lease agreement. [NCGA Statement 5]

Five percent criterion. Second of two tests used to determine whether a given governmental fund or enterprise fund must be reported as a major fund in the basic financial statements. This test is applied to the combined total assets, liabilities, revenues or expenses/expenditures of all governmental and enterprise funds for which the 10 percent criterion has been met.

Fixed budgets. Budgets that embody estimates of specific (fixed) dollar amounts, in contrast with *flexible budgets.* [NCGA Statement 1]

Fixed coupon repurchase/reverse repurchase agreement. A repurchase agreement or a reverse repurchase agreement where the parties agree that the securities returned will have the same stated interest rate as, and maturities similar to, the securities transferred. [SGAS 3]

Flexible budgets. Budgets that embody dollar estimates that vary according to demand for the goods or services provided, in contrast with *fixed* budgets. [NCGA Statement 1]

Food stamps. Federal award program intended to improve the diets of members of low-income households by increasing their ability to purchase food. The term itself harkens back to a time when paper coupons were used to distribute benefits, as opposed to the electronic benefit transfer systems now in place. [SGAS 24]

Foreign currency risk. Risk that changes in exchange rates will adversely affect the fair value of an investment or a deposit. [SGAS 40]

Formula grants. Government-mandated or voluntary nonexchange transactions involving the provision of resources based upon established criteria (e.g., number of full-time equivalent students) other than the incurrence of qualifying expenditures. Also referred to as "shared revenues."

Function. Group of related activities aimed at accomplishing a major service or regulatory program for which a government is responsible (e.g., public safety).

Fund. Fiscal and accounting entity with a self-balancing set of accounts recording cash and other financial resources, together with all related liabilities and residual equities or balances, and changes therein, that are segregated for the purpose of carrying on specific activities or attaining certain objectives in accordance with special regulations, restrictions, or limitations. [NCGA Statement 1]

Fundamental analysis. In the context of investment valuation, a method of estimating the fair value of a security when it is thinly traded or when quoted market prices are not available. Fundamental analysis considers assets, liabilities, operating statement performance, management, and economic environment of the issuer in estimating a fair value. [SGAS 31, Q&A]

Fund balance. Difference between assets and liabilities reported in a governmental fund.

Fund classifications. One of the three categories (governmental, proprietary, and fiduciary) used to classify fund types.

Fund financial statements. Basic financial statements presented on the basis of funds, in contrast to *government-wide* financial statements.

Fund type. One of eleven classifications into which all individual funds can be categorized. Governmental fund types include the general fund, special revenue funds, debt service funds, capital projects funds, and permanent funds. Proprietary fund types include enterprise funds and internal service funds. Fiduciary fund types include pension (and other employee benefit) trust funds, investment trust funds, private-purpose trust funds, and agency funds.

Funded mandate. Also known as a government-mandated nonexchange transaction. A situation where a higher level government requires performance of a lower level government and provides it full or partial funding to do so. [SGAS 33]

Funded ratio. In the context of defined benefit pension and other postemployment benefit plans, the actuarial value of assets expressed as a percentage of the actuarial accrued liability. [SGAS 25 and SGAS 43]

Funding excess. In the context of defined benefit pension and other postemployment benefit plans, the excess of the actuarial value of plan assets over the actuarial accrued liability. [SGAS 45]

GAAFR. Acronym for *Governmental Accounting, Auditing, and Financial Reporting*, a publication of the Government Finance Officers Association. Also known as the "Blue Book," various editions of this book have been published since the mid 1930s.

GAAP hierarchy. Identification and ranking of the sources of GAAP set forth in SAS No. 69, *The Meaning of "Present Fairly in Conformity with Generally Accepted Accounting Principles" in the Independent Auditor's Report* and SAS No. 91, *Federal GAAP Hierarchy.*

General Accounting Office (GAO). Former name of the Government Accountability Office. (See below.)

General fund. One of five governmental fund types. The general fund typically serves as the chief operating fund of a government. The general fund is used to account for all financial resources except those required to be accounted for in another fund. [NCGA Statement 1]

General revenues. All revenues that are *not* required to be reported as program revenues in the government-wide statement of activities. [SGAS 34]

Generally accepted accounting principles (GAAP). Conventions, rules, and procedures that serve as the norm for the fair presentation of financial statements.

Generally accepted auditing standards (GAAS). Rules and procedures that govern the conduct of a financial audit.

Generally accepted government auditing standards (GAGAS). Standards for the conduct and reporting of both financial and performance audits in the public sector promulgated by the Government Accountability Office through its publication *Government Auditing Standards*, commonly known as the "Yellow Book."

Government Accountability Office (GAO). Investigative arm of the U.S. Congress charged with improving the performance and accountability of the federal government. The GAO issues the publication *Government Auditing Standards*, commonly known as the "Yellow Book," which sets generally accepted government auditing standards.

Government Finance Officers Association of the United States and Canada (GFOA). Association of public finance professionals founded in 1906 as the Municipal Finance Officers Association. The GFOA has played a major role in the development and promotion of GAAP for state and local government since its inception and has sponsored the Certificate of Achievement for Excellence in Financial Reporting Program since 1946. It also publishes *Governmental Accounting, Auditing, and Financial Reporting*, commonly known as the "Blue Book."

Governmental Accounting Standards Advisory Council (GASAC). Advisory body established to assist the GASB. The membership of the GASAC represents all major groups with an interest in accounting and financial reporting for state and local governments.

Governmental Accounting Standards Board (GASB). Ultimate authoritative accounting and financial reporting standard-setting body for state and local governments. The GASB was established in June 1984 to replace the NCGA.

Governmental Accounting, Auditing, and Financial Reporting (GAAFR). Publication of the Government Finance Officers Association. Also known as the "Blue Book," various editions have been published since the mid 1930s.

Governmental activities. Activities generally financed through taxes, intergovernmental revenues, and other nonexchange revenues. These activities are usually reported in governmental funds and internal service funds. [SGAS 34]

Governmental entity. For accounting and financial reporting purposes, an entity subject to the hierarchy of GAAP applicable to state and local governmental units.

Governmental external investment pool. Arrangement that commingles (pools) the moneys of more than one legally separate entity and invests, on the participants' behalf, in an investment portfolio; one or more of the participants not being part of the sponsor's reporting entity. An external investment pool can be sponsored by an individual government, jointly by more than one government, or by a nongovernmental entity. An investment pool that is sponsored by an individual state or local government is an external investment pool only if it includes participation by a legally separate entity that is not part of the same reporting entity as the sponsoring government. [SGAS 31]

Governmental financial reporting model. Minimum combination of financial statements, note disclosures, and required supplementary information prescribed for state and local governments by the GASB.

Governmental funds. Funds generally used to account for tax-supported activities. There are five different types of governmental funds: the general fund, special revenue funds, debt service funds, capital projects funds, and permanent funds.

Government-mandated nonexchange transactions. Situation where a higher level government requires performance of a lower level government and provides it full or partial funding to do so.

Government-wide financial statements. Financial statements that incorporate all of a government's governmental and business-type activities, as well as its nonfiduciary component units. There are two basic government-wide financial statements: the statement of net assets and the statement of activities.

Grant anticipation note. Short-term, interest-bearing note issued by a government in anticipation of a grant to be received at a later date. The note is retired from proceeds of the grant to which it is related.

Guaranteed investment contract. Group annuity contract designed to provide guarantees of principal and interest on funds deposited with an insurance company for a specified period.

Healthcare cost trend rate. In connection with other postemployment benefit healthcare plans, the rate of change in per capita health claims costs over time as a result of factors such as medical inflation, utilization of healthcare services, plan design, and technological developments. [SGAS 43]

Impact fees. Fees charged to developers to cover, in whole or in part, the anticipated cost of improvements that will be necessary as a result of the development (e.g., parks, sidewalks).

Impairment. Significant, unexpected decline in the service utility of a capital asset. [SGAS 42]

Implementation guides. Guidance on the proper implementation of authoritative accounting and financial reporting standards issued by the staff of the GASB. Implementation guides use a question-and-answer format and enjoy "level 4" status on the hierarchy of GAAP for state and local governments. The GASB annually issues a *Comprehensive Implementation Guide* that consolidates, updates, and expands upon the guidance offered in the individual publications.

Imposed nonexchange revenues. Revenues that result from assessments imposed on nongovernmental entities, including individuals, other than assessments on exchange transactions (for example, property taxes and fines). [SGAS 33]

Improvement. Addition made to, or change made in, a capital asset, other than maintenance, to prolong its life or to increase its efficiency or capacity. The cost of the addition or change normally is added to the book value of the asset.

"In-relation-to" opinion. Indication in the independent auditor's report that the auditor does *not* render an opinion on the fair presentation *per se* of certain information contained in the financial report (e.g., combining and individual fund financial statements), but does assert that the information in question is fairly presented *in relation to* the audited financial statements.

Incurred but not reported (IBNR) claims. In connection with risk financing, claims for insured events that have occurred but have not yet been reported to the governmental entity, public entity risk pool, insurer, or reinsurer as of the date of the financial statements. IBNR claims include (a) known loss events that are expected to be presented later as claims, (b) unknown loss events that are expected to become claims, and (c) expected future development on claims already reported. [SGAS 10]

Independent auditor. Auditors who are independent, both in fact and appearance, of the entities they audit. Both GAAS and GAGAS set specific criteria that must be met for an auditor to be considered independent.

Independent auditor's report. Official written communication of the results of an audit. In a financial audit, the independent auditor's report typically will offer (or disclaim) an opinion on whether a set of financial statements is fairly presented in conformity with GAAP (or some other comprehensive basis of accounting).

Indirect expenses. Expenses that cannot be specifically associated with a given service, program, or department and thus, cannot be clearly associated with a particular functional category. [SGAS 34]

Individual investment accounts. Investment service provided by a governmental entity for other, legally separate entities that are not part of the same reporting entity. With individual investment accounts, specific investments are acquired for individual entities and the income from and changes in the value of those investments affect only the entity for which they were acquired. [SGAS 31]

Infrastructure. Long-lived capital assets that normally are stationary in nature and normally can be preserved for a significantly greater number of years than most capital assets. Examples of infrastructure assets include roads, bridges, tunnels, drainage systems, water and sewer systems, dams, and lighting systems. [SGAS 34]

In-substance defeasance of debt. Situation that occurs when debt is considered defeased for accounting and financial reporting purposes, even though a legal defeasance has not occurred. When debt is defeased, it is no longer reported as a liability on the face of the statement of position; only the new debt, if any, is reported as a liability. [SGAS 7]

Insured benefit. In the context of pension and other postemployment benefits, a financing arrangement whereby an employer accumulates funds with an insurance company, while employees are in active service, in return for which the insurance company unconditionally undertakes a legal obligation to pay the benefits of those employees or their beneficiaries, as defined in the employer's plan. From an employer perspective, an insured benefit resembles a defined contribution plan, while from an employee perspective it resembles a defined benefit plan. [SGAS 27 and SGAS 45]

Integrated budget. Situation where the accounting system has been designed to automatically provide timely budgetary information concerning the uncommitted balance of appropriations and unrealized revenues.

Interest rate risk. Risk that changes in interest rates will adversely affect the fair value of an investment. [SGAS 40]

Interfund activity. Activity between funds of the primary government, including blended component units. Interfund activities are divided into two broad categories: reciprocal and nonreciprocal. Reciprocal interfund activity comprises interfund loans and interfund services provided and used. Nonreciprocal interfund activity comprises interfund transfers and interfund reimbursements.

Interfund loans. Amounts provided between funds and blended component units of the primary government with a requirement for repayment. [SGAS 34]

Interfund reimbursements. Repayments by one fund or blended component unit of a primary government to another for expenditures or expenses incurred on its behalf. [SGAS 34]

Interfund services provided and used. Sales and purchases of goods and services between funds and blended component units of the primary government for a price approximating their external exchange value. [SGAS 34]

Interfund transfers. Flows of assets (such as cash or goods) between funds and blended component units of the primary government without equivalent flows of assets in return and without a requirement for repayment. [SGAS 34]

Internal auditing. Appraisal of the diverse operations and controls within a government entity to determine whether acceptable policies and procedures are followed, established standards are met, resources are used efficiently and economically, and the organization's objectives are being achieved. The term covers all forms of appraisal of activities undertaken by auditors working for and within an organization.

Internal control framework. Integrated set of policies and procedures designed to assist management to achieve its goals and objectives. To be truly comprehensive, a government's internal control framework must (a) provide a favorable control environment, (b) provide for the continuing assessment of risk, (c) provide for the design, implementation, and maintenance of effective control-related policies and procedures, (d) provide for the effective communication of information, and (e) provide for the ongoing monitoring of the effectiveness of control-related policies and procedures as well as the resolution of potential problems identified by controls.

Internal financial reporting. Financial reporting specifically designed to meet the needs of management.

Internal service funds. Proprietary fund type that may be used to report any activity that provides goods or services to other funds, departments, or agencies of the primary government and its component units, or to other governments, on a cost-reimbursement basis. [SGAS 34]

Introductory section. First of three essential components of any comprehensive annual financial report. The introductory section typically provides general information on a government's structure and personnel as well as information useful in assessing the government's economic condition. The key element of the introductory section is the letter of transmittal.

Invested in capital assets, net of related debt. One of three components of net assets that must be reported in both government-wide and proprietary fund financial statements. Related debt, for this purpose, includes the outstanding balances of any bonds, mortgages, notes, or other borrowings that are attributable to the acquisition, construction, or improvement of capital assets of the government.

Investing activities. In the context of cash flows reporting, cash flows from making and collecting loans (except program loans) and from acquiring and disposing of debt or equity instruments. [SGAS 9]

Investment section. One of the sections of a comprehensive annual financial report of an investment pool or public employee retirement system.

Investment trust funds. Fiduciary fund type used to report governmental external investment pools in separately issued reports and the external portion of these same pools when reported by the sponsoring government. [SGAS 34]

Invitation to comment. Due-process document that may be released by the GASB to solicit the views of interested parties on a topic under study by the board prior to the release of an exposure draft.

Issuer. In the context of investment disclosure, the entity that has the authority to distribute a security or other investment. A bond issuer is the entity that is legally obligated to make principal and interest payments to bondholders. In the case of mutual funds, external investment pools, and other pooled investments, "issuer" refers to the entity invested in, not the investment company manager or pool sponsor. [SGAS 40]

Joint venture. Legal entity or other organization that results from a contractual arrangement and that is owned, operated, or governed by two or more participants as a separate and specific activity subject to joint control, in which the participants retain (a) an ongoing financial interest or (b) an ongoing financial responsibility. Generally, the purpose of a joint venture is to pool resources and share the costs, risks, and rewards of providing goods or services to the joint venture participants directly, or for the benefit of the public or specific service recipients. [SGAS 14]

Jointly governed organization. Regional government or other multi-governmental arrangement that is governed by representatives from each of the governments that create the organization, but that is not a joint venture because the participants do not retain an ongoing financial interest or responsibility. [SGAS 14]

Landfill closure and postclosure care costs. Costs incurred to provide for the protection of the environment that occur near or after the date that a municipal solid-waste landfill stops accepting solid waste and during the postclosure period. Closure and postclosure care costs include the cost of equipment and facilities (e.g., leachate collection systems and final cover) as well as the cost of services (e.g., postclosure maintenance and monitoring costs). [SGAS 18]

Lapse period. Specified time at the beginning of a given budget period during which encumbrances outstanding at the end of the prior budget period may be liquidated using the prior year's budgetary authority. Many governments avoid the use of a lapse period by automatically appropriating as part of each new budget an amount sufficient to cover encumbrances outstanding at the end of the prior budget period (a process known as "reappropriation").

Legal debt margin. Excess of the amount of debt legally authorized over the amount of debt outstanding.

Legal defeasance. Situation that occurs when debt is legally satisfied based on certain provisions in the debt instrument even though the debt is not actually paid. When debt is defeased, it is no longer reported as a liability on the face of the statement of position; only the new debt, if any, is reported as a liability. [SGAS 7]

Legal level of budgetary control. Level at which a government's management may not reallocate resources without special approval from the legislative body.

Lent securities. Securities lent to the borrower in a securities lending transaction. Also referred to as *underlying securities*. [SGAS 28]

Level (1-4) guidance. In the context of the hierarchy of GAAP for state and local governments, a reference to the relative authority of a given source of GAAP guidance.

Level of effort requirement. Requirement that a grant recipient not use grant resources to reduce its own participation in a given program or activity.

Lien date. For property (ad valorem) taxes, the date when an enforceable legal claim to taxable property arises. Generally the lien date is specified in the relevant enabling legislation. Many governments use the term *lien date* even though a lien is not formally placed on the property at that date. Alternatively, the term *assessment date* is used to describe this same date. [SGAS 33]

Loan premium or fee. In connection with securities lending arrangements, payments from the borrower to the lender as compensation for the use of the underlying securities when the securities lending arrangement is backed either by a letter of credit, or by securities that cannot be pledged or sold absent a default. [SGAS 28]

Major fund. Governmental fund or enterprise fund reported as a separate column in the basic fund financial statements and subject to a separate opinion in the independent auditor's report. The general fund is always a major fund. Otherwise, major funds are funds whose revenues, expenditures/expenses, assets, or liabilities (excluding extraordinary items) are at least 10 percent of corresponding totals for all governmental *or* enterprise funds and at least 5 percent of the aggregate amount for all governmental *and* enterprise funds for the same item. Any other government or enterprise fund may be reported as a major fund if the government's officials believe that fund is particularly important to financial statement users. [SGAS 34]

Major program. Term used in the context of Single Audits. As part of the Single Audit, the independent auditor must gain an understanding of internal control over compliance for each major federal award program and then test it. In addition, the independent auditor must render an opinion on whether the government complied with laws, regulations, and provisions of contracts or grant agreements that could have a direct and material effect on each major federal award program.

Management letter. In the context of the independent audit of the financial statements, a formal communication by the auditor to management that focuses on internal control weaknesses discovered in the course of the audit of the financial statements. A management letter typically would be redundant in an audit conducted in accordance with GAGAS, which require that the independent auditor publish internal control weaknesses and instances of noncompliance in conjunction with a formal report on internal control and compliance. The management letter, as just described, should be distinguished from the management *representation* letter. The latter is a communication by management to the independent auditor in which management takes formal responsibility for the fair presentation of the financial statements and makes certain specific representations regarding their contents and circumstances.

Management's discussion and analysis. Component of required supplementary information used to introduce the basic financial statements and provide an analytical overview of the government's financial activities. [SGAS 34]

Market-access risk. In the context of disclosures for derivatives, the risk that arises when a government enters into a derivative in anticipation of entering the credit market at a later date, but may ultimately be prevented from doing so, thereby frustrating the purpose of the derivative.

Matching requirement. Requirement that a grant recipient contribute resources to a program that equal or exceed a predetermined percentage of amounts provided by the grantor.

Material weakness. Reportable condition (internal control weakness) of such magnitude that it could potentially result in a material misstatement of the financial statements.

Materiality. In the context of financial reporting, the notion that an omission or misstatement of accounting information is of such significance as to make it probable that the judgment of a reasonable person relying on the information would be changed or influenced by the omission or misstatement.

Matrix pricing. In the context of investment valuation, a method of estimating the fair value of a security when it is thinly traded or when quoted market prices are not available. Matrix pricing estimates a security's fair value by considering coupon interest rates, maturity, credit rating, and market indexes as they relate to the security being valued and to similar issues for which quoted prices are available. [Q&A]

Measurement focus. Types of balances (and related changes) reported in a given set of financial statements (i.e., economic resources, current financial resources, assets and liabilities resulting from cash transactions).

Modified accrual basis of accounting. Basis of accounting used in conjunction with the current financial resources measurement focus that modifies the accrual basis of accounting in two important ways 1) revenues are not recognized until they are measurable and available, and 2) expenditures are recognized in the period in which governments in general normally liquidate the related liability rather than when that liability is first incurred (if earlier).

Modified approach. Election *not* to depreciate infrastructure assets that are part of a network or subsystem of a network that meets two requirements. First, the government manages the eligible infrastructure assets using an asset management system that has certain specified characteristics; second, the government documents that the eligible infrastructure assets are being preserved approximately at (or above) a condition level established and disclosed by the government. [SGAS 34]

Money market investment. Short-term, highly liquid debt instrument, including commercial paper, banker's acceptances, and U.S. Treasury and agency obligations. Asset-backed securities, derivatives, and structured notes are *not* included in this term. [SGAS 31]

Multi-purpose grants. In connection with the identification of program revenues, grants intended to finance activities reported in different functional categories in the government-wide statement of activities. [SGAS 34]

Municipal Finance Officers Association. Original name of the Government Finance Officers Association of the United States and Canada.

Municipal solid-waste landfill. Discrete area of land or an excavation that receives household waste, and that is not a land application unit, surface impoundment, injection well, or waste pile, as those terms are defined in regulations of the Environmental Protection Agency. It may also receive other types of Resource Conservation and Recovery Act Subtitle D wastes, such as commercial solid waste, nonhazardous sludge, and industrial solid waste. The term *municipal* indicates the primary type of solid waste received by the landfill, not its ownership. [SGAS 18]

National Advisory Council on State and Local Budgeting (NACSLB). Working group created by eight public-sector organizations to establish a comprehensive framework for public-sector budgeting that could be used by state and local governments as an ideal against which to measure and improve the quality of their own budget practices. The Government Finance Officers Association has formally recommended the NACSLB's guidelines to its members.

National Committee on Governmental Accounting. Committee of the Municipal Finance Officers Association that served as the authoritative accounting and financial reporting standard-setting body for local governments from 1946 until the establishment of the National Council on Governmental Accounting in the 1970s.

National Council on Governmental Accounting (NCGA). Immediate predecessor of the GASB as the authoritative accounting and financial reporting standard-setting body for state and local governments.

National Committee on Municipal Accounting (NCMA). Committee of the Municipal Finance Officers Association that served as the authoritative accounting and financial reporting standard-setting body for local governments prior to 1946. The NCMA was one of the predecessors of the GASB.

Negotiable certificates of deposit. Transferable certificates of deposit normally sold in $1 million units that can be traded in a secondary market. (Q&A)

Net cost. In the context of the government-wide statement of activities, the difference between functional expenses and program revenues.

Net general obligation debt. General obligation debt reduced by the amount of any accumulated resources restricted to repaying the principal of such debt. [SGAS 44]

Net pension/OPEB obligation. In the context of defined benefit pension and other postemployment benefit plans, the cumulative difference between annual pension cost and the employer's contributions to the plan, including the pension/OPEB liability (asset) at transition, if any, and excluding (a) short-term differences and (b) unpaid contributions that have been converted to pension-related/OPEB-related debt. [SGAS 27 and SGAS 45]

No-commitment special assessment debt. Special assessment debt that is secured solely by liens on assessed properties and resources provided from bond proceeds and is not backed by either the full faith and credit of the government or by any other type of general government commitment.

Noncapital financing activities. Term used in connection with cash flows reporting. Noncapital financing activities include borrowing money for purposes other than to acquire, construct, or improve capital assets and repaying those amounts borrowed, including interest. This category includes proceeds from all borrowings (such as revenue anticipation notes) not clearly attributable to acquisition, construction, or improvement of capital assets, regardless of the form of the borrowing. Also included are certain other interfund and intergovernmental receipts and payments. [SGAS 9]

Nonexchange transaction. Transaction in which a government (including the federal government, as a provider) either gives value (benefit) to another party without directly receiving equal value in exchange or receives value (benefit) from another party without directly giving equal value in exchange. [SGAS 33]

Nonfinancial assets. In the context of the current financial resources measurement focus and the modified accrual basis of accounting, assets that are expected to be used in the provision of goods or services rather than converted to cash. Financial statement preparers have the option of treating prepaid items and inventories of supplies as either a financial asset (consumption method) or as a nonfinancial asset (purchases method).

Nonoperating revenues and expenses. In the context of the proprietary fund operating statement, revenues and expenses not qualifying as operating items (e.g., taxes, grants that are not equivalent to contracts for services, and most interest revenue and expense).

Nonparticipating interest-earning investment contracts. Investment contracts whose value is not affected by market (interest rate) changes (e.g., nonnegotiable certificates of deposit with redemption terms that do not consider market rates). This definition excludes investment contracts that are negotiable or transferable, or whose redemption value considers market rates. [SGAS 31]

Nonreciprocal interfund activity. Counterpart of nonexchange transactions within the primary government. This category includes both interfund transfers and interfund reimbursements. [SGAS 34]

Normal cost. In the context of defined benefit pension and other postemployment benefit plans, that portion of the actuarial present value of plan benefits and expenses which is allocated to a valuation year by the actuarial cost method. [SGAS 25 and SGAS 43]

Normal costing. Method of estimating the historical cost of a capital asset by taking the value of acquiring the same asset new today and then discounting that amount by an appropriate inflation factor back to the date of acquisition.

Notional amount. In the context of a derivative, the number (e.g., current units, shares, bushels) to which an underlying is applied.

Number of funds principle. Principle that only the minimum number of funds consistent with legal and operating requirements should be established, since unnecessary funds result in inflexibility, undue complexity, and inefficient financial administration. [NCGA Statement 1]

Object (of expenditure). In the context of the classification of expenditures, the article purchased or the service obtained, rather than the purpose for which the article or service was purchased or obtained (e.g., personal services, contractual services, materials and supplies).

Office of Management and Budget (OMB). Agency of the federal government with regulatory oversight of Single Audits.

On-behalf payments of fringe benefits and salaries. Direct payments of fringe benefits or salaries made by one entity (the paying entity or paying government) to a third-party recipient for the employees of another, legally separate entity (the employer entity or employer government). [SGAS 24]

Open amortization period. In the context of defined benefit pension and other postemployment benefit plans, an open amortization period (open basis) is one that begins again or is recalculated at each actuarial valuation date. Within a maximum number of years specified by law or policy (for example, 30 years), the period may increase, decrease, or remain stable. [SGAS 25 and SGAS 43]

Open-end mutual fund. An open-end mutual fund is one that continuously offers its shares for sale to the public, compared with a closed-end company, which may issue only a limited number of shares. Mutual funds generally do not issue share certificates; instead, they send out periodic statements showing deposits, withdrawals, and dividends credited to the investor's account. [SGAS 3]

Operating activities. Term used in connection with cash flows reporting. Operating activities generally result from providing services and producing and delivering goods, and include all transactions and other events that are not defined as capital and related financing, noncapital financing, or investing activities. [SGAS 9]

Operating revenues and expenses. Cost of goods sold and services provided to customers and the revenue thus generated.

Operational accountability. Governments' responsibility to report the extent to which they have met their operating objectives efficiently and effectively, using all resources available for that purpose, and whether they can continue to meet their objectives for the foreseeable future. [SGAS 34]

Option-adjusted spread models. Method of estimating the fair value of an option when it is thinly traded or when quoted market prices are not available. Such models measure the spread provided from a security that is an option or includes an option. Using a benchmarked yield curve, separate cash flows are discounted according to their maturity. The result is a spread when compared to yields for risk-free investments. [Q&A]

Option contract. Contract giving the buyer (owner) the right, but not the obligation, to purchase from (call option) or sell to (put option) the seller (writer) of the contract a fixed number of items (such as shares of equity securities) at a fixed or determinable "strike" price on a given date or at any time on or before a given date. [SGAS 31]

Option-pricing models. Method of estimating the fair value of an option when it is thinly traded or when quoted market prices are not available. Under one such model (i.e., the Black-Scholes model) consideration is given to a security's return, the-risk free interest rate, the time remaining until the option expires, and the relationship of the underlying security's price to the strike price of the option. [SGAS 31, Q&A]

Original budget. First complete appropriated budget. The original budget may be adjusted by reserves, transfers, allocations, supplemental appropriations, and other legally authorized legislative and executive changes before the beginning of the fiscal year. The original budget should also include actual appropriation amounts automatically carried over from prior years by law. For example, a legal provision may require the automatic rolling forward of appropriations to cover prior-year encumbrances. [SGAS 34]

Other financing source. Increase in current financial resources that is reported separately from revenues to avoid distorting revenue trends. The use of the *other financing sources* category is limited to items so classified by GAAP.

Other financing use. Decrease in current financial resources that is reported separately from expenditures to avoid distorting expenditure trends. The use of the *other financing uses* category is limited to items so classified by GAAP.

Other postemployment benefits (OPEB). Postemployment benefits other than pension benefits. Other postemployment benefits (OPEB) include postemployment healthcare benefits, regardless of the type of plan that provides them, and all postemployment benefits provided separately from a pension plan, excluding benefits defined as termination offers and benefits. [SGAS 43]

Outcome measures. In the context of service efforts and accomplishments reporting, indicators that measure accomplishments or results that occur (at least partially) because of services provided. Results also include measures of public perceptions of outcomes. [SGAC 2]

Output measures. Term used in connection with service efforts and accomplishments reporting. Indicators that measure the quantity of services provided. Output measures include both measures of the *quantity of service provided* and measures of the *quantity of a service provided that meets a certain quality requirement.* [SGAC 2]

Overlapping debt. In the context of the statistical section, the outstanding long-term debt instruments of governments that overlap geographically, at least in part, with the government preparing the statistical section information. That is, debt of another government that at least some of the reporting government's taxpayers will also have to pay in whole or in part. Lower levels of government are not required to treat debt of the state as overlapping debt, even though it technically meets this definition. Furthermore, states, regional governments, and counties are exempted from the requirement to present overlapping debt, although counties are still encouraged to do so. [SGAS 44]

Overlapping governments. In the context of the statistical section, all local governments located wholly or in part within the geographic boundaries of the reporting government. [SGAS 44]

Overlapping rate. In the context of the statistical section, an amount or percentage applied to a unit of a specific revenue base by governments that overlap geographically, at least in part, with the government preparing the statistical section information. [SGAS 44]

Own-source revenues. In the context of the statistical section, revenues that are generated by a government itself (e.g., tax revenues; water and sewer charges; investment income) rather than provided from some outside source (e.g., intergovernmental aid and shared revenues). [SGAS 44]

Participating interest-earning investment contracts. Interest-earning investment contracts whose value is affected by market (interest rate) changes (e.g., contracts that are negotiable or transferable, or whose redemption value considers market rates). [SGAS 31]

Passenger facilities charge (PFC). Fixed fee authorized by the Federal Aviation Administration that airports may impose on each departing passenger for use in eligible construction projects or for related debt service. This charge is collected by whoever sells the ticket and then remitted to the airport.

Pass-through grants. Grants and other financial assistance received by a governmental entity to transfer to, or spend on behalf of, a secondary recipient. [SGAS 24]

Payment in lieu of taxes (PILOT). Payment that a property owner not subject to taxation makes to a government to compensate it for services that the property owner receives that normally are financed through property taxes.

Pension (and other employee benefit) trust funds. Fiduciary fund type used to report resources that are required to be held in trust for the members and beneficiaries of defined benefit pension plans, defined contribution plans, other postemployment benefit plans, or other employee benefit plans. [SGAS 34]

Pension benefits. Retirement income and all other benefits (e.g., disability benefits, death benefits, life insurance) except healthcare benefits, that are provided through a defined benefit pension plan to plan members and beneficiaries after termination of employment or after retirement. Postemployment healthcare benefits are considered other postemployment benefits, regardless of how they are provided. [SGAS 43]

Pension cost. Accrual measure of the periodic cost of an employer's participation in a defined benefit pension plan. [SGAS 27]

Pension obligation bonds. Bonds issued by employers to finance one or more elements of their pension obligation to employees. Pension obligation bonds may be used, for example 1) to reduce or eliminate the employer's net pension obligation, 2) to pay the employer's annual required contribution for the year, or 3) to reduce or eliminate the plan's unfunded actuarial accrued liability.

Pension plan. Arrangement for the provision of pension benefits in which all assets accumulated for the payment of benefits may legally be used to pay benefits (including refunds of member contributions) to any of the plan members or beneficiaries, as defined by the terms of the plan. [SGAS 25]

Pension-related debt. All long-term liabilities of an employer to a pension plan, the payment of which is not included in the annual required contributions of a sole or agent employer or the actuarially determined required contributions of a cost-sharing employer. Payments generally are made in accordance with installment contracts that usually include interest. Examples include contractually deferred contributions and amounts assessed to an employer upon joining a multiple-employer plan. [SGAS 27]

Pension trend data. Actuarial data on trends involving 1) the funding progress of a defined benefit pension plan and 2) employers' actual and annual required contributions to the plan.

Performance auditing. Auditing designed to evaluate the effectiveness or efficiency of an organization, program, or activity.

Performance measurement. Commonly used term for service efforts and accomplishments reporting.

Permanent accounts. Accounts that appear on the statement of position (i.e., assets, liabilities, and equity/net assets).

Permanent funds. Governmental fund type used to report resources that are legally restricted to the extent that only earnings, and not principal, may be used for purposes that support the reporting government's programs (i.e., for the benefit of the government or its citizenry). [SGAS 34]

Perspective differences. Differences between the basis of budgeting and GAAP that result when the structure used for budgeting differs from the fund structure used for GAAP financial reporting. [NCGA Interpretation 10]

Policyholder dividends. In the context of public-entity risk pools, payments made or credits extended to the insured by the insurer, usually at the end of a policy year, that result in reducing the net insurance cost to the policyholder. These dividends may be paid in cash to the insured or applied by the insured to reduce premiums due for the next policy year. [SGAS 10]

Popular annual financial reporting. Supplementary financial reporting designed to meet the special needs of interested parties who are either unable or unwilling to use the more detailed financial information provided in traditional comprehensive annual financial reports.

Popular Annual Financial Reporting Award Program. Awards program sponsored by the Government Finance Officers Association with the objective of encouraging and assisting governments to prepare and publish high quality popular annual financial reports.

Postemployment. Period following termination of employment, including the time between termination and retirement. [SGAS 43]

Postemployment healthcare benefits. Medical, dental, vision, and other health-related benefits provided to terminated employees, retired employees, dependents, and beneficiaries. [SGAS 43]

Preliminary project stage. In the context of computer software developed or obtained for internal use, costs incurred prior to the development stage of computer software (e.g., the conceptual formulation of alternatives, the evaluation of alternatives, the determination of the existence of needed technology, and the final selection of alternatives).

Preliminary views. Due-process document issued by the GASB soliciting comments from interested parties on a proposed authoritative pronouncement prior to the issuance of an exposure draft.

Premium deficiency. In the context of public-entity risk pools, a situation that occurs if the sum of 1) expected claims costs (including incurred but not reported claims) and all expected claim adjustment expenses, 2) expected dividends to policyholders or pool participants, and 3) unamortized acquisition costs exceeds related unearned premiums. [SGAS 30]

Primary government. Term used in connection with defining the financial reporting entity. A state government or general purpose local government. Also, a special-purpose government that has a separately elected governing body, is legally separate, and is fiscally independent of other state or local governments. The primary government is the focus of the financial reporting entity. [SGAS 14]

Primary users of general-purpose external financial reports. Types of financial statement users whose needs guide the development of GAAP. For state and local governments, the primary users of general-purpose external financial reports are (a) those to whom government is primarily accountable (the citizenry), (b) those who directly represent the citizens (legislative and oversight bodies), and (c) those who lend or who participate in the lending process (investors and creditors). [SGAC 1]

Private-purpose trust funds. Fiduciary trust fund type used to report all trust arrangements, other than those properly reported in pension trust funds or investment trust funds, under which principal and income benefit individuals, private organizations, or other governments. [SGAS 34]

Program. Group activities, operations or organizational units directed to attaining specific purposes or objectives.

Program loan. In connection with cash flows reporting, a loan made and collected as part of a governmental program that provides a *direct* benefit to *individual* constituents. [SGAS 9 and Q&A]

Program revenue. In the context of the government-wide statement of activities, revenues that derive directly from the program itself or from parties outside the reporting government's taxpayers or citizenry, as a whole; they reduce the net cost of the function to be financed from the government's general revenues. [SGAS 34]

Proprietary funds. Funds that focus on the determination of operating income, changes in net assets (or cost recovery), financial position, and cash flows. There are two different types of proprietary funds: enterprise funds and internal service funds.

Public employee retirement system (PERS). State or local governmental entity entrusted with administering one or more pension plans; it also may administer other postemployment benefit plans and deferred compensation plans. [SGAS 25]

Public-entity risk pool. Cooperative group of governmental entities joining together to finance an exposure, liability, or risk. Risk may include property and liability, workers' compensation, or employee health care. A pool may be a stand-alone entity or included as part of a larger governmental entity that acts as the pool's sponsor. [SGAS 10]

Pure cash conduit. In the context of pass-through grants, a grantor that merely transmits grantor-supplied moneys without having administrative or direct financial involvement in the program. [SGAS 24]

Purpose restrictions. In the context of government-mandated and voluntary nonexchange transactions, legal limitations that specify the purpose or purposes for which resources are required to be used (as distinguished from eligibility requirements). [SGAS 33]

Put option. Option contract giving the buyer (owner) the right, but not the obligation, to sell to the writer of the contract a fixed number of items (such as shares of equity securities) at a fixed or determinable "strike" price on a given date or at any time on or before a given date. [SGAS 31]

Qualified opinion. In the context of financial audits, a modification of the independent auditor's report on the fair presentation of the financial statements indicating that there exists one or more specific exceptions to the auditor's general assertion that the financial statements are fairly presented.

Questioned cost. In the context of Single Audits, a determination by the independent auditor that an expenditure under a federal grant does not meet all of the grantor's requirements and therefore may be subject to refund to the grantor.

Realized gains and losses. Difference between the carrying value of an asset and its price at the time of sale if the asset had been reported at other than fair value. (The term *unrealized gains and losses* is used to describe the difference between carrying value and fair value prior to sale).

Reappropriation. Inclusion of a balance from the prior year's budget as part of the budget of the subsequent fiscal year. Reappropriation is common for encumbrances outstanding at the end of a fiscal year that a government intends to honor in the subsequent fiscal year.

Reasonable assurance. Principle that the goal of the independent audit of the financial statements is to ensure that those statements are free from *material* misstatement (based upon the assumption that it is not cost beneficial to attempt to ensure that financial statements are free of *immaterial* misstatements).

Rebatable arbitrage. Requirement to remit to the federal government interest revenue in excess of interest costs when the proceeds from the sale of tax-exempt securities are reinvested in a taxable money market instrument with a materially higher yield.

Reciprocal interfund activity. Interfund counterpart to exchange and exchange-like transactions. This category includes both interfund loans and interfund services provided and used. [SGAS 34]

Refunding. Issuance of new debt whose proceeds are used to repay previously issued debt. The proceeds may be used immediately for this purpose (a current refunding), or they may be placed with an escrow agent and invested until they are used to pay principal and interest on the old debt at a future time (an advance refunding). [SGAS 23]

Regulated enterprises. Enterprises for which (a) rates for regulated services or products are either established by, or subject to approval by an independent, third-party regulator (or the governing board itself if it is empowered by statute or contract to establish rates that bind customers), (b) the regulated rates are designed to recover the specific enterprise's costs of providing regulated services or products, and (c) it is reasonable to assume that the regulated activity can set and collect charges sufficient to recover its costs. Regulated enterprises have the *option* of adopting certain specialized guidance issued by the FASB. In practice, the term "regulated enterprise" normally is applied only to enterprises that elect this option.

Reimbursement grant. Grant for which a potential recipient must first incur qualifying expenditures to be eligible. Reimbursement grants are also referred to as *expenditure-driven grants*.

Reinsurance. Transaction in which an assuming enterprise (reinsurer), for a consideration (premium), assumes all or part of a risk undertaken originally by another insurer (ceding enterprise). However, the legal rights of the insured are not affected by the reinsurance transaction, and the ceding enterprise issuing the original insurance contract remains liable to the insured for payment of policy benefits. [SGAS 10]

Related organization. In the context of defining the financial reporting entity, an organization for which a primary government appoints a voting majority of the board, but for which it is not *financially* accountable. [SGAS 14]

Related party transaction. Transaction that an informed observer might reasonably believe reflects considerations other than economic self interest based upon the relationship that exists between the parties to the transaction. The term often is used in contrast to an *arm's-length transaction*.

Relative order of liquidity. Practice of arranging assets and liabilities on the government-wide statement of net assets based upon the relative liquidity of each account taken as a whole, rather than separately reporting the current and noncurrent portions of each. [SGAS 34]

Relevance. Principle that there should be a close logical relationship between the financial information provided and the purpose for which it is needed. Information is relevant if it is capable of making a difference in a user's assessment of a problem, condition, or event. [SGAC 1]

Reliability. Principle that financial information should be verifiable, free from bias, and faithfully represent what it purports to represent. [SGAC 1]

Reportable condition. Significant deficiency in internal controls discovered in the course of the financial statement audit that must be communicated by the independent auditor to the entity's audit committee or its equivalent.

Reporting date. Date of the financial statements; the last day of the fiscal year.

Reporting package. In the context of a Single Audit, the package that the independent auditor must communicate to the Federal Audit Clearing House that includes (a) the government's financial statements, (b) the government's supplementary schedule of expenditures of federal awards, (c) the auditor's reports, (d) a summary schedule of prior audit findings, and (e) a corrective action plan. The reporting package must be accompanied by a special data collection form that summarizes the information contained in the reporting package.

Repurchase agreement. Transaction in which the governmental entity (buyer-lender) transfers cash to a broker-dealer or financial institution (seller-borrower); the broker-dealer or financial institution transfers securities to the governmental entity and promises to repay the cash plus interest in exchange for the return of the same securities. [SGAS 3]

Required supplementary information. Statements, schedules, statistical data, or other information that the GASB has determined to be necessary to supplement, although not required to be a part of, the basic statements of a governmental entity. [SGAS 43]

Reserved fund balance. Portion of a governmental fund's net assets that is not available for appropriation.

Reset date. Time that a bond's variable coupon is repriced to reflect changes in a benchmark index. [SGAS 40]

Restoration cost approach. Method for measuring the impairment of a capital asset as a result of physical damage that uses estimated restoration costs to establish a ratio (restoration cost/replacement cost or deflated restoration cost/original cost) for determining the portion of the book value of the asset that should be written off.

Restricted assets. Assets whose use is subject to constraints that are either (a) externally imposed by creditors (such as through debt covenants), grantors, contributors, or laws or regulations of other governments or (b) imposed by law through constitutional provisions or enabling legislation. [SGAS 34]

Restricted net assets. Component of net assets calculated by reducing the carrying value of restricted assets by amounts repayable from those assets, excluding capital-related debt.

Retrospectively (experience) rated policy. Term used in connection with public-entity risk pools. An insurance policy for which the final amount of the premium is determined by adjusting the initial premium based on actual experience during the period of coverage (sometimes subject to maximum and minimum limits). A retrospectively rated policy is designed to encourage safety by the insured and to compensate the insurer if larger-than-expected losses are incurred. [SGAS 10]

Revenue and claims development trend data. Required supplementary information mandated by the GASB for public-entity risk pools.

Revenue anticipation note. Short-term, interest-bearing note issued by a government in anticipation of revenues to be received at a later date. The note is retired from the revenues to which it is related.

Reverse repurchase agreement. Agreement in which a broker-dealer or financial institution (buyer-lender) transfers cash to a governmental entity (seller-borrower); the entity transfers securities to the broker-dealer or financial institution and promises to repay the cash plus interest in exchange for the same securities or for different securities. [SGAS 3]

Risk-sharing pool. One of four different types of public-entity risk pool. An arrangement by which governments pool risks and funds and share in the cost of losses. [SGAS 10]

Roll-over risk. In the context of disclosures for derivatives, the risk that arises when a derivative associated with a government's variable-rate debt does not extend all the way to the maturity date of the associated debt, thereby creating a gap in the protection otherwise afforded by the derivative.

Salary-related payments. In the context of compensated absences, payments by an employer that are directly and incrementally associated with payments made for compensated absences on termination. Such salary-related payments include the employer's share of Social Security and Medicare taxes and also might include, for example, the employer's contributions to pension plans. [SGAS 16]

Schedule of employer contributions. In the context of defined benefit pension plans and other postemployment benefit plans, trend data on employers' annual required contribution to a plan and actual contributions.

Schedule of funding progress. In the context of defined benefit pension plans and other postemployment benefit plans, trend data on the relationship between the actuarial value of plan assets and the related actuarial accrued liability.

SEC 2a7-like pool. External investment pool that is not registered with the Securities and Exchange Commission (SEC) as an investment company, but nevertheless has a policy that it will, and does, operate in a manner consistent with the SEC's Rule 2a7 of the Investment Company Act of 1940 (17 Code of Federal Regulations §270.2a-7). Rule 2a7 allows SEC-registered mutual funds to use amortized cost rather than market value to report net assets to compute share prices if certain conditions are met. Those conditions include restrictions on the types of investments held, restrictions on the term-to-maturity of individual investments and the dollar-weighted average of the portfolio, requirements for portfolio diversification, requirements for divestiture considerations in the event of security downgrades and defaults, and required actions if the market value of the portfolio deviates from amortized cost by a specified amount. [SGAS 31]

Securities lending transactions. Transactions in which governmental entities transfer their securities to broker-dealers and other entities for collateral—which may be cash, securities, or letters of credit—and simultaneously agree to return the collateral for the same securities in the future. [SGAS 28]

Segment. Identifiable activity (or grouping of activities) reported as or within an enterprise fund or an other stand-alone entity that has one or more bonds or other debt instruments outstanding, with a revenue stream pledged in support of that debt. In addition, the activity's revenues, expenses, gains and losses, assets, and liabilities are required to be accounted for separately.

Segmented time distribution. In the context of investment disclosure, segmented time distribution groups investment cash flows into sequential time periods in tabular form. [SGAS 40]

Segregation of incompatible duties. In the context of an evaluation of internal control, the principle that no single employee should be placed in a position that allows that employee both to commit and conceal an irregularity in the ordinary course of the employee's duties.

Service efforts and accomplishments reporting. Term used by the GASB to describe the presentation of performance measures in connection with general purpose external financial reporting.

Service units approach. Method of measuring capital asset impairments resulting from either 1) changes in environmental factors (e.g., laws, regulations), 2) technological developments and obsolescence, or 3) a change in the manner or expected duration of use of the asset. The method is based on a comparison of service units before and after an impairment occurs.

Simulation models. Models that estimate changes in an investment's or a portfolio's fair value, given hypothetical changes in interest rates. Various models or techniques are used, such as "shock tests" or value-at-risk. [SGAS 40]

Single Audit. Audit designed to meet the needs of all federal grantor agencies and performed in accordance with the Single Audit Act of 1984 (as amended) and Office of Management and Budget (OMB) Circular A-133, *Audits of States, Local Governments, and Non-Profit Organizations.*

Single Audit Act of 1984. Federal legislation that provides for state and local government recipients of federal financial awards to have one audit performed to meet the needs of all federal grantor agencies. The Single Audit Act was amended in 1996.

Single-program government. In the context of financial reporting, a government that budgets, manages, and accounts for its activities as a single program. Single-program governments that use only governmental funds have the option to combine their fund financial statements and their government-wide financial statements into a single, combining presentation.

Solvency test. In the context of pension plan financial reporting, the comparison of a pension plan's present assets to the aggregate accrued liabilities classified into the following categories: (a) liability for active member contributions on deposit, (b) liability for future benefits to present retired lives, and (c) liability for service already rendered by active members. In preparing this schedule, valuation assets are arbitrarily allocated first to the liability for active member contributions on deposit, second to the liability for future benefits to present retired lives, and third to the liability for service already rendered by active members, regardless of the method used for asset allocation.

Special assessment. Compulsory levy made against certain properties to defray all or part of the cost of a specific capital improvement or service deemed to benefit primarily those properties.

Special funding situation. Situation in which a governmental entity is legally responsible for contributions to pension plans or other postemployment benefit plans that cover the employees of another governmental entity or entities. For example, a state government may be legally responsible for the annual "employer" contributions to a pension plan that covers employees of school districts within the state. [SGAS 27 and SGAS 45]

Special items. Significant transactions or other events within the control of management that are either unusual in nature or infrequent in occurrence. [SGAS 34]

Special revenue fund. Governmental fund type used to account for the proceeds of specific revenue sources (other than for major capital projects) that are legally restricted to expenditure for specified purposes. [NCGA Statement 1]

Special termination benefits. Benefits offered by an employer for a short period of time as an inducement to employees to hasten the termination of services. For example, to reduce payroll and related costs, an employer might offer enhanced pension benefits or OPEB to employees as an inducement to take early termination, for employees who accept the offer within a sixty-day window of opportunity. [SGAS 43]

Specific identification. In the context of the interest rate risk disclosure for investments, the listing of each investment, its amount, its maturity date, and any call options. [SGAS 40]

Sponsor. In the context of pension and other postemployment benefits, the entity that established the plan. [SGAS 43]

Stand-alone plan financial report. In the context of pension and other postemployment benefits, a report that contains the financial statements of a plan and is issued by the plan or by the public employee retirement system that administers the plan. The term *stand-alone* is used to distinguish such a financial report from plan financial statements that are included in the financial report of the plan sponsor or employer. [SGAS 43]

Standard costing. Method of estimating the historical cost of a capital asset by establishing the average cost of obtaining the same or a similar asset at the time of acquisition.

Statistical section. Third of three essential components of any comprehensive annual financial report, it 1) provides information on financial trends, 2) provides information on revenue capacity, 3) provides information on debt capacity, 4) provides demographic and economic information, and 5) provides operating information.

Stock rights. Rights given to existing stockholders to purchase newly issued shares in proportion to their holdings at a specific date. [SGAS 31]

Stock warrants. Certificates entitling the holder to acquire shares of stock at a certain price within a stated period. Warrants often are made part of the issuance of bonds or preferred or common stock. [SGAS 31]

Street or nominee name. Securities that are issued in or endorsed to the name of a securities depository, broker-dealer, or other financial services company, on behalf of the true beneficial owners of the securities. [Q&A]

Strike price. Fixed or determinable price on a given date or at any time on or before a given date at which the buyer (owner) may purchase from (call option) or sell to (put option) the seller (writer) of an option contract a fixed number of items (such as shares of equity securities). [SGAS 31]

Structured settlement. In the context of risk financing, a means of satisfying a claim liability, consisting of an initial cash payment to meet specific present financial needs combined with a stream of future payments designed to meet future financial needs, generally funded by annuity contracts. [SGAS 10]

Subobject. Subdivision within an expenditure object classification (e.g., *regular employees* is a possible subobject classification within the *personal services—salaries and wages* expenditure object classification).

Substantive plan. Terms of an OPEB plan as understood by the employer(s) and plan members [SGAS 43]

Summary of significant accounting policies (SSAP). First of the notes to the financial statements or a separate section immediately preceding the notes to the financial statements. The basic contents should include a discussion of 1) any selection of an accounting treatment when GAAP permit more than one approach, 2) accounting practices unique to state and local governments, and 3) unusual or innovative applications of GAAP.

Supplementary information. Financial information presented together with basic financial statements that is not included within the scope of the audit of those statements. When the presentation of certain supplementary information is mandated by the GASB it is referred to as *required supplementary information.*

Susceptible to accrual. In the context of the modified accrual basis of accounting, revenues that are collectible within the current period or soon enough thereafter to be used to pay liabilities of the current period. [NCGA Statement 1]

Swap (principal/interest). Contract in which the parties agree to make future payments to each other designed to achieve a net effect equivalent to each assuming the debt service burden of the other.

System development fees. Fees charged to join or to extend an existing utility system. Also referred to as *tap fees* or *connection fees.*

Take-out agreement. In the context of demand bonds, an arrangement with a financial institution to convert those bonds to an installment loan payable over a specified period, sometimes as long as ten years or more. A take-out agreement is used to provide long-term financing in the event the remarketing agent is unable to resell demand bonds within a specified period (usually three to six months) subsequent to the exercise of the "demand" feature by bondholders. [IGAS 1]

Tap fees. Fees charged to join or to extend an existing utility system. Also referred to as *system development fees* or *connection fees.*

Tax anticipation note. Short-term, interest-bearing note issued by a government in anticipation of tax revenues to be received at a later date. The note is retired from the tax revenues to which it is related.

Tax-increment financing. Financing secured by the anticipated incremental increase in tax revenues, resulting from the redevelopment of an area.

Technical agenda. In the context of the GASB's due-process procedures, a list of research projects formally undertaken by the GASB as part of its development of authoritative standards of accounting and financial reporting.

Technical bulletin. Document issued by the staff of the GASB to provide guidance for applying GASB statements and interpretations and resolving accounting issues not directly addressed by them. [TB 84-1]

Temporary accounts. Accounts that close to net assets at the end of an accounting period (e.g., revenues and expenses).

Ten percent criterion. First of two tests used to determine whether a given governmental fund or enterprise fund must be reported as a major fund in the basic financial statements. For governmental funds, this test is applied to the total assets, liabilities, revenues, and expenditures of all governmental funds. For enterprise funds, this test is applied to the total assets, liabilities, revenues, and expenses of all enterprise funds. The test need be met for only one of these four items.

Termination payments method. Method of calculating the liability for earned sick leave for which it is probable that the benefits will result in termination payments. Under this method, the amount of the liability is estimated based on a governmental entity's past experience of making termination payments for sick leave, adjusted for the effect of changes in its termination policy and other factors. [SGAS 16]

Termination risk. In the context of disclosures for derivatives, the risk that an unscheduled termination of a derivative could have an adverse effect on the government's asset or liability strategy or could lead to potentially significant unscheduled payments.

Timeliness. Principle that financial statements must be issued soon enough after the reported events to affect decisions. [SGAC 1]

Timing differences. Differences between the basis of budgeting and GAAP that occur when the period used for budgeting differs from the period used for GAAP reporting (e.g., a special revenue fund that uses a grant-year budget rather than a fiscal-year budget).

Total direct rate. In the context of the statistical section, the weighted average of all individual direct rates applied by the government preparing the statistical section information. [SGAS 44]

Tri-party arrangement. In the context of repurchase agreements, an arrangement in which the custodian serves as agent both of the buyer-lender and of the seller-borrower by agreeing, in the event of default by one, to protect the interests of the other. The custodian holds the securities underlying the agreement in the names of both repurchase agreement parties (the buyer-lender as pledgee and the seller-borrower as owner). [Q&A]

Type A program. Term used in connection with the determination of major programs for purposes of Single Audits. Type A programs are defined on the basis of the relationship between program expenditures and total federal awards expended.

Type B program. Term used in connection with the determination of major programs for purposes of Single Audits. A Type B program is any program with insufficient program expenditures to qualify as a Type A program.

Unallocated claim adjustment expenses. In the context of risk financing, costs that cannot be associated with specific claims, but are related to claims paid or in the process of settlement, such as salaries and other internal costs of the pool's claims department. [SGAS 10]

Unallocated depreciation. In the context of the government-wide statement of activities, depreciation not properly reported as a direct expense of a functional category.

Uncommitted balance of appropriations. Portion of an appropriation remaining after the deduction of expenditures and encumbrances.

Underlying. In the context of a derivative, a variable that is applied to a notional amount (e.g., a specified interest rate, price index, foreign exchange rate, commodity price), or is associated with a payment provision.

Understandability. Principle that information in financial reports should be expressed as simply as possible. [SGAC 1]

Undesignated unreserved fund balance. Available expendable financial resources in a governmental fund that are not the object of tentative management plans (i.e., designations).

Undivided interest. Arrangement (also known as a *joint operation*) that resembles a joint venture, but no entity or organization is created by the participants. An undivided interest is an ownership arrangement in which two or more parties own property in which title is held individually to the extent of each party's interest. Implied in that definition is that each participant is also liable for specific, identifiable obligations (if any) of the operation. [SGAS 14]

Unearned revenue. Specific type of deferred revenue that does *not* involve the application of the availability criterion, and therefore applies equally to both accrual and modified accrual financial statements.

Unfunded actuarial accrued liability. Excess of the actuarial accrued liability over the actuarial value of assets. This value may be negative, in which case it may be expressed as a *negative unfunded actuarial accrued liability*, the *excess of the actuarial value of assets over the actuarial accrued liability*, or the *funding excess*. [SGAS 43]

Unqualified opinion. Opinion rendered without reservation by the independent auditor that financial statements are fairly presented.

Unrealized gains and losses. Difference between the carrying value of an asset and its fair value prior to sale.

Unrealized revenues. In the context of budgeting, the difference between estimated revenues and actual revenues.

Unrestricted net assets. That portion of net assets that is neither restricted nor invested in capital assets (net of related debt).

Variable-rate investment. In the context of investment disclosure, an investment with terms that provide for the adjustment of its interest rate on set dates (such as the last day of a month or calendar quarter) and that, upon each adjustment until the final maturity of the instrument or the period remaining until the principal amount can be recovered through demand, can reasonably be expected to have a fair value that will be unaffected by interest rate changes. [SGAS 40]

Vesting method. Method of calculating the liability for earned sick leave for which it is probable that the benefits will result in termination payments. Under this method, the amount of the liability is estimated based on the sick leave accumulated at the date of the statement of position for those employees who currently are eligible to receive termination payments as well as other employees who are expected to become eligible in the future to receive such payments. In calculating the liability, these accumulations are reduced to the maximum amount allowed as a termination payment. Accruals for those employees who are expected to become eligible in the future are based on assumptions concerning the probability that individual employees or classes or groups of employees will become eligible to receive termination payments. [SGAS 16]

Voluntary nonexchange transactions. Transactions that result from legislative or contractual agreements, other than exchanges, entered into willingly by the parties to the agreement (for example, certain grants and private donations). [SGAS 33]

Voting majority. In the context of defining the financial reporting entity, a situation in which the number of the primary government's appointees to a component unit's board is sufficient to control decisions of the component unit. [SGAS 14, Q&A]

Vulnerability assessment. In the context of an evaluation of internal control, the risk-based systematic prioritization of what is to be evaluated.

Weighted average maturity. In the context of investment disclosure, a weighted average maturity measure that expresses investment time horizons—the time when investments become due and payable—in years or months, weighted to reflect the dollar size of individual investments within an investment type. [SGAS 40]

Widely recognized and prevalent practice. In the context of the GAAP hierarchy, the principle that accounting and financial reporting practice should itself serve as a source of GAAP in the absence of higher level guidance.

Yellow Book. Term commonly used to describe the Government Accountability Office's publication *Government Auditing Standards*, the source of GAGAS.

Yield maintenance repurchase/reverse repurchase agreement. A repurchase agreement or a reverse repurchase agreement where the parties agree that the securities returned will provide the seller-borrower with a yield as specified in the agreement. [SGAS 3]

General Index

..